MARKET
SHARE
REPORTER

ISSN 1052-9578

MARKET SHARE REPORTER

AN ANNUAL COMPILATION
OF REPORTED MARKET SHARE
DATA ON COMPANIES,
PRODUCTS, AND SERVICES

1 9 9 7

ROBERT S. LAZICH

GALE

DETROIT · NEW YORK · TORONTO · LONDON

Robert S. Lazich, *Editor*

Editorial Code & Data Inc. Staff

Marlita A. Reddy and Susan Turner, *Contributing Editors*
Gary Alampi, *Programmer/Analyst*

Gale Research Inc. Staff

Donna Wood, *Coordinating Editor*

Mary Beth Trimper, *Production Manager*
Deborah Milliken, *Production Assistant*

Cynthia D. Baldwin, *Product Design Manager*
Barbara Yarrow, *Graphic Services Supervisor*
Sherrell Hobbs, *Macintosh Artist*

The paper used in this publication meets the minimum requirements of American National Standard for Information Sciences—Permanence Paper for Printed Library Materials, ANSI Z39.48-1984.

This book is printed on recycled paper that meets Environmental Protection Agency Standards.

Copyright © 1997
Gale Research Inc.
835 Penobscot Building
Detroit, MI 48226-4094

ISBN 0-8103-0209-8
ISSN 1052-9578

Printed in the United States of America

TABLE OF CONTENTS

TABLE OF TOPICS

The *Table of Topics* lists all topics used in *Market Share Reporter* in alphabetical order. One or more page references follow each topic; the page references identify the starting point where the topic is shown. The same topic name may be used under different SICs; therefore, in some cases, more than one page reference is provided.

INTRODUCTION

Market Share Reporter (MSR) is a compilation of market share reports from periodical literature. The seventh edition covers the period 1993 through 1996; while dates overlap slightly with the sixth edition, the seventh edition of *MSR* has completely new and updated entries. As shown by reviews of previous editions plus correspondence and telephone contact with many users, this is a unique resource for competitive analysis, diversification planning, marketing research, and other forms of economic and policy analysis. Features of the 1997 edition include—

- More than 2,000 entries, all new or updated.

- SIC classification, with entries arranged under 462 SIC codes.

- Corporate, brand, product, service and commodity market shares.

- Coverage of private and public sector activities.

- North American coverage.

- Comprehensive indexes, including products, companies, brands, places, sources, and SICs.

- Table of Topics showing topical subdivisions of chapters with page references.

- Graphics.

- Annotated source listing—provides publishers' information for journals cited in this edition of *MSR*.

MSR is a one-of-a-kind resource for ready reference, marketing research, economic analysis, planning, and a host of other disciplines.

Categories of Market Shares

Entries in *Market Share Reporter* fall into four broad categories. Items were included if they showed the relative strengths of participants in a market or provided subdivisions of economic activity in some manner that could assist the analyst.

- *Corporate market shares* show the names of companies that participate in an industry, produce a product, or provide a service. Each company's market share is shown as a percent of total industry or product sales for a defined period, usually a year. In some cases, the company's share represents the share of the sales of the companies shown (group total)—because shares of the total market were not cited in the source or were not relevant. In some corporate share tables, brand information appears behind company names in parentheses. In these cases, the tables can be located using either the company or the brand index.

- *Institutional shares* are like corporate shares but show the shares of other kinds of organizations. The most common institutional entries in *MSR* display the shares of states, provinces, or regions in an activity. The shares of not-for-profit organizations in some economic or service functions fall under this heading.

- *Brand market shares* are similar to corporate shares with the difference that brand names are shown. Brand names include equivalent categories such as the names of television programs, magazines, publishers' imprints, etc. In some cases, the names of corporations appear in parentheses behind the brand name; in these cases, tables can be located using either the brand or the company index.

- *Product, commodity, service, and facility* shares feature a broad category (e.g. household appliances) and show how the category is subdivided into components (e.g. refrigerators, ranges, washing machines, dryers, and dishwashers). Entries under this category cover products (autos, lawnmowers, polyethylene, etc.), commodities (cattle, grains, crops), services (telephone, child care), and facilities (port berths, hotel suites, etc.). Subdivisions may be products, categories of services (long-distance telephone, residential phone service, 800-service), types of commodities (varieties of grain), size categories (e.g., horsepower ranges), modes (rail, air, barge), types of facilities (categories of hospitals, ports, and the like), or other subdivisions.

- *Other shares.* MSR includes a number of entries that show subdivisions, breakdowns, and shares that do not fit neatly into the above categorizations but properly belong in such a book because they shed light on public policy, foreign trade, and other subjects of general interest. These items include, for instance, subdivisions of governmental expenditures, environmental issues, and the like.

Coverage

The seventh edition of *Market Share Reporter* covers essentially the same range of industries as previous editions. However, all tables are *new* or represent *updated* information (more recent or revised data). Also, coverage in detail is different in certain industries, meaning that more or fewer SICs are covered or product details *within* SICs may be different. For these reasons, it is recommended that

previous editions of *MSR* be retained rather than replaced.

Changes in Coverage. Beginning with the sixth edition, *MSR*'s geographic area of coverage became North America—Canada, the United States, and Mexico. As in all past editions, the vast majority of entries are for the United States. In the first four editions of *MSR*, international data were included at greater or lesser intensity depending on availability of space. This necessitated, among other things, frequent exclusion of data organized by states or regions of the United States—which are propular with users.

In order to provide better service to users, a companion publication, called *World Market Share Reporter* (*WMSR*), is available. *WMSR* features global market share information as well as country-specific market share and/or market size information outside North America. At the same time, *MSR* will feature more geographical market shares in the North American area.

MSR reports on *published* market shares rather than attempting exhaustive coverage of the market shares, say, of all major corporations and of all products and services. Despite this limitation, *MSR* holds share information on nearly 5,400 companies, more than 1,650 brands, and more than 2,500 product, commodity, service, and facility categories. Several entries are usually available for each industry group in the SIC classification; omitted groups are those that do not play a conventional role in the market, e.g., Private Households (SIC 88).

Coverage by SIC is comparable with the sixth edition: 462 SIC categories versus 479 last year. Variation in coverage from previous editions is due in part to publication cycles of sources and a different mix of brokerage house reports for the period covered (due to shifting interests within the investment community).

As pointed out in previous editions, *MSR* tends to reflect the current concerns of the business press. In addition to being a source of market share data, it mirrors journalistic preoccupations, issues in the business community, and events abroad. Important and controversial industries and activities get most of the ink. Heavy coverage is provided in those areas that are—

- large, important, basic (autos, chemicals)
- on the leading edge of technological change (computers, electronics, software)
- very competitive (toiletries, beer, soft drinks)
- in the news because of product recalls, new product introductions, mergers and acquisitions, lawsuits, and for other reasons
- relate to popular issues (environment, crime), or have excellent coverage in their respective trade press.

In many cases, several entries are provided on a subject each citing the same companies. No attempt was made to eliminate such seeming duplication if the publishing and/or original sources were different and the market shares were not identical. Those who work with such data know that market share reports are often little more than the "best guesses" of knowledgeable observers rather than precise measurements. To the planner or analyst, variant reports about an industry's market shares are useful for interpreting the data.

Publications appearing in the June 1995 to August 1996 period were used in preparing *MSR*. As a rule, material on market share data for 1996 were used by preference; in response to reader requests, we have included historical data when available. In some instances, information for earlier years was included if the category was unique or if the earlier year was necessary for context. In a few other cases, projections for 1997 and later years were also included.

"Unusual" Market Shares

Some reviewers of the first edition questioned—sometimes tongue-in-cheek, sometimes seriously—the inclusion of tables on such topics as computer crime, endangered species of fish, children's allowances, governmental budgets, and weapons system stockpiles. Indeed, some of these categories do not fit the sober meaning of "market share." A few tables on such subjects are present every edition—because they provide market information, albeit indirectly, or because they are the "market share equivalents" in an industrial classification which is in the public sector or dominated by the public sector's purchasing power.

Organization of Chapters

Market Share Reporter is organized into chapters by 2-digit SIC categories (industry groups). The exception is the first chapter, entitled *General Interest and Broad Topics*; this chapter holds all entries that bridge two or more 2-digit SIC industry codes (e.g. retailing in general, beverage containers, advanced materials, etc.) and cannot, therefore, be classified using the SIC system without distortion. Please note, however, that a topic in this chapter will often have one or more additional entries later—where the table could be assigned to a detailed industry. Thus, in addition to two tables on food containers in the first chapter, numerous tables appear later on glass containers, metal cans, etc.

Within each chapter, entries are shown by 4-digit SIC (industry level). Within blocks of 4-digit SIC entries, entries are sorted alphabetically by topic, then alphabetically by title.

SIC and Topic Assignments

MSR's SIC classifications are based on the coding as defined in the *Standard Industrial Classification Manual* for 1987, issued by the Bureau of the Census, Department of Commerce. This 1987 classification system introduced significant revisions to the 1972 classification (as slightly modified in 1977); the 1972 system is still in widespread use (even by the Federal government); care should be used in comparing data classified in the new and in the old way.

The closest appropriate 4-digit SIC was assigned to each table. In many cases, a 3-digit SIC had to be used because the substance of the table was broader than the nearest 4-digit SIC category. Such SICs always end with a zero. In yet other cases, the closest classification possible was at the 2-digit level; these SICs terminate with double-zero. If the content of the table did not fit the 2-digit level, it was assigned to the first chapter of *MSR* and classified by topic only.

Topic assignments are based on terminology for commodities, products, industries, and services in the SIC Manual; however, in many cases phrasing has been simplified, shortened, or updated; in general, journalistically succinct rather than bureaucratically exhaustive phraseology was used throughout.

Organization of Entries

Entries are organized in a uniform manner. A sample entry is provided below. Explanations for each

part of an entry, shown in boxes, are provided on the facing page.

1   *Entry Number.* A numeral between star symbols. Used for locating an entry from the index.

2   *Topic.* Second line, small type. Gives the broad or general product or service category of the entry. The topic for Raisin Market - 1995 is Raisins.

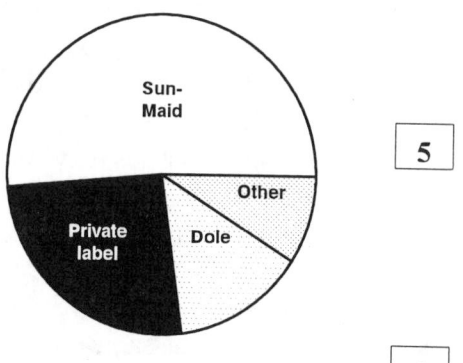

★ 255 ★   **1**   **2**   **3**

Raisins (SIC 2034)

Raisin Market - 1995   **4**

5

6

Sales are shown by brand for the 52 weeks ended March 24, 1996. Shares are shown based on a $218.3 million market.   **7**

	($ mil.)	Share
Sun-Maid	$ 112.7	51.6%
Private label	57.4	26.3
Dole	29.4	13.5	**8**
Other	18.8	8.6

Source: *Brandweek*, May 27, 1996, p. 16, from Information Resources Inc.

9

3   *SIC Code.* Second line, small type, follows the topic. General entries in the first chapter do not have an SIC code.

4 *Title.* Third line, large type. Describes the entry with a headline.

5 *Graphic.* When a graphic is present, it follows the title. Some entries will be illustrated with a pie or bar chart. The information used to create the graphic is always shown below the pie or bar chart.

6 *Note Block.* When present, follows the title and is in italic type. The note provides contextual information about the entry to make the data more understandable. Special notes about the data, information about time periods covered, market totals, and other comments are provided. Self-explanatory entries do not have a note block.

7 *Column headers.* Follow the note block. Some entries have more than one column or the single column requires a header. In these cases, column headers are used to describe information covered in the column. In most cases, column headers are years (1995) or indicators of type and magnitude ($ mil.). Column headers are shown only when necessary for clarity of presentation.

8 *Body.* Follows the note block or the column header and shows the actual data in two or more columns. In most cases, individual rows of data in the body are arranged in descending order, with the largest market share holder heading the list. Collective shares, usually labelled ''Others'' are placed last.

9 *Source.* Follows the body. All entries cite the source of the table, the date of publication, and the page number (if given). In many cases, the publisher obtained the information from another source (original source); in all such cases, the original source is also shown.

Continued entries. Entries that extend over two adjacent columns on the same page are not marked to indicate continuation but continue in the second column. Entries that extend over two pages are marked *Continued on the next page.* Entries carried over from the previous page repeat the entry number, topic (followed by the word *continued*), title, and column header (if any).

Use of Names

Company Names. The editors reproduced company names as they appeared in the source unless it was clearly evident from the name and the context that a name had been misspelled in the original. Large companies, of course, tend to appear in a large number of entries and in variant renditions. General Electric Corporation may appear as GE, General Electric, General Electric Corp., GE Corp., and other variants. No attempt was made to enforce a uniform rendition of names in the entries. In the Company Index, variant renditions were reduced to a single version or cross-referenced.

Use of Numbers

Throughout *MSR*, tables showing percentage breakdowns may add to less than 100 or fractionally more than 100 due to rounding. In those cases where only a few leading participants in a market are shown, the total of the shares may be substantially less than 100.

Numbers in the note block showing the total size of the market are provided with as many significant digits as possible in order to permit the user to calculate the sales of a particular company by multiplying the market total by the market share.

In a relatively small number of entries, actual unit or dollar information is provided rather than share information in percent. In such cases, the denomination of the unit (tons, gallons, $) and its magnitude (000 indicates multiply by 1,000; mil., multiply by 1,000,000) are mentioned in the note block or shown in the column header.

Data in some entries are based on different kinds of currencies and different weight and liquid measures. Where necessary, the unit is identified in the note block or in the column header. Examples are long tons, short tons, metric tons or Canadian dollars, etc.

Graphics

Pie and bar charts are used to illustrate some of the entries. The graphics show the names of companies, products, and services when they fit on the charts. When room is insufficient to accommodate the label, the first word of a full name is used followed by three periods (...) to indicate omission of the rest of the label.

In the case of bar charts, the largest share is always the width of the column, and smaller shares are drawn in proportion. Two bar charts, consequently, should not be compared to one another.

Sources

The majority of entries were extracted from newspapers and from general purpose, trade, and technical periodicals normally available in larger public, special, or university libraries. All told, 1,120 sources were used; of these, 399 were primary print sources. Many more were reviewed but lacked coverage of the subject. These primary sources, in turn, used 721 original sources.

In many cases, the primary source in which the entry was published cites another source for the data, the original source. Original sources include other publications, brokerage houses, consultancies and research organizations, associations, government agencies, special surveys, and the like.

Since many primary sources appear as original sources elsewhere, and vice-versa, primary and original sources are shown in a single Source Index under two headings. Primary sources included in *MSR* almost always used the market share data as illustrative material for narratives covering many aspects of the subject. We hope that this book will also serve as a guide to those articles.

Indexes

Market Share Reporter features five indexes and two appendices.

- **Source Index.** This index holds 1,120 references in two groupings. *Primary sources* (399) are publications where the data were found. *Original sources* (721) are sources cited in the primary sources. Each item in the index is followed by one or more entry numbers arranged sequentially, beginning with the first mention of the source.

- **Place Names Index.** This index provides references to cities, states, and regions in North America and elsewhere. References are to entry numbers.

- **Products, Services, and Issues Index.** This index holds more than 2,500 references to products and services in alphabetical order. The index also lists subject categories that do not fit the definition of a product or service but properly belong in the index. Examples include *budgets, conglomerates, crime, defense spending, economies, lotteries*, and the like. Some listings are abbreviations for chemical substances, computer software, etc. which may not be meaningful to those unfamiliar with the industries. Wherever possible, the full name is also provided for abbreviations commonly in use. Each listing is followed by one or more references to entry numbers.

- **Company Index.** This index shows references to nearly 5,400 company names by entry number. Companies are arranged in alphabetical order. In some cases, the market share table from which the company name was derived showed the share for a combination of two or more companies; these combinations are reproduced in the index.

- **Brand Index.** The Brand Index shows references to more than 1,650 brands by entry number. The arrangement is alphabetical. Brands include names of publications, computer software, operating systems, etc., as well as the more conventional brand names (Coca Cola, Maxwell House, Budweiser, etc.)

- **Appendix I - SIC Coverage.** The first appendix shows SICs covered by *Market Share Reporter*. The listing shows major SIC groupings at the 2-digit level as bold-face headings followed by 4-digit SIC numbers, the names of the SIC, and a *page* reference (rather than a reference to an entry number, as in the indexes). The page shows the first occurrence of the SIC in the book. *MSR*'s SIC coverage is quite comprehensive, as shown in the appendix. However, many 4-digit SIC categories are further divided into major product

groupings. Not all of these have corresponding entries in the book.

- **Appendix II - Annotated Source List.** The second appendix provides publisher names, addresses, telephone and fax numbers, and publication frequency of primary sources cited in *Market Share Reporter*, 7th Edition. As a new feature in this edition, the costs of the publications are also provided in some of the entries.

Acknowledgements

Market Share Reporter is something of a collective enterprise which involves not only the editorial team but also many users who share comments, criticisms, and suggestions over the telephone. Their help and encouragement is very much appreciated. *MSR* could not have been produced without the help of many people in and outside of Gale Research. The editors would like to express their special appreciation to Ms. Donna Wood (Senior Editor, Gale Research) and to the staff of Editorial Code and Data, Inc.

Comments and Suggestions

Comments on *MSR* or suggestions for improvement of its usefulness, format, and coverage are always welcome. Although every effort is made to maintain accuracy, errors may occasionally occur; the editors will be grateful if these are called to their attention. Please contact:

Editors
Market Share Reporter
Gale Research Inc.
835 Penobscot Building
Detroit, Michigan 48226-4094
Phone: (313) 961-2242 or (800) 347-GALE
Fax: (313) 961-6815

General Interest and Broad Topics

★1★

Assembly Plants

Maquiladoras by Region

Maquiladoras are foreign owned assembly plants operating in Mexico. This table shows the number of companies per border area. The 1,427 maquiladoras shown employ 456,573 workers.

Tijuana	476
Cd. Juarez	282
Mexicali	119
Matamoros	104
Tecate	81
Nogales	76
Reynosa	75
Nuevo Laredo	51
Cd. Acuna	49
Piedras Negras	42
San Luis Rio Colorado	30
Agua Prieta	23
Valle Hermoso	13
Palomas	5
Ojinaga	1

Source: *Dallas Morning News*, February 27, 1996, p. Mexican Ministry of Commerce and Industrial Development, from maquiladora associations, & economic development organizations in Mexico, Brownsville, McAllen and Laredo, and *Twin Plant News*.

★2★

Building Materials

Leading Building Materials Makers

Firms are ranked by 1995 revenues in millions of dollars.

Corning	$ 5,346
Owens-Illinois	3,763
Owens-Corning	3,612
Manville	2,734
Armstrong World Ind.	2,635
USG	2,444

Source: *Fortune*, April 29, 1996, p. 44.

★3★

Collectibles

Leading Collectibles Marketers

Ad spending is shown for the first four months of 1996. Figures are in millions of dollars.

Bradford Exchange	$ 21.9
Roll (Franklin Mint)	21.3
MBI (Danbury Mint)	5.5
Stanhome (Hamilton Collection)	5.3
Brown-Forman (Lenox Collections)	1.8

Source: *Advertising Age*, August 5, 1996, p. 32, from Competitive Media Reporting.

★ 4 ★
Collectibles

Top Collectibles Marketers

Shares are for 1994. Producers are shown in parentheses.

Roll Intl. (Franklin Mint)	10.5%
Bradford Exchange	6.6
MBI Inc. (Danbury Mint)	4.2
Stanhome (Hamilton)	1.8
Brown-Forman (Lenox)	1.2
Other	75.7

Source: *Advertising Age*, September 27, 1995, p. 30.

★ 5 ★
Federal Contracting

Top Federal Contractors

Firms are ranked by the value of federal contracts awarded to them in 1995. Data are in thousands.

IBM	$ 699,573
Computer Sciences Corp.	576,990
TRW Inc.	430,504
PRC Corp.	358,969
EDS	319,676
Johns Hopkins	271,094
Lockheed	245,259
Mitre Corp.	239,989
AT&T	221,928
Bell Atlantic Network	213,847

Source: *Washington Post*, April 1, 1996, p. 13.

★ 6 ★
Foreign Trade

Chinese Goods in the U.S. Market

The table shows the share of selected markets represented by Chinese goods.

Dolls and parts	70.0%
Toys	69.0
Christmas decorations	66.0
Rubber/fabric shoes	66.0
Nonrubber shoes	55.0

Source: *Wall Street Journal*, May 17, 1996, p. A10, from American Chamber of Commerce, U.S. and Chinese governments, and Footwear Distributors and Realtors of America.

★ 7 ★
General Merchandise

Top General Merchandise Makers

Sales are shown in millions of dollars for the 52 weeks ended February 29, 1996.

Ambassador	$ 364.2
Eastman Kodak	294.3
General Electric	293.7
American Greetings	291.0
Eveready Battery	215.3
Duracell	215.1
L'Eggs Products	213.7
Gibson Greetings	183.8
Murdoch Magazines	155.3
Time Inc.	149.9

Source: *Supermarket Business*, April 1996, p. 58, from industry reports.

Languages

Foreign Languages at Home

	($ bil.)	Share
Housewares	$ 2.40	3.4%
Infant products	2.38	3.4
Footwear	2.15	3.1
Other	3.41	4.9

Spanish/Spanish creole

French/French creole

German

Chinese

Italian

Tagalog

Polish

Source: *Nonfoods Merchandising*, June 1996, p. 21, from *The Licensing Letter*.

The table shows the millions of people 5 years or older who speak a language other than English at home.

Spanish/Spanish creole	17.35
French/French creole	1.93
German	1.54
Chinese	1.31
Italian	1.30
Tagalog	0.84
Polish	0.72

Source: *HR Magazine*, June 1996, p. 75, from United States Bureau of the Census.

Licensed Merchandise

Licensed Product Sales - 1995

Sales are shown in billions of dollars in the United States and Canada. "Other" includes music/video and electronics.

	($ bil.)	Share
Apparel	$ 11.03	15.8%
Toys/games	7.46	10.7
Gifts/novelties	6.74	9.6
Accessories	6.55	9.4
Food/beverage	5.78	8.3
Domestics	4.63	6.6
Publishing	4.35	6.2
Health & beauty	4.12	5.9
Stationery & paper	3.36	4.8
Video games & software	3.13	4.5
Sporting goods	2.46	3.5

Media

Largest Entertainment Firms

Firms are ranked by 1995 revenues in millions of dollars.

Walt Disney	$ 12,112
Viacom	11,780
Time Warner	8,067
Turner Broadcasting	3,437

Source: *Fortune*, April 29, 1996, p. F50.

Media

Top Media Firms

Firms are ranked by 1995 media revenues in millions of dollars.

Time Warner	$ 9,884.7
Disney Capital Cities/ABC	7,391.5
Tele-Communications Inc.	5,118.0
CBS (Westinghouse Co.)	4,318.2
Gannett Co.	3,998.7
NBC TV (General Electric Co.)	3,919.0
Advance Publications	3,217.0
News Corp.	2,945.0
Cox Enterprises	2,749.8
Hearst Corp.	2,513.0
New York Times Co.	2,409.4
Times Mirror Co.	2,307.1
Knight-Ridder	2,250.2
Viacom	2,136.1
Tribune Co.	2,022.0

Source: *Advertising Age*, August 19, 1996, p. S2.

★ 12 ★
Packaging

Egg Packaging by Type

The table shows the type of container used for gradeable nest run eggs for 1992 and 1994. Gradeable nest run eggs refers to eggs sold to be graded into loose eggs or cartons.

	1992	1994
Pallets	29.2%	58.7%
Cases	63.6	32.9
Racks	7.1	8.4

Source: *Egg Industry*, November 1995, p. 16, from Egg Clearinghouse Inc.

★ 13 ★
Packaging

Food/Beverage Closure Market

Data for 1995 are based on 64.5 billion units.

Soft drinks	28.0%
Beer	22.0
Food	22.0
Fun drinks	12.0
Milk	8.0
Wine & liquor	5.0
Water	3.0

Source: *Beverage World*, September 1995, p. 75.

★ 14 ★
Packaging

Sterile Packaging Demand

The market for sterile packaging is expected to increase from $1.75 billion to $2.84 billion in 2000.

	1994	2000
Thermoformed trays	53.1%	54.5%
Blister packs and clamshells	5.9	8.8
Sterile pouches	9.8	8.8
Sterilization wrap	8.1	6.2
Sterile bags	6.4	6.5
Plastic IV containers	6.5	5.8
Ampuls & vials	4.0	3.2
Other	6.2	6.2

Source: *Plastics News*, November 27, 1995, p. 3, from Freedonia Group Inc.

★ 15 ★
Pallets

Pallet Sales by Type

In 1995, U.S. companies purchased 500 million wooden pallets.

Wood	91.0%
Plastic	3.0
Wood composite	3.0
Cardboard/corrugated	1.0
Metal	1.0
Other	1.0

Source: *Modern Materials Handling*, February 1996, p. 12, from National Wooden Pallet and Container Association.

★ 16 ★
Patents

University Patent Income

Royalties are shown in millions of dollars.

U. of California System	$ 50.2
Stanford U.	37.7
Michigan State U	26.7
U of Washington/Washington Research Foundation	12.3
Iowa State U	9.6
Wisconsin Alumni Research Foundation	8.3
Florida State U	6.7
Harvard U	5.8
U of Florida	5.1

Source: *Chronicle of Higher Education*, January 26, 1996, p. A24, from Association of University Technology Managers Inc.

★ 17 ★
Plumbing Fixtures

Plumbing Fixture Shipments

Shares of manufacturer shipments are shown for the first nine months of 1995.

Fiberglass	33.1%
Vitreous china	30.4
Metal	19.5
Plastics	11.1
Other nonmetal	5.9

Source: *Contractor*, February 1996, p. 3, from United States Department of Commerce and Cahners Economics.

★ 18 ★
Private Label

Private Label Grocery Categories

The leading private label categories shown are based on volume of sales in millions of dollars.

Milk	$ 5,900.0
Fresh bread & rolls	1,800.0
Cheese	1,600.0
Fresh eggs	1,300.0
Ice cream	934.0
Carbonated beverages	825.0
Frozen plain vegetables	748.0
Sugar	640.0
Vegetables, shelf stable	610.0
Juices, shelf stable	563.0
Juices, refrigerated	545.0
Cold cereal	492.0
Frozen juices	464.0
Diapers	451.0
Fruit, shelf stable	444.0
Cookies	396.0
Deli luncheon meats	394.0
Food & trash bags	350.0
Chips & snacks	350.0
Pickles/relish/olives	298.0

Source: *Grocery Marketing*, November 1995, p. 12, from Information Resources Inc. and Private Label Manufacturers Association.

★ 19 ★
Promotional Products

Promotional Product Sales - 1994

Norwood Promotional Products Inc. is the leading producer of promotional products with a 3% share of the $7.0 billion market. The table shows the types of products distributed in 1994.

Wearables	22.5%
Writing instruments	12.3
Glassware/ceramics	9.7
Calendars	8.7
Desk/office/business accessories	8.5
Trophies, awards, jewelry	8.2
Buttons, badges, magnets, stickers, ribbons	5.7
Textiles	5.6
Other	18.8

Source: *Investor's Business Daily*, February 22, 1996, p. A6, from Promotional Products Association International.

★ 20 ★
R&D

Who Performs R&D

Data are for 1996. Total research & development expenditures is expected to reach $174 billion.

Industry	71.4%
Colleges/universities	15.8
Federal government	9.3
Other nonprofit	3.5

Source: *Water Environment & Technology*, February 1996, p. 13, from Battelle.

★ 21 ★

R&D

Who Provides R&D Funds

Data are for 1996.

Industry	60.2%
Federal government	34.7
Colleges & universities	3.2
Other nonprofit	1.9

Source: *American Ceramic Society Bulletin*, March 1996, p. 40, from Battelle.

★ 22 ★

Window Frames

Window Frame Market

Wood
Vinyl
Aluminum
Other

The market for residential windows is shown by framing material. Market is based on 44.9 million units.

Wood	59.3%
Vinyl	37.1
Aluminum	2.5
Other	1.1

Source: *Building Supply Business*, January 1996, p. 47, from National Wood Window and Door Association.

SIC 01 - Agricultural Production - Crops

★ 23 ★

Crops (SIC 0110)

U.S. Crop Plantings

Data are shown in millions of acres.

Corn	79.2
Wheat	70.3
Soybeans	61.7
Cotton	13.7
Sorghum	9.8
Sunflowers	3.6
Rice	3.4

Source: *Agricultural Outlook*, May 1996, p. 2, from United States Department of Agriculture.

★ 24 ★

Grain (SIC 0110)

Grain Production - North America

Data are in thousands of metric tons for 1992-94.

United States	245,500
Canada	22,300
Mexico	19,400

Source: *NAFTA. International Agriculture and Trade Reports*, May 1995, p. 23, from United States Department of Agriculture.

★ 25 ★

Grain (SIC 0111)

Grain Industry - Canada

The grain handling industry is shown by company.

Saskatchewan Wheat Pool	31.0%
Alberta Wheat	19.0
United Grain Growers	17.0
Pioneer Grain Co.	10.0
Cargill Canada	9.0
Manitoba Pool Elevators	7.0
Others	7.0

Source: *Globe & Mail's Report on Business*, December 1995, p. 83, from Canadian Grain Commission and 1994 annual reports.

★ 26 ★

Wheat (SIC 0111)

Wheat Production - North America

Data are in thousands of metric tons for 1992-94.

United States	65,100
Canada	26,800
Mexico	3,100

Source: *NAFTA. International Agriculture and Trade Reports*, May 1995, p. 23, from United States Department of Agriculture.

★ 27 ★

Corn (SIC 0115)

Seed Corn Market - North America

Shares are for 1994.

Pioneer Hi-Bred	44.9%
DEKALB Genetics	8.7
Northup-King (Sandoz)	4.1
Cargill	3.4
ICI	3.3
Mycogen(TM) brand seed corn	2.0
Other	33.6

Source: *Investext,* Thomson Financial Services, December 14, 1995, p. 3, from Pioneer Hi-Bred.

★ 28 ★

Oilseeds (SIC 0119)

Oilseed Production - North America

Data are in thousands of metric tons for 1992-94.

United States	59,100
Canada	7,500
Mexico	500

Source: *NAFTA. International Agriculture and Trade Reports*, May 1995, p. 23, from United States Department of Agriculture.

★ 29 ★

Cotton (SIC 0131)

Cotton Production

Production for 1995-96 is shown in thousands of bales.

Mid-South	5,935
Southwest	4,626
Southeast	3,880
West	3,169

Source: *Textile Asia*, March 1996, p. 139, from National Agricultural Statistics Service and United States Department of Agriculture.

★ 30 ★

Cotton (SIC 0131)

Cotton Seed Producers

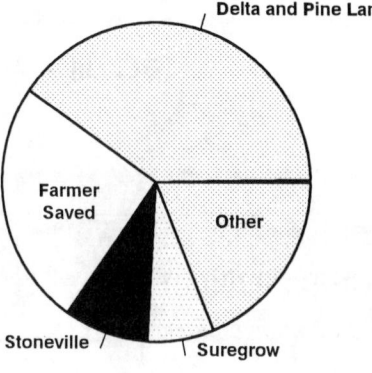

Shares are shown in percent.

Delta and Pine Land	40.0%
Farmer Saved	25.0
Stoneville	9.0
Suregrow	7.0
Other	19.0

Source: *Investor's Business Daily*, February 26, 1996, p. A4, from NatWest Securities Inc.

★ 31 ★

Tobacco (SIC 0132)

Tobacco Production by State

States are ranked by acreage devoted to tobacco.

North Carolina	283,900
Kentucky	268,140
Tennessee	75,621
Virginia	55,419
South Carolina	50,196
Georgia	40,403
Ohio	11,006
Indiana	9,170
Maryland	8,470
Pennsylvania	8,445

Source: *USA TODAY*, July 27, 1995, p. A10, from United States Department of Agriculture.

★ 32 ★

Sugarbeets (SIC 0133)

Sugarbeet Production

Production is shown in thousands of short tons in 1994.

	(000)	Share
Minnesota	8,652	27.3%
Idaho	5,226	16.5
North Dakota	4,222	13.3
California	4,089	12.9
Michigan	3,024	9.5
Nebraska	1,453	4.6
Montana	1,298	4.1
Wyoming	1,116	3.5
Colorado	942	3.0
Texas	564	1.8
Oregon	437	1.4
Ohio	248	0.8
Others	433	1.4

Source: *Sugar and Sweetener. U.S. Department of Agriculture*, December 1994, p. 14, from National Agricultural Statistics Service.

★ 33 ★

Sugarcane (SIC 0133)

Top Sugarcane Producing States

States are ranked by 1995 acreage devoted to sugarcane production. Figures are estimates based on the calender year except Hawaii.

	Acres	Share
Florida	427,000	47.0%
Louisiana	368,000	40.5
Hawaii	46,000	5.1
Texas	41,000	4.5
Puerto Rico	26,000	2.9

Source: *Agricultural Outlook*, March 1996, p. 17, from National Agricultural Statistics Service and Economic Research Service, United States Department of Agriculture.

★ 34 ★

Potatoes (SIC 0134)

Potato Production by State

Production is shown in thousands of Cwt (hundredweight) for 1994.

Idaho	134.340
Washington	88.920
North Dakota	28.200
Colorado	25.795
Oregon	25.784
Wisconsin	25.740
Minnesota	17.755
Missouri	12.150
New York	7.805
California	4.400
New England	3.888
Pennsylania	3.780
Montana	3.200

Source: *Potato Stocks. National Agricultural Statistics Service*, April 13, 1995, p. 3, from United States Department of Agriculture.

★ 35 ★

Vegetables (SIC 0161)

Cantaloupe Production by State

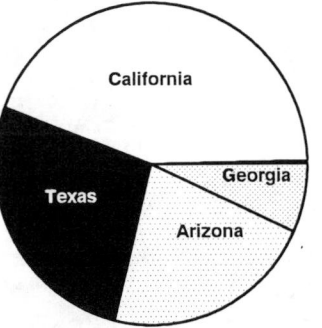

Distribution is shown based on 25,100 acres expected to be harvested in 1995.

California	43.7%
Texas	27.0
Arizona	21.9
Georgia	7.4

Source: *Vegetables*, April 1995, p. 4, from National Agricultural Statistics Service, U.S. Dept. of Agriculture.

★ 36 ★
Vegetables (SIC 0161)

Head Lettuce Production by State

Distribution is shown based on 39,850 acres expected to be harvested in 1995.

New Mexico 50.0%
California 45.8
Florida 1.6
New Jersey 1.1
Arizona and other 1.5

Source: *Vegetables*, April 1995, p. 4, from National Agricultural Statistics Service, U.S. Dept. of Agriculture.

★ 37 ★
Vegetables (SIC 0161)

North Carolina's Vegetable Production

Production is shown by acreage.

Sweet potatoes 38,682
Irish potatoes 18,775
Cucumbers & pickles 15,987
Watermelon 7,762
Cabbage 6,453
Sweet corn 5,689
Peppers 4,215
Snap beans 3,411
Squash 2,578
Tomatoes 1,357

Source: *American Vegetable Grower*, April 1996, p. 11, from United States Department of Agriculture.

★ 38 ★
Vegetables (SIC 0161)

Northern U.S. Vegetable Farms

This table shows the leading vegetable growers ranked by total acreage under cultivation in 1994. Shares of the group are shown based on 131,313 acres managed by the top 25 firms.

	Acres	% of Group
Hartung Brothers Inc.	23,034	17.5%
Crystal Fruit co.	8,950	6.8
A & W Farms	8,040	6.1
Paramount Farms Inc.	7,100	5.4
Heartland Farms Inc.	6,635	5.1

	Acres	% of Group
Charles H. West Farms Inc. . . .	6,473	4.9%
Okray Family Farms	5,444	4.1
Wysocki Farms Inc.	5,186	3.9
Borzynski Farms Inc.	5,000	3.8
Torrey Farms Inc.	4,567	3.5
Anthony Farms Inc.	4,450	3.4
Twin Garden Farms	4,437	3.4
Empire Farms Inc.	4,330	3.3
Dean Kincaid Inc.	3,810	2.9
MY-T Acres Inc.	3,740	2.8
Other	30,117	22.9

Source: *American Vegetable Grower*, October 1995, p. 12.

★ 39 ★
Vegetables (SIC 0161)

Tomato Production by State

Distribution is shown based on 31,850 acres expected to be harvested in 1995.

Florida 57.8%
California 17.6
South Carolina 11.0
Texas 10.4
Arizona 1.7
Alabama 1.6

Source: *Vegetables*, April 1995, p. 4, from National Agricultural Statistics Service, U.S. Dept. of Agriculture.

★ 40 ★
Vegetables (SIC 0161)

U.S. Vegetable Farms - Southeast

This table shows the leading vegetable growers ranked by total acreage under cultivation in 1994. Shares of the group are shown based on 191,572 acres managed by the top 25 firms.

	Acres	% of Group
A. Duda & Sons Inc.	30,000	15.7%
Dimare-Homestead	18,820	9.8
Pacific Tomato Growers/Triple E. Produce Corp.	15,600	8.1
Six L's Packing Co. Inc.	13,550	7.1
Hundley Farms Inc.	10,484	5.5
Thomas Produce Co.	10,365	5.4
Zellwin Farms Co.	8,569	4.5
Roger Harloff Farms	7,265	3.8
NTGargiulo, L.P.	7,000	3.7
Pero Family Farms Inc.	5,770	3.0
Mecca Farms Inc.	5,760	3.0
Long Farms Inc.	5,750	3.0
R.C. Hatton Inc.	5,700	3.0
DuBois Farms Inc.	5,186	2.7
Barnes Farming Corp.	4,800	2.5
Other	36,953	19.3

Source: *American Vegetable Grower*, October 1995, p. 12.

★ 41 ★
Vegetables (SIC 0161)

U.S. Vegetable Farms - Southwest

This table shows the leading vegetable growers ranked by total acreage under cultivation in 1994. Shares of the group are shown based on 113,720 acres managed by the top 25 firms.

	Acres	% of Group
Navajo Agricultural Products Industry	15,920	14.0%
Griffin and Brand Inc.	15,600	13.7
Martori Farms	8,000	7.0
Sharyland Plantation	6,800	6.0
Greer Farms	6,350	5.6
J.S. McManus Produce Co. Inc.	5,550	4.9
Rousseau Farming Co.	4,900	4.3
Pasquinelli Produce Co.	4,747	4.2
Holden Wallace Inc.	4,562	4.0

	Acres	% of Group
Starr Produce Co.	4,100	3.6%
Texas Hill Farms	3,695	3.2
Barkley Co.	3,500	3.1
Sakata Farms Inc.	3,300	2.9
Everkrisp Vegetables Inc.	3,300	2.9
Pecos Cantaloupe Co. Inc.	3,230	2.8
Other	20,166	17.7

Source: *American Vegetable Grower*, October 1995, p. 16.

★ 42 ★
Vegetables (SIC 0161)

U.S. Vegetable Shipments

Data are for 1994 in thousands of CWT (hundredweight).

Potatoes	170,446
Lettuce, iceberg	46,370
Onions, dry	39,404
Tomatoes	34,537
Watermelon	23,287
Carrots	16,127
Celery	14,795
Cantaloupe	12,292
Cabbage	10,637
Cucumbers	9,505
Broccoli	8,896
Peppers, bell	6,874
Corn, sweet	5,803
Cauliflower	5,075
Squash	4,566

Source: *Vegetables and Specialties. Situation and Outlook Yearbook*, July 1995, p. 17, from United States Department of Agriculture.

★ 43 ★
Vegetables (SIC 0161)

Watermelon Production by State

Florida
Texas
Arizona
California
Alabama

Distribution is shown based on 84,000 acres expected to be harvested in 1995.

Florida	42.9%
Texas	40.5
Arizona	8.3
California	5.8
Alabama	2.5

Source: *Vegetables*, April 1995, p. 4, from National Agricultural Statistics Service, U.S. Dept. of Agriculture.

★ 44 ★
Vegetables (SIC 0161)

Western U.S. Vegetable Farmers

This table shows the leading vegetable growers ranked by total acreage under cultivation in 1994. Shares of the group are shown based on 289,022 acres managed by the top 25 firms.

	Acres	% of Group
Tanimura and Antle	29,417	10.2%
D'Arrigo Bros. Co. of California Inc.	20,890	7.2
Bruce Church Inc.	20,330	7.0
Boskovich Farms, Inc.	16,050	5.6
Blain Larsen Farms	15,500	5.4
Mike Yurosek & Son L.P.	15,500	5.4
Grimmway Farms	15,040	5.2
Rio Farms	14,350	5.0
Sea Mist Farms/Boutonnet Farms	13,098	4.5
AgriNorthwest	13,000	4.5
Merrill Farms	12,898	4.5
Nunes Vegetables Inc.	12,800	4.4
P.J. Taggares Co.	11,565	4.0
Dresick Farms Inc.	10,300	3.6
Tom Bengard Ranch Inc.	8,145	2.8
Other	60,139	20.8

Source: *American Vegetable Grower*, October 1995, p. 18.

★ 45 ★
Fruit (SIC 0170)

Fruit Producers in the Columbia Basin

The table shows who is producing fruit in Washington's Columbia Basin.

	Acres	Share
Broetje Fruit Co.	4,000	30.5%
Evans Fruit Co.	1,500	11.5
AgriNorthwest	1,300	9.9
Borton Fruit	1,000	7.6
Chief Wenatchee	1,000	7.6
Stemlit Growers	1,000	7.6
Douglas Fruit Co.	800	6.1
Hanson Fruit Co.	750	5.7
Dovex Fruit	500	3.8
Monson Farms	450	3.4
Snake River Farms	300	2.3
Zerkle Fruit Co.	300	2.3
Larson Fruit	200	1.5

Source: *Fruit Grower*, April 1996, p. 39.

★ 46 ★
Berries (SIC 0171)

Blueberry Harvest - Canada

Production of lowbush berries is shown in tons.

Nova Scotia	13,460
Quebec	7,200
New Brunswick	4,700
Prince Edward Island	900
Newfoundland	500

Source: *Canadian Geographic*, January/February 1995, p. 42.

★ 47 ★
Berries (SIC 0171)

Strawberry Farms - Tampa Bay Area

Firms are ranked by number of planted acres.

Astin Farms	145
G&D Farms	140
Wilson & Son Sales	95
Parkesdale Farms	86
Hinton Farms Produce Inc.	80
McDonald Farms	80
Favorite Farms	79

Continued on next page.

★ 47 ★ *Continued*
Berries (SIC 0171)

Strawberry Farms - Tampa Bay Area

Firms are ranked by number of planted acres.

Three Star Farms	78
Fancy Farms	75
Strawberry Station	74

Source: *Tampa Bay Business Journal*, February 9, 1996, p. 21.

★ 48 ★
Berries (SIC 0171)

Top Berry Growers

Growers are ranked by acreage devoted to berry crops.

Cherryfield Foods Inc.	8,022
Jasper Wyman & Son	7,009
Northland Cranberries Inc.	2,265
A.D. Makepeace Co.	1,475
Atlantic Blueberry Co.	1,320
Gargiulo	1,300
Haines & Haines	1,156
Reiter Affiliated Cos.	820
Beaton Cranberries Inc.	814
Adkin Blue Ribbon Pkg. Co.	790
A.R. Demarco Enterprises Inc.	725
Sandy Farms Inc.	635
Habelman Brothers Co.	566
Variety Farms Inc.	556
Reenders Blueberries Farms	530
Edgewood Trust	519
All Natural Farms Inc.	510
Bertino Brothers	510
Fuji Farms	480
Joseph J. White Co.	335

Source: *Fruit Grower*, August 1995, p. 12.

★ 49 ★
Grapes (SIC 0172)

California Grape Production

Thompson	36.7%
Flame	23.9
Rudy/red	9.8
Redglobe	8.4
Perlette	5.4
Emperor	4.3
Chris Rose	1.9
Ribier	1.8
Other color	6.0
Other white	1.7

Source: *World Horticultural Trade & U.S. Export Opportunities*, 1994, p. 22, from United States Department of Agriculture.

★ 50 ★
Grapes (SIC 0172)

Grape Planting in California

Data are for 1995.

	Acres	Share
Raisin	277,516	39.0%
Wine grapes, red	176,518	24.8
Wine grapes, white	171,843	24.2
Table	85,650	12.0

Source: *Wines & Vines*, June 1996, p. 15, from California Agricultural Statistics Service.

★ 51 ★
Grapes (SIC 0172)

Top Grape Producers

The top growers are ranked by acreage devoted to grapes in 1995.

Delicato Vineyards	12,520
Simpson Farm Co.	12,004
Giumarra Vineyards Corp.	10,000
Dole Food Co.	8,000
Golden State Vintners	7,800
Sun World International	7,500
Wine World Estates	6,663
E&J Gallo Winery	6,200
Met West Agribusiness	5,400
Vino Farms Inc.	4,800
Royal Madera Vineyards	4,300
The McCarty Co.	4,200
Frank A. Logolusco Farms Inc.	4,100
Sutter Home Winery	4,052
Pandol & Sons	3,773
Stimson Lane Vineyards & Estates	3,360
Scheid Vineyards & Management Co.	3,200
J&L Farms	3,100
Gerewan Farming	3,040
Tejon Ranch Co.	1,449

Source: *Fruit Grower*, August 1995, p. 13.

★ 52 ★
Nuts (SIC 0173)

Top Nut Producers

The top growers are ranked by acreage devoted to nuts.

Paramount Farming Co.	34,360
Diamond Agraindustries	8,619
Dole Food Co.	8,200
Farmland Management Services	7,375
Farmers Investment Co.	6,787
Ka'u Agribusiness Co. Inc.	6,320
Lassen Land Co.	5,610
Braden Farms Inc.	4,954
Big Valley	4,265
MacFarms of Hawaii, Inc.	3,800
Montpelier Orchard Management	3,760
Stahmann Farms Inc.	3,750
Nuts Unlimited Inc.	3,295
Blackwell Land Co.	2,547
Horstville Ranch	2,438
Belridge Farms	2,441

Met West Agribusiness	2,300
Tejon Ranch Co.	2,223
Mockingbird Hill Farms	2,100
Wetherbee Farms	2,034

Source: *Fruit Grower*, August 1995, p. 12.

★ 53 ★
Fruit (SIC 0174)

Top Citrus Growers

Growers are ranked by acreage devoted to citrus products.

Ben Hill Griffin	30,000
Evans Properties Inc.	30,000
Turner Foods Corp.	25,063
Jack M. Berry Inc.	20,000
Lykes Citrus Management	20,000
U.S. Sugar Corp.	18,843
VIA Tropical Fruits	16,480
A. Duda & Sons Inc.	16,405
Orange-Co. of Florida	16,391
Becker Holding Corp.	15,015
Crittenden Fruit Co. Inc.	14,000
Running W. Citrus	14,000
Sun Ag Inc.	14,000
Gracewood Inc.	11,854
Barron Collier Co./Silver Strand	10,423

Source: *Fruit Grower*, August 1995, p. 13.

★ 54 ★
Fruit (SIC 0175)

Apple Production by State

Washington

Michigan

New York

California

Pennsylvania

Virginia

North Carolina

West Virginia

Oregon

Ohio

Other

Distribution is shown based on 266.321 million units produced in 1995.

Washington	46.5%
Michigan	10.8
New York	10.1
California	8.9
Pennsylvania	4.7
Virginia	3.6
North Carolina	2.1
West Virginia	1.7
Oregon	1.3
Ohio	1.0
Other	9.3

Source: *Fruit Grower*, September 1995, p. 8, from United States Department of Agriculture.

★ 55 ★
Fruit (SIC 0175)

Peach Production by State

The value of production is shown for 1994 in millions of dollars.

California	$ 67.68
Georgia	32.24
South Carolina	27.57
New Jersey	22.68
Washington	8.95
Michigan	1.80

Source: *Fruit Grower*, April 1996, p. 14, from Noncitrus Fruits Summary.

★ 56 ★
Fruit (SIC 0175)

Top Stone Fruit Growers

The top growers are ranked by acreage. The fruit crops grown include nectarines, grapes, apples, cherries, and peaches.

Gerawan Farming	4,600
Lane Packing Co.	4,000
Taylor Orchard	3,510
Evans Farm	3,200
California Prune Packing	3,162
J.W. Yonce & Sons Farms Inc.	2,675
Fowler Packing Co.	2,660
Ito Packing Co.	2,163
Miami Valley Fruit Farm Inc.	2,075
R.W. Dubose & Sons Inc.	2,000
Big Six Farm	1,994
J.R. Wood Inc.	1,997
Sun World International	1,800
Valley View Packing Co.	1,800
Chappel Farms Inc.	1,800

Source: *Fruit Grower*, August 1995, p. 11.

★ 57 ★
Floriculture (SIC 0181)

Green Goods Sales

Shares are shown based on $44.6 billion in retail sales in 1994.

Nursery crops & turfgrass	59.0%
Cut flowers & greens	15.6
Bedding plants	10.7
Potted flowering plants	8.0
Foliage plants	6.7
Other	10.0

Source: *Agricultural Outlook*, September 1995, p. 30.

★ 58 ★

Floriculture (SIC 0181)

Nursery Sales in Georgia

Illinois		9.492
Massachusetts		8.368
Alabama		8.270
Wisconsin		8.224

Source: *Floriculture Crops*, April 1995, p. 8, from Agricultural Statistics Board, United States Department of Agriculture.

Data are for 1993.

	($ mil.)	Share
Greenhouse-grown stock	$ 65.0	38.7%
Container plants	58.0	34.5
Sod and/or sprigs	27.4	16.3
B&B stock	11.0	6.5
Bare-root stock	4.9	2.9
Other plant material	1.7	1.0

Source: *American Nurseryman*, October 15, 1995, p. 10, from *Georgia Green Industry Association Journal*.

★ 59 ★

Greenhouses (SIC 0181)

Greenhouse Cover by State

Total greenhouse cover is shown in thousands of square feet for 1994.

California	115.800
Florida	51.386
Michigan	29.750
Ohio	26.372
Texas	24.273
New York	19.731
Pennsylvania	18.762
New Jersey	12.192
North Carolina	11.193
Oregon	11.111
Colorado	10.410

SIC 02 - Agricultural Production - Livestock

★ 60 ★

Livestock (SIC 0210)

Livestock Production - Mexico

Production is shown in thousands of tons.

	1992	1993
Cattle	2,335	2,362
Poultry	1,088	1,299
Pork	1,130	1,103
Goats	93	85
Sheep	68	62

Source: *National Trade Data Bank*, March 2, 1996, p. IS9411.037.

★ 61 ★

Livestock (SIC 0210)

U.S. Cattle Imports

	1995	1996
Slaughter cattle		
Canada	131,413	187,820
Mexico	4,886	456
Feeder cattle		
Mexico	306,617	92,610
Canada	7,182	78,456

Source: *Farm Journal*, May/June 1996, p. 33, from United States Department of Agriculture and Animal and Plant Health Inspection Service.

★ 62 ★

Cattle (SIC 0212)

Leading Cattle Producers

Market shares for feed cattle production are shown in percent for 1995.

IBP	35.0%
ConAgra	21.0
Cargill	20.0
Other	24.0

Source: *Investext*, Thomson Financial Services, April 8, 1996, p. 64.

★ 63 ★

Hogs (SIC 0213)

Leading Pork Producers

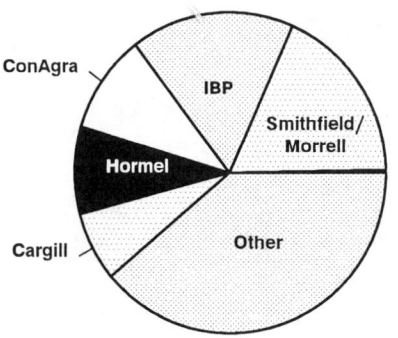

Data are for 1995.

Smithfield/Morrell	18.0%
IBP	17.0
ConAgra	10.0
Hormel	9.0
Cargill	7.0
Other	39.0

Source: *Investext*, Thomson Financial Services, April 8, 1996, p. 64.

★ 64 ★

Hogs (SIC 0213)

U.S. Pork Producers

Firms are ranked by total sows in production as of August 1, 1995. Data refer to companies with more than 10,000 heads.

Murphy Family Farms	227,500
Carrol's Foods	110,000
Tyson Foods	107,000
Premium Standard Farms	96,800
Prestage Farms	96,000
Smithfield Farms	95,000
Cargill	80,000
DeKalb Swine Breeders	72,000
Goldsboro Milling Co.	52,000
Seabeard Corporation	50,000
Iowa Select Farms	42,000
Continental Grain Co.	35,000
National Farms	34,000
Sand Systems	27,000
Louis Dreyfus Corp.	20,000
Heartland Pork Enterprises	18,000
Clougherty Packing Co.	17,600
PIC, USA	17,000
Gold Kist	16,500
Farmland Industries	16,000

Source: *Successful Farming*, October 1995, p. 21.

★ 65 ★

Goats (SIC 0214)

Dairy Goats by State

States are ranked by dairy goat population. The United States had 124,718 dairy goats in 1993.

California	16,593
Texas	11,727
Wisconsin	7,677
New York	5,746
Ohio	4,953
Missouri	4,406
Michigan	4,184
Oregon	4,133
Washington	3,731
Oklahoma	3,393
Indiana	3,247
Tennessee	3,154
Pennsylvania	2,956
Iowa	2,955
Illinois	2,905

Virginia	2,863
Colorado	2,827
Minnesota	2,718
Maryland	2,389
Arkansas	2,273

Source: *Dairy Goat Journal*, March 1996, p. 28.

★ 66 ★

Dairy Farms (SIC 0241)

Dairy Goat Farms by State

There were 11,559 dairy goat farms in the United States in 1993.

Texas	902
California	694
Ohio	634
Missouri	506
Pennsylvania	496
Indiana	435
New York	426
Oregon	413
Michigan	404
Oklahoma	401

Source: *Dairy Goat Journal*, March 1996, p. 28.

★ 67 ★

Dairy Farms (SIC 0241)

Milk Cows by State

Population is shown by state in thousands of heads for December 1995.

Wisconsin	1,478
California	1,259
New York	702
Pennsylvania	647

Continued on next page.

★ 67 ★ *Continued*
Dairy Farms (SIC 0241)

Milk Cows by State

Population is shown by state in thousands of heads for December 1995.

Minnesota	600
Texas	400
Michigan	326
Ohio	287
Washington	264
Iowa	260

Source: *Dairy Herd Management*, February 1996, p. 58, from United States Department of Agriculture.

★ 68 ★
Poultry (SIC 0251)

Largest Poultry Producers

Companies are ranked by average weekly ready-to-cook production in millions of pounds.

Tyson Foods Inc.	117.20
Gold Kist Inc.	46.17
Perdue Farms Inc.	44.95
ConAgra Poultry Company	38.27
Pilgrim's Pride Corporation	28.00
Wayne Poultry Div./Continental Grain	21.52
Hudson Foods Inc.	19.70
Seaboard Farms Inc.	14.30
Gagle's Inc.	14.09
Townsends Inc.	12.64
Foster Farms	12.53
Fieldale Farms	12.00
Wampler-Longacre Inc./Chicken Div.	11.00
Sanderson Farms Inc.	10.98
Allen Family Foods Inc.	10.43

Source: *Broiler Industry*, January 1996, p. A26.

★ 69 ★
Poultry (SIC 0251)

Leading Broiler Producers

Data are for 1995.

Tyson	25.0%
Gold Kist	10.0
Perdue	10.0
ConAgra	8.0
Pilgrim's Pride	6.0
Cont. Grain	5.0
Hudson Foods	4.0
Other	33.0

Source: *Investext,* Thomson Financial Services, April 8, 1996, p. 64.

★ 70 ★
Poultry (SIC 0251)

Poultry Production - North America

Data are in thousands of metric tons for 1992-94.

United States	11,500
Mexico	1,100
Canada	800

Source: *NAFTA. International Agriculture and Trade Reports*, May 1995, p. 23, from United States Department of Agriculture.

★ 71 ★
Eggs (SIC 0252)

Top Egg Producers

Companies are ranked by millions of layers as of December 31, 1995. The top 53 companies had 168.2 million layers in 1995.

	(mil.)	Share
Cal-Maine Foods Inc.	15.6	9.6%
Michael Foods Inc.	14.8	9.1

Continued on next page.

★ 71 ★ *Continued*
Eggs (SIC 0252)

Top Egg Producers

Companies are ranked by millions of layers as of December 31, 1995. The top 53 companies had 168.2 million layers in 1995.

	(mil.)	Share
Rose Acre Farms Inc.	12.6	7.7%
DeCoster Egg Farms Inc.	9.0	5.5
Fort Recovery Equity	6.8	4.2
ISE America	6.0	3.7
Agri-General Corp.	5.6	3.4
Papetti Hygrade Eggs	5.1	3.1
Mahard Egg Farms	4.2	2.6
Midwest Poultry Services Inc.	4.1	2.5
Wabash Valley Produce/Brown Produce	4.1	2.5
Hillandale Farms	4.0	2.4
National Food Corp.	3.5	2.1
Smith Farms Inc.	3.3	2.0
Sparboe Companies	2.9	1.8
McAnally Enterprises Inc.	2.8	1.7
Cypress Foods Inc.	2.7	1.7
Gemperle Enterprises Inc.	2.7	1.7
Kofkoff Egg Farms	2.5	1.5
Valley Fresh Foods	2.5	1.5
Vaughan Bros.	2.5	1.5
Boomsma	2.4	1.5
Demler Egg Ranches	2.4	1.5
Sunbest Foods	2.4	1.5
Pilgrim's Pride Corp.	2.1	1.3
Tampa Farm Service Inc.	2.1	1.3
Other	34.6	21.2

Source: *Egg Industry*, January 1996, p. 7.

★ 72 ★

Turkeys (SIC 0253)

Leading Turkey Producers

Data are for 1995.

ConAgra	18.0%
WRL	14.0
Hormel	11.0
Rocco	10.0
Cargill	9.0%
Carolina	9.0
Sara Lee	8.0
Other	21.0

Source: *Investext,* Thomson Financial Services, April 8, 1996, p. 64.

★ 73 ★

Turkeys (SIC 0253)

Turkey Production by State

| North Carolina |
| Minnesota |
| Arkansas |
| Virginia |
| California |
| Other |

Production is shown in millions of turkeys. A total of 295.9 million turkeys was produced in 1995.

	(mil.)	Share
North Carolina	63.0	21.3%
Minnesota	41.0	13.9
Arkansas	25.0	8.4
Virginia	24.0	8.1
California	22.0	7.4
Other	120.9	40.9

Source: *USA TODAY*, November 9, 1995, p. A4, from National Turkey Federation.

★ 74 ★

Horses (SIC 0272)

Horse Population by Province - Canada

Ontario	340,000
Alberta	150,000
British Columbia	114,000
Quebec	60,000
Saskatchewan	45,000
Nova Scotia	21,000
Manitoba	15,000
New Brunswick	12,000
Prince Edward Island	7,000

Source: *National Trade Data Bank*, September 1, 1995, p. 111096781, from *Saddle and Harnesses Market in Canada Report*.

★75★

Pets (SIC 0279)

Dog Registrations - 1994

Labrador retriever	126,393
Rottweiler	102,596
German shepard	78,999
Golden retriever	64,322
Poodle	61,775
Cocker spaniel	60,888
Beagle	59,215
Dachschund	46,129
Dalmatian	39,497
Pomeranian	39,947
Yorkshire terrier	38,628
Shik Tzu	37,017
Shetland sheepdog	36,853
Miniature schnauzer	33,344
Chihuahau	32,705
Boxer	30,629
Chow chow	25,415
Siberian husky	24,804
Doberman pinscher	19,822
Basset hound	18,043

Source: *USA TODAY*, August 24, 1995, p. A2, from American Kennel Club.

★76★

Pets (SIC 0279)

Our Favorite Pets

Percentage of households with each pet.

Dogs	36.0%
Cats	30.0
Fresh water fish	10.0
Birds	6.0
Small animals	5.0
Reptiles	3.0
Marine fish	1.0

Source: *Supermarket Business*, June 1996, p. 77, from APPMA Pet Ownership Study, 1995.

★77★

Farms (SIC 0291)

Farms by State

There were 2,073,320 farms in the United States as of July 1995.

Texas	202,000
Montana	106,000
Iowa	100,000
Kentucky	89,000
Minnesota	87,000
Tennessee	82,000
California	80,000
Wisconsin	80,000
Illinois	77,000
Ohio	74,000
Oklahoma	71,000

Source: *Farms and Land in Farms*, July 1995, p. 4, from United States Department of Agriculture.

★78★

Farms (SIC 0291)

Farms by Type - Canada

The table shows the types of farms in Canada.

	No.	Share
Cattle	66,282	26.3%
Small grains	47,460	18.8
Wheat	42,988	17.0
Dairy	28,910	11.5
Pigs	10,461	4.1
Fruits	6,525	2.6
Poultry	4,211	1.7
Vegetables	3,505	1.4
Other specialty	22,933	9.1

Continued on next page.

★ 78 ★ *Continued*

Farms (SIC 0291)

Farms by Type - Canada

The table shows the types of farms in Canada.

	No.	Share
Other field crops	11,861	4.7%
Livestock combination	7,034	2.8

Source: *Forces*, no. 110, 1995, p. 63, from Statistics Canada.

SIC 07 - Agricultural Services

★ 79 ★

Farm Management (SIC 0762)

Farm Management Companies

The top 15 companies are ranked by total acreage managed. Locations are shown in parentheses.

Nations Bank (TX)	2,040,000
Farmers National Co. (NE)	1,244,031
Texas Pacific Land Trust (TX) . . .	1,110,000
InterWest Ranch & Farm Mgmt. Inc. (OR)	1,005,122
Norwest Bank NE (NE)	1,003,837
Bank One Texas N.A., Trust Dept. (TX)	900,000
Boatman's Trust Co. (MO)	699,860
AmSouth Bank of Alabama (AL) . . .	612,938
Capital Agricultural Property Services Inc. (IL)	601,889
First Bank Trust Farm Division (ND) . .	450,000
Hall and Hall Incorporated (MT) . . .	276,911
First of America Agricultural Services (IL)	264,050
Hertz Farm Management Co. (IA) . . .	240,680
Southern Plantations Group Inc. (GA) .	240,000
First Trust Company of North Dakota (ND)	225,000

Source: *Agri Finance*, November 1995, p. 44.

★ 80 ★

Landscape Services (SIC 0783)

Landscaping Tree Shipments

Shipments are shown by type in thousands of units.

	1995	1996
Evergreen trees	51,868	60,280
Shade trees	37,477	46,595
Flowering trees	26,963	32,960
Fruit/nut trees	11,162	13,016

Source: *Grounds Maintenance*, November 1995, p. 10, from *U.S. Landscape Tree Planting Survey, 1994-95*.

SIC 08 - Forestry

★ 81 ★

Timber (SIC 0811)

Midwest Forests

Data show that forests comprise an estimated 33% of land area in the United States. The table shows the states in the Midwest with the greatest amount of forests. Figures include, in thousands of acres, the total land area and the percent of forested acres.

	Area	Forest
Michigan	36,358	50.0%
Wisconsin	34,761	45.0
Minnesota	50,955	33.0

Source: *Chicago Tribune*, June 16, 1996, p. C1, from United States Forest Service.

★ 82 ★

Timber (SIC 0811)

Top Timber Companies

International Paper

Georgia-Pacific

Weyerhaeuser

Champion International

Boise Cascade

Plum Creek Timber

Temple-Inland

Willamette Industries

Potlatch

Firms are ranked by holdings in millions of forest acreage.

International Paper	6.4
Georgia-Pacific	5.7
Weyerhaeuser	5.5
Champion International	5.3
Boise Cascade	3.1
Plum Creek Timber	2.6
Temple-Inland	1.9
Willamette Industries	1.8
Potlatch	1.5

Source: *Wall Street Journal*, August 8, 1996, p. A3.

★ 83 ★

Timber (SIC 0811)

Who Plants America's Trees

Data show who planted 2.5 million acres.

Individuals	42.3%
Forest industry	39.1
Government	14.6
Other	4.0

Source: *Builder*, August 1996, pp. S-49, from Tree Planting in the United States and United States Forest Service.

SIC 09 - Fishing, Hunting, and Trapping

★ 84 ★

Fishing (SIC 0910)

Top Cities - Fresh Water Fishing

Data show the percentage of population that fishes.

Detroit	18.7%
Chicago	18.6
Atlanta	15.4
Houston	14.6
Riverside/Bernadino	13.4

Source: *Lakeland Boating*, July 1996, p. 18, from National Sporting Goods Association.

★ 85 ★

Fishing (SIC 0910)

Top Cities - Salt Water Fishing

| Houston |
| Philadelphia |
| Los Angeles/Long Beach |
| Washington D.C. |
| Boston |

Data show the percentage of population that fishes.

Houston	15.4%
Philadelphia	11.3
Los Angeles/Long Beach	5.3
Washington D.C.	4.7
Boston	4.6

Source: *Motor Boating and Sailing*, June 1996, p. 34, from National Sporting Goods Association.

★ 86 ★

Finfish (SIC 0912)

Finfish Production - Canada

Aquaculture production is shown in tons.

Salmon	33,325
Trout	5,892
Steelhead	96
Char	71

Source: *National Trade Data Bank*, May 27, 1996, p. IM960509.032, from Canadian Aquaculture Alliance.

★ 87 ★

Shellfish (SIC 0913)

Shellfish Production - Canada

Aquaculture production is shown in tons.

Oysters	7,787
Mussels	6,898
Clams	397
Scallops	40

Source: *National Trade Data Bank*, May 27, 1996, p. IM960509.032, from Canadian Aquaculture Alliance.

★ 88 ★

Fish Hatcheries (SIC 0921)

Fish Hatching in Illinois

The table shows the types of fish harvested in 1995. Data are in thousands of fish.

Walleyes	61,000.0
Saugers	1,500.0
Largemouth bass	757.2
Bluegills	715.2
Channel catfish	408.0
Chinook salmon	362.7
Coho salmon	308.2
White crappies	302.6

Source: *Field & Stream*, April 1996, p. 76.

SIC 10 - Metal Mining

★ 89 ★
Mining (SIC 1000)

Mining Companies - Denver Area

Firms are ranked by number of employees.

Newmont Mining\Gold Cos.	220
Cyprus Amax Minerals Co.	175
Echo Bay Mines Ltd.	150
Arco Coal Co.	101
Pittsburgh & Midway Coal Mining Co.	78
Cotter Corp.	42
Independence Mining Co. Inc.	34
ASARCO Inc.	33
USMX, Inc.	22
Canyon Resources Corp.	17

Source: *Denver Business Journal*, April 4, 1996, p. 29A.

★ 90 ★
Mining (SIC 1000)

Top Canadian Mining Companies

Companies are ranked by revenues as of December 31, 1994. Alcan Aluminum, Inco Ltd., Placer Dome Inc, and Barrick Gold Corp.'s figures are in U.S. dollars.

Alcan Aluminum	$ 8,325,000
Noranda Mining & Metals Group	4,602,000
Inco Ltd.	2,205,200
Dofasco	2,261,700
Falconbridge Ltd.	1,960,335
Suncor Inc.	1,637,000
Syncrude Canada Ltd.	1,519,000
Placer Dome Inc.	966,000
Barrick Gold Corp.	954,000
Rio Algon Ltd.	1,212,087
Cominco Ltd.	1,138,569

Algoma Steel	$ 1,090,900
Inmetal Mining Corp.	929,745
Fording Coal	639,516
Potash Corp. of Saskatchewan	613,560

Source: *Canadian Mining Journal*, August 1995, p. 8.

★ 91 ★
Iron (SIC 1011)

Iron Ore Production in Canada

Production is shown in thousands of metric tons in 1994.

QCM (Quebec)	16,351.3
IOC (Newfoundland)	15,902.2
Wabush Mines (Newfoundland)	5,064.1
Algoma Ore (Ontario)	674.1

Source: *Skillings Mining Review*, April 6, 1996, p. 4.

★ 92 ★
Copper (SIC 1021)

Copper Producers - Mexico

Percentage of total output in shown by company.

Mexicana de Cobre	53.0%
Mexicana de Canenca	29.0
Other	18.0

Source: *Mineral Industries of Latin America and Canada*, 1993, p. 195.

★ 93 ★

Copper (SIC 1021)

Largest U.S. Copper Producers

Production is shown in thousands of metric tons.

Phelps Dodge	480.2
Kennecott	335.5
Cyprus Amax	293.9
Magma Copper	270.2

Source: *New York Times*, June 15, 1996, p. 16, from Copper Development Association and American Bureau of Metal Statistics.

★ 94 ★

Lead (SIC 1031)

Lead Production - Mexico

Shares are shown based on total output.

Penoles	34.2%
MEDIMSA Inc.	28.4
Frisco	23.7
Other	13.7

Source: *Mineral Industries of Latin America and Canada*, 1993, p. 196.

★ 95 ★

Zinc (SIC 1031)

Zinc Mining - North America

Mine production is shown in metric tons.

	1993	1994	1995
Canada	1,004	1,008	1,130
Mexico	359	382	378
United States	119	101	96

Source: *Engineering & Mining Journal*, March 1996, p. 32, from International Lead & Zinc Study Group, *Metals Week*, and Cominco.

★ 96 ★

Zinc (SIC 1031)

Zinc Production - Mexico

MEDIMSA Inc.	51.5%
Penoles	28.7
Frisco	14.3
Other	5.5

Source: *Mineral Industries of Latin America and Canada*, 1993, p. 196.

★ 97 ★

Gold (SIC 1041)

Gold Production by State

Data are in kilograms for 1995.

	Kg.	Share
Nevada	221,000	70.8%
California	20,300	6.5
Montana	13,800	4.4
Idaho	2,940	0.9
Arizona	2,810	0.9
Other	51,500	16.5

Source: *American Metal Market*, July 25, 1996, p. 4, from United States Bureau of Mines.

★ 98 ★
Gold (SIC 1041)

Gold Production by State - Mexico

Mine production reached 9,792 kilograms in 1993.

Durango 29.0%
Guanajuato 26.0
Sonora 18.0
Sinaloa 6.0
Chihuahua 5.0
Zacatecas 4.0
Other 12.0

Source: *Mineral Industries of Latin America and Canada*, 1993, p. 196.

★ 99 ★
Gold (SIC 1041)

Top Gold Producers - Canada

Firms are ranked by revenues in millions of dollars.

Barrick Gold . . . . $ 1,307.2
Placer Domes Inc. 1,098.0
Teck Corp. 714.2
Placer Dome Canada 466.0
Echo Bay Mines 375.9
Homestake Canada 366.4
Pegasus Gold 259.1
Cambior Inc. 347.8
TVX Gold 175.5

Source: *Globe and Mail's Report on Business*, July 1996, p. 160.

★ 100 ★
Silver (SIC 1044)

Silver Production by State - Mexico

Mine production reached 2.136 million kilograms in 1993. The leading producer was Penoles with 796,437 kilograms.

Zacatecas 39.0%
Durango 16.4
Chihuahua 15.8
Guanajuanto 7.3
Sonora 4.6
Hidalgo 4.2
Other 12.7

Source: *Mineral Industries of Latin America and Canada*, 1993, p. 197.

★ 101 ★
Silver (SIC 1044)

Top Silver Firms - Canada

Production is shown in millions of ounces.

Noranda 15.7
Echo Bay 11.9
Prime Resources 10.0

Source: *Globe and Mail*, May 16, 1996, p. B10, from *World Silver Survey, 1994*.

★ 102 ★
Silver (SIC 1044)

Top Silver Firms - Mexico

Production is shown in millions of ounces.

	1994	1995
Penoles	27.0	29.7
Frisco	10.0	11.0
IMMSA	10.7	10.8

Source: *Globe and Mail*, May 16, 1996, p. B10, from *World Silver Survey, 1994*.

★ 103 ★
Molybdenum (SIC 1061)

Molybdenum Consumption

Data are for 1993.

	Kg.	Share
Steel	90,159	50.6%
Chemical/ceramic uses	21,437	12.0
Mill products made from metal powder	17,604	9.9
Superalloys	8,885	5.0
Cast irons	8,367	4.7
Alloys	1,556	0.9
Other	30,147	16.9

Source: *Molybdenum. U.S. Dept. of the Interior*, 1993, p. 9, from United States Bureau of the Census.

★ 104 ★

Uranium (SIC 1094)

Uranium Production Centers - 1995

White Mesa

Highland

Crow Butte

Uncle Sam

Rosita

El Mesquite

Irigaray/Christensen

Donaldsonville

Ambrosia Lake

Centers are ranked by production in estimated millions of pounds. Principal owners are in parentheses.

	(mil.)	Share
White Mesa (Energy Fuels) . . .	2.00	32.3%
Highland (Nuclear Electric) . . .	0.81	13.1
Crow Butte (Uranerz)	0.76	12.3
Uncle Sam (IMC-Agrico) . . .	0.63	10.2
Rosita (U.R.I.)	0.50	8.1
El Mesquite (COGEMA) . . .	0.49	7.9
Irigaray/Christensen (COGEMA)	0.45	7.3
Donaldsonville (Louisiana)	0.40	6.5
Ambrosia Lake (Rio Algom) . . .	0.15	2.4

Source: *Engineering & Mining Journal*, March 1996, p. 30.

★ 105 ★

Vanadium (SIC 1094)

U.S. Vanadium Consumption

Consumption is shown for the first seven months of 1995.

Carbon	36.1%
High-strength low-alloy	26.0
Full alloy	19.6
Steel, tool	8.8
Steel, stainless and heat resisting	0.7
Superalloys	0.4
Other	8.4

Source: *Vanadium. Mineral Industry Surveys*, July 1995, p. 2, from United States Bureau of Mines.

★ 106 ★

Mercury (SIC 1099)

How We Use Mercury

Consumption is shown in metric tons for 1994.

Chemical and allied products	
Mercury cell chloralkali process	139
Laboratory uses	24
Other chemical uses	24
Electrical and electronics	
Wiring devices and switches	77
Electric lights	29
Batteries	6
Instruments and related products	
Measuring/control instruments	53
Dental	22
Other	481

Source: *Environmental Progress*, November 1995, p. 233, from Bureau of Mines.

★ 107 ★

Platinum (SIC 1099)

Platinum Metal Consumption

Consumption is shown for the third quarter of 1994.

Automotive	58.3%
Electrical	21.2
Dental/medical	12.1
Jewelry/decorative	3.8
Other	4.6

Source: *Platinum Group Metals. Mineral Industry Surveys*, July 1995, p. 4, from United States Bureau of Mines.

SIC 12 - Coal Mining

★ 108 ★

Coal (SIC 1220)

Coal Consumption - 1996

Domestic coal consumption is shown for 1996 in millions of tons.

Electric utilities 839.0
Nonutility (except cogen) 80.0
Coking coal 31.0
Industrial & retail 14.0

Source: *Mining Engineering*, April 1996, p. 11, from National Mining Association.

★ 109 ★

Coal (SIC 1220)

Coal Production - 1993

Production is shown by coalbed in millions of short tons. Coalbeds shown represent 46.8% of U.S. production.

Wyodak 185.7
Pittsburgh 49.5
No. 9 . . . . 34.8
Hazard No. 5-A 32.4
No. 6 . . . . 30.7
Beulah-Zap 27.7
Hazard No. 4 . . . . 24.5
Lower Kittanning 22.6
Lower Elkhorn 18.0
Rosebud 16.2

Source: *Coal Data: A Reference*, February 1995, p. 8, from Energy Information Administration and *Coal Industry Annual, 1993*.

★ 110 ★

Coal (SIC 1220)

Top Coal Producing States

| Wyoming |
| West Virginia |
| Kentucky |

Data are in millions of tons.

	1993	1994	1995
Wyoming	210.1	231.3	263.7
West Virginia	130.5	156.8	162.9
Kentucky	156.3	158.9	150.6

Source: *Public Utilities Fortnightly*, April 1, 1996, p. 35, from U.S. Energy Information Administration.

★ 111 ★

Coal (SIC 1220)

Top U.S. Coal Producers

Production is shown in millions of short tons.

	Prod.	Share
Peabody Holding Co. Inc.	69.7	7.4%
Cyprus Minerals Co.	65.3	6.9
Consol Energy Inc.	50.7	5.4
Zeigler Coal Holding Co.	37.5	4.0
ARCO Coal Co.	37.4	4.0
Kennecott Energy Co.	36.7	3.9
Exxon Coal USA Inc.	28.1	3.0
Texas Utilities Co.	27.6	2.9
Montana Power Co.	26.4	2.8
North American Coal Corp. . . .	26.3	2.8

Source: *Coal Data: A Reference*, February 1995, p. 20, from Energy Information Administration and *Coal Industry Annual, 1993*.

SIC 13 - Oil and Gas Extraction

★ 112 ★

Natural Gas (SIC 1311)

Natural Gas Production by State

Data are for 1995 in millions of cubic feet daily.

	(mil.)	Share
Alabama	1,017	1.9%
Alaska	1,280	2.4
Arkansas	517	1.0
California	787	1.5
Colorado	1,177	2.2
Kansas	1,952	3.6
Louisiana	14,390	26.6
Michigan	711	1.3
Mississippi	257	0.5
New Mexico	4,357	8.1
Ohio	364	0.7
Oklahoma	5,325	9.8
Pennsylvania	414	0.8
Texas	17,405	32.2
West Virginia	502	0.9
Wyoming	2,308	4.3
Others	1,346	2.5

Source: *Oil & Gas Journal*, January 29, 1996, p. 64.

★ 113 ★

Natural Gas (SIC 1311)

Natural Gas Reserves - Canada

Reserves are shown in trillions of cubic feet.

	1992	1993	1994
Alberta	57.56	56.04	54.93
British Columbia	8.78	8.77	8.60
Saskatchewan	2.50	2.87	3.03
Other	0.61	0.95	0.81

Source: *Petroleum Economist*, January 1996, p. 13, from Canadian Association of Petroleum Producers.

★ 114 ★

Natural Gas (SIC 1311)

U.S. Natural Gas Producers

The top gas producing companies shown are based on production in billions of cubic feet.

Amoco Corp.	893.0
Exxon Corp.	787.0
Chevron Corp.	761.0
Texaco Inc.	645.0
Mobil Corp.	572.0
Shell Oil Co.	570.0
Unocal Corp.	421.0
Meridian Oil Inc.	384.0
Phillips Petroleum Co.	370.0
ARCO	350.0

Source: *Oil & Gas Journal*, September 4, 1995, p. 58.

★ 115 ★

Oil (SIC 1311)

Leading Crude Oil Firms

The leading firms involved in crude oil mining and production are ranked by 1995 revenues in millions of dollars. Shares of the group are shown in percent.

	Rev. ($ mil.)	% of Group
Cyprus Amax Minerals	$ 3,207	24.9%
Asarco	3,198	24.8
Freeport-McMoran C&G	1,834	14.2
Vulcan Materials	1,461	11.3
Oryx Energy	1,129	8.8
Mitchell Energy	1,072	8.3
Freeport & McMoran	996	7.7

Source: *Fortune*, April 29, 1996, p. F57.

★ 116 ★
Oil (SIC 1311)
Leading Oil Firms

The table compares second quarter revenues for 1995 and 1996. Data are in billions of dollars.

	1995	1996
Exxon	$ 32.21	$ 31.67
Mobil	18.85	19.55
Texaco	9.26	11.26
Chevron	9.40	10.51
Amoco	7.71	8.76

Source: *Financial Times*, July 23, 1996, p. 16, from agency reports.

★ 117 ★
Oil (SIC 1311)
Oil Consumption by End Use

Percentages are based on the 17.7 million barrels of oil consumed daily in 1995. Other uses include industry, businesses, and homes.

Highway transportation	53.4%
Plastics and fertilizers	10.2
Jet fuel	6.5
Railroad, boat and some constr. equip.	4.8
Electric utilities	1.4
Other uses	23.7

Source: *New York Times*, July 23, 1996, p. C6, from America's Petroleum Institute from Energy Department Data.

★ 118 ★
Oil (SIC 1311)
Oil Production - North America

Production is shown in thousands of barrels per day.

	1993	1994
United States	8,585	8,355
Mexico	3,240	3,265
Canada	2,185	2,280

Source: *Oil & Gas Journal*, April 22, 1996, p. 46, from BP Statistical Review.

★ 119 ★
Oil (SIC 1311)
Oil Production by State

Production is shown in thousands of barrels annually by state. Data are for 1995. California, Louisiana, and Texas include offshore figures.

Alabama	18,468.0
Alaska	542,104.0
Arkansas	8,694.0
California	352,217.0
Colorado	27,225.0
Florida	5,840.0
Illinois	16,150.0
Indiana	2,251.0
Kansas	44,649.0
Kentucky	3,370.0
Louisiana	419,434.0
Michigan	11,467.0
Mississippi	19,500.0
Montana	15,845.0
Nebraska	3,831.0
Nevada	1,460.0
New Mexico	65,191.0
New York	1,945.0
North Dakota	28,932.0
Ohio	8,119.0
Oklahoma	87,674.0
Pennsylvania	365.0
South Dakota	1,429.0
Tennessee	365.0
Texas	195,175.0
Utah	19,828.0
West Virginia	1,839.0
Wyoming	75,254.0

Source: *World Oil*, February 1996, p. 69, from American Petroleum Institute.

★ 120 ★
Oil & Gas (SIC 1311)

Oil & Gas Cos. - Louisiana

Firms are ranked by 1995 revenues in thousands of dollars.

Louisiana Land & Exploration	$ 830,500
Flores & Rucks Inc.	127,970
Newpak Resources Inc.	97,982
Stone Energy Corp.	40,551
Amber Inc.	38,457
Crystal Oil Co.	11,518

Source: *Times Picayune*, May 18, 1996, p. I18, from TopBiz Network Inc.

★ 121 ★
Oil & Gas (SIC 1311)

Top 20 Oil & Gas Producers

The top companies are ranked by revenues in millions of dollars. Shares of the group are shown in percent.

	($ mil.)	% of Group
Exxon Corp.	$ 113,904.0	25.9%
Mobil Corp.	67,383.0	15.3
Chevron Corp.	35,854.0	8.2
Texaco Inc.	33,353.0	7.6
Amoco Corp.	30,362.0	6.9
Shell Oil Co.	21,581.0	4.9
Conoco Inc.	17,203.0	3.9
ARCO	17,199.0	3.9
BP (USA)	14,220.0	3.2
USX-Marathon Group	12,757.0	2.9
Phillips Petroleum Co.	12,367.0	2.8
Ashland Oil Inc.	10,404.0	2.4
Coastal Corp.	10,215.3	2.3
Occidental Petroleum Corp.	9,416.0	2.1
Enron Corp.	9,022.9	2.1
Unocal Corp.	7,965.0	1.8
Amerada Hess Corp.	6,698.8	1.5
FINA Inc.	3,437.1	0.8
Kerr-McGee Corp.	3,376.0	0.8
Consolidated Natural Gas Co.	3,045.7	0.7

Source: *Oil & Gas Journal*, September 4, 1995, p. 52.

★ 122 ★
Oil & Gas (SIC 1311)

Top Oil & Gas Producers - Canada

Firms are ranked by revenues in billions of dollars.

Aoco Canada Petroleum	$ 3.61
Imperial Oil Resources	2.29
PanCanadian Petroleum	2.01
Norcen Energy Resources	1.40
Chevron Canada Resources	1.35

Source: *Globe and Mail's Report on Business*, July 1996, p. 159.

★ 123 ★
Gas Liquids (SIC 1321)

U.S. Liquid Gas Producers

The top liquid gas producing companies shown are ranked by production in billions of barrels.

BP (USA)	220.8
ARCO	216.0
Exxon Corp.	206.0
Shell Oil Co.	151.0
Texaco Inc.	148.0
Chevron Corp.	134.0
Mobil Corp.	110.0
Amoco Corp.	93.0
Unocal Corp.	50.0
Phillips Petroleum Co.	45.0
USX-Marathon Group	40.2
Conoco Inc.	33.0

Source: *Oil & Gas Journal*, September 4, 1995, p. 58.

★ 124 ★

Oil Wells (SIC 1381)

Land Drilling Contractors

The largest contractors are ranked by number of wells in 1995.

Nabors Drilling USA Inc.	939
UTI Energy Corp.	611
Exeter Drilling Co.	501
Wes-Tex	498

Source: *Investor's Business Daily*, June 6, 1996, p. A6, from *Land Rig Newsletter*.

★ 125 ★

Oil Wells (SIC 1381)

Oil Rig Operators - Gulf of Mexico

The leading operators in the Gulf of Mexico are ranked by oil wells drilled. Shares are shown based on 858 wells drilled in 1995; 915 are expected to be drilled in 1996.

	No.	Share
Shell (shelf)	103	12.0%
Chevron	54	6.3
Vastar Res.	44	5.1
Mobil	29	3.4
Unocal	27	3.1
Exxon	22	2.6
Samedan	22	2.6
Texaco	22	2.6
Oryx Energy	21	2.4
Amoco	20	2.3
Marathon	19	2.2
Flores & Rucks	19	2.2
Kerr McGee	18	2.1
Newfield Explor.	18	2.1
Seagull Energy	16	1.9
Walter O&G	14	1.6
Zilkha Energy	14	1.6
Coastal Oil & Gas	13	1.5
Conoco	13	1.5
Pennzoil	12	1.4
Other	338	39.4

Source: *World Oil*, February 1996, p. 63, from Offshore Data Services.

★ 126 ★

Oil Wells (SIC 1381)

Oil Well Drilling by State

Data show the total wells expected to be drilled in 1996.

Alabama	158
Alaska	202
Arizona	5
Arkansas	163
California	998
Colorado	720
Florida	5
Illinois	285
Indiana	90
Kansas	1,490
Kentucky	417
Louisiana	1,320
Maryland	1
Michigan	680
Mississippi	190
Missouri	7
Montana	220
Nebraska	39
Nevada	32
New Mexico	1,535
New York	40
North Dakota	145
Ohio	585
Oklahoma	2,100
Pennsylvania	595
South Dakota	25
Tennessee	65
Texas	8,105
Utah	105
Virginia	290
Washington	1
West Virginia	357
Wyoming	705

Source: *Oil & Gas Journal*, January 29, 1996, p. 76.

★ 127 ★

Oil Wells (SIC 1381)

U.S. Deep Drilling Oil Barges

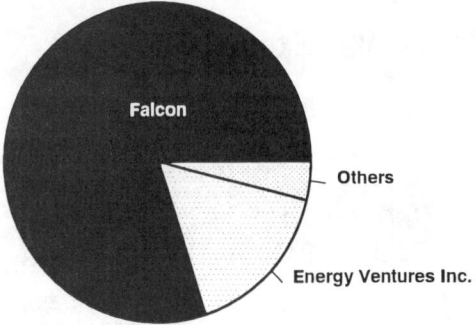

Companies leading the barge rig market are shown based on percent of barges owned or operated. There are 115 barge rigs worldwide.

Falcon 80.0%
Energy Ventures Inc. 16.0
Others 4.0

Source: *Investor's Business Daily*, January 17, 1996, p. A4.

★ 128 ★

Oil & Gas Services (SIC 1389)

Oil & Gas Service Providers - Canada

Firms are ranked by revenues in millions of dollars.

Nowsco Well Service . . . . $ 483.0
Canadian Fracmaster 333.4
Ensign Resource Service Group 180.6
Precision Drilling 179.3
Enserv Corp. 174.6
Dreco Energy Services 90.4

Source: *Globe and Mail's Report on Business*, July 1996, p. 159.

★ 129 ★

Oil & Gas Services (SIC 1389)

Oilfield Service Providers

The leading companies in oilfield services are ranked by 1995 revenues in millions of dollars.

Schlumberger . . . . $ 7,339
Halliburton 5,602
Dresser Industries 5,392
Western Atlas 2,191
BJ Services 574
Tidewater 561

Source: *Forbes*, January 1, 1996, p. 124, from Value Line Data Base Service and OneSource Information Services.

SIC 14 - Nonmetallic Minerals, Except Fuels

★ 130 ★

Nonfuel Mining (SIC 1400)

Nonfuel Mineral Production by State

Nevada	
Michigan	
Utah	
Texas	
Minnesota	
Missouri	
Pennsylvania	
New Mexico	
Ohio	
New York	

Production is shown in millions of dollars for 1994.

Nevada	$ 2,761.4
Michigan	1,621.3
Utah	1,428.0
Texas	1,408.6
Minnesota	1,351.6
Missouri	1,003.2
Pennsylvania	963.8
New Mexico	913.8
Ohio	893.2
New York	870.9

Source: *Mineral Commodity Summaries. U.S. Dept. of the Interior*, 1995, p. 12.

★ 131 ★

Nonfuel Mining (SIC 1400)

Nonfuel Mining in Manitoba

The value of production is shown in millions of dollars in 1994.

Sand & gravel	28.0
Cement	13.0
Peat moss	11.5
Building stone	9.0
Lime	8.0
Gypsum	1.2

Source: *National Trade Data Bank*, March 2, 1996, p. IM951109.016.

★ 132 ★

Crushed Stone (SIC 1420)

Crushed Stone Producers - 1994

Top crushed stone companies are ranked by production in millions of tons per year (tpy). Data are for 1994. Shares of the group are shown in percent.

	TPY	% of Group
Vulcan Materials (KY)	10.00	11.1%
Rinker Materials	9.95	11.0
Redland Stone Products	9.70	10.8
Preque Isle Corp.	8.54	9.5
Texas Crushed Stone	8.30	9.2
Michigan Limestone	7.80	8.7
Vulcan Materials (IL)	7.34	8.1
Material Service Corp.	7.00	7.8
Vecellio & Grogan	6.90	7.7
Specialty Minerals	5.10	5.7
Sunbelt Asphalt & Material	4.90	5.4
Texas Industries	4.60	5.1

Source: *Rock Products*, August 1995, p. 26, from company reports.

★ 133 ★
Crushed Stone (SIC 1420)

Crushed Stone Production by State

Production is shown in millions of metric tons for the first nine months of 1995.

Texas	63.4
Pennsylvania	60.2
Missouri	50.8
Florida	50.2
Georgia	45.4
Ohio	42.5
North Carolina	42.4
Virginia	41.9
Illinois	41.2
Tennessee	38.0

Source: *Rock Products*, January 1996, p. 21, from United States Bureau of Mines.

★ 134 ★
Sand & Gravel (SIC 1440)

Industrial Sand/Gravel Use

Distribution is shown based on 27.3 million metric tons in 1994.

Glass sands	39.2%
Foundry sands	24.6
Hydraulic fracturing sand	6.0
Abrasives	5.5
Ceramics	0.9
Other	23.7

Source: *American Ceramic Society Bulletin*, June 1996, p. 152.

★ 135 ★
Sand & Gravel (SIC 1440)

Sand & Gravel Company Leaders

Quarry production is shown in millions of tons per year (tpy) for 1994. Companies in the top 20 without available figures are CalMat Co., A. Teichert & Son, RMC Lonestar, and Meyer Material. Shares of the group are shown in percent.

	TPY	% of Group
Salt River Sand & Rock	3.68	10.6%
Lone Star Northwest	3.50	10.1
Kaiser/Beazer USA	3.18	9.1
Nugent Sand Co.	3.00	8.6
Kaiser Materials	3.00	8.6
Fordyce Co.	2.50	7.2
United Rock Products	2.42	7.0
Owl Rock Products	2.20	6.3
Southdown/Transit Mix Concrete .	2.03	5.8
Amboy Aggregate Joint Venture . .	2.00	5.8
Pioneer Concrete of America . . .	1.99	5.7
Hilltop Basic Resources	1.92	5.5
Vulcan Materials	1.80	5.2
Livingston-Graham/Blue Diamond Materials/Beazer . . .	1.54	4.4

Source: *Rock Products*, August 1995, p. 27.

★ 136 ★
Sand & Gravel (SIC 1440)

Sand & Gravel Production by State

Production is shown in millions of metric tons for the first nine months of 1995.

Arkansas	68.8
Texas	44.5
Michigan	38.1
Ohio	36.1
Arizona	29.8
Washington	29.6
Illinois	25.1
Minnesota	24.7
Wisconsin	22.1
Colorado	21.2

Source: *Rock Products*, January 1996, p. 21, from United States Bureau of Mines.

★ 137 ★
Clay (SIC 1455)

China Clay Producers

The table shows the shares of the market represented by the top 3 companies.

Nalco/Betz	20.0%
Calgon	8.0
Other	72.0

Source: *Management Today*, October 1995, p. 51.

★ 138 ★
Clay (SIC 1459)

Clay/Shale Consumption by State

Data are in thousands of dollars for 1993.

Texas	$ 17,441
Alabama	15,659
Georgia	11,559
North Carolina	11,165
New York	9,250
California	8,431
Ohio	7,887
Michigan	4,848
South Carolina	4,499
Mississippi	4,475

Source: *Clay. U.S. Dept. of the Interior*, 1993, p. 16, from United States Bureau of the Census.

★ 139 ★
Chemical Minerals (SIC 1470)

Chemical/Fertilizer Mineral Production

Production is shown in thousands of tons for 1996.

Phosphate rock	47,948
Lime	20,617
Sulfur	13,228
Sodium carbonate	11,138
Potash	1,641
Bromine	233

Source: *Chemical & Engineering News*, June 24, 1996, p. 43, from United States Bureau of Mines, United States Bureau of the Census, and United States Geological Survey.

★ 140 ★
Potash (SIC 1474)

Potash Producers - Canada

Production is shown in metric tons (m.t.).

	M.t.	Share
Potash Corp. of Saskatchewan . . .	3.20	39.3%
Kalium	1.80	22.1
IMC Global	1.70	20.9
Agrium Ltd.	0.72	8.8
Potacan	0.72	8.8

Source: *Engineering & Mining Journal*, March 1996, p. 66.

★ 141 ★
Perlite (SIC 1499)

U.S. Perlite Consumption

Distribution is shown based on 636,000 metric tons.

Formed products	67.9%
Filter aid	10.9
Horticultural aggregate	8.7
Fillers	6.8
Insulation	2.0
Concrete/plaster aggregate	1.8
Other	1.8

Source: *American Ceramic Society Bulletin*, June 1996, p. 146.

SIC 15 - General Building Contractors

Building Construction (SIC 1500)

Building Permits - Philadelphia

Data for 1995 are for the first five months.

	1994	1995
New residential units		
Single-family	13,678	4,422
2- to 4- bedroom buildings	223	92
buildings 5 or more units	690	224
New nonresidential buildings		
Stores	251	85
Offices	111	57
Hotels	21	51
Industrial	99	44
Other	4,707	1,950
Additions and alterations		
Residential	33,566	12,787
Other	8,423	3,656

Source: *Urban Land*, October 1995, p. 36.

Building Construction (SIC 1500)

Leading Design Companies

Design contractors are ranked by U.S. billings in millions of dollars for 1995.

The Parsons Corp.	$ 927.7
Brown & Root Inc.	872.8
Raytheon Engineers & Constructors Intl.	846.0
Fluor Daniel Inc.	786.0
CH2M Hill Cos. Ltd.	721.3
Jacobs Engineering Group Inc.	698.0
Stone & Webster Engineering Corp.	654.5
Rust International Inc.	572.0
ABB Lummus Global Inc.	559.0
Parsons Brinckerhoff Inc.	521.3

Source: *ENR*, April 1, 1996, p. 52.

Building Construction (SIC 1500)

Leading Engineer/Construction Firms

Firms are ranked by 1995 revenues in millions of dollars.

Fluor	$ 9,301
Halliburton	5,951
Turner Corp.	3,281
Centex	3,278
Foster Wheeler	3,082
Peter Kiewit Sons	2,902
Morrison Knudsen	2,531
Pulte	2,050
Jacobs Engineering Group	1,723
Ryland Group	1,596

Source: *Fortune*, April 29, 1996, p. F50.

Building Construction (SIC 1500)

Top Designers/Builders

Firms are ranked by 1995 revenues in millions of dollars.

Bechtel Group Inc.	$ 6,642.0
Fluor Daniel Inc.	5,487.0
Jacobs Engineering Group Inc.	2,366.0
Trafalgar House Engineering & Const.	1,789.0
Raytheon Engineers & Construction	1,775.0
McDermott Intl. Inc.	1,729.5
Foster Wheeler Corp.	1,021.1
The M.W. Kellogg Co.	836.7
Kiewit Construction Group Inc.	815.5
Black & Veatch	708.0

Source: *ENR*, June 10, 1996, p. 36.

★ 146 ★
Residential Construction (SIC 1520)

Housing Permits by State

Data are for the second quarter of 1995.

Texas	26,336
California	22,902
Arizona	14,350
Washington	11,759
Colorado	10,522
Nevada	9,140
Oregon	8,015
Missouri	6,086
Utah	5,735
Arkansas	3,229
New Mexico	3,005
Idaho	2,860
Kansas	2,532
Nebraska	2,325
Hawaii	1,405

Source: *Building Material Retailer*, October 1995, p. 8, from United States Bureau of the Census.

★ 147 ★
Residential Construction (SIC 1520)

Leading Residential Construction Market

The value of the top markets are shown in thousands of dollars for 1995.

Atlanta	$ 1,927,538
Phoenix-Mesa	1,868,679
Chicago	1,664,244
Washington D.C.	1,251,058
Dallas	1,241,180
Las Vegas	1,185,750
Detroit	866,655
Portland-Vancouver	859,538
Minneapolis-St. Paul	844,800
Denver	794,322
Houston	770,970

Source: *Construction Equipment*, January 1996, p. 36, from United States Department of Commerce.

★ 148 ★
Residential Construction (SIC 1520)

Top Metro Areas - 1996

The value of residential construction permits are shown for the first three months of 1996. Data are in millions of permits.

Phoeniz/Mesa	1,133.0
Atlanta	1,003.8
Chicago	704.0
Dallas	688.3
Las Vegas	626.7
Washington D.C.	535.6
Denver	516.8
Houston	470.0
Portland/Vancouver OR-WA	438.4
Riverside-San Bernadino, CA	406.5

Source: *Professional Builder*, June 1996, p. 148, from United States Department of Commerce and Cahners Economics.

★ 149 ★
Residential Construction (SIC 1521)

Chicago's Leading Homebuilders

The top builders are ranked by home sales in the Chicago area. Over 10,000 new homes were sold during the first half of 1995. The Northwest area was the leading region of the city for construction with a 25.8% share.

Town & Country Homes	942
Lakewood Homes Inc.	520
Pulte Home Corp.	507
Kimball Hill Homes Inc.	447
Lexington Homes Inc.	372
Concord Development Corp.	309
Cambridge Homes Inc.	294

Continued on next page.

★ 149 ★ *Continued*
Residential Construction (SIC 1521)

Chicago's Leading Homebuilders

The top builders are ranked by home sales in the Chicago area. Over 10,000 new homes were sold during the first half of 1995. The Northwest area was the leading region of the city for construction with a 25.8% share.

Pasquinelli Construction Co.	238
Hartz Construction Co.	188
Wiseman-Hughes Enterprises Inc.	175

Source: *Crain's Chicago Business*, August 7, 1995, p. 16, from Tracy Cross & Associates Inc.

★ 150 ★

Residential Construction (SIC 1521)

Housing Starts - Canada

Data are for 1994.

	No.	Share
Ontario	66,500	34.9%
British Columbia	45,000	23.6
Quebec	43,600	22.9
Alberta	18,400	9.7
Nova Scotia	4,800	2.5
New Brunswick	3,650	1.9
Manitoba	3,150	1.7
Newfoundland	2,550	1.3
Saskatchewan	2,100	1.1
Prince Edward Island	630	0.3

Source: *National Trade Data Bank*, May 27, 1996, p. ISA9309.

★ 151 ★

Residential Construction (SIC 1521)

Leading Residential Builders

Firms are ranked by 1995 sales in millions of dollars.

Centex	$ 3,077
Pulte	1,888
Ryland Group	1,583
Walter Industries	1,445
Kaufman & Broad Home	1,322
US Home	1,082
MDC Holdings	887
NVR	885
Del Webb	847
Oakwood Homes	$ 821
Lennar	816

Source: *Forbes*, January 1, 1996, p. 106, from Value Line Data Base Service and OneSource Information Services.

★ 152 ★

Residential Construction (SIC 1521)

Top Builders - Arizona

The top builders are ranked by number of construction permits in 1995.

Del Webb	2,250
Continental Homes	2,045
Hancock Homes	1,617
Shea Homes	1,517
UDC Homes	1,169

Source: *Arizona Republic*, May 5, 1996, p. AI8, from *Phoenix Housing Market Letter*.

★ 153 ★

Residential Construction (SIC 1521)

Top Builders - Atlanta

Companies are ranked by number of single family closings. Shares are shown based on 34,944 single family closings in the Atlanta area in 1995.

	No.	Share
Torrey Homes	1,040	3.0%
John Wieland Homes	790	2.3
Pulte Home Corp.	700	2.0
Colony Homes	607	1.7
Ryland Homes	510	1.5
Other	31,297	89.6

Source: *Builder*, May 1996, p. 219.

★ 154 ★

Residential Construction (SIC 1521)

Top Builders - Charlotte

Companies are ranked by number of single family closings. Shares are shown based on 10,056 single family closings in 1995.

	No.	Share
Centex/Crosland	557	5.5%
Squires Homes	435	4.3
Pulte Home Corp.	343	3.4
Ryland Homes	342	3.4
Ryan Homes	270	2.7
Other	8,109	80.6

Source: *Builder*, May 1996, p. 220, from M.O.R.E.

★ 155 ★

Residential Construction (SIC 1521)

Top Builders - W. Palm Beach

Companies are ranked by number of single family closings. Shares are shown based on 7,473 single family closings in 1995.

	No.	Share
Lennar Homes	418	5.6%
Engle Homes	366	4.9
Centex Homes	255	3.4
G.L. Homes	241	3.2
Oriole Homes	241	3.2
Other	5,952	79.6

Source: *Builder*, May 1996, p. 226, from *Real Estate Market Profiles*.

★ 156 ★

Residential Construction (SIC 1521)

Top Single-Family Builders

Firms are ranked by 1995 gross revenues in millions of dollars.

Centex	$ 3,074
Pulte	1,936
Ryland	1,590
Kaufman and Brand	1,397
U.S. Home	1,108
Lincoln Property	1,082
NVR	910
Del Webb	910
Lennar	870
M.D.C.	866

Trammell Crow	$ 831
Hovnanian	778
Weyerhaeuser	723
Beazer	705
Toll Brothers	646

Source: *Builder*, May 1996, p. 186.

★ 157 ★

Residential Construction (SIC 1522)

Apartment Building Construction

States are ranked by the value of construction awards for the first 11 months of 1995. Data are in millions of dollars.

Florida	$ 1,987
California	920
Texas	903
New York	883
Georgia	570
Ohio	480
Arizona	471
Illinois	447
Michigan	407
Colorado	396

Source: *ENR*, January 29, 1996, p. 36, from ENR-F.W. Dodge Division.

★ 158 ★

Nonresidential Construction (SIC 1540)

Commercial Building Construction

States are ranked by value of commercial building contracts for the first 11 months of 1995. Data are in millions of dollars.

California	$ 4,084
Florida	2,889
Texas	2,856
New York	2,490
Ohio	2,308
Georgia	1,994
North Carolina	1,480
Pennsylvania	1,462
Illinois	1,355
New Jersey	1,184
Nevada	1,057
Michigan	1,151
Virginia	1,101

Continued on next page.

★ 158 ★ *Continued*

Nonresidential Construction (SIC 1540)

Commercial Building Construction

States are ranked by value of commercial building contracts for the first 11 months of 1995. Data are in millions of dollars.

Tennessee . . . . $ 1,063
Massachusetts 1,026

Source: *ENR*, January 29, 1996, p. 36, from ENR-F.W. Dodge Division.

★ 159 ★

Nonresidential Construction (SIC 1540)

Leading Commercial Builders

Builders are ranked by 1995 sales in millions of dollars.

Fluor . . . . $ 9,111
Turner 3,108
Foster Wheeler 2,755
Morrison Knudsen 2,118
Jacobs Engineering 1,723
Perini 1,093
Stone & Webster 902
Apogee Enterprises 833
Butler Manufacturing 818
Granite Construction 811
Forest City Enterprises 484

Source: *Forbes*, January 1, 1996, p. 106, from Value Line Data Base Service and OneSource Information Services.

★ 160 ★

Nonresidential Construction (SIC 1540)

Nonresidential Construction Spending

Data are in billions of dollars for 1995.

Commercial
  Retail . . . . $ 35.3
  Office 20.4
   Hotel/motel 5.7
Industrial 25.7

Institutional
  Education . . . . $ 30.3
  Hospital 14.5
  Other 38.0

Source: *Rural Builder*, February 1996, p. 48, from United States Department of Commerce.

★ 161 ★

Nonresidential Construction (SIC 1542)

College Construction

The table shows the millions of dollars in construction scheduled to be completed in 1995-97 at two-year and four-year schools. In 1994, a total of $3.6 billion in new construction was completed; the retrofit category followed with $2.17 billion in total construction; the added construction followed with $619 million.

	2yr	4yr
New	3,227	8,168
Retrofit	891	2,443
Add	505	842

Source: *Buildings*, January 1996, p. 24, from Association of Higher Education Facilities Officers.

★ 162 ★

Nonresidential Construction (SIC 1542)

Construction Market - 1991-95

Educational 23.6%
Retail 22.4
Manufacturing/distribution 18.4
Office 15.8
Health care 12.9
Public 6.8

Source: *Architectural Record*, June 1996, p. 36, from F.W. Dodge and American Institute of Architects.

★ 163 ★

Nonresidential Construction (SIC 1542)

Hospital/Health Building Construction

States are ranked by value of contract awards for the first 11 months of 1995. Data are in millions of dollars.

Illinois	$ 957
California	855
New York	736
Florida	641
Texas	495
Ohio	475
North Carolina	429
Pennsylvania	422
Michigan	333
Missouri	285
Massachusetts	272
Tennessee	235
Georgia	225
Louisiana	210
New Jersey	206

Source: *ENR*, January 29, 1996, p. 36, from ENR-F.W. Dodge Division.

★ 164 ★

Retail Construction (SIC 1542)

Top Contractors of Interior Space

The top retail contractors of interior space are ranked by millions of square feet constructed from December 1990 - December 1995.

EMJ Corp.	16.455
Walbridge Contracting Inc.	13.540
Fisher Development Inc.	13.132
Miller Building Corp.	12.982
Tony Crawford Construction	10.070
The Whiting-Turner Contracting Co.	9.886
The Pepper Companies Inc.	8.551
Hale-Mills Construction Inc.	8.406
The Stewart/Perry Co. Inc.	7.768
L.M.B. Construction Co. Inc.	7.700
Inland Construction Co.	7.670
Keene Construction Co.	7.658
Hoar Construction	7.643
S.D. Deacon	7.355
Coastland Construction Inc.	7.245

Source: *Shopping Center World*, February 1996, p. 40.

★ 165 ★

Retail Construction (SIC 1542)

Top Contractors of Shell Space

The leading retail contractors of shell space are ranked by square footage constructed from December 1990 - December 1995. Figures are in millions of square feet.

EMJ Corp.	17.237
Walbridge Contracting Inc.	16.394
The Whiting-Turner Contracting Co.	14.123
Miller Building Corp.	11.035
IMC (International Management Consultants Inc.)	10.605
Hoar Construction	9.808
Hale-Mills Construction Inc.	8.947
The Stewart/Perry Co. Inc.	8.353
L.F. Jennings Inc.	8.212
Keene Construction Co.	7.891
Inland Construction	7.760
S D Deacon Corp.	7.673
Pinkerton & Laws Inc.	7.648
Vratsinas Construction Co.	7.520
Lyle Parks Jr. Inc.	7.300

Source: *Shopping Center World*, February 1996, p. 41.

SIC 16 - Heavy Construction, Except Building

★ 166 ★

Heavy Construction (SIC 1600)

Major Contractors - St. Louis

The biggest contractors are ranked by 1995 revenues in millions of dollars.

McCarthy	$ 950.0
J.S. Alberici	647.4
Fru-Con	335.9
Sverdrup	207.2
HBE	188.5
Clayco	128.1
Fred Weber	122.0
Nooter	93.0
Lionmark	80.1
Korte	71.4
Tariton	60.9
BSI	51.9

Source: *St. Louis Post-Dispatch*, July 10, 1996, p. 1C, from *Engineering News Record*.

★ 167 ★

Heavy Construction (SIC 1600)

Top Contractors

Firms are ranked by 1995 revenues in millions of dollars.

Fluor Daniel Inc.	$ 7,501.0
Bechtel Group Inc.	7,407.0
Jacobs Engineering Group Inc.	3,610.0
Trafalgar House Engineering & Const. . .	3,387.0
Centex Construction Group	2,968.7
Brown & Root Inc.	2,742.6
The Turner Corp.	2,727.0
Raytheon Engineers & Constructors Intl. .	2,467.0
Kiewit Construction Group Inc.	2,212.0
Foster Wheeler Corp.	2,132.6
The Parsons Corp.	1,870.6
McDermott International Inc.	1,729.5
Morrison Knudsen Corp.	1,706.8
The Clark Construction Group Inc. . . .	1,485.0
Gilbane Building Co.	1,370.5

Source: *ENR*, May 20, 1996, p. 48.

★ 168 ★

Street and Highway Construction (SIC 1611)

Heavy/Highway Construction Awards

States are ranked by value of heavy and highway construction contract awards for the first 11 months of 1995. Data are in millions of dollars.

California	$ 7,191
Texas	4,662
New York	4,004
Florida	3,524
Illinois	2,569
Massachusetts	2,246

Continued on next page.

45

★ 168 ★ *Continued*

Street and Highway Construction (SIC 1611)

Heavy/Highway Construction Awards

States are ranked by value of heavy and highway construction contract awards for the first 11 months of 1995. Data are in millions of dollars.

Ohio	$ 2,004
Pennsylvania	1,590
Virginia	1,563
Michigan	1,476

Source: *ENR*, January 29, 1996, p. 41, from ENR-F.W. Dodge Division.

★ 169 ★

Heavy Construction (SIC 1620)

Top Commercial Contractors

Firms are ranked by revenues in millions of dollars.

The Turner Crop.	$ 2,125.94
BE&K Inc.	1,746.00
Clark Construction Group Inc.	1,180.63
Centex Construction Group	1,077.52
Flour Daniel Inc.	886.78
Bechtel Group Inc.	831.00
Austin Co.	751.39
Hensel Phelps Construction Co.	693.00
Perini Corp.	616.40
M.A. Mortenson Co.	588.62
Huber, Hunt & Nichols	573.00
Hoffman Corp.	514.92

Source: *Building Design & Construction*, July 1995, p. 29.

★ 170 ★

Heavy Construction (SIC 1620)

Top Heavy Contractors

Firms are ranked by 1995 revenues in millions of dollars. Data include transportation, sewer, water, and hazardous waste construction.

Kiewit Construction Group Inc.	$ 1,553.8
Bechtel Group Inc.	1,527.1
Granite Construction Co.	895.0
Jacobs Engineering Group Inc.	688.6
Morrison Knudsen Corp.	663.9
OHM Corp.	507.7
Spectrum Construction Group	500.5
The Parsons Corp.	455.6

ICF Kaiser International Inc.	$ 359.4
Tutor-Saliba Corp.	357.7
Fluor Daniel Inc.	348.8
Raytheon Engineers & Constructors Intl.	330.1
Modern Continental Const. Co.	293.9
Perini Corp.	291.2
J.A. Jones Inc.	281.1

Source: *ENR*, May 20, 1996, p. 82.

★ 171 ★

Bridge Construction (SIC 1622)

Bridge Construction by State

Data are in millions of dollars for 1996.

Georgia	$ 176
Mississippi	144
West Virginia	120
Florida	117
Pennsylvania	105
Louisiana	69
Wisconsin	65
Hawaii	60
Idaho	50
Nevada	47

Source: *ENR*, January 29, 1996, p. 46, from ENR Construction Economics Department.

SIC 17 - Special Trade Contractors

★ 172 ★

Remodeling (SIC 1700)

Kitchen Remodeling Spending

Data show the percentage of dollars spent in 1995.

Under $5,000 . . . . 49.0%
$5,000-$6,999 . . . . 18.0
$10,000-$14,999 . . . . 11.0
$7,000-$9999 . . . . 10.0
$15,000-$19,999 . . . . 5.0
$20,000 + ... 7.0

Source: *Home Mechanix*, November 1995, p. 12, from *Kitchen & Bath Business*.

★ 173 ★

Remodeling (SIC 1700)

Renovation Spending - Canada

Ontario
British Columbia
Newfoundland
Nova Scotia
Quebec
Alberta
Prince Edward Island
New Brunswick
Manitoba
Saskatchewan

Per capita spending is shown for 1993.

Ontario . . . . $ 1,583
British Columbia 1,567
Newfoundland 1,434
Nova Scotia 1,412
Quebec 1,355
Alberta 1,336
Prince Edward Island 1,324
New Brunswick 1,113

Manitoba . . . . $ 1,099
Saskatchewan 838

Source: *National Trade Data Bank*, September 1, 1995, p. IS9503.168.

★ 174 ★

Remodeling (SIC 1700)

Residential Remodeling Market

Ciites are ranked by value of permits in millions of dollars.

Los Angeles . . . . $ 316.2
Washington D.C. 211.0
Chicago 197.3
Boston 174.3
New York City 170.9
Minneapolis 155.2
Philadelphia 143.8
San Francisco 124.3
Nassau-Suffolk N.Y. 116.1
Detroit 115.2
Newark 98.8
Bergen-Passaic 90.5
Oakland 88.6
Miami 87.5
Atlanta 74.8

Source: *Contractor*, October 1995, p. 3, from United States Department of Commerce and Cahners Economics.

★ 175 ★
Remodeling (SIC 1700)

Window/Door Remodeling

Data shows the market for window and door replacement and remodeling in 1994. Figures are in millions of dollars and compare the rental property and owner occupied markets.

	Rental	Occ.
Window/door alterations	$ 910	$ 2,487
Window replacement	288	1,157
Door replacement	769	703

Source: *Building Supply Business*, February 1996, p. 33, from Regis J. Sheehan and United States Department of Commerce.

★ 176 ★
Contracting - Piping (SIC 1711)

Top Piping Contractors

Firms are ranked by sales in millions of dollars.

Kinetic Systems Inc.	$ 202.04
Corrigan Co.	118.88
Murphy Co. Mechanical Contractors . . .	101.52
Harder Mechanical Contractors	95.34
MMC Corp.	92.02
Sanders Bros. Inc.	85.50
The Poole & Kent Co.	77.15
J.H. Kelly Co.	67.46
Limbech Constructors Inc.	65.67
Fischbach Corp.	64.85

Source: *Contractor*, May 1996, p. 54.

★ 177 ★
Contracting - Paint (SIC 1721)

Top Painting Contractors

Painting contractors are ranked by 1994 revenues in millions of dollars.

J.L. Manta Inc.	$ 32.9
Robison-Prezioso Inc.	23.9
Avalotis Painting Co. Inc.	22.7
M.L. McDonald Co.	22.1
Swanson & Youngdale Inc.	17.1
Irvin H. Whitehouse & Sons Co.	12.1

Hartman Walsh Painting Co.	$ 11.5
Vulcan Painters Inc.	11.2
Ascher Bros. Co. Inc.	11.0
Certified Coatings of Calfornia	10.6

Source: *ENR*, October 2, 1995, p. 44.

★ 178 ★
Contracting - Electrical (SIC 1731)

Top Electrical Contractors - 1994

The top firms are ranked by 1994 revenues in millions of dollars.

EMCOR Group Inc.	$ 1,004.9
Fischbach Corp.	430.5
The L.E. Myers Co. Group	214.7
SASCO Group	214.3
Mass. Electric Construction Co.	163.3
L.K. Comstock & Co. Inc.	157.7
Sachs Electric Co.	134.2
Fisk Electric Co.	109.7
Cupertino Electric Inc.	88.9
Rosendin Electric Inc.	88.5

Source: *ENR*, October 2, 1995, p. 32.

★ 179 ★
Contracting - Fire Protection (SIC 1742)

Top Fire Protection Contractors

Firms are ranked by sales in millions of dollars.

VSC Corp.	$ 35.74
COSCO Fire Protection	31.25
J.F. Aher Co.	27.41
Shambaugh & Sons Inc.	25.85
J.A. Croson Co.	16.45
Great Lakes Plumbing & Heating Co. . . .	12.29
F&G Mechanical Corp.	11.80
Eckert Mechanical Group	8.14
Scott Co. of California	7.10
John E. Green Co.	7.02

Source: *Contractor*, May 1996, p. 54.

★ 180 ★
Contracting - Sheet Metal (SIC 1761)

Sheet Metal Contractors - 1994

The top sheet metal contractors are ranked by 1994 revenues shown in millions of dollars.

Kirk & Blum	$ 55.8
EMCOR Group Inc.	52.9
Hill Mechanical Group	50.0
McKinstry Co.	35.7
Tougher Industries Inc.	31.4
The Egan Cos.	25.0
Bright Sheet Metal Co. Inc.	24.2
Bonland Industries Inc.	23.0
TDIndustries Inc.	22.1
B.H.W. Sheet Metal Co.	16.4

Source: *ENR*, October 2, 1995, p. 41.

★ 181 ★
Roofing (SIC 1761)

Roofing Market - 1993-95

The market was $16.5 billion in 1993, $16.1 billion in 1994, $15.8 billion in 1995.

	1993	1994	1995
Commercial	74.9%	71.5%	71.1%
Residential	25.1	28.5	28.9

Source: *Rural Builder*, May 1995, p. 14, from National Roofing Contractors Association.

★ 182 ★
Roofing (SIC 1761)

Roofing Preferences - South

Built-up	36.5%
Single-ply	24.0
Modified-bitumin	23.5
Other	16.0

Source: *Buildings & Operation Management*, August 1995, p. 10, from National Roofing Contractors Association.

★ 183 ★
Roofing (SIC 1761)

Roofing Preferences - West

Built-up	39.5%
Modified-bitumen	23.0
Single-ply	17.0
Other	29.5

Source: *Buildings & Operation Management*, August 1995, p. 10, from National Roofing Contractors Association.

★ 184 ★
Contracting - Concrete (SIC 1771)

Top Concrete Contractors - 1994

The top contractors specializing in concrete work are ranked by 1994 revenues shown in millions of dollars.

Baker Concrete Construction Inc.	$ 186.0
Ceco Concrete Construction	73.6
Miller & Long Co. Inc.	67.0
VSL Corp.	47.5
Structural Preservation Systems Inc.	33.5
Bomel Construction Co. Inc.	31.5
Capform Inc.	31.0
Colasanti Corp.	30.9
Cleveland Cement Contractors Inc.	28.9
Western Group	28.9

Source: *ENR*, October 2, 1995, p. 38.

★ 185 ★
Contracting - Water Work (SIC 1781)

Water/Waste Water Contractors

Firms are ranked by sales in millions of dollars.

The Poole & Kent Co.	$ 108.01
Emcor Group Inc.	96.00
Monterey Mechanical Co.	39.81
Harris Contracting Co.	38.80
J.F. Afhern Co.	21.32
H. Sand & Co. Inc.	15.00
Scott Co. of California	14.20
Fischbach Corp.	12.01

Source: *Contractor*, May 1996, p. 56.

★ 186 ★

Contracting - Glazing & Curtain Wall (SIC 1793)

Glazing & Curtain Wall Specialists

Contractors specializing in curtain wall erection and concrete surface glazing are ranked by 1994 revenues shown in millions of dollars.

Harmon Contract WSA Inc.	$ 314.0
Flour City Architectural Metals Inc.	40.0
WALTEK Inc.	37.7
MTH Industries	18.5
Atlantic Plate Glass Co. Inc.	16.6
Masonry Arts Inc.	14.3
American Glass & Metals Corp.	12.1
Tri-State Glass Inc.	12.0
National Glass & Mirror Co. Inc.	12.0
Ajay Glass & Mirror Co. Inc.	10.2

Source: *ENR*, October 2, 1995, p. 43.

★ 187 ★

Contracting - Excavation (SIC 1794)

Top Excavation and Foundation Contractors - 1994

The top contractors specializing in excavations and foundation building are ranked by 1994 revenues shown in millions of dollars.

Ryan Inc. Central	$ 80.2
Christensen Boyles Corp.	65.4
Hayward Baker Inc.	52.5
Malcolm Drilling Co. Inc.	48.5
Geo-Con Inc.	45.8
Borderland Construction Co. Inc.	42.1
Beaver Excavating Co.	40.0
AGRA Foundation Group	39.3
Ground Improvement Techniques Inc.	33.2
Independence Excavating Inc.	32.2

Source: *ENR*, October 2, 1995, p. 36.

★ 188 ★

Contracting - Demolition Work (SIC 1795)

Wrecking & Demolition Contractors

Leading contractors are ranked by 1994 revenues shown in millions of dollars.

Penhall International Inc.	$ 81.0
Cleveland Wrecking Co.	69.1
Bierlein Demolition Contractors Inc.	28.7
U.S. Dismantlement Corp.	$ 27.2
Olshan Demolishing Co. Inc.	22.5
Allied Erecting & Dismantling Co. Inc.	21.4
Best Group Inc.	20.4
Plant Reclamation/F. Scott Industries	20.3
Midwest Steel & Alloy Corp.	18.0
Integrated Wastes Special Services Inc.	14.1

Source: *ENR*, October 2, 1995, p. 46.

SIC 20 - Food and Kindred Products

★ 189 ★

Food (SIC 2000)

Clinical Nutrition Market

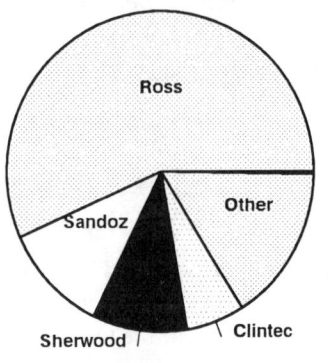

Shares are shown in percent.

Ross	57.0%
Sandoz	11.0
Sherwood	10.0
Clintec	6.0
Other	16.0

Source: *Investext,* Thomson Financial Services, January 9, 1996, p. 22, from company reports.

★ 190 ★

Food (SIC 2000)

Diet Aids/Food Supplement Market

The protein supplement and weight control market reached $652.3 million for the year ended October 8, 1995. Brand shares are shown in percent.

	Sales ($ mil.)	Market Share
Ultra Slim Fast	$ 173.4	26.6%
Ensure	161.0	24.7
Ensure Plus	142.3	21.8
Sweet Success	56.7	8.7
Slim Fast	20.6	3.2
Sustacal	6.4	1.0

	Sales ($ mil.)	Market Share
Boost	$ 2.8	0.4%
Ultra Slim Fast Plus	1.4	0.2
Sustacal Plus	1.2	0.2
Others	86.5	13.3

Source: *Nonfoods Merchandising*, April 1996, p. 23, from Information Resources Inc.

★ 191 ★

Food (SIC 2000)

Food Processing Market - Mexico

The food processing market in Mexico is shown in millions of dollars.

	1992 ($ mil.)	1993 ($ mil.)	Share
Beverages	$ 234.948	$ 296.983	32.1%
Vegetables	215.042	212.800	23.0
Chili peppers	209.079	201.186	21.7
Sauces	84.629	90.494	9.8
Fruit in syrup	58.419	56.879	6.1
Tomato paste	31.094	37.128	4.0
Marmalades	31.257	31.141	3.4

Source: *National Trade Data Bank*, January 1, 1996, p. IS9508.630, from Canned Food Industry National Chamber.

★ 192 ★

Food (SIC 2000)

Largest Food Producers

Firms are ranked by 1995 revenues in millions of dollars. Shares of the group are shown in percent.

	Rev. ($ mil.)	% of Group
ConAgra	$ 24,109	13.6%
Sara Lee	17,719	10.0
RJR Nabisco	16,008	9.0

Continued on next page.

51

★ 192 ★ *Continued*

Food (SIC 2000)

Largest Food Producers

Firms are ranked by 1995 revenues in millions of dollars. Shares of the group are shown in percent.

	Rev. ($ mil.)	% of Group
Archer Daniels Midland	$ 12,672	7.2%
IBP	12,668	7.2
CPC International	8,431	4.8
General Mills	8,394	4.7
H.J. Heinz	8,087	4.6
Campbell Soup	7,278	4.1
Farmland Industries	7,257	4.1
Ralston Purina	7,210	4.1
Kellogg	7,004	4.0
Quaker Oats	6,365	3.6
Tyson Foods	5,511	3.1
Dole Food	4,133	2.3
Chiquita Brands	4,037	2.3
Hershey Foods	3,691	2.1
Hormel Foods	3,046	1.7
Dean Foods	2,630	1.5
Agway	2,083	1.2
Specialty Foods	1,975	1.1
McCormick	1,859	1.0
Wm. Wrigley Jr.	1,770	1.0
Gold Kist	1,689	1.0
Smithfield Foods	1,527	0.9

Source: *Fortune*, April 29, 1996, p. F50.

★ 193 ★

Food (SIC 2000)

Popular Breakfast Foods

The table shows the percentage of households that consume each product for breakfast.

Cereals	37.0%
Bread products/baked sweet goods	28.0
Fruit	9.0
Eggs	8.0
Breakfast meats	7.0
Pancakes, waffles, french toast	6.0
Others	5.0

Source: *U.S. News & World Report*, April 29, 1996, p. 18, from Kraft Foods, National Eating Trends, National Consumers League, and Nielsen Consumer Information Services.

★ 194 ★

Food (SIC 2000)

Processed Food Market in Mexico

The table shows the market share of processed food sales at stores in Mexico.

Ante	18.0%
Aurrera	16.0
Comercial Mexicana	12.0
Superama	8.0
Sumesa	6.0
ISSSTE	4.0
Tiendas IMSS	4.0
Cadena Comerical Oxxo	4.0
Cadena Valso	3.0
Casa Ley	2.0
Tiendas Chedraui	2.0
Neighborhood stores	9.0
Restaurants	7.0
Public markets	5.0

Source: *National Trade Data Bank*, September 1, 1995, p. 111090815.

★ 195 ★

Food (SIC 2000)

Processed Vegetables Market

The market was valued at $201.19 million in 1993.

Frozen vegetables	58.2%
Mushrooms	16.0
Corn	7.6
Peas	6.2
Mixed vegetables	5.3
Nopal	1.4
Asparagus	1.1
String beans	0.1
Other	4.0

Source: *National Trade Data Bank*, January 1, 1996, p. IS9508.630, from Canned Food Industry National Chamber.

★ 196 ★

Food (SIC 2000)

Top Food Companies - Mexico

The top 20 food firms in Mexico are ranked by 1994 sales in millions of dollars.

	($ mil.)	% of Group
Grupo Industrial Bimbo	$ 1,787.0	20.2%
CIA Nestle	1,416.0	16.0
Gruma	1,190.0	13.4
Grupo Industrial Marseca	625.0	7.1
Grupo Industrial Lala	454.0	5.1
Sigma Alimentos	435.0	4.9
Industrial Bachoco	418.0	4.7
Anderson Clayton	409.0	4.6
Ganaderos Productores De Leche Pura	338.0	3.8
Grupo Herdez	305.0	3.4
Agribios	218.0	2.5
Pasteurizadora Laguna	192.0	2.2
Jugos Del Valle	164.0	1.9
Grupo Quan	154.0	1.7
Promotora Industrial Azucarero	153.0	1.7
Donone De Mexico	141.0	1.6
Lechera Guadolajara	139.0	1.6
Tablex	136.0	1.5
Helados Holanda	96.0	1.1
Pasteurizadora Del Nazas	94.0	1.1

Source: *Food Engineering*, January 1996, p. 63, from *Chilton's Expansion Magazine*.

★ 197 ★

Food (SIC 2000)

Top Public Food Firms

The top companies in the United States and Canada are ranked by food and beverage sales in millions of dollars for 1995.

Philip Morris Companies Inc.	$ 33,378.0
PepsiCo. Inc.	19,093.0
ConAgra Inc.	18,309.0
Coca-Cola Co.	17,963.0
IBP Inc.	12,668.0
Anheuser-Busch Companies Inc.	9,586.0
Sara Lee Corp.	8,887.0
Nabisco Inc.	8,294.0
H.J. Heinz Co.	8,087.0
Campbell Soup Co.	7,278.0
CPC International Inc.	7,199.0
Kellogg Co.	7,004.0
Seagram Co.	6,694.0
Quaker Oats Co.	6,365.0
Tyson Foods Inc.	5,511.0

Source: *Prepared Foods*, July 1996, p. 12.

★ 198 ★

Food (SIC 2000)

Top Shelf Stable Foods

The top items are ranked by sales in millions of dollars.

Dry dinners	$ 1,100
Mexican tortillas	485
Rice mixes	450
Beans with meat	433
Chili	297
Rice cakes	242
Canned spaghetti	222
Canned ravioli	190
Macaroni products	160
Beef stew	144

Source: *DM*, August 1995, p. 70, from A.C. Nielsen.

★ 199 ★

Meat Packing (SIC 2011)

Leading Meat Packing Houses

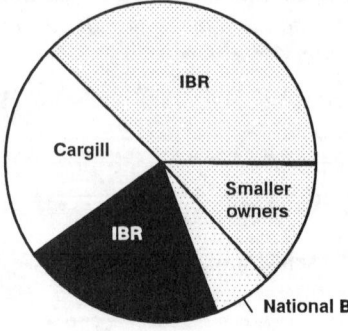

Shares of the market are shown in percent.

IBR 38.0%
Cargill 22.0
IBR 21.0
National Beef 6.0
Smaller owners 13.0

Source: *New York Times*, October 17, 1995, p. C6, from National Association Livestock Marketing Information Center, United States Department of Agriculture, and *Cattle Buyers Weekly*.

★ 200 ★

Meat Products (SIC 2011)

Beef Production - North America

Data are in thousands of metric tons for 1992-94.

United States 10,700
Mexico 1,700
Canada 900

Source: *NAFTA. International Agriculture and Trade Reports*, May 1995, p. 23, from United States Department of Agriculture.

★ 201 ★

Meat Products (SIC 2011)

Meat Production - Mexico

Production is shown in thousands of tons.

	1992	1993
Beef	1,247	1,256
Pork	820	822
Goats	43	42
Mutton/lamb	28	29

Source: *National Trade Data Bank*, March 2, 1996, p. IS9411.037.

★ 202 ★

Meat Products (SIC 2011)

Pork Production - North America

Data are in thousands of metric tons for 1992-94.

United States 7,700
Canada 1,200
Mexico 900

Source: *NAFTA. International Agriculture and Trade Reports*, May 1995, p. 23, from United States Department of Agriculture.

★ 203 ★

Meat Products (SIC 2013)

Hot Dog Producers

Shares are shown based on sales of $1.4 billion for the 52 weeks ended July 16, 1995.

	Sales ($ mil.)	Share
Oscar Mayer	$ 261.3	18.7%
Hygrade	187.2	13.4
ConAgra	161.9	11.6
Hillshire Farms	68.2	4.9
Private label	108.7	7.8
Others	612.7	43.8

Source: *Brandweek*, September 25, 1995, p. 22, from Information Resources Inc.

★ 204 ★

Meat Products (SIC 2013)

Meat Alternatives Market

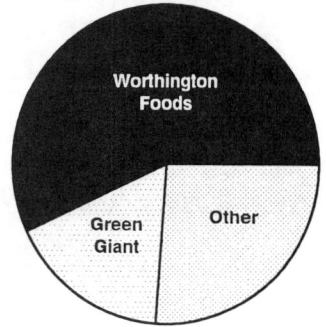

Shares are for 1995.

Worthington Foods 57.0%
Green Giant 17.0
Other 26.0

Source: *Financial World*, February 26, 1996, p. 20.

★ 205 ★

Meat Products (SIC 2013)

Meat Snack Market

Supermarket sales are shown by type for 1994. New flavors this year include turkey jerky, venison jerky, and buffalo jerky.

Regular 38.5%
Smoked 18.0
Teriyaki . . . . ⸲ 6.0
Meat & cheese 5.8
BBQ 0.2
Other 17.3

Source: *U.S. Distribution Journal*, July 15, 1995, p. 22, from *Snack Food Association's Industry Report, 1995.*

★ 206 ★

Slaughter Houses (SIC 2015)

Beef Slaughter Houses

Shares of the beef slaughtering market are shown in percent.

IBP 32.0%
ConAgra 21.0
Cargill 17.0
Other 30.0

Source: *Investext,* Thomson Financial Services, May 19, 1995, p. 9, from federally inspected slaughter numbers.

★ 207 ★

Slaughter Houses (SIC 2015)

Pork Slaughter Houses

Shares of the pork slaughtering market are shown in percent.

IBP 20.0%
ConAgra 12.0
Hormel 10.0
Smithfield 10.0
Other 48.0

Source: *Investext,* Thomson Financial Services, May 19, 1995, p. 9, from federally inspected slaughter numbers.

★ 208 ★

Dairy Products (SIC 2020)

Dairy Product Market - Saskatchewan

The market for milk, sour cream, yogurt, cottage cheese and ice cream in Saskatchewan is shown by company.

Dairyworld Foods 83.0%
Other 17.0

Source: *Marketing Magazine*, April 15, 1996, p. 4.

★ 209 ★

Dairy Products (SIC 2020)

Leading Dairy Cooperatives

The top cooperatives are ranked by sales in millions of dollars.

Land O'Lakes Inc.	$ 1,468.0
Mid-America Dairymen Inc.	1,371.0
Associated Milk Producers Inc.	1,291.0
Prairie Farms Dairy Inc.	763.0
Darigold Inc.	738.0
Dairyman's Coop Creamery Association	558.0
Wisconsin Dairies Cooperative	491.0
Milk Marketing Inc.	317.0
Alto Dairy Cooperative	246.0
Swiss Valley Farms Co.	220.0
Danish Creamery Association	210.0
San Joaquin Valley Dairymen's Assoc.	208.0
Golden Guernsey Dairy Cooperative	188.0
Upstate Milk Cooperative Inc.	162.0
California Gold Dairy Products	132.0

Source: *Dairy Foods*, July 1995, p. 14, from Datamonitor.

★ 210 ★

Dairy Products (SIC 2020)

Leading Dairy Food Makers

Leading dairy companies are ranked by 1994 sales in millions of dollars. ConAgra's figure includes Beatrice Cheese Co. and Healthy Choice frozen dessert sales. Some of the data are estimates.

Kraft USA	$ 3,200.0
Dean Foods Co.	1,469.0
Borden Inc.	1,300.0
Schreiber Foods Inc.	975.0
ConAgra Inc.	900.0
Good Humor-Breyers Ice Cream	900.0
Bols Wessanen USA Inc.	820.0
Stella Foods Inc.	750.0
Leprino Foods Co.	735.0
Baskin-Robbins USA Co.	580.0
Dreyer's/Edy's Grand Ice Cream Inc.	564.0
H.P. Hood Inc.	550.0
Besnier America	495.0
Dannon Co.	490.0
Wells' Dairy Inc.	450.0

Source: *Dairy Foods*, July 1995, p. 13.

★ 211 ★

Dairy Products (SIC 2020)

Top Dairy Processors

The top companies are ranked by 1994 sales in millions of dollars.

Kraft Foods	$ 3,300
Associated Milk Producers	2,600
Mid-America Dairymen Inc.	2,500
Land O'Lakes Inc.	1,480
Dean Foods Co.	1,440
Borden Inc.	1,280
Schreiber Foods Green Bay	1,280
Kroger Co.	1,260
ConAgra Inc.	1,100
Leprino Foods	1,100
Prairie Farms Dairy Inc.	1,100
Milk Marketing Co.	1,000
Baskin-Robbins Co.	925
Darigold Inc.	903
Good Humor-Breyers Ice Cream	900

Source: *Hoard's Dairyman*, December 1995, p. 801.

★ 212 ★

Butter (SIC 2021)

Butter Makers - Mexico

The table shows who leads the Mexican butter market. "Other" includes its largest competitors Cremeria Americana and Chalco. Leading producers of margarine include Anderseon Clayton and Carrencedo.

Prolesa	50.0%
Other	50.0

Source: *National Trade Data Bank*, March 2, 1996, p. IS9508.639.

★ 213 ★

Butter (SIC 2021)

Top Butter Brands

Shares are shown for the 52 weeks ended December 3, 1995.

Private label	41.4%
Land O'Lakes	35.9
Other	22.7

Source: *Brandweek*, February 26, 1996, p. 24, from Information Resources Inc.

★ 214 ★

Cheese (SIC 2022)

Cheese Production by Type

The table shows the variation of cheese produced by manufacturer, based on a survey of 100 respondents.

Flavored cheese	31.0%
Blended cheese	21.0
Smoked cheese	20.0
Spiced cheese	13.0
Mixed cheese	10.0
Other	5.0

Source: *School Foodservice & Nutrition*, May 1996, p. 12, from FoodTrends.

★ 215 ★

Cheese (SIC 2022)

Natural Cheese Leaders

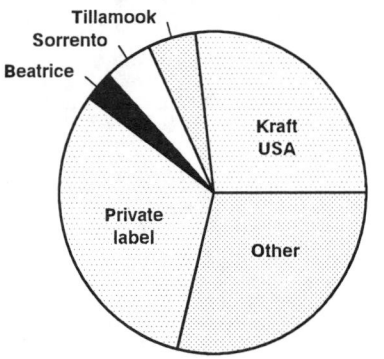

Shares of the $1.6 billion market are shown in percent for 1995.

Kraft USA	26.8%
Tillamook	4.9
Sorrento	4.9
Beatrice	3.3
Private label	30.8
Other	29.3

Source: *Dairy Foods*, April 1996, p. 7, from Information Resources Inc.

★ 216 ★

Cheese (SIC 2022)

Processed American Cheese Leaders

Shares of the $1.6 billion market are shown in percent for 1995.

	($ mil.)	Share
Kraft USA	$ 1,008.0	61.3%
Private label	384.3	23.4
Borden	136.9	8.3
Land O'Lakes	25.0	1.5
Beatrice	19.4	1.2
Other	26.4	4.3

Source: *Dairy Foods*, April 1996, p. 7, from Information Resources Inc.

★ 217 ★

Cheese (SIC 2022)

Shredded Cheese Leaders

Shares of the $1.1 billion market are shown in percent for 1995.

Kraft USA	25.1%
Sargento	22.6
Beatrice	6.5
Sorrento	2.7
Private label	34.5
Other	8.6

Source: *Dairy Foods*, April 1996, p. 7, from Information Resources Inc.

★ 218 ★

Baby Formula (SIC 2023)

Infant Formula Makers

Shares of the $2.62 billion market are shown for the 52 weeks ended June 1995.

Abbott	50.0%
Bristol Myers Squibb	32.0
American Home Products	10.0
Nestle	6.0
Sandoz	2.0

Source: *Investext,* Thomson Financial Services, May 10, 1996, p. 6, from A.C. Nielsen.

★ 219 ★
Egg Nog (SIC 2023)

Leading Egg Nog Brands

Shares are shown for the 52 weeks ended June 10, 1995 based on total sales of $76.3 million.

Private label	29.8%
Borden	10.2
Hood Golden	4.5
Dean	4.0
Darigold	2.1
Meadow Gold	2.1
Kemps	2.0
Sealtest	1.9
Southern Comfort	1.6
Hood Golden Light	1.5
C.F. Burger	1.5
Quality Chek'd	1.4
Other	37.4

Source: *Beverage World's Periscope*, December 31, 1995, p. 8, from A.C. Nielsen.

★ 220 ★
Infant Formula (SIC 2023)

Top Formula Brands - Canada

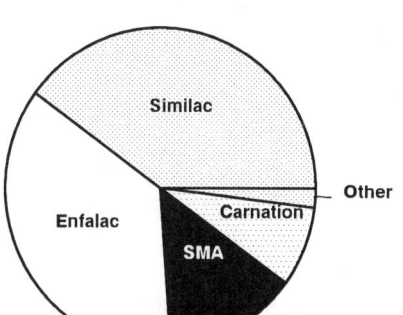

Shares of the $175 million market are shown in percent. Data are based on tonnage sales.

Similac	40.0%
Enfalac	36.0
SMA	14.0
Carnation	8.0
Other	2.0

Source: *Marketing Magazine*, July 15, 1996, p. 4.

★ 221 ★
Frozen Desserts (SIC 2024)

Frozen Yogurt Brands

Shares of the $585 million market are shown in percent for the 52 weeks ended December 5, 1995.

Private label	15.5%
Dreyer's/Edy's	8.5
Kemps	8.4
Ben & Jerry's	7.0
Breyer's	6.5
Other	54.1

Source: *Dairy Foods*, March 1996, p. 70, from Information Resources Inc.

★ 222 ★
Frozen Desserts (SIC 2024)

Leading Frozen Novelty Brands

Brands are ranked by sales in millions of dollars for the 52 weeks ended December 3, 1995.

	Sales ($ mil.)	Share
Private label	$ 225.9	14.8%
Klondike	91.9	6.0
Popsicle	87.3	5.7
Drumstick	57.8	3.8
Haagen-Dazs	3.6	1.6

Source: *Dairy Foods*, March 1996, p. 69, from Information Resources Inc.

★ 223 ★
Frozen Desserts (SIC 2024)

Leading Sherbert/Sorbet Brands

Shares of the $161 million market are shown for the 52 weeks ended December 5, 1995.

Private label	29.3%
Haagen-Dazs	21.6
Dreyer's/Edy's	4.5
Real Fruit	4.5
Blue Bell	2.9
Other	37.2

Source: *Dairy Foods*, March 1996, p. 67, from Information Resources Inc.

★ 224 ★
Ice Cream (SIC 2024)

Ice Cream Makers

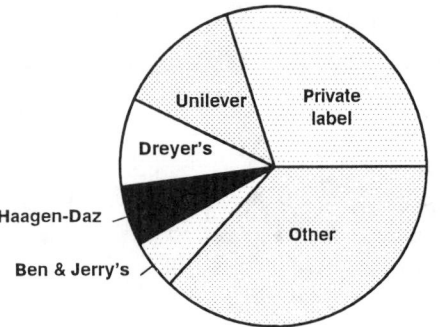

Shares of the $3.3 billion market are shown for the 52 weeks ended May 21, 1995.

Private label	30.0%
Unilever	13.0
Dreyer's	9.3
Haagen-Daz	5.6
Ben & Jerry's	5.2
Other	36.9

Source: *Advertising Age*, September 11, 1995, p. 45, from Information Resources Inc.

★ 225 ★
Ice Cream (SIC 2024)

Leading Ice Cream Brands

Shares of the $2.6 billion market are shown for the 52 weeks ended December 3, 1995.

Breyers	12.7%
Dreyer's/Edy's	9.6
Haagen-Dazs	4.7
Ben & Jerry's	3.8
Private label	28.1
Other	41.1

Source: *Dairy Foods*, March 1996, p. 68, from Information Resources Inc.

★ 226 ★
Ice Cream (SIC 2024)

Top Ice Cream Brands

Shares are shown for the 52 weeks ended December 3, 1995.

Private label	28.1%
Good Humor-Breyers	13.1
Edy's-Dreyer's	12.2
Blue Bell	5.8
Haagen-Dazs	5.2
Other	35.6

Source: *Brandweek*, February 19, 1996, p. 20, from Information Resources Inc.

★ 227 ★
Milk (SIC 2026)

Premium Milk Market - Ontario

Premium milk refers to milk produced with a double pasteurization process. It also refers to milk with increased levels of calcium and protein. Company shares of the market are shown in percent.

Ault Foods of Toronto	34.0%
Beatrice Foods of Toronto	33.0
Neilson Dairy	33.0

Source: *Marketing Magazine*, April 22, 1996, p. 2.

★ 228 ★
Yogurt (SIC 2026)

Nutritional Yogurt Market - Quebec

The nutritional yogurt market is shown by company. It has a 26% share across all of Canada. This yogurt is advertised as having germ fighting properties and helps prevent various infections.

Delisle Foods	50.0%
Others	50.0

Source: *Marketing Magazine*, February 26, 1996, p. 3.

★ 229 ★

Yogurt (SIC 2026)

Yogurt Producers

Yogurt market reached $1.6 billion as of November 5, 1995. Shares are shown in percent.

	($ mil.)	Share
Danon	$ 607.6	38.0%
Yoplait	321.1	20.0
Private label	238.7	15.0
Other	432.6	27.0

Source: *Dairy Foods*, March 1996, p. 29, from Information Resources Inc.

★ 230 ★

Baby Food (SIC 2032)

Baby Food Makers

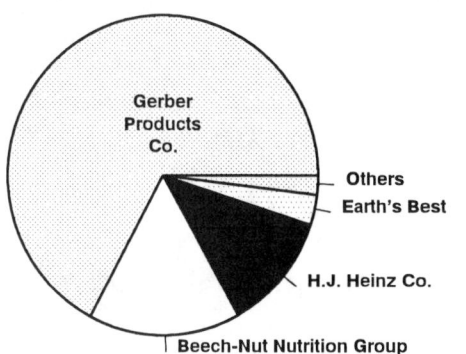

Shares are shown based on total sales of $740.3 million in 1995.

Gerber Products Co.	68.3%
Beech-Nut Nutrition Group	15.8
H.J. Heinz Co.	11.5
Earth's Best	2.9
Others	1.5

Source: *Advertising Age*, April 1, 1996, p. 17, from Information Resources Inc.

★ 231 ★

Canned Food (SIC 2032)

Canned Pasta Makers

Shares of the market are shown for the 52 weeks ended March 24, 1996.

American Home	58.5%
Campbell Soup Co.	35.6
Private label	4.6
Other	1.3

Source: *Advertising Age*, July 1, 1996, p. 6, from Information Resources Inc.

★ 232 ★

Canned Food (SIC 2032)

Refrigerated Pudding Market

Shares of the $380 million market are shown in percent.

Jell-O	60.0%
Swiss Miss	28.0
Other	12.0

Source: *Chicago Tribune*, November 17, 1995, p. C3, from Information Resources Inc.

★ 233 ★

Canned Food (SIC 2032)

Shelf-Stable Pudding Market

Shares of the $170 million market are shown in percent.

Hunt's Snack Pack	60.0%
Del Monte Pudding Cup	27.0
Other	13.0

Source: *Chicago Tribune*, November 17, 1995, p. C3, from Information Resources Inc.

★ 234 ★
Canned Food (SIC 2033)
Canned Fruit Market - Mexico

The market for fruit in syrup in Mexico reached $56.87 million in 1993.

Peaches	59.6%
Pineapples	21.6
Mangoes	5.3
Mixed fruit & others	13.4

Source: *National Trade Data Bank*, January 1, 1996, p. IS9508.630, from Canned Food Industry National Chamber.

★ 235 ★
Canned Food (SIC 2033)
Canned Fruit Sales

Sales reached $1.96 billion in 1994. Sales are shown by segment.

Peaches	19.7%
Applesauce	16.6
Fruit cocktail	14.8
Pineapple	12.1
Pears	9.3
Cranberries	6.2
Citrus fruit	2.9
Apricots	1.7
Other	16.6

Source: *Supermarket Business*, September 1995, p. 58.

★ 236 ★
Canned Food (SIC 2033)
Canned Vegetable Brands

Brands are ranked by 1995 sales in millions of dollars. Shares of the group are shown in percent.

	Sales ($ mil.)	% of Group
Private label	$ 599.0	45.9%
Del Monte	333.0	25.5
Green Giant	304.0	23.3
Larsen	68.0	5.2

Source: *Wall Street Journal*, February 20, 1996, p. B4, from Information Resources Inc.

★ 237 ★
Canned Food (SIC 2033)
Canned Vegetables Market

Sales reached $3.602 billion for 1994.

Corn	17.7%
Beans with pork or sauce	13.4
Tomatoes	12.9
Beans (waxed & green)	12.3
Tomato sauce	10.6
Peas	8.7
Mushrooms	6.8
Tomato paste	4.6
Potatoes	3.5
Asparagus	2.4
Beets	2.2
Sauerkraut	2.0
Tomato puree	1.4
Other	1.4

Source: *Supermarket Business*, September 1995, p. 58.

★ 238 ★
Canned Food (SIC 2033)
Ketchup Makers

Shares of the $427.6 million market are shown in percent for the year ended November 6, 1994.

Heinz	57.6%
Hunt-Wesson	21.0
Private label	13.5
Del Monte	6.6
Other	1.3

Source: *Investext,* Thomson Financial Services, January 5, 1995, p. 3, from Information Resources Inc. and PaineWebber estimates.

★ 239 ★
Canned Food (SIC 2033)

Tomato Paste/Sauce Makers

Shares of the $409.3 million market are shown in percent for the year ended November 6, 1994.

Hunt Wesson	39.5%
Private label	27.4
Nestle	17.8
Del Monte	4.7
Tri-Valley Growers	3.3
Pet Inc.	2.2
Other	5.1

Source: *Investext,* Thomson Financial Services, January 5, 1995, p. 2, from Information Resources Inc. and PaineWebber estimates.

★ 240 ★
Juices (SIC 2033)

Apple Juice Leaders

Shares are shown based on $586.9 million in sales at food stores for the year ended December 9, 1995.

Mott's	14.0%
Tree Top	9.0
Seneca	7.8
Lucky Leaf	4.5
Musselman's	4.5
White House	3.5
Langers	3.4
Minute Maid	3.2
Apple & Eve	2.1
Red Cheek	1.9
Juicy Juice	1.8
Private label	29.0
Other	15.3

Source: *Beverage World's Periscope*, June 30, 1996, p. 10, from A.C. Nielsen.

★ 241 ★
Juices (SIC 2033)

Aseptic Juice Market

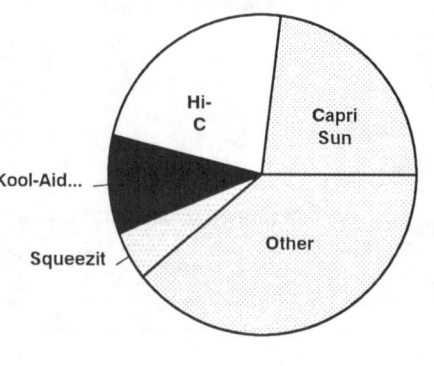

Brand shares of the $564.8 million category are shown in percent.

Capri Sun (Kraft Foods)	23.3%
Hi-C (Coca-Cola Foods)	22.6
Kool-Aid Kool Bursts (Kraft's)	9.7
Squeezit (General Mills)	5.4
Other	39.0

Source: *Advertising Age*, July 29, 1996, p. 7, from Information Resources Inc.

★ 242 ★
Juices (SIC 2033)

Chilled/Shelf-Stable Orange Juices

Brand shares of the $2.09 billion market are shown for the 52 weeks ended December 9, 1995.

Tropicana	39.4%
Private label	21.2
Minute Maid	19.6
Florida's Natural	6.3
Floridagold	1.4
Donald Duck	1.2
Just Squeezed	0.8
Floridagold Premium Select	0.6
Old South	0.5
Sealtest	0.4
Quality Chekd	0.4
Hood	0.3
Anderson Erickson	0.3

Continued on next page.

★ 242 ★ *Continued*

Juices (SIC 2033)

Chilled/Shelf-Stable Orange Juices

Brand shares of the $2.09 billion market are shown for the 52 weeks ended December 9, 1995.

Dean Foods	0.3%
Juice Harvest	0.3
Odwalla	0.3
Other	6.7

Source: *Beverage World's Periscope*, June 30, 1996, p. 14, from A.C. Nielsen.

★ 243 ★

Juices (SIC 2033)

Cranberry Juice/Drink Market

Shares of the $700.7 million market are shown for the year ended March 11, 1995.

Ocean Spray	70.2%
Private label	16.8
Tropicana Twister	4.0
Apple & Eve	3.0
Minute Maid	1.5
Ocean Spray Refresher	1.4
Langers	1.0
Tropicana	0.5
Veryfine	0.5
Ruby Kist	0.2
R W Knudsen	0.2
Other	0.7

Source: *Beverage World's Periscope*, August 31, 1995, p. 14, from A.C. Nielsen.

★ 244 ★

Juices (SIC 2033)

Frozen Fruit Beverage Leaders

The market for frozen fruit beverages (non-O.J.) is shown for the year ended December 9, 1995. Total sales in foodstores reached $350 million. By volume, Seneca lead the market with a 14.9% share.

Dole	15.7%
Seneca	14.4
Welch's	11.1
Welch's 100's	8.7
Minute Maid	5.7
Tree Top	3.6
Chiquita	2.8
Old Orchard	1.9
Donald Duck	0.4
Lucky Leaf	0.4
Private label	21.5
Other	13.8

Source: *Beverage World's Periscope*, May 31, 1996, p. 15, from A.C. Nielsen.

★ 245 ★
Juices (SIC 2033)

Frozen Orange Juice Brands

Shares are shown for the year ended December 3, 1995.

	Sales ($ mil.)	Share
Minute Maid	$ 251.7	38.7%
Tropicana	44.7	6.9
Citrus World	14.8	2.3
Private label	273.7	42.0
Other	66.1	10.2

Source: *Advertising Age*, February 5, 1996, p. 12, from Information Resources Inc.

★ 246 ★
Juices (SIC 2033)

Fruit Beverage Market

The market is shown by segment.

	1992	1993	1994
Fruit juices	64.8%	63.6%	61.1%
Fruit drinks	35.2	36.4	38.9

Source: *Dairy Foods*, March 1996, p. 35, from Beverage Marketing Corp.

★ 247 ★
Juices (SIC 2033)

Juice Market by Type - 1995

Shares are shown based on $4.18 billion in supermarket sales.

Apple juice/cider	14.7%
Cranberry juice	9.8
Grape juice	5.1
Grapefruit	4.2
Orange	2.4
Nectars	2.2
Prune	2.2
Tomato	2.0
Pineapple	1.5
Lemon/lime	1.2
Other vegetable	5.3
Other juices	2.2

Source: *Progressive Grocer*, July 1996, p. 60.

★ 248 ★
Juices (SIC 2033)

Leading Refrigerated O.J. Brands

Shares are shown for the year ended December 3, 1995.

	Sales ($ mil.)	Share
Tropicana	$ 823.7	39.2%
Private label	502.9	23.9
Minute Maid	404.1	19.2
Citrus World	161.7	7.7
Other	207.6	9.9

Source: *Advertising Age*, February 5, 1996, p. 12, from Information Resources Inc.

★ 249 ★
Juices (SIC 2033)

Popular Apple Juice Brands

Shares are shown based on shelf-stable apple juice sales of $584.4 million. Data are for the 52 weeks ended June 10, 1995.

	($ mil.)	Share
Mott's	$ 79.5	13.4%
Tree Top	55.0	9.3
Seneca	43.0	7.2
Lucky Leaf	27.3	4.6
Musselman's	26.1	4.4
Langers	20.4	3.4
White House	19.5	3.3
Minute Maid	19.5	3.3
Apple & Eve	13.3	2.2
Private label	179.3	30.2
Others	111.5	18.8

Source: *Beverage World's Periscope*, December 31, 1995, p. 10, from A.C. Nielsen.

★ 250 ★
Juices (SIC 2033)

Popular Chilled/Shelf-Stable Juices

Brand shares of the $2.37 billion market are shown for the 52 weeks ended December 9, 1995.

Gatorade	15.9%
Sunny Delight	15.8
Hi-C	7.7
Ocean Spray	6.9
Minute Maid	6.3

Continued on next page.

★ 250 ★ *Continued*

Juices (SIC 2033)

Popular Chilled/Shelf-Stable Juices

Brand shares of the $2.37 billion market are shown for the 52 weeks ended December 9, 1995.

Capri Sun	6.0%
Private label	4.8
Snapple	4.1
Hawaiian Punch	3.9
Tropicana Twister	2.5
Tampico	2.5
Kool-Aid Bursts	1.9
Squeezit	1.8
Powerade	1.5
Mistic	1.1
Other	17.3

Source: *Beverage World's Periscope*, June 30, 1996, p. 14, from A.C. Nielsen.

★ 251 ★

Juices (SIC 2033)

Popular Shelf-Stable Juices

Shares are shown based on $2.22 billion in sales for the 52 weeks ended June 6, 1995.

Gatorade	15.5%
Sunny Delight	15.4
Hi-C	8.4
Minute Maid	7.2
Ocean Spray	6.7
Capri Sun	5.6
Snapple	4.6
Hawaiian Punch	3.8
Tropicana Twister	2.6
Tampico	2.3
Kool-Aid Bursts	2.2
Squeezit	2.0
Mondo	1.2
PowerAde	1.2
Tropicana	1.2
Veryfine	1.1
Five Alive	1.0
Fruitopia	0.8
Welch's Orchard	0.7
Private label	4.6
Other	11.9

Source: *Beverage World's Periscope*, November 30, 1995, p. 10, from A.C. Nielsen.

★ 252 ★

Juices (SIC 2033)

Refrigerated Fruit Drink Market

Shares of the market are shown in percent.

Sunny Delight	54.4%
Other	45.6

Source: *Advertising Age*, June 24, 1996, p. S24, from Information Resources Inc.

★ 253 ★

Juices (SIC 2033)

Tomato Juice Leaders

Shares are shown based on total sales of $84.8 million for the 52 weeks ended March 11, 1995.

Campbell's	53.0%
Private label	23.8
Sacramento	6.1
Hunt's	6.0
Del Monte	4.5
Red Gold	1.6
Stokely	1.0
Welch's	0.9
Generic	0.7
Glorietta	0.4
Snow Floss	0.4
Heinz	0.3
S&W	0.3
Beckman's	0.2
Libby's	0.1
Other	0.7

Source: *Beverage World's Periscope*, August 31, 1995, p. 16, from A.C. Nielsen.

★ 254 ★

Powdered Milk (SIC 2033)

Powdered Milk Market - Mexico

Nestle	75.0%
Other	25.0

Source: *National Trade Data Bank*, March 2, 1996, p. IS9508.639.

★ 255 ★

Raisins (SIC 2034)

Raisin Market - 1995

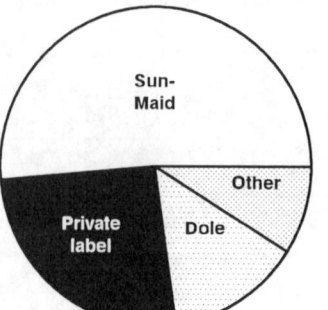

Sales are shown by brand for the 52 weeks ended March 24, 1996. Shares are shown based on a $218.3 million market.

	($ mil.)	Share
Sun-Maid	$ 112.7	51.6%
Private label	57.4	26.3
Dole	29.4	13.5
Other	18.8	8.6

Source: *Brandweek*, May 27, 1996, p. 16, from Information Resources Inc.

★ 256 ★

Soups (SIC 2034)

Canned Soups by Brand

Shares are shown for the year ended October 29, 1995. Campbell has a 79.2% share of the canned soup market; its traditional line is under "Red and white"; their Chunky, Home Cookin' brand is included under "ready to serve"; "Broth" is also a Campbell product.

Red and white	64.5%
Ready to serve	11.0
Progresso	5.6
Broth	3.7
Healthy Choice	2.0
Private label	7.6
All others	5.6

Source: *New York Times*, November 17, 1995, p. C1, from Information Resources Inc.

★ 257 ★

Soups (SIC 2034)

Ready-to-Serve Soup Market

In the condensed segment, Campbell holds an 88% share.

Campbell Soup Co.	56.4%
ConAgra	10.5
Other	33.1

Source: *Advertising Age*, June 24, 1996, p. 47, from Sachs & Co.

★ 258 ★

Mayonnaise (SIC 2035)

Mayonnaise Market - Mexico

McCormick	50.0%
Hellman's	27.0
Other	23.0

Source: *Investext*, Thomson Financial Services, January 25, 1995, p. 2.

★ 259 ★

Pickles and Olives (SIC 2035)

Pickle and Olive Spending

Pickles, dill	33.9%
Pickles, sweet	13.7
Olives, black	13.3
Olives, green	10.9
Peppers	7.2
Relishes	5.3
Chilies	2.6
Pimentos	1.2
Other	1.5

Source: *Progressive Grocer*, July 1996, p. 62.

★ 260 ★
Salad Dressings (SIC 2035)
Salad Dressing Market

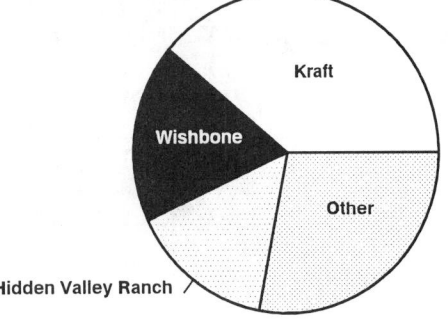

Brand shares are shown in percent. Unilever produces Wishbone; Clorox Co. produces Hidden Valley Ranch.

Kraft	39.3%
Wishbone	17.7
Hidden Valley Ranch	15.1
Other	27.9

Source: *Advertising Age*, April 29, 1996, p. 17, from Information Resources Inc.

★ 261 ★
Sauces (SIC 2035)
Mexican Sauce Brands

Shares of the $747.3 million market are shown for the year ended September 9, 1995. Campbell Soup Co. is the leading salsa producer with a 25.5% share.

	Sales ($ mil.)	Market Share
Pace	$ 193.4	25.9%
Old El Paso	117.2	17.7
Tostitos	116.3	15.6
Chi Chi's	62.1	8.3
Ortega	42.5	5.7
La Victoria	34.5	4.6
Taco Bell	22.0	2.9
Las Palmas	15.8	2.1
Eagle	9.7	1.3
Private label	32.5	4.4
Other	101.3	11.5

Source: *Snack Food*, February 1996, p. 20, from Information Resources Inc.

★ 262 ★
Sauces (SIC 2035)
Pasta Sauce Producers

Companies are ranked by 1995 sales in millions of dollars. Unilever makes Ragu and Five Brothers; Campbell makes Prego.

	Sales ($ mil.)	Share
Unilever	$ 465.9	36.0%
Campbell	325.7	25.2
Hunt-Wesson	137.0	10.6
Borden	125.6	9.7
Private label	44.3	3.4
Other	194.5	15.0

Source: *Advertising Age*, March 25, 1996, p. 49, from Information Resources Inc.

★ 263 ★
Sauces (SIC 2035)
Sauce Market - Mexico

The market grew from $84.629 million in 1992 to $90.49 million in 1993.

	1992	1993
Ketchup	43.2%	45.8%
Semi-solid	32.7	34.3
Liquid	24.2	19.9

Source: *National Trade Data Bank*, January 1, 1996, p. IS9508.630, from Canned Food Industry National Chamber.

★ 264 ★
Sauces (SIC 2035)
Steak Sauce Market

Shares of the meat sauce market are shown in percent.

A-1	65.0%
Other	35.0

Source: *Prepared Foods*, September 1995, p. 36.

★ 265 ★

Sauces (SIC 2035)

Steak Sauce Producers

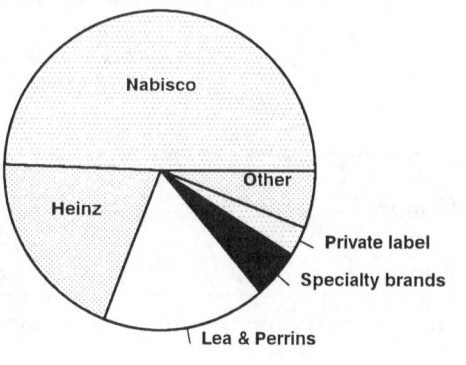

Data are for 1994.

Nabisco	49.9%
Heinz	19.8
Lea & Perrins	16.6
Specialty brands	4.5
Private label	3.4
Other	5.8

Source: *Investext,* Thomson Financial Services, February 22, 1995, p. 26, from Information Resources Inc. InfoScan.

★ 266 ★

Frozen Fruits (SIC 2037)

Frozen Fruit Market

The retail and institutional fruit market is shown for 1994.

	Lbs. (000)	Share
Strawberries	436,431.0	39.9%
Blueberries	130,584.0	11.9
Peaches	102,073.0	9.3
Apples	91,709.0	8.4
Purees, non-citrus	63,122.0	5.8
Red raspberries	28,754.0	2.6
Blackberries	24,226.0	2.2
Cherries, sweet	18,480.0	1.7
Apricots	18,192.0	1.7
Boysenberries	5,105.0	0.5

	Lbs. (000)	Share
Plums & prunes	1,181.0	0.1%
Black raspberries	1,146.0	0.1
Loganberries	59.0	0.0
Miscellaneous	173,099.0	15.8

Source: *Quick Frozen Foods International*, October 1995, p. A16.

★ 267 ★

Frozen Vegetables (SIC 2037)

Frozen Vegetables

The retail and institutional vegetable market is shown for 1994.

	Lbs. (000)	Share
Potato products	7,934,849.0	71.0%
Corn products	1,131,554.0	10.1
Green peas	444,953.0	4.0
Green beans	322,049.0	2.9
Carrots	304,196.0	2.7
Spinach	207,390.0	1.9
Broccoli	149,178.0	1.3
Onions	100,138.0	0.9
Lima beans	91,960.0	0.8
Okra	65,114.0	0.6
Summer squash	54,887.0	0.5
Brussel sprouts	37,983.0	0.3
Peppers, bell	33,588.0	0.3
Black-eyed peas	33,427.0	0.3
Cauliflower	31,802.0	0.3
Celery	28,504.0	0.3
Pumpkin/cooked squash	27,356.0	0.2
Turnips	21,998.0	0.2
Mushrooms	21,177.0	0.2
Collards	20,871.0	0.2
Turnip greens	19,834.0	0.2
Sweet potatoes/yams	19,506.0	0.2
Asparagus	14,967.0	0.1
Wax beans	9,144.0	0.1
Rhubarb	7,525.0	0.1
Butter beans	7,491.0	0.1
Mustard green	4,987.0	0.0
Kale	3,212.0	0.0
Artichokes	1,364.0	0.0
Miscellaneous	24,718.0	0.2

Source: *Quick Frozen Foods International*, October 1995, p. A15.

★ 268 ★

Frozen Vegetables (SIC 2037)

Leading Frozen Vegetable Brands

Brands are ranked by 1995 sales in millions of dollars. Shares of the group are shown in percent.

	Sales ($ mil.)	% of Group
Private label	$ 733.0	52.1%
Green Giant	311.0	22.1
Birds Eye	259.0	18.4
Pictsweet	104.0	7.4

Source: *Wall Street Journal*, February 20, 1996, p. B4, from Information Resources Inc.

★ 269 ★

Frozen Food (SIC 2038)

Frozen Dinner Makers

Shares of the $3.63 billion market are shown in percent for the year ended November 6, 1994.

Stouffer Foods (Nestle) 26.9%
ConAgra 26.5
Heinz 15.3
Campbell Soup 11.8
Other 19.5

Source: *Investext,* Thomson Financial Services, January 5, 1995, p. 2, from Information Resources Inc. and PaineWebber estimates.

★ 270 ★

Frozen Food (SIC 2038)

Frozen Dinner Sales

	($ mil.)	Share
Stouffer	$ 1,000.0	29.4%
Healthy Choice	317.2	9.3
Banquet	243.2	7.2
Other	1,839.6	54.1

Source: *Brandweek*, August 5, 1996, p. 6, from Information Resources Inc.

★ 271 ★

Frozen Food (SIC 2038)

Frozen Pasta Brands

Shares of the $224 million market are shown in percent for the 52 weeks ended September 30, 1995.

Rosetto 25.0%
Mrs. T's 14.7
Celantano 9.8
Italian Village 8.5
Reames 5.4
Other 36.6

Source: *Brandweek*, January 1, 1996, p. 3, from Information Resources Inc.

★ 272 ★

Frozen Food (SIC 2038)

Private Label Frozen Foods

The table shows the share of sales represented by private label for selected frozen foods.

Fish/seafood 11.5%
Pasta 3.2
Breakfast foods 3.1
Dinners/entrees 0.7

Source: *Quick Frozen Foods International*, April 1996, p. 100, from Information Resources Inc.

★ 273 ★
Frozen Food (SIC 2038)

Top 10 Frozen Pizza Brands

Brand shares are shown based on supermarket sales of $1.581 billion for the year ended March 11, 1995. Tony's figure excludes Tony's Creations, Tony's Kidstuff, Tony's Our Choice, and Tony's Personal Pizza and under Stouffer's Extra and Stouffer's Lunch Express are not included.

Tombstone	21.5%
Tony's	12.8
Red Baron	11.6
Totino's	9.2
Jack's	7.5
Stouffer's	5.2
Celesta	5.1
Pappalo's	3.2
Jeno's	2.8
Private label	5.3
Other	15.8

Source: *Snack Food*, July 1995, p. 20, from A.C. Nielsen.

★ 274 ★
Frozen Food (SIC 2038)

Top Frozen Dinner/Entree Brands

Shares of the $3.43 billion market are shown for 1994.

Healthy Choice	15.4%
Lean Cuisine	14.5
Stouffers	13.6
Swanson	12.4
Budget Gourmet	10.5
Weight Watchers	7.5
Banquet	6.7
Michelinas	4.5
Marie Callendar	3.1
Tyson	2.6
Other	9.1

Source: *Advertising Age*, November 27, 1995, p. 6, from Information Resources Inc.

★ 275 ★
Cereals (SIC 2043)

Cereal Makers - 1996

Market leaders are shown for the 52 weeks ended July 6, 1996.

Kellogg	35.0%
General Mills	26.7
Post	13.1
Quaker	7.6
Private label	6.7
Other	10.9

Source: *New York Times*, August 7, 1996, p. C4, from Quaker Oats Company.

★ 276 ★
Cereals (SIC 2043)

Cereal Makers - Canada

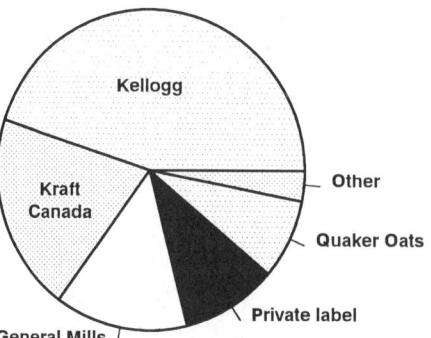

Shares of the market are shown in percent. "Other" includes Weetabix and Lifestream.

Kellogg	45.0%
Kraft Canada	20.0
General Mills	14.0
Private label	10.0
Quaker Oats	8.0
Other	3.0

Source: *Marketing Magazine*, April 29, 1996, p. 6.

★ 277 ★
Cereals (SIC 2043)

Cereal Market Leaders

Shares are shown for the 52 weeks ended February 25, 1996.

Kellogg	36.3%
General Mills	26.4
General Foods (Post brand)	12.7
Quaker	7.6
Nabisco	3.4
Other	13.6

Source: *New York Times*, April 16, 1996, p. C1, from Information Resources Inc.

★ 278 ★
Cereals (SIC 2043)

Hot Cereal Makers

Shares of the $672.5 million market are shown for the year ended December 4, 1994.

Quaker Oats	64.2%
Nabisco	16.4
Private label	11.8
Malt-O Meal	2.6
National Oats	0.9
Other	4.1

Source: *Investext,* Thomson Financial Services, February 22, 1995, p. 25, from Information Resources Inc. InfoScan.

★ 279 ★
Cereals (SIC 2043)

Hot Cereal Makers

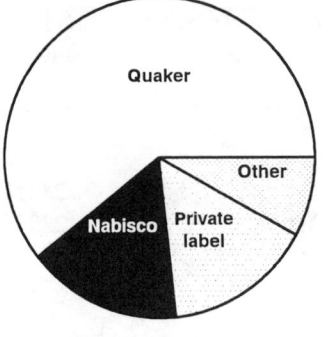

Market leaders are shown for the 52 weeks ended July 6, 1996.

Quaker	60.1%
Nabisco	16.1
Private label	15.4
Other	8.4

Source: *New York Times*, August 7, 1996, p. C4, from Quaker Oats Company.

★ 280 ★
Cereals (SIC 2043)

Ready-to-Eat Cereal Market

The table shows who leads the $2.6 billion cereal market. Shares are shown for the year ended April 1996.

Kellogg	35.4%
General Mills	23.3
Post	15.5
Store brands	10.4
Quaker	7.9
Ralston	3.4
Other	4.1

Source: *Advertising Age*, June 17, 1996, p. 10, from Information Resources Inc.

★ 281 ★
Cereals (SIC 2043)

Top 10 Breakfast Cereals

Shares are shown based on $8.0 billion in sales for the 52 weeks ended December 3, 1995.

	Sales ($ mil.)	Market Share
Frosted Flakes	$ 339.5	4.3%
Cheerios	289.3	3.6
Corn Flakes	240.5	3.0
Honey Nut Cheerios	220.5	2.8
Rice Krispies	220.0	2.8
Raisin Bran	214.9	2.7
Fruit Loops	191.6	2.4
Special K	167.7	2.1
Corn Pops	166.5	2.1
Lucky Charms	157.5	2.0
Other	5,792.0	72.2

Source: *Star Tribune*, January 28, 1996, p. D4, from Information Resources Inc. and Goldman Sachs.

★ 282 ★
Cereals (SIC 2043)

Top Cereal Brands - Ontario

Shares of the $270 million market are shown in percent.

Kellogg's Corn Flakes	7.3%
GM Honey Nut Cheerios	5.8
Kellogg's Rice Krispies	5.6
Kellogg's Raisin Bran	5.3
GM Regular Cheerios	5.1
Kellogg's Frosted Flakes	4.5
Post Shreddies	4.2
Kellogg's Special K	3.2
Post Shredded Wheat	3.2
Kellogg's Bran Flakes	3.1
Raisin Bran	2.6
Corn Flakes	2.1
Crispy Rice	0.6
Other	47.4

Source: *Toronto Star*, July 9, 1996, p. D1, from Kellogg Canada Inc.

★ 283 ★
Cereals (SIC 2043)

Top Cereal Makers

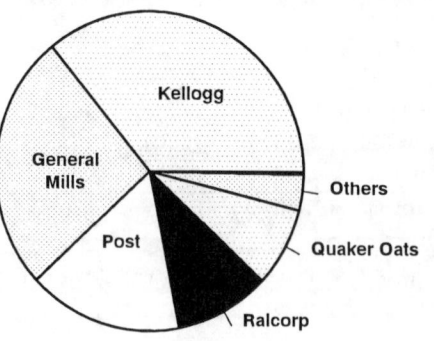

Shares are shown of the $7.9 billion market for the 52 weeks ended April 21, 1996.

Kellogg	36.2%
General Mills	26.4
Post	16.1
Ralcorp	10.0
Quaker Oats	7.6
Others	3.7

Source: *St. Louis Post-Dispatch*, June 11, 1996, p. 1A, from Information Resources Inc., Kellogg Co., and Ralcorp.

★ 284 ★
Rice (SIC 2044)

Rice Cake Market

Quaker
Hain Food Group Inc.
Other

Market leaders are shown for the 52 weeks ended July 6, 1996.

Quaker	77.6%
Hain Food Group Inc.	8.9
Other	13.5

Source: *New York Times*, August 7, 1996, p. C4, from Quaker Oats Company.

★ 285 ★

Rice (SIC 2044)

Rice Cake Producers

Rice cake sales grew from $209.4 million in 1994 to $257.4 million in 1995. Shares are shown for the 52 weeks ended March 26 of each year.

	1994	1995
Quaker Oats	69.3%	76.5%
Pet Inc.	12.6	10.3
Others	18.1	13.2

Source: *Investor's Business Daily*, May 31, 1995, p. A4, from Information Resources Inc.

★ 286 ★

Baking Needs (SIC 2045)

Refrigerated Cookie Dough Market

Shares of the market are shown in percent.

Pillsbury	73.0%
Other	27.0

Source: *USA TODAY*, November 6, 1995, p. B2.

★ 287 ★

Pet Food (SIC 2047)

Bird Food Sales by Region

Midwest	$ 68,109,180
South	60,685,143
West	48,565,421
East	47,923,111

Source: *Pet Product News*, December 1995, p. 22.

★ 288 ★

Pet Food (SIC 2047)

Cat Food Brands

Shares of the wet cat food market are shown for the 52 weeks ended September 9, 1995. Total sales reached $1.1385 billion.

Fancy Feast (Friskies)	8.6%
Nine-Lives (Heinz)	8.6
Friskies Buffet (Friskies)	8.2
Whiskas (Kal Kan)	7.9
Alpo (Friskies)	5.7
Private label	5.7
Sheba (Kal Kan)	3.8
Kal Kan Optimum (Kal Kan)	3.2
Purina Premium (Ralston Purina)	2.5
Amore (Heinz)	2.5
Other	43.3

Source: *Nonfoods Merchandising*, May 1996, p. 33, from A.C. Nielsen.

★ 289 ★

Pet Food (SIC 2047)

Dog Food Sales by Region

Midwest	$ 84,708,397
West	78,043,048
East	77,338,457
South	65,305,909

Source: *Pet Product News*, December 1995, p. 22.

★ 290 ★

Pet Food (SIC 2047)

Dog Treat Makers

Data are for 1994.

Nabisco	33.0%
Private label	26.0
Heinz	9.8
Ralston	8.4
Alpo	4.3
Quaker Oats	3.8
Other	14.7

Source: *Investext*, Thomson Financial Services, February 22, 1995, p. 27, from Information Resources Inc. InfoScan.

★ 291 ★

Pet Food (SIC 2047)

Dry Dog Food Leaders

The dry dog food market reached $1.30 billion for the 52 weeks ended September 9, 1995. Brand shares are shown in percent.

Purina Dog Chow	9.9%
Pedigree Mealtime	9.0
Purina Puppy Chow	7.8
Private label	7.6
Purina One	6.5
Ken-L Ration Kibbles N Bits	5.6
Purina Kibbles & Chunks	3.5
Purina Fit & Trim	3.0
Friskies Come N Get It	2.8
Purina High Protein	2.6
Other	41.6

Source: *Nonfoods Merchandising*, May 1996, p. 33, from A.C. Nielsen.

★ 292 ★

Pet Food (SIC 2047)

Popular Dog Treats

Pet specialty retailers sold $90 million in dog treats and chews in 1994. The table shows the most popular brands. Sales are in millions of dollars. Producers are shown in parentheses.

Milk Bones and others (RJR Nabisco)	$ 122.3
Jerky Treats (Heinz)	55.0
Cheweez, Master Choice (Friskies)	51.5
Meaty Bones (Heinz)	35.0
Pup-peroni (Quaker Oats)	33.0
Purina Biscuits (Ralston Purina)	26.7
Beggin Strips (Ralston Purina)	24.5
Snausages (Quaker Oats)	18.2
Bonz (Ralston Purina)	14.1
Beef Bites (Alpo)	11.0
Alpo Snaps (Alpo)	10.6
Beef Burgers (Alpo)	6.2
Alpo Jerky (Alpo)	5.8
Attaboy (American Nutrition)	5.4
Alpo Beef Biscuit (Alpo)	4.4
Hartz Jerky Treats (Hartz)	3.5

Source: *Pet Product News*, December 1995, p. 40, from *Petfood Industry*.

★ 293 ★

Pet Food (SIC 2047)

Top Pet Food Makers - 1994

Ralston Purina	17.1%
Nestle	10.9
Colgate-Palmolive	8.1
Mars Inc.	7.7
H.J. Heinz Co.	7.4
Quaker Oats Co.	6.0
Doane's	5.8
Grand Metropolitan	5.0
Iams Pet Food	2.2
Other	25.6

Source: *Advertising Age*, September 27, 1995, p. 22, from Information Resources Inc.

★ 294 ★

Pet Food (SIC 2047)

Wet Dog Food Leaders

The wet dog food market had sales of $745.2 million for the 52 weeks ended September 9, 1995. Brand shares are shown in percent.

Pedigree (Kal Kan)	15.3%
Pedigree Choice Cuts (Kal Kan)	10.5
Alpo Prime Cuts (Heinz)	9.5
Mighty Dog (Friskies)	7.9
Alpo (Heinz)	7.2
Skippy Premium (Heinz)	5.8
Private label	5.3
Pedigree Select Dinners (Kal Kan)	4.6
Ken-L Ration (Heinz)	4.5
Reward (Heinz)	3.5
Other	25.8

Source: *Nonfoods Merchandising*, May 1996, p. 33, from A.C. Nielsen.

★ 295 ★
Bakery Products (SIC 2050)
Bakery Product Sales

Sales are shown by category in millions of dollars for 1995.

Bread	$ 4,652.7
Cookies	3,469.0
Crackers	2,737.9
Buns/rolls	1,377.0
Baked snacks	918.9
Pastries/danish	516.2
English muffins	394.5
Bagels/bialys	251.3
Muffins	184.7

Source: *Snack Food*, May 1996, p. 31, from Information Resources Inc. InfoScan.

★ 296 ★
Bakery Products (SIC 2051)
Bagel Sales

Americans are expected to purchase $2.3 billion in bagels in 1995. The market is shown in percent by segment.

	($ mil.)	Share
Supermarket bakeries	$ 708.0	30.8%
Retail bakeries	450.0	19.6
Bagel shops	450.0	19.6
Packaged	300.0	13.0
Frozen	250.0	10.9
Other	142.0	6.2

Source: *Business Week*, November 13, 1995, p. 82, from *Bakery Production and Marketing*.

★ 297 ★
Bakery Products (SIC 2051)
Fresh Bagel Market

Shares are shown based on total sales of $245.6 million for the 52 weeks ended November 5, 1995.

	Sales ($ mil.)	Share
Lenders Bagel Bakery	$ 76.0	30.9%
Private label	41.0	16.7
Sara Lee Bakery	26.4	10.7
International Baking	23.4	9.5
Best Foods Baking	18.0	7.3
Other	60.8	24.8

Source: *Bakery Production and Marketing*, March 15, 1996, p. 40, from Information Resources Inc. InfoScan.

★ 298 ★
Bakery Products (SIC 2051)
Fresh Pie Market

Shares of the $123.9 million market are shown for the year ended February 25, 1996. Data exclude snack pies.

Entenmann's	15.1%
Plush Pippin	2.6
Table Talk	2.0
Private-label	57.7
Other	22.6

Source: *Bakery Production and Marketing*, June 15, 1996, p. 42, from Information Resources Inc.

★ 299 ★
Bakery Products (SIC 2051)

Leading Bakery Snacks

The market had sales of $883.3 million for the 52 weeks ended June 18, 1995.

McKee Foods	39.5%
Continental	25.2
Tastykake	7.1
Drake Bakeries	5.7
Private label	4.4
Other	18.1

Source: *Brandweek*, July 24, 1995, p. 6, from Information Resources Inc.

★ 300 ★
Bakery Products (SIC 2051)

Muffin Sales Leaders

Muffin sales in supermarkets are shown for the 52 weeks ended August 14, 1994 and August 13, 1995.

	1994 ($ mil.)	1995 ($ mil.)	Share
Otis Spunkmeyer . . .	$ 22.0	$ 28.7	15.6%
Hostess Breakfast Bake Shop	25.6	20.5	11.1
Hostess	11.8	9.8	5.3
Entenmann's	10.0	9.3	5.1
Private label	66.5	62.4	33.9
Other	43.5	53.2	28.9

Source: *Bakery Production and Marketing*, November 24, 1995, p. 40, from Information Resources Inc. InfoScan.

★ 301 ★
Bakery Products (SIC 2051)

Popular Donut Brands

Shares of the $428.8 million market are shown for the year ended April 23, 1995.

Entenmann's	19.8%
Hostess	17.4
Dolly Madison	8.9
Krispy Kreme	8.5
Freihofer	2.0
Rainbow Break Cake	1.8
Merita	1.8
Tastykake	1.4
Mickey	1.2
Private label	18.3
Other	18.9

Source: *Investext,* Thomson Financial Services, September 5, 1995, p. 7, from Information Resources Inc.

★ 302 ★
Bakery Products (SIC 2051)

Popular Snack Cake Brands

Shares of the $888.2 million market are shown for the year ended April 23, 1995.

Little Debbie	27.0%
Tastykake	6.9
Hostess	6.5
Hostess Light	4.5
Hostess Twinkies	4.3
Little Debbie Nutty Bar	4.3
Drake	2.9
Entenmann's	2.6
Hostess Twinkie Lights	2.2

Continued on next page.

★ 302 ★ *Continued*
Bakery Products (SIC 2051)

Popular Snack Cake Brands

Shares of the $888.2 million market are shown for the year ended April 23, 1995.

Private label	4.3%
Other	34.6

Source: *Investext,* Thomson Financial Services, September 5, 1995, p. 6, from Information Resources Inc.

★ 303 ★
Bakery Products (SIC 2051)

Refrigerated Bakery Product Sales

Bakery good retail sales are projected to reach $34.4 billion in 1996. This table shows the refrigerated segment of the market in millions of dollars.

	Sales	Share
Biscuits/dough	$ 1,022.6	53.7%
Desserts	382.8	20.1
Pies	375.5	19.7
Bread/baked goods	111.9	5.9
Cheesecakes	9.8	0.5

Source: *Bakery Production and Marketing*, May 15, 1996, p. 28, from Food Institute Analysis and Information Resources Inc. InfoScan.

★ 304 ★
Bakery Products (SIC 2051)

Toaster Pastry Market

Brand shares are shown based on total sales of $602.9 million for the 52 weeks ended October 9, 1995.

Pop-Tarts (Kellogg's)	56.3%
Toaster Strudel (Pillsbury)	14.9
Private label	10.9
Toastettes (Nabisco)	9.3
Toast 'em (Schulze & Burch)	3.5
Pop-Tarts Minis (Kellogg's)	2.8
Other	2.3

Source: *Snack Food*, March 1996, p. 18, from A.C. Nielsen.

★ 305 ★
Bakery Products (SIC 2051)

Toaster Pastry Producers

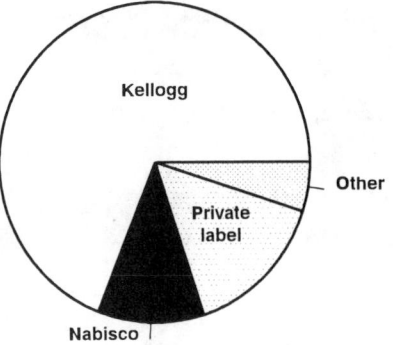

Shares of the $487.3 million market are shown in percent for the year ended June 16, 1996.

Kellogg	68.9%
Nabisco	11.0
Private label	15.0
Other	5.1

Source: *Advertising Age*, August 5, 1996, p. 6, from Information Resources Inc.

★ 306 ★
Bread (SIC 2051)

Bread Makers - Mexico

Shares are shown in percent.

Grupo Industrial Bimbo	90.0%
Other	10.0

Source: *Mexico Business*, January/February 1996, p. 55.

★ 307 ★
Bread (SIC 2051)

Bread Makers - Texas

Shares of the bread market are shown in percent.

Mrs. Baird's Bakeries	50.0%
Other	50.0

Source: *Mexico Business*, January/February 1996, p. 56.

★ 308 ★
Bread (SIC 2051)

Frozen Bread Brands

Brands are ranked by sales in millions of dollars for the 52 weeks ended August 13, 1995.

	Sales ($ mil.)	Share
Pepperidge Farm	$ 38.49	31.9%
Cole's	27.44	22.7
Mamma Bella	9.48	7.8
New York	9.17	7.6
Sara Lee	8.91	7.4
Private label	5.36	4.4
Orlando	4.37	3.6
Earth Grains	3.21	2.7
Joseph Campione	2.85	2.4
Other	11.52	9.5

Source: *Snack Food*, March 1996, p. 45, from Information Resources Inc. InfoScan.

★ 309 ★
Cookies (SIC 2052)

Cookie Brands

Shares are for the year ended August 1995.

Nabisco	35.0%
Keebler	11.0
Sunshine	5.0
Private label	11.0
Others	38.0

Source: *New York Times*, September 13, 1995, p. C2, from Goldman, Sachs & Company.

★ 310 ★
Cookies (SIC 2052)

Popular Cookie Brands

Brand shares are shown for the year ended March 11, 1995.

	Sales ($ mil.)	Share
Chips Ahoy	$ 292.9	8.0%
Oreo	264.0	7.3
Newtons	253.0	7.0
SnackWell's	242.6	6.7
Archways	142.8	4.0
Little Debbie	122.7	3.4
Mother's	97.3	2.7
Chips Deluxe	79.7	2.2
Pepperidge Farm Distinctive . .	78.1	2.2
Private label	339.0	9.4
Other	1,698.8	47.1

Source: *Snack Food*, August 1995, p. 28, from A.C. Nielsen.

★ 311 ★
Crackers (SIC 2052)

Cracker Market

Shares of the $2.6 billion market are shown in percent.

Nabisco	46.2%
Keebler	16.3
Sunshine	8.5
Private label	7.9
Other	21.1

Source: *Brandweek*, July 24, 1995, p. 6, from Information Resources Inc.

★ 312 ★
Crackers (SIC 2052)

Cracker Sandwich Brands

Brand shares of the $313.2 million market are shown in percent.

Handi Snacks	29.4%
Ritz	20.0
Lance	14.9
Mootown Snackers	6.5
Little Debbie	6.4
Frito-Lay	5.5
Austin	5.0

Continued on next page.

★ 312 ★ *Continued*
Crackers (SIC 2052)

Cracker Sandwich Brands

Brand shares of the $313.2 million market are shown in percent.

Keebler	4.5%
Nabs	1.9
Private label	1.8
Other	4.1

Source: *Snack Food*, January 1996, p. 18, from A.C. Nielsen.

★ 313 ★

Pretzels (SIC 2052)

Leading Pretzel Brands

Sales at food stores are shown by brand for 1994. Shares of the group are shown in percent.

	($ mil.)	% of Group
Frito-Lay, Rold Gold	$ 152.0	35.4%
Snyders	83.0	19.3
Nabisco	57.0	13.3
Eagle	38.0	8.9
Bachman	27.0	6.3
Keebler	22.0	5.1
Private label	50.0	11.7

Source: *Food Technology*, June 1995, p. 46.

★ 314 ★

Pretzels (SIC 2052)

Pretzel Market - Canada

Market shares are shown in percent.

Hostess/Frito-Lay	27.0%
Old Dutch Ltd.	19.0
Others	54.0

Source: *Snack Food*, April 1996, p. 22.

★ 315 ★

Frozen Bakery Products (SIC 2053)

Frozen Bagel Market

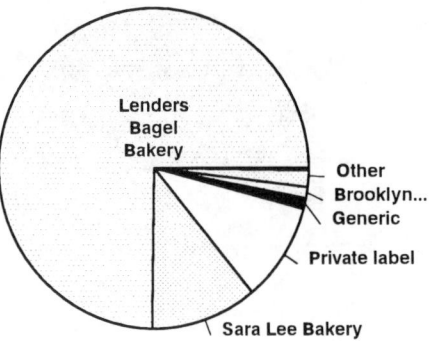

Shares of the $236.9 million frozen bagel market are shown for the 52 weeks ended November 5, 1995.

Lenders Bagel Bakery	75.1%
Sara Lee Bakery	10.7
Private label	9.7
Generic	1.4
Brooklyn Bagel Boys	1.2
Other	1.9

Source: *Bakery Production and Marketing*, March 15, 1996, p. 40, from Information Resources Inc. InfoScan.

★ 316 ★

Frozen Bakery Products (SIC 2053)

Frozen Bakery Product Sales

The top categories are ranked by sales in millions of dollars.

Sweet goods	$ 326.1
Pies	266.0
Bagels	233.9
Cheesecake	67.7
Pretzels	37.9
Muffins	18.3

Source: *Snack Food*, May 1996, p. 31, from Information Resources Inc. InfoScan.

★ 317 ★

Frozen Bakery Products (SIC 2053)

Frozen Pie Brands

Shares of the $265 million market are shown in percent.

Mrs. Smith's	54.0%
Sara Lee	22.0
Other	24.0

Source: *Chicago Tribune*, January 24, 1996, p. C2, from Information Resources Inc.

★ 318 ★

Frozen Bakery Products (SIC 2053)

Popular Frozen Pie Brands

Shares are shown for the year ended February 25, 1996. Data exclude snack pies.

	Sales ($ mil.)	Share
Mrs. Smith's	$ 137.5	52.0%
Sara Lee	60.9	23.1
Christopher Edwards	45.4	5.8
Mountain Top	10.8	4.1
Banquet	10.2	3.9
Edwards	7.2	2.7
Pet Ritz	5.8	2.2
Private-label	5.7	2.1
Mrs. Smith's Smart Style	2.8	1.1
Weight Watchers	2.8	1.1

Source: *Bakery Production and Marketing*, June 15, 1996, p. 42, from Information Resources Inc.

★ 319 ★

Confectionery Products (SIC 2064)

Confectionery Leaders

Shares are shown for the year ended May 28, 1995.

Hershey	34.2%
Mars	26.1
Nestle	9.2
Brach	7.1
Leaf	3.8
Nabisco	3.5
Other	16.1

Source: *Investext,* Thomson Financial Services, July 24, 1995, p. 2, from Information Resources Inc. InfoScan.

★ 320 ★

Confectionery Products (SIC 2064)

Hard Sugar & Roll Candy Sales

Sales are shown for the third quarter of 1995 in thousands of dollars by brand.

	Sales ($000)	Share
Werthers	$ 15,761.0	17.2%
Jolly Rancher	13,336.6	14.5
LifeSavers	11,153.0	12.1
Pearson Nips	5,182.3	5.6
Tootsie Roll Pops	3,747.0	4.1
Charms Blow Pop	3,223.2	3.5
Brachs	3,130.0	3.4
Ocean Spray Fruit Waves	3,047.0	3.3
Juicefuls	2,597.3	2.8
Private label	6,555.6	7.1
Other	24,111.0	25.4

Source: *Manufacturing Confectioner*, January 1996, p. 22, from Information Resources Inc.

★ 321 ★

Confectionery Products (SIC 2064)

Leading Cough Drops

Shares are shown for the 12 months ended September 9, 1995.

Halls	46.6%
Robitussin	14.2
Luden's	11.7
Control	9.1
Ricola	8.8

Continued on next page.

★ 321 ★ *Continued*
Confectionery Products (SIC 2064)

Leading Cough Drops

Shares are shown for the 12 months ended September 9, 1995.

Vicks Chloraseptic	2.7%
Vicks	2.6
Sucrets	1.6
Fisherman's Friend	1.5
Other	1.2

Source: *Nonfoods Merchandising*, May 1996, p. 24, from A.C. Nielsen.

★ 322 ★
Confectionery Products (SIC 2064)

Mint Brand Shares

Sales are shown for the third quarter of 1995 in thousands of dollars by brand.

	Sales ($000)	Share
LifeSavers Plainmint	$ 11,265.5	30.5%
Brachs Plainmint	5,112.6	13.8
Van Melles Mentos	4,710.7	12.7
Brock Plainmint	4,448.3	12.0
Sathers Plainmint	1,724.0	4.7
Farleys Plainmint	1,526.2	4.1
Richardson After Dinner	1,277.6	3.5
NECCO Plainmint	581.8	1.6
Kraft Plainmint	488.2	1.3
Private Label Plainmint	3,538.4	9.6
Others	2,284.3	6.2

Source: *Manufacturing Confectioner*, January 1996, p. 23, from Information Resources Inc.

★ 323 ★
Confectionery Products (SIC 2064)

Non-Chocolate Candy

Brand shares are shown based on total sales of $784.0 million for the year ended March 11, 1995.

	Sales ($ mil.)	Share
Brach's	$ 120.3	15.3%
LifeSavers	48.7	6.2
Twizzlers	46.6	5.9
Jolly Rancher	30.5	3.9
Starburst	29.6	3.8

	Sales ($ mil.)	Share
Werther's	$ 28.8	3.7%
Farley	28.1	3.6
Skittles	27.0	3.4
Tootsie Roll	18.7	2.4
Private label	33.9	4.3
Other	371.8	47.5

Source: *Snack Food*, September 1995, p. 19, from A.C. Nielsen.

★ 324 ★
Confectionery Products (SIC 2064)

Popular Breath Fresheners

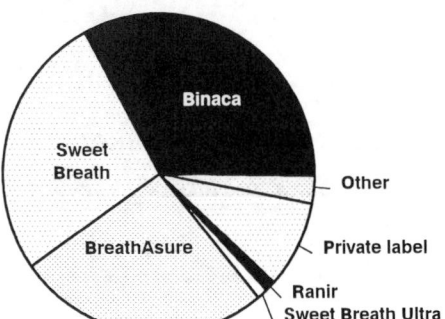

Dollar shares are shown for the 52 weeks ended November 5, 1995.

Binaca	33.4%
Sweet Breath	26.6
BreathAsure	26.4
Sweet Breath Ultra	0.9
Ranir	0.8
Private label	8.9
Other	3.0

Source: *Supermarket Business*, February 1996, p. 77, from Information Resources InfoScan.

★ 325 ★
Confectionery Products (SIC 2064)

Popular Cough Drop Brands

Sales are shown for the second quarter of 1995.

	Sales	Share
Halls	$ 21,682,216	29.1%
Ricola	7,291,388	9.8
Robitussin	7,089,365	9.5

Continued on next page.

★ 325 ★ *Continued*

Confectionery Products (SIC 2064)

Popular Cough Drop Brands

Sales are shown for the second quarter of 1995.

	Sales	Share
Ludens	$ 6,690,264	9.0%
Sucrets	6,328,570	8.5
Nice	4,494,016	6.0
Vicks Chloraseptic	4,466,854	6.0
Halls Plus	3,702,641	5.0
Celestial Seasonings	2,742,277	3.7
Private label	1,776,220	2.4
Other	8,136,594	11.0

Source: *Manufacturing Confectioner*, September 1995, p. 26.

★ 326 ★

Confectionery Products (SIC 2064)

U.S. Confectionery Makers

Shares are shown for the 52 weeks ended February 29, 1996.

Hershey	31.1%
Mars	22.8
Nestle	8.6
Russell Stover	7.6
Brace & Brick	5.8
Leaf	3.8
RJR Nabisco	3.4
Other	16.9

Source: *Investext,* Thomson Financial Services, May 21, 1996, p. 5, from Hershey Foods.

★ 327 ★

Granola Bars (SIC 2064)

Granola Bar Makers

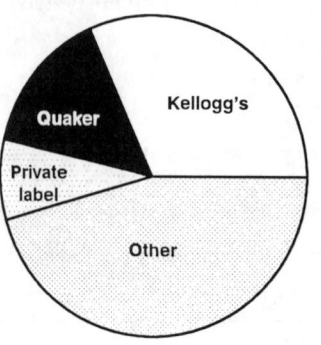

Market leaders are shown for the 52 weeks ended July 6, 1996.

Kellogg's	31.9%
Quaker	14.5
Private label	7.6
Other	46.0

Source: *New York Times*, August 7, 1996, p. C4, from Quaker Oats Company.

★ 328 ★

Granola Bars (SIC 2064)

Granola Snack Bars

Shares are shown based on $821.6 million in supermarket sales for the 52 weeks ended May 12, 1996.

Kellogg's Nutri Grain Bar	17.6%
Quaker Chewy	13.4
SnackWell's	13.2
Kellogg's Rice Krispies Treats	11.1
Kudos	5.8
Nature Valley	5.8
Sunbelt	4.5
Private label	3.3
Betty Crocker Sweet Rewards	2.6
Powerbar	2.5
Other	20.2

Source: *Snack Food*, July 1996, p. 17, from Information Resources Inc.

★ 329 ★

Candy (SIC 2066)

Candy Market

Shares of the market are shown for the year ended May 28, 1995.

Hershey	34.2%
M&M/Mars	26.1
Other	39.7

Source: *Advertising Age*, September 11, 1995, p. 3, from Information Resources Inc.

★ 330 ★

Candy (SIC 2066)

Miniature Chocolate Market

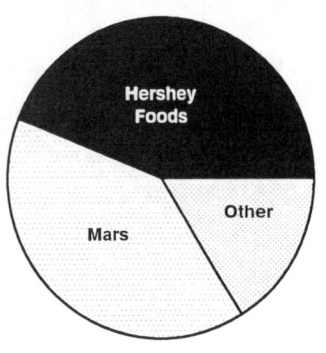

Shares of the $801.3 million market are shown for the year ended June 16, 1996.

Hershey Foods	43.8%
Mars	39.8
Other	16.4

Source: *Advertising Age*, August 19, 1996, p. 1, from Information Resources Inc.

★ 331 ★

Chewing Gum (SIC 2067)

Chewing Gum Sales

Shares are shown for the second quarter of 1995.

Wrigleys Double Mint	11.1%
Freedent	8.8
Wrigleys Big Red	7.8
Wrigleys Spearmint	6.7
Wrigleys Juicy Fruit	6.6
Wrigleys	5.9
Bubble Yum	5.2

Bubblicious	4.4%
Cinn a Burst	4.0
Mint A Burst	3.3
Other	36.2

Source: *Manufacturing Confectioner*, September 1995, p. 26.

★ 332 ★

Chewing Gum (SIC 2067)

Leading Sugarless Gum Brands

Sugarless gum brand shares are shown for the third quarter of 1995.

Wrigley's Extra	38.4%
Trident	27.7
Carefree	21.4
Stick Free	5.4
Dentyne	3.1
Bubble Yum	2.7
Topps Bazooka	0.6
Leaf Xylifresh	0.5
Source	0.2

Source: *Manufacturing Confectioner*, January 1996, p. 23, from Information Resources Inc.

★ 333 ★

Nuts (SIC 2068)

Snack Nut Makers

Shares are shown based on $568.2 million for the 52 weeks ended January 1, 1995.

Planters	36.4%
Private label	20.2
Eagle Snacks	7.8
Procter & Gamble	5.3
Other	30.3

Source: *Investext,* Thomson Financial Services, February 22, 1995, p. 25, from Information Resources Inc. InfoScan.

★ 334 ★

Nuts (SIC 2068)

Snack Nut Market

Supermarket sales are shown by type in 1994.

Peanuts	66.0%
Mixed nuts	15.7

Continued on next page.

★ 334 ★ *Continued*
Nuts (SIC 2068)
Snack Nut Market

Supermarket sales are shown by type in 1994.

Walnuts	3.7%
Pistachios	2.9
Almonds	1.9
Hazelnuts	0.7
Pecans	0.6
Brazil nuts	0.5
Pine nuts	0.1

Source: *U.S. Distribution Journal*, July 15, 1995, p. 20, from *Snack Food Association's Industry Report, 1995.*

★ 335 ★
Nuts (SIC 2068)
U.S. Nut Consumption

Per person consumption is shown in ounces by type. "Other" includes Brazil nuts, pine nuts, chesnuts, and cashews.

Almonds	12.0
Walnuts	7.0
Pecans	6.0
Pistachios	2.0
Filberts	1.0
Macadamias	1.0
Others	9.0

Source: *Sunday Journal Sentinel*, December 17, 1995, p. 1G, from Knight-Ridder Tribune.

★ 336 ★
Fats and Oils (SIC 2070)
Fat and Shortening Sales

Sales reached $21.62 billion in 1994.

Cooking & salad oils	55.3%
Shortening	16.2
Cooking sprays	16.8
Olive oil	9.2
Lard	2.6

Source: *Supermarket Business*, September 1995, p. 60.

★ 337 ★
Fats and Oils (SIC 2079)
Cooking/Salad Oil Makers

Shares of the $812.17 million market are shown in percent for the year ended November 6, 1994.

Procter & Gamble	24.9%
Private label	24.5
Hunt-Wesson	23.7
Best Foods	17.9
Pet Inc.	2.5
Other	6.5

Source: *Investext,* Thomson Financial Services, January 5, 1995, p. 2, from Information Resources Inc. and PaineWebber estimates.

★ 338 ★
Fats and Oils (SIC 2079)
Leading Oil Producers

Data are for 1995.

Procter & Gamble	24.0%
ConAgra	21.0
Other	55.0

Source: *Investext,* Thomson Financial Services, March 15, 1996, p. 26, from Information Resources Inc.

★ 339 ★
Fats and Oils (SIC 2079)
Top Margarines/Spreads

Shares are shown for the 52 weeks ended December 3, 1995.

Van den Bergh	47.6%
Nabisco	33.8
Private label	7.7
Land O'Lakes	5.8
Other	5.1

Source: *Brandweek*, February 26, 1996, p. 24, from Information Resources Inc.

★ 340 ★

Beverages (SIC 2080)

Leading Alcoholic Beverage Makers - Canada

Firms are ranked by revenues in millions of dollars.

Molson Cos.	$ 2,656.7
Vincor International	114.5
Andres Wines	70.6
Corby Distilleries	46.9

Source: *Globe and Mail's Report on Business*, July 1996, p. 164.

★ 341 ★

Beverages (SIC 2080)

Nutritional Beverage Market

The table shows the leading brands of nutritional beverages marketed to senior citizens. Ensure leads with an 80% share. Brands are ranked by supermarket sales in millions of dollars. Total sales of Ensure were approximately $500 million.

Ensure (Abbott Laboratories)	$ 167.4
Nutrament (Mead Johnson)	5.7
Sustacal (Mead Johnson)	1.6

Source: *Detroit News*, April 28, 1996, p. A7.

★ 342 ★

Beverages (SIC 2080)

Top U.S. Beverage Companies

Firms are ranked by worldwide 1995 sales in millions of dollars.

Coca-Cola Co.	$ 18,018
Nestle	13,300
PepsiCo.	10,548
Anheuser-Busch Inc.	9,600
The Seagram Co.	6,694
Miller Brewing Co.	4,304
Cadbury Beverages	4,270
IDV North America	2,827
Quaker Oats Beverages	1,959
Coors Brewing Co.	1,675
American Brands Inc.	1,290
Brown-Forman Corp.	$ 1,138
Ocean Spray Cranberries Inc.	1,114
E&J Gallo	1,000
The Stroh Brewery Co.	1,000

Source: *Beverage Industry*, July 1996, p. 28.

★ 343 ★

Beer (SIC 2082)

Beer Market - Mexico

Beer production is shown by company in Mexico. "Other" includes Grupo Femsa, its largest competitor.

Grupo Modelo	54.0%
Others	46.0

Source: *Mexico Business*, January/February 1996, p. 58.

★ 344 ★

Beer (SIC 2082)

Imported Beer Brands

Shares are for the 52 weeks ended March 11, 1995.

Heineken	2.3%
Corona Extra	2.0
Molson Ice	1.4
Foster's Lager	0.6
Labatt Blue	0.6
Tecate	0.5
Molson Golden	0.5
Moosehead	0.5
Labatt Ice	0.4
St. Pauli Girl	0.3
Dos Equis	0.3
Grolsch	0.2
Other	90.4

Source: *Beverage World's Periscope*, October 31, 1995, p. 8, from A.C. Nielsen.

★ 345 ★

Beer (SIC 2082)

Malt Beverage Leaders

Shares of the $2.79 billion malt beverage (full-calorie) market are shown in percent for the year ended March 9, 1996.

Budweiser	28.0%
Miller Genuine Draft	6.8
Busch	5.9
Miller High Life	4.3
Milwaukee's Best	4.0
Corona Extra	2.7
Heineken	2.6
Original Coors	2.5
Michelob	2.4
Old Milwaukee	2.4
Red Dog	2.3
Ice House	2.1
Bud Ice	1.9
Other	32.1

Source: *Beverage World's Periscope*, July 31, 1996, p. 10, from A.C. Nielsen.

★ 346 ★

Beer (SIC 2082)

Popular Domestic Beers - Mexico

Shares are for 1994.

Corona	30.1%
Tecata	14.1
Carta Blanca	12.8
Superior	12.3
Modelo Especial	11.2
Victoria	6.7%
Pacifico	4.9
XX Lager	3.2
Others	4.7

Source: *Investext*, Thomson Financial Services, September 7, 1995, p. 14, from Femsa and Modelo.

★ 347 ★

Beer (SIC 2082)

Top Brewers - 1995

Total domestic production reached 189.4 million gallons.

Anheuser-Busch	46.4%
Miller	22.8
Coors	10.7
Stroh	5.8
G. Heileman	4.0
S&P Industries	4.0
Genesee	1.0
Latrobe	0.6
Boston Brewing	0.5
Pittsburgh Brewing	0.3
Other	3.9

Source: *Beverage World*, March 1996, p. 43, from Beverage Marketing Corporation.

★ 348 ★

Beer (SIC 2082)

Top Brewing Companies

	1994	1995
Anheuser-Busch	39.5%	39.7%
Miller Brewing	25.7	25.6
Adolph Coor Company	11.1	11.0
Stroh Brewery Co.	6.4	5.8
G. Heileman Brewing Company	4.9	4.6
Pabst Brewing	4.3	4.0
Other	8.1	9.2

Source: *Investext*, Thomson Financial Services, December 14, 1995, p. 5, from industry sources.

★ 349 ★

Beer (SIC 2082)

Top Light Beers

Data show the share of the overall beer market and the lite beer market for 1995.

	Overall Share	Light Share
Bud Light	9.7%	26.5%
Miller Lite	8.4	23.1
Coors Light	7.0	19.2
Natural Light	3.6	9.9
Busch Light Draft	2.2	6.1
Michelob Light	1.3	3.5
Keystone Light	1.0	2.8
Milwaukee's Best Light	1.0	2.6
Miller Genuine Draft Light . . .	0.7	1.9
Old Milwaukee Light	0.5	1.5
Others	64.6	2.9

Source: *Beverage World*, March 1996, p. 48, from Beverage Marketing Corp.

★ 350 ★

Beer (SIC 2082)

Top U.S. Beer Brands

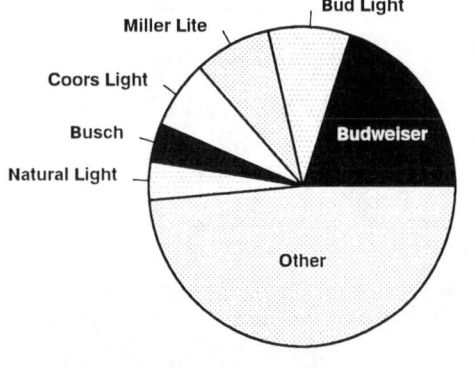

Miller Lite
Bud Light
Coors Light
Busch
Natural Light
Budweiser
Other

Shares are shown for 1995. Producers are shown in parentheses.

Budweiser (Anheuser-Busch)	19.8%
Bud Light (Anheuser-Busch)	9.3
Miller Lite (Miller)	8.0
Coors Light (Coors)	6.7
Busch (Anheuser-Busch)	4.2
Natural Light (Anheuser-Busch)	3.5
Other	48.5

Source: *Business Week*, February 12, 1996, p. 37, from *Beer Marketer's Insights*.

★ 351 ★

Wine (SIC 2084)

Charity Wine Auctions

The top wine auctions in the United States are shown based on total bids in 1995.

Napa Valley Wine Auction	$ 1,796,250
Un Ete du Vin	690,000
Auction of Northwest Wines	431,140
Florida Winefest	380,000
Sonoma County Showcase	308,879
High Museum Atlanta Wine Auction . .	308,000
Sun Valley (Idaho) Wine Auction . . .	303,000
KCBX Central Coast Wine Classic . . .	273,682
Jackson Hole (Wyo.) Wine Auction . .	264,779
Sanoma Valley Harvest Wine Auction .	258,045

Source: *Wine Spectator*, March 31, 1996, p. 25.

★ 352 ★

Wine (SIC 2084)

Popular Wine Brands

Shares are shown based on $2.12 billion in sales at food stores for the year ended March 9, 1996.

E&J Gallo Wine Cellars	5.7%
Gallo Livingston Cellars	5.3
Sutter Home	4.5
Carlo Rossi	4.4
Franzia	4.4
Glen Ellen Proprietor's Reserve	3.3
Almaden	3.1
Robert Mondavi Woodbridge	3.1
Beringer	3.0
Kendall-Johnson	2.7
Inglenook Vineyards	2.6
August Sebastiana	2.5
Fetzer	2.3
Vendage	2.0
Other	51.1

Source: *Beverage World's Periscope*, July 31, 1996, p. 14, from A.C. Nielsen.

★ 353 ★
Wine (SIC 2084)

Top 10 Wine Brands

The leading wine brands shown are ranked by 9-liter case depletions in 1994.

Gallo Livingston Cellars	11,700
Carlo Rossi	11,600
Franzia	11,500
Wine Cellars of E&J Gallo	9,100
Inglenook Vineyards	7,000
Almaden	6,900
Sutter Home	4,700
August Sebastiani	4,240
Woolbridge	3,355
Glen Ellen	3,265

Source: *Brandweek*, November 20, 1995, p. 40, from *Impact Wine Market Study, 1995.*

★ 354 ★
Wine (SIC 2084)

Top Wine Cooler Brands

Shares of the $261.9 million market are shown in percent for the 52 weeks ended December 9, 1995.

Bartles & James	35.2%
Seagram's	26.6
Tropical Freezes	12.2
Boone's Orchard & Vineyard	7.0
Bacardi Breezer	6.2
Richards	2.6
MD 20-20	1.9
Thunderbird	1.6
Riunite	1.0
Boone's	0.9
Night Train Express	0.7
Other	5.7

Source: *Beverage World's Periscope*, May 31, 1996, p. 14, from A.C. Nielsen.

★ 355 ★
Wine (SIC 2084)

U.S. Wine Auction Houses

The table shows the revenues generated by auction houses for 1994-95. Figures are in millions of dollars.

Christie's London	$ 13.3
Chicago Wine Co.	4.8
Sotheby's London	4.4
Butterfield & Butterfield	3.6
Davis & Co.	3.5
Morrell & Co.	1.9
Sherry-Lehmann with Sotheby's	1.6

Source: *Wine Spectator*, September 15, 1995, p. 60.

★ 356 ★
Wine (SIC 2084)

U.S. Wine Shipments by Type

Wine shipments in millions of gallons are shown for 1995 and 1996.

	1995 (mil.)	1996 (mil.)	Share
Table wine	372.0	388.0	79.7%
Sparkling wine	31.0	30.0	6.2
Wine coolers	18.0	16.0	3.3
All other	52.0	53.0	10.9

Source: *Wines & Vines*, February 1996, p. 15, from Jon Fredrikson.

★ 357 ★
Liquors (SIC 2085)

Canadian Whisky Market

The Canadian whisky market is shown in the United States for 1992.

Seagram	23.0%
Allied	13.0
IDV	11.0
Other	53.0

Source: *Investext*, Thomson Financial Services, February 27, 1996, p. 12.

★ 358 ★
Liquors (SIC 2085)

Cognac Market

Shares are shown based on total depletions of 21.61 million cases, valued at $1.61 billion.

Hennessey	40.2%
Courvoisier	24.1
Martell	13.7
Remy Martin	13.4
Other	8.6

Source: *Investext,* Thomson Financial Services, August 14, 1995, p. 23, from Impact International.

★ 359 ★
Liquors (SIC 2085)

Liquor Consumption by Type

U.S. consumption is shown in thousands of 9-liter cases in 1994. Bourbon includes blended bourbons and blended whiskey is counted under whiskey.

Whiskey	32,434
Vodka	31,565
Cordial & specialties	14,915
Bourbon	13,043
Gin	11,582
Rum	10,613
Brandy	5,830
Cocktails	5,116
Tequila	4,481

Source: *Beverage Industry,* April 1996, p. 16, from Distilled Spirits Council of the United States.

★ 360 ★
Liquors (SIC 2085)

Popular Cocktail Mixes

Shares of the $70.3 million market are shown in percent for the 52 weeks ended December 9, 1995.

Mr. And Mrs. T	29.4%
Jose Cuervo	21.1
Holland House	10.6
Daily's	8.5
Coco Lopez	6.4
Tabasco	3.2
Master of Mixes	2.9
Major Peter's	2.5
La Paz	2.3

Goya	1.6%
Other	11.5

Source: *Beverage World's Periscope,* May 31, 1996, p. 13, from A.C. Nielsen.

★ 361 ★
Liquors (SIC 2085)

Top Liquor Brands

Brand shares are shown for 1994. Top producers include Bacardi imports, Heublein Inc., Seagram Co., Jim Beam Brands, Brown-Forman Corp., and Carillon Importers.

Bacardi	4.7%
Smirnoff	4.1
Seagram's Gin	2.8
Jim Beam	2.6
Popov	2.5
7 Crown	2.3
Jack Daniels	2.1
Canadian Mist	2.1
Absolute	2.0
De Kuypers	1.5
Gordon's Vodka	1.5
Jose Cuervo	1.5
E&J Gallo Brandy	1.5
V.O.	1.4
Windsor Supreme	1.4
Other	66.0

Source: *Beverage Industry,* April 1996, p. 18, from Adams-Joson 1995 Handbook Advance.

★ 362 ★
Liquors (SIC 2085)

Top Liquor Firms

Data are for 1994.

Heublein Inc.	15.4%
James Beam	13.4
Seagram Co.	13.3
United Distillers Glenmore	9.6
Brown Forman Corp.	8.1
Bacardi Corp.	6.2
Hiram Walker	5.7

Continued on next page.

★ 362 ★ *Continued*
Liquors (SIC 2085)

Top Liquor Firms

Data are for 1994.

Schieffelein & Somerset 3.6%
Barton Inc. 2.9
Paddington 2.7
Other 20.9

Source: *Beverage Industry*, June 1996, p. 40.

★ 363 ★
Liquors (SIC 2085)

Top Selling Distilled Liquors

Bacardi rum	
Smirnoff Vodka	
Seagram gin	
Jim Beam	
Popov vodka	
Jack Daniels Black	
Seagram 7 Crown	
Absolut vodka	
Canadian Mist	
	Jose Cuervo tequila

Brands are ranked by 1995 shipments in millions of 9-liter cases.

Bacardi rum 6.35
Smirnoff Vodka 5.99
Seagram gin 3.90
Jim Beam 3.70
Popov vodka 3.00
Jack Daniels Black 3.00
Seagram 7 Crown 2.99
Absolut vodka 2.98
Canadian Mist 2.97
Jose Cuervo tequila 2.28

Source: *Chicago Tribune*, January 22, 1996, p. 2, from Adams/Jobson Group.

★ 364 ★
Liquors (SIC 2085)

U.S. Scotch Market

Scotch whiskey market shares are shown in percent. Dewar's is the leading brand.

Guinness 67.0%
Other 33.0

Source: *Forbes*, December 4, 1995, p. 254.

★ 365 ★
Liquors (SIC 2085)

Vodka Producers

Shares are for 1992. Allied and Seagram have less than 5% of the market.

IDV 35.0%
UB 14.0
Other 51.0

Source: *Investext,* Thomson Financial Services, February 27, 1996, p. 12.

★ 366 ★
Bottled Water (SIC 2086)

Bottled Water - Leading Brands

Brand shares are shown based on wholesale revenues of $3.375 billion for 1995.

Arrowhead 6.9%
Poland Spring 6.0
Evian 5.0
Sparkletts 4.7
Hinkley & Schmitt 3.4
Ozarka 2.6
Crystal Geyser 2.5
Zephyrhills 2.4
Mountain Valley 2.0
Deer Park 2.0
All others 62.8

Source: *Beverage World*, March 1996, p. 50, from Beverage Marketing Corporation.

★ 367 ★
Bottled Water (SIC 2086)

Bottled Water Industry

Shares are shown based on wholesale revenues of $3.375 billion in 1995.

Perrier Group	25.2%
McKesson Corp.	7.6
Great Brands of Europe	5.3
Anjou International	5.0
Suntory Water Group	4.7
Sammons	2.6
Crystal Geyser	2.5
Culligan	1.7
Nora Beverages	1.0
Black Mountain	0.8
All others	43.6

Source: *Beverage World*, March 1996, p. 52, from Beverage Marketing Corporation.

★ 368 ★
Bottled Water (SIC 2086)

Top Water Brands

Evian
Arrowhead
Poland Spring
Sparkletts
Zephyrhills
Deer Park
Hickley & Schmitt
Crystal Geyser
Ozark
Other

Evian	10.7%
Arrowhead	9.2
Poland Spring	6.7
Sparkletts	3.7
Zephyrhills	3.0
Deer Park	2.9
Hickley & Schmitt	2.6
Crystal Geyser	2.5
Ozark	2.1
Other	56.6

Source: *Beverage Industry*, June 1996, p. 41.

★ 369 ★
Bottled Water (SIC 2086)

Where We Buy Bottled Water

Grocery store	44.7%
Home/office delivery	39.0
Vending machines/restaurants	16.3

Source: *The Baltimore Sun*, August 18, 1996, p. E1, from Beverage Marketing Corp.

★ 370 ★
Soft Drinks (SIC 2086)

Bottled/Canned Tea Market

Market leaders are shown for the 52 weeks ended July 6, 1996.

Pepsico (Lipton)	30.0%
Quaker(Snapple)	24.7
Coca-Cola (Nestea)	16.4
Arizona	10.2
Private label	4.7
Other	14.0

Source: *New York Times*, August 7, 1996, p. C4, from Quaker Oats Company.

★ 371 ★
Soft Drinks (SIC 2086)

Liquid Tea Brands

Tea brand sales are shown for the 52 weeks ended March 24, 1996.

	($ mil.)	Share
Snapple	$ 101.159	28.2%
Lipton Brisk	66.997	18.7
Lipton Original	47.970	13.4
Arizona	40.995	11.4
Nestea Cool	25.773	7.2
Nestea	24.086	6.7
Ssips	5.796	1.6
All Brand	5.419	1.5
Royal Mistic	3.395	0.9
Private label	14.870	4.1
Others	22.028	6.1

Source: *Beverage Industry*, June 1996, p. 48, from Information Resources Inc. InfoScan.

★ 372 ★

Soft Drinks (SIC 2086)

RTD Brand Shares

Ready-to-drink (RTD) tea brand shares are shown based on total sales of $378.5 million for the 52 weeks ended June 10, 1995.

Lipton	29.9%
Snapple	26.4
Nestea	16.3
Arizona	10.1
Ssips	1.4
Turkey Hill	1.3
Mistic	1.1
Tropicana Twister	0.8
Clover Farms	0.7
Community	0.6
Milo's	0.6
Private label	4.1
Other	6.7

Source: *Beverage World's Periscope*, October 31, 1995, p. 1, from A.C. Nielsen.

★ 373 ★

Soft Drinks (SIC 2086)

Ready-to-Drink Tea Leaders

The market generated $1.7 billion in wholesale sales in 1995.

Pepsi/Lipton	30.0%
Snapple	17.5
Nestea	16.6
Other	35.9

Source: *Advertising Age*, June 17, 1996, p. 4.

★ 374 ★

Soft Drinks (SIC 2086)

Root Beer Market - 1994

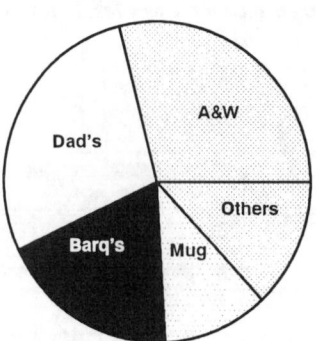

Data include diet drinks.

A&W	28.5%
Dad's	28.2
Barq's	19.4
Mug	11.0
Others	12.9

Source: *Beverage World's Periscope*, August 31, 1995, p. 18, from Beverage Marketing Corporation.

★ 375 ★

Soft Drinks (SIC 2086)

Smooth Beverage Market

Market leaders are shown for the 52 weeks ended July 6, 1996. Data does not refer to juices.

Ocean Spray	39.5%
Private label	17.5
Quaker (Snapple)	6.1
Seagram (Tropicana)	5.1
Other	31.8

Source: *New York Times*, August 7, 1996, p. C4, from Quaker Oats Company.

★ 376 ★
Soft Drinks (SIC 2086)
Soda Brand Shares - 1995

Brand shares of the soft drink market are shown for 1994 and 1995. Diet Coke* and Diet Pepsi* indicates caffeine free soda brands.

	1994	1995
Coke Classic	19.8%	20.2%
Pepsi-Cola	15.7	15.5
Diet Coke	8.8	8.8
Dr. Pepper	5.8	6.1
Diet Pepsi	5.8	5.7
Mountain Dew	5.2	5.6
Sprite	4.3	4.9
7UP	2.9	2.8
Diet Coke*	2.3	2.2
Diet Pepsi*	1.2	1.1
Other	28.2	27.1

Source: *Advertising Age*, February 12, 1996, p. 14, from *Beverage Digest* and Maxwell Report.

★ 377 ★
Soft Drinks (SIC 2086)
Soft Drink Industry - 1995

Parent companies are ranked by millions of gallons produced in 1995.

	(mil.)	Share
Coca-Cola	5,915.4	42.9%
Pepsi-Cola	4,201.8	30.6
Dr. Pepper/Cadbury	2,208.1	16.1
Cott	336.8	2.4
Royal Crown	268.6	2.0
National Beverage	233.5	1.7
Monarch	147.5	1.1
Double-Cola	51.5	0.4
Big Red	30.8	0.2
All other	358.6	2.6

Source: *Beverage World*, March 1996, p. 67, from Beverage Marketing Corp.

★ 378 ★
Soft Drinks (SIC 2086)
Soft Drink Market - 1996

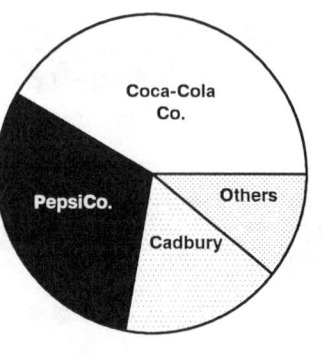

Shares are estimated.

Coca-Cola Co.	41.8%
PepsiCo.	31.1
Cadbury	16.5
Others	10.6

Source: *Investext*, Thomson Financial Services, May 4, 1995, p. 11.

★ 379 ★
Soft Drinks (SIC 2086)
Sports Drink Distribution

Industrial	92.6%
Athletic	6.6
Retail	0.8

Source: *Beverage World*, March 1996, p. 82, from Beverage Marketing Corporation.

★ 380 ★
Soft Drinks (SIC 2086)
Sports Drink Makers

Market leaders are shown for the 52 weeks ended July 6, 1996.

Quaker	81.2%
Pepsico	7.4
Coca-Cola	7.0
Other	4.4

Source: *New York Times*, August 7, 1996, p. C4, from Quaker Oats Company.

★ 381 ★
Soft Drinks (SIC 2086)

Sports Drink Market

Gatorade 80.0%
Other 20.0

Source: *Business Week*, July 22, 1996, p. 40.

★ 382 ★
Soft Drinks (SIC 2086)

Top Soft Drinks - Chicago

The top 10 brands in Chicago are shown for 1994.

Pepsi 15.7%
Coca-Cola Classic 9.9
Diet Coke 6.6
Diet Pepsi 6.5
RC 5.4
7Up 5.4
Diet Rite 4.3
Sprite 2.3
Mountain Dew 2.2
Coke II, Dr. Pepper, Caffeine-Free Coke . . 2.1
Other 39.6

Source: *Beverage Industry*, September 1995, p. 42, from Coca-Cola Bottling Co. of Chicago.

★ 383 ★
Soft Drinks (SIC 2087)

Powdered Drink Market

Shares are shown based on total sales of $582.6 million in 1995.

Kool-Aid (unsweetened) 24.9%
Kool-Aid 13.9
Crystal Light 12.3
Country Time 11.2
Crystal Light Tropical Passion 6.1
Gatorade 6.0
Kool-Aid Island Twist (unsweetened) 4.7
Kool-Aid (sugar-free) 4.5
Kool-Aid Island Twist 3.4
Other 13.0

Source: *Beverage World's Periscope*, May 31, 1996, p. 12, from A.C. Nielsen.

★ 384 ★
Sweeteners (SIC 2087)

Sweeteners & Flavoring Market

Sales reached $2.99 billion in 1994.

Sugar 59.7%
Table syrup 22.8
Synthetic sweeteners 9.7
Flavoring extracts 6.5
Packaged molasses 0.9
Marshmallow cream 0.4

Source: *Supermarket Business*, September 1995, p. 62.

★ 385 ★
Seafood (SIC 2091)

Canned Fish Sales

Shares of $1.653 billion in supermarket sales are shown in percent.

Tuna 77.2%
Salmon 6.9
Clams 3.8
Sardines 3.2
Crab 2.9
Oysters 1.9
Shrimp 1.4
Anchovies 0.8
Other 1.9

Source: *Progressive Grocer*, July 1996, p. 59.

★ 386 ★
Seafood (SIC 2091)

Fish Products

Sales of fish and seafood in supermarkets are shown by product.

Fish 44.0%
Shrimp 33.0
Prepared entrees (cooked) 9.0
Prepared entrees (uncooked) 6.0
Lobster 3.0
Clams, other shell fish 2.0
Scallops 2.0
Soups 1.0

Source: *Supermarket Business*, November 1995, p. 74.

★ 387 ★
Coffee (SIC 2095)

Coffee Drink Sales

Shares of the $21.144 million market are shown in percent based on sales for the 52 weeks ended March 11, 1995.

Maxwell House Cappio	92.0%
Prince Jamaican Gold	3.1
Hillside	2.2
Chock O'Chino	1.9
Aspire	0.3
Millstone Java Cooler	0.3
Victorian House	0.1
Other	0.1

Source: *Beverage World's Periscope*, October 31, 1995, p. 16, from A.C. Nielsen.

★ 388 ★
Coffee (SIC 2095)

Coffee Market Leaders

Shares of the $2.852 billion market are shown for the 52 weeks ended December 9, 1995.

Folgers	30.8%
Maxwell House	20.0
Private label	7.6
Hills Bros.	6.2
Master Blend	5.3
Eight O'Clock	4.4
Chock Full O'Nuts	3.2
MJB	2.5
Yuban	2.1
Community	1.7
Chase & Sanborn	1.7
Boyer Bros.	1.0
S&W	0.8
Sanka	0.8
JFG	0.7
Other	11.2

Source: *Beverage World's Periscope*, May 31, 1996, p. 11, from A.C. Nielsen.

★ 389 ★
Coffee (SIC 2095)

Coffee Producers - 1994

Procter & Gamble	32.2%
General Foods	29.0
Nestle	15.2
Chock Full O'Nuts	3.4
Other	20.2

Source: *Investext*, Thomson Financial Services, March 22, 1995, p. 14.

★ 390 ★
Coffee (SIC 2095)

Instant Coffee Leaders

Shares of the market are shown as of December 1995.

General Foods	36.0%
Procter & Gamble	30.0
Nestle	23.0
Other	11.0

Source: *Investext*, Thomson Financial Services, March 15, 1996, p. 36, from Information Resources Inc.

★ 391 ★

Snacks (SIC 2096)

Leading Potato Chip Brands

Shares are shown for the year ended July 16, 1995.

Lay's	18.5%
Ruffles	16.0
Pringles	8.8
Eagle Thins	5.3
Private label	6.9
Other	44.5

Source: *Brandweek*, September 19, 1995, p. 28, from Information Resources Inc.

★ 392 ★

Snacks (SIC 2096)

Popcorn/Popcorn Oil Producers

Shares of the $587 million market are shown in percent for the year ended November 6, 1994.

Hunt Wesson	42.8%
General Mills	29.4
Private label	12.2
American Popcorn Co.	5.3
Golden Valley	1.2
Other	9.1

Source: *Investext,* Thomson Financial Services, January 5, 1995, p. 3, from Information Resources Inc. and PaineWebber estimates.

★ 393 ★

Snacks (SIC 2096)

Potato Chip Makers - Canada

Market shares are shown in percent.

Old Dutch Ltd.	36.0%
Hostess/Frito-Lay	16.0
Others	48.0

Source: *Snack Food*, April 1996, p. 22.

★ 394 ★

Snacks (SIC 2096)

Potato Chip Market - Chicago

Shares are shown for the 52 weeks ended October 15, 1995.

Eagle	33.4%
Jay's	19.5
Frito Lay's	12.4
Other	34.7

Source: *Crain's Chicago Business*, November 20, 1995, p. 3, from Information Resources Inc.

★ 395 ★

Snacks (SIC 2096)

Potato Crisp Brands

Shares are shown based on sales of $292 million for the year ended September 9, 1995.

Pringles	68.4%
O'Boises	11.3
Mr. Phipps Tater Crisp	6.8
Tato Wilds	4.5
Tato Skins	3.4
Other	2.6

Source: *Snack Food*, April 1996, p. 17, from A.C. Nielsen.

★ 396 ★

Snacks (SIC 2096)

Snack Food Consumption

Consumption is shown in pounds per person per year.

Potato chips	6.60
Corn/tortilla chips	5.78

Continued on next page.

★ 396 ★ *Continued*
Snacks (SIC 2096)

Snack Food Consumption

Consumption is shown in pounds per person per year.

Pretzels	2.55
Popcorn	2.50
Nuts	1.60
Party mix	0.39
Meat snacks	0.23
Pork rinds	0.18
Other	1.89

Source: *Business North Carolina*, November 1995, p. 84, from Snack Food Association.

★ 397 ★
Snacks (SIC 2096)

Snack Food Makers - 1996

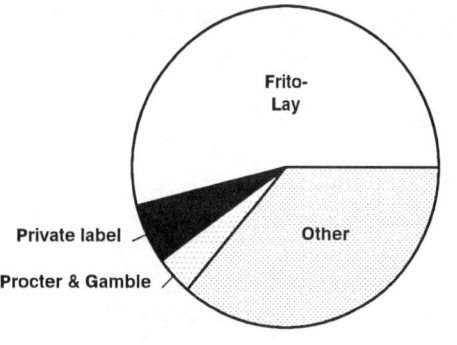

Shares of the $6.6 billion market are shown for the year ended June 16, 1996.

Frito-Lay	53.5%
Private label	5.8
Procter & Gamble	4.4
Other	36.3

Source: *Chicago Tribune*, July 29, 1996, p. C1, from Information Resources Inc., Perception Research Services, and *Progressive Grocer*.

★ 398 ★
Snacks (SIC 2096)

Snack Food Market

Shares of the $5.9 billion market for chips and snack foods are shown in percent.

Frito-Lay	49.4%
Private label	5.8
Eagle Snacks	4.9
Procter & Gamble	4.2
Borden Snacks	3.1
Keebler	2.0
Snyder's of Hanover	1.5
Nabisco Foods	1.4
General Foods	1.2
UTZ Potato Chip	1.0
Other	25.5

Source: *Brandweek*, September 19, 1995, p. 28, from Information Resources Inc.

★ 399 ★
Snacks (SIC 2096)

Snack Food Producers

Firms are ranked by 1995 snack food sales in millions of dollars.

Nabisco Inc.	$ 6,450.0
Frito-Lay Inc.	5,010.0
Hershey Chocolate North America	2,300.0
M&M/Mars	2,200.0
Kraft Foods Inc.	2,177.0
Campbell Soup Co.	1,875.0
Wm. Wrigley Jr. Co.	1,750.0
Keebler Co.	1,700.0
Nestle USA Inc.	1,697.0
General Mills Inc.	1,500.0
Pillsbury Co.	1,500.0
Warner-Lambert Co.	1,365.0

Source: *Snack Food*, December 1995, p. 84, from Valueline Investment Survey and company reports.

★ 400 ★

Snacks (SIC 2096)

Snack Foods Market - Canada

Consumption is shown in millions of dollars for 1995.

	($ mil.)	Share
Potato chips	$ 236.9	57.2%
Taco/tortilla chips	83.6	20.2
Cheesies	43.4	10.5
Pretzels	19.8	4.8
Corn chips	5.4	1.3
Popcorn	5.2	1.3
Others	20.0	4.8

Source: *Macleans*, February 5, 1996, p. 49, from Nielsen Marketing Research.

★ 401 ★

Snacks (SIC 2096)

Top Potato Chip Makers

Shares are shown for the $2.2 billion market in 1995.

Frito-Lay	47.3%
Procter & Gamble	12.5
Eagle Snacks	8.1
Borden Snacks	5.1
Private label	6.7
Other	20.3

Source: *Snack Food*, May 1996, p. 30, from Information Resources Inc.

★ 402 ★

Snacks (SIC 2096)

Top Tortilla Chips

Shares of the $3.3 billion market are shown in percent for the 52 weeks ended November 4, 1995.

Doritos	37.0%
Tostitos	31.7
Eagle El Grande	5.0
Santitos	4.6
Private label	4.6
Mission	1.5
Padrinos	1.3
Guiltless Gourmet	1.0
Chi-Chi's	0.9
Keebler's ChaCho's	0.7
Other	11.7

Source: *Advertising Age*, December 11, 1995, p. 42, from Snack Food Association and A.C. Nielsen.

★ 403 ★

Pasta (SIC 2098)

Dry Pasta Producers

Shares are shown for the 52 weeks ended February 29, 1996.

Hershey	28.4%
Borden	23.2
Private label	16.3
CPC International	11.2
Imports	10.8
Quaker Oats	3.1
Archer Daniels Midland	1.0
Other	6.0

Source: *Investext,* Thomson Financial Services, May 21, 1996, p. 5, from Hershey Foods.

★ 404 ★

Pasta (SIC 2098)

Pasta Brands

Shares of the $1.277 billion dry pasta market are shown in percent. Data are for the 52 weeks ended September 30, 1995.

Hershey Foods	27.3%
Borden	22.7
CPC/Best Foods	11.4
Private label	15.3
Other	23.3

Source: *Brandweek*, January 1, 1996, p. 3, from Information Resources Inc.

★ 405 ★

Pasta (SIC 2098)

Pasta Market by Type

Shares are shown based on $2.46 billion in supermarket sales.

Pasta dinners	44.1%
Noodles	17.8
Spaghetti	15.7
Macaroni	15.0
Pasta, shelf-stable	6.4
Pizza/crust mixes	1.0

Source: *Progressive Grocer*, July 1996, p. 60.

★ 406 ★

Pasta (SIC 2098)

Refrigerated Pasta Market

Shares of the $181 million market are shown for the year ended September 30, 1995.

Nestle's Contadina	55.2%
Kraft Foods DiGiorgio	20.6
Private label	8.8
Other	15.3

Source: *Brandweek*, January 1, 1996, p. 3, from Information Resources Inc.

★ 407 ★

Food Preparations (SIC 2099)

Chili Pepper Processing - Mexico

The market decreased from $215.04 million in 1992 to $212.8 million in 1993.

	1992	1993
Jalapeno	73.4%	71.4%
Chipotle	17.0	19.8
Serrano	5.4	4.6
Others	4.2	4.2

Source: *National Trade Data Bank*, January 1, 1996, p. IS9508.630, from Canned Food Industry National Chamber.

★ 408 ★
Food Preparations (SIC 2099)

Egg Substitute Market

Shres are shown for the 52 weeks ended Janaury 1, 1995 based on total sales of $76.3 million.

Nabisco	46.7%
Avoset Foods	31.2
Worthington Foods	14.1
Papetti	2.8
Crystal Farms	2.3
Private label	1.8
Other	1.1

Source: *Investext,* Thomson Financial Services, February 22, 1995, p. 25, from Information Resources Inc. InfoScan.

★ 409 ★
Food Preparations (SIC 2099)

Popular Lunch Kit Brands

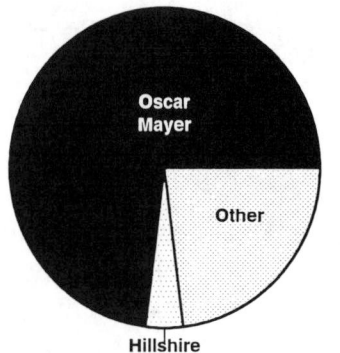

Shares of the $442.4 million market are shown in percent.

Oscar Mayer	73.4%
Hillshire	4.0
Other	22.6

Source: *Brandweek,* July 22, 1996, p. 6, from Information Resources Inc.

★ 410 ★
Food Preparations (SIC 2099)

Retail Spice Market

Specialty brands refer to Dunkee-French and Spice Islands.

McCormick	37.0%
Private label	25.0
Specialty brands	14.0
Lawry's	7.0
Sauer's	3.0
Other	17.0

Source: *Spice Market in the United States,* July 1995, p. 15, from United States Department of Agriculture.

★ 411 ★
Food Preparations (SIC 2099)

Sugar-Substitute Market

Shares of the $226 million market are shown for the year ended November 1995.

	Sales ($ mil.)	Share
Equal	$ 107.0	47.3%
Sweet 'N Low	60.0	26.5
NutraSweet Spoonful	15.0	6.6
SugarTwin	10.0	4.4
Other	34.0	15.0

Source: *Chicago Tribune,* January 9, 1995, p. C3, from Information Resources Inc.

★ 412 ★
Peanut Butter (SIC 2099)

Popular Peanut Butter Brands

Data are current as of December 1995.

Jif	31.0%
Skippy	19.0
Peter Pan	16.0
Other	34.0

Source: *Investext,* Thomson Financial Services, March 15, 1996, p. 26, from Information Resources Inc.

★ 413 ★

Syrup (SIC 2099)

Top Maple Syrup Makers

Production is shown in thousands of gallons in 1995.
The United States produced 1.096 million gallons;
Canada produced 4.017 gallons.

Quebec, Canada	3,020
Vermont	365
Ontario, Canada	290
New York	208
Maine	162
Wisconsin	98
Ohio	65
New Hampshire	64
Michigan	55

Source: *Detroit Free Press*, March 29, 1996, p. D16, from
Michigan Maple Syrup Association, Michigan State
University, North American Maple Syrup Council,
Michigan Department of Agriculture, and Statistics
Canada.

★ 414 ★

Tortillas (SIC 2099)

Tortilla Market

The table shows the leaders in the tortilla market in
the United States.

Gruma	15.0%
Tyson Foods	8.0
Other	77.0

Source: *Wall Street Journal*, May 10, 1996, p. A6.

SIC 21 - Tobacco Products

★ 415 ★
Cigarettes (SIC 2111)
Cigarette Brands - 1995

Marlboro	30.1%
GPC	5.8
Winston	5.8
Doral	5.7
Newport	5.6
Basic	4.7
Camel	4.4
Kool	3.6
Benson & Hedges	2.4
Merit	2.4
Virginia Slims	2.4
Other	27.1

Source: *U.S. Distribution Journal*, April 15, 1996, p. 13, from *Tobacco Reporter* and John C. Maxwell.

★ 416 ★
Cigarettes (SIC 2111)
Cigarette Makers - Canada

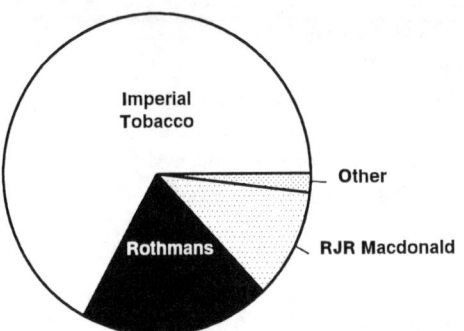

Shares are shown for 1993.

Imperial Tobacco	67.1%
Rothmans	20.0
RJR Macdonald	10.8
Other	2.1

Source: *Marketing Magazine*, October 2, 1995, p. 4, from *Beverage and Tobacco Guidebook, 1995* and Levesque Beaubien Goffrion Inc.

★ 417 ★
Cigarettes (SIC 2111)
Cigarette Market - Mexico

Cigarera La Moderna	54.6%
Other	35.4

Source: *Mexico Business*, January/February 1996, p. 56.

★ 418 ★
Cigarettes (SIC 2111)

Cigarette Producers

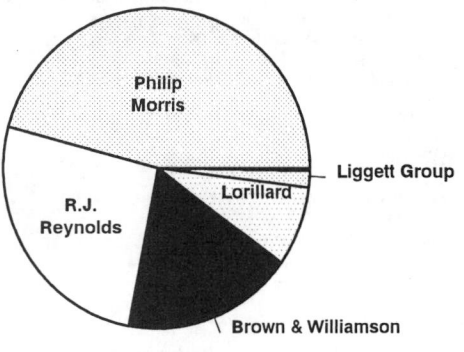

Shares are for 1995. Philip Morris produces Benson & Hedges and Marlboro; R.J. Reynolds produces Camel, Salem, and Winston; Brown & Williamson produces Kool and Raleigh; Lorillard produces Newport and True; Liggett Group produces Chesterfield and Eve.

Philip Morris	46.1%
R.J. Reynolds	25.7
Brown & Williamson	18.0
Lorillard	8.0
Liggett Group	2.2

Source: *U.S. News & World Report*, March 25, 1996, p. 17, from Maxwell Consumer Reports.

★ 419 ★
Cigarettes (SIC 2111)

Discount Cigarette Makers

Shares of the discount cigarette market are shown for 1995.

Brown & Williamson	34.8%
R.J. Reynolds	31.9
Philip Morris	26.6
Liggett	5.5
Lorillard	1.2

Source: *U.S. Distribution Journal*, April 15, 1996, p. 13, from *Tobacco Reporter* and John C. Maxwell.

★ 420 ★
Cigarettes (SIC 2111)

Discount Cigarette Market

The table shows the market for 1995. Data include the share of the market and the share of the discount market.

	Mkt. Share	Dsc. Share
Branded discounts	23.5%	78.3%
Private label	6.0	19.9
Price-off	0.4	1.3
Value	0.1	0.5

Source: *DM*, June 1996, p. 102, from John C. Maxwell and *Tobacco Reporter*.

★ 421 ★
Cigarettes (SIC 2111)

Leading Cigarette Brands

The top cigarette brands are ranked by billions of units sold in 1995. PM - Philip Morris; RJR - RJR Nabisco; B&M - Brown & Williamson.

	Cigarettes	Market Share
Marlboro (PM)	36.46	29.7%
GPC (B&W)	7.34	6.0
Doral (RJR)	6.93	5.8
Newport (Lorillard)	7.04	5.7
Winston (RJR)	7.05	5.7
Basic (PM)	5.77	4.7
Camel (RJR)	5.69	4.6
Salem (RJR)	4.56	3.7
Kool (B&W)	4.46	3.6
Virginia Slims (PM)	2.96	2.4
Merit (PM)	2.84	2.3
Benson & Hedges (PM)	2.83	2.3
Other	0.03	21.7

Source: *Nonfoods Merchandising*, February 1996, p. 30, from Maxwell Consumer Report; Wheat First Butcher Singer.

★ 422 ★
Cigars (SIC 2121)

Cigar/Cigarillo Makers

Data are for 1994.

Swisher International Inc.	32.1%
King Edward	22.5

Continued on next page.

★ 422 ★ *Continued*
Cigars (SIC 2121)
Cigar/Cigarillo Makers

Data are for 1994.

Optimo	22.5%
Bering	0.7
Other	6.7
Consolidated Cigar Corp.	22.3
Muriel	5.2
Dutch Masters	4.5
Antonio y Cleopatra	4.2
El Producto	2.4
Backwoods	2.2
La Corona	0.5
Roi-Tan	0.4
Other	2.8
H.A.T. Holding Co.	25.2
Phillies	13.0
Havatampa	10.2
Erik Filter Menthol	2.0
General Cigar Co.	16.8
White Owl	5.4
Garcia y Vega	4.6
Robert Burns	2.2
William Penn	2.0
Tijuana Small	1.7
Other	1.0
House of Windsor	2.3
M&N Standard Cigar	1.9
Other	0.6

Source: *U.S. Distribution Journal*, January 15, 1996, p. 14, from John C. Maxwell and Tobacco Reporter.

★ 423 ★
Cigars (SIC 2121)
Imported Cigar Market

The table shows the millions of cigars imported from each country by the United States.

Dominican Republic	81.1
Honduras	53.5
Jamaica	15.3
Mexico	9.7
Cuba	5.0
Nicaragua	3.5
Canary Islands/Spain	0.4
Panama	0.3

Source: *New York Times*, April 17, 1996, p. C1, from Cigar Association of America, based on U.S. Customs data.

★ 424 ★
Smokeless Tobacco (SIC 2131)
Smokeless Tobacco Makers

	1993	1994
U.S. Tobacco Co.	36.5%	37.4%
Conwood Co.	24.4	24.0
Pinkerton Tobacco Co.	22.2	22.2
National Tobacco Co.	9.1	9.1
Swisher International	6.7	6.2
Brown & Williamson	0.7	0.6
R.C. Owen	0.4	0.4

Source: *U.S. Distribution Journal*, December 15, 1995, p. 12, from John C. Maxwell and *Tobacco Reporter*.

★ 425 ★

Smokeless Tobacco (SIC 2131)

Top Loose Leaf Brands

Shares are for 1994. Pinkerton Tobacco Co. is the leading loose leaf producer, with 43% of the market; Conwood follows with 31% of the market.

Red Man	24.0%
Levi Garrett	22.0
Beech Nut Regular	12.0
Golden Blend	10.0
Taylor's Pride	0.7
Other	31.3

Source: *U.S. Distribution Journal*, December 15, 1995, p. 14, from John C. Maxwell.

★ 426 ★

Smokeless Tobacco (SIC 2131)

Top Moist Snuff Brands

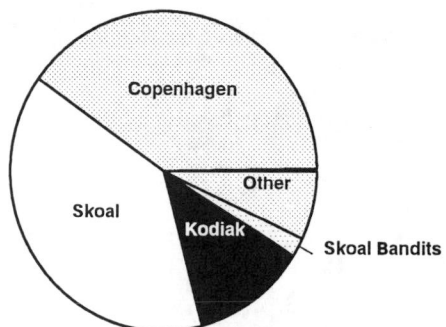

Shares are shown for 1994. U.S. Tobacco is the top producer of moist snuff, with 82% of the market.

Copenhagen	40.0%
Skoal	39.0
Kodiak	12.0
Skoal Bandits	2.0
Other	7.0

Source: *U.S. Distribution Journal*, December 15, 1995, p. 14, from John C. Maxwell.

SIC 22 - Textile Mill Products

★ 427 ★
Textiles (SIC 2200)

Leading Textile Firms

Firms are ranked by 1995 revenues in millions of dollars. Shares of the group are shown in percent.

	Rev. ($ mil.)	% of Group
Shaw Industries	$ 2,870	17.1%
Springs Industries	2,233	13.3
Burlington Industries	2,209	13.2
Westpoint Stevens	1,650	9.8
Mohawk Industries	1,555	9.3
UNIFI	1,555	9.3
Collins & Aikman	1,497	8.9
Triarc	1,184	7.1
Fieldcrest	1,095	6.5
Cone Mills	910	5.4

Source: *Fortune*, April 29, 1996, p. F62.

★ 428 ★
Textiles (SIC 2200)

Leading Textile Mills

Textile mill sales are shown in millions of dollars for 1995.

Spring Industries	$ 2,233.1
Burlington Industries	2,207.0
Westpoint Stevens	1,649.9
Unifi	1,596.9
Wellman	1,109.4
Cone Mills	910.2
Guilford Mills	774.2
Dixie Yarns	670.8
Galey & Lord	460.1

Dan River	$ 384.8
Johnston Industries	296.0
Texfi	262.9
Thomaston Mills	204.5

Source: *DNR*, March 19, 1996, p. 12, from Morgan Stanley & Co.

★ 429 ★
Textiles (SIC 2200)

Leading Textile Producers

Textile mills shown are ranked by 1994 sales in millions of dollars.

Burlington Industries	$ 2,127.1
UNIFI	1,384.8
Cone Mills Corp.	806.2
Guilford Mills	703.7
Dixie Yarns	688.5
Delta Woodside Industries	613.8
JPS Textile Group	603.4
Galey and Lord	451.1
Texfi Industries	282.9
Thomaston Mills	279.5
CULP	245.0
Forstmann & Co.	237.0
Synthetic Industries	235.0
Concord Fabrics	197.8
FAB Industries	189.8
Quaker Fabric Corp.	180.8
Dyersburg Corp.	180.5
Johnstone Industries	159.9

Source: *Apparel Industry Magazine*, August 1995, p. 32, from Kurt Salmon Associates.

★ 430 ★
Hosiery (SIC 2250)

Hosiery Market

The hosiery market is shown in millions of dollars.
Data for 1995 are for the first six months.

	1994	1995	Share
Women's	$ 4,083	$ 1,982	66.8%
Men's	1,518	618	20.8
Girl's	488	187	6.3
Boy's	451	178	6.0

Source: *Bobbin*, December 1995, p. 60, from NPD
Group Inc. and AAMA Apparel Market Monitor.

★ 431 ★
Hosiery (SIC 2250)

Women's Legwear Market

The market for women's legwear is shown by
classification. Alternative legwear refers to tights,
socks, and trouser socks.

	($ bil.)	Share
Sheer hosiery	$ 2.6	61.9%
Alternative	1.6	38.1

Source: *Discount Store News*, May 6, 1996, p. A22, from
Information Resources Inc. and NPD Group.

★ 432 ★
Hosiery (SIC 2251)

Women's Hosiery Market by Type

The sheer hosiery market reached $2.681 billion in
1994 and $2.745 billion in 1995. Figures are based
on sales at supermarket, drugstore, and discount
stores.

	1994	1995
All nylon non-control top	36.4%	35.0%
All nylon control top	29.0	28.2
Below the knee	8.1	10.6
Spandex: 19% and above	10.4	9.9
Spandex: up to 18%	9.4	9.6
Stockings	6.6	6.7

Source: *Nonfoods Merchandising*, July 1996, p. 12, from
National Association of Hosiery Manufacturers.

★ 433 ★
Knitting Mills (SIC 2253)

U.S. Knit Shirt Imports

The table shows the value of men's and boy's cotton
knit shirts for the first four months of 1995. Data are
in millions of U.S. dollars.

Pakistan	$ 67.3
Thailand	42.8
Hong Kong	32.5
Philippines	30.8
China	27.7
India	24.2
Indonesia	21.5
Turkey	15.9
Honduras	15.3

Source: *Textile Asia*, August 1995, p. 178, from United
States Department of Commerce.

★ 434 ★
Carpets (SIC 2273)

Carpet Market Leaders

Shares are shown based on $7.8 billion in sales in
1993.

Shaw	32.0%
Mohawk	20.0
Beaulieu	11.0
Queen	6.0
Other	31.0

Source: *Investext*, Thomson Financial Services, March 5,
1995, p. 4, from *Focus Magazine* and Smith Barney.

★ 435 ★
Carpets (SIC 2273)

U.S. Carpet Shipments

Data are shown in millions of square yards.

	1994	1995	Share
Tufted broadloom	1,317	1,325	81.5%
Automotive and industrial .	90	90	5.5
Artificial grass	10	10	0.6
Needlepunch and other . .	115	115	7.1
Rugs and others	82	85	5.2

Source: *Textile World*, May 1996, p. 30, from United
States Department of Commerce.

★ 436 ★

Technical Fabrics (SIC 2295)

Needled Fabric Market

Market revenues are shown by product based on U.S. sales in 1993.

	Rev. ($ mil.)	Share
Geotextiles	$ 300.0	32.9%
Automotive	197.0	21.6
Filtration	115.0	12.6
Interlining	90.0	9.9
Substrates	65.0	7.1
Roofing	50.0	5.5
Furniture/bedding	41.0	4.5
Shoes/art, leather	20.0	2.2
Miscellaneous	35.0	3.8

Source: *Textile Asia*, August 1995, p. 115.

SIC 23 - Apparel and Other Textile Products

★ 437 ★
Apparel (SIC 2300)

Activewear Fleece Makers

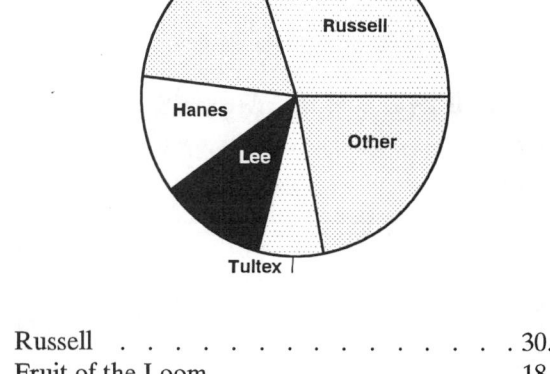

Russell	30.0%
Fruit of the Loom	18.0
Hanes	12.0
Lee (VF Corp.)	11.0
Tultex	7.0
Other	22.0

Source: *Investext,* Thomson Financial Services, December 21, 1995, p. 6, from Prudential Securities estimates.

★ 438 ★
Apparel (SIC 2300)

Apparel Market Leaders

Apparel companies are ranked by 1995 sales shown in millions of dollars.

Sara Lee Apparel	$ 7,150.0
VF Corp.	5,062.3
Fruit of the Loom	2,403.1
Liz Claiborne	2,081.6
Phillips-Van Heusen	1,464.1
Kellwood Co.	1,451.1
Nike Inc.	1,168.6
Russell Corp.	1,152.6
Waranco Group	$ 916.2
Jones Apparel Group	776.4
Oxford Industries	675.8
Hartmarx Corp.	595.3

Source: *Bobbin,* June 1996, p. 62.

★ 439 ★
Apparel (SIC 2300)

Discount Apparel Sales

Sales at discount stores are shown in billions of dollars.

	($ bil.)	Share
Men's	$ 9.94	26.6%
Women's	9.54	25.6
Boy's	3.26	8.7
Girl's	3.18	8.5
Shoes	2.83	7.6
Infant's	2.78	7.5
Accessories	2.63	7.0
Intimates	2.43	6.5
Other	0.72	1.9

Source: *Discount Store News,* August 7, 1995, p. 50.

★ 440 ★
Apparel (SIC 2300)

Fleece Market - 1995

Shares include both printed and unprinted clothing.

Russell	9.0%
Hanes	8.0
Tultex	7.0
Bassett-Walker	6.0
Imports	11.0
Other	53.0

Source: *Investext,* Thomson Financial Services, November 7, 1995, p. 21.

★ 441 ★
Apparel (SIC 2300)

Jeans Makers

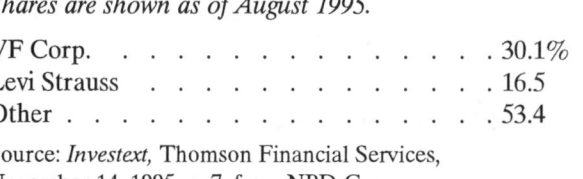

Shares are shown as of August 1995.

VF Corp.	30.1%
Levi Strauss	16.5
Other	53.4

Source: *Investext,* Thomson Financial Services, November 14, 1995, p. 7, from NPD Group.

★ 442 ★
Apparel (SIC 2300)

Private Label Apparel Market

Private label shares for the year ended August 1995 are shown for selected apparel markets.

Girl's bottoms	36.0%
Women's bottoms	36.0
Women's tops	36.0
Boy's tops	35.0
Girl's tops	33.0
Boy's bottoms	32.0
Men's tops	32.0
Men's bottoms	25.0

Source: *Apparel Industry Magazine*, January 1996, p. 54, from NPD Group.

★ 443 ★
Apparel (SIC 2300)

Top Apparel Firms

Firms are ranked by 1995 revenues in millions of dollars.

Levi Strauss	$ 6,708
VF	5,062
Fruit of the Loom	2,403
Liz Claiborne	2,082
Kellwood	1,365
Russell	1,153
Warnaco Group	916

Source: *Fortune*, April 29, 1996, p. 44.

★ 444 ★
Apparel (SIC 2300)

Top Children's Wear Makers

Companies are ranked by sales in millions of dollars.

Oshkosh B'Gosh Inc.	$ 432
William Carter Co.	295
Gerber Childrenswear	186
Buster Brown Apparel	150
Garan Inc.	141

Source: *Apparel Industry Magazine*, June 1996, p. 21.

★ 445 ★
Apparel (SIC 2300)

Top Rugged Outerwear Makers

Firms are ranked by 1995 sales in millions of dollars.

Woolrich	$ 170.0
Patagonia	150.0
Timberland	114.6
Walls	83.5
Pacific Trail	70.0
Columbia	88.0
The North Face	62.0
JanSport	35.0
Helly-Hansen	29.0
Nike ACG	25.0

Source: *Sportstyle*, May 1996, p. 40.

★ 446 ★

Apparel (SIC 2300)

Top U.S. Clothing Makers

| Levi Strauss |
| VF Corp. |
| Fruit of the Loom |
| Liz Claiborne |
| Kelwood |
| Russell Corporation |

Firms are ranked by revenues in billions of dollars for fiscal year 1995.

Levi Strauss	$ 6.5
VF Corp.	5.3
Fruit of the Loom	2.4
Liz Claiborne	2.3
Kelwood	1.4
Russell Corporation	1.1

Source: *Economist*, June 8, 1996, p. 66, from UBS Global Research.

★ 447 ★

Apparel (SIC 2311)

Wool Suit Sales by Canada

The table shows Canada's sales of men's wool suits to the United States by year. Data are in thousands of Canadian dollars.

1991	67,931
1992	100,968
1993	135,531
1994	179,941
1995	233,908

Source: *Financial Times*, August 16, 1996, p. 4, from Industry Canada.

★ 448 ★

Apparel (SIC 2320)

Men's Apparel Sales by Province - Canada

Ontario	38.0%
Quebec	27.0
Prairie Provinces	17.0
British Columbia	12.0
Atlantic Provinces	6.0

Source: *National Trade Data Bank*, March 2, 1996, p. ISA9409.

★ 449 ★

Apparel (SIC 2320)

Top Men's Apparel Makers

The top men's wear makers are ranked by sales in millions of dollars.

Polo/Ralph Lauren Corp.	$ 4,400
Phillips-Van Heusen Corp.	1,464
Oxford Industries Inc.	656
Hartmarx Corp.	595
Salant Corp.	502

Source: *Apparel Industry Magazine*, June 1996, p. 26.

★ 450 ★

Apparel (SIC 2321)

T-Shirt Market - 1995

Shares include both printed and unprinted clothing.

Fruit of the Loom	17.0%
Hanes	13.0
Russell	6.0
Bassett-Walker	4.0
Oneita	4.0
Tultex	3.0
Imports	22.0
Other	32.0

Source: *Investext,* Thomson Financial Services, November 7, 1995, p. 21.

★ 451 ★

Apparel (SIC 2321)

Who Makes T-Shirts

Unit shares are for 1994.

Fruit of the Loom	35.0%
Hanes	22.0
Russell	11.0
Oneita	8.0
Anvil	4.0
Lee	2.0
Tultex	1.0
Other	17.0

Source: *Investext,* Thomson Financial Services, December 21, 1995, p. 7, from Prudential Securities estimates.

★ 452 ★

Apparel (SIC 2330)

Bodywear Producers

The leading makers of women's workout apparel are ranked by 1995 sales in millions of dollars. Shares of the group are shown in percent.

	Sales ($ mil.)	% of Group
Jacques Monet	$ 88.0	20.1%
Sara Lee Bodywear	77.0	17.6
Rainbeau Flyte	70.0	16.0
Danskin	65.0	14.8
Marika	30.0	6.8
Gilda Marx	27.0	6.2
S.F. City Lights	20.0	4.6
Active Apparel Group	15.0	3.4
Body Wrappers	13.0	3.0
Activewear Corp. of America	11.0	2.5
Carushka	9.0	2.1
Guess Activewear	7.5	1.7
Eurotard	5.0	1.1
Crunch	1.2	0.3

Source: *Sportstyle*, May 1996, p. 24.

★ 453 ★

Apparel (SIC 2330)

Top Women's Wear Makers

Companies are ranked by sales in millions of dollars.

Liz Claiborne	$ 2,081
Jones Apparel Group Inc.	776
Cygne Designs Inc.	540
Donna Karan	510
Avon Products	501

Source: *Apparel Industry Magazine*, June 1996, p. 21.

★ 454 ★

Bras (SIC 2342)

Bra Makers

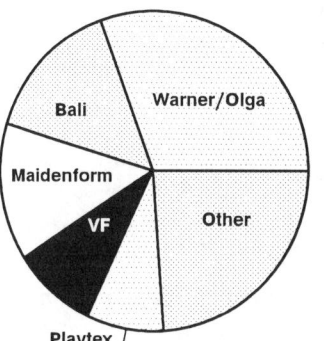

Market shares are shown in percent. Figures are for department store sales.

	1993	1994
Warner/Olga (Warnaco)	34.7%	31.1%
Bali	14.0	14.7
Maidenform	15.0	13.8
VF	7.7	8.6
Playtex	7.0	8.0
Other	21.6	23.8

Source: *Investext,* Thomson Financial Services, October 20, 1995, p. 2, from company data.

★ 455 ★
Home Furnishings (SIC 2392)
Bedding Market

Shares are estimated for 1995.

Sealy 17.5%
Serta 15.0
Simmons 15.0
Spring Air 10.0
Other 42.5

Source: *Furniture Today*, September 4, 1995, p. 20.

★ 456 ★
Home Furnishings (SIC 2392)
Domestics Sales by Type

*Distribution is shown based on $8.14 billion in sales
at discount stores.*

Bed 48.3%
Bath 23.8
Kitchen 7.2
Window 6.1
Other 14.5

Source: *Discount Store News*, August 5, 1996, p. 66.

★ 457 ★
Home Furnishings (SIC 2392)
Leading Sheet Makers

Data are for 1994.

WestPoint Stevens 35.0%
Springs 32.0
Fieldcrest Cannon 14.0
Bibb 11.0
Dan River 8.0

Source: *Investext,* Thomson Financial Services, August 9,
1995, p. 3, from *Home Textiles Today* and industry
reports.

★ 458 ★
Home Furnishings (SIC 2392)
Leading Towel Makers

Data are for 1994.

Fieldcrest Cannon 45.0%
WestPoint Stevens 32.0
Springs 14.0
Bibb 8.0

Source: *Investext,* Thomson Financial Services, August 9,
1995, p. 3, from *Home Textiles Today* and industry
reports.

★ 459 ★
Home Furnishings (SIC 2392)
Sheet/Pillowcase Producers

Westpoint Stevens 35.0%
Springs Industries 32.0
Fieldcrest Cannon 15.0
Bibb Company 8.0
Other 10.0

Source: *Investext,* Thomson Financial Services, October
18, 1995, p. 7, from *Seidman News Bulletin* and
Prudential Securities Inc. estimates.

★ 460 ★

Home Furnishings (SIC 2392)

Terrycloth Towel Market

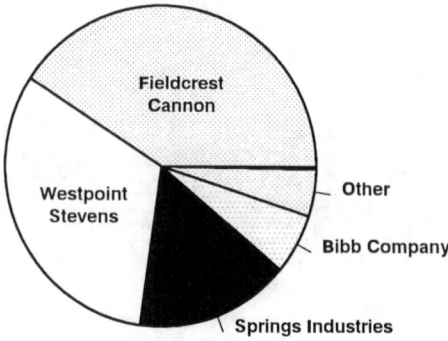

	1994 ($ mil.)	1999 ($ mil.)	% of Group
Boston - Lawrence - Lowell -Brockton . .	$ 625.9	$ 717.6	3.5%
Orange County, CA . .	624.0	712.0	3.4
Dallas	640.5	711.4	3.4
San Diego	585.9	700.8	3.4
Seattle - Bellevue - Everett	563.3	690.8	3.3
Minneapolis - St. Paul	561.1	688.0	3.3

Source: *Furniture Today*, December 25, 1995, p. 25, from Market Statistics.

Fieldcrest Cannon 41.0%
Westpoint Stevens 32.0
Springs Industries 16.0
Bibb Company 6.0
Other 5.0

Source: *Investext,* Thomson Financial Services, October 18, 1995, p. 7, from *Seidman News Bulletin* and Prudential Securities Inc. estimates.

★ 461 ★

Home Furnishings (SIC 2392)

Top Cities for Homefurnishings

Cities are ranked by millions of dollars in bedding and furniture sales. Shares of the group are shown in percent for 1999.

	1994 ($ mil.)	1999 ($ mil.)	% of Group
Chicago	$ 1,988.8	$ 2,727.5	13.1%
Washington D.C. . . .	1,312.1	1,887.4	9.1
New York City	1,300.7	1,566.4	7.5
Detroit	1,028.8	1,372.9	6.6
Los Angeles - Long Beach	1,370.3	1,319.8	6.4
Atlanta	822.7	1,148.1	5.5
Philadelphia	924.1	1,108.3	5.3
Phoenix - Mesa . . .	611.2	867.9	4.2
Nassau - Suffolk, NY .	652.2	822.9	4.0
Houston	662.6	774.3	3.7
Cleveland - Lorain - Elyria	502.4	749.3	3.6
Denver	523.3	735.4	3.5
Miami	619.1	729.4	3.5
Baltimore	558.5	717.7	3.5

★ 462 ★

Automotive Trimmings (SIC 2396)

Interior Trim Suppliers - North America

The leading firms are ranked by trim sales to automakers in North America. Data are in millions of dollars for 1994. Ford Automotive Components Division is ranked second but figures are not available.

Delphi Interior and Lighting Systems . . $ 5,289.0
Textron Automotive Co. 962.0
United Technologies Automotive 675.0
Prince Corp. 481.0
Becker Group Inc. 420.0
Automotive Industries 380.0
Manchester Plastics 169.0
Cambridge Industries 120.0

Source: *Automotive News*, November 7, 1995, p. 35.

★ 463 ★

Automotive Restraints (SIC 2399)

Airbags and Seatbelt Makers

| Delphi Interior and Lighting Systems |
| Takata Inc. |
| AlliedSignal Automotive |
| Breed Technologies Inc. |
| Autoliv North America Inc. |

Airbag and seatbelt systems suppliers to the North American automotive industry are ranked by sales in millions of dollars. Morton Automotive Safety Products and TRW Vehicle Safety Systems Inc. were ranked first and second with sales of $1.226 billion and $2.5 billion worldwide, but their 1994 data for North America are not available.

Delphi Interior and Lighting Systems . .	$ 750.0
Takata Inc.	701.0
AlliedSignal Automotive	560.0
Breed Technologies Inc.	234.0
Autoliv North America Inc.	99.0

Source: *Automotive News*, December 25, 1995, p. 27.

SIC 24 - Lumber and Wood Products

★ 464 ★

Lumber (SIC 2411)

U.S. Lumber Production

Production is shown by region in billions of board feet.

	1994	1995
Western U.S.	17.473	15.671
Southern U.S.	15.010	14.800
Canadian imports	16.062	16.900
Other	1.624	1.520

Source: *Home Improvement Market*, April 1996, p. 22, from Western Wood Products Association.

★ 465 ★

Lumber (SIC 2421)

Softwood Lumber Production - Canada

Production is shown in millions of board feet.

	1994	1995
British Columbia	14,269	13,819
Eastern Canada	8,952	9,038
Prairies	2,356	2,291

Source: *Wood Technology*, May 1996, p. 25, from Statistics Canada.

★ 466 ★

Hardwood (SIC 2426)

Hardwood Flooring Providers

Triangle Pacific	29.0%
Robbins	8.0
Tibbals	8.0
Masco	6.0
Memphis	6.0
28 others	43.0

Source: *Investext,* Thomson Financial Services, December 19, 1994, p. 2, from *Floor Covering Weekly*, Floor Focus, National Oak Flooring Manufacturers Association, and company reports.

★ 467 ★

Hardwood (SIC 2426)

Hardwood Use by Species

The table shows the most popular species of wood used by hardwood dimension manufacturers. Figures are based on a survey.

Red oak	39.0%
Poplar	16.4
White oak	15.0
Maple	10.5
Cherry	5.6

Source: *Forest Products Society*, Vol. 46, no. 5, p. 39.

★ 468 ★
Millwork (SIC 2431)

Engineered Wood Demand

Data are in millions of board feet. LVL stands for laminated veneer lumber.

	1995	2000	Share
Wood I-Jist	430	840	64.5%
Glulam	280	418	32.1
LVL	26	45	3.5

Source: *Building Supply Business*, January 1996, p. 43, from Engineered Lumber Association.

★ 469 ★
Millwork (SIC 2431)

U.S. Wood Panel Production

Panel production is shown by type in thousands of square feet for 1993 and 1994. MDF stands for medium-density fiberboard.

	1993	1994	Share
Structural panels . . .	26,317,000	27,124,000	71.0%
Hardboard . . .	5,248,074	5,300,000	13.9
Particleboard . .	4,241,146	4,542,073	11.9
MDF	1,161,040	1,250,539	3.3

Source: *Wood Technology*, September 1995, p. 35, from National Particleboard Association, American Hardboard Association, and American Particleboard Association.

★ 470 ★
Millwork (SIC 2431)

Wood Panel Production - Canada

Panel production is shown by type in thousands of square feet for 1993 and 1994. OSB stands for oriented-strand board.

	1993	1994	Share
Waferboard/OSB .	2,751,389	3,016,257	45.1%
Const. plywood .	1,824,004	1,833,915	27.5
Particleboard . .	1,421,972	1,477,461	22.1
Fiberboard . . .	320,027	353,057	5.3

Source: *Wood Technology*, September 1995, p. 35, from Statistics Canada.

★ 471 ★
Millwork (SIC 2431)

Wood Patio Door Market

The market for residential patio doors is shown by application. Data are in thousands of units.

	(000)	Share
Remodel/replacement	680	52.1%
New construction	625	47.9

Source: *Building Supply Business*, March 1996, p. 32, from Wood Window & Door Marketplace and National Window and Door Association.

★ 472 ★
Cabinets (SIC 2434)

Top Cabinet Makers

Companies are ranked by 1995 sales in millions of dollars.

Masco Corp. Cabinet Group	$ 675.0
Aristokraft Inc.	230.0
Schrock Cabinet Co.	200.0
American Woodmark	195.0
Triangle Pacific Corp.	183.2
Omega Cabinets	130.0
Wood-Mode Inc.	105.0
Canac Kitchens	100.0
Texwood Industries	96.5
Elkay Mfg. Co. Cabinet Group	93.0
Kitchen Kompact Inc.	75.0
Norcraft Cos. Inc.	73.5
General Marble	66.0
Cardell Kitchen & Bath Cabinetry	65.0
HomeCrest Corp.	65.0

Source: *Wood & Wood Products*, May 1996, p. 52.

★ 473 ★
Manufactured Homes (SIC 2452)

Modular Home Producers

Firms are ranked by sales volume in millions of dollars. Shares are shown based on the top 30 firms in North America reporting sales of $458.7 million.

	($ mil.)	Share
All American Homes Inc.	$ 83.2	18.1%
Nanticoke Homes Inc.	42.0	9.2
Nationwide Homes	36.8	8.0
DeLuxe Homes of PA Inc. . . .	34.1	7.4
Ritz Craft Corp.	33.0	7.2

Continued on next page.

★ 473 ★ *Continued*
Manufactured Homes (SIC 2452)

Modular Home Producers

Firms are ranked by sales volume in millions of dollars. Shares are shown based on the top 30 firms in North America reporting sales of $458.7 million.

	($ mil.)	Share
Excel Homes	$ 29.0	6.3%
Wisconsin Homes Inc.	26.6	5.8
Kan Build Inc.	23.0	5.0
Avis America	19.0	4.1
Stratford Homes	16.2	3.5
Other	115.8	25.2

Source: *Automated Builder*, May 1996, p. 36.

★ 474 ★
Manufactured Homes (SIC 2452)

Top Panelized/Pre-Cut Home Makers

Firms are ranked by sales volume in millions of dollars. Shares are shown based on top 53 firms in North America generating total gross sales of $568.8 million.

	($ mil.)	Share
Wausau Homes Inc.	$ 150.7	26.5%
Davidson Industries	55.0	9.7
Lindal Cedar Homes	42.3	7.4
Eagle Building Products	29.0	5.1
Barden & Robeson Corp.	27.0	4.7
Bartow Homes Inc.	26.5	4.7
Linwood Homes	21.7	3.8
Deck House Inc.	15.0	2.6
AmerLink Ltd.	14.0	2.5
Town & Country Cedar Homes .	12.0	2.1
Other	175.7	30.9

Source: *Automated Builder*, June 1996, p. 36.

★ 475 ★
Preserved Wood (SIC 2491)

Laminated Log Industry

A total of 622,000 lineal feet of laminated logs was sold in 1994. The sales were primarily domestic, with 81.7% of sales staying within the United States, 11.9% going to the Pacific Rim, and 6.4% going to Europe. The distribution shown is based on the 508,174 lineal feet that were sold domestically.

Rocky Mts.	35.4%
West Coast	25.0
Midwest	24.0
East Coast	15.7

Source: *Forest Products Journal*, March 1996, p. 81.

★ 476 ★
Photo Frames (SIC 2499)

Photo Frame Producers

Newell's share of the photo frame market in mass merchants and drug stores is shown in percent. Newell Co. recently made a deal to acquire Holson Burnes Group Inc., the second largest frame maker, to give it a 40% share of the entire photo frame market.

Newell Co.	60.0%
Other	40.0

Source: *HFN*, December 18, 1995, p. 1.

SIC 25 - Furniture and Fixtures

★ 477 ★
Furniture (SIC 2500)

Contract Furniture Makers

Firms are ranked by 1995 sales in millions of dollars. Shares of the group are shown in percent.

	($ mil.)	% of Group
Steelcase Inc.	$ 2,500.0	29.8%
Haworth Inc.	1,150.0	13.7
Herman Miller	1,080.0	12.9
HON Industries	845.0	10.1
Kimball Intl.	650.8	7.7
Knoll Group	567.0	6.7
KI (Krueger Intl.)	363.0	4.3
Virco Mfg. Corp.	215.0	2.6
Allsteel	180.0	2.1
Shelby Williams	168.0	2.0
American Seating	110.0	1.3
GF Office Furniture	100.0	1.2
Falcon Products	90.0	1.1
American of Martin.	65.0	0.8
Trendway Corp.	64.1	0.8
Hunt Mfg. Co.	60.0	0.7
Thomasville Furniture	57.0	0.7
La-Z-Boy Chair	55.0	0.7
Styline Industries	42.0	0.5
WinsLoew Furniture	40.0	0.5

Source: *Wood & Wood Products*, February 1996, p. 59.

★ 478 ★
Furniture (SIC 2500)

Furniture Demand by City - Canada

Montreal	13.0%
Toronto	13.0
Vancouver	6.0
Other	71.0

Source: *National Trade Data Bank*, March 2, 1996, p. 111091772, from Statistics Canada.

★ 479 ★
Furniture (SIC 2500)

Furniture Market - Canada

The market is shown by segment. "Other" includes hotel, restaurant, and institutional.

Household	43.0%
Office	24.0
Other	33.0

Source: *National Trade Data Bank*, March 2, 1996, p. 111091772, from Statistics Canada.

★ 480 ★
Furniture (SIC 2500)

Furniture Sales by Segment

Distribution is shown based on $4.7 billion in sales at discount stores.

Living room	38.0%
Juvenile	25.4
Office	15.8
Decorative	12.6
Bedroom	2.6
Other	5.8

Source: *Discount Store News*, August 5, 1996, p. 82.

★ 481 ★

Furniture (SIC 2500)

RTA Furniture Makers

The leading manufacturers of RTA (ready-to-assemble) furniture are ranked by 1995 sales in millions of dollars. Shares of the group are shown in percent.

	Sales ($ mil.)	% of Group
Sauder	$ 465.0	43.9%
O'Sullivan	274.2	25.9
Bush	220.0	20.8
Ameriwood	100.8	9.5

Source: *Furniture Today*, May 13, 1996, p. 30, from company reports.

★ 482 ★

Furniture (SIC 2500)

RTA Furniture Sales by Region

RTA stands for ready-to-assemble.

South Atlantic	18.8%
Pacific	17.4
Great Lakes	17.3
Middle Atlantic	12.3
Other	45.8

Source: *HFN*, March 18, 1996, p. 10, from Tactical Retail Solutions Inc.

★ 483 ★

Furniture (SIC 2500)

Top Furniture Makers - Canada

Dorel Inds.
Palliser Furniture
Shermag Inc.
Sealy Canada
La-Z-Boy Canada
El Ran Furniture
Canadel Furniture
Dutalier
Dynasty Wood Products
Sklar-Peppler

The top manufacturers of furniture and bedding are ranked by 1995 sales in millions of Canadian dollars. The top 10 firms had 31.5% share of the market.

Dorel Inds.	387.8
Palliser Furniture	253.0
Shermag Inc.	61.7
Sealy Canada	56.0
La-Z-Boy Canada	54.0
El Ran Furniture	50.0
Canadel Furniture	48.0
Dutalier	47.8
Dynasty Wood Products	42.4
Sklar-Peppler	37.8

Source: *Furniture Today*, June 10, 1996, p. 9.

★ 484 ★

Furniture (SIC 2500)

Top Residential Furniture Makers

Firms are ranked by 1995 sales in millions of dollars.

Furnishings International Inc.	$ 2,000.0
Furniture Brands International	1,600.0
La-Z-Boy	900.0
Ethan Allen	737.6
Klaussner Furniture Industries	715.0
LADD Furniture Inc.	614.5
Bassett Furniture Industries	500.0
Sauder Woodworking	430.0
Ashley Furniture Industries	370.0
Dorel Industries Inc.	298.0
O'Sullivan Industries	280.0

Continued on next page.

★ 484 ★ *Continued*
Furniture (SIC 2500)

Top Residential Furniture Makers

Firms are ranked by 1995 sales in millions of dollars.

Bush Industries Inc.	$ 220.0
Flexsteel Industries Inc.	208.0
Stanley Furniture	190.0
Palliser Furniture Ltd.	185.0

Source: *Wood & Wood Products*, June 1996, p. 50.

★ 485 ★
Furniture (SIC 2500)

Top U.S. Furniture Producers

The top manufacturers are ranked by estimated 1995 revenues in millions of dollars. Shares of the group are shown in percent.

	Rev. ($ mil.)	% of Group
Masco Home Furnishings	$ 2,014.0	21.2%
Furniture Brands International	1,073.9	11.3
La-Z-Boy	914.9	9.6
Klaussner	655.0	6.9
Ladd	614.5	6.5
Thomasville	550.2	5.8
Bassett	490.8	5.2
Ethan Allen	482.4	5.1
Sauder Woodworking	465.0	4.9
Ashley	370.0	3.9
O'Sullivan	274.2	2.9
Bush	220.0	2.3
Natuzzi	203.0	2.1
Flexsteel	202.7	2.1
Consolidated Furniture	176.8	1.9
Stanley	174.2	1.8
Pulaski	173.5	1.8
Chromcraft Revington	152.6	1.6
The Jackson Companies	152.0	1.6
WinsLoew	147.2	1.5

Source: *Furniture Today*, May 13, 1996, p. 24.

★ 486 ★
Furniture (SIC 2511)

Wood Furniture Market - Mexico

Data show the types of wood furniture makers in Mexico.

Home furniture	75.0%
Office furniture	10.0
Hotel, school, hospital	8.0
Kitchen furniture	7.0

Source: *National Trade Data Bank*, March 2, 1996, p. 111091758.

★ 487 ★
Furniture (SIC 2511)

Wood Furniture Producers

The leading wood furniture manufacturers are ranked by sales in millions of dollars. The top 28 companies shipped $9.9 billion worth of residential furniture or 47% of the $21 billion market.

Masco Corp.	$ 1,900.0
Interco Inc.	1,100.0
La-Z-Boy	850.0
Ethan Allen	710.0
Klaussner Furniture Ind.	615.0
LADD Furniture Inc.	591.6
Thomasville Furniture Ind. Inc.	526.6
Bassett Furniture Ind.	503.0
Sauder Woodworking	415.0
Ashley Furniture Ind.	307.0

Source: *Wood & Wood Products*, August 1995, p. 52, from American Furniture Manufacturers Association.

★ 488 ★
Furniture (SIC 2520)

Largest Office Furniture Firms - Columbus

Firms are ranked by number of full-time employees in Greater Columbus.

Continental Office Furniture	200
Thomas W. Ruff & Co.	129
Boise Cascade	82
Howard's Office Supplies Inc.	68
Wasserstrom Co.	55
Staples Inc.	45
Corporate Environments of Ohio Inc.	43

Continued on next page.

★ 488 ★ *Continued*
Furniture (SIC 2520)

Largest Office Furniture Firms - Columbus

Firms are ranked by number of full-time employees in Greater Columbus.

Corporate Express	40
Globe Furniture Rentals	26
Cort Furniture Rental	26

Source: *Business First - Columbus*, February 26, 1996, p. A10, from company reports.

★ 489 ★
Furniture (SIC 2520)

Office Furniture Dealers - Portland

Dealers are ranked by office furniture sales in millions of dollars. Office Depot revenues are between $8 and $10 million.

Smith Brothers Office Environments Inc.	$ 24.5
Commercial Furnishings Inc.	15.1
Environetics Inc.	8.5
Office Depot	8.0
City Liquidators	7.4
Pacific Office Furnishings	5.1
B&I Furnishings	5.0
Peter's Office Supply Co.	4.8
Corporate Environments of Oregon Inc.	4.0
Total Office Products & Printers Inc.	3.7

Source: *Business Journal*, May 5, 1995, p. 14, from representative of each company.

★ 490 ★
Furniture (SIC 2521)

Wood Office Furniture

Furniture shipments by category are shown for 1994. The industry showed a 7.4% increase in 1995 reaching a total market of $9.4 billion.

Systems	34.4%
Seating	24.8
Files	15.7
Desks	9.5
Tables	6.7
Storage	5.3
Other	3.6

Source: *Wood & Wood Products*, February 1996, p. 58, from Business & Institutional Furniture Manufacturing Assn.

★ 491 ★
Store Fixtures (SIC 2541)

Wooden Store Fixture Producers

Firms are ranked by sales in millions of dollars for 1995. Shares of the group are shown in percent.

	Sales ($ mil.)	% of Group
Ontario Store Fixtures	$ 150.0	24.7%
Hamilton Fixture	76.0	12.5
Oklahoma Fixture Co.	68.0	11.2
Store Kraft Mfg. Co.	40.0	6.6
Monarch Ind.	32.6	5.4
Russell William Ltd.	30.0	4.9
Barnett Millworks	28.0	4.6
Imperial Wdwking (1994 fig.)	27.0	4.5
Tarrant Interiors	26.0	4.3
Wigand Corp.	25.0	4.1
Columbia Showcase	24.0	4.0
Dayton Showcase	23.0	3.8
Valley City Mfg. Co.	19.4	3.2
Famous Fixtures	19.1	3.2
Midhattan Woodworking	18.0	3.0

Source: *Wood & Wood Products*, March 1996, p. 75.

SIC 26 - Paper and Allied Products

★ 492 ★
Pulp & Paper (SIC 2600)

Business Paper Market

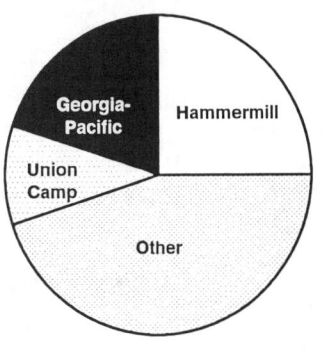

The retail business paper market is estimated in percent by company.

Hammermill	25.0%
Georgia-Pacific	20.0
Union Camp	10.0
Other	45.0

Source: *PIMA Magazine*, November 1995, p. 8, from industry reports.

★ 493 ★
Pulp & Paper (SIC 2600)

Paper Companies - Canada

The leading pulp and paper companies shown are ranked by 1995 net sales in millions of dollars.

Avenor Inc.	$ 2,824.0
Abitibi-Price Inc.	2,782,0
Stone Consolidated	2,539.0
Cascades	2,271.0
Domtar Inc.	2,206.0
Recap Enterprises Inc.	2,077.0
MacMillan Bloedel Ltd.	1,953.0
Fletcher Challenge Canada	1,590.0

Noranda Forets Inc.	$ 1,544.0
Cantor Corp.	767.0

Source: *PIMA Magazine*, June 1996, p. 35.

★ 494 ★
Pulp & Paper (SIC 2600)

Paper Companies - U.S.

The leading pulp and paper companies shown are ranked by 1995 net sales in millions of dollars.

International Paper Co.	$ 14,397.0
Kimberly-Clark Corp.	13,789.0
Procter & Gamble Corp.	9,291.0
Stone Container Corp.	7,351.0
Alco Standard Corp.	6,987.0
Georgia-Pacific Corp.	6,943.0
James River Corp.	6,163.0
Champion International Corp.	6,007.0
Weyerhaeseur Co.	5,682.0
Mead Corp.	5,179.0

Source: *PIMA Magazine*, June 1996, p. 35.

★ 495 ★
Pulp & Paper (SIC 2600)

Paper/Paperboard Market - Mexico

Shares of the market are shown in percent.

	1993	1994
Packaging	51.0%	49.1%
Writing/printing	20.0	21.0
Sanitary tissue	13.5	12.8
Newsprint	11.7	11.9
Special	3.8	5.2

Source: *National Trade Data Bank*, March 2, 1996, p. IS9506.360, from Cellulose and Paper Industries National Chamber.

★ 496 ★

Pulp & Paper (SIC 2600)

Paper/Paperboard Production

Annual paper and paperboard production reached 86.61 million short tons for the year ended January 1996.

	(000)	Share
Unbleached kraft paperboard	. . 22,052	25.5%
Recycled paperboard	13,720	15.8
Uncoated freesheet	12,128	14.0
Coated paper	7,527	8.7
Newsprint	7,150	8.3
Tissue paper	6,380	7.4
Semichemical medium	5,035	5.8
Bleached paperboard	5,030	5.8
Uncoated groundwood	1,925	2.2
Packaging and other paper	4,129	4.8
Other printing/writing	1,533	1.8

Source: *Pulp & Paper*, May 1996, p. 11, from American Forest & Paper Association.

★ 497 ★

Pulp & Paper (SIC 2600)

Pulp & Paper Production - Canada

Production is shown by region in millions of tons. Total annual production in Canada was 14.83 billion tons in paper, 3.48 billion tons in paperboard, and 9.61 billion tons in market pulp.

Quebec	8.8
British Columbia	7.5
Ontario	5.5
Atlantic	3.2
Prairie	2.9

Source: *National Trade Data Bank*, May 27, 1996, p. IMI960403.

★ 498 ★

Paper (SIC 2621)

Coated Groundwood Producers

Market shares of North American companies are shown in percent. Total capacity was 5.319 million tons, with the United States comprising 4.524 million tons and Canada 795,000 tons.

Consolidated Papers	17.0%
Champion International	14.2
International Paper	12.0

Repap	11.2%
Bowater	9.2
Fletcher Challenge Canada	8.6
Mead	6.3
Boise Cascade	5.8
Crown Vantage	5.0
Weyerhaeuser	4.0
Kruger	3.0
Noranda Forest	2.4
Other	6.7

Source: *Pulp & Paper*, May 1996, p. 13.

★ 499 ★

Paper (SIC 2621)

Corrugated Medium Makers

Shares are shown based on a total capacity of 9.037 million short tons.

Stone Container	10.9%
Weyerhaeuser	9.7
Packaging Corp.	9.2
Georgia-Pacific	8.1
Temple-Inland	7.3
Jefferson Smurfit	5.9
Mead	4.6
Grief/Virginia Fibre	4.3
International Paper	4.1
Willamette Industries	4.0
Other	31.8

Source: *Pulp & Paper*, October 1995, p. 13.

★ 500 ★
Paper (SIC 2621)

Major Newsprint Makers - 1995

Shares are shown based on total capacity of 16.304 million tons in North America.

Abitibi-Price	9.6%
Stone Consolidated	8.8
Avenor	7.5
Bowater	6.5
Quno	5.3
Champion International	5.2
Kruger	5.2
Fletcher Challenge Canada	4.3
Weyerhaeuser	3.7
Jefferson Smurfit	3.2
Other	40.9

Source: *Investext,* Thomson Financial Services, October 5, 1995, p. 5.

★ 501 ★
Paper (SIC 2621)

Paper Consumption in Mexico

Consumption is shown in thousands of tons.

	1995	1996	1997
Packaging	1,453	1,500	1,556
Writing/printing	738	723	727
Sanitary tissue	483	502	527
Newspaper/textbook	390	382	384
Cardboard	312	312	320
Special	190	186	187

Source: *National Trade Data Bank*, March 2, 1996, p. IS9506.360, from Cellulose and Paper Industries National Chamber.

★ 502 ★
Paper (SIC 2621)

Paper Producers - Mexico

Data are for 1993.

Kimberly-Clark de Mexico	58.8%
Smurfit Cartan Papel de Mexico	12.6
Grupo Industrial de Atenquique	6.1
Empaques Ponderosa	5.1
Compaeia Papelera Maldonado	4.8
Envases Especializados de la Laguna	3.7
Papelera de Chihuahua	3.6
Celulosa y Papel Ponderosa	2.6

Aluprint	2.1%
Forma Todo	0.6

Source: *National Trade Data Bank*, March 2, 1996, p. IS9506.360, from Cellulose and Paper Industries National Chamber.

★ 503 ★
Paper (SIC 2621)

Top Kraft Paper Makers

Shares are shown based on total capacity of 2.45 million short tons.

Stone Container	22.5%
Longview Fibre	17.6
Georgia-Pacific	12.0
Gaylord Container	11.0
International Paper	10.6
Union Camp	8.2
Port Townsend Paper	5.1
Chesapeake	4.1
Ivex Packaging	4.1
Champion International	4.0
Other	0.9

Source: *Pulp & Paper*, November 1995, p. 3.

★ 504 ★
Paper (SIC 2621)

U.S. Tissue Paper Makers

Shares are shown based on a total capacity of 6.62 million tons in 1994.

Scott	17.2%
James River	16.6
Fort Howard	15.8

Continued on next page.

★ 504 ★ *Continued*

Paper (SIC 2621)

U.S. Tissue Paper Makers

Shares are shown based on a total capacity of 6.62 million tons in 1994.

Procter & Gamble	13.0%
Georgia-Pacific	8.6
Kimberly-Clark	7.3
Chesapeake Corp.	3.3
Potlatch	2.1
Pope & Talbot	1.7
Mosinee	1.4
Other	13.0

Source: *Investext,* Thomson Financial Services, May 1, 1995, p. 4.

★ 505 ★

Paper (SIC 2621)

Uncoated Free-Sheet Market

The market is shown by end use based on estimated shipments of 13.3 million short tons in 1994, 13.0 million short tons in 1995, and 13.43 million short tons in 1996.

	1994	1995	1996
Reprographic	29.3%	30.9%	31.5%
Offset papers	25.7	25.8	25.8
Forms bond	15.4	14.8	14.0
Envelopes	10.3	10.0	9.9
Carbonless	6.7	6.2	6.3
Cover & text	3.9	4.0	3.9
Tablets	3.4	3.1	3.1
Other	5.4	5.3	5.4

Source: *High Volume Printing,* February 1996, p. 23, from American Forest & Paper Association and United Bank of Switzerland.

★ 506 ★

Paper (SIC 2621)

Uncoated Free-Sheet Paper Producers

Uncoated free-sheet paper is used for office and computer printing, stationery and envelopes, and business forms. The top North American producers are shown ranked by 1995 production capacity in thousands of metric tons.

	Cap. (000)	Share
International Paper Co.	2,520.0	15.9%
Georgia-Pacific Corp.	2,124.0	13.4
Champion International . . .	1,491.0	9.4
Boise Cascade Corp.	1,340.0	8.5
Union Camp Corp.	1,155.0	7.3
Willamette Industries	980.0	6.2
Weyerhaeuser Co.	830.0	5.3
Domtar Inc.	826.0	5.2
James River Corp.	710.0	4.5
Appleton Papers Inc.	575.0	3.6
Other	3,277.0	20.0

Source: *Pulp & Paper,* April 1996, p. 13, from American Forest & Paper Association.

★ 507 ★

Paper (SIC 2621)

Uncoated Groundwood Paper Producers

Leading North American uncoated groundwood paper producers are ranked by annual capacity in thousands of tons.

	Tons (000)	Share
Abitibi-Price	563.0	11.5%
Stone-Consolidated	500.0	10.2
MacMillan Bloedel	500.0	10.2
Bowater	345.0	7.1
Rainy River	333.0	6.8
Champion International	320.0	6.5
Fletcher Challenge	254.0	5.2
Lake Superior Paper	240.0	4.9
Madison Paper	225.0	4.6
Daishowa	200.0	4.1
Other	1,400.0	28.9

Source: *Pulp & Paper,* September 1995, p. 13, from company data, industry analysts and *Pulp & Paper Company Profiles.*

★ 508 ★
Paperboard (SIC 2631)
Mottled White Paperboard Makers

Jefferson Smurfit

Chesapeake Corp.

International Paper

Green Bay Packaging

St. Joe Paper

Stone Container

Temple-Inland

Simpson

Champion International

Market shares are shown based on an estimated capacity of 1.77 million tons in 1995.

Jefferson Smurfit	17.8%
Chesapeake Corp.	17.5
International Paper	12.9
Green Bay Packaging	12.7
St. Joe Paper	11.0
Stone Container	10.1
Temple-Inland	9.8
Simpson	4.5
Champion International	3.7

Source: *Investext,* Thomson Financial Services, October 17, 1995, p. 6.

★ 509 ★
Paperboard (SIC 2631)
Top Linerboard Producers

Shares of the market are shown based on a total capacity of 24.56 million short tons.

Stone Container	14.0%
International Paper	9.3
Georgia-Pacific	9.0
Temple-Inland	8.1
Union Camp	7.4
Weyerhaeuser	7.2
Jefferson Smurfit	7.1
Packaging Corp. of America	5.3
Gaylord Container	4.8
Willamette Industries	4.8
Other	22.9

Source: *Pulp & Paper,* January 1996, p. 13.

★ 510 ★
Paperboard (SIC 2631)
U.S. Containerboard Makers

Market shares are shown based on an estimated capacity of 32.99 million tons in 1995.

Stone Container	13.1%
Georgia-Pacific	9.4
Temple-Inland	7.8
Weyerhaeuser	7.2
International Paper	7.0
Packaging Corporation of America	6.2
Jefferson Smurfit	5.9
Union Camp	5.6
Willamette Industries	4.7
Gaylord Container	3.6
Other	29.6

Source: *Investext,* Thomson Financial Services, October 17, 1995, p. 6.

★ 511 ★
Packaging (SIC 2650)
Rigid Bulk Packaging

Shipments are estimated to grow from $3.38 billion in 1994 to $4.69 billion in 2000.

	1994	2000
Drums	39.2%	34.1%
Rigid intemediate bulk containers	13.8	22.4
Pails	17.5	16.0
Bulk boxes	17.8	15.8
Materials handling containers	11.7	11.6

Source: *Purchasing,* October 19, 1995, p. 45, from Freedonia Group.

★ 512 ★
Paper Tubing (SIC 2655)
Paper Tube and Core Market

Data are for the first six months of each year.

	1994	1995
Paper mill cores	23.8%	25.4%
Film cores	16.5	17.6
Yarn carriers	14.3	15.0
Cloth/floor covering cores	13.5	13.4
Tape/label cores	6.4	6.0
Metal foil & strapping cores	4.0	4.4
Convertor cores	3.7	3.6
Mailing & packaging tubes	3.4	3.4

Continued on next page.

★ 512 ★ *Continued*
Paper Tubing (SIC 2655)

Paper Tube and Core Market

Data are for the first six months of each year.

	1994	1995
Construction tubes & concrete molds	2.2%	2.0%
Household cores	2.4	1.9
Spools/reels	0.9	1.0
Roofing cores	0.9	0.9
Other uses	7.9	5.4

Source: *Paperboard Packaging*, October 1995, p. 24, from Composite Can and Tube Institute.

★ 513 ★

Paper Plates (SIC 2656)

Top Disposable Dishes Brands

The top brands are ranked by volume of sales in thousands of dollars for the 52 weeks ended September 9, 1995. Shares of the group are shown in percent.

	($000)	% of Group
Private label	$ 229,288	46.4%
Hefty (Mobil Chemical)	88,182	17.8
Dixie Livingware (James River)	87,236	17.6
Chinet (Keyes Fibre)	48,238	9.8
Solo (NSB)	41,585	8.4

Source: *Nonfoods Merchandising*, April 1996, p. 12, from A.C. Nielsen.

★ 514 ★

Folding Boxes (SIC 2657)

Folding Carton Market

Shares of the $8.0 billion market are shown in percent.

Dry food	14.0%
Wet food	12.0
Beverages/carriers	11.0
Medicinal/cosmetics	9.0
Paper goods	7.0
Hardware	6.0
Tobacco	6.0
Soaps	5.0
Carryout retail food	5.0
Bakery	4.0
Biscuits & crackers	3.0%
Candy	3.0
Toys & sporting goods	3.0
Other	12.0

Source: *Paperboard Packaging*, August 1995, p. 24.

★ 515 ★

Paper Products (SIC 2670)

Converted Product Producers

	Tons (000)	Share
Procter & Gamble	780	23.0%
Scott	680	20.0
James River	610	18.0
Kimberly-Clark	373	11.0
Georgia-Pacific	340	10.0
Fort Howard	306	9.0
Other	306	9.0

Source: *Investext,* Thomson Financial Services, May 1, 1995, p. 4.

★ 516 ★

Paper Products (SIC 2670)

Leading Paper Product Makers

The leading manufacturers are ranked by 1995 revenues in millions of dollars. Shares of the group are shown in percent.

	Rev. ($ mil.)	% of Group
International Paper	$ 19,797	15.8%
Georgia-Pacific	14,292	11.4
Kimberly-Clark	13,789	11.0
Weyerhaeuser	11,788	9.4
Stone Container	7,351	5.9
Champion International	6,972	5.6
James River Corp.	6,800	5.4
Mead	5,179	4.1

Continued on next page.

★ 516 ★ *Continued*
Paper Products (SIC 2670)

Leading Paper Product Makers

The leading manufacturers are ranked by 1995 revenues in millions of dollars. Shares of the group are shown in percent.

	Rev. ($ mil.)	% of Group
Boise Cascade	$ 5,058	4.0%
Union Camp	4,212	3.4
Jefferson Smurfit	4,093	3.3
Willamette Industries	3,874	3.1
Temple-Inland	3,460	2.8
Westvaco	3,303	2.6
Avery Dennison	3,114	2.5
Fleetwood Enterprises . . .	2,856	2.3
Louisiana-Pacific	2,843	2.3
Sonoco Products	2,706	2.2
Bowater	2,001	1.6
Federal Paper Board	1,913	1.5

Source: *Fortune*, April 29, 1996, p. F52.

★ 517 ★
Coated Paper (SIC 2672)

Coated Free-Sheet Paper Makers

Leading North American coated free-sheet paper producers are ranked by annual capacity in thousands of tons. U.S. capacity reached 4,166,000 tons and Canadian capacity reached 340,000 tons in 1995.

	Tons (000)	Share
S.D. Warren	1,045.0	20.8%
Westvaco	680.0	13.6

	Tons (000)	Share
Champion International	574.0	11.4%
Simpson	495.0	9.9
Consolidated Papers	450.0	9.0
Repap	405.0	8.1
Mead	375.0	7.5
Potlatch	333.0	6.6
Boise Cascade	140.0	2.8
Appleton Papers	130.0	2.6
Other	539.0	7.7

Source: *Pulp & Paper*, March 1996, p. 13.

★ 518 ★
Coated Paper (SIC 2672)

Coated Paper Market

Production is shown in thousands of tons for 1995.

Groundwood	4,725
Freesheet	4,185

Source: *Graphic Arts Monthly*, January 1996, p. 46.

★ 519 ★
Tape (SIC 2672)

Noncellophane Tape Market

Manco	48.0%
Other	52.0

Source: *Forbes*, November 6, 1995, p. 78.

★ 520 ★
Trash Bags (SIC 2673)

Trash Bag Brands

Brands are ranked by sales in millions of dollars for the 52 weeks ended September 10, 1995. Data do not include lawn or leaf bags.

	($ mil.)	Share
Private label	$ 198.389	20.5%
Glad	198.244	20.5
Hefty Cinch Sak	78.960	8.2
Hefty	44.390	4.6
Glad Stress Flex	20.460	2.1
Hefty Basics	16.680	1.7
Hefty Handle Sak	13.480	1.4
Good Sense	11.730	1.2
Hefty Steel Sak	9.070	0.9

Continued on next page.

★ 520 ★ *Continued*
Trash Bags (SIC 2673)

Trash Bag Brands

Brands are ranked by sales in millions of dollars for the 52 weeks ended September 10, 1995. Data do not include lawn or leaf bags.

	($ mil.)	Share
Ruffies Color Scents	$ 8.020	0.8%
Other	368.593	38.1

Source: *Nonfoods Merchandising*, January 1996, p. 14, from Information Resources Inc.

★ 521 ★

Trash Bags (SIC 2673)

Trash Bag Market

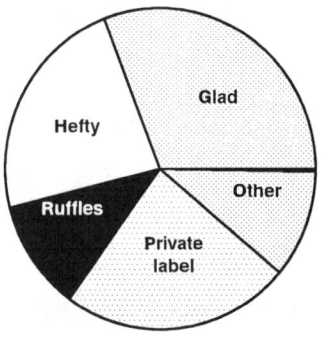

Shares of the $1.0 billion market are shown for the year ended June 16, 1996.

Glad	31.0%
Hefty	23.0
Ruffles	11.0
Private label	24.0
Other	11.0

Source: *Wall Street Journal*, August 12, 1996, p. A3, from Information Resources Inc.

★ 522 ★
Sanitary Paper Products (SIC 2676)

Bathroom Tissue Makers

Shares are shown as of December 1995.

Procter & Gamble	32.0%
James River	14.0
Kimberly-Clark	7.0
Other	47.0

Source: *Investext,* Thomson Financial Services, March 15, 1996, p. 31, from Information Resources Inc.

★ 523 ★
Sanitary Paper Products (SIC 2676)

Bathroom Tissue Makers - Mexico

Kimberly-Clark	50.0%
Crisoba (Scott Paper)	40.0
Lypps	10.0

Source: *Investext,* Thomson Financial Services, March 15, 1996, p. 2, from company reports and CS First Boston.

★ 524 ★
Sanitary Paper Products (SIC 2676)

Diaper Makers

Data are for 1995.

Kimberly-Clark	39.4%
Procter & Gamble	37.2
Other	23.4

Source: *Advertising Age*, April 1, 1996, p. 16, from Dean Witter Reynolds.

★ 525 ★
Sanitary Paper Products (SIC 2676)

Diaper Market Leaders - 1996

Shares are shown for the first five months of 1996.

Kimberly-Clark	38.7%
Procter & Gamble	38.5
Drypers	3.2
Private label	17.3
Other	2.1

Source: *Advertising Age*, July 29, 1996, p. 6, from Dean Witter Reynolds.

★ 526 ★
Sanitary Paper Products (SIC 2676)

Facial Tissue Brands

Data are current as of December 1995.

Kleenex	44.0%
Puffs	28.0
Scotties	7.0
Other	21.0

Source: *Investext,* Thomson Financial Services, March 15, 1996, p. 26, from Information Resources Inc.

★ 527 ★
Sanitary Paper Products (SIC 2676)

Facial Tissue Makers

Kimberly-Clark	46.6%
Procter & Gamble	32.1
Other	2.1

Source: *Dallas Morning News*, July 16, 1995, p. H1, from *Bloomberg Business News* and Dean Witter Reynolds.

★ 528 ★
Sanitary Paper Products (SIC 2676)

Feminine Hygiene Products - Mexico

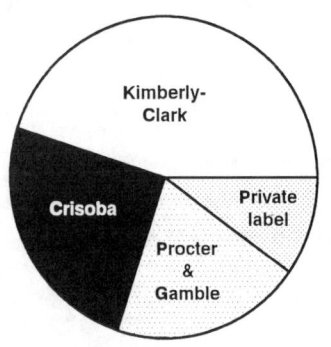

Shares are estimated for 1995.

Kimberly-Clark	45.0%
Crisoba	25.0
Procter & Gamble	20.0
Private label	10.0

Source: *Investext,* Thomson Financial Services, March 15, 1996, p. 2, from company reports and CS First Boston.

★ 529 ★
Sanitary Paper Products (SIC 2676)

Incontinence Product Market

Shares are shown for the third quarter of 1995. Kimberly-Clark makes Depends and Poise; P&G makes Attends; J&J makes Serenity.

Kimberly-Clark	53.1%
J&J	14.3
P&G	8.9
Private label	22.7
Other brands	1.0

Source: *Investext,* Thomson Financial Services, November 30, 1995, p. 10, from Information Resources Inc.

★ 530 ★
Sanitary Paper Products (SIC 2676)

Leading Tampon Brands

Shares are for October - December 1995.

Tampax	54.9%
Playtex	22.7
Kotex	10.7
OB	8.4
Private label	3.2
Other	9.9

Source: *Investext,* Thomson Financial Services, August 8, 1995, p. 10, from Information Resources Inc.

★ 531 ★
Sanitary Paper Products (SIC 2676)

Paper Napkin Brands

Sales are shown by brand for the 52 weeks ended September 9, 1995. Shares of the group are shown in percent.

	($000)	% of Group
Private label	$ 95,747	37.3%
Mardi Gras	48,445	18.9
Northern	38,790	15.1
Scott Family	38,252	14.9
Vanity Fair	35,591	13.9

Source: *Nonfoods Merchandising*, April 1996, p. 12, from A.C. Nielsen.

★ 532 ★

Sanitary Paper Products (SIC 2676)

Paper Towel Makers

Shares of the $2.0 billion market are shown in percent for 1995.

Procter & Gamble 38.4%
Kimberly-Clark 17.7
James River 12.9
Fort Howard 5.4
Private label 13.2
Other 2.0

Source: *Advertising Age*, March 4, 1996, p. 13, from Dean Witter Reynolds.

★ 533 ★

Sanitary Paper Products (SIC 2676)

Paper Towel Makers - Mexico

Shares are estimated for 1995.

Kimberly-Clark 65.0%
Crisoba (Scott Paper) 30.0
Lypps 5.0

Source: *Investext*, Thomson Financial Services, March 15, 1996, p. 2, from company reports and CS First Boston.

★ 534 ★

Sanitary Paper Products (SIC 2676)

Tampon Market - 1996

Shares are shown based on unit sales for the year ended June 30, 1996.

Tambrands 51.5%
Playtex 23.6
Naturals 5.0
Other 19.9

Source: *Wall Street Journal*, August 14, 1996, p. B6, from A.C. Nielsen.

★ 535 ★

Sanitary Paper Products (SIC 2676)

Tampon Market Leaders

Dollar shares are estimated.

	1994	1995
Tambrands	49.9%	44.3%
Playtex	28.7	25.1
Kimberly-Clark	8.2	20.0
Johnson & Johnson	10.7	8.6
Private label	2.5	2.0

Source: *Investext*, Thomson Financial Services, March 13, 1995, p. 3, from Information Resources Inc. InfoScan and Prudential Securities.

★ 536 ★

Sanitary Paper Products (SIC 2676)

Top Diaper Brands

Shares of the market are shown in percent for the 52 weeks ended February 25, 1996.

Huggies 39.6%
Pampers 26.8
Private label 17.8
Luvs 10.5
Drypers 2.3
Others 2.8

Source: *Supermarket Business*, June 1996, p. 81, from Information Resources Inc.

★ 537 ★
Sanitary Paper Products (SIC 2676)

Top Paper Towel Brands

Shares are shown based on total sales of $1.356 billion for the 52 weeks ended September 9, 1995.

Bounty (Procter & Gamble)	31.5%
Brawny (James River)	13.0
Scottowels (Scott)	10.0
Bounty Microwave (Procter & Gamble)	9.7
Sparkle (Georgia-Pacific)	5.8
Viva (Scott)	4.8
Private label	4.7
Hi-Dri (Kimberly Clark)	3.6
Mardi Gras (Fort Howard)	3.5
Coronet Thirsty (Georgia-Pacific)	2.2
Other	11.2

Source: *Nonfoods Merchandising*, April 1996, p. 12, from A.C. Nielsen.

★ 538 ★
Sanitary Paper Products (SIC 2676)

Top Paper Towel Makers

Shares of the $2.0 billion market are shown in percent.

Procter & Gamble	36.7%
Kimberly-Clark	16.5
Other	46.8

Source: *Advertising Age*, June 17, 1996, p. 38, from Dean Witter, Discover & Co.

★ 539 ★
Sanitary Paper Products (SIC 2676)

Top Toilet Tissue Brands

Shares are shown based on sales of $2.183 billion for the 52 weeks ended September 9, 1995.

Charmin (P&G)	24.4%
Scott 1000 (Scott)	16.1
Northern (James River)	13.5
Private label	10.4
Cottonelle (Scott)	6.8
Angel Soft (Georgia-Pacific)	6.7
Kleenex (Kimberly Clark)	6.1

Soft 'N Gentle (Barcolene Penn Champ)	4.2%
M.D. (Georgia-Pacific)	2.3
Charmin Plus (P&G)	1.5
Other	8.0

Source: *Nonfoods Merchandising*, April 1996, p. 12, from A.C. Nielsen.

★ 540 ★
Sanitary Paper Products (SIC 2676)

Training Pants Leaders

Shares are shown for the third quarter of 1995. The retail market is valued at $485 million.

Kilmberly-Clark Pull-Ups	91.2%
P&G Pampers Trainers	8.8

Source: *Investext,* Thomson Financial Services, November 30, 1995, p. 10, from Information Resources Inc.

★ 541 ★
Stationery (SIC 2678)

Stationery Producers - Mexico

Kimberly-Clark	42.0%
Crisoba	25.0
Berol	10.0
Goba	0.8
Acme-Lamusa	0.6
Others	0.9

Source: *National Trade Data Bank*, January 2, 1996, p. IS9509.645, from industry sources.

★ 542 ★
Stationery (SIC 2678)

Stationery Sales by Segment

Distribution is shown based on $5.32 billion in sales at discount stores.

Back-to-school	31.0%
Greeting cards	30.5
Office supplies	19.0
Party goods	6.2
Other	13.3

Source: *Discount Store News*, August 5, 1996, p. 94.

★ 543 ★

Stationery (SIC 2678)

Who Uses Stationery in Mexico

Students 53.0%
Secretaries/office workers 31.0
Professionals 9.0
General public 7.0

Source: *National Trade Data Bank*, January 2, 1996, p. IS9509.645, from industry sources.

SIC 27 - Printing and Publishing

★ 544 ★

Printing (SIC 2700)

Canadian Printing Market

The 1992 printing market is shown by province, ranked by revenues in millions of U.S. dollars.

	($ mil.)	Share
Ontario	$ 1,800.0	59.8%
Quebec	718.6	23.9
British Columbia	215.9	7.2
Alberta	111.3	3.7
Manitoba	107.1	3.6
Nova Scotia	24.5	0.8
Saskatchewan	23.3	0.8
New Brunswick	11.0	0.4

Source: *National Trade Data Bank*, March 2, 1996, p. 111092513.

★ 545 ★

Printing (SIC 2700)

Leading Printing Markets

Categories are ranked by size of printing market in 1996. Figures are shown in billions of dollars. The top 25 industries represent a $8,047 billion market.

Healthcare	$ 1,295.0
Motor vehicles	1,200.0
Commercial banking	725.0
Heavy machinery	550.0
Travel	525.0
Real estate	490.0
Consumer electronics	480.0
Chemicals/petroleum	464.0
Packaged foods	396.0
Telecommunications equipment/services	348.0
Restaurants, clubs	318.0
Discount retailing	246.0
Home improvements	228.0
Fashion	175.0
Beverages	118.0
Leisure activity products	79.0
Medical products/pharmaceuticals	$ 78.0
Computer software	73.0
Tobacco	68.0
Amusements	59.0

Source: *American Printer*, December 1995, p. 38, from American Management Financial Corp.

★ 546 ★

Publishing (SIC 2700)

Leading Publishers

Companies are ranked by revenues in millions of dollars for 1995.

Time Warner Inc.	$ 2,010.5
Hearst Magazines	901.7
Conde Nast	750.0
Hachette Filipacchi	696.8
Meredith Corp.	562.0
Parade Publications	515.6
Ziff-Davis	472.6
Gruner + Jahr	423.7
News America	406.9
Newsweek Inc.	331.9

Source: *Brandweek*, March 4, 1996, p. 27, from Competitive Media Reporting.

★ 547 ★

Publishing (SIC 2700)

Leading Publishers/Printers

Firms are ranked by 1995 revenues in millions of dollars.

R.R. Donnelley & Sons	$ 6,512
Gannett	4,007
Times Mirror	3,491
Reader's Digest Assn.	3,069
McGraw-Hill	2,935
Tribune	2,864
Knight-Ridder	2,752

Continued on next page.

★ 547 ★ *Continued*

Publishing (SIC 2700)

Leading Publishers/Printers

Firms are ranked by 1995 revenues in millions of dollars.

New York Times	$ 2,409
Dow Jones	2,284
American Greetings	1,878
Deluxe	1,858
Washington Post	1,719
E.W. Scripps	1,309
World Color Press	1,296
K-III Communications	1,046

Source: *Fortune*, April 29, 1996, p. F59.

★ 548 ★

Newspapers (SIC 2711)

Canada's Newspaper Companies

Southam

Hollinger

Thomson Corporation

Toronto Sun Publishing

Torstar Corporation

Quebecor

Independents

Power Corporation

Irving

Newfoundland Capital

Shares are shown based on an average daily circulation of 5,286,774.

Southam	27.8%
Hollinger	14.0
Thomson Corporation	12.3
Toronto Sun Publishing	11.1
Torstar Corporation	9.8
Quebecor	8.4
Independents	7.0
Power Corporation	5.9
Irving	2.7
Newfoundland Capital	0.9

Source: *Financial Times*, May 31, 1996, p. 21, from Canadian Daily Newspaper Association.

★ 549 ★

Newspapers (SIC 2711)

Largest Newspapers - Milwaukee

Papers are ranked by total paid circulation.

Milwaukee Journal Sentinel	309,137
Milwaukee Labor Press	68,860
The Journal Times	36,259
Catholic Herald	27,496
The Freeman	23,863
The Business Journal	13,193
Wisconsin Senior Advocate	11,000
West Bend Daily News	10,891
Ozaukee County News Graphic	10,000
North Shore Herald	9,569

Source: *Business Journal*, December 30, 1995, p. 18.

★ 550 ★

Newspapers (SIC 2711)

Largest Newspapers - San Diego

Papers are ranked by average paid circulation.

San Diego Union Tribune	382,804
North County Blade Citizen	52,596
Times-Advocate	40,262
Daily Californian	22,507
San Diego Jewish Times	15,183
San Diego Business Journal	12,812
San Diego Daily Transcript	6,195

Source: *San Diego Business Journal*, August 14, 1995, p. 16.

★ 551 ★

Newspapers (SIC 2711)

Leading New York Dailies

Daily circulation is shown for 1995.

New York Times	1,170,869
Daily News	725,599
Newsday	550,342
Star Ledger	450,316
New York Post	408,204

Source: *Crain's New York Business*, September 25, 1995, p. 26, from Audit Bureau of Circulations.

★ 552 ★
Newspapers (SIC 2711)

Leading Newspapers

Papers are ranked by circulation for the six months ended September 30, 1995. USA TODAY's Friday paper is not included and Houston Chronicle's figure includes the Saturday paper.

Wall Street Journal	1,763,140
USA TODAY	1,523,610
New York Times	1,081,541
Los Angeles Times	1,012,189
Washington Post	793,660
Daily News	738,091
Chicago Tribune	684,366
Newsday	634,627
Houston Chronicle	541,478
Dallas Morning News	524,640
Boston Globe	498,853
San Francisco Chronicle	489,238
Chicago Sun-Times	488,405
Philadelphia Inquirer	469,398
Newark Star-Ledger	436,634

Source: *Advertising Age*, November 6, 1995, p. 34.

★ 553 ★
Newspapers (SIC 2711)

Leading Newspapers - Canada

The top newspapers are ranked by circulation.

Toronto Star	519,070
Globe and Mail	314,972
Le Journal de Montreal	287,986
Toronto Sun	250,695
La Presse	212,527
Vancouver Sun	210,964
Ottawa Citizen	164,120
Gazette (Montreal)	159,108
Province (Vancouver)	156,687
Edmonton Journal	157,873

Source: *Globe and Mail*, September 20, 1995, p. B9, from Canadian Daily Newspaper Association.

★ 554 ★
Newspapers (SIC 2711)

Leading Sunday Newspapers

The top 25 Sunday papers are ranked by circulation for the six months ended March 31, 1996.

New York Times	1,746,707
Los Angeles Times	1,391,076
Washington Post	1,140,564
Chicago Tribune	1,066,393
New York Daily News	1,010,504
Philadelphia Inquirer	901,891
Dallas Morning News	803,610
Boston Globe	777,902
Houston Chronicle	764,443
Atlanta Journal & Constitution	715,397
Minneapolis/St. Paul Star Tribune	682,318
San Francisco Examiner & Chronicle	646,171
Newsday	643,421
Newark Star-Ledger	641,393
Phoenix Arizona Republic	597,255
St. Louis Post-Dispatch	541,991
Cleveland Plain Dealer	528,818
Seattle Times/Post-Intelligencer	506,216
Miami Herald	500,654
Baltimore Sun	488,562
Milwaukee Journal Sentinel	462,168
Chicago Sun-Times	469,161
St. Petersburg Times	462,103
Denver Post	456,057
San Diego Union-Tribune	453,891

Source: *Editor & Publisher*, May 11, 1996, p. 13, from Audit Bureau of Circulations.

★ 555 ★
Newspapers (SIC 2711)

Newspaper Circulation - 1996

Circulation is shown for the six months ended March 31, 1996.

Wall Street Journal	1,841,188
USA Today	1,617,743
New York Times	1,157,656
Los Angeles Times	1,021,121
Washington Post	834,641
Daily News (New York)	758,509
Chicago Tribune	667,908
Newsday	555,203
Houston Chronicle	551,553
Chicago Sun-Times	501,115

Continued on next page.

★ 555 ★ *Continued*
Newspapers (SIC 2711)

Newspaper Circulation - 1996

Circulation is shown for the six months ended March 31, 1996.

Dallas Morning News	494,266
San Francisco Chronicle	439,942
Boston Globe	486,403

Source: *New York Times*, April 30, 1996, p. C5, from Audit Bureau of Circulations.

★ 556 ★
Newspapers (SIC 2711)

Tabloid News Circulation

Circulation is shown in millions. Data for 1995 are for the first six months.

	1994	1995
National Enquirer	3.15	2.70
Star	2.78	2.51
Globe	1.00	0.91

Source: *USA TODAY*, October 4, 1995, p. 5B, from Audit Bureau of Circulations.

★ 557 ★
Newspapers (SIC 2711)

Top Newspaper Companies

Companies are ranked by average daily circulation for the six months ended September 30, 1995.

Gannett Co. Inc.	6,109,223
Knight-Ridder Inc.	3,669,580
Newhouse Newspapers	2,910,012
Times Mirror Co.	2,514,298
Dow Jones & Co. Inc.	2,334,696
New York Times Co.	2,309,594
Thomson Newspapers Inc.	1,707,449
Hearst Newspapers	1,352,594
Cox Enterprises	1,325,352
Tribune Co.	1,297,824
E.W. Scripps Co.	1,260,610
Hollinger International	1,196,180
McClatchy Newspapers	973,279
Freedom Newspapers Inc.	961,436
MediaNews Group	878,678

Source: *Facts About Newspapers*, 1996, p. 22, from Thomas Vander Poel, Lynch, Jones & Ryan and Audit Bureau of Circulations.

★ 558 ★
Magazines (SIC 2721)

Consumer Magazines - Canada

Canadian consumer magazines are ranked by total advertising pages in 1995. Data refer to english-language magazines only.

Women's	6,118
General interest	5,180
Business	3,209
Lifestyle	2,896
City/regional	2,120
Special interest	880
Entertainment	533

Source: *Marketing Magazine*, April 15, 1996, p. 15, from Auditor, Inquiry Management Systems.

★ 559 ★
Magazines (SIC 2721)

Leading Magazines - Ad Revenues

The top 25 magazines are ranked by 1995 advertising revenues in millions of dollars.

Parade	$ 515.6
People Weekly	437.7
Sports Illustrated	435.7
TV Guide	406.9
Time	404.5
Newsweek	331.9
PC Magazine	331.1
Better Homes & Gardens	274.4
Business Week	267.6
Good Housekeeping	238.7
USA Weekend	229.6
U.S. News & World Report	222.4
Forbes	205.7
Woman's Day	197.5
Reader's Digest	186.6
Fortune	179.5
Family Circle	164.0
Cosmopolitan	159.7
Ladies' Home Journal	158.5
New York Times Magazine	119.3
Vogue	116.4
Redbook	112.5
Money	105.3
McCall's	104.1
Glamour	103.7

Source: *Adweek*, March 4, 1996, p. 26, from Competitive Media Reporting.

★ 560 ★

Magazines (SIC 2721)

Magazine Circulation Leaders

The top 25 magazines are ranked by average paid circulation for the six months ended December 31, 1995.

Reader's Digest	15,103,830
TV Guide	13,175,549
National Geographic	8,988,444
Better Homes & Gardens	7,603,207
Good Housekeeping	5,372,786
Ladies' Home Journal	5,045,644
Family Circle	5,007,542
Woman's Day	4,707,330
McCall's	4,520,186
Time	4,083,105
People Weekly	3,321,198
Playboy	3,283,272
Prevention	3,252,115
Redbook	3,173,313
Sports Illustrated	3,157,303
Newsweek	3,155,155
Cosmopolitan	2,569,186
Southern Living	2,471,170
U.S. News & World Report	2,220,327
Seventeen	2,172,923
YM	2,165,079
Smithsonian	2,151,172
Glamour	2,141,752
Field & Stream	2,001,875
Ebony	1,927,675

Source: *Adweek*, March 4, 1996, p. 26, from Audit Bureau of Circulations.

★ 561 ★

Magazines (SIC 2721)

Men's Magazines by Ad Pages

Magazines are ranked by ad pages for the year ended April 1995 and 1996.

	1995	1996
GQ	463.94	468.17
Rolling Stones	508.78	458.56
Out	241.65	301.64
Details	307.66	295.98
Outside	387.99	263.26
Spin	289.43	258.98
Men's Health	173.48	206.36
Men's Journal	229.69	184.21

	1995	1996
Vibe	164.37	181.18
Esquire	235.47	181.05
Playboy	175.50	178.60

Source: *Women's Wear Daily*, March 29, 1996, p. 14, from *Media Industry Newsletter*.

★ 562 ★

Magazines (SIC 2721)

Top Computer Magazines

Average circulation is shown for 1994.

PC Magazine	1,044,227
PC World	929,084
PC Computing	881,917
Macworld	568,142
Computer Shopper	505,461

Source: *Washington Post*, March 29, 1996, p. F2, from Simba Information and *San Jose Mercury News*.

★ 563 ★

Books (SIC 2731)

Book Sales - 1994

The table shows who purchased $17 billion in books from publishers in 1994.

Bookstores	38.0%
Consumers directly	19.0
Colleges/universities	17.0
Schools	15.0
Libraries/institutions	10.0
Other	1.0

Source: *USA TODAY*, April 24, 1996, p. D1, from Book Industry Study Group.

★ 564 ★

Books (SIC 2731)

Book Sales - U.S./Canada

The table compares per capita book sales in the United States and Canada for 1995.

United States . . . . $ 106
Canada 56

Source: *Macleans*, July 8, 1996, p. 30.

★ 565 ★

Books (SIC 2731)

Book Sales by Format - 1996

Data are in millions of units. A total of 2.31 billion units are expected to be published, valued at $20.11 billion.

Trade 869.5
  Adult 492.4
  Juvenile 377.1
Mass market 489.3
Elhi 248.0
Professional 166.8
Religious 157.7
College 151.0
Book clubs 121.4
Mail order 93.9
University press 17.8
Sub. reference 1.2

Source: *Publishers Weekly*, July 8, 1996, p. 12, from Book Industry Study Group.

★ 566 ★

Books (SIC 2731)

Book Sales by Type

By format, mass market lead with a 37% share; hardcover and trade followed with 29% shares each.

Fiction 50.0%
Cooking/crafts 11.0
Nonfiction 10.0
Religion 7.0
Psychology/self-help 6.0
Art 5.0
Technical/scientific/education 5.0
Reference 2.0
Travel 1.0
Other 3.0

Source: *Publishers Weekly*, October 16, 1995, p. 10, from *Consumer Research Study on Book Purchasing, 1994*.

★ 567 ★

Books (SIC 2731)

Children's Book Sales by Category

Paperback sales lead the market with a 63% share in 1994.

Fiction reading books 45.0%
Coloring/activity 32.0
Nonfiction reading books 10.0
Religious 4.0
Educational 4.0
Electronic 2.0
Book/record tape 2.0
Reference 1.0

Source: *Publishers Weekly*, October 30, 1995, p. 31, from *Consumer Research Study on Book Purchasing, 1994*.

★ 568 ★
Books (SIC 2731)

Hardcover Book Publishers

Data are shown based on publisher's share of the 1,530 best-seller positions in 1995. Bantam lead the paperback market with a 20.8% share of the market.

	Books	Share
Random House Inc.	54	29.2%
Bantam Doubleday Dell	28	12.9
Simon & Schuster	32	12.7
Time Warner	11	11.6
HarperCollins	15	10.5
Putnam Berkley	15	4.9
St. Martin's	5	3.1
Running Press	1	2.9
New World	1	2.8
Hyperion	5	2.5
Penguin USA	5	1.9
Hearst	5	1.7
Andrews & McMeel	1	0.2

Source: *Publishers Weekly*, January 1, 1996, p. 50.

★ 569 ★
Books (SIC 2731)

Leading Book Publishers

| Simon & Schuster |
| Reader's Digest |
| McGraw-Hill Ed. |
| HarperCollins |
| Times Mirror |
| Harcourt Brace |

Firms are ranked by revenues in millions of dollars for 1995.

Simon & Schuster	$ 2,171.1
Reader's Digest	2,099.8
McGraw-Hill Ed.	1,235.6
HarperCollins	1,096.0
Times Mirror	1,091.0
Harcourt Brace	1,017.6

Source: *Publishers Weekly*, July 1, 1996, p. 11.

★ 570 ★
Books (SIC 2731)

Popular Children's Books

The all-time best sellers are ranked by hardcover sales.

The Poky Little Puppy	14,000,000
The Tale of Peter Rabbit	9,331,266
Tootle	8,055,500
Saggy Baggy Elephant	7,098,000
Scuffy the Tugboat	7,065,000
Pat the Bunny	6,146,543
Green Eggs and Ham	6,065,197
The Cat in the Hat	5,643,731
The Littlest Angel	5,424,709
One Fish, Two Fish, Red Fish, Blue Fish	4,822,331

Source: *Business and Society Review*, July 1, 1996, p. 74, from *Publisher's Weekly*.

★ 571 ★
Books (SIC 2731)

Top Small Publishers - 1994

Small publishing houses are ranked by sales in millions of dollars for 1994. Companies whose sales figures were confidential include General Pub. Grp., Element Books, Adams Media, Charlesbridge Pub., Avery Pub. Grp., Paul H. Brooks Pub. Co., Mountaineers Books, Nolo Press, Falcon Press, Stackpole Books, and Jist Works.

Educational Develop. Corp.	$ 12.5
Llewellyn	9.2
That Patchwork Place	8.0
New World Library	6.6
Taylor Publishing Co.	5.8
Gibbs Smith, Publisher	3.6
Timber Press	3.4
Chapters Publishers & Booksellers	3.1
Conari Press	3.1
Career Press	2.9
Bear & Co.	2.5
Great Quotations	2.5
Island Press	2.5
Northland Publishing	1.8
Reference Press Inc.	1.6

Source: *Publishers Weekly*, November 20, 1995, p. 45.

★ 572 ★
Commercial Printing (SIC 2750)

Printing Companies - Denver

Firms are ranked by 1994 revenues in millions of dollars.

Intermountain Color Inc.	$ 20.4
A.B. Hirschfeld Press Inc.	20.0
American Web Inc.	19.1
VIP Communications Group	14.1
Johnson Printing	12.6
Klatler Inc.	12.4
Frederic Printing	12.0
Publication Printers Corp.	11.5
Eastwood Printing	9.3
Eagle Direct	8.5

Source: *Denver Business Journal*, August 24, 1995, p. 16A.

★ 573 ★
Commercial Printing (SIC 2750)

Top Printing Companies

Firms are ranked by 1995 sales in millions of dollars.

R.R. Donnelley & Sons	$ 6,500.0
Quebecor Printing Inc.	3,004.0
Moore Corp.	2,600.0
Deluxe Corp.	1,858.0
World Color	1,300.0
Banta Corp.	1,023.0
Quad/Graphics Inc.	1,002.0
Standard Register	903.0
Big Flower Press Holdings Inc.	897.0
Wallace Computer Services Inc.	712.8
UARCO Inc.	675.0
American Business Products	634.0
Valassis Communications Inc.	613.8
Taylor Corp.	600.0
AT&T Systemedia Group	600.0

Source: *American Printer*, July 1996, p. 32.

★ 574 ★
Labels (SIC 2759)

Office Label Market

Shares of the market are shown in percent.

Avery	85.0%
Others	15.0

Source: *Forbes*, September 25, 1995, p. 88.

★ 575 ★
Business Forms (SIC 2761)

U.S. Form Shipments

Shipments are shown in millions of dollars.

	1995	1996	Share
Custom continuous forms	$ 3,153	$ 3,046	38.8%
Unit sets	1,405	1,350	17.2
Cutsheet	1,061	1,119	14.2
Stock continous	1,173	1,106	14.1
Labels, pressure-sensitive	865	939	11.9
Salesbooks/pegbooks	310	300	3.8

Source: *Purchasing*, April 25, 1996, p. S12, from International Business Forms Industries.

★ 576 ★
Greeting Cards (SIC 2771)

Top Card-Giving Occasions

Holidays are ranked by millions of cards.

Christmas	2,650
Valentine's Day	925
Mother's Day	154
Easter	133
Father's Day	99
Graduation	67
Thanksgiving	34

Continued on next page.

Greeting Cards (SIC 2771)

Top Card-Giving Occasions

Holidays are ranked by millions of cards.

Halloween	26
St. Patrick's Day	15
Rosh Hashanah and Yom Kippur	12

Source: *Detroit Free Press*, June 7, 1996, p. A2.

SIC 28 - Chemicals and Allied Products

Chemicals (SIC 2800)

Canadian Chemical Output

Production is shown in thousands of metric tons for 1995.

Ammonia	4,696
Sulfuric acid	4,180
Ethylene	3,422
Urea	3,405
Polyethylene, low-density	1,390
Sodium hydroxide	1,205
Chlorine	1,150
Ammonium nitrate	1,055
Sodium chlorate	1,053
Nitric acid	1,015
Benzene	847
Polyethylene, high-density	798
Propylene	738
Xylenes	465
Toulene	280

Source: *Chemical & Engineering News*, December 11, 1995, p. 58, from Statistics Canada.

★ 578 ★
Chemicals (SIC 2800)

Chemical Process Catalysts

The total market reached 216 million pounds in 1993.

Organic synthesis	44.0%
Polymerization	31.0
Synthetic gas	11.0
Oxidation	7.0
Hydrogenation	5.0
Dehydrogenation	3.0

Source: *Chemical Engineering*, August 1995, p. 59, from Freedonia Group.

★ 579 ★
Chemicals (SIC 2800)

Chemical Production - 1995

Data are in billions of pounds.

Sulfuric acid	95.36
Nitrogen	68.04
Oxygen	53.48
Ethylene	46.97
Lime	41.23
Ammonia	35.60
Phosphoric acid	26.19
Sodium hydroxide	26.19
Propylene	25.69
Chlorine	25.09
Sodium carbonate	22.28
Methyl tert-butyl ether	17.62
Ethylene dichloride	17.26
Nitric acid	17.24
Ammonium nitrate	15.99
Benzene	15.97
Urea	15.99
Vinyl chloride	14.98
Ethylbenzene	13.66
Styrene	11.39
Methanol	11.29
Carbon dioxide	10.89
Xylene	9.37
Formaldehyde	8.11
Terephthalic acid	7.95

Source: *Chemical & Engineering News*, April 8, 1996, p. 17.

★ 580 ★
Chemicals (SIC 2800)

Flame Retardant Market

	1993	1998	Share
Additive flame retardants	810	1,050	43.8%
alumina trihydrate	432	565	23.5
phosphorous compounds	97	127	5.3

Continued on next page.

★ 580 ★ *Continued*
Chemicals (SIC 2800)

Flame Retardant Market

	1993	1998	Share
bromine compounds . . .	88	112	4.7%
antimony oxide	62	78	3.3
chlorinated compounds . .	55	66	2.8
baron compounds	16	20	0.8
other additives	60	82	3.4
Reactive flame retardants . .	120	150	6.3
epoxy intermediates . . .	36	44	1.8
polyester intemediates . .	27	32	1.3
urethane intermediates . .	20	24	1.0
polycarbonate intermediates	16	22	0.9
other intermediates	21	28	1.2

Source: *Chemical Engineering*, September 1995, p. 65, from Freedonia Group.

★ 581 ★
Chemicals (SIC 2800)

Fluorchemical Demand

Demand reached 954 million pounds in 1994.

Fluorocarbons	63.7%
Inorganics	25.5
Fluoropolymers	7.3
Organic chemical specialties	3.5

Source: *InTech*, November 1995, p. 32, from Freedonia Group.

★ 582 ★
Chemicals (SIC 2800)

Leading Chemical Companies

Firms are ranked by 1995 revenues in millions of dollars. Shares of the group are shown in percent.

	($ mil.)	% of Group
E.I. Du Pont De Nempours . . .	$ 37,607	25.8%
Dow Chemical	20,957	14.4
Occidental Petroleum	10,423	7.1
Monsanto	8,962	6.1
PPG Industries	7,058	4.8
Union Carbide	5,888	4.0
W.R. Grace	5,784	4.0
Eastman Chemical	5,040	3.5
Lyondell Petrochemical	4,936	3.4

	($ mil.)	% of Group
FMC	$ 4,567	3.1%
Air Products	3,891	2.7
Rohm & Haas	3,884	2.7
Morton International	3,355	2.3
Sherwin Williams	3,274	2.2
Olin	3,150	2.2
Praxair	3,146	2.2
Engelhard	2,840	1.9
Hercules	2,427	1.7
Witco	2,374	1.6
Great Lakes Chemical	2,361	1.6
Valhi	1,994	1.4
IMC Global	1,924	1.3

Source: *Fortune*, April 29, 1996, p. 45.

★ 583 ★
Chemicals (SIC 2800)

N-Paraffin Makers

Production capacity is shown in millions of pounds. Shares of the group are shown in percent.

	(mil.)	% of Group
Exxon	500	60.2%
Vista	330	39.8

Source: *Chemical Marketing Reporter*, October 16, 1995, p. 45.

★ 584 ★
Chemicals (SIC 2800)

Top Chemical Firms

Firms are ranked by 1995 chemical sales in millions of dollars.

Dow Chemical	$ 19,234.0
DuPont	18,433.0
Exxon	11,737.0
Hoechst Celanese	7,395.0
Monsanto	7,251.0
General Electric	6,628.0
Mobil	6,155.0
Union Carbide	5,888.0
Amoco	5,655.0
Occidental Petroleum	5,410.0
Eastman Chemical	5,040.0
BASF Corp.	4,847.0

Continued on next page.

★ 584 ★ *Continued*
Chemicals (SIC 2800)

Top Chemical Firms

Firms are ranked by 1995 chemical sales in millions of dollars.

Shell Oil	$ 4,841.0
Huntsman Chemical	4,300.0
Arco Chemical	4,282.0

Source: *Chemical & Engineering News*, June 24, 1996, p. 48.

★ 585 ★
Chemicals (SIC 2800)

U.S. Aerosol Production

Personal products

Household products

Automotive/industrial

Paint and finishes

       Food products

       Insect sprays

| Animal products

■ Other

Production is shown in millions of units. Hair sprays lead the personal products category with 297.6 million units; Room sprays lead the household products category with 183.9 million units; Lubricants/silicones lead the automotive/industrial category with 123.0 million units.

	(mil.)	Share
Personal products	1,007.0	33.5%
Household products	725.0	24.1
Automotive/industrial	420.0	14.0
Paint and finishes	374.0	12.5
Food products	252.0	8.4
Insect sprays	184.0	6.1
Animal products	6.5	0.2
Other	34.1	1.1

Source: *Spray Technology & Marketing*, June 1996, p. 22, from CPC International.

★ 586 ★
Chemicals (SIC 2800)

Water Treatment Chemical Makers

Nalco Chemical	22.0%
Betz Laboratories	19.0
Calgon	6.0
Dearborn	5.0
Cytec Industries	4.0
Drew Industrial	4.0
Rhone-Poulenc	4.0
Chemtreat	3.0
Diversey	3.0
Garrett-Callahan	3.0
Western Chemical	3.0
Dow Chemical USA	2.0
Rohm and Hass	2.0
American Norit	1.0
Calgon Carbit	1.0
Elf Atochem North America	1.0
Others	17.0

Source: *Chemicalweek*, May 8, 1996, p. 42, from SRI International.

★ 587 ★
Chemicals (SIC 2800)

Water Treatment Chemicals

The top producers of water treatment chemicals are ranked by sales in millions of dollars for 1994. Calgon is the subsidiary of English China Clays, Drew Industrial is part of Ashland Chemical, and Diversey is a subsidiary of Molson. Shares of the group are shown in percent.

	($ mil.)	% of Group
Nalco	$ 1,346.0	43.9%
Betz	708.0	23.1
Grace Dearborn	363.0	11.8
Calgon	254.0	8.3
Buckman Laboratories	240.0	7.8
Drew Industrial	90.0	2.9
Diversey	67.0	2.2

Source: *Chemicalweek*, October 11, 1995, p. 10, from company reports.

★ 588 ★
Chemicals (SIC 2800)

Water Treatment by Application

Cooling 27.0%
Waste 22.0
Process 20.0
Boiler 19.0
Municipal supply 12.0

Source: *Chemicalweek*, May 8, 1996, p. 45, from Kline & Co.

★ 589 ★
Chemicals (SIC 2800)

Wet Chemical Market Leaders

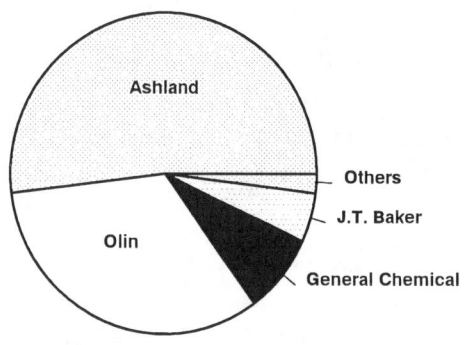

Shares of the $180 million market are shown for 1994.

Ashland 52.0%
Olin 33.0
General Chemical 8.0
J.T. Baker 5.0
Others 2.0

Source: *Chemicalweek*, August 22, 1995, p. 35, from Rose Associates.

★ 590 ★
Alkalies and Chlorine (SIC 2812)

Caustic Potash Makers

Capacity is shown in thousands of short tons per year.

OxyChem 350
Ashta 74
Vulcan 62

Source: *Chemical Marketing Reporter*, January 22, 1996, p. 41.

★ 591 ★
Alkalies and Chlorine (SIC 2812)

Caustic Soda Market

The market is shown by end use for 1994.

Pulp & paper 24.0%
Organic compounds 21.0
Inorganic compounds 13.0
Soaps and detergents 7.0
Water treatment 5.0
Alumina 4.0
Other 26.0

Source: *Chemistry & Industry*, October 16, 1995, p. 832, from Chem Systems.

★ 592 ★
Alkalies and Chlorine (SIC 2812)

Chlorine Production - North America

Companies are ranked by production in thousands of metric tons.

	(000)	Share
Dow Chemical	3,100	24.0%
OxyChem	2,950	22.9
PPG	1,450	11.2
Olin	700	5.4
Formosa	600	4.7
Dow Canada	550	4.3
Vulcan	550	4.3
Mexico(state)	550	4.3
Georgia Gulf	405	3.1
ICI Canada	300	2.3
Pioneer	280	2.2
B.F. Goodrich	200	1.6
Niachlor	200	1.6
LaRoche	180	1.4
Elf Atochem	175	1.4

Continued on next page.

★ 592 ★ *Continued*
Alkalies and Chlorine (SIC 2812)

Chlorine Production - North America

Companies are ranked by production in thousands of metric tons.

	(000)	Share
Holtrachem	160	1.2%
Weyerhauser	135	1.0
Georgia-Pacific	85	0.7
Other U.S.	240	1.9
Other Canada	80	0.6

Source: *Chemicalweek*, March 13, 1996, p. 38, from SRI Consulting.

★ 593 ★
Alkalies and Chlorine (SIC 2812)

Potassium Carbonate Makers

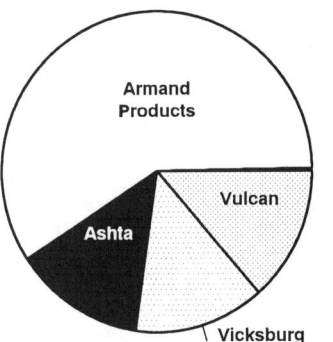

Shares are shown based on total capacity of 185,000 short tons.

Armand Products	59.5%
Ashta	13.5
Vicksburg	13.5
Vulcan	13.5

Source: *Chemical Marketing Reporter*, April 15, 1996, p. 16, from United States Bureau of the Census.

★ 594 ★
Alkalies and Chlorine (SIC 2812)

Soda Ash Demand

Total demand reached 7.155 million short tons in 1995.

Glass containers	27.4%
Chemicals	25.1
Flat glass	15.9
Detergents	12.5
Fiberglass	3.4
Other	15.7

Source: *Chemical Marketing Reporter*, March 11, 1996, p. 24, from FMC Corporation.

★ 595 ★
Alkalies and Chlorine (SIC 2812)

U.S. Soda Ash Producers

The leading companies are ranked by production capacities in million of tons per year in 1994 and 1995.

	1994	1995
FMC Corp.	2.85	2.85
General Chem.	2.40	2.40
Rhone Poulenc	2.30	2.30
Solvay Minerals	2.00	2.00
TG Soda Ash	1.30	1.30
North American	1.25	1.25

Source: *Engineering & Mining Journal*, March 1996, p. 38WW.

★ 596 ★
Industrial Gases (SIC 2813)

Industrial Gas Consumption

Consumption of the $2.0 billion market is shown by industry.

Nitrogen	25.0%
Oxygen	18.0
Hydrogen	13.0
Mixed/specialty gases	13.0
Hydrogen (in refining)	10.0
Oxygen (in refining)	9.0
Carbon dioxide	8.0
Nitrogen	4.0

Source: *Chemicalweek*, February 28, 1996, p. 22, from BOC.

★ 597 ★

Inorganic Pigments (SIC 2816)

Colored Inorganic Pigment Use

Consumption is shown in thousands of metric tons in 1995.

Iron oxide	77.9%
Lead chromate	8.3
Complex inorganics	4.9
Chromium oxide	4.4
Ultramarines	2.5
Iron blues	1.5
Cadmiums	0.5

Source: *Chemical Engineering*, June 1996, p. 67, from SRI Consulting.

★ 598 ★

Inorganic Pigments (SIC 2816)

Titanium Dioxide Makers

Production is shown in thosuands of metric tons.

DuPont	479
SCM	299
Kemira	145
Kerr-McGee	145
Louisiana Pigment	110
Kronos	75

Source: *Chemicalweek*, May 22, 1996, p. 31, from *Interior Board of Mine Operations Appeals*.

★ 599 ★

Inorganic Chemicals (SIC 2819)

Folic Acid Consumption

Consumption is estimated to grow from 100,000 kilos to 150,000 kilos.

	1995	1998
Animal feed	70.0%	50.0%
Food	15.0	35.0
Nutrients	15.0	15.0

Source: *Chemical Marketing Reporter*, March 11, 1996, p. 14.

★ 600 ★

Inorganic Chemicals (SIC 2819)

Hydrogen Peroxide Makers

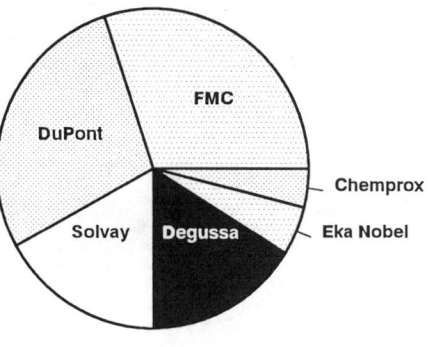

Capacity shares are shown for North America, based on a total production capacity of 1.5 billion pounds.

FMC	30.0%
DuPont	27.6
Solvay	16.9
Degussa	16.0
Eka Nobel	5.1
Chemprox	4.4

Source: *Chemical Marketing Reporter*, August 21, 1995, p. 19.

★ 601 ★

Inorganic Chemicals (SIC 2819)

Mexican HF Producers

Shares are shown based on the 92,000 tons produced annually.

Quimica Fluor SA	70.7%
Norfluor SA de CV	13.0
Industrias Quimicas de Mexico	10.9
Quimobasicos	5.4

Source: *Industrial Minerals*, September 1995, p. 40.

★ 602 ★

Inorganic Chemicals (SIC 2819)

Pool Sanitizer Market

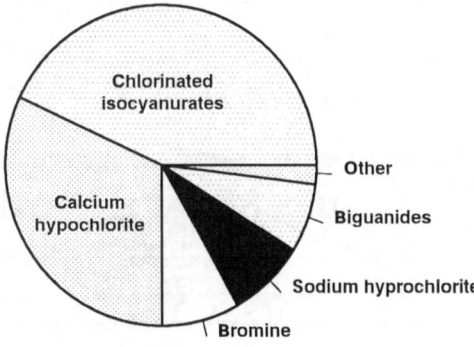

The leading producers of chlorinated isocyanuates are OxyChem, Great Lakes/ BioLab, and Israel Chemicals; Calcium hyprchlorite is produced by Olin and PPG.

Chlorinated isocyanurates	43.0%
Calcium hypochlorite	32.0
Bromine	8.0
Sodium hyprochlorite	8.0
Biguanides	7.0
Other	2.0

Source: *Chemical Marketing Reporter*, June 12, 1995, p. 21.

★ 603 ★

Inorganic Chemicals (SIC 2819)

Sodium Dioxide Makers

The top firms in North America are ranked by production in thousands of short tons. Shares are shown based on a total of 498,000 short tons.

	(000)	Share
Marsulex	144.0	28.9%
Rhone-Poulenc	105.0	21.1
Cominco American	88.0	17.7
Hoechst Celanese	65.0	13.1
Bolinden Intertrade	45.0	9.0
Peridot Chemicals	15.0	3.0
Coulton Chemicals	13.0	2.6
Industrias Penoles	13.0	2.6
Thatcher	10.0	2.0

Source: *Chemical Marketing Reporter*, January 8, 1996, p. 21.

★ 604 ★

Inorganic Chemicals (SIC 2819)

Sodium Silicate Makers

Shares are shown based on production capacity of 1.26 million short tons per year.

PG	34.4%
OxyChem	16.8
J.M. Huber	16.8
PPG	9.2
W.R. Grave	9.2
Power Silicates	6.2
Crosfield	5.4
Chemical Products	1.9
Z-Tech	0.2

Source: *Chemical Marketing Reporter*, December 18, 1995, p. 27.

★ 605 ★

Plastics (SIC 2821)

ABS Makers - North America

Companies are ranked by production in thousands of metric tons. ABS stands for acrylonitrile-butadiene-styrene.

	M.t. (000)	% of Group
GE Plastics	415	41.3%
Monsanto	355	35.4
Dow Chemical	190	18.9
Resistol	24	2.4
Diamond Polymers	20	2.0

Source: *Chemicalweek*, August 23, 1995, p. 40, from Schroder Wertheim.

★ 606 ★

Plastics (SIC 2821)

ABS Market - 1995

The total market reached 1.454 billion pounds in 1995. ABS stands for acrylonitrile butadiene styrene.

	(mil.)	Share
Injection molding	720	27.6%
Appliances	92	3.5
Business machines	86	3.3
Construction	32	1.2
Consumer electronics	22	0.8
Furniture	10	0.4
Luggage	3	0.1

Continued on next page.

★ 606 ★ *Continued*
Plastics (SIC 2821)

ABS Market - 1995

The total market reached 1.454 billion pounds in 1995. ABS stands for acrylonitrile butadiene styrene.

	(mil.)	Share
Recreation	24	0.9%
Telecommunications	35	1.3
Transportation	293	11.2
Other injection molding	123	4.7
Extrusion	448	17.2
Appliances	168	6.4
Construction	127	4.9
Leisure products	11	0.4
Luggage	11	0.4
Packaging	9	0.3
Recreational vehicles	32	1.2
Other	78	3.0
Export	207	7.9
Modifiers	50	1.9
Other	29	1.1

Source: *Modern Plastics*, January 1996, p. 71.

★ 607 ★
Plastics (SIC 2821)

Acrylic Resin Market

Shares are shown based on a 546 million pound market.

Extruded sheet	35.1%
Molding	31.8
Cast sheet	24.1
Dispersions kitchen/bathroom	9.0

Source: *Modern Plastics*, January 1996, p. 71.

★ 608 ★
Plastics (SIC 2821)

Automotive Industry Plastic Suppliers

Firms are ranked by 1994 plastic sales to auto companies in North America. Data are shown in millions of dollars. GE Plastics figure is an estimate.

DuPont Automotive	$ 848.0
GE Plastics	800.0
Automotive Materials Group of Dow Chemical Co.	750.0
LNP Engineering Plastics Inc.	120.0

Source: *Automotive News*, August 21, 1995, p. 42, from company reports.

★ 609 ★
Plastics (SIC 2821)

Canadian Resin Market

Production is shown in kilotons for the first quarter of 1995. LDPE stands for low-density polyethylene; HDPE stands for high-density polyethylene; ABS stands for acylonitrile butadiene styrene.

LDPE	355.7
HDPE	196.6
Polyvinyl chloride	116.8
Polystyrene & ABS	48.2
Polyesters, unsaturated	15.3

Source: *Canadian Plastics*, July 1995, p. 4, from Statistics Canada.

★ 610 ★
Plastics (SIC 2821)

Composite Shipments by Market

Shipments are expected to grow from 3.04 billion pounds in 1994 to 3.174 billion pounds in 1995.

	1994	1995
Transportation	31.1%	31.1%
Construction	19.6	19.7
Corrosion-resistant equipment . . .	12.4	12.4
Marine	11.9	11.8
Electrical/electronics	9.8	9.8
Consumer products	5.7	5.7
Appliances/business equipment . . .	5.3	5.2
Aircraft/aerospace/defense	0.8	0.8
Other	3.3	3.4

Source: *Modern Plastics*, October 1995, p. 38, from SPI Composites Institute.

★ 611 ★

Plastics (SIC 2821)

EPDM Market - North America

The ethylene-propylene-diene-monomer (EPDM) market is shown by end use, based on the 590 million pounds in 1995 and 689 million pounds in 2000.

	1995	2000
Auto parts	24.6%	24.8%
Single-ply roofing	16.9	18.1
TPOs/TPVs	15.6	16.3
Rubber goods	13.6	12.8
Oil additives	8.5	8.0
Wire & cable	7.1	6.8
Tires & tubes	4.1	3.9
Appliance parts	2.7	2.8
Hoses	2.5	2.5
Others	4.4	4.1

Source: *Chemicalweek*, April 3, 1996, p. 41, from Chemical Market Resources.

★ 612 ★

Plastics (SIC 2821)

HDPE Makers - North America

Companies are ranked by capacity in millions of pounds per year.

	(mil.)	Share
Exxon-Paxon	1,920	15.7%
Phillips	1,700	13.9
Quantum	1,660	13.6
Lyondell	1,500	12.3
Solvay	1,480	12.1
Union Carbide	1,275	10.5
Chevron	1,145	9.4
Mobil	560	4.6
Formosa	440	3.6
Fina	420	3.4
Dow Chemical	100	0.8

Source: *Chemicalweek*, January 17, 1996, p. 7.

★ 613 ★

Plastics (SIC 2821)

HDPE Market - 1995

The market for high-density polyethylene (HDPE) is shown in millions of pounds for 1995. The total market was 11.645 billion pounds.

Blow molding	3,488
Extrusion	
Packaging film	302
Non-packaging film	
Grocery sacks	530
Trash bags and liners	382
Other	168
Other retail bags	140
Pipe and conduit	
Industrial/sewer	340
Gas distribution	196
Corrugated	176
Other	44
Sheet	680
Wire & cable	133
Coating	64
Other extrusion	116
Injection molding	1,932
Exports	1,330
Resellers and compounders	1,140
Rotomolding	110

Source: *Modern Plastics*, January 1996, p. 70.

★ 614 ★

Plastics (SIC 2821)

Injection Molded Plastics Market

Demand is shown by segment.

	1994	2000
Consumer & institutional	30.1%	29.7%
Packaging	26.1	26.9
Electrical/electronic	17.3	17.4
Other	26.5	25.9

Source: *Sales & Marketing Management*, January 1996, p. 16, from Freedonia Group Inc.

★ 615 ★

Plastics (SIC 2821)

LLDPE Makers - North America

The leading makers of linear low-density polyethylene (LLDPE) are ranked by production in millions of pounds.

Union Carbide 2,500
Dow Chemical 1,820
Novacor 1,750
Mobil 1,200
Exxon 990
Quantum Chemical 935
Imperial Oil (Exxon) 540
Chevron 500
Dow (Canada) 450
Montell 440
Petromont (Canada) 440
Eastman Chemical 260
Solvay Polymers 120
Phillips 100

Source: *Chemicalweek*, April 10, 1996, p. 9, from SRI International and Wertheim Schroder.

★ 616 ★

Plastics (SIC 2821)

Leading Markets for LDPE

The market for low-density polyethylene (LDPE) is shown by segment.

Film & sheet 61.0%
Extrusion coating 13.0
Injection coating 7.0
Wire & cable 5.0
Other 14.0

Source: *Chemicalweek*, April 10, 1996, p. 10, from SRI International.

★ 617 ★

Plastics (SIC 2821)

Leading Window Extruders

Companies are ranked by 1995 sales in millions of dollars.

Royal Plastics Group Ltd. . . . . $ 156.0
Mikron Industries Inc. 76.0
Veka Inc. 58.0
Chelsea Building Products 55.0
Dayton Technologies 50.0
CertainTeed Corp. 44.0
Silver Line Building Products Corp. 41.0
Vinyl Building Products Inc. 32.0
Weather Shield Manufacturing Inc. 25.0
Spectus Systems Midwest 20.0

Source: *Plastics News*, June 17, 1996, p. 13, from industry estimates.

★ 618 ★

Plastics (SIC 2821)

Low-Density Polyethylene Makers

The leading U.S. manufacturers are ranked by production in thousands of metric tons. Shares of the group are shown in percent.

	(000)	% of Group
Quantum	706	19.2%
Dow Chemical	520	14.1
Chevron	418	11.4
Westlake	386	10.5
DuPont	367	10.0
Eastman	295	8.0
Exxon	283	7.7
Mobil	227	6.2
Union Carbide	227	6.2

Continued on next page.

★ 618 ★ *Continued*
Plastics (SIC 2821)

Low-Density Polyethylene Makers

The leading U.S. manufacturers are ranked by production in thousands of metric tons. Shares of the group are shown in percent.

	(000)	% of Group
Rexene	187	5.1%
Lyondell	64	1.7

Source: *Chemicalweek*, April 10, 1996, p. 10, from SRI International.

★ 619 ★
Plastics (SIC 2821)

Mexican Resin Market

Domestic demand is shown in millions of pounds. LDPE - low-density polyethylene; HDPE - high-density polyethylene; PP - polypropylene; PS - polystyrene; PVC - polyvinyl chloride; PET - polyethylene terephthalate.

	1994	1995
LDPE	924	910
HDPE	675	620
PP	520	560
PS	398	415
PVC	561	530
PET	148	205

Source: *Modern Plastics*, January 1996, p. 73, from Instituto Mexicano del Plastico Industrial.

★ 620 ★
Plastics (SIC 2821)

PET Makers - North America

Production is shown in thousands of metric tons per year. PET stands for polyethylene terephthalate.

Eastman Chemical	625.0
Shell Chemical	265.0
Hoechst Celanese	200.0
ICI Americas	165.0
Eastman (Mexico)	120.0
Wellman	110.0
Nan Ya Plastics	100.0
Hoechst Celanese (Mexico)	70.0

Source: *Chemicalweek*, April 10, 1996, p. 8, from SRI International.

★ 621 ★
Plastics (SIC 2821)

Polvinyl Chloride Makers - North America

Production capacity is shown in thousands of metric tons.

	(000)	Share
Shintech	1,225.0	19.7%
Geon	925.0	14.9
OxyChem	920.0	14.8
Formosa	915.0	14.7
Georgia Gulf	405.0	6.5
Vista Chemical	375.0	6.0
Borden Chemicals	372.0	6.0
Westlake PVC	226.0	3.6
Imperial (Exxon)	147.0	2.4
CertainTeed	118.0	1.9

Continued on next page.

★ 621 ★ *Continued*
Plastics (SIC 2821)

Polvinyl Chloride Makers - North America

Production capacity is shown in thousands of metric tons.

	(000)	Share
Union Carbide	64.0	1.0%
Vygen	64.0	1.0
Keysor-Century	27.0	0.4
Mexico (country)	442.0	7.1

Source: *Chemicalweek*, April 10, 1996, p. 11, from SRI International.

★ 622 ★
Plastics (SIC 2821)

Polypropylene Makers

The leading companies in the United States are ranked by capacity in thousands of metric tons (m.t.). Shares of the group are shown in percent.

	M.t. (000)	% of Group
Montell	840.0	18.8%
Amoco	750.0	16.8
Exxon Chemical	477.0	10.7
Fina	455.0	10.2
Huntsman	350.0	7.8
Aristech (Mitsubishi)	315.0	7.1
Shell (with Union Carbide) . . .	245.0	5.5
Phillips	238.0	5.3
Solvay Polymer	200.0	4.5
Epsilon	182.0	4.1
Lyondell Petrochemical	137.0	3.1
Quantum Chemical	137.0	3.1
Rexene	82.0	1.8
Novacor	57.0	1.3

Source: *Chemicalweek*, April 10, 1996, p. 5, from SRI International.

★ 623 ★
Plastics (SIC 2821)

Polystyrene Makers

The top producers in North America are ranked by output in millions of pounds.

	(mil.)	Share
Dow Chemical	1,310	18.7%
Huntsman Chemical	1,240	17.7
BASF	835	11.9
Novacor Chemicals	720	10.3
Fina	700	10.0
Arco Chemical	515	7.3
Chevron Chemical	480	6.8
Amoco Chemical	295	4.2
Deltech	144	2.1
Resistol	120	1.7
Scott Polymers	115	1.6
Polidesa	110	1.6
Others	430	6.1

Source: *Chemicalweek*, August 9, 1995, p. 30, from SRI International and Wertheim Schroder.

★ 624 ★
Plastics (SIC 2821)

Polyvinyl Chloride Market - 1995

The total market reached 11.799 billion pounds in 1995.

	(mil.)	Share
Extrusion (total)	7,531	39.6%
Pipe & conduit	4,560	24.0
Siding	1,408	7.4
Wire & cable	392	2.1
Packaging	348	1.8
Non-packaging	55	0.3
Other	471	2.5
Calendering	1,122	5.9
Molding	533	2.8
Coatings	398	2.1
Exports	1,366	7.2
Compounders & resellers	501	2.6
Paste processes	220	1.2
Other	128	0.7

Source: *Modern Plastics*, January 1996, p. 70.

★ 625 ★
Plastics (SIC 2821)

Resin Consumption - Canada

Synthetic resin consumption is shown by market. Leading resin makers include B.F. Goodrich, Dow Chemical, DuPont Canada, Esso Chemical, G.E. Plastics, and Himont Canada.

Packaging	39.5%
Building and construction	29.0
Transportation	12.9
Home and commercial furnishings	4.7
Agriculture/environment	3.1
Communications/electronics	2.7
Institutional/retail serviceware	2.2
Recreation	2.0
Housewares	1.8
Apparel/accessories/personal care	1.4
Advertising/publications	0.6

Source: *National Trade Data Bank*, March 2, 1996, p. 111092697.

★ 626 ★
Plastics (SIC 2821)

Synthetic Polymer Market

Segmentation is shown based on a 2.7 billion pound market.

Tackifiers	29.0%
SB rubber/styrene block copolymer	29.0
Acrylics	13.0
Vinyl acetate	10.0
Polyurethane	7.0
Ethylvinyl acetate	4.0
Polyvinyl acetate	4.0
Vinyl acrylic	4.0

Source: *Chemicalweek*, March 27, 1996, p. 26, from ChemQuest Group.

★ 627 ★
Plastics (SIC 2821)

Top PET Makers

Eastman
Hoechst
Shell
Wellman
ICI
Nan Ya/Formosa
Other

Total capacity is expected to grow from 4.63 million pounds in 1996 to 6.34 million pounds in 1998.

	1996	1998
Eastman	36.7%	31.0%
Hoechst	27.5	24.0
Shell	15.2	17.4
Wellman	7.1	15.8
ICI	7.8	7.6
Nan Ya/Formosa	5.4	3.9
Other	0.3	0.2

Source: *Chemicalweek*, April 24, 1996, p. 8, from Bonner & Moore Associates.

★ 628 ★
Plastics (SIC 2821)

U.S. Polypropylene Producers

Production capacity is shown in millions of pounds. A 25% expansion is planned by the industry.

Montell Polyolefins	1,950
Amoco	1,710
Exxon Chemical	1,030
Huntsman Chemical	1,010
Fina	995
Aristech Chemical	810
Shell Polypropylene	575
Formosa Plastics	500
Phillips/Sumika	480
Solvay Polymers	440
Epsilon Products	360
Lyondell Petrochemical	350
Quantum Chemical	280
Rexene	180

Source: *Chemical & Engineering News*, August 7, 1995, p. 19, from Fina.

★ 629 ★

Synthetic Rubber (SIC 2822)

Crumb Rubber Market

The market is shown by segment in 1995.

Asphalt 44.0%
Pneumatic tires 20.0
Bound rubber 18.0
Athletic 8.0
Friction material 4.0
Molded/extruded rubber 3.0
Rubber/plastic 3.0

Source: *Rubber & Plastics News*, February 12, 1996, p. 1, from Baker Rubber Co. and Scrap Tire Management Council.

★ 630 ★

Synthetic Rubber (SIC 2822)

Rubber Industry Leaders

Companies are ranked by rubber sales in millions of dollars. Data are for 1994.

Goodyear . . . . $ 10,700.0
Michelin North America 4,100.0
Bridgestone/Firestone Inc. 3,900.0
Kelly-Springfield Tire Co. 1,480.0
Cooper Tire & Rubber Co. 1,403.2
Continental General Tire Inc. 1,400.0
Gates Rubber Co. 1,241.0
Mark IV Industries Inc. 1,000.0
Standard Products Co. 771.0
Dunlop Tire Corp. 664.0
Bandag Inc. 596.5
Gen Corp. Inc. 574.2
Trinova Corp. 448.7
Rubbermaid Inc. 433.9
Yokohama Tire Corp. 411.0

Source: *Rubber & Plastics News*, July 17, 1995, p. 20.

★ 631 ★

Synthetic Rubber (SIC 2822)

Synthetic Rubber Consumption - North America

Data are in thousands of metric tons. SBR stands for styrene butadiene rubber. TPE stands for thermoplastic elastomer. Natural rubber consumption is expected to fall from 1.116 billion metric tons in 1995 to 1.112 billion metric tons in 1996.

	1995	1996	Share
SBR solid	881.0	886.0	26.2%
Carboxylated latex . . .	616.0	625.0	18.5
Polybutadiene	529.0	533.0	15.7
TPEs	377.0	397.5	11.7
Ethylene propylene . . .	267.0	268.0	7.9
SBR latex	90.2	91.3	2.7
Nitrile solid	84.0	84.0	2.5
Polychloroprene	70.0	70.0	2.1
Other synthetics	427.4	431.4	12.7

Source: *Rubber & Plastics News*, March 25, 1996, p. 6, from International Institute of Synthetic Rubber Producers.

★ 632 ★
Synthetic Rubber (SIC 2822)

Synthetic Rubber Shipments

Shipments grew from 2.18 million metric tons in 1994 to 2.25 million metric tons in 1995.

	1994	1995
Styrene-butadiene rubber	38.9%	39.0%
Polybutadiene	23.1	23.4
Ethylene-propylene	12.0	11.8
Nitrile-solid	3.8	3.7
Polychloroprene	3.5	3.1
Other	18.7	18.9

Source: *Chemical & Engineering News*, June 24, 1996, p. 44, from International Institute of Synthetic Rubber Producers.

★ 633 ★
Synthetic Rubber (SIC 2822)

Top Rubber Product Companies

Firms are ranked by 1995 rubber sales in millions of dollars. Products include tires, belts, hoses, inner tubes, and sealing systems.

Goodyear	$ 11,849.0
Bridgestone/Firestone Inc.	4,605.8
Michelin North America Inc.	4,218.0
Cooper Tire & Rubber Co.	1,493.0
Gates Rubber Co.	1,484.0
Continental General Tire Inc.	1,464.0
Mark IV Industries	1,253.0
Standard Products Co.	896.0
Bandag Inc.	677.8
Dunlop Tire Corp.	632.0
GenCorp Inc.	584.0
Trinova Corp.	471.0
Freudenberg-NOK G.P.	453.0
Dana Corp.	425.0
Parker Hannifin Corp.	417.0

Source: *Rubber & Plastics News*, July 15, 1996, p. 14.

★ 634 ★
Synthetic Fibers (SIC 2823)

Cellulosic Fiber Production

While the level of production remained constant at 50 million pounds, the table shows the shift in production by type.

	1994	1995
Rayon	56.3%	55.8%
Acetate	43.8	44.2

Source: *Chemical & Engineering News*, April 8, 1996, p. 22, from Society of the Plastics Industry and Fiber Economics Bureau.

★ 635 ★
Synthetic Fibers (SIC 2823)

Manmade Filament Shipments

Shipments are shown in millions of pounds.

Olefin	1,901.3
Nylon carpet	1,202.4
Polyester textile	1,166.1
Polyester industrial	422.7
Nylon textiles	372.0
Nylon industrial	256.1

Source: *America's Textile International*, May 1996, p. 6, from Fiber Economics Bureau.

★ 636 ★
Synthetic Fibers (SIC 2824)

Noncellulosic Fiber Production

	1994	1995
Polyester	40.8%	41.2%
Nylon	29.0	28.6
Olefin	25.6	25.7
Acrylic	4.7	4.6

Source: *Chemical & Engineering News*, April 8, 1996, p. 22, from Society of the Plastics Industry and Fiber Economics Bureau.

★ 637 ★

Medicinals (SIC 2833)

Makers of Herbal Supplements

Producers of herbal supplements are ranked by share of the market for the 12 months ended May 1995.

Sunsource Health Products	25.5%
Pharmavite	20.4
Leiner	7.1
Lichtwer Pharma	6.4
Nature's Bounty	4.2
Bayer	2.4
Kyolic	1.4
Other	32.6

Source: *Nonfoods Merchandising*, October 1995, p. 50, from Towne-Oller & Associates.

★ 638 ★

Medicinals (SIC 2833)

Supplement Market - 1996

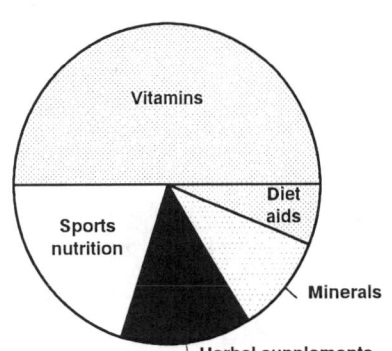

Sales are estimated by segment in millions of dollars for 1996.

	($ mil.)	Share
Vitamins	$ 3,535	49.5%
Sports nutrition	1,429	20.0
Herbal supplements	1,007	14.1
Minerals	720	10.1
Diet aids	453	6.3

Source: *Newsweek*, May 6, 1996, p. 67.

★ 639 ★

Medicinals (SIC 2833)

Top Vitamin and Tonic Brands

Vitamin and tonic brand shares shown reflect sales of $1.259 billion in 1994 and $1.371 billion in 1995.

	1994	1995
Nature Made	10.3%	11.1%
Centrum	10.4	9.5
Your Life	7.6	7.4
Nature's Bounty	4.1	3.7
One-A-Day	3.2	3.1
Flintstones	2.4	2.2
Theragran	3.0	2.1
Private label	34.0	33.4
Other	25.0	27.5

Source: *Advertising Age*, January 1, 1996, p. 20, from Towne-Oller & Associates.

★ 640 ★

Medicinals (SIC 2833)

Vitamin Sales by Type

Multivitamins	32.1%
Children's	13.3
Vitamin C	11.6
Vitamin E	10.5
Calcium	8.4
Herbal supplements	6.5
Vitamin B	6.5
Iron	3.5
Vita-A (Beta)	1.9
Vitamin packs	1.9
Zinc	0.6
Fiber	0.1
Other	3.2

Source: *Nonfoods Merchandising*, October 1995, p. 48.

★ 641 ★

Drugs (SIC 2834)

Adult Cold Remedy Brands

Shares are shown for the year ended September 9, 1995.

Control	15.5%
Vicks NyQuil	11.1
Sudafed	7.4
Alka-Seltzer Plus	6.4

Continued on next page.

★ 641 ★ *Continued*

Drugs (SIC 2834)

Adult Cold Remedy Brands

Shares are shown for the year ended September 9, 1995.

Dimetapp	4.9%
Benadryl 25	4.4
Tavist D	4.3
Theraflu	3.8
Vicks DayQuil	2.9
Tylenol Cold	2.9
Other	36.4

Source: *Nonfoods Merchandising*, May 1996, p. 24, from A.C. Nielsen.

★ 642 ★

Drugs (SIC 2834)

Allergy Relief Drugs

Market share is shown based on total prescriptions.

	1993	1996
Claritin	9.0%	48.3%
Seldane	51.0	21.4
Hismanal	14.0	5.4
Zyrtec	--	6.6
Other	26.0	18.3

Source: *Wall Street Journal*, May 23, 1996, p. B1, from IMS America Ltd.

★ 643 ★

Drugs (SIC 2834)

Antacid Brands

Brand shares are shown for the 52 weeks ended November 26, 1995.

Mylanta	13.5%
Tums	12.8
Private label	11.0
Immodium	8.3
Pepcid AC	8.2
Pepto Bismol	8.1
Maalox	7.4
Alka Seltzer	5.5
Rolaids	5.4
Tagamet HB	4.3
Other	15.5

Source: *Supermarket Business*, March 1996, p. 96, from Information Resources Inc.

★ 644 ★

Drugs (SIC 2834)

Antidepressant Prescriptions

Share of total prescriptions is shown by year.

	1993	1995
Prozac	56.2%	44.2%
Zoloft	32.0	33.5
Paxil	11.8	21.2
Other	-	1.1

Source: *Wall Street Journal*, May 9, 1996, p. B1, from IMS America.

★ 645 ★
Drugs (SIC 2834)

Antipsychotic Drugs

The top 12 antipsychotics are ranked by number of prescriptions issued for the 12 months ended March 1995.

	RX (000)	Share
Haloperidol	2,797	38.5%
Clozaril	1,291	17.8
Thiothixene	1,144	15.7
Risperdal	1,007	13.8
Loxapine	265	3.6
Haldol	237	3.1
Navane	170	2.3
Haldol Decanoate	130	1.8
Moban	103	1.4
Loxitane	73	1.0
Orap	62	0.9
Taractan	2	0.0

Source: *Drug Topics*, November 20, 1995, p. 48, from Scott-Levin Associates, Source Prescription Audit.

★ 646 ★
Drugs (SIC 2834)

Aspirin Makers

Production is shown in millions of pounds per year.

Rhone-Poulenc	20.0
Dow	12.0
P&G Pharmaceuticals	4.0

Source: *Chemical Marketing Reporter*, January 8, 1996, p. 37.

★ 647 ★
Drugs (SIC 2834)

Children's Analgesic Market

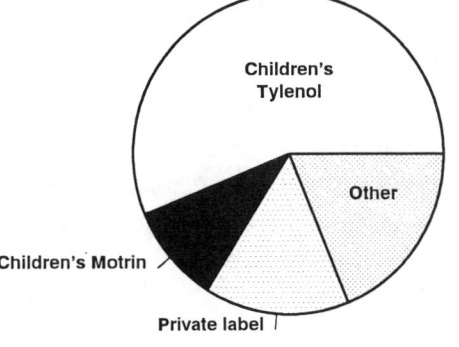

Shares of the $300 million market are shown in percent.

Children's Tylenol	56.0%
Children's Motrin	10.0
Private label	15.0
Other	19.0

Source: *Wall Street Journal*, July 1, 1996, p. B6, from Information Resources Inc.

★ 648 ★
Drugs (SIC 2834)

Cold & Cough Remedies

The market is shown by segment, based on food store sales for the 52 weeks ended December 31, 1995. In the overall trade class, drug stores lead with a 44.8% share.

	Sales ($ mil.)	Share
Cold & sinus tabs. cough drops	$ 703.33	34.3%
Cold/allergy liquids	190.88	36.5
Cough syrup	126.64	31.1
Nasal spray	94.01	28.3

Source: *Nonfood Merchandising*, May 1996, p. 16, from Information Resources Inc. InfoScan.

★ 649 ★

Drugs (SIC 2834)

Cold Market - Canada

The $724 million market is shown by segment.

Cold & sinus remedies	35.5%
Headache remedies	29.1
Antihistimines	18.8
Non-prescription cough syrups	11.0
Throat lozenges	3.5
Nasal decongestants	2.2

Source: *Globe and Mail*, January 11, 1996, p. B13, from Nielsen Marketing Research.

★ 650 ★

Drugs (SIC 2834)

Cold Remedies for Children

Shares are shown based on sales for the year ended September 9, 1995.

Tylenol Cold	27.7%
Benadryl Elixir	19.2
Pedia Care	14.8
Vicks NyQuil	7.7
Control	7.4
Triaminic Nite Light	3.7
Triaminic AM	3.2
Dimetapp Cold & Allergy	3.1
Robitussin Pediatric Nt. Relief	2.7
Pedia Care Night Rest	2.5
Other	8.0

Source: *Nonfoods Merchandising*, May 1996, p. 24, from A.C. Nielsen.

★ 651 ★

Drugs (SIC 2834)

Cough/Cold Medicines - Solid Form

Data refer to the oral, non-analgesic form of the medication. Brand shares are shown in percent.

Claritin D	27.2%
Seldane-D	16.9
Trinalin	3.6
R-Tannate	3.3
Poly-Histine-D	2.4
Semprex-D	2.1
Bromfed-PD	2.1
Deconamine SR	1.9
Bromfed	1.8

Phanchlor S.B.A.	1.7%
Chlorphenir/Pseudo	1.6
Dura-Vent/DA	1.5
Nalspan	1.4
Triotann	1.2
Rynatan	1.2
Resaid	1.2
Atrohist Plus	1.1
Poly-Histine-D PED	1.1
All others	26.9

Source: *Drug Topics*, January 8, 1996, p. 17, from Source Prescription Audit and Scott-Levin Associates.

★ 652 ★

Drugs (SIC 2834)

Drug Purchases by Type - North America

Drug sales are shown by application for the first 11 months of 1995.

	($ mil.)	Share
Central nervous system	$ 9,182.0	17.6%
Alimentary/metabolism	8,482.0	16.3
Cardiovascular	8,179.0	15.7
Respiratory	5,604.0	10.7
Anti-infectives	4,849.0	9.3
Blood agents	2,476.0	4.7
Musculo-skeletal	2,104.0	4.0
Others	11,302.0	21.7

Source: *Financial Times*, January 22, 1996, p. 4, from IMS International.

★ 653 ★

Drugs (SIC 2834)

Eye Drops - Allergy Relief

Sales are shown in millions of dollars for the 52 weeks ended February 25, 1996. The market is estimated at $45 million.

	($ mil.)	Share
Naphcon-A (Alcon Laboratories)	$ 7.5	16.7%
Opcon-A (Bausch & Lomb) . . .	6.6	14.7
Clear Eyes ACR (Abbott Laboratories)	5.5	12.2
Vasocon-A (Ciba-Geigy Corp.) .	2.5	5.6
Other	22.9	50.9

Source: *Advertising Age*, May 13, 1996, p. 17, from Information Resources Inc.

★ 654 ★

Drugs (SIC 2834)

Headache Remedies

Leading pain relievers are ranked by sales in millions of dollars for the 52 weeks ended February 17, 1996. Shares are shown based on an estimated $3.0 billion market.

	($ mil.)	Share
Tylenol	$ 530.3	17.7%
Advil	343.9	11.5
Aleve	141.8	4.7

	($ mil.)	Share
Tylenol PM	$ 106.3	3.5%
Excedrin	104.8	3.5
Motrin IB	83.4	2.8
Bayer	63.2	2.1
Children's Tylenol	63.1	2.1
Excedrin PM	49.8	1.7
Anacin	45.3	1.5
Bufferin	27.7	0.9
Excedrin Aspirin Free	26.5	0.9
Nuprin	24.3	0.8
BC Powder	17.8	0.6
Other	1,371.8	45.7

Source: *Commercial Appeal*, March 24, 1996, p. C6, from listed companies and A.C. Nielsen.

★ 655 ★

Drugs (SIC 2834)

Herbal Ecstacy Market

Herbal ecstacy, a counterpart to the illicit drug ecstacy, has been described as "synergistically blended to insure visionary vibrations" by its manufacturer. Global World Media Corp. claims to have 90% of the market after having sold more than 150 million pills in the last four years.

Global World Media Corp.	90.0%
Other	10.0

Source: *Newsweek*, May 6, 1996, p. 64.

★ 656 ★

Drugs (SIC 2834)

Inhaled Nasal Steroid Market

Shares are shown as of June 1995.

Glaxo-Welcome	48.5%
Schering	45.2
Other	6.3

Source: *Investext*, Thomson Financial Services, August 1, 1995, p. 20.

★ 657 ★
Drugs (SIC 2834)

Laxative Market

Selected shares of the $168.1 million market are shown in percent.

Fibercon	5.2%
Citrucel	3.6
Fleet	2.5
Senokot	2.4
Surfak	0.8
Colace	0.7
Private label	17.2
Other	67.6

Source: *Supermarket Business*, July 1996, p. 61, from A.C. Nielsen.

★ 658 ★
Drugs (SIC 2834)

Leading Antiarthritics

Brand shares are shown for the first nine months of 1995.

Ibuprofen	26.5%
Naproxen	14.2
Relafen	10.0
Lodine	7.8
Daypro	6.8
Voltaren	5.7
Indomethacin	5.5
Feldene	3.9
Naprosyn + EC	3.3
Oruvail	3.3
Clinoril	2.5
Ansaid	2.4
Motrin	2.4
Diclofenac Sodium	1.5
Ketoprofen	1.3
Others	3.2

Source: *Drug Topics*, November 20, 1995, p. 31, from Source Prescription Audit and Scott-Levin Associates.

★ 659 ★
Drugs (SIC 2834)

Leading Pain Relievers

Shares are shown based on total sales of $2.7 billion for the 12 months ended February 25, 1996.

Tylenol	29.3%
Advil	12.7
Excedrin	6.7
Aleve	5.3
Bayer	4.3
Motrin	3.9
Private label	22.1
Others	15.2

Source: *Economist*, March 30, 1996, p. 60, from Information Resources Inc.

★ 660 ★
Drugs (SIC 2834)

Leading Pharmaceutical Products

The table shows the top prescription pharmaceuticals ranked by sales in millions of dollars for 1995.

Zantac	$ 2,145
Prozac	1,472
Prilosec	1,191
Procardia XL	1,110
Epogen	964
Zoloft	894
Vasotec	858
Mevacor	849
Cardizem CD	758
Premarin	711
Cipro	656

Continued on next page.

★ 660 ★ *Continued*
Drugs (SIC 2834)

Leading Pharmaceutical Products

The table shows the top prescription pharmaceuticals ranked by sales in millions of dollars for 1995.

Biaxin	$ 620
Augmentin	607
Neupogen	601
Pepcid	600

Source: *Medical Marketing & Media*, May 1996, p. 60, from Retail Perspective and Provider Prospective.

★ 661 ★
Drugs (SIC 2834)

Leading Pharmaceuticals - Federal Hospitals

The top pharmaceuticals are ranked by volume in millions of dollars for 1995.

Ranitidine	$ 65.6
Nifedipine	57.7
Omeprazole	42.7
Diltiazem	38.5
Lovastatin	37.2
Fluoxetine	31.0
Setraline	29.9
Amlodipine	27.9
Lisinopril	27.8
Pravastatin	25.9

Source: *Hospital Pharmacy*, June 1996, p. 641.

★ 662 ★
Drugs (SIC 2834)

Leading Pharmaceuticals - Nonfederal Hospitals

The top pharmaceuticals are ranked by volume in millions of dollars for 1995.

Erthropoietein alpha	$ 347.6
Cefriaxone	338.2
Filgrastim	283.3
Alteplase	267.3
Immune globulin	228.4
Midazolam	225.2
Paclitaxel	215.6
Propofol	194.9

Ondanstetron	$ 182.5
Ciprofloxacin	181.1

Source: *Hospital Pharmacy*, June 1996, p. 638.

★ 663 ★
Drugs (SIC 2834)

Most Advertised Surgical/Medical Products

The table shows the most advertised medical and surgical products. Shares are shown based on total advertising expenditures.

	1994	1995
Cardizem CD	2.38%	2.54%
Adalat CC	1.47	2.47
Cozzar & Hyzaar	-	2.09
Norvasc	1.77	1.82
Prilosec	0.86	1.68
Ultram tablets	0.05	1.63
Serevent	1.07	1.53
Effexor	2.08	1.31
Procardia XL	1.58	1.30
Ziac	1.66	1.23
Flonase	-	1.19
Cipro	1.52	1.14
Plendil	0.72	1.13
Serzone	-	1.06
Zoloft	1.32	1.05
Zovirax	1.54	0.95
Lescol	1.67	0.94
Propulsid	1.23	0.92
Cataflam tablets	1.11	0.92
Famvir	1.01	0.90
Glucophage	-	0.89
Rocephin IV/IM	0.92	0.87
Prevacid	-	0.86
Ambien tablets	1.10	0.84
Vantin	0.91	0.83
Other	74.03	67.91

Source: *Medical Marketing & Media*, March 1996, p. 56, from HCI Medical Promotion Audit (MPA).

★ 664 ★

Drugs (SIC 2834)

Nicotine Patch Market

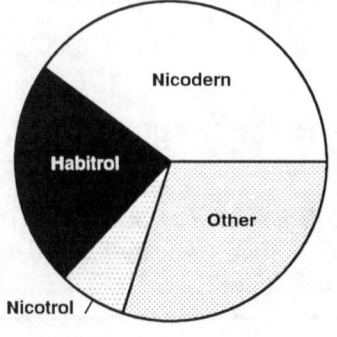

Shares of the market are shown in percent.

Nicodern 39.8%
Habitrol 23.0
Nicotrol 6.8
Other 30.4

Source: *Advertising Age*, April 22, 1996, p. 2.

★ 665 ★

Drugs (SIC 2834)

OTC Drug Market

Shares of the over-the-counter (OTC) pharmaceutical market are shown for 1994.

	($ mil.)	Share
Vitamin/nutrtional supplements	$ 2,111	16.9%
Cough & cold combinations . . .	2,100	16.8
Acetominophen	986	7.9
Antacids	834	6.7
Ibuprophen	682	5.5
Aspirin	457	3.7
Naproxen	65	0.5
Other	5,261	42.1

Source: *Investor's Business Daily*, May 16, 1996, p. A6, from Kline & Company and Lehman Brothers Inc.

★ 666 ★

Drugs (SIC 2834)

OTC Medications Market

This table shows the change in sales between branded and generic over-the-counter (OTC) drugs. Data are based on total sales of $55.65 billion in 1992, $58.57 billion in 1993, and $62.69 billion in 1994.

	1992	1993	1994
Branded	93.3%	92.2%	89.9%
Generic	6.7	7.8	10.1

Source: *Chemicalweek*, March 10, 1996, p. 34, from Dillon Read Equity Research.

★ 667 ★

Drugs (SIC 2834)

Pain Relief Market by Segment

Acetaminophen 43.0%
Aspirin 28.0
Ibuprofen 26.0
Naproxen/sodium 3.0

Source: *American Health*, January/February 1996, p. 67.

★ 668 ★

Drugs (SIC 2834)

Pharmaceutical Market - Canada

Distribution is shown based on 220 million prescriptions issued in 1994. Apotex and Novopharm control 70% of the $900 million generic drug market in Canada; the generic drug market has a 12% share of the entire prescription drug market.

Branded 63.0%
Generic 27.0

Source: *Financial Post*, March 16, 1996, p. 1, from IMS Canada.

★ 669 ★
Drugs (SIC 2834)

Popular Cough Syrup/Tablet Brands

Shares are shown based on supermarket sales for the year ended September 9, 1995.

Robitussin DM	20.0%
Control	13.9
Robitussin CF	10.9
Vicks 44D	5.7
Vicks 44M	4.4
Halls	4.7
Robitussin	4.6
Vicks 44E	3.3
Triaminic	3.2
Vicks 44	3.2
Other	26.1

Source: *Nonfoods Merchandising*, May 1996, p. 24, from A.C. Nielsen.

★ 670 ★
Drugs (SIC 2834)

Popular Diabetes Drugs

Brand shares are shown for the first seven months of 1995.

Glyburide	29.9%
Glipizide	11.1
Glynase Prestab	11.1
DiaBeta	10.3
Glucotrol XL	9.9
Micronase	9.9
Glucotrol	8.9
Chloropropamide	3.6
Glucophage	1.9
Tolazamide	1.1

Diabinese	1.0%
Tolbutamide	0.7
Tolinase	0.2
Orinase	0.2
Dymelor	0.1
Acetohexamide	0.1

Source: *Drug Topics*, September 18, 1995, p. 20, from Scott-Levin Associates.

★ 671 ★
Drugs (SIC 2834)

Stomach Remedy Market

Shares are shown for the 52 weeks ended January 28, 1996.

Mylanta	12.3%
Tums	12.1
Pepcid AC	11.8
Immodium	8.1
Pepto-Bismol	7.5
Maalox	6.7
Tagamet HB	6.1
Alka-Seltzer	5.2
Rolaids	5.1
Other	25.1

Source: *Advertising Age*, March 11, 1996, p. 4, from Information Resources Inc.

★ 672 ★
Drugs (SIC 2834)

Top Antacids

Shares of the $1.45 billion market are shown for the year ended May 26, 1996.

Pepcid AC	16.8%
Tums	11.0
Mylanta	10.5
Tagamet	8.5
Imodium	7.6
Pepto	6.8
Maalox	5.9
Alka-Seltzer	4.6
Rolaids	4.6
Other	23.7

Source: *Advertising Age*, July 1, 1996, p. 3, from Information Resources Inc.

★ 673 ★
Drugs (SIC 2834)

Top Cough/Cold Remedies

Shares are shown for 1994 based on a $2.43 billion market.

Private label	18.3%
Tylenol	8.6
Robitussin	8.2
Benadryl	6.1
Nyquil	6.1
Sufafed	6.0
Dimetapp	4.4
Alka-Seltzer	4.2
Tavist	4.0
Vicks Formula 44	2.9
Other	31.2

Source: *Advertising Age*, September 27, 1995, p. 6, from Information Resources Inc.

★ 674 ★
Drugs (SIC 2834)

Top Generic Drug Firms - 1995

Firms are ranked by millions of prescriptions dispensed in 1995.

	(mil.)	Share
Mylan	108.0	5.0%
Rugby Labs Inc.	67.4	3.1
Geneva Generics	65.9	3.1
Apothecon	64.1	3.0
Schein	60.7	2.8
Lemmon Co.	44.4	2.1
Qualitest	32.3	1.5
Biocraft Labs	31.4	1.5
Goldline	31.3	1.5
Purepac	27.3	1.3
Others	1,615.4	75.2

Source: *Medical Marketing & Media*, April 1996, p. 54, from Walsh America/Prime Medical Services Inc.

★ 675 ★
Drugs (SIC 2834)

Top Pharmaceutical Firms - 1995

Firms are ranked by millions of prescriptions dispensed in 1995.

American Home Products	136.3
Hoechst Marion Roussel	130.5
Bristol-Myers Squibb	122.7
Mylan	108.1
Ciba-Geigy Corp.	102.8
Glaxo Wellcome	98.1
Schering-Plough Corp.	79.1
Bayer	77.0
SmithKline Beecham	72.9
Johnson & Johnson	72.3
Pfizer Inc.	65.9
Merck & Company	65.8
Eli Lilly	56.3
Pharmacia & Upjohn	53.7
Abbott Labs	47.9

Source: *Medical Marketing & Media*, April 1996, p. 50, from Walsh America/Prime Medical Services Inc.

★ 676 ★
Drugs (SIC 2834)

Who Makes Insulin

The $820 million market is shown by company.

Lilly	82.0%
Other	18.0

Source: *Forbes*, June 3, 1996, p. 154, from IMS America.

★ 677 ★
Diagnostic Substances (SIC 2835)

Diagnostic Substance Centers by State

Firms are ranked by number of diagnostic substance firms.

California	66
New Jersey	17
Massachusetts	17
Texas	17
New York	16
Florida	12
Minnesota	10
Illinois	9
Ohio	5
Indiana	4

Source: *Site Selection*, February 1996, p. 102, from Dun & Bradstreet.

★ 678 ★
Diagnostic Substances (SIC 2835)

Home Testing Kits by Type

Sales are shown for the first quarter of 1995.

Blood glucose strips/meters	53.0%
Pregnancy kits	40.7
Ovulation kits	1.7
Cholesterol kits	1.0
Other	3.6

Source: *Nonfoods Merchandising*, May 1996, p. 48, from Towne-Oller & Associates.

★ 679 ★
Biological Products (SIC 2836)

Blood-Clotting Market

Shares of the market are shown for 1979-83. The Red Cross also had a small percentage of the market.

Bayer AG	45.0%
Baxter International	25.0
Rhone-Polenc	25.0
Green Cross	15.0

Source: *New York Times*, June 10, 1996, p. C1, from Rhone-Polenc and Centers for Disease Control.

★ 680 ★
Biological Products (SIC 2836)

Leading Biotech Firms

Firms are ranked by 1994 sales in millions of dollars. Leading biotechnology drugs include Epogen, Neupogen, and Humulin.

Amgen	$ 1,550
Genentech	601
Genzyme	290
ALZA	279
Chiron	276
Biogen	140
Immunex	136
IDEXX	126
Centocor	67

Source: *Chemistry & Industry*, May 6, 1996, p. 334.

★ 681 ★
Detergent Chemicals (SIC 2840)

Chemical Product Makers

The top makers of cleaning products and personal care products are ranked by sales in billions of dollars.

Procter & Gamble	$ 16.73
Colgate-Palmolive	7.56
S.C. Johnson Wax	4.00
Amway	3.15
Estee Lauder	2.89
Avon Products	2.78
Revlon	1.93
Sara Lee	1.70
Bristol-Myers Squibb	1.56
Clorox	1.40

Continued on next page.

★ 681 ★ *Continued*
Detergent Chemicals (SIC 2840)

Chemical Product Makers

The top makers of cleaning products and personal care products are ranked by sales in billions of dollars.

Dial . . . .$ 1.40
Alberto-Culver 1.36
Ecolab 1.34
Helene Curtis 1.25
Gillette 1.24

Source: *Household and Personal Products Industry*, July 1996, p. 71.

★ 682 ★
Detergent Chemicals (SIC 2840)

Glycerine Producers

Production is shown based on a total capacity of 522.5 million pounds per year.

Procter & Gamble 28.7%
Dow 26.8
Henkel 12.4
Unilever 11.5
Witco 7.7
Dial 6.7
Colgate 3.8
Lonza 1.9
Marietta 0.5

Source: *Chemical Marketing Reporter*, January 15, 1996, p. 41.

★ 683 ★
Detergent Chemicals (SIC 2840)

Personal Care Chemicals Market

Shares are shown based on a $4.0 billion market in 1995. "Other" includes shaving products, deodorants, and bubble bath.

Surfactants 22.0%
Synthetic aromas/blends 20.0
Fat-based products 16.0
Natural products 9.0
Petroleum products 7.0
Other 26.0

Source: *Chemical & Engineering News*, July 1, 1996, p. 15, from Freedonia Group.

★ 684 ★
Detergent Chemicals (SIC 2840)

Personal Care Chemicals Use

Shares are shown based on a $4.0 billion market in 1995. "Other" includes shaving products, deodorants, and bubble bath.

Skin care 40.0%
Hair care 23.0
Perfumes 13.0
Cosmetics 5.0
Oral hygiene 5.0
Other 14.0

Source: *Chemical & Engineering News*, July 1, 1996, p. 15, from Freedonia Group.

★ 685 ★
Detergent Chemicals (SIC 2840)

Surfactant Demand

	1994	2000
Anionic	64.5%	63.8%
Nonionic	25.4	25.5
Cationic	9.4	9.8
Amphoteric	0.7	0.9

Source: *Chemicalweek*, January 24, 1996, p. 33, from Freedonia Group.

★ 686 ★
Detergents (SIC 2841)

Dishwasher Detergent Market

Data are for 1994.

Cascade 45.7%
Sunlight 18.1
Jet Dry 8.2
Electra Sol 6.7
All Free N Clear 3.0
Private label 6.5
Other 11.8

Source: *Investext*, Thomson Financial Services, June 23, 1995, p. 98, from Information Resources Inc. and PaineWebber estimates.

★ **687** ★

Detergents (SIC 2841)

Fabric Softener Makers

Shares are shown as of December 1995.

Procter & Gamble 57.0%
Unilever 19.0
Other 24.0

Source: *Investext,* Thomson Financial Services, March 15, 1996, p. 27, from Information Resources Inc.

★ **688** ★

Detergents (SIC 2841)

Fabric Softener Sheet Brands

Shares are shown based on the $400.2 million category in 1994.

Bounce 33.9%
Snuggle Singles 14.0
Downy 11.9
Other 40.2

Source: *Investext,* Thomson Financial Services, June 23, 1995, p. 125, from Information Resources Inc. and PaineWebber estimates.

★ **689** ★

Detergents (SIC 2841)

Laundry Product Makers - North America

Procter & Gamble 56.0%
Unilever 21.0
Colgate-Palmolive 17.0
Other 17.0

Source: *Soap/Cosmetics/Chemical Specialties*, June 1996, p. 72, from Euromonitor.

★ **690** ★

Detergents (SIC 2841)

Leading Dishwasher Detergent Makers

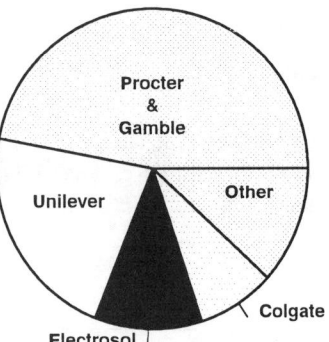

Data are for the first six months of 1995.

Procter & Gamble 47.0%
Unilever 22.0
Electrosol 11.0
Colgate 8.0
Other 12.0

Source: *Investext,* Thomson Financial Services, September 22, 1995, p. 26, from Information Resources Inc.

★ **691** ★

Detergents (SIC 2841)

Liquid Fabric Softener Market

Shares are shown for the first quarter of 1995.

Procter & Gamble 63.0%
  Ultra Downy 57.8
  Downy 5.2
Unilever 21.7
  Ultra Snuggle 11.0
  Snuggle 5.8
  Final Touch 2.7
  Ultra Final Touch 2.3
Dial 4.0
  Stapuf 1.8
  Ultra Purex Rinse and Soft 1.7
  Ultra Purex 0.4
Benckiser 2.0
Continued on next page.

★ 691 ★ *Continued*
Detergents (SIC 2841)

Liquid Fabric Softener Market

Shares are shown for the first quarter of 1995.

Ultra Clingfree	2.0%
Nice N Fluffy	1.6
USA Detergents	1.6
Private label	6.4

Source: *Investext,* Thomson Financial Services, June 23, 1995, p. 168, from Information Resources Inc. and PaineWebber estimates.

★ 692 ★
Detergents (SIC 2841)

Powdered Detergent Market

Shares of the powdered detergent market are shown based on total sales of $2.2 billion. Procter & Gamble also commands a 48% share of the liquid detergent market.

Procter & Gamble	65.0%
Lever Brothers	16.0
Dial	6.0
Church & Dwight	5.0
Other	8.0

Source: *Chemicalweek,* January 24, 1996, p. 32, from Information Resources Inc.

★ 693 ★
Detergents (SIC 2841)

Stain Remover Brands

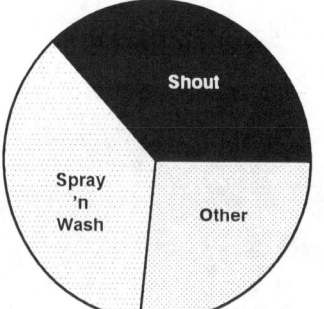

Shares of the $189 million laundry pretreatment category are shown in percent.

Shout	37.0%
Spray 'n Wash	36.5
Other	26.5

Source: *Brandweek,* May 27, 1996, p. 18, from Information Resources Inc.

★ 694 ★
Detergents (SIC 2841)

Top Brands of Liquid Detergent

Sales at mass merchants, drugstores, and foodstores are shown in millions of dollars. Liquid detergent shares are shown in percent.

	Sales ($ mil.)	Share
Tide	$ 510.5	29.8%
Wisk	195.6	11.4
All	193.8	11.3
Purex	142.0	8.3
Cheer	122.3	7.1
Other	535.8	32.1

Source: *Nonfoods Merchandising,* February 1996, p. 11, from Information Resources Inc.

★ 695 ★

Detergents (SIC 2841)

Top Detergent Producers

| Procter & Gamble |
| Unilever |
| Dial |
| Colgate |
| Church & Dwight |
| Private label |
| Others |

Shares of the liquid and powdered detergent market are shown for the year ended August 1995.

Procter & Gamble	58.0%
Unilever	19.5
Dial	6.6
Colgate	4.5
Church & Dwight	4.0
Private label	2.9
Others	4.1

Source: *Advertising Age*, January 8, 1996, p. 12, from Dean Witter Reynolds.

★ 696 ★

Detergents (SIC 2841)

Top Liquid Detergent Brands

Shares are shown for the year ended June 10, 1995.

Tide	18.3%
Tide With Bleach	10.3
All	6.8
Wisk Double Power	6.4
Era	5.6
Purex	4.3
Cheer	4.1
Yes Ultra	3.8
Purex With Bleach	3.5
Private label	3.7
Other	33.2

Source: *Household and Personal Products Industry*, January 1996, p. 76, from A.C. Nielsen.

★ 697 ★

Soaps (SIC 2841)

Bar Soap Market

Data are for 1994.

Dove	16.3%
Dial	9.4
Lever 2000	8.4
Ivory	6.6
Irish Spring	6.3
Zest	5.7
Oil of Olay	5.3
Shield	5.1
Andrew Jergens	4.0
Coast	3.9
Safeguard	3.9
Jergens	3.8
Other	21.3

Source: *Investext*, Thomson Financial Services, June 23, 1995, p. 98, from Information Resources Inc. and PaineWebber estimates.

★ 698 ★

Soaps (SIC 2841)

Leading Bath/Shower Gels

Shares are for the 12 months ended August 1995.

Jergens	15.9%
Caress	11.4
Dove	11.0
Nivea	8.1
Neutrogena	6.7
Sarah Michaels	5.1
Vitabath	3.7
Dial	3.7
Naturistics	3.4
Alpha Hydrox	3.4
Other	27.6

Source: *Nonfoods Merchandising*, January 1996, p. 34, from Towne-Oller.

★ 699 ★
Soaps (SIC 2841)
Leading Body Washes

Brand shares are shown based on food store sales for the 52 weeks ended December 9, 1995.

Jergens	37.4%
Oil of Olay	33.6
Dove	23.7
Dial	1.5
Vaseline Intensive Care	1.4
Other	2.4

Source: *Household and Personal Products Industry*, June 1996, p. 106, from A.C. Nielsen.

★ 700 ★
Soaps (SIC 2841)
Liquid Soap Brands

Data are for 1994.

Softsoap	17.2%
Jergens	14.7
Dial	13.6
Lever 2000	3.9
Caress	3.6
Other	47.0

Source: *Investext,* Thomson Financial Services, June 23, 1995, p. 178, from Information Resources Inc. and PaineWebber estimates.

★ 701 ★
Soaps (SIC 2841)
Popular Shower Gels

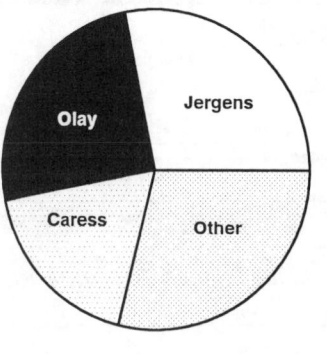

The market had $285 million in sales in 1995.

Jergens	28.3%
Olay	24.8
Caress	17.5
Other	29.4

Source: *Advertising Age*, August 28, 1995, p. 2, from Information Resources Inc.

★ 702 ★
Cleaning Preparations (SIC 2842)
All-Purpose Cleaner Makers - Mexico

	1993	1994
Productos Allen	37.7%	36.9%
Colgate-Palmolive	34.7	36.2
P&G	13.4	13.6
Other	14.2	15.3

Source: *Investext,* Thomson Financial Services, February 15, 1996, p. 30, from company data and trade sources.

★ 703 ★
Cleaning Preparations (SIC 2842)
Car Wax Market

Shares of the $220 market are estimated by company.

Turtle Wax	50.0%
Other	50.0

Source: *Brandweek*, July 22, 1996, p. 16.

★ 704 ★

Cleaning Preparations (SIC 2842)

Floor Maintenance Products

Data show the thousands of gallons manufactured in 1994. Maintenance compounds such as spray-buff media, mop-on maintainers, and restorers are designed to be used in combination with buffing or burnishing operations. Stone/mineral surfaces include concrete and terrazano floors.

Floor polish	19,897.6
Polish/wax stripper products	9,305.9
Maintenance compounds	1,854.7
Stone/mineral surface cleaners	1,778.5

Source: *Soap/Cosmetics/Chemical Specialties*, March 1996, p. 56.

★ 705 ★

Cleaning Preparations (SIC 2842)

Hard Surface Cleaner Brands

Shares are shown for the year ended May 28, 1995. Total sales reached $446.2 million.

Lysol (L&F)	19.4%
Pine Sol (Clorox)	18.6
Mr. Clean (P&G)	15.7
Spic & Span (P&G)	8.9
Clean Up (Clorox)	7.5
Other	29.9

Source: *Household and Personal Products Industry*, November 1995, p. 70, from Information Resources Inc.

★ 706 ★

Cleaning Preparations (SIC 2842)

Household Cleaner Makers

Shares are shown as of December 1995.

Clorox	29.0%
Procter & Gamble	18.0
Colgate	4.0
Other	49.0

Source: *Investext,* Thomson Financial Services, March 15, 1996, p. 27, from Information Resources Inc.

★ 707 ★

Cleaning Preparations (SIC 2842)

Popular Disinfectants

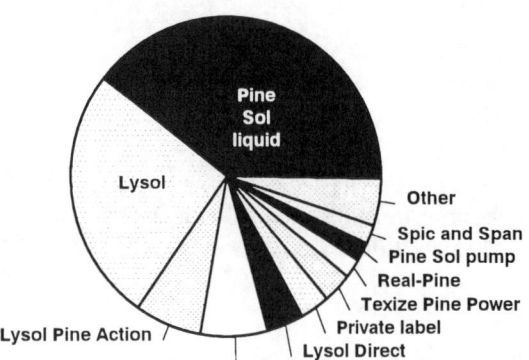

Shares of the $154.5 million market are shown for the 52 weeks ended September 9, 1995.

Pine Sol liquid	40.2%
Lysol	25.5
Lysol Pine Action	6.7
Xtra Pine	6.6
Lysol Direct	4.0
Private label	3.2
Texize Pine Power	2.9
Real-Pine	2.4
Pine Sol pump	2.2
Spic and Span	1.6
Other	4.7

Source: *Household and Personal Products Industry*, April 1996, p. 80, from A.C. Nielsen.

★ 708 ★

Cleaning Preparations (SIC 2842)

Popular Dry Bleach Brands

Shares are for 1994.

Clorox 2	46.0%
Biz	18.1
Mule 20 Teram Borax	8.8
Vivid	4.8
Borateem	4.6
Purex	2.9
Clorox 2 For Colors	1.7

Continued on next page.

★ 708 ★ *Continued*
Cleaning Preparations (SIC 2842)

Popular Dry Bleach Brands

Shares are for 1994.

La France	1.4%
Snowy	1.3
Private label	7.5
Other	2.9

Source: *Investext,* Thomson Financial Services, March 2, 1995, p. 90, from Information Resources Inc. and PaineWebber Inc.

★ 709 ★
Cleaning Preparations (SIC 2842)

Popular Tub/Mildew Cleaners

Shares are shown for the third quarter of 1995.

Tilex	18.7%
Lysol	17.1
Dow	16.4
Comet	14.8
X-14	8.1
Lime A Way Extra	4.4
Scrubb Free One	3.1
Other	17.4

Source: *Investext,* Thomson Financial Services, November 30, 1995, p. 190, from Information Resources Inc. and PaineWebber estimates.

★ 710 ★
Cleaning Preparations (SIC 2842)

Top Abrasive Cleaners

Shares of the $198.4 million market are shown in percent for 1994.

Comet	39.0%
Soft Scrub	37.5
Ajax	11.9
Private label	4.0
Dow Smart Scrub	1.0
Other	6.6

Source: *Advertising Age*, September 27, 1995, p. 6, from Information Resources Inc.

★ 711 ★
Cleaning Preparations (SIC 2842)

Top Furniture Polish Brands

Pledge	
Endust	
Old English	
Scott Liquid Gold	
Favor	
Other	

Brand shares are shown based on an estimated $250 million market for the year ended March 11, 1995.

	($ mil.)	Share
Pledge	$ 68.0	27.2%
Endust	19.7	7.9
Old English	18.0	7.2
Scott Liquid Gold	8.7	3.5
Favor	6.4	2.6
Other	129.2	51.7

Source: *Household and Personal Products Industry*, September 1995, p. 60, from A.C. Nielsen and Kline & Company.

★ 712 ★
Cleaning Preparations (SIC 2842)

Top Spray Cleaners

Shares of the $720.4 million market are shown in percent for 1994.

Windex	16.2%
Formula 409	10.5
Lysol	9.6
Tilex	8.3
Dow	7.9
Other	47.5

Source: *Advertising Age*, September 27, 1995, p. 6, from Information Resources Inc.

★ 713 ★

Baby Care (SIC 2844)

Baby Care Market

Shares are shown based on total sales of $125.5 million in 1995.

Baby powder	24.8%
Petroleum jelly	18.4
Baby ointments/creams	18.2
Baby oils	15.0
Baby soaps	14.2
Baby lotions	9.3

Source: *Nonfoods Merchandising*, June 1996, p. 27, from Information Resources Inc.

★ 714 ★

Baby Care (SIC 2844)

Baby Wipes Market

Brand shares are shown for the first quarter of 1996.

Baby Fresh/Kid Fresh	32.9%
Huggies	29.1
Other	38.0

Source: *Advertising Age*, May 27, 1996, p. 8, from Dean, Witter, Discover & Co.

★ 715 ★

Cosmetics (SIC 2844)

Cosmetics Market by Segment - Mexico

The leading mass market brands in 1993 were Max Factor, Maybelline, Cover Girl, and Renova.

Lipstick	25.6%
Nail polish/care	16.5
Liner pencil	12.3
Face powder	12.2
Mascara	8.5
Blush	6.5
Eyeshadow	4.1
Makeup base	3.2
Liner pencil	2.4
Lips/gel	2.2
Other	6.5

Source: *National Trade Data Bank*, March 2, 1996, p. IS9412.040.

★ 716 ★

Cosmetics (SIC 2844)

Cosmetics Sales by Type

Skin	41.0%
Eye	32.0
Lip	27.0

Source: *Household and Personal Products Industry*, March 1996, p. 20, from Packaged Facts.

★ 717 ★

Cosmetics (SIC 2844)

Eye Makeup Producers

Shares are shown for the 12 weeks ended June 18, 1995.

Maybelline	32.7%
Cover Girl	23.3
L'Oreal	12.5
Revlon	10.9
Max Factor	7.3
Almay	7.2
Other	6.1

Source: *Investext,* Thomson Financial Services, August 17, 1995, p. 66, from Information Resources Inc. and PaineWebber estimates.

★ 718 ★

Cosmetics (SIC 2844)

Leading Cosmetics Brands

Shares are for the year ended September 9, 1995.

	Dol. Share	Unit Share
Cover Girl	23.1%	24.5%
Maybelline	18.9	18.9
CoverStay	19.2	12.1
Other	38.8	44.5

Source: *Household and Personal Products Industry*, November 1995, p. 56, from A.C. Nielsen.

★ 719 ★
Cosmetics (SIC 2844)

Lipstick Market

Shares of the $466.1 million market are shown for 1995.

Revlon	38.3%
Cover Girl	12.3
L'Oreal	12.3
Other	37.2

Source: *Household and Personal Products Industry*, March 1996, p. 61, from Information Resources Inc.

★ 720 ★
Cosmetics (SIC 2844)

Popular Cosmetics Brands

Cover Girl	23.0%
Revlon	19.0
Other	58.0

Source: *Women's Wear Daily*, June 1996, p. 6, from A.C. Nielsen.

★ 721 ★
Cosmetics (SIC 2844)

Popular Lipsticks

The top brands are ranked by sales in thousands of dollars for the year ended December 9, 1995.

Revlon ColorStay	$ 6,730
Revlon Super Lustrous	6,094
Maybelline Moisture Whip	5,987
Cover Girl Continuous Color	5,579
Cover Girl Luminesse	3,704
Wet N' Wild	3,206
Revlon Moon Drops	3,164

L'Oreal Colour Riche	$ 2,678
Cover Girl Remarkable	2,345
Bonne Bell Lip Smacker	2,266

Source: *Nonfoods Merchandising*, June 1996, p. 10, from A.C. Nielsen.

★ 722 ★
Cosmetics (SIC 2844)

Top Cosmetics Brands

Shares are for 1995.

Cover Girl	21.9%
Revlon	19.8
Maybelline	16.2
L'Oreal	11.1
Max Factor	6.5
Alamy	4.9
Sally Hansen	3.1
Wet n' Wild	2.3
Coty	1.6
Bonne Bell	1.3
Other	11.3

Source: *Brandweek*, June 3, 1996, p. 44, from Information Resources Inc.

★ 723 ★
Cosmetics (SIC 2844)

Top Facial Makeup Brands

The top brands are ranked by sales in thousands of dollars for the year ended December 9, 1995.

Cover Girl Clean	$ 12,041
Cover Girl Moisture Wear	6,856
Cover Girl Fr Complexion O-C	5,000
Cover Girl Replenishing	4,913
Revlon Age Defying	3,829
Maybelline Shine Free	3,636
Cover Girl Clarifying	3,517
Cover Girl Ultimate Finish	3,481
Cover Girl Cheekers	2,722
Maybelline Revitalizing	2,596

Source: *Nonfoods Merchandising*, June 1996, p. 10, from A.C. Nielsen.

★ 724 ★

Cosmetics (SIC 2844)

U.S. Cosmetics Marketers

The top companies are ranked by 1994 revenues in millions of dollars. The top 50 companies generated $28.96 billion in revenues in 1994. Some figures are industry estimates. Shares of the group are shown in percent.

	Rev. ($ mil.)	% of Group
Procter & Gamble	$ 4,700.0	18.2%
Estee Lauder Cos.	2,850.0	11.1
Revlon/Almay	1,730.0	6.7
Cosmair/L'Oreal	1,630.0	6.3
Colgate/Mennen	1,610.0	6.2
Avon Products	1,410.0	5.5
Unilever/Chesebrough/Arden	1,390.0	5.4
Bristol Myers/Clairol/Matrix . .	1,290.0	5.0
Helene Curtis	1,200.0	4.7
Alberto-Culver/Sally Beauty . .	1,100.0	4.3
Gillette/Jafra/Oral B	1,080.0	4.2
Mary Kay Cosmetics	850.0	3.3
Johnson & Johnson/ Neutrogena	770.0	3.0
Warner-Lambert	590.0	2.3
Benckiser/Coty/Lancaster . . .	560.0	2.2
Schering/Coppertone	377.0	1.5
Maybelline	349.0	1.4
Carter/Wallace	348.0	1.3
NuSkin	345.0	1.3
Sanofi/YSL	337.0	1.3
Amway	320.0	1.2
Bath & Body Works	261.0	1.0
Merle Norman	250.0	1.0
Jergens/Kao	220.0	0.9
Pfizer	219.0	0.8

Source: *DCI*, June 1995, p. 43.

★ 725 ★

Deodorants (SIC 2844)

Deodorant Producers

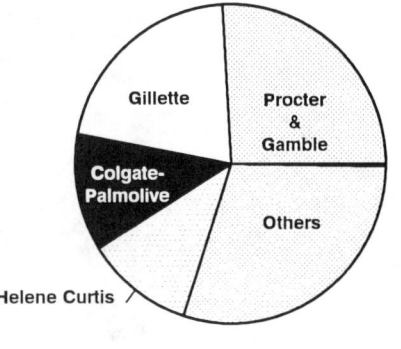

Shares of the $1.46 billion market are shown in percent for 1995.

Procter & Gamble	25.8%
Gillette	20.8
Colgate-Palmolive	12.4
Helene Curtis	11.4
Others	29.6

Source: *New York Times*, February 15, 1996, p. C4, from Information Resources Inc.

★ 726 ★

Deodorants (SIC 2844)

Top Deodorant Brands

Shares are shown for the 52 weeks ended August 27, 1995.

Secret	14.0%
Right Guard	9.9
Arrid	8.0
Sure	7.3
Ban	7.2
Other	53.6

Source: *Nonfoods Merchandising*, February 1996, p. 12, from Information Resources Inc.

★ 727 ★

Deodorants (SIC 2844)

Top Deodorant Brands - 1995

Brand shares are shown for 1995.

Secret	14.2%
Right Guard	10.3

Continued on next page.

★ 727 ★ *Continued*
Deodorants (SIC 2844)

Top Deodorant Brands - 1995

Brand shares are shown for 1995.

Arrid	7.7%
Sure	7.3
Ban	7.1
Degree	6.9
Mennen	6.8
Ladies Mennen	4.9
Soft & Dri	4.7
Old Spice	4.6
Other	25.5

Source: *Brandweek*, June 3, 1996, p. 44, from
Information Resources Inc.

★ 728 ★
Eye Care (SIC 2844)

Top Contact Lens Solutions

*The top 10 brands are ranked by sales at all food
stores with sales of $2.0 million and over. Figures are
for the 52 weeks ended March 9, 1996. The total eye
contact lens care market was valued at $1.2 billion.
Shares of the group are shown in percent.*

	Sales ($000)	% of Group
Alcon Opti-Free	$ 6,428	15.9%
Allergon Ultrazyme	6,004	14.8
Alcon Opti-zyme	4,533	11.2
Reny	4,260	10.5
CIBC Vision AODISC	4,168	10.3
Bausch & Lomb Moisture Drops	3,726	9.2
Alcon Tears Naturals II	3,314	8.2
Renu 1 Stop	2,776	6.9
Sensitive Eyes	2,666	6.6
Murine	2,627	6.5

Source: *Nonfoods Merchandising*, August 1996, p. 12,
from A.C. Nielsen.

★ 729 ★
Eye Care (SIC 2844)

Top Eye Drops/Solutions

*The top 10 brands are ranked by sales at all food
stores with sales of $2.0 million and over. Figures are
for the 52 weeks ended March 9, 1996. The total eye
contact lens care market was valued at $1.2 billion.
Pfizer makes the Visine brand; Abbott Laboratories
makes Clear Eyes. Shares of the group are shown in
percent.*

	Sales ($000)	% of Group
Visine Regular	$ 9,888	21.7%
Clear Eyes	7,058	15.5
Visine Extra	6,241	13.7
Visine A.C.	5,422	11.9
Private label	4,568	10.0
Hypotears	3,110	6.8
Visine L.R.	3,047	6.7
Bausch & Lomb Allergy Drops . .	2,533	5.6
Clear Eyes ACR	1,959	4.3
Opcon-A	1,673	3.7

Source: *Nonfoods Merchandising*, August 1996, p. 12,
from A.C. Nielsen.

★ 730 ★
Fragrances (SIC 2844)

Fragrance Market - 1995

*The table compares the per capita spending on
fragrances and women's fragrances in the United
States and Mexico. In 1995, the men's fragrance
market reached $507.1 million and the women's
fragrance market reached $785 million.*

	Overall	Women
United States	$ 5.40	$ 17.00
Mexico	8.40	12.60

Source: *Household and Personal Products Industry*, April
1996, p. 58, from Information Resources Inc.

★ 731 ★

Fragrances (SIC 2844)

Fragrance Market by Segment - Mexico

The top selling mass market brands for women in 1993 were Clyo, Le Jardin, and Charmis; the prestige category was lead by Chanel 5, Madame Rochas, and Poison. The top mass market brands for men were Old Spice, English Leather, and Brut; in the prestige segment was Azzaro, Cool Water, and Obsession for Men.

Cologne, feminine 51.2%
Cologne, men 39.3
Aftershave 9.0
Perfume/extract 0.5

Source: *National Trade Data Bank*, March 2, 1996, p. IS9412.040.

★ 732 ★

Fragrances (SIC 2844)

Leading Fragrance Brands

Shares are shown for October - December 1995, based on a survey of more than 1,000 retailers.

CK One 9.7%
Beautiful 4.7
Pleasures 4.6
Tommy 3.4
Chanel No. 5 . . . . 2.8
Eternity for Men 2.6
Eternity 2.4
Obsession for Men 2.3
Hugo 1.9
Design for Men 1.8
Other 63.8

Source: *Advertising Age*, April 22, 1996, p. 20, from NPD Group.

★ 733 ★

Fragrances (SIC 2844)

Top Fragrances for Men

| Old Spice |
| Stetson |
| Jovan |
| Preferred Stock |
| Brut |
| Skin Bracer |
| Aspen |
| Drakkar Noir |
| Gillette Series |
| Other |

Brand shares of the men's fragrance market are shown for 1995.

Old Spice 10.2%
Stetson 10.0
Jovan 5.5
Preferred Stock 5.3
Brut 5.2
Skin Bracer 5.0
Aspen 4.1
Drakkar Noir 3.5
Gillette Series 3.4
Other 47.8

Source: *Brandweek*, June 3, 1996, p. 44, from Information Resources Inc.

★ 734 ★

Fragrances (SIC 2844)

Top Fragrances for Women

Brand shares of the women's fragrance market are shown for 1995.

Vanilla Fields 4.7%
Jovan 4.2
Vanderbilt 3.1
Lady Stetson 2.6
Exclamation 2.3
Sand & Sable 2.2
White Diamond 2.1
Continued on next page.

★ 734 ★ *Continued*
Fragrances (SIC 2844)

Top Fragrances for Women

Brand shares of the women's fragrance market are shown for 1995.

Vanilla Musk	2.1%
Charlie	2.0
Longing	1.9
Other	72.8

Source: *Brandweek*, June 3, 1996, p. 44, from Information Resources Inc.

★ 735 ★
Hair Care (SIC 2844)

Hair Care Market - Mexico

Shampoo	57.5%
Dyes/bleaches	19.2
Lacquers	13.4
Balsam and conditioners	7.0
Special treatments	1.7
Permanent waving	1.3

Source: *National Trade Data Bank*, May 27, 1996, p. ISA951101.

★ 736 ★
Hair Care (SIC 2844)

Hair Care Market by Segment

Data are for 1995. Total sales reached $1.36 billion.

Shampoo	42.8%
Hair conditioners	19.8
Hair sprays	14.7
Hair coloring	12.0
Hair styling gels/mousse	9.3
Home permanent kits	0.5
Other	0.8

Source: *Nonfoods Merchandising*, May 1996, p. 14, from Information Resources Inc. InfoScan.

★ 737 ★
Hair Care (SIC 2844)

Hair Coloring Market

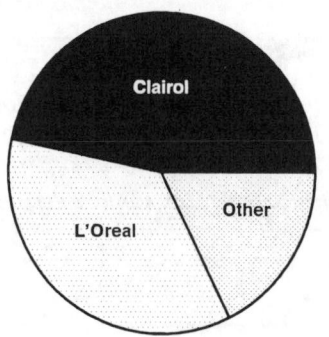

Shares are shown for the year ended February 25, 1996.

Clairol	46.6%
L'Oreal	35.8
Other	17.6

Source: *Advertising Age*, June 24, 1996, p. S14, from Information Resources Inc.

★ 738 ★
Hair Care (SIC 2844)

Hair Conditioner Makers

Shares of the $807 million market are shown in percent for 1995.

Helene Curtis	18.9%
Procter & Gamble	16.5
Alberto-Culver	10.0
Bristol-Myers Squibb	7.6
Johnson & Johnson	4.5
Others	33.8

Source: *New York Times*, February 15, 1996, p. C4, from Information Resources Inc.

★ 739 ★
Hair Care (SIC 2844)

Hair Styling Brands

Shares are shown for the first quarter of 1995.

Pantene Pro V	10.1%
Suave	6.6
Finesse	5.3
Alberto VO 5	5.0

Continued on next page.

★ 739 ★ *Continued*

Hair Care (SIC 2844)

Hair Styling Brands

Shares are shown for the first quarter of 1995.

Salon Selectives	4.6%
Infusium 23	4.2
Vidal Sasson	3.6
Alberto VO5 Hot Oil	2.0
Johnsons	1.8
Neutrogena Heatsafe	1.7
Other	55.1

Source: *Investext,* Thomson Financial Services, June 23, 1995, p. 149, from Information Resources Inc. and PaineWebber estimates.

★ 740 ★

Hair Care (SIC 2844)

Hairspray Makers

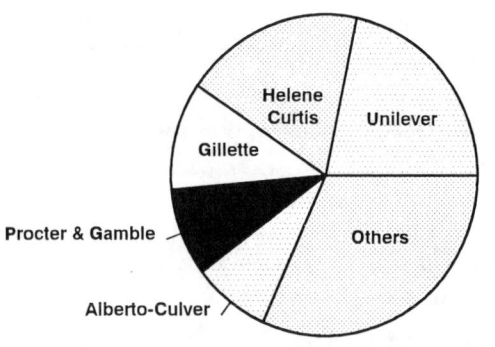

Shares of the $610 million market are shown in percent for 1995.

Unilever	21.6%
Helene Curtis	18.5
Gillette	11.0
Procter & Gamble	8.7
Alberto-Culver	7.9
Others	32.2

Source: *New York Times,* February 15, 1996, p. C4, from Information Resources Inc.

★ 741 ★

Hair Care (SIC 2844)

Leading Shampoo Brands

Shares of the market are shown for 1995.

Pantene	13.5%
Pert Plus	8.8
Head & Shoulders	7.6
Suave	7.4
Neutrogena	4.4
Finesse	4.0
Salon Selectives	3.8
Vidal Sassoon	3.5
White Rain	3.5
Revlon	3.0
Other	40.5

Source: *Brandweek,* June 3, 1996, p. 44, from Information Resources Inc.

★ 742 ★

Hair Care (SIC 2844)

Medicated Shampoo Brands

Shares of the $347 million medicated shampoo market are shown in percent.

Head & Shoulders	24.0%
Neutrogena	19.0
Selsun Blue	11.0
Denorex	10.0
Scalpicin	6.0
All other	30.0

Source: *NARD Journal,* November 1995, p. 52, from DPH & A Image Database.

★ 743 ★

Hair Care (SIC 2844)

Men's Hair Coloring Brands

Just for Men	59.0%
Grecian Formula 16	14.6
Men's Choice	13.3
Other	13.1

Source: *Advertising Age,* September 25, 1995, p. 12, from Information Resources Inc.

★ 744 ★

Hair Care (SIC 2844)

Professional Hair Product Makers

The leading makers of salon and professional hair care products are ranked by 1995 sales in millions of dollars.

Matrix/Logics/Clairol . . . . $ 390
L'Oreal/Redken 195
Nexxus 165
JPMS 150
Wella/Sebastian 135
Helene Curtis 75
Aveda 72
Zotos 62
Revlon 50
Tressa 40

Source: *DCI*, June 1996, p. 60, from Audits and Surveys.

★ 745 ★

Hair Care (SIC 2844)

Top Shampoo Brands

Brand shares are shown for the year ended June 10, 1995.

Pantene (P&G) 10.6%
Pert Plus (P&G) 10.4
Suave (Helene Curtis) 9.1
Head & Shoulders (P&G) 7.8
Salon Selectives (Helene Curtis) 3.7
Vidal Sassoon (P&G) 3.5
Alberto VO5 (Alberto-Culver) 3.5
Finesse (Helene Curtis) 3.2
Private label 2.8
White Rain (Gillette) 2.3
Other 43.1

Source: *Household and Personal Products Industry*, December 1995, p. 80, from A.C. Nielsen.

★ 746 ★

Hair Care (SIC 2844)

Top Shampoo Makers

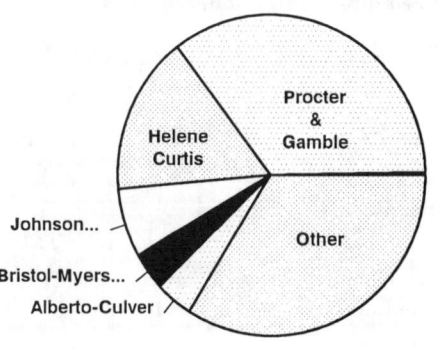

Shares of the $1.49 billion market are shown in percent for 1995.

Procter & Gamble 34.9%
Helene Curtis 16.2
Johnson & Johnson 7.2
Bristol-Myers Squibb 4.0
Alberto-Culver 3.9
Other 33.8

Source: *New York Times*, February 15, 1996, p. C4, from Information Resources Inc.

★ 747 ★

Nail Care (SIC 2844)

Nail Polish Producers

Shares are of the $309.8 million category for 1994.

Revlon 22.2%
Del Labs 20.1
L'Oreal 12.6
Cover Girl 8.7
Jean Phillipe 6.9
Maybelline 5.4
Pavlon 4.1
Max Factor 3.1
Arthur Matney 2.9
CCA Industries 1.8
Almay 1.7
Nutra Nail 1.6
Bari Cosmetics 1.1
Other 7.8

Source: *Investext*, Thomson Financial Services, June 23, 1995, p. 187, from Information Resources Inc. and PaineWebber estimates.

★ 748 ★

Nail Care (SIC 2844)

Nail Products Producers

Shares are shown for the 12 weeks ended June 18, 1995.

Revlon	22.9%
L'Oreal	11.8
Cover Girl	7.4
Maybelline	5.6
Max Factor	2.9
Almay	2.0
Other	47.4

Source: *Investext,* Thomson Financial Services, August 17, 1995, p. 66, from Information Resources Inc. and PaineWebber estimates.

★ 749 ★

Oral Care (SIC 2844)

Dentifrice Makers

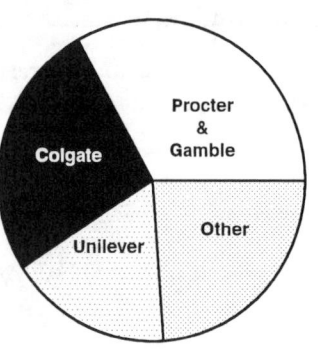

Shares are shown as of December 1995.

Procter & Gamble	33.0%
Colgate	26.0
Unilever	17.0
Other	24.0

Source: *Investext,* Thomson Financial Services, March 15, 1996, p. 33, from Information Resources Inc.

★ 750 ★

Oral Care (SIC 2844)

Denture Cleaners

Selected shares of the $137.4 million market are shown in percent.

Polident	20.3%
Fixodent Fresh	8.3
Dentu-Creme	4.8
Sea-Bond	3.1
Poli-Grip Freee	1.3
Dentu-Gel	1.1
Private-label	4.5
Other	56.6

Source: *Supermarket Business*, July 1996, p. 60, from A.C. Nielsen.

★ 751 ★

Oral Care (SIC 2844)

Oral Care Market by Segment

Shares are shown based on total sales of $1.4 billion.

Toothpaste	51.3%
Mouthwash	20.1
Toothbrush/dental accessories	18.9
Denture products	8.9
Breath aids	0.8

Source: *Nonfoods Merchandising*, May 1996, p. 14, from Information Resources Inc. InfoScan.

★ 752 ★

Oral Care (SIC 2844)

Popular Toothpastes

Shares are shown for the first quarter of 1995.

Crest	29.9%
Colgate	17.6
Mentadent	13.6
Aqua Fresh	5.9
Other	33.0

Source: *Investext,* Thomson Financial Services, June 23, 1995, p. 220, from Information Resources Inc. and PaineWebber estimates.

★ 753 ★

Oral Care (SIC 2844)

Toothpaste Brand Leaders

Shares are shown for the 52 weeks ended December 9, 1995.

Crest Tartar Control	13.6%
Metadent	11.5
Crest Advanced Formula	6.6
Colgate Original Paste	6.1
Colgate Tartar Control	6.1
Aqua-Fresh Triple Protection	3.5
Colgate Baking Soda	3.4
Arm & Hammer Dental Care	3.1
Sensodyne	2.9
Arm & Hammer Dental TC	2.6
Other	40.6

Source: *Supermarket Business*, July 1996, p. 79, from A.C. Nielsen.

★ 754 ★

Oral Care (SIC 2844)

Toothpaste Market - Canada

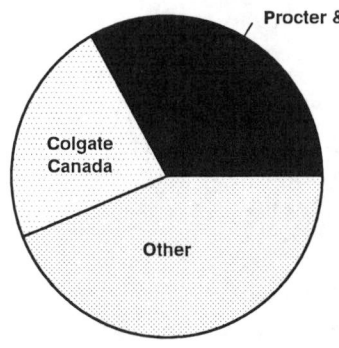

Procter & Gamble Canada

Colgate Canada

Other

Market shares are shown based on unit sales.

	1994	1995
Procter & Gamble Canada	33.9%	33.3%
Colgate Canada	21.6	23.0
Other	44.5	43.7

Source: *Investext*, Thomson Financial Services, March 5, 1996, p. 3.

★ 755 ★

Oral Care (SIC 2844)

Toothpaste Producers

Data are for 1994.

Procter & Gamble	31.4%
Colgate-Palmolive	21.5
Unilever	17.1
Church & Dwight	8.1
SmithKline Beecham	8.1
Block Drug	3.6
Den-Mat	3.4
Rembrandt	3.4
Gillette	1.1
Other	0.3

Source: *Investext*, Thomson Financial Services, June 23, 1995, p. 220, from Information Resources Inc. and PaineWebber estimates.

★ 756 ★

Oral Care (SIC 2844)

Top Antiseptic Brands

Brand shares of the $631.9 million market are shown in percent for the 52 weeks ended June 18, 1995.

Listerine	36.9%
Scope	19.6
Plax	8.7
Act	2.2
Cepacol	1.9
Viadent	1.4
Mentadent	1.4
Listermint	1.3
Oral B	1.1
Other	25.5

Source: *Nonfoods Merchandising*, December 1995, p. 58, from Information Resources Inc. InfoScan.

★ 757 ★

Oral Care (SIC 2844)

Top Dentifrices

Brand shares of the $1.447 billion market are shown in percent for the 52 weeks ended June 18, 1995.

Crest	29.4%
Colgate	18.4
Mentadent	11.9
Aquafresh	8.3
Arm & Hammer	6.4

Continued on next page.

★ 757 ★ *Continued*
Oral Care (SIC 2844)

Top Dentifrices

Brand shares of the $1.447 billion market are shown in percent for the 52 weeks ended June 18, 1995.

Closeup	3.3%
Sensodyne	3.3
Rembrandt	2.9
UltraBrite	2.0
PeroxiCare	1.7
Other	12.4

Source: *Nonfoods Merchandising*, December 1995, p. 57, from Information Resources Inc. InfoScan.

★ 758 ★
Oral Care (SIC 2844)

Top Toothpastes

Shares are shown based on total sales of $1.46 billion.

Crest	24.0%
Colgate	18.0
Mentadent	10.0
Arm & Hammer	9.0
Aquafresh	7.0
Rembrandt	5.0
Sensodyne	5.0
Close-Up	3.0
Other	19.0

Source: *NARD Journal*, June 1996, p. 52, from DPH&A Image Database.

★ 759 ★
Personal Care Products (SIC 2844)

Feminine Hygiene Products

Feminine hygiene products brand shares are shown ranked by supermarket sales for the 52 weeks ended September 9, 1995. Company names are included in parentheses.

	($000)	Share
Monistat 7 (Ortho-McNeil) . .	$ 26,059	20.6%
Massengil (SmithKline Beecham)	25,497	20.1
Summer's Eve (C.B. Fleet) . .	13,636	10.8
Mycelex-7 (Miles)	10,553	8.3
Gyne-Lotrimin (Schering-Plough)	9,255	7.3
Johnson & Johnson K-Y (Johnson & Johnson)	7,769	6.1
FDS (Alberto-Culver)	5,789	4.6
Vagisil cream (Combe)	4,015	3.2
Betadine (Blair)	1,579	1.2
Private label	9,701	7.7
Other	12,864	10.2

Source: *Nonfoods Merchandising*, April 1996, p. 14, from A.C. Nielsen.

★ 760 ★
Personal Care Products (SIC 2844)

Health & Beauty Care Sales

Distribution is shown based on $9.37 billion in sales at discount stores.

Hair care	15.5%
Analgesics	15.2
Dental care	12.3
Sanitary	12.0
Cold/cough	11.1
Shaving	10.7
Vitamins/health	7.0
External	6.7
Skin care	6.3
Other	3.2

Source: *Discount Store News*, August 5, 1996, p. 73.

★ 761 ★
Personal Care Products (SIC 2844)
Men's Grooming Market

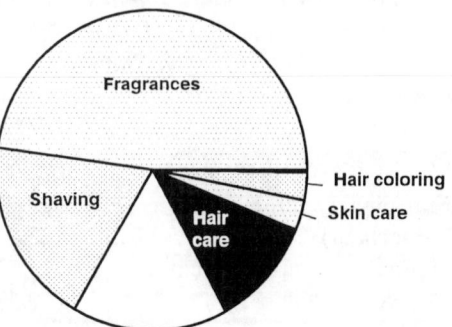

Data are based on $3.33 billion in spending.

Fragrances	48.0%
Shaving	19.0
Deodorants	16.1
Hair care	10.9
Skin care	3.0
Hair coloring	3.0

Source: *Fortune*, September 9, 1996, p. 74, from Packaged Facts.

★ 762 ★
Personal Care Products (SIC 2844)
Toiletries Market - Mexico

Data are for 1994.

Deodorants, roll-on	36.5%
Deodorants, non-alcohol bar	19.1
Bath preparations	15.7
Talc	11.9
Normal aerosol	9.4
Anti-perspirant aerosol	2.9
Shaving preparations	2.2
Deodorants, anti-perspirants aerosol	1.8
Deodorants, cream	0.5

Source: *National Trade Data Bank*, May 27, 1996, p. ISA951101.

★ 763 ★
Personal Care Products (SIC 2844)
Toiletries Market by Segment - 1995

Fragrances	22.0%
Hair care	17.0
Personal hygiene	17.0
Makeup	13.0
Skin care	13.0
Oral hygiene	11.0
Male toiletries	7.0

Source: *DCI*, June 1996, p. 28.

★ 764 ★
Personal Care Products (SIC 2844)
Women's Anti-Fungal Products

Shares of the $233 million market are shown in percent for the year ended May 26, 1996.

Monistat-7	48.4%
Femstat-3	4.0
Other	47.6

Source: *Advertising Age*, June 17, 1996, p. 10, from Information Resources Inc.

★ 765 ★
Personal Care Products (SIC 2844)
Women's Contraceptive Market

Shares of the $9.2 million market are shown for the 52 weeks ended December 9, 1995.

Contraceptol	27.1%
Gynol II	14.8
Clearplan Easy	11.5
Other	46.6

Source: *Supermarket Business*, June 1996, p. 63, from Nielsen Marketing Research.

★ 766 ★

Shaving Preparations (SIC 2844)

Top Shaving Cream Brands

Shaving cream sales through mass market outlets are shown for the 52 weeks ended July 16, 1995. Brand shares are shown in percent.

	Sales ($ mil.)	Share
Edge	$ 75.05	29.1%
Colgate	36.27	14.0
Soft Sense	34.45	13.3
Gillette Foamy	27.79	10.8
Barbasol	24.33	9.4
Gillette Series	16.67	6.5
Noxzema	13.20	5.1
Skintimate	8.43	3.3
Soft Shave	3.78	1.5
Old Spice	2.44	0.9
Other	15.86	6.1

Source: *Supermarket Business*, October 1995, p. 93, from Information Resources Inc.

★ 767 ★

Skin Care (SIC 2844)

Face Moisturizer Market

Shares are shown for the first quarter of 1995.

Procter & Gamble	41.4%
Unilever	14.4
Revlon	11.1
Johnson & Johnson	10.3
Beiersdorf	4.3
St. Ives	2.0
Helene Curtis	1.3
Suave	1.3
Maybelline	0.9
Owen Labs	0.9
Other	12.1

Source: *Investext*, Thomson Financial Services, June 23, 1995, p. 137, from Information Resources Inc. and PaineWebber estimates.

★ 768 ★

Skin Care (SIC 2844)

Hand/Body Lotion Makers

Data are for 1994.

Unilever	20.9%
Andrew Jergens	11.3
Beiersdorf	10.6
Warenr Lambert	10.4
Bausch & Lomb	6.2
Bristol-Myers	6.1
Helene-Curtis	4.8
Johnson & Johnson	4.7
St. Ives	4.2
J.N. Mitchell	1.4
E.T. Browne Drug	1.2
Revlon	1.1
Other	17.1

Source: *Investext*, Thomson Financial Services, March 2, 1995, p. 90, from Information Resources Inc.

★ 769 ★

Skin Care (SIC 2844)

Popular Skin/Body Lotions

Brand shares of the market are shown for 1995.

Intensive Care (Chesebrough-Ponds)	18.6%
Jergens (Andrew Jergens)	11.2
Lubriderm (Warner-Wellcome)	9.7
Nivea (Beiersdorf)	5.5
Suave (Warner-Wellcome)	5.3
Eucerin (Beiersdorf)	5.1
Curel (Bausch & Lomb)	4.6
Neutrogena (Neutrogena)	4.3
St. Ives (St. Ives)	4.3
Other	31.4

Source: *Brandweek*, June 3, 1996, p. 44, from Information Resources Inc.

★ 770 ★

Skin Care (SIC 2844)

Skin Care Market by Segment - Mexico

The market is shown by category. Leading brands in 1993 were Plenitude, Oil of Olay, Nivea Visage, and Pond's.

Solid creams	22.8%
Liquid creams	21.3
Special treatments	16.3
Moisturizers	14.2
Cleaners	13.0
Tonic lotions	2.7
Other	9.7

Source: *National Trade Data Bank*, March 2, 1996, p. IS9412.040.

★ 771 ★

Skin Care (SIC 2844)

Top Acne Remedies

Shares are shown for the 52 weeks ended December 9, 1995. Data are based on a $300 million category. Drug stores have a 37% share of acne product sales.

	($000)	Share
Clearasil	$ 22,644	7.5%
Oxy Clean	11,363	3.8
Stri-Dex	8,916	3.0
Neutrogena	8,805	2.9
Oxy Ten	5,529	1.8
Noxzema	4,643	1.5
Clean & Clear	2,305	0.8
Clearasil Clearstick	2,190	0.7
Clearasil Adult Care	2,151	0.7
Oxy Ten Cover	2,062	0.7
Other	229,392	76.5

Source: *Nonfoods Merchandising*, July 1996, p. 10, from A.C. Nielsen.

★ 772 ★

Sun Care (SIC 2844)

Leading Sunscreen Brands

Sunscreen brand shares are shown based on supermarket sales for the 52 weeks ended September 9, 1995. Only supermarkets with sales of $2.0 million and over are included. The total market for sun care products reached $393.8 million.

Coppertone (Schering-Plough)	26.9%
Banana Boat (Sun Pharmaceuticals)	15.3
Water Babies (Schering-Plough)	9.2
Coppertone Sport (Schering-Plough)	9.0
Hawaiian Tropic (Tanning Research Lab) . .	6.8
No-Ad (Solar Suncare)	4.3
Shade (Schering-Plough)	4.3
Bain de Soleil (Procter & Gamble)	3.4
Bullfrog (Chattem)	3.2
Vaseline Intensive Care (Chesebrough-Pond's)	2.5
Neutrogena (Neutrogena Corp/J&J)	1.7
Private label	7.0
Other	6.4

Source: *Nonfoods Merchandising*, March 1996, p. 8, from A.C. Nielsen.

★ 773 ★

Sun Care (SIC 2844)

Popular Sun Care Products

The sale of sun care products reached $393.4 million in 1995, with drug stores carving out a 44% share of total sales. The table compares the unit and dollar share at drug stores only. It is important to note that the product mix is often more varied at drug stores than at food stores and mass merchandisers.

	Unit Share	Dol. Share
Coppertone	30.3%	30.5%
Pre-Sun	13.9	11.9
Banana Boat	6.5	8.2
Shade	6.8	8.1
Bain de Soleil	6.5	6.6
Durascreen	4.0	5.8
Hawaiian Tropic	5.7	5.7
Neutrogena	5.0	5.5

Continued on next page.

★ 773 ★ *Continued*
Sun Care (SIC 2844)

Popular Sun Care Products

The sale of sun care products reached $393.4 million in 1995, with drug stores carving out a 44% share of total sales. The table compares the unit and dollar share at drug stores only. It is important to note that the product mix is often more varied at drug stores than at food stores and mass merchandisers.

	Unit Share	Dol. Share
Solbar	4.1%	4.9%
Sundown	3.4	3.5
Bullfrog	2.6	2.7
Other	11.2	6.6

Source: *Drug Topics*, April 22, 1996, p. 46, from Information Resources Inc.

★ 774 ★
Sun Care (SIC 2844)

Sun Screen Market

Data refer to suntan lotion and oil market. The total sun care market generated sales of $393.8 million for the 52 weeks ended December 3, 1995.

Sunblock SPF 15-30	30.0%
Suntan SPF 0-4	26.0
Babies/kids	13.0
Self-tanning	10.0
Sunscreen SPF 5-14	8.0
Sport	6.0
After-sun/sunburn	4.0
Face/lips	3.0

Source: *NARD Journal*, April 1996, p. 43, from Information Resources Inc.

★ 775 ★
Sun Care (SIC 2844)

Top Suntan Lotion Brands

Shares are shown for the 52 weeks September 9, 1995. Schering-Plough is the top sun care product producer with 30% share of the market.

Coppertone	29.8%
Hawaiian Tropic	18.7
Bain de Soleil	14.9
Banana Boat	14.2
Tropical Blend	9.5
Private label	5.9
Australian Gold	4.0
Neutrogena	2.3
Panama Jack	2.0
No Ad	1.8
Other	5.9

Source: *Household and Personal Products Industry*, March 1996, p. 68, from A.C. Nielsen.

★ 776 ★
Paints and Coatings (SIC 2851)

Coatings Industry

Shipments are shown for the first six months of each year. OEM stands for original equipment manufacturers.

	1994 ($ mil.)	1995 ($ mil.)	Share
Architectural	$ 2,952.8	$ 3,049.8	42.2%
OEM	2,521.2	2,760.4	38.2
Special purpose	1,532.4	1,411.7	19.5

Source: *American Paint & Coatings Journal*, September 11, 1995, p. 12, from United States Bureau of the Census.

★ 777 ★

Paints and Coatings (SIC 2851)

Environmentally Safe Coatings Market

The market for environmentally acceptable coatings in the United States is expected to grow from $1.14 billion gallons in 1994 to $1.3 billion gallons in 1999.

	1994	1999
Waterbornes	50.9%	62.0%
High-solids	9.6	10.6
Powders	6.1	8.7
Radiation-cure	0.6	0.8
Other	32.9	17.9

Source: *Industrial Paint & Powder*, October 1995, p. 8, from Business Communications.

★ 778 ★

Paints and Coatings (SIC 2851)

Linings and Coatings Market Shares

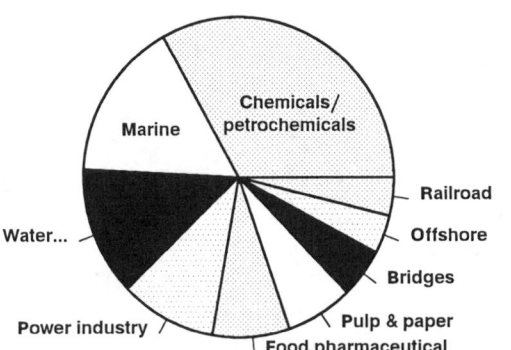

The market for protective linings and coatings is shown by sector in percent.

Chemicals/petrochemicals	33.0%
Marine	16.0
Water & waste water	13.0
Power industry	10.0
Food pharmaceutical	8.0
Pulp & paper	7.0
Bridges	5.0
Offshore	4.0
Railroad	4.0

Source: *Chemical Marketing Reporter*, October 2, 1995, p. SR10, from P.D. Lovett & Co.

★ 779 ★

Paints and Coatings (SIC 2851)

Paint Materials Market

The total market is estimated to grow from 11.5 million pounds in 1994 to 12.55 million pounds in 1998.

	1994	1998
Solvents	41.7%	35.8%
Synthetic resins	24.3	26.3
Pigments	12.2	13.7
Additives	1.7	1.8
Other chemicals	20.0	22.3

Source: *Industrial Paint & Powder*, November 1995, p. 9, from Decision Resources Inc. and G.A. Habib & Associates Inc.

★ 780 ★

Paints and Coatings (SIC 2851)

Paint and Coatings Market - Mexico

Shares are shown for 1993. The domestic use market was lead by vinyls and acrylics; industrial paints market was lead by wood varnishes and primary auto painting.

Domestic use	59.0%
Industrial	19.2
Solvents and thinners	16.6
Automotive refinishing	5.7

Source: *National Trade Data Bank*, March 2, 1996, p. IS9505.324.

★ 781 ★

Paints and Coatings (SIC 2851)

Popular Full-Size Auto Colors

Shipments are shown by color in North America.

	1994	1995
White	18.1%	18.9%
Dark green	19.4	17.3
Medium red	10.0	11.2
Light brown	10.0	9.7
Black	5.7	5.9
Silver	5.7	5.4
Teal/aqua	5.5	4.6

Continued on next page.

★ 781 ★ *Continued*
Paints and Coatings (SIC 2851)

Popular Full-Size Auto Colors

Shipments are shown by color in North America.

	1994	1995
Medium blue	4.0%	4.4%
Bright red	4.2	4.4
Light blue	2.7	4.3
Other	14.7	13.9

Source: *Purchasing*, March 7, 1996, p. 55, from DuPont Automotive.

★ 782 ★
Paints and Coatings (SIC 2851)

Popular Luxury Car Colors

Data are for 1995.

White	14.9%
Tan	13.4
Green	13.0
Black	9.7
Red	9.1
Others	39.9

Source: *WARD's Auto World*, March 1996, p. 20, from DuPont Automotive.

★ 783 ★
Paints and Coatings (SIC 2851)

Popular Sport Car Colors

Shipments are shown by color in North America.

Dark green	15.2%
White	14.4
Medium red	11.3
Black	11.2
Bright red	9.5
Other	38.4

Source: *USA TODAY*, December 26, 1995, p. 2B, from DuPont Automotive.

★ 784 ★
Paints and Coatings (SIC 2851)

Top 5 Truck Colors

Data are for 1995.

White	23.8%
Green	15.9
Black	9.1
Red	8.5
Burgandy	7.5
Others	35.2

Source: *WARD's Auto World*, March 1996, p. 20, from DuPont Automotive.

★ 785 ★
Paints and Coatings (SIC 2851)

Top Coatings Firms

The top firms are ranked by sales in billions of dollars. Shares of the group are shown in percent.

	Sales ($ bil.)	% of Group
Sherwin-Williams	$ 1.80	22.5%
PPG Industries	1.70	21.3
DuPont	0.85	10.6
ICI	0.75	9.4
BASF	0.70	8.8
Akzo Nobel	0.60	7.5
Courtaulds	0.60	7.5
Morton	0.60	7.5
Benjamin Moore	0.40	5.0

Source: *Chemicalweek*, May 31, 1995, p. 7, from Kusumager & Nelfi Inc.

★ 786 ★
Paints and Coatings (SIC 2851)

Waterproofing Market

Shares of the exterior cleaning/waterproofing market are shown in percent.

Thompson's Water Seal	57.4%
Other	42.6

Source: *Advertising Age*, July 1, 1996, p. 15.

★ 787 ★

Charcoal (SIC 2861)

Charcoal Brands

Kingsford

Private label

Royal Oak

Embers

Royal Oak Plus

Other

Shares of the $423.1 million market are shown in percent for the 52 weeks ended September 9, 1995.

Kingsford (Clorox) 58.8%
Private label 23.5
Royal Oak (Royal Oak Enterprises) 7.5
Embers (TS Ragsdale) 3.5
Royal Oak Plus (Royal Oak Enterprises) . . 1.3
Other 5.4

Source: *Nonfoods Merchandising*, March 1996, p. 10, from A.C. Nielsen.

★ 788 ★

Organic Chemicals (SIC 2865)

Orthoxylene Makers

Companies are ranked by capacity in millions of pounds.

	(mil.)	Share
Exxon	280	24.2%
Koch	270	23.4
Lyondell	270	23.4
Phillips	180	15.6
Mobil	155	13.4

Source: *Chemical Marketing Reporter*, August 7, 1995, p. 45.

★ 789 ★

Organic Chemicals (SIC 2865)

Paraxylene Makers

Production is shown in thousands of metric tons.

Amoco Chemical 1,400
Koch Industries 590
Exxon Chemical 455
Phillips Chemical 340
Chevron Chemical 260
Lyondell Petrochemical 195
Mobil Chemical 75

Source: *Chemicalweek*, April 10, 1996, p. 45, from company reports.

★ 790 ★

Organic Chemicals (SIC 2865)

Phthalic Anhydride Makers

Production in North America is shown in millions of pounds annually.

Exxon Chemical 260
Aristech 250
Sterling Chemicals 180
Koppers Industries 175
Stepan 175
Grupo Celanese 70
Grupo Primex 60
Grupo Idesa 50

Source: *Chemicalweek*, December 6, 1995, p. 64, from SRI International.

★ 791 ★

Organic Chemicals (SIC 2865)

Styrene Producers

North American firms are ranked by capacities shown in millions of pounds. Cos-Mar's figures represent a joint venture of Fina and GE Plastics.

	(mil.)	Share
Arco Chemical	2,335.0	18.3%
Cos-Mar	2,000.0	15.7
Chevron	1,700.0	13.3
Dow Chemical	1,560.0	12.2
Sterling Chemicals	1,500.0	11.8

Continued on next page.

★ 791 ★ *Continued*
Organic Chemicals (SIC 2865)

Styrene Producers

North American firms are ranked by capacities shown in millions of pounds. Cos-Mar's figures represent a joint venture of Fina and GE Plastics.

	(mil.)	Share
Huntsman	1,250.0	9.8%
Shell Canada Chem.	990.0	7.8
Amoco	825.0	6.5
Novacor	600.0	4.7

Source: *Chemicalweek*, April 24, 1996, p. 12, from company reports.

★ 792 ★
Organic Chemicals (SIC 2865)

Textile Dye Sales

Colorant sales to the textile industry were projected to reach $920 million in 1995. Shares are shown by type of dye.

Reactive dyes	29.0%
Dispersive dyes	22.0
Acid & premetalized dyes	12.0
Sulfur dyes	11.0
Pigments	10.0
Direct dyes	6.0
Basic dyes	6.0
Vat dyes	3.0
Naftol dyes	1.0

Source: *Chemical & Engineering News*, January 15, 1996, p. 11, from industry estimates.

★ 793 ★
Organic Chemicals (SIC 2865)

Toluene Diisocyanate Makers

Production is shown in thousands of metric tons (m.t.) per year. The largest end use market is flexible foam, with an 89% share.

	(000)	Share
Bayer	105	26.6%
BASF	100	25.3
Olin	100	25.3
Dow Chemical	65	16.5
Rubicon	25	6.3

Source: *Chemicalweek*, September 13, 1995, p. 39, from Schroder Wertheim and SRI International.

★ 794 ★
Organic Chemicals (SIC 2865)

Top Maleic Anhydride Producers

The top companies in North America are ranked by production in millions of pounds.

Huntsman	220
Bayer	185
Ashland	140
Amoco	90
Bartek Chemical	40
Derivados Maleicos	15

Source: *Chemicalweek*, October 25, 1995, p. 38, from SRI International, company reports, and Schroder Wertheim.

★ 795 ★
Organic Chemicals (SIC 2869)

Acrylonitrile Producers

Capacity in North America is shown by company. Data are in thousands of tons. Pemex is in Mexico.

BP Chemicals	495
Sterling Chemicals	330
Monsanto	225
Cytec Industries	220
DuPont	170
Pemex	160

Source: *Chemicalweek*, March 27, 1996, p. 36, from SRI Consulting.

★ 796 ★
Organic Chemicals (SIC 2869)

Caprolactam Makers

Producers are ranked by capacity in millions of pounds.

AlliedSignal	660
BASF	510
DSM	360

Source: *Chemical Marketing Reporter*, October 2, 1995, p. 57.

★ 797 ★

Organic Chemicals (SIC 2869)

Citric Acid Production

Citric acid production capacity is shown in millions of pounds per year.

Archer Daniels Midland 180.0
Cargill 160.0
Haarmann & Reimer 150.0

Source: *Chemical Marketing Reporter*, April 1, 1996, p. 37.

★ 798 ★

Organic Chemicals (SIC 2869)

Corrosion Inhibitor Demand

	1994 ($ mil.)	2000 ($ mil.)	Share
Motor vehicles . . .	$ 1,344.0	$ 1,970.0	27.7%
Water treatment . . .	690.0	1,115.0	15.7
Containers and closures	719.0	905.0	12.7
Industrial maintenance	515.0	805.0	11.3
Machinery and equipment	530.0	730.0	10.3
Petroleum industry . .	642.0	710.0	10.0
Other transportation equipment	403.0	560.0	7.9
Heat transfer fluids and other	296.0	325.0	4.6

Source: *InTech*, April 1996, p. 22, from Freedonia Group.

★ 799 ★

Organic Chemicals (SIC 2869)

Cyclohexane Makers

Producers are ranked by capacity in millions of gallons per year. Shares are shown based on a total capacity of 545 million gallons.

	(mil.)	Share
Phillips	290	53.2%
Huntsman	75	13.8
Caribbean Petroleum	50	9.2
Chevron	40	7.3
Sun Refining	35	6.4
Citgo	30	5.5
Koch	25	4.6

Source: *Chemical Marketing Reporter*, November 13, 1995, p. 45.

★ 800 ★

Organic Chemicals (SIC 2869)

Dipropylene Glycol

Production capacity is shown in millions of pounds per year.

Arco 50
Dow 40
Huntsman 12
Eastman 8
Olin 8

Source: *Chemical Marketing Reporter*, February 19, 1996, p. 45.

★ 801 ★

Organic Chemicals (SIC 2869)

Formaldehyde Producers

North American leading formaldehyde producers are ranked by capacity shown in millions of pounds per year.

Hoechst Celanese 2,290.0
Georgia-Pacific 2,065.0
Borden 1,925.0
DuPont 900.0
Borden Chemicals 640.0
Continued on next page.

★ 801 ★　*Continued*
Organic Chemicals (SIC 2869)

Formaldehyde Producers

North American leading formaldehyde producers are ranked by capacity shown in millions of pounds per year.

Neste Resin	600.0
Mexico	405.0
Dyne Polymers	300.0
Perstorp	220.0

Source: *Chemicalweek*, October 4, 1995, p. 18, from Schroder Wertheim and company reports.

★ 802 ★
Organic Chemicals (SIC 2869)

Solvents Demand

Distribution is based on 13.738 billion pounds in 1994.

Hydrocarbons	31.9%
Ether	23.8
Alcohol	21.2
Ketone	7.7
Chlorinated	7.4
Ester	5.4
Other	2.6

Source: *Chemicalweek*, November 8, 1995, p. 54, from Freedonia Group.

★ 803 ★
Organic Chemicals (SIC 2869)

Sorbitol Makers

Production capacity is shown in millions of pounds per year.

	(mil.)	Share
ADM	150	24.4%
Roquette America	150	24.4
SPI	125	20.3
Lonza	100	16.3
Hoffmann-La Roche	60	9.8
Ethichem	30	4.9

Source: *Chemical Marketing Reporter*, October 30, 1995, p. 27.

★ 804 ★
Organic Chemicals (SIC 2869)

U.S. Solvents Market

The market is shown based on 34 billion pounds in 1995 and 38 billion pounds in 2000.

	1995	2000
Oxygenated	58.0%	65.0%
Aromatic	19.0	18.0
Aliphatic	19.0	18.0
Other	4.0	1.0

Source: *Chemicalweek*, August 2, 1995, p. 31, from Dieter Stoye.

★ 805 ★
Organic Chemicals (SIC 2869)

Who Makes Methanol

The top manufacturers in North America are ranked by production in thousands of metric tons (m.t.).

	M.t. (000)	Share
Methanex	2,290	22.9%
Hoechst Celanese	1,900	19.0
Terra Industries	970	9.7
Borden Chemicals & Plastics	900	9.0
Lyondell Petrochemical	732	7.3
Quantum Chemical	600	6.0
Georgia Gulf	480	4.8
Ashland Chemical	460	4.6
Sterling-BP Chemicals	450	4.5
Enron Methanol	375	3.7
Pemex	210	2.1
Eastman Chemical	195	1.9
Air Products & Chemicals	180	1.8
Others	260	2.6

Source: *Chemicalweek*, June 5, 1996, p. 39, from Chemical Market Associates Incorporated and DeWitt & Co.

★ 806 ★
Agrichemicals (SIC 2870)

Insecticide Producers

Firms are ranked by sales in millions of dollars.

Bayer	$ 1,065
AgrEvo	699
Rhone-Poulenc	670
Dow Elanco	520

Continued on next page.

★ 806 ★ *Continued*
Agrichemicals (SIC 2870)

Insecticide Producers

Firms are ranked by sales in millions of dollars.

Zeneca	$ 510
FMC	500
DuPont	230
Ciba	180
BASF	80

Source: *Chemicalweek*, August 7, 1996, p. 29, from Lehman Brothers.

★ 807 ★
Agrichemicals (SIC 2870)

Leading Agrichemical Firms

Firms are ranked by estimated 1995 sales in millions of dollars.

Monsanto	$ 8,960
Ciba-Geigy	1,725
Pioneer Hi-Bred	1,530
DeKalb Genetics	319
Mycogen	113
Delta & Pine Land	79
Calgene	57
Ecogen	12

Source: *Forbes*, May 20, 1996, p. 160, from IBES Inc.

★ 808 ★
Agrichemicals (SIC 2870)

Pesticide Production

Data are in millions of pounds for 1994.

Herbicides	868
Insecticides	253
Nematicides	86
Fungicides	72
Plant growth regulators	8

Source: *Chemical & Engineering News*, June 24, 1996, p. 46, from American Crop Protection Association.

★ 809 ★
Agrichemicals (SIC 2870)

Pesticide Sales

Shares are shown based on total sales of $6.16 billion in 1995.

Herbicides	56.1%
Insecticides	25.6
Fungicides	9.6
Biopesticides	1.3
Other conventional pesticides	7.5

Source: *Chemical & Engineering News*, April 29, 1996, p. 36, from Freedonia Group.

★ 810 ★
Agrichemicals (SIC 2873)

Fertilizer Users in Canada

Farmers	80.0%
Commercial landscapers	17.0
Consumers	3.0

Source: *National Trade Data Bank*, March 2, 1996, p. 111089980.

★ 811 ★
Phosphates (SIC 2874)

Ammonium Phosphate Makers

Companies are ranked by capacity in thousands of short tons per year. Shares are shown based on a capacity of 9.21 million short tons.

	(000)	Share
IMC Agrico	3,280	36.7%
Cargill	1,375	15.4
CF Industries	1,100	12.3
Farmland Hydro	650	7.3
PCS	460	5.1
OxyChem	390	4.4
US Agri-Chemicals	350	3.9
Mississippi Phosphate	335	3.7
Mulberry Phosphates	320	3.6
Mobil Mining	275	3.1
J.R. Simplot	200	2.2
SF Phosphates	200	2.2

Source: *Chemical Marketing Reporter*, September 18, 1995, p. 53.

★ 812 ★
Phosphates (SIC 2874)

Industrial Phosphate Production

Phosphate production is shown by end use in thousands of short tons. Total production in 1998 is expected to reach 445,000-534,000 tons.

	(000)	Share
Food, beverages	118.0	21.3%
I&I cleaners	88.0	15.9
Autodish	65.0	11.8
Metal/plastics	32.0	5.8
Water treatment	31.3	5.7
Laundry detergent	26.0	4.7
Dentifrices	4.4	0.8
Other consumer	10.0	1.8
Other	178.0	32.2

Source: *Chemical Marketing Reporter*, October 16, 1995, p. 22, from SRI International.

★ 813 ★
Phosphates (SIC 2874)

Phosphoric Acid Capacity by State - 1995

Production is shown in metric tons (m.t.) by state.

	M.t.	Share
Florida	7,865	66.2%
Louisiana	1,533	12.9
North Carolina	1,146	9.6
Idaho	599	5.0
Mississippi	315	2.7
Texas	220	1.9
Wyoming	200	1.7

Source: *Engineering & Mining Journal*, March 1996, p. 71.

★ 814 ★
Fertilizers (SIC 2879)

Fertilizer Production

Phosphate rock	42,657
Diammonium phosphate	15,722
Ammonia	15,670
Phosphoric acid	12,272
Urea	5,177
Ammonium nitrate	2,643
Monoammonium phosphate	2,617
Ammonium sulfate	2,579

Potassium chloride	1,840
Concentrated superphosphate	1,631

Source: *Chemical & Engineering News*, June 24, 1996, p. 46.

★ 815 ★
Pesticides (SIC 2879)

Corn Herbicide Market

Shares are for 1995.

Atrazine	13.8%
Dual II	8.0
Banvel	7.8
Accent	7.1
24-D	6.2
Buctril	5.7
Harness	5.0
Extrazine	4.3
Bicep	3.8
Lasso/Lasso MT	2.7
Other	35.6

Source: *Investext*, Thomson Financial Services, February 22, 1996, p. 34.

★ 816 ★
Pesticides (SIC 2879)

Pesticides Market

Spending reached $765.56 million in 1994.

Aerosols	43.6%
Non-chemical pest control	27.6
Personal insect repellants	16.5
Pastes, solids, strips	6.6
Liquid (non-aerosol)	5.7

Source: *Supermarket Business*, September 1995, p. 70.

★ 817 ★

Rat Poison (SIC 2879)

Rat Poison Sales by City

New York City

Los Angeles

Houston

Philadelphia

Dallas

San Antonio

Cities are ranked by supermarket sales of rodent killers in millions of dollars in 1995. Data are for the 52 weeks ended November 25, 1995.

New York City	$ 1.6
Los Angeles	1.2
Houston	1.1
Philadelphia	1.0
Dallas	0.8
San Antonio	0.7

Source: *USA TODAY*, March 27, 1995, p. A1, from A.C. Nielsen Scanfact.

★ 818 ★

Adhesives (SIC 2891)

Adhesives Market - 1995

The market was valued at $7.1 billion in 1995.

Construction	20.0%
Packaging	16.0
Transportation	15.0
Textile	13.0
Primary wood bonding	10.0
Other	26.0

Source: *Chemicalweek*, March 27, 1996, p. 29, from Kusumgar & Nerlfi.

★ 819 ★

Adhesives (SIC 2891)

Adhesives Market by Type

The market was valued at $9.4 billion.

Waterborne	38.0%
Hot melt	16.0
Solventborne	16.0
Other	30.0

Source: *Chemicalweek*, March 27, 1996, p. 28, from ChemQuest.

★ 820 ★

Printing Ink (SIC 2893)

Gravure Ink Use

Consumption is shown in millions of dollars.

	($ mil.)	Share
Advertising supplements	$ 110.0	16.7%
Magazines	90.0	13.6
Catalogs	70.0	10.6
Folding cartons	70.0	10.6
Giftwrap & decorative	70.0	10.6
Flexible cartons	65.0	9.8
Newspaper magazines	40.0	6.1
Flexible film	25.0	3.8
Flexible foil	25.0	3.8
Labels	15.0	2.3
Household paper	10.0	1.5
Wallcoverings and others	70.0	10.6

Source: *American Ink Maker*, November 1995, p. 46.

★ 821 ★

Printing Ink (SIC 2893)

Largest Ink Companies

Companies are ranked by sales in millions of dollars. Shares of the group are shown in percent.

	($ mil.)	% of Group
Sun Chemical	$ 800	33.5%
Flint	600	25.2
INX International	275	11.5
Ink Company	115	4.8
Zeneca	115	4.8
SICPA	85	3.6
Heritage	70	2.9
Superior Printing Ink	70	2.9
Thrall	70	2.9
Progressive Printing Ink	65	2.7
Seigwerk	65	2.7
CZ Inks	55	2.3

Source: *Graphic Arts Monthly*, March 1996, p. 62.

★ 822 ★

Printing Ink (SIC 2893)

Printing Ink Producers

| Sun Chemical |
| Flin Ink Corp. |
| INX Intl Ink Co. |
| BASF Corp., Graphics Group |
| Zeneca Specialty Ink. |
| Ink Company |
| Superior Printing Ink Co., Inc. |
| CZ Inks Div., James River |
| Heritage Inks International |
| Siegwerk, Inc. |
| Scipa Securink |
| Progressive Ink Co. |
| Others |

Shares are shown in percent for 1994. Data are for North America.

	Sales ($ mil.)	Share
Sun Chemical	$ 850.0	25.2%
Flin Ink Corp.	500.0	14.8
INX Intl Ink Co.	240.0	7.1
BASF Corp., Graphics Group	155.0	4.6
Zeneca Specialty Ink.	120.0	3.6
Ink Company	100.0	3.0
Superior Printing Ink Co., Inc.	70.0	2.1
CZ Inks Div., James River	65.0	1.9
Heritage Inks International	65.0	1.9
Siegwerk, Inc.	65.0	1.9
Scipa Securink	60.0	1.8
Progressive Ink Co.	50.0	1.5
Others	1,030.0	30.6

Source: *American Ink Maker*, December 1995, p. 18, from *Leading Edge Reports*.

★ 823 ★

Printing Ink (SIC 2893)

Printing Ink Use - 1995

Data show how printing ink is used in North America.

	($ mil.)	Share
Lithography (offset)	$ 1,673	45.8%
Flexography	730	20.0
Gravure	687	18.8
Specialty - plate	260	7.1
Specialty - plateless	200	5.5
Letterpress	100	2.7

Source: *American Ink Maker*, February 1996, p. 14.

★ 824 ★

Carbon Black (SIC 2895)

U.S. Carbon Black Makers

Capacity is shown in millions of pounds.

Cabot	780
Columbian Chemicals	595
Ameripol-Synpol	535
Sid Richardson Carbon	535
Degussa	532
China Synthetic Rubber	435
Chevron Chemical	20
Ebonex	8
General Carbon	1
Hoover Color	1

Source: *Chemical & Engineering News*, July 17, 1995, p. 33, from SRI International.

★ 825 ★

Lighter Fluid (SIC 2899)

Top Charcoal/Wood Lighter Brands

Shares are shown for the 52 weeks ended September 9, 1995.

Private label	42.9%
Kingsford	18.8
Gulf Lite Charcoal Starter	14.8
Royal Oak	7.2
Wizard	7.1
Other	9.2

Source: *Nonfoods Merchandising*, March 1996, p. 10, from A.C. Nielsen.

★ 826 ★

Salt (SIC 2899)

Leading U.S. Salt Producers

Companies are ranked by production in thousands of short tons per year.

	(000)	Share
Akzo Salt	10,255.0	20.3%
Morton International	6,260.0	12.4
Cargill	3,875.0	7.7
Carey Salt	1,700.0	3.4
Great Lake Minerals	3,000.0	5.9
Hutchinson Salt	600.0	1.2
Corpus Christi Brine	525.0	1.0
United Salt	525.0	1.0
Independent Salt	500.0	1.0
North American Salt	300.0	0.6
Lyons Salt	250.0	0.5
Moab Salt	200.0	0.4
Pacific Salt & Chemical	200.0	0.4
Western Salt	125.0	0.2
Redmond Clay & Salt	80.0	0.2
New Mexico Salt & Mineral	30.0	0.1
Huck Salt	15.0	0.0
Don McKibben Trucking	10.0	0.0
Salt Products	10.0	0.0
Others	22,069.0	43.7

Source: *Industrial Minerals*, September 1995, p. 85.

SIC 29 - Petroleum and Coal Products

★ 827 ★

Fuels (SIC 2911)

U.S. Gasoline Imports

Imports of finished gasoline are shown in thousands of barrels per day in 1995.

	(000)	Share
Virgin Islands	102.0	38.8%
Canada	61.0	23.2
Western Europe	53.0	20.2
Venezuela	28.0	10.6
Saudi Arabia	8.0	3.0
Others	6.0	2.3
Other Western Hemisphere	5.0	1.9

Source: *Oil & Gas Journal*, April 22, 1996, p. 25, from Energy Information Administration.

★ 828 ★

Petroleum Refining (SIC 2911)

Leading Petroleum Refiners

Leading refiners are ranked by 1995 revenues in millions of dollars. Shares of the group are shown in percent.

	Rev. ($ mil.)	% of Group
Exxon	$ 110,009	29.2%
Mobil	66,724	17.7
Texaco	36,787	9.8
Chevron	32,094	8.5
Amoco	27,665	7.3
USX	18,214	4.8
Atlantic Richfield	16,739	4.4
Phillips Petroleum	13,521	3.6
Ashland	11,251	3.0
Coastal	10,223	2.7
Sun	8,370	2.2

	Rev. ($ mil.)	% of Group
Unocal	$ 7,527	2.0%
Amerada Hess	7,525	2.0
Tosco	7,284	1.9
Mapco	3,310	0.9

Source: *Fortune*, April 29, 1996, p. F58.

★ 829 ★

Lubricants (SIC 2992)

Industrial Lubricant Demand

	1994	2000
Nondurable manufacturing	24.2%	25.3%
Process oils	18.5	20.3
General industrial oils	19.2	18.6
Durable manufacturing	16.3	15.4
Non-manufacturing	9.5	9.3
Industrial engine oils	5.4	5.0
Metalworking fluids	4.4	3.9
Greases and other	2.4	2.2

Source: *Purchasing*, July 11, 1996, p. 152, from Freedonia Group.

★ 830 ★

Lubricants (SIC 2992)

Motor Oil Market

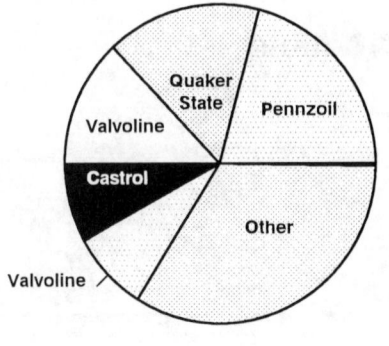

Data are for 1995.

Pennzoil	21.0%
Quaker State	16.0
Valvoline	13.0
Castrol	8.0
Valvoline	8.0
Other	34.0

Source: *Aftermarket Business*, March 1996, p. 15, from Pennzoil.

SIC 30 - Rubber and Misc. Plastics Products

Tires (SIC 3011)

Replacement Passenger Tire Makers

Replacement tire market share leaders are shown based on sales. Private label tires are excluded.

Goodyear	16.0%
Michelin	9.0
Firestone	8.0
General	6.0
Kelly-Springfield	5.0
Bridgstone	4.0
Cooper	4.0
B.F. Goodrich	4.0
Uniroyal	3.0
Dayton	2.0
Dunlop	2.0
Mastercraft	2.0
Yokohama	2.0
Lee	2.0
Others	31.0

Source: *Tire Business*, December 11, 1995, p. 12.

Tires (SIC 3011)

Tire Market - 1995

The replacement market is shown by company, based on a total of 166.5 million tires.

Goodyear	16.0%
Michelin/Uniroyal/B.F. Goodrich	15.0
Bridgestone/Firestone	12.0
General Tire	4.5
Cooper Tires	4.0
Kelly Tires	4.0
Sears	4.0
Other	40.5

Source: *New York Times*, July 20, 1996, p. 21, from *Modern Tire Dealer*.

★ 833 ★

Tires (SIC 3011)

Tire Market - North America

Data are for 1995.

Goodyear	33.0%
Michelin/Uniroyal/Goodrich	22.5
Bridgestone/Firestone	14.5
Continental General Tire	6.0
Cooper Tire & Rubber Co.	2.0
Other	22.0

Source: *Rubber & Plastics News*, August 14, 1995, p. 24, from Fundamental Research Inc.

★ 834 ★

Tires (SIC 3011)

Tire Market Leaders - North America

Data are for 1994.

Goodyear	28.9%
Michelin/Uniroyal/Goodrich	22.6
Bridgestone/Firestone	20.0
Continental General Tire	7.4
Cooper	6.4
Others	15.0

Source: *Tire Business*, December 11, 1995, p. 12.

★ 835 ★

Tires (SIC 3011)

Tire Shipments

Data are in millions of units.

	1994	1995	1996
Passenger replacement	170.0	167.0	171.0
Passenger OE	58.5	57.8	58.2
Light truck replacement	26.4	27.5	28.5
Light truck OE	5.9	6.2	6.2

Source: *Rubber World*, September 1995, p. 14, from Rubber Manufacturers Association.

★ 836 ★

Athletic Footwear (SIC 3021)

Men's Athletic Shoe Market

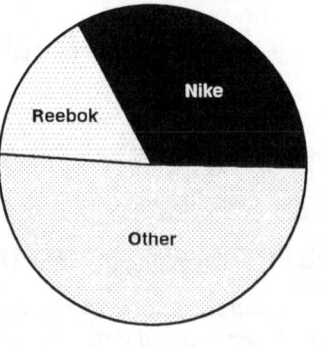

Shares are shown for the year ended April 1995.

Nike	33.0%
Reebok	16.0
Other	51.0

Source: *USA TODAY*, October 11, 1995, p. B1, from ADS/Target Research.

★ 837 ★

Athletic Footwear (SIC 3021)

Sports Shoe Market

Data are for 1995.

Nike	36.98%
Reebok	20.40
Fila	5.56
Adidas	5.19
Keds	3.58
L.A. Gear	3.00
Converse	2.92
Air Walk	2.71
New Balance	2.21
Other	17.45

Source: *Investext,* Thomson Financial Services, March 13, 1996, p. 9, from Sporting Goods Intelligence.

★ 838 ★
Athletic Footwear (SIC 3021)

Top Sports Shoe Makers

Athletic shoe manufacturers are ranked by 1995 sales in millions of dollars. Champion includes golf shoes. Nike lead the market with an estimated 37% share.

Nike	$ 2,309.4
Reebok	1,404.8
Fila	398.8
Adidas	350.0
Converse	208.0
L.A. Gear	192.5
New Balance	151.0
Asics Tiger	121.9
Foot-Joy	115.0
Spalding	114.0
K-Swiss	89.2
British Knights	85.0
Avia	73.0
Etonic	56.0
Saucony	47.0
Puma	42.0
Turntec-Nevados-OP	40.0
Mizuno	32.5
Brooks	27.0
Mitre	24.0

Source: *Sportstyle*, May 1996, p. 28.

★ 839 ★
Athletic Footwear (SIC 3021)

Women's Sports Shoe Market

Shares are for 1994.

Reebok	25.0%
Nike	15.0
Other	60.0

Source: *Investext,* Thomson Financial Services, August 22, 1995, p. 9, from Sporting Goods Manufacturers Association, Footwear Manufacturers Institute, Sporting Goods Intelligence, and Donaldson, Lufkin & Jenrette.

★ 840 ★
Hoses (SIC 3050)

Hose Shipments by Segment

Total shipments rose from $1.55 billion in 1993 to $2.07 billion in 1998.

	1993	1998
Hydraulic	39.8%	41.8%
Nonhydraulic	19.6	19.3
Wrapped & reinforced	5.5	4.6
Circular woven textile	3.2	2.9
Braided	2.3	1.9
Other	29.6	29.5

Source: *Purchasing*, May 23, 1996, p. S14, from Freedonia Group.

★ 841 ★
Belts (SIC 3052)

Synchronous Belt Users

Production is shown in North America for 1993.

	No.	Share
GM	3,379	47.1%
Ford	2,302	32.1
Chrysler	1,500	20.9

Source: *European Rubber Journal*, June 1996, p. 42.

★ 842 ★
Rubber Seals (SIC 3053)

Bonded Piston Seal Market

Federal-Mogul	75.0%
Other	25.0

Source: *Rubber & Plastics News*, May 20, 1996, p. 1.

★ 843 ★
Rubber Products (SIC 3069)

Best-Selling Condoms

Shares of the $41.3 million market are shown for the 52 weeks ended December 9, 1995.

Trojan	30.7%
Trojan-Enz	22.7
LifeStyles	13.6
Sheik Super Thin	4.4
Sheik Elite	3.1
Class Act	3.0

Continued on next page.

Rubber Products (SIC 3069)

Best-Selling Condoms

Shares of the $41.3 million market are shown for the 52 weeks ended December 9, 1995.

Touch	2.5%
Ramses Extra	2.4
Other	17.6

Source: *Supermarket Business*, June 1996, p. 63, from Nielsen Marketing Research.

★ 844 ★
Plastic Products (SIC 3080)

Canadian Plastic Product Use - Building Materials

Pipes and fittings	34.6%
Insulation	23.0
Siding and soffit	19.0
Cladding	14.5
Flooring, wire and cable	8.9

Source: *National Trade Data Bank*, March 2, 1996, p. 111092697.

★ 845 ★
Plastic Products (SIC 3080)

Plastic Packaging Industry - Canada

Injection molded thinwall containers/ closures	22.5%
Bags	22.5
Blow molded bottles/containers	14.4
Cases/crates	11.1
Thermoformed containers/lids	5.2
Food wrap and other wrap	5.1
Coextrustion, lamination, and extrusion coating	4.7
Ovenable trays and containers	2.4
Other	12.1

Source: *National Trade Data Bank*, March 2, 1996, p. 111092697.

★ 846 ★
Plastic Products (SIC 3081)

Plastic Film & Sheet Makers

North American leading manufacturers are ranked by sales in millions of dollars for their latest fiscal year.

DuPont Co.	$ 1,300.0
Mobile Chemical Co.	1,000.0
Bemis Co. Inc.	653.5
First Brands Corp.	619.7
American National Can Co.	500.0
Cryovac Division	500.0
Printpack Inc.	465.0
Huntsman Packaging Corp.	437.0
ICI Americas Inc.	433.2
James River Corp. Packaging Business . .	420.0

Source: *Plastics News*, September 18, 1995, p. 23.

★ 847 ★
Plastic Products (SIC 3081)

Plastic Sheet Producers

North American companies are ranked by plastic sheet sales in millions of dollars. Some of the figures are estimates. DuPont Co., GenCorp Plastic Films Division, Pentaplast of America Inc., and Twinpak Inc. figures were not included.

Spartech Plastics	$ 262.9
AtoHaas North America Inc.	205.0
Primex Plastics Corp.	197.4
ICI Americas Inc.	181.9
GSE Lining Technology Inc.	180.0
Cyro Industries	161.0
GE Plastics Structured Prod. Div.	154.0
O'Sullivan Corp.	142.2
Kama Corp.	127.5
Uniroyal Technology Corp.	105.6
Packaging Corp. of America Spec. Pack. Grp.	91.2
HPG International Inc.	81.0

Source: *Plastics News*, September 18, 1995, p. 20.

★ 848 ★
Laminates (SIC 3083)

Leading Laminate Brands

Shares of the decorative laminates market are shown in percent.

Wilsonart	48.0%
Other	52.0

Source: *Chicago Tribune*, January 22, 1996, p. D4.

★ 849 ★
Plastic Pipes (SIC 3084)

Polyethylene Pipe Market

Gas distribution	
Industrial/mining	
Oil/gas production	
Sewer/drain	
Water	
Other	

Distribution is shown based on 626 million pounds of polyethylene pipe used in 1994. Data refer to pressure rated materials only and do not include corrugated drainage pipe.

Gas distribution	31.9%
Industrial/mining	16.8
Oil/gas production	14.7
Sewer/drain	12.0
Water	10.9
Other	13.7

Source: *Modern Plastics*, October 1995, p. 51.

★ 850 ★
Plastic Pipes (SIC 3084)

Top Pipe Extruders - North America

Firms are ranked by pipe sales in millions of dollars.

JM Manufacturing Co.	$ 420.0
North American Pipe Co.	248.0
Pacific Western Extruded Plastics Co. . . .	222.0
Advanced Drainage Systems Inc.	206.0
Lamson & Sessions Co.	201.6
Ipex Inc.	195.0

Charlotte Pipe & Foundry Co.	$ 170.0
Hancor Inc.	160.0
Uponor US Inc.	152.0
Phillips Driscopipe Inc.	143.0

Source: *Plastics News*, June 17, 1996, p. 33, from industry estimates.

★ 851 ★
Plastic Bottles (SIC 3085)

Non-PET Bottle Makers

Data refer to polyethylene and all non-PET containers. Total sales reached $4.0 billion in 1994.

Owens-Illinois	15.9%
Graham	8.8
Continental Plastics	5.6
Constar (Crown Cook)	2.8
Plastipak	2.5
American National-Can	1.3
Others	63.3

Source: *Investext*, Thomson Financial Services, January 27, 1995, p. 34, from industry sources and PaineWebber estimates.

★ 852 ★
Plastic Bottles (SIC 3085)

PET Container Market

PET (polyethylene terephthalate) container manufacturers are ranked by share of the market for 1995.

Crown Cork & Seal	31.5%
Johnson Controls Inc.	19.4
Coca-Cola Co. Co-ops	14.6
Continental PET Technologies	9.7
Plastipak Packaging Inc.	7.9
Brunswick Container Corp.	3.6
Graham Packaging Co.	2.3
Silgan Plastics	2.0
Other	9.0

Source: *Plastics News*, October 9, 1995, p. 3, from Containers Consulting Inc. and CS First Boston.

★ 853 ★
Packaging (SIC 3089)

Flexible Packaging Makers

Data are for 1994.

Bemis Co.	6.4%
James River	4.6
American National Can	3.5
Printpak	3.2
Reynolds	2.7
Archer	2.5
Bryce	1.4
Others	75.7

Source: *Investext*, Thomson Financial Services, January 27, 1995, p. 37, from industry sources and PaineWebber estimates.

★ 854 ★
Plastic Connectors (SIC 3089)

Thermoplastic Connector Makers

AMP Intl.

Molex

Amphenol

Berg Electronics

ITT Canon

3M

Other

Data are for 1995.

AMP Intl.	19.4%
Molex	4.5
Amphenol	4.2
Berg Electronics	3.7
ITT Canon	3.5
3M	2.9
Other	61.8

Source: *Modern Plastics*, January 1996, p. 27, from Freck Research.

★ 855 ★
Plastic Containers (SIC 3089)

Plastic Container Makers

The market for plastic containers is shown by company. Rubbermaid has an estimated 80% share of the food storage container market.

Rubbermaid	50.0%
Other	50.0

Source: *HFN*, August 28, 1995, p. 6.

★ 856 ★
Plastic Molding (SIC 3089)

Injection Molding Industry Leaders

The top 10 injection molding companies in North America are ranked by sales in millions of dollars.

Textron Automotive Co.	$ 1,400.0
Lear Corp.	610.5
United Technologies Automotive Inc.	514.0
Decoma International Inc.	436.1
Becker Group Inc.	375.0
LDM Technologies	350.0
Donnelly Corp.	341.2
Owens-Illinois Inc.	315.0
Worthington Custom Plastics Inc.	302.0
Mack Molding Co. Inc.	298.0

Source: *Plastics News*, April 15, 1996, p. 1, from industry estimates.

★ 857 ★
Vinyl Siding (SIC 3089)

Vinyl Siding Market

Shares are estimated for 1996.

Alcoa/Mastic	25.0%
Certainteed/Wolverine	22.0
Jannock (Canada)	14.0
Ply-Gem	10.0
Fibreboard	9.0
Other	20.0

Source: *Investext*, Thomson Financial Services, April 11, 1996, p. 10, from WFBS.

SIC 31 - Leather and Leather Products

Saddles (SIC 3111)

Saddle and Harness Preferences - Canada

The table shows the preferences for saddle and harnesses by type. Eastern Canada holds a 75% share of the market for saddles and harnesses.

Eastern Canada
english-style 70.0%
western-style 30.0
Western Canada
western style 70.0
eastern style 30.0

Source: *National Trade Data Bank*, September 1, 1995, p. 111096781, from *Saddle and Harnesses Market in Canada Report*.

★ 859 ★
Footwear (SIC 3140)

Casual Footwear Makers

Companies are ranked by 1995 sales in millions of dollars.

Timberland . . . . $ 344.5
Rockport 331.0
Keds 251.9
Airwalk 190.0
Skechers USA 130.0
Hush Puppies 93.0
Vans 75.1
Birkenstock 58.0
Teva 55.9
Sperry 45.0
Guess 42.0
N.Y. Lugz 25.0
Simple 23.6
Ugg 20.3
Trettorn 8.0

Source: *Sportstyle*, May 1996, p. 32.

★ 860 ★
Footwear (SIC 3140)

Rugged Footwear Makers

Firms are ranked by 1995 sales in millions of dollars.

Nike ACG . . . . $ 227.0
Wolverine 133.0
LaCrosse 77.0
Rocky 60.4
Hi-Tec USA 58.0
Reebok 44.0
Vasque 29.0
Adidas 29.0
Merrell 28.0
Danner 20.0
Northlake 15.0
Dunham 13.5
Asolo 12.9
Columbia 9.0
Tecnica 6.5

Source: *Sportstyle*, May 1996, p. 32.

★ 861 ★
Footwear (SIC 3143)

Men's Casual Shoe Producers

Shares are shown for the 12 months ended April 1995.

Rockport 7.2%
Bass 6.6
Dexter 5.4
Timberland 4.8
Florsheim 2.1
Other 73.9

Source: *New York Times*, December 23, 1995, p. A2, from Footwear Market Insight.

★ 862 ★

Footwear (SIC 3143)

Men's Dress Shoe Producers

| Florsheim |
| Dexter |
| Rockport |
| Bass |
| Johnston & Murphy |
| Other |

Shares are for the 12 months ended April 1995.

Florsheim 15.0%
Dexter 8.1
Rockport 5.9
Bass 4.7
Johnston & Murphy 2.9
Other 63.4

Source: *New York Times*, December 23, 1995, p. A2, from Footwear Market Insight.

★ 863 ★

Footwear (SIC 3144)

Women's Casual Shoe Producers

Shares are for 1994.

Bass 5.5%
Easy Spirit 2.9
Dexter 2.5
SAS 2.4
Rockport 1.5
Other 85.2

Source: *New York Times*, December 23, 1995, p. A2, from Footwear Market Insight.

SIC 32 - Stone, Clay, and Glass Products

★ 864 ★

Glass (SIC 3200)

Glass Industry Leaders

Firms are ranked by total sales in millions of dollars.

PPG Industries Inc.	$ 7,100
Corning Inc.	5,300
Owens-Illinois	3,800
Owens Corning	3,600

Source: *Glass Industry*, July 1996, p. 28, from annual reports.

★ 865 ★

Gypsum and Cement (SIC 3200)

Gypsum and Cement Makers

Firms are ranked by 1995 sales in millions of dollars.

USG	$ 2,443
Lafarge	1,507
Vulcan Materials	1,449
Martin Marietta Materials	622
Southdown	586

Source: *Forbes*, January 1, 1996, p. 106, from Value Line Data Base Service and OneSource Information Services.

★ 866 ★

Glass Containers (SIC 3221)

Glass Container Makers

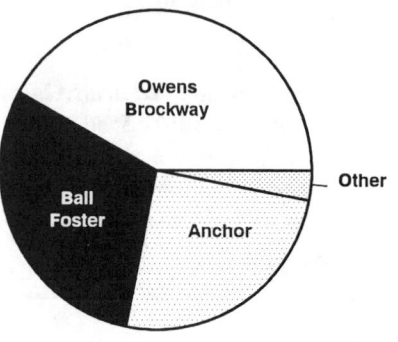

Producer shares are shown in percent.

Owens Brockway	42.0%
Ball Foster	30.0
Anchor	25.0
Other	3.0

Source: *Financial Times*, February 22, 1996, p. 16, from Salomon Brothers and company reports.

★ 867 ★

Glass Containers (SIC 3221)

Glass Container Producers

Shares of the estimated $5.1 billion market are shown in percent.

Owens-Illinois	39.9%
Anchor Glass	25.0
Ball-InCon Glass Packaging	13.8
Foster-Forbes Glass Division	12.1
Other	9.2

Source: *Glass Industry*, October 1995, p. 12, from PaineWebber.

★ 868 ★

Glass Containers (SIC 3221)

Wine Bottle Producers

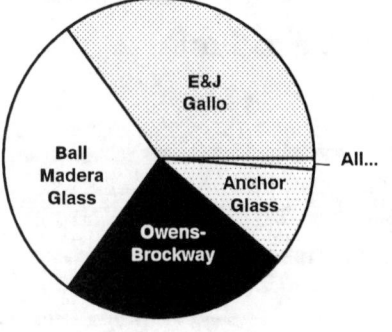

Wine bottle producers supplied nearly 2.0 billion bottles for an estimated $450 - $550 million market. Shares of the market are shown in percent.

E&J Gallo 35.0%
Ball Madera Glass 30.0
Owens-Brockway 24.0
Anchor Glass 10.0
All imported glass 1.0

Source: *Wines & Vines*, October 1995, p. 27, from industry sources and company reports.

★ 869 ★

Glassware (SIC 3229)

Popular Glassware Brands

Data show the preferred brands of glassware, based on a survey.

Libbey 13.0%
Anchor Hocking 5.0
Corning 3.0
Corelle 2.0
Other 4.0

Source: *Stores*, January 1996, p. 93, from Leo J. Shapiro & Associates.

★ 870 ★

Cement (SIC 3241)

Cement Makers - Mexico

Data are for 1993.

CEMEX 68.1%
Apasco 17.5
Cruz Azul 10.0
Cementos Chihuahua 3.2
Cementos Moctezuma 1.2

Source: *Mineral Industries of Latin America and Canada*, 1993, p. 198.

★ 871 ★

Cement (SIC 3241)

Cement Market - Canada

Market shares are shown in percent.

Lafarge Canada 34.0%
Stl Lawrence Cement (Holderbank) 21.0
CBR Cement Canada (Heidelberger/CBR) . 20.0
St. Mary's Cement Company 12.0
Ciment Quebec 6.0
Lake Ontario Cement 5.0
North Star Cement 2.0

Source: *Investext,* Thomson Financial Services, March 29, 1996, p. 63, from ICR.

★ 872 ★

Cement (SIC 3241)

Cement Market - Mexico

Cemex 62.0%
Apasco 25.0
Cruz Azul 10.0
Others 3.0

Source: *Investext,* Thomson Financial Services, March 29, 1996, p. 69, from Apasco/SBC Warburg.

★ 873 ★

Cement (SIC 3241)

Leading Cement Suppliers

Shares are for 1993.

Holnam 13.0%
Lafarge 8.8
Southdown 6.0
Continued on next page.

★ 873 ★ *Continued*
Cement (SIC 3241)

Leading Cement Suppliers

Shares are for 1993.

Ash Grove Cement	5.7%
Lone Star Industries	5.2
Blue Circle	5.1
Lehigh Portland Cement	4.7
Medusa	4.4
ESSROC Materials	4.3
California Portland Cement	3.9
Other	38.9

Source: *Investext,* Thomson Financial Services, February 24, 1995, p. 19, from Portland Cement Association.

★ 874 ★

Ceramics (SIC 3250)

Advanced Ceramics Market

The market for advanced ceramics is expected to grow from $4.86 billion in 1994 to $8.53 billion in 2000.

	1994	2000
Electronic ceramics	79.4%	77.0%
Structural ceramics	9.8	12.0
Ceramic coatings	10.8	11.0

Source: *Ceramic Forum International*, July 1995, p. 376.

★ 875 ★

Ceramics (SIC 3250)

Ceramic Products Market - Mexico

The market is shown by sector for 1996.

	($ mil.)	Share
Bathroom, sanitaryware	$ 174.6	35.0%
Ceramic floor/wall coverings . .	125.8	25.0
Tableware, incl. porcelain	89.9	18.0
Advanced indust. ceramic prod. .	79.9	16.6
Artistic/decorative items	29.1	6.0

Source: *National Trade Data Bank*, May 27, 1996, p. IS960319.096.

★ 876 ★

Ceramics (SIC 3250)

Electronic Ceramics Market

The market is expected to increase from $3.86 billion in 1994 to $6.57 billion in 2000.

	1994	2000
Substrated and IC packages	56.5%	55.6%
Capacitors	23.3	24.0
Ferrite magnets	10.2	9.8
Insulators	6.5	5.3
Piezoelectric ceramics	3.3	3.5
Superconductors	0.2	1.5

Source: *American Ceramic Society Bulletin*, February 1996, p. 49, from Business Communications Company.

★ 877 ★

Clay Refractories (SIC 3255)

U.S. Refractory Clay Producers

Production capacity is shown in tons per year by company.

C-E Minerals	500,000.0
National Refractories & Minerals . . .	150,000.0
Christy Minerals Co.	100,000.0
AFC Co.	6,000.0

Source: *Industrial Minerals*, March 1996, p. 62.

★ 878 ★

Ceramic Powders (SIC 3259)

Ceramic Powder Market

The market is shown in millions of dollars.

	($ mil.)	($ mil.)	Share
Electronic	$ 613	$ 977	89.6%
Structural	45	83	7.6
Thermal spray	26	31	2.8

Source: *American Ceramic Society Bulletin*, August 1995, p. 63, from Business Communications Co.

★ 879 ★

Ceramic Toilets (SIC 3261)

Ceramic Toilet Makers

Shares are estimated.

American Standard	15.0%
Eljer	15.0
Kohler	15.0
Mansfield	15.0
Briggs	10.0
Other	30.0

Source: *Investext,* Thomson Financial Services, July 17, 1995, p. 20.

★ 880 ★

Magnets (SIC 3264)

Permanent Magnet Market

The market increased from $455 million in 1992 to $763 million in 1997.

	1992	1997
Metallic	39.1%	38.6%
Bonded	30.8	33.7
Ceramic	30.1	27.7

Source: *International Journal of Powder Metallurgy*, no. 2, 1995, p. 135.

★ 881 ★

Gypsum (SIC 3275)

Gypsum Tile Makers

The ceiling tile market is estimated in percent.

Armstrong World	50.0%
USG Corp.	35.0
Celotex	15.0

Source: *Investext,* Thomson Financial Services, January 19, 1995, p. 2, from Smith Barney.

★ 882 ★

Gypsum (SIC 3275)

Gypsum Wallboard Makers

Shares are estimated.

USG	32.0%
National Gypsum	23.0
Georgia-Pacific	12.0
Domtar	9.0
Celotex	6.0
Others	18.0

Source: *Investext,* Thomson Financial Services, January 19, 1995, p. 2, from U.S. Gypsum.

★ 883 ★

Abrasives (SIC 3291)

Cleaning Products Market

Soap-filled pads	26.0%
Sponges	25.0
Scouring sponges	23.0
Other	26.0

Source: *HFN*, March 25, 1996, p. 32, from Information Resources Inc. InfoScan.

★ 884 ★

Abrasives (SIC 3291)

Coated Abrasives Market - Northeast Central

The top markets for Northeast Central states are ranked in millions of dollars.

Vehicles and vehicle bodies	$ 31.5
Vehicle parts	31.0
Millwork	15.2
Automotive stamping plants	12.8
Wood kitchen cabinets	10.1

Source: *Industrial Distribution*, February 1996, p. 63, from Industrial Market Information Inc.

★ 885 ★

Treated Minerals (SIC 3295)

Exfoliated Vermiculite Market

Data are for 1995, based on 130,000 tons.

Agricultural	56.2%
Insulation	24.6
Aggregates	15.4
Other	3.8

Source: *American Ceramic Society Bulletin*, June 1996, p. 161.

★ 886 ★

Treated Minerals (SIC 3295)

U.S. Kaolin Consumption

Consumption of airfloated kaolin is shown in percent.

Fiberglass	29.3%
Rubber/elastomeric	25.6
Sanitaryware	13.2
Filler/extender	12.8
Refractories	5.9

Dinnerware	2.9%
Ceramic tile	1.8
Electrical porcelain	1.1
Other	7.3

Source: *American Ceramic Society Bulletin*, June 1996, p. 130.

SIC 33 - Primary Metal Industries

★ 887 ★

Metals (SIC 3300)

Leading Metal Companies

Firms are ranked by 1995 revenues in millions of dolalrs. Shares of the group are shown in percent.

	Rev. ($ mil.)	% of Group
Alcoa	$ 12,655	20.9%
Reynolds Metals	7,252	12.0
Bethlehem Steel	4,868	8.1
Inland Steel Industries	4,781	7.9
LTV	4,283	7.1
Phelps Dodge	4,185	6.9
Nucor	3,462	5.7
Alumax	2,926	4.8
Maxxam	2,565	4.2
Ak Steel Holdings	2,257	3.7
Commercial Metals	2,117	3.5
Armco	1,960	3.2
Allegheny Ludlum	1,494	2.5
Worthington Industries	1,484	2.5
Walter Industries	1,442	2.4
WHX	1,365	2.3
Weirton Steel	1,352	2.2

Source: *Fortune*, April 29, 1996, p. F57.

★ 888 ★

Metals (SIC 3300)

Top Metal Cos. - U.S./Canada

The U.S. and Canadian firms are ranked by 1995 sales in millions of dollars.

Alcan Aluminium Ltd.	$ 8,234.0
Aluminum Co. of America	8,034.0
Reynolds Metals Co.	6,509.0
USX Corp.	6,456.0
Inland Steel Industries Inc.	4,782.0
Bethlehem Steel Corp.	4,768.6
LTV Corp.	4,283.2

Noranda Inc.	$ 4,228.2
Inco Ltd.	3,471.0
Nucor Corp.	3,462.0
National Steel Corp.	2,954.3
Alumax Inc.	2,926.1

Source: *American Metal Market*, June 25, 1996, p. 3A.

★ 889 ★

Metals (SIC 3300)

Top Metals Companies - North America

Companies are ranked by sales in billions of dollars for 1995.

Alcan Aluminum Ltd.	$ 8.23
Aluminum Co. of America	8.03
Reynolds Metals Co.	6.50
USX Corp.	6.45
Inland Steel Industries Inc.	4.78
Bethlehem Steel Corp.	4.76
LTV Corp.	4.28
Noranda Inc.	4.22
Inco Ltd.	3.47
Nucor Corp.	3.46
National Steel Corp.	2.95
Alumax Inc.	2.92
Asarco Inc.	2.81
Phelps Dodge Corp.	2.49
AK Steel Corp.	2.30

Source: *American Metal Market*, May 1, 1996, p. 8, from company reports.

★ 890 ★
Steel (SIC 3312)

Coated Steel Use

Data are based on 23.35 million net tons in 1994, 22.13 million net tons in 1995, and 21.69 million net tons in 1996.

	1994	1995	1996
Galvanized	69.9%	71.3%	71.8%
Tinplate	19.7	18.5	18.1
Other coated	10.4	10.2	10.1

Source: *Purchasing*, April 11, 1996, p. 34B.

★ 891 ★
Steel (SIC 3312)

Largest Steel Makers - Mexico

Data are in millions of metric tons.

Altos Hornos de Mexico (AHMSA)	2.59
Hysla de Mexico	2.03
IMEXA	1.35
SICARTSA	1.17

Source: *Mineral Industries of Latin America and Canada*, 1993, p. 196.

★ 892 ★
Steel (SIC 3312)

Raw Steel Shipments - North America

The top companies are ranked by thousands of tons of steel shipped in 1994.

U.S. Steel Group	10,568.0
Bethlehem Steel	9,251.0
LTV Steel	7,969.0
Nucor	5,980.0
National Steel	5,208.0
Inland Steel	5,170.0
Stelco	4,421.0
AK Steel	3,878.0
Dofasco	3,076.0
Rouge Steel	2,640.0
Weirton Steel	2,606.0
Wheeling-Pittsburgh	2,388.0

Source: *American Metal Market*, March 29, 1996, p. 4.

★ 893 ★
Steel (SIC 3312)

Sheet Steel Market

Sales are shown by end market.

Distributors & processors	42.0%
Transportation	20.0
Construction products	9.0
Containers & packaging	8.0
Machinery & equipment	6.0
Major appliances	5.0
Export & other uses	10.0

Source: *Purchasing*, May 9, 1996, p. 32B4, from American Iron and Steel Institute.

★ 894 ★
Steel (SIC 3312)

Steel Market Shares - 1995

Shares are estimated.

USX	9.7%
Bethlehem	7.9
Nucor	7.0
LTV	6.9
National	4.7
Inland	4.5
Armco AKST	3.5
Other	62.9

Source: *Investext*, Thomson Financial Services, June 28, 1995, p. 37, from annual reports.

★ 895 ★
Steel (SIC 3312)

Steel Producers - North America

Firms are ranked by 1995 steel shipments in tons.

U.S. Steel Group	11,378,000
Bethlehem Steel Corp.	8,970,000
LTV Steel Corp.	7,961,000
National Steel Corp.	5,564,000
Inland Steel Co.	5,117,000
Stelco Inc.	4,380,000
AK Steel Corp.	4,051,000
Dofasco Inc.	3,181,000
Weirton Steel Corp.	2,718,000
Rouge Steel Co.	2,542,000
Wheeling-Pittsburgh Steel Corp. . . .	2,514,631
Geneva Steel Co.	2,432,000
Algoma Steel Co.	2,009,000

Continued on next page.

★ 895 ★ *Continued*
Steel (SIC 3312)

Steel Producers - North America

Firms are ranked by 1995 steel shipments in tons.

WCI Steel Inc.	1,221,940
Acme Steel Co.	619,052

Source: *American Metal Market*, February 19, 1996, p. 3, from company reports.

★ 896 ★
Steel (SIC 3316)

Cold-Rolled Stainless Steel Makers

	Tons (000)	Share
Armco	370	24.0%
Allegheny Ludlum	325	21.0
J&L	262	17.0
Lukens	122	8.0
North American Stainless	105	7.0
Imports	362	23.0

Source: *Investext,* Thomson Financial Services, September 6, 1995, p. 47, from annual reports and Specialty Steel Industry of North America.

★ 897 ★
Steel Tubes (SIC 3317)

U.S./Mexico Steel Tube Trade

The table shows the net tons of steel tubing and pipe traded between Mexico and the United States. Data indicate the tons shipped to each country. OCTG stands for Oil Country Tubular Goods.

	Mexico	U.S.
Line pipe	4,536	57,086
Mechanical	24,263	45,990
OCTG	4,275	32,377
Structural	5,431	18,626
Standard	7,995	10,635
Pressure	1,278	1,383
Stainless	4,978	1,337

Source: *American Metal Market*, March 29, 1996, p. A13, from Preston Report.

★ 898 ★
Copper (SIC 3331)

Copper Smelter Production - Mexico

Mexicana de Cobre	64.0%
Other	36.0

Source: *Mineral Industries of Latin America and Canada*, 1993, p. 195.

★ 899 ★
Alumina (SIC 3334)

Alumina Demand - 1993

U.S. alumina demand is shown by product in thousands of metric tons.

	(000)	Share
Flame retardents fillers	200.0	27.0%
Detergent zeolites	125.0	16.9
Aluminum sulfate	120.0	16.2
Catalysts dessicants	120.0	16.2
Sodium aluminate	75.0	10.1
Aluminum fluoride	57.0	7.7
Other	43.0	5.8

Source: *Chemical Marketing Reporter*, December 11, 1995, p. 20, from SRI International.

★ 900 ★
Alumina (SIC 3334)

Leading Alumina Plants

Capacity is shown in thousands of metric tons per year for 1993.

Aluminum Co. of America	1,735
Reynolds Metals Co.	1,700
Kaiser Aluminum & Chemical Corp.	1,000
Virgin Islands Alumina	635
Ormet Corp.	600

Source: *Aluminum, Bauxite, and Alumina*, 1993, p. 19, from Bureau of Mines.

★ 901 ★

Aluminum (SIC 3334)

Aluminum Producers

Sales are shown for the first nine months of 1995 in billions of dollars.

Aluminum Co. of America	$ 9.39
Alcan Aluminum Ltd.	7.10
Reynolds Metal Co.	5.35
Alumax Inc.	2.18
Kaiser Aluminum Corp.	1.64

Source: *American Metal Market*, October 27, 1995, p. 1, from company reports.

★ 902 ★

Cadmium (SIC 3339)

Cadmium by End Use

Distribution is shown for 1994 based on annual consumption of 600 tons.

Batteries	63.0%
Pigments	15.0
Plastic	10.0
Coatings	7.0
Alloys	2.0
Other	3.0

Source: *Purchasing*, October 5, 1995, p. 32B15, from International Cadmium Association.

★ 903 ★

Silver (SIC 3341)

Silver Use in Photography

End use is shown in millions of ounces.

	(mil.)	Share
Commercial photography	110.6	50.3%
Medical X-rays	51.1	23.3
Graphic arts	40.2	18.3
Dental/industrial x-rays	17.8	8.1

Source: *American Metal Market*, April 3, 1996, p. 5, from CPM Group.

★ 904 ★

Brass Rods (SIC 3351)

Brass Rod Producers

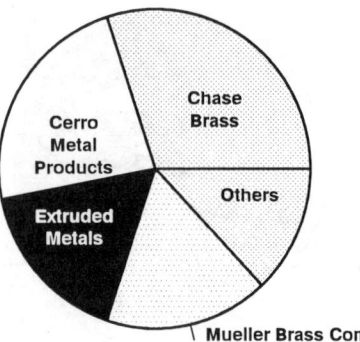

Data are shown based on 1995 shipments.

Chase Brass	30.0%
Cerro Metal Products	23.0
Extruded Metals	17.0
Mueller Brass Company	17.0
Others	13.0

Source: *Investor's Business Daily*, April 30, 1996, p. A6, from Copper and Brass Servicenter Association.

★ 905 ★

Copper (SIC 3351)

Copper Use - 1995

End use is shown in thousands of metric tons. Shares of the group are shown in percent.

	(000)	% of Group
Building wire	541.8	19.4%
Plumbing, heating	468.6	16.8
Power utilities	296.7	10.6
Air conditioning	290.3	10.4
Telecommunications	249.5	8.9
Automobile electronics	238.1	8.5
Plant equipment	225.9	8.1
Electronics	223.6	8.0
Automobiles	140.2	5.0
Appliances, extension cords . . .	114.3	4.1

Source: *New York Times*, June 15, 1996, p. 16, from Copper Development Association and American Bureau of Metal Statistics.

★ 906 ★

Copper Rods (SIC 3351)

Copper-Alloy Rod Makers

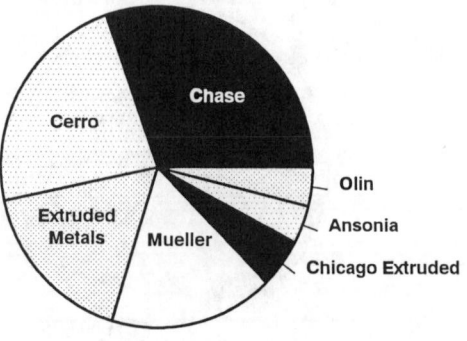

Shares are shown based on 810 ,illion pounds sold in 1993.

Chase 30.0%
Cerro 23.0
Extruded Metals 17.0
Mueller 17.0
Chicago Extruded 5.0
Ansonia 4.0
Olin 4.0

Source: *Investext,* Thomson Financial Services, December 19, 1994, p. 4, from company reports.

★ 907 ★

Metal Tubing (SIC 3356)

Metal Tubing Market

Distribution is shown based on 5.7 million net tons in 1995 and 5.68 million net tons in 1996.

	1995	1996
Mechanical steel	71.1%	69.8%
Structural steel	14.1	15.0
Copper & brass	9.1	9.4
Aluminum	3.3	3.3
Press-use steel	1.5	1.4
Stainless steel	1.0	1.0

Source: *Purchasing*, June 6, 1996, p. 32B9, from Metal Market Strategies.

SIC 34 - Fabricated Metal Products

★ 908 ★
Metal Products (SIC 3400)

Leading Metal Product Makers

The leading firms are ranked by 1995 revenues in millions of dollars.

Gillette	$ 6,795
Crown Cork & Seal	5,054
Masco	4,779
Tyco International	4,535
Illinois Tool Works	4,152
U.S. Industries	2,908
Johnson Controls	8,330
Dana	7,795
Eaton	6,822
Navistar International	6,342
Paccar	4,848
Lear Seating	4,714
Echlin	2,718
Varity	2,419
Federal-Mogul	1,996

Source: *Fortune*, April 29, 1996, p. F56.

★ 909 ★
Hardware (SIC 3420)

Hardware Market - Canada

"Other" includes firms in the lock and latch subsector, including locks, lock parts, and non-automatic door closures.

Hand tools and accessories	53.0%
Furniture cabinet, casket hardware/fittings	13.0
Hinges and butts	7.0
Other	20.0

Source: *National Trade Data Bank*, March 2, 1996, p. 111099252.

★ 910 ★
Hardware (SIC 3420)

Hardware Sales by Segment

Distribution is shown based on $4.53 billion in sales at discount stores.

Accessories	45.0%
Paint supplies	20.1
Power tools	9.9
Hand tools	8.4
Other	16.6

Source: *Discount Store News*, August 5, 1996, p. 70.

★ 911 ★
Razors (SIC 3421)

Canadian Disposable Market

Shares are as of March 1995.

Gillette	42.1%
Bic	29.3
Wilkinson	3.4
Schick	0.4
Other	24.8

Source: *Investext*, Thomson Financial Services, August 2, 1995, p. 12.

★ 912 ★
Razors (SIC 3421)

Razor and Blade Brand Shares

Razor and razor blade sales through mass market outlets are shown for the 52 weeks ended July 16, 1995. Gillette leads the $987 million market with a 66.1% share.

	Sales ($ mil.)	Share
Gillette Sensor	$ 176.99	17.9%
Gillette Sensor for Women . . .	69.93	7.1
Gillette SensorExel	60.75	6.2

Continued on next page.

★ 912 ★ *Continued*
Razors (SIC 3421)
Razor and Blade Brand Shares

Razor and razor blade sales through mass market outlets are shown for the 52 weeks ended July 16, 1995. Gillette leads the $987 million market with a 66.1% share.

	Sales ($ mil.)	Share
Bic	$ 59.00	6.0%
Gillette Atra	54.60	5.5
Private label	54.44	5.5
Gillette Good News	52.38	5.3
Schick Tracer	36.73	3.7
Gillette Trac II Plus	35.86	3.6
Gillette Good News Plus	33.86	3.4
Other	352.45	35.8

Source: *Supermarket Business*, October 1995, p. 93, from Information Resources Inc.

★ 913 ★
Razors (SIC 3421)
Razor/Razor Blade Producers

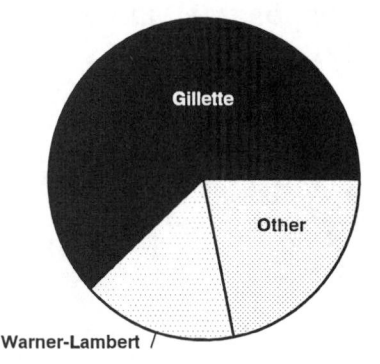

Shares of the $1.0 billion market are shown in percent.

Gillette	62.2%
Warner-Lambert	15.5
Other	22.3

Source: *Advertising Age*, July 29, 1996, p. 2, from Information Resources Inc.

★ 914 ★
Hardware (SIC 3429)
Builders' Hardware Market

Locks	60.0%
Mountings and fittings	15.0
Hinges	11.0
Other	14.0

Source: *Builders Hardware. Industry & Trade Summary*, March 1994, p. 2, from United States Department of Commerce.

★ 915 ★
Lock Sets (SIC 3429)
Lock/Latch Set Users - Canada

The total demand for locks and latches reached $161.2 million in Canada in 1992. Data show demand by end user. DIY stands for do-it-yourselfer.

Building contractors/new construction . . .	65.0%
Locksmiths/DIYers	35.0

Source: *National Trade Data Bank*, March 2, 1996, p. 111099252.

★ 916 ★
Solar Equipment (SIC 3433)
Solar Equipment Producers

The largest producers of solar energy equipment are ranked by capacity of solar panels sold in 1995. Data are in megawatts.

Siemens Solar	17.0
Solarex	9.5
Solec International	2.6
Astropower	2.5
Ase Americas	2.0
USSC	0.6
Entech	0.2
Advanced PV Systems	0.1

Source: *New York Times*, June 5, 1996, p. C18, from *PV News*.

★ 917 ★

Metal Doors (SIC 3442)

Metal Patio Door Market

The market for residential patio doors is shown by application. Data are shown in thousands of units for 1995.

	(000)	Share
New construction	1,000	66.0%
Remodel/replacement	515	34.0

Source: *Building Supply Business*, March 1996, p. 32, from Wood Window & Door Marketplace and National Window and Door Association.

★ 918 ★

Boilers (SIC 3443)

Boiler Producers

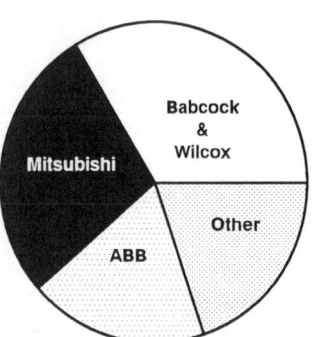

Shares are for 1995.

Babcock & Wilcox	33.6%
Mitsubishi	27.7
ABB	19.0
Other	19.7

Source: *Investext,* Thomson Financial Services, May 8, 1996, p. 4, from McCoy Power Reports and Smith Barney estimates.

★ 919 ★

Boilers (SIC 3443)

Boiler Shipments by Type

Shipents are shown for the first quarter of 1995.

Cast iron, gas-fired	38,578
Cast-iron, oil-fired	25,667
Steel (all types)	5,560

Source: *Contractor*, July 1995, p. 5, from Hydronics Institute.

★ 920 ★

Heat Exchangers (SIC 3443)

Heat Exchange Market by End Use

Shipments of heat exchangers in 1995 reached 267 million units and are forecast to rise to 282 million units by the year 2000. HVAC stands for heating, ventilating, and air conditioning.

HVAC equipment	32.0%
Chemical processing	24.0
Petroleum refining	18.0
Electric power industry	14.0
Food & beverages	5.0
Other	7.0

Source: *InTech*, January 1996, p. 17, from Frost & Sullivan.

★ 921 ★

Prefabricated Buildings (SIC 3448)

Manufactured Home Shipments by State

The top 10 states shipped 164,075 units in 1994.

North Carolina	9.3%
Texas	8.7
Georgia	6.0
Florida	5.9
South Carolina	5.0
Alabama	5.0
Tennessee	4.4
Kentucky	3.4
Michigan	3.3
Mississippi	3.0
Other	46.0

Source: *Investext,* Thomson Financial Services, April 24, 1995, p. 3, from Manufactured Housing Industry.

★ 922 ★

Prefabricated Buildings (SIC 3448)

Manufactured Homes Producers

Shares of the market are shown in percent.

Fleetwood 21.5%
Champion 8.6
Other 69.9

Source: *Financial World*, February 26, 1996, p. 50.

★ 923 ★

Prefabricated Buildings (SIC 3448)

Prefab Building Makers

Shares are for 1994.

Butler Manufacturing 22.0%
United Dominion Industries 16.5
Robertson-Ceco 12.5
American Buildings Co. 10.2
NCI Building System 9.0
Other 29.8

Source: *Investext,* Thomson Financial Services, October 3, 1995, p. 5, from Metal Buildings Manufacturers Association and Wheat First Butcher Singer estimates.

★ 924 ★

Fasteners (SIC 3450)

Industrial Fasteners by End Use

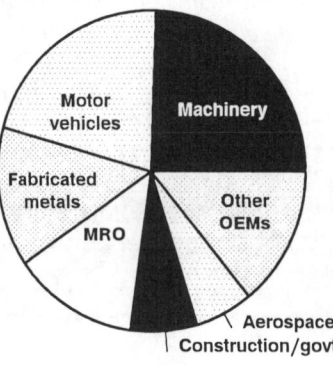

Market shares shown for 1994 represent a $7.5 billion industrial fastener market. MRO stands for maintenance, repair, and operation. OEM stands for original equipment manufacturers.

Machinery 24.0%
Motor vehicles 21.0
Fabricated metals 14.0
MRO 13.0
Construction/govt. 7.0
Aerospace 6.0
Other OEMs 14.0

Source: *Assembly*, October 1995, p. 12, from Freedonia Group Inc.

★ 925 ★

Cookware (SIC 3469)

Cookware Shipments by Type

Shipments are shown by segment.

	1994 ($ mil.)	1995 ($ mil.)	Share
Aluminum cookware . .	$ 387.0	$ 394.0	39.4%
Stainless cookware . .	299.0	312.0	31.2
Bakeware	220.0	227.0	22.7
Cast iron, porcelain on steel and other . .	27.0	34.0	3.4
Kitchenware	25.0	33.0	3.3

Source: *HFN*, February 19, 1996, p. 44, from Cookware Manufacturers Association.

★ 926 ★

Lunch Boxes (SIC 3469)

Lunch Box Preferences

Data show the top three lunch box characters preferred by 5-10 year olds. Figures are based on a survey.

Pochahontas	36.0%
Power Rangers	21.0
Batman	8.0

Source: *USA TODAY*, September 18, 1995, p. D1, from Veryfine Products Inc.

★ 927 ★

Valves (SIC 3491)

Valve Shipments by End Use

Shipments are shown by end use for 1996.

Chemical	17.5%
Water & sewage	17.1
Petroleum production	12.4
Petroleum refining	10.8
Power generation	10.8
Pulp & paper	7.1
Oil & gas transmission	5.4
Commercial construction	5.1
Gas distribution	2.3
Food & beverage	2.2
Iron & steel	1.9
Co-generation	1.8
Marine	1.5
Miscellaneous	4.1

Source: *Contractor*, January 1996, p. 5, from Valve Manufacturers Association of America.

★ 928 ★

Powdered Metal (SIC 3499)

P/M Parts by End Use

Distribution of the powder metallurgy (P/M) parts market is shown by application.

Automotive	63.8%
Recreation, hand tools, & hobby	13.0
Household appliances	6.4
Hardware	3.7
Industrial motors/controls, hydraulics . . .	3.7
Business machines	2.0
All other	7.4

Source: *Design News*, December 4, 1995, p. 48, from Powder Metallurgy Parts Association.

★ 929 ★

Powdered Metal (SIC 3499)

Powdered Metal Makers - Canada

Quebec Metal Powders Limited

Domfer Metal Powders Ltd.

Sherritt Inc.

Metachimie Canada Ltd.

Production is shown in metric tons per year. Sherritt Inc. includes a production of 2,000 metric tons of cobalt powder; the rest is for nickel based powder. Figures for INCO SPP and Kennametal Inc. were not available.

Quebec Metal Powders Limited	137,000
Domfer Metal Powders Ltd.	31,800
Sherritt Inc.	26,000
Metachimie Canada Ltd.	1,250

Source: *International Journal of Powder Metallurgy*, no. 2, 1996, p. 106.

SIC 35 - Industry Machinery and Equipment

Industrial Machinery (SIC 3500)

Largest Industrial/Farm Equipment Makers

Firms are ranked by 1995 revenues in millions of dollars. Shares of the group are shown in percent.

	Rev. ($ mil.)	% of Group
Caterpillar	$ 16,072	20.6%
Deere	10,291	13.2
Ingersoll-Rand	5,729	7.3
Dresser Industries	5,629	7.2
Black & Decker	5,566	7.1
Cummins Engine	5,245	6.7
American Standard	5,221	6.7
CASE	5,105	6.5
Dover	3,746	4.8
Parker Hannifin	3,214	4.1
York International	2,930	3.8
Baker Hughes	2,637	3.4
Harnischfeger Ind.	2,254	2.9
Timken	2,231	2.9
Western Atlas	2,226	2.9

Source: *Fortune*, April 29, 1996, p. F52.

★ 931 ★

Engines (SIC 3519)

Gas Engine Production - North America

Shares are shown based on 31.772 million engines produced in 1995.

<5	77.2%
5.1-20	15.7
21-50	1.2
51-100	5.9
101-300	0.1
301-700	0.0
701-2,000	0.0%
2,001+	0.0

Source: *Diesel Progress Engines & Drives*, July 1995, p. 28, from Power Systems Research.

★ 932 ★

Engines (SIC 3519)

Heavy-Duty Diesel Engine Makers

Shares of the North American market are shown for 1995.

Cummins	35.5%
DDC	26.2
Caterpillar	25.2
Mack	12.2
Other	0.9

Source: *Investext*, Thomson Financial Services, April 25, 1996, p. 12, from Motor Vehicle Manufacturers Association.

★ 933 ★

Engines (SIC 3519)

Lawn Care Equipment Engines

This table shows the leading producer of 2-20 horsepower lawn and garden equipment engines.

Briggs & Stratton	65.0%
Others	35.0

Source: *Financial World*, October 30, 1995, p. 35, from Smith Barney.

★ 934 ★

Farm Equipment (SIC 3523)

Crawler Tractor Makers

Shares are for the first six months of 1995.

Caterpillar 56.8%
Deere 18.6
Komatsu-Dresser 14.9
Case 9.1
Other 1.4

Source: *Investext,* Thomson Financial Services, November 30, 1995, p. 8, from Manfredi & Associates Inc.

★ 935 ★

Farm Equipment (SIC 3523)

Tractor Makers - North America

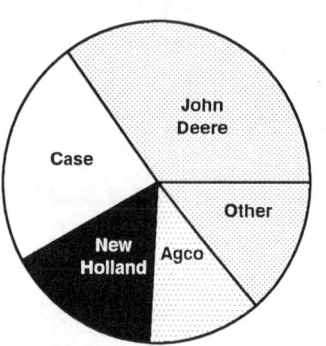

John Deere 35.0%
Case 23.0
New Holland 16.0
Agco 12.0
Other 14.0

Source: *Financial Times*, June 27, 1996, p. 16.

★ 936 ★

Farm Equipment (SIC 3523)

Tractor Manufacturers

Shares of the North American tractor market are shown in percent. Data refer to row crop tractors only. These tractors are used for planting and cultivating crops grown in rows.

Deere 50.0%
Case 35.0
Other 15.0

Source: *Wall Street Journal*, July 16, 1996, p. A8.

★ 937 ★

Farm Equipment (SIC 3523)

Who Makes Loader Backhoes

Shares are for the first six months of 1995.

Caterpillar 39.2%
Case 27.5
Deere 18.7
JCB 5.7
Other 12.9

Source: *Investext,* Thomson Financial Services, November 30, 1995, p. 8, from Manfredi & Associates Inc.

★ 938 ★

Lawn & Garden Equipment (SIC 3524)

Gas-Powered Landscaping Tools

Unit shipments are shown for 1994.

Trimmers and brushcutters 3,906,272
Chain saws 1,918,915
Hand held blowers 922,130
Hedge trimmers 204,165
Back pack blowers 163,284
Cut-off saws 84,032

Source: *Grounds Maintenance*, July 1995, p. 8, from Portable Power Equipment Manufacturers Association.

★ 939 ★
Lawn & Garden Equipment (SIC 3524)

Leaf Blower Makers

Market shares for hand-held leaf blowers are shown based on 4.1 million units shipped in 1995.

Poulan/Weed Eater	37.0%
Toro (Lawn-Boy)	18.0
Homelite	11.0
Black & Decker	10.0
McCulloch	7.0
Ryobi	6.0
Echo	3.0
Stihl	2.0
Husqvarna	1.0
Other	5.0

Source: *Appliance Manufacturer*, April 1996, p. 31, from industry reports.

★ 940 ★
Lawn & Garden Equipment (SIC 3524)

Mower Market Leaders - 1995

Shares are shown based on shipments of 5.95 million units. Data refer to walk-behind gas mowers.

MTD Products	35.0%
Murray	35.0
American Yard Products	20.0
Southland	4.0
Snapper	3.0
Toro (Lawn-Boy)	3.0

Source: *Appliance Manufacturer*, April 1996, p. 31, from industry reports.

★ 941 ★
Lawn & Garden Equipment (SIC 3524)

Outdoor Power Equipment Shipments

	1995	1996
Walk-behind mowers	5,984,325	6,079,043
Front engine lawn tractors	1,247,360	1,316,457
Tillers	352,559	356,986
Riding garden tractors	226,868	239,435
Rear engine riding mowers	168,137	158,088

Source: *Implement & Tractor*, November/December 1995, p. 15, from Outdoor Power Equipment Institute.

★ 942 ★
Lawn & Garden Equipment (SIC 3524)

String Trimmer Makers

Market shares are shown based on 6.9 million units shipped in 1995.

Poulan/Weed Eater	35.0%
Ryobi	14.0
McCulloch	12.0
Toro (Lawn-Boy)	11.0
Home Lite	10.0
Black & Decker	7.0
Stihl	4.0
Echo	2.0
Husqvarna	2.0
Other	3.0

Source: *Appliance Manufacturer*, April 1996, p. 31, from industry reports.

★ 943 ★
Construction Equipment (SIC 3531)

Hydraulic Excavator Market

Shares are for the first six months of 1995.

Caterpillar	35.7%
Komatsu-Dresser	20.7
Deere	12.1
Hitachi	8.0
Case	5.2
Other	17.7

Source: *Investext,* Thomson Financial Services, November 30, 1995, p. 8, from Manfredi & Associates Inc.

★ 944 ★
Mining Machinery (SIC 3532)

Electric Cable Shovel Market

The table shows the top brand's share of the electric cable shovel market. P&H is produced by Harnischfeger Industries.

P&H 75.0%
Other 25.0

Source: *Financial World*, February 26, 1996, p. 54.

★ 945 ★
Industrial Lifts (SIC 3537)

Forklift Market - Canada

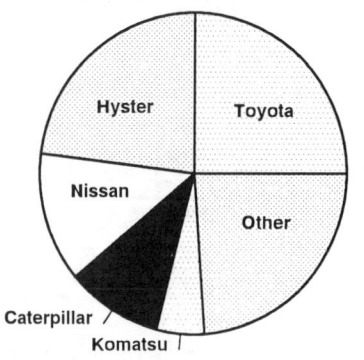

Toyota 25.0%
Hyster 23.0
Nissan 13.0
Caterpillar 10.0
Komatsu 5.0
Other 24.0

Source: *National Trade Data Bank*, May 27, 1996, p. IS960130.049.

★ 946 ★
Industrial Lifts (SIC 3537)

Industrial Lift Trucks

Production is shown by year.

	1996	1997	1998
Riders	110,000	90,000	98,000
Pedestrian	40,500	38,000	40,000

Source: *Purchasing*, February 15, 1996, p. 108, from Industrial Truck Association.

★ 947 ★
Machine Tools (SIC 3540)

Machine Tool Leaders - Canada

Shares are shown based on total installations in 1995.

Mazak 14.0%
Fadal 8.5
Matsurra 4.0
Mori Selki 4.0
Toshiba 4.0
Other 65.5

Source: *National Trade Data Bank*, May 27, 1996, p. IM960517.019.

★ 948 ★
Machine Tools (SIC 3540)

Top Machine Tool Firms

Firms are ranked by estimated value of 1996 production in millions of British pounds.

Cincinnati Milacron 95.0
Western Atlas 90.0
Bridgeport Machines 70.0
Giddings & Lewis 50.0

Source: *Financial Times*, April 30, 1996, p. 10, from industry reports.

★ 949 ★
Machine Tools (SIC 3541)

Cutting Tool Market - North America

Shares of the $1.2 billion market are estimated in percent.

Kennametal 35.0%
Sandvik/SECO 25.0
Valenite 17.0
Mitsubishi 3.0
Sumitomo 3.0
Toshiba 3.0
Other 14.0

Source: *Investext,* Thomson Financial Services, October 30, 1995, p. 3, from Lehman Brothers and Kennametal Inc.

★ 950 ★
Machine Tools (SIC 3541)

Machine Tool Market by End Use

Consumption is shown by industry.

Automotive 50.0%
Non-mechanical 25.0
Aerospace 7.0
Defense 5.0
Other 13.0

Source: *Tooling & Production*, May 1995, p. 12, from
Association for Manufacturing Technology.

★ 951 ★
Power Tools (SIC 3546)

Power Hand Tool/Tool Box Market

*The table shows the leading markets in Northeast
Central states in millions of dollars.*

Motor vehicle parts . . . . $ 33.5
Motor vehicles 21.8
Plumbing, heating & air conditioning 16.3
Special dies and tools 15.9
Industrial machinery 14.3

Source: *Industrial Distribution*, May 1996, p. 55, from
Industrial Market Information Inc.

★ 952 ★
Welding Equipment (SIC 3548)

Engine-Driven Welder Makers

Miller Electric Manufacturing Co.

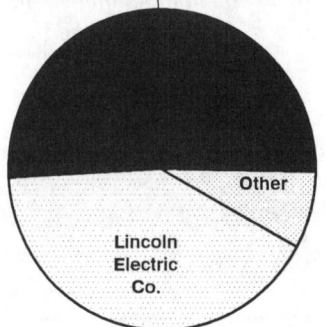

The North American market is shown by company.

Miller Electric Manufacturing Co. 51.0%
Lincoln Electric Co. 41.0
Other 8.0

Source: *Welding Design & Fabrication*, January 1996, p.
49, from industry estimates.

★ 953 ★
Welding Equipment (SIC 3548)

Who Uses Welding Equipment - Canada

The market is shown by end user.

Rolling stock 60.0%
Mining, oil drilling, maintenance 20.0
Pulp & paper machinery 10.0
Marine and aircraft 7.0
Other 3.0

Source: *National Trade Data Bank*, September 1, 1995,
p. IS9501.096.

★ 954 ★

Assembly Equipment (SIC 3549)

AMH Equipment Market

The table shows the share of the automated material handling market (AMH) represented by international firms. AGV stands for automatic guided vehicle. AS/RS stands for automated storage/retrieval systems.

Robots	90.0%
Monorial	60.0
Sorting conveyors	45.0
Vertical carousels	35.0
Horizontal carousels	30.0
AS/RS	25.0
AGV	15.0

Source: *Assembly*, April 1996, p. 8, from Advanced Technology Advisor.

★ 955 ★

Assembly Equipment (SIC 3549)

Wireline Market Shares

Data are for 1994.

Schlumberger	48.0%
Halliburton	21.0
Western Atlas	14.0
Other	16.0

Source: *Investext,* Thomson Financial Services, February 21, 1995, p. 9, from PaineWebber estimates.

★ 956 ★

Printing Equipment (SIC 3555)

Popular Printing Presses

Data show the types of presses in use at Fortune 500 companies, based on a survey of 61 respondents.

Small sheetfed offset	87.0%
Large sheetfed offset	51.0
Electronic/digital printers	49.0
Web offset	31.0
Envelope press	10.0
Label press	7.0
Other	5.0

Source: *In-Plant Graphics*, January 1996, p. 32.

★ 957 ★

Food Machinery (SIC 3556)

Who Uses Meat Machinery in Canada

Industrial packers/processing plants	45.0%
Grocery store chains	30.0
Independent delicatessans/meat shops	25.0

Source: *National Trade Data Bank*, March 2, 1996, p. IS9503.167.

★ 958 ★

Plastics Machinery (SIC 3559)

Plastics Machinery Demand

Demand is expected to increase from $2.1 billion in 1994 to $3.15 billion in 2000.

	1994	2000
Injection molding	61.6%	58.2%
Extrusion	11.5	10.9
Blow molding	12.5	15.6
Thermoforming	4.1	3.7
Other	10.3	11.6

Source: *Plastics News*, January 1, 1996, p. 9, from Freedonia Group Inc.

★ 959 ★

Semiconductor Equipment (SIC 3559)

U.S. Semiconductor Equipment Makers

Companies are ranked by 1995 sales in millions of dollars.

Applied Manufacturers	$ 3,500
Lam Research	1,030
Teradyne	675
Vanan	606

Source: *Electronic News*, March 4, 1996, p. 24, from VLSI Research Inc.

★ 960 ★

Pumps (SIC 3561)

Positive Displacement Pump Market - Canada

The end market is shown for 1992. The leading producers are John Brooks Company, Ingersoll - Dresser Pump, Viking Pump of Canada Inc., Wheatley Canada Ltd., and Wilron Equipment Ltd.

Oil & gas	60.0%
Food processing	20.0
Forestry equipment	10.0
Automotive parts	5.0
Pharmaceuticals	5.0

Source: *National Trade Data Bank*, March 2, 1996, p. 111089978.

★ 961 ★

Bearings (SIC 3562)

Bearing Shipments by Type

	1994	2000
Roller bearings	43.8%	45.1%
Ball bearings	36.2	36.3
Other bearing/parts	20.0	18.6

Source: *Purchasing*, June 6, 1996, p. 71, from Freedonia Group.

★ 962 ★

Office Equipment (SIC 3570)

Office Equipment Shipments - 1996

Shipments are shown in thousands of units.

Calculators	55,750
Disk drives	37,500
Computers	24,468
Computer printers	14,555
Modems	7,200
Fax machines	4,900
Display terminals	3,480
Typewriters	2,065
Copiers	1,650

Source: *Appliance Manufacturer*, January 1996, p. 107, from Information Technology Industry Council.

★ 963 ★

Computers (SIC 3571)

Computer Bases in Schools

Data show the brands of computers installed in public schools from grades K-12.

	93-94	94-95
Apple/Mac	59.0%	57.0%
IBM/clone	36.0	10.0
Others	5.0	33.0

Source: *Computer Reseller News*, February 26, 1996, p. 81, from Market Data Retrieval.

★ 964 ★

Computers (SIC 3571)

Computer Market Leaders

Shares are shown in percent.

	1994	1995
Compaq	10.3%	10.0%
IBM	8.5	8.0
Apple	8.5	7.8
Packard Bell	4.9	5.3
NEC	4.0	4.8
Others	63.8	64.1

Source: *Purchasing*, March 7, 1996, p. 7.

★ 965 ★

Computers (SIC 3571)

Computer Users by Age

Penetration is shown for 1995.

Under 30	34.6%
30-39	45.5
40-49	51.9
50-60	43.2
60 or older	20.0

Source: *Wall Street Journal*, May 21, 1996, p. B6, from Computer Intelligence InfoCorp.

★ 966 ★
Computers (SIC 3571)

Desktop PC Makers

Shares of the desktop personal computer (PC) market are shown for the first quarter of 1996.

Packard Bell	13.5%
Compaq	13.3
Apple	8.1
IBM	5.9
NEC	1.3
Other	57.9

Source: *New York Times*, June 5, 1996, p. C1, from Dataquest Inc., Packard Bell, and NEC.

★ 967 ★
Computers (SIC 3571)

Home Computer Market

The table shows who lead the home computer market in the first quarter of 1996.

Packard Bell	32.0%
Compaq	13.0
Apple	7.0
Gateway 2000	6.0
IBM	6.0
Other	36.0

Source: *USA TODAY*, June 27, 1996, p. 1, from Dataquest Inc.

★ 968 ★
Computers (SIC 3571)

Multimedia Computer Market

Multimedia machines had a 48% share of all personal computer sales in the United States in the last 18 months. Market shares are shown in percent.

Apple	19.0%
Packard Bell Electronics	14.0
Compaq	9.3
International Business Machines	7.4
NEC Corp.	7.0
Other	43.0

Source: *Investor's Business Daily*, June 11, 1996, p. A9, from Dataquest Inc.

★ 969 ★
Computers (SIC 3571)

Notebook Computer Market

Data are for 1994.

Toshiba	14.0%
Compaq	10.0
IBM	10.0
NEC	9.0
Apple	7.0
Other	50.0

Source: *Investor's Business Daily*, October 12, 1995, p. H1, from Dataquest Inc.

★ 970 ★
Computers (SIC 3571)

Notebook Computer Market - Canada

Dollar shares are shown for the second quarter of 1995.

Toshiba	13.2%
Compaq	11.5
IBM	11.0
AST	8.1
Apple	6.2
NEC	5.1
Digital Equipment	3.7
Dell	2.9
Other	38.2

Source: *Globe and Mail*, December 5, 1995, p. C4, from International Data Corp. Canada.

★ 971 ★
Computers (SIC 3571)

PC Market Shares

Shares are for the second quarter of 1996.

Compaq 12.4%
IBM 9.0
Packard Bell 8.7
Apple 7.4
Dell Computer 7.2
Other 55.3

Source: *Investor's Business Daily*, July 31, 1996, p. A6, from Dataquest Inc.

★ 972 ★
Computers (SIC 3571)

PC Shipments - 1995

	Units	Share
Compaq	2,669,000	11.7%
Packard Bell	2,656,000	11.6
Apple	2,636,000	11.5
IBM	1,885,000	8.2
Gateway 2000	1,175,000	5.1
Dell	1,145,000	5.0
Hewlett-Packard	1,023,000	4.5
Acer	824,000	3.6
Toshiba	750,000	3.3
AST	566,000	2.5
Others	7,521,000	32.9

Source: *Philadelphia Inquirer*, December 9, 1995, p. C1, from International Data Corp.

★ 973 ★
Computers (SIC 3571)

PC Shipments - 1996

Data are for the first quarter of 1996.

Compaq 12.9%
Packard Bell 10.8
Hewlett-Packard 7.0
Apple 6.5
Gateway 2000 . . . . 6.0
Other 43.2

Source: *Computerworld*, May 6, 1996, p. 32, from International Data Corp.

★ 974 ★
Computers (SIC 3571)

PCs in Public Schools

This table shows the share of the installed bases of educational computers in public schools. Data show 1995-96 estimates.

Apple 54.0%
IBM 26.0
Other IBM compatible 15.0
Other 5.0

Source: *Wall Street Journal*, November 13, 1995, p. R31, from Quality Education Data Inc.

★ 975 ★
Computers (SIC 3571)

PDA Market Leaders

Shares are shown based on a total market of 514,000 units in 1995. PDA stands for personal digital assistants.

Hewlett-Packard 34.0%
Apollo 18.0
Psion 14.0
Sharp 12.0
Sony 6.0
Motorola 4.0
Other 12.0

Source: *Informationweek*, July 22, 1996, p. 48, from Yankee Group.

★ 976 ★
Computers (SIC 3571)

Portable Computer Market

Toshiba 26.0%
Compaq 9.0
IBM 8.0
Texas Instruments 8.0
NEC 6.0
Apple 5.0
Dell 4.0
Micro Electronics 3.0
Sharp 2.0
AST 2.0
Other 27.0

Source: *Informationweek*, June 17, 1996, p. 18, from International Data Corp.

★ 977 ★

Computers (SIC 3571)

Portable PC Market

Company shares are shown as percentage of 3.8 million portable PCs (personal computers) shipped in 1995. Data are estimated.

Toshiba	19.9%
Compaq	11.4
Apple	9.9
IBM . . . . ·	9.8
NEC	4.3
AST	2.4
Other	42.3

Source: *PC Week*, February 26, 1996, p. 31, from Workgroup Strategic Services.

★ 978 ★

Computers (SIC 3571)

Top Computer Firms - 1994

Firms are ranked by revenues in billions of dollars. Shares of the group are shown in percent.

	Rev. ($ mil.)	% of Group
IBM	$ 64.1	44.5%
Hewlett-Packard	25.0	17.3
Digital Equipment	13.5	9.4
Compaq	10.9	7.6
Apple	9.2	6.4
AT&T G.I.S.	8.5	5.9
Unisys	7.4	5.1
Olivetti	5.6	3.9

Source: *New York Times*, September 21, 1995, p. C5, from *Hoover's Guide to Computer Companies*.

★ 979 ★

Computers (SIC 3571)

Top PC Brands - Mexico

Brand shares are shown in percent.

	1993	1994
Acer	22.5%	29.0%
Compaq	8.2	16.0
Hewlett-Packard	11.9	15.0
IBM	15.9	10.0
Lanix	3.9	5.0
Apple	5.0	4.0
Printaform	6.6	4.0
Olivetti	1.8	1.0
Toshiba	1.5	1.0
Others	20.0	11.0

Source: *National Trade Data Bank*, September 1, 1995, p. IMI950531, from Grupo Serfin.

★ 980 ★

Computers (SIC 3571)

Top PC Vendors - Mexico

Shares are shown for the first quarter of each year. Data are based on unit shipments.

	1Q 1995	1Q 1996
Acer	39.7%	23.7%
IBM	8.0	16.9
Compaq	8.7	10.9
Other	43.6	48.5

Source: *Computer Reseller News*, July 15, 1996, p. 19, from Dataquest Inc.

★ 981 ★

Computers (SIC 3571)

U.S. Computer Market by Type

Consumption is shown by segment in millions of dollars.

	1995 ($ mil.)	1996 ($ mil.)	Share
PC desk tops . . .	$ 45,418.0	$ 48,213.0	47.1%
Multiuser PCs . . .	26,385.0	28,888.0	28.2
Notebooks	12,922.0	15,131.0	14.8
Workstations . . .	7,081.0	7,388.0	7.2
Subnotebooks . . .	1,054.0	2,537.0	2.5
Laptops	225.0	132.0	0.1
Handheld computers	84.0	123.0	0.1

Source: *Electronic Business Today*, January 1996, p. 39, from Computer Intelligence InfoCorp.

★ 982 ★

Computers (SIC 3571)

Who Shipped PCs in 1995

Market shares are shown based on unit shipments in 1995. Figures are based on the recent agreement by Packard Bell to purchase much of the PC operations of NEC Corp.

Packard Bell and NEC	13.8%
Compaq	11.4
Apple	10.3
IBM	10.2
Dell	5.7
Gateway 2000	4.9
HP	3.2
AST	3.0
Acer	2.8
Other	34.6

Source: *San Jose Mercury News*, June 5, 1996, p. C1, from Computer Intelligence Infocorp.

★ 983 ★

Workstations (SIC 3571)

X Terminal Market Leaders

X terminal market shares are shown by company based on 237,426 units shipped in 1995.

Hewlett-Packard	25.2%
NCD	23.7
Tektronix	19.7
DEC	7.7
IBM	4.3
Other	19.4

Source: *PC Week*, February 19, 1996, p. 31, from Zona Research Inc.

★ 984 ★

Computer Data Storage (SIC 3572)

CD-ROM Drive Market - Canada

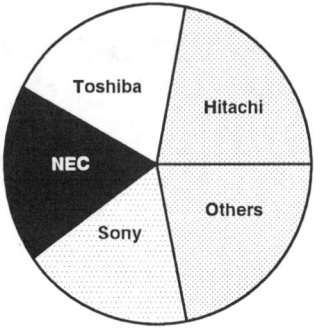

Market shares are shown in percent.

Hitachi	22.0%
Toshiba	20.0
NEC	18.0
Sony	18.0
Others	22.0

Source: *National Trade Data Bank*, March 2, 1996, p. 111093104, from industry sources.

★ 985 ★
Computer Data Storage (SIC 3572)

DASD Market

Direct-access storage device (DASD) market shares are shown based on the estimated 1,325 terabytes shipped in 1995.

EMC	38.0%
IBM	37.0
Hitachi Data Systems	12.0
StorageTek	9.0
Others	4.0

Source: *Informationweek*, November 6, 1995, p. 22, from Gartner Group.

★ 986 ★
Computer Data Storage (SIC 3572)

Data Storage Subsystem Market

Data are for 1995.

IBM	21.6%
EMC	7.4
Digital Equipment	5.6
NEC	5.5
Compaq	5.2
Fujitsu	5.0
Other	9.7

Source: *Wall Street Journal*, April 22, 1996, p. B4, from International Data Corp.

★ 987 ★
Computer Data Storage (SIC 3572)

Disk Drive Makers

Data are for 1995.

Quantum	22.3%
Seagate	19.3
Western Digital	14.2
Conner	13.5
IBM	12.2
Maxtor	8.1
Other	10.4

Source: *Electronic News*, January 15, 1996, p. 50, from Dataquest Inc.

★ 988 ★
Computer Data Storage (SIC 3572)

Low-End Tape Drive Producers

Shares of the low-end tape drive market are shown in percent. Data are for 1994.

Hewlett-Packard	31.0%
Conner	26.0
Tandberg	21.0
Rexon	12.0
Iomega	5.0
Others	5.0

Source: *Investor's Business Daily*, February 26, 1996, p. A8, from Freeman Associates Inc.

★ 989 ★
Computer Data Storage (SIC 3572)

Mainframe-Backup Market

The mainframe-backup market is shown by vendor for 1995.

Interlink (Harbor)	29.2%
Network Systems	21.7
IBM	20.5
Others	28.6

Source: *PC Week*, March 4, 1996, p. 39, from Strategic Research.

★ 990 ★
Computer Peripherals (SIC 3577)

Computer Keyboard Market

Shares are shown based on the $620 million market in 1993.

Lexmark 24.0%
Key Tronic 17.0
NMB 10.0
Other 49.0

Source: *Electronic Business Today*, October 1995, p. 71, from Venture Development Corp.

★ 991 ★
Computer Peripherals (SIC 3577)

Computer Monitor Makers

Firms are ranked by 1995 revenues in millions of dollars.

NEC Technologies Inc., MultiSync Display
   Division . . . . $ 745.0
Sony Electronics Inc., Information
   Technology of America 730.0
Samsung Electronics America 728.0
Phillips Consumer Electronics Co. . . . 551.0
ADI Systems Inc. 548.0
LG Electronics USA Inc. 507.0
Acer Peripherals Inc. 440.0
MAG InnoVision 379.0
CTX International Inc. 305.0
Tatung Company of America 295.0

Source: *PC Magazine*, July 1996, p. 258, from Stanford Resources.

★ 992 ★
Computer Peripherals (SIC 3577)

Intelligent Printer Market

Shares are shown based on 267,519 units shipped in 1995. Figures are for 13-ppm to 20-ppm monochrome laser printers. Intelligent printers not only have the ability to coordinate large jobs but they can also respond to remote inquiries. This allows companies to monitor all their printers from one central location.

Hewlett-Packard 55.0%
Lexmark 17.0
Apple 16.0
Kyocera 2.0
Xerox 2.0
Other 8.0

Source: *Informationweek*, August 5, 1996, p. 70, from International Data Corp.

★ 993 ★
Computer Peripherals (SIC 3577)

Multifunctional Peripheral Units

The table shows the all-in-one multifunction peripheral unit market by producer. Data are for 1995.

Hewlett-Packard 50.74%
Brother 19.03
Canon 13.74
Lexmark 8.46
Xerox 6.77
Panasonic 1.27

Source: *Computer Reseller News*, April 1, 1996, p. 71, from International Data Corp.

★ 994 ★
Computer Peripherals (SIC 3577)

Top Motherboard Vendors

Companies are ranked by 1995 sales in millions of dollars.

Intel . . . . $ 1,500
SCI Systems 1,000
First International 800
Acer 600
Elitegroup 440
Asus 305
Maxtech/GVC 250
Continued on next page.

★ **994** ★ *Continued*
Computer Peripherals (SIC 3577)

Top Motherboard Vendors

Companies are ranked by 1995 sales in millions of dollars.

Micronics	$ 234
Mitac	180
A-Trend	100

Source: *Computer Reseller News*, June 3, 1996, p. 134, from industry analysts and company reports.

★ **995** ★
Computer Peripherals (SIC 3577)

Top PC Monitor Makers

Companies are ranked by 1995 sales in millions of dollars.

Samsung	$ 2,750
NECT	1,800
Philips	1,360
LG Electronics	1,200
Sony	840
Acer	790
ADI	680
Lite-On	642
Tatung	550
Mag Innovision	512

Source: *Computer Reseller News*, June 3, 1996, p. 130, from industry analysts and company reports.

★ **996** ★
Computer Peripherals (SIC 3577)

Video/Graphics Board Producers

Firms are ranked by 1995 revenues in millions of dollars.

Diamond Multimedia Systems Inc.	$ 227
ATI Technologies	147
Matrox Graphics Inc.	123
STB Systems Inc.	99
Number Nine Visual Technology Corp. . . .	82

Source: *PC Magazine*, July 1996, p. 260, from International Data Corp. and John Peddie Associates.

★ **997** ★
Computer Printers (SIC 3577)

Color Laser Printer Makers

Shares are shown based on unit shipments in 1994 and 1995.

	1994	1995
Hewlett-Packard	49.0%	36.0%
Apple	-	30.0
Xerox	19.0	11.0
Tektronix	2.0	9.0
Others	30.0	14.0

Source: *Computer Reseller News*, March 11, 1996, p. 12, from International Data Corp.

★ **998** ★
Computer Printers (SIC 3577)

Computer Printer Makers

Market shares are shown based on unit sales of color printers.

Hewlett-Packard	59.4%
Canon	21.1
Epson	10.1
Apple	4.1
Lexmark	3.3
Others	2.0

Source: *New York Times*, May 20, 1996, p. C3, from Computer Intelligence and Hard Copy Observer.

★ **999** ★
Computer Printers (SIC 3577)

Dot Matrix Printers

Shares of dot matrix printer shipments are shown in percent.

	1993	1994	1995
Epson	26.0%	24.0%	29.0%
Okidata	15.0	18.0	22.0
Panasonic	25.0	25.0	19.0
Lexmark	5.0	5.0	6.0
Other	29.0	28.0	24.0

Source: *Computer Reseller News*, March 4, 1996, p. 97, from International Data Corp.

★ 1000 ★

Computer Printers (SIC 3577)

Laser Printer Makers

Xerox Corp.

IBM Corp.

Hewlett-Packard Co.

QMS Inc.

Digital Equipment Corp.

Printronix, Inc.

Siemens Nixdorf Printer Systems

Others

The departmental market is shown by company.

Xerox Corp.	34.0%
IBM Corp.	23.0
Hewlett-Packard Co.	9.0
QMS Inc.	7.0
Digital Equipment Corp.	5.0
Printronix, Inc.	5.0
Siemens Nixdorf Printer Systems	5.0
Others	12.0

Source: *Computer Reseller News*, December 11, 1995, p. 99, from BIS Strategic Resources.

★ 1001 ★

Computer Printers (SIC 3577)

U.S. Computer Printer Makers

Market shares refer to printers that can print 1-14 pages per minute.

HP	57.5%
Okidata	7.8
Apple	5.6
Panasonic	4.6
Epson	4.6
Lexmark	3.2
Other	16.7

Source: *Computer Reseller News*, December 25, 1995, p. 115, from Venture Marketing Strategies.

★ 1002 ★

Automated Banking Machines (SIC 3578)

ATMs by Installed Base

	1994	1995
Commercial banks	72.0%	69.0%
Non-financial companies	13.0	18.0
Thrifts	13.0	12.0
Credit unions	2.0	1.0

Source: *USBanker*, October 1995, p. 20, from Mentis Corp.

★ 1003 ★

Heating and Cooling (SIC 3585)

A/C and Heat Pump Makers

Shares of the unitary air conditioning and heat pump market are shown in percent for 1993.

United Technologies	22.0%
Lennox (Armstrong)	15.0
American Standard	13.0
Inter-City	13.0
Rheem	12.0
Goodman	10.0
York	9.0
Nordyne (Interthem)	3.0
Coleman/Evcon	2.0
Other	5.0

Source: *Investext*, Thomson Financial Services, April 12, 1995, p. 17, from *Appliance Manufacturer*.

★ 1004 ★

Heating and Cooling (SIC 3585)

Air Terminal Units

Shares are estimated for 1994. Data refer to terminal units sent to mechanical and sheet metal contractors for commercial and industrial applications. The market was valued at $75-$85 million.

Trane	25.0%
Titus	20.0
Environmental Technologies	15.0
Metal Aire	7.0
Hart & Cooley	3.0
Other	30.0

Source: *Investext*, Thomson Financial Services, July 17, 1995, p. 20.

★ 1005 ★

Heating and Cooling (SIC 3585)

Central Air Conditioner Makers

Residential air conditioner market is shown for 1995.

United Technologies	20.0%
Goodman	15.0
Rheem	14.0
American Standard	12.0
Lennox	10.0
Inter-City	9.0
York	7.0
Nordyne	5.0
Coleman	3.0
Raytheon	3.0
Others	2.0

Source: *Appliance Manufacturer*, April 1996, p. 30, from industry reports.

★ 1006 ★

Heating and Cooling (SIC 3585)

Gas Furnace Makers

Market shares of the residential gas furnace market are shown in percent for 1993.

United Technologies	24.0%
American Standard (Trane)	15.0
Lennox (Armstrong)	15.0
Inter-City	15.0
Rheem	10.0
Goodman	9.0
York	6.0

Ducane	3.0%
Nordyne	2.0
Raytheon (Amana)	2.0
Othr	4.0

Source: *Investext,* Thomson Financial Services, April 12, 1995, p. 17, from *Appliance Manufacturer*.

★ 1007 ★

Heating and Cooling (SIC 3585)

HVAC Equipment Shipments - 1994

Shares are shown based on $16.6 billion in shipments. HVAC stands for heating, ventillating, and air conditioning.

Heating Xfer equipment	33.0%
Unitary	26.0
Compressors	22.0
Furnaces	9.0
Room units	7.0
Refrigeration equipment	3.0

Source: *Air Conditioning, Heating & Refrigeration News*, November 13, 1995, p. 3, from United States Bureau of the Census.

★ 1008 ★

Heating and Cooling (SIC 3585)

HVAC Shipments - 1995

Water heaters	8,491,088
Air conditioners	8,363,176
Furnaces (central)	3,138,073
Heat pumps	1,024,000
Heaters (room)	576,222
Boilers	300,991
Heaters (unit)	171,256
Furnaces (wall)	168,502
Furnaces (duct)	16,812
Furnaces (gas floor)	13,111

Source: *Appliance Manufacturer*, March 1996, p. 12, from Air Conditioning and Refrigeration Institute and Appliance Manufacturers Association.

★ 1009 ★

Heating and Cooling (SIC 3585)

Room Air Conditioner Market

Shares are shown based on shipments of 4.3 million units in 1995.

Kenmore	17.3%
Fedders	15.9
GE/GE Profile	9.7
Whirlpool	9.3
White-Westinghouse	5.9
Amana	5.4
Carrier	4.8
Emerson Quiet Kool	4.8
Friedrich	4.2
Frigidaire	3.5
Roper	2.9
Sharp	2.2
Montgomery Ward	2.1
Pansonic	1.7
Airtemp	1.4
Goldstar	1.3
Quasar	1.2
Gibson	1.1
Climatrol	0.8
Crosley	0.8
Other	3.7

Source: *HFN*, March 11, 1996, p. 86, from Association of Home Appliance Manufacturers and company reports.

★ 1010 ★

Water Filters (SIC 3589)

Water Filter Market

Shares of the filtered water carafe market are shown in percent.

Brita Products Co.	85.0%
Other	15.0

Source: *Advertising Age*, July 1, 1996, p. 10.

★ 1011 ★

Water Filters (SIC 3589)

Water Filtration Market

Filter pitcher	
Faucet mount	
Filter dispenser	
Under-the-sink	
Whole house	
Countertop	

Water filtration unit sales reached $5.54 million in 1995.

Filter pitcher	53.5%
Faucet mount	17.0
Filter dispenser	8.1
Under-the-sink	7.9
Whole house	7.7
Countertop	5.8

Source: *DM*, July 1996, p. 57, from industry reports.

★ 1012 ★

Components (SIC 3590)

Hydraulic Power Components

Sales of hydraulic power components reached $5.65 billion in 1994.

Fluid connectors and filters	44.0%
Pumps, motors, hydrostatic transmissions	22.0
Hydraulic cylinders, rotary actuators	17.0
Hydraulic valves	16.0
Other	1.0

Source: *InTech*, October 1995, p. 18, from Frost & Sullivan.

★ 1013 ★

Fluid Power (SIC 3590)

Fluid Power Market - South Atlantic

The leading markets are ranked by value in millions of dollars.

Road construction	$ 17.9
Heavy construction	9.2
Water, sewer, utility	8.9
Concrete work	8.7
Excavation work	6.4

Source: *Industrial Distribution*, June 1996, p. 109, from Industrial Market Information Inc.

SIC 36 - Electronic and Other Electric Equipment

★ 1014 ★

Electronics (SIC 3600)

Top Electronics Firms

The top 10 companies are ranked by 1994 sales in billions of dollars. Shares of the group are shown in percent.

	Sales ($ bil.)	% of Group
IBM	$ 64.05	29.4%
AT&T	28.55	13.1
Hewlett-Packard	26.61	12.2
Motorola	22.25	10.2
Xerox	15.09	6.9
GM Hughes	14.10	6.5
Digital	13.78	6.3
Intel	11.52	5.3
Lockheed Martin	10.90	5.0
Compaq Computer	10.87	5.0

Source: *Purchasing*, August 17, 1995, p. 7, from Cahners Economics.

★ 1015 ★

Carbon Fibers (SIC 3624)

Carbon Fiber Producers

Share of total production capacity is estimated by company.

Hercules	47.2%
Amoco	33.3
Mitsubishi	19.4

Source: *Interavia*, December 1995, p. 25, from *Air & Cosmos*.

★ 1016 ★

Control Equipment (SIC 3625)

Motion Control Industry

Motion control industry is shown by segment. The market is led by Allied Signal with a 9.3% share and Parker Hannifin Corp. with a 9.0% share.

	Sales ($ mil.)	Share
Hydraulic actuators	$ 702	20.6%
Electric actuators	273	8.0
Motion controllers	249	7.3
Brushless motors & controls . . .	248	7.3
CNCs	240	7.0
Servo motors	233	6.8
Motion control semiconductors .	183	5.4
Encoders	179	5.2
Servo drivers & amplifiers . . .	176	5.2
Pneumatic actuators	166	4.9
Servovalves	165	4.8
Stepping motors	132	3.9
Positioning systems, tables . . .	104	3.0
Synchros & resovers	92	2.7
S/D converters	65	1.9
Stepmotor controllers	55	1.6
Steppers (can-types)	35	1.0
Others	114	3.3

Source: *Industrial Distribution*, December 1995, p. 14, from Ross Associates.

★ 1017 ★

Household Appliances (SIC 3630)

Household Product Shipments

Shipments are shown in thousands of units for 1996.

Cooking equipment	15,965
Microwave ovens	8,965
Electric ranges	4,070
Gas ranges	2,930
Surface cooktops	333
Laundry equipment	12,165

Continued on next page.

★ 1017 ★ *Continued*
Household Appliances (SIC 3630)
Household Product Shipments

Shipments are shown in thousands of units for 1996.

Washers	6,921
Electric dryers	4,019
Gas dryers	1,225
Cleanup equipment	9,356
Disposers	4,724
Dishwashers	4,505
Compactors	127
Food preservation	10,321
Comfort equipment	4,978

Source: *Appliance Manufacturer*, January 1996, p. 104, from Association of Home Appliance Manufacturers.

★ 1018 ★
Cooking Equipment (SIC 3631)
Electric Range Brands

Shares are shown based on 4.048 million units shipped in 1995.

GE/GE Profile	25.3%
Whirlpool	16.4
Kenmore	15.8
Hotpoint	5.5
Frigidaire	4.8
Maytag	4.7
Tappan	4.3
Magic Chef	4.2
Roper	3.3
White-Westinghouse	2.7
KitchenAid	2.1
Caloric	1.7
Jenn-Air	1.7
Amana	1.6
Gibson	1.1
Other	4.8

Source: *HFN*, March 11, 1996, p. 84, from Association of Home Appliance Manufacturers and company reports.

★ 1019 ★
Cooking Equipment (SIC 3631)
Electric Range Market

Shares are shown by retail value. The most popular color shipped was white, with 55% of all shipments.

General Electric	24.50%
Sears/Kenmore	17.50
Whirlpool	15.25
Tappan	5.60
Frigidaire	4.35
Hotpoint	4.25
Maytag	4.00
Jenn-Air	3.75
Magic Chef	3.30
Amana	2.50
Kitchen Aid	2.10
White Westinghouse	2.00
Roper	2.00
Caloric	1.60
Montgomery Ward	1.00
RCA	0.50
Other	5.80

Source: *Dealerscope*, May 1996, p. 55, from Hudson Valley Editorial Services.

★ 1020 ★
Cooking Equipment (SIC 3631)
Gas Grill Makers

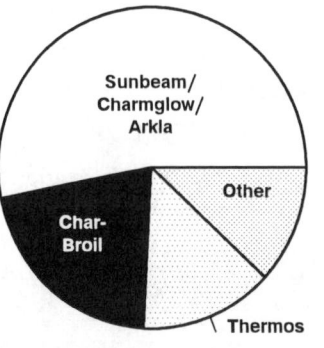

Shares are for 1993.

Sunbeam/Charmglow/Arkla	53.0%
Char-Broil	21.0
Thermos	14.0
Other	12.0

Source: *Investext,* Thomson Financial Services, May 8, 1995, p. 8, from Sunbeam-Oster.

★ 1021 ★

Cooking Equipment (SIC 3631)

Gas Range Brands

Shares are shown based on 2.853 million units shipped in 1995.

GE/GE Profile	16.7%
Kenmore	16.5
Tappan	13.3
Magic Chef	9.4
Caloric	8.3
Whirlpool	6.5
Maytag	5.5
Hotpoint	3.6
Roper	2.7
Frigidaire	2.3
White-Westinghouse	2.0
Amana	1.3
Premier	1.1
Jenn-Air	0.9
KitchenAid	0.9
Sunray	0.9
Brown	0.8
RCA	0.8
Other	6.5

Source: *HFN*, March 11, 1996, p. 84, from Association of Home Appliance Manufacturers and company reports.

★ 1022 ★

Cooking Equipment (SIC 3631)

Outdoor Grill Makers

Shares of the $100 million market are shown in percent.

Weber	46.0%
Sunbeam Outdoor Products	19.0
Other	35.0

Source: *Advertising Age*, September 11, 1995, p. 4.

★ 1023 ★

Cooking Equipment (SIC 3631)

Top Microwave Brands

Shares are shown based on 8.596 million units shipped in 1995.

Sharp	23.6%
GE/GE Profile	14.7
Panasonic	10.5
Kenmore	10.0

Tappan	6.1%
Whirlpool	5.1
Magic CHef	4.9
Goldstar	4.8
Emerson	4.3
Samsung	3.3
Amana	2.7
Sanyo	2.2
Quasar	1.5
Other	6.3

Source: *HFN*, March 11, 1996, p. 86, from Association of Home Appliance Manufacturers and company reports.

★ 1024 ★

Refrigerators and Freezers (SIC 3632)

Built-In Refrigerator Makers

The built-in refrigerator market has an estimated 1%- 2% of the 8.5 million unit refrigerator market. Shares of the built-in market are shown in percent.

Sub-Zero	70.0%
Other	30.0

Source: *Forbes*, April 8, 1996, p. 98.

★ 1025 ★

Refrigerators and Freezers (SIC 3632)

Leading Freezer Brands

Shares are shown based on retail value.

Sears	34.85%
GE Appliances	12.25
Whirlpool	7.75
Frigidaire	7.25
White Westinghouse	5.80
Kelvinator	5.60

Continued on next page.

★ 1025 ★ *Continued*

Refrigerators and Freezers (SIC 3632)

Leading Freezer Brands

Shares are shown based on retail value.

Tappan	5.25%
Amana Refrigeration	4.20
Gibson	4.10
Roper	4.00
Holiday	1.60
W.C. Wood & Co.	1.40
Crosley	0.75
Other	5.20

Source: *Dealerscope*, May 1996, p. 57, from Hudson Valley Editorial Services.

★ 1026 ★

Refrigerators and Freezers (SIC 3632)

Top Refrigerator Brands

Shares are shown based on 8.67 million units shipped in 1995.

Kenmore	20.1%
GE/GE Profile	19.6
Whirlpool	11.5
Amana	8.5
Frigidaire	6.3
Hotpoint	4.8
Roper	4.4
Maytag	3.4
Admiral	3.0
KitchenAid	2.7
White-Westinghouse	2.6
Magic Chef	2.5
Gibson	1.0
RCA	1.0
Kelvinator	0.9
Other	7.4

Source: *HFN*, March 11, 1996, p. 84, from Association of Home Appliance Manufacturers and company reports.

★ 1027 ★

Laundry Equipment (SIC 3633)

Dryer Market - 1995

Shares are shown by retail value.

Sears/Kenmore	28.00%
Whirlpool	20.25
Maytag	13.10

General Electric	12.50%
Hotpoint	3.90
Amana	3.75
White Westinghouse	3.25
Frigidaire	2.75
Roper	2.25
Admiral	1.50
Magic Chef	1.50
Montgomery Ward	1.50
Speed Queen	1.25
RCA	0.50
Tappan	0.50
Crosley	0.40
Kelvinator	0.40
Norge	0.40
Gibson	0.30

Source: *Dealerscope*, May 1996, p. 60, from Hudson Valley Editorial Services.

★ 1028 ★

Laundry Equipment (SIC 3633)

Washer Market - 1995

Shares are shown by retail value.

Sears/Kenmore	28.50%
Whirlpool	20.00
Maytag	13.25
General Electric	10.50
Amana	3.50
Frigidaire	3.00
Hotpoint	2.90
White Westinghouse	2.60
Roper	2.30
Admiral	2.00
Kitchen Aid	2.00
Magic Chef	1.75
Speed Queen	1.60
Montgomery Ward	1.30
Kelvinator	0.90
Gibson	0.75
Tappan	0.70
RCA	0.50
Norge	0.40
Crosley	0.30
Other	1.25

Source: *Dealerscope*, May 1996, p. 60, from Hudson Valley Editorial Services.

★ 1029 ★

Laundry Equipment (SIC 3633)

Washing Machine Producers

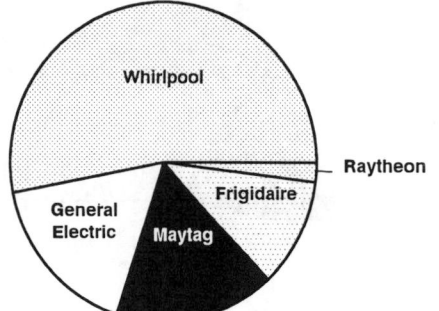

Market shares shown are based on shipments. Whirlpool produces both Sears' Kenmore brand (30% share) and its own brand Whirlpool (23% share).

Whirlpool	53.0%
General Electric	17.0
Maytag	17.0
Frigidaire	11.0
Raytheon	2.0

Source: *Business Week,* November 20, 1995, p. 97, from *Appliance* and Sears Roebuck & Co.

★ 1030 ★

Small Appliances (SIC 3634)

Can Opener Makers

Shares are shown based on 6.9 million units shipped in 1995.

Hamilton Beach/Proctor-Silex	26.0%
Black & Decker	25.0
Rival	25.0
Sunbeam-Oster	9.0
Presto	5.0
Toastmaster	2.0
Farberware	1.0
Waring	1.0
Others	6.0

Source: *Appliance Manufacturer,* April 1996, p. 31, from industry reports.

★ 1031 ★

Small Appliances (SIC 3634)

Dehumidifier Market Leaders - 1995

Shares are shown based on shipments of 1.003 million units.

Holmes	25.0%
Whirlpool	25.0
GEA	5.0
Royal Sovereign	2.0
Sanyo Fisher	2.0
Others	41.0

Source: *Appliance Manufacturer,* April 1996, p. 30, from industry reports.

★ 1032 ★

Small Appliances (SIC 3634)

Electric Knives Market

Shares are shown based on 1.62 million units shipped in 1995.

Hamilton Beach/Proctor-Silex	32.0%
Black & Decker	29.0
Toastmaster	15.0
Regal	12.0
Presto	5.0
Sunbeam-Oster	4.0
Other	3.0

Source: *Appliance Manufacturer,* April 1996, p. 31, from industry reports.

★ 1033 ★

Small Appliances (SIC 3634)

Iron Makers

Shares of the $265 million market are shown in percent.

Black & Decker	50.0%
Subeam	20.0
Other	30.0

Source: *Investext,* Thomson Financial Services, May 8, 1995, p. 14.

★ 1034 ★

Small Appliances (SIC 3634)

Men's Shaver Market

Shares are shown based on 7.065 million units shipped in 1995.

North American Philips (Norelco, Shick)	48.0%
Remington	32.0
Braun	14.0
Matsushita (Panasonic)	5.0
Others	1.0

Source: *Appliance Manufacturer*, April 1996, p. 31, from industry reports.

★ 1035 ★

Small Appliances (SIC 3634)

Mixer Market Shares

Shares are shown based on 5.42 million units shipped in 1995.

Hamilton Beach/Proctor-Silex	22.0%
Black & Decker	19.0
Sunbeam-Oster	17.0
KitchenAid	10.0
West Bend	7.0
Betty Crocker	6.0
Rival	5.0
Toastmaster	3.0
Waring	3.0
Farberware	1.0
Others	7.0

Source: *Appliance Manufacturer*, April 1996, p. 31, from industry reports.

★ 1036 ★

Small Appliances (SIC 3634)

Popular Hair Dryers

Data show the preferred brands of hair dryers, based on a survey.

Conair	54.0%
Vidal Sassoon	12.0
General Electric	10.0
Clairol	4.0
Sunbeam	4.0
Norelco	2.0
Other	14.0

Source: *Stores*, May 1996, p. 86, from Leo J. Shapiro & Associates.

★ 1037 ★

Small Appliances (SIC 3634)

Portable Kitchen Appliance Makers - Canada

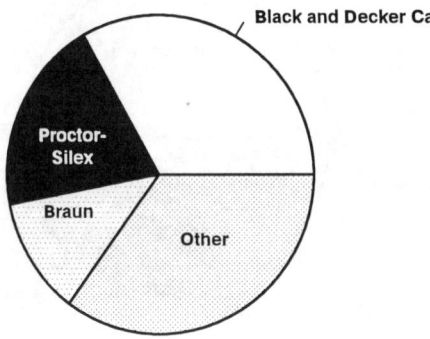

Black and Decker Canada

Proctor-Silex

Braun

Other

Producers of small electrical kitchen appliances are shown in percent.

Black and Decker Canada	33.0%
Proctor-Silex	20.0
Braun	12.0
Other	35.0

Source: *National Trade Data Bank*, March 2, 1996, p. 111092698.

★ 1038 ★

Small Appliances (SIC 3634)

Who Makes Coffeemakers

Shares are shown based on 13.67 million units shipped in 1995.

North American Systems	29.0%
Hamilton Beach/Proctor-Silex	23.0
Black & Decker	15.0
Braun	9.0
West Bend	7.0
Bunn-O Matic	5.0
Regal	5.0
Krups	4.0
Melitta	2.0
Other	1.0

Source: *Appliance Manufacturer*, April 1996, p. 31, from industry reports.

★ 1039 ★
Small Appliances (SIC 3634)

Women's Shaver Market

Shares are shown based on 2.335 million units shipped in 1995.

Remington	38.0%
North American Philips (Norelco, Schick) . .	32.0
Matsushita (Panasonic)	19.0
Others	11.0

Source: *Appliance Manufacturer*, April 1996, p. 31, from industry reports.

★ 1040 ★
Vacuum Cleaners (SIC 3635)

Hand-Held Vacuum Makers

Shares are shown based on shipments of 6.0 million units in 1995.

Royal	43.0%
Black & Decker	31.0
Hoover	10.0
Eureka	4.0
Bissell	3.0
Douglas	3.0
Ryobi (Singer)	3.0
Other	3.0

Source: *Appliance Manufacturer*, April 1996, p. 31, from industry reports.

★ 1041 ★
Vacuum Cleaners (SIC 3635)

Popular Vacuum Brands

Shares are shown based on retail value. Data show that consumers purchased 30.5% of them in discount department stores. By type, upright vacuums lead with a 71% share, sticks followed with an 18.7% share and canisters with a 10.3% share.

Hoover	27.25%
Eureka	19.25
Sears/Kenmore	10.80
Royal	10.40
Kirby	5.00
Oreck	3.00
Singer	3.00
Electrolux	2.90
Regina	2.80
Black & Decker	2.50
Panasonic	2.50
Shop Vac	2.10
Rainbow	2.00
Bissell	1.80
Sharp	0.80
Other	30.9

Source: *Dealerscope*, May 1996, p. 60, from Hudson Valley Editorial Services.

★ 1042 ★
Dishwashers (SIC 3639)

Leading Dishwashers

Shares are shown by retail value.

Sears/Kenmore	26.00%
General Electric	17.75
Whirlpool	16.00
Maytag	15.00
Kitchen Aid	9.25
Frigidaire	3.50
Hotpoint	3.00
White Westinghouse	2.50
Magic Chef	1.50
Tappan	1.25
Gibson	0.75
Amana	0.50
Bosch	0.50

Continued on next page.

★ 1042 ★ *Continued*
Dishwashers (SIC 3639)

Leading Dishwashers

Shares are shown by retail value.

Caloric 0.50%
Roper 0.50
Jenn Air 0.25
Other 1.25

Source: *Dealerscope*, May 1996, p. 56, from Hudson
Valley Editorial Services.

★ 1043 ★
Dishwashers (SIC 3639)

Top Dishwasher Brands

*Shares are shown based on 4.553 million units
shipped in 1995.*

Kenmore 22.5%
GE/GE Profile 18.1
Maytag 17.6
Whirlpool 15.7
KitchenAid 8.1
Frigidaire 3.6
Hotpoint 2.8
Roper 1.6
White-Westinghouse 1.5
Magic Chef 1.3
Tappan 1.1
Caloric 0.8
Jenn-Air 0.8
Other 4.5

Source: *HFN*, March 11, 1996, p. 86, from Association of
Home Appliance Manufacturers and company reports.

★ 1044 ★
Lamps (SIC 3641)

U.S. Lamp Shipments

*Shipments are shown for 1992 and estimated for
1997 in millions of dollars.*

	1992	1997	Share
Fluorescents	$ 965	$ 1,380	37.8%
Large incandescents . . .	1,047	1,275	34.9
Miniature incandescents . .	483	530	14.5
HID and other electrical discharge	306	435	11.9
Photographic incandescents	52	35	1.0

Source: *Purchasing*, March 7, 1996, p. 70, from
Freedonia Group.

★ 1045 ★
Switches (SIC 3643)

Switch Market - 1995

Microswitches 23.1%
Lever/rocker 18.3
Pushbutton 18.0
Keylock 17.3
Slide 10.0
Rotary 9.4
Thumbwheel 3.9

Source: *Purchasing*, May 23, 1996, p. S16, from Frost &
Sullivan.

★ 1046 ★
Spotlights (SIC 3648)

Long-Range Spotlight Market

*Shares of the market are shown in percent. The most
popular brand is the Super Trouper.*

Ballantyne of Omaha Inc. 85.0%
Other 15.0

Source: *Forbes*, May 6, 1995, p. 65.

★ 1047 ★
Consumer Electronics (SIC 3651)

CD Player Market

Shares are shown based on 32.3 million units shipped in 1995.

Sony	42.0%
Matsushita	9.0
Pioneer	8.0
Sanyo Fisher	7.0
JVC	6.0
Kenwood	5.0
Thomson	5.0
Sharp	4.0
NAP	3.0
Emerson	1.0
Samsung	1.0
Other	9.0

Source: *Appliance Manufacturer*, April 1996, p. 31, from industry reports.

★ 1048 ★
Consumer Electronics (SIC 3651)

Camcorder Suppliers

The top three suppliers are ranked by market share.

Sony	22.0%
RCA	17.0
JVC/Panasonic	15.0
Other	46.0

Source: *Dealerscope*, July 1995, p. 38.

★ 1049 ★
Consumer Electronics (SIC 3651)

Color TV Makers

Shares are shown based on 25.2 million units shipped in 1995.

Thomson	21.0%
NAP	14.0
Zenith	13.0
Sony	7.0
Sharp	6.0
Emerson	5.0
Sanyo Fisher	5.0
Toshiba	5.0
Matsushita	4.0
Mitsubishi	3.0
Samsung	3.0

Goldstar	2.0%
Others	12.0

Source: *Appliance Manufacturer*, April 1996, p. 32, from industry reports.

★ 1050 ★
Consumer Electronics (SIC 3651)

Electronic Entertainment Products

Consumption is shown by segment for 1995 in millions of dollars.

	($ mil.)	Share
Televisions	$ 8,170.0	34.7%
Radios	5,012.0	21.3
VCRs	3,500.0	14.9
Camcorders	2,238.0	9.5
Electronic watches	1,615.0	6.9
CDs	1,335.0	5.7
Tape record/players	853.0	3.6
Car units	841.0	3.6

Source: *Electronic Business Today*, January 1996, p. 42, from Elsevier Advanced Technology.

★ 1051 ★
Consumer Electronics (SIC 3651)

Electronic Products - 1996

Shipments are shown in thousands of units for 1996.

Audio equipment	146,598
CD players	34,450
Portable headset audio	34,013
Portable CD equipment	21,100
Tape and radio/tape players	18,870
Home radios	17,300
Tape and radio/tape recorders	13,450
Compact audio systems	6,300
Rack audio systems	1,115
Video products	66,100
TVs, direct view color	25,900
VCR decks	13,700
TVs, direct-view with stereo	11,760
VCR decks with stereo	5,320
Camcorders	3,550
TV/VCR combos	2,400
TVs, projection	915
VCRs	610
TVs, LCD monochrome	540
TVs monochrome	460

Continued on next page.

★ 1051 ★ *Continued*
Consumer Electronics (SIC 3651)

Electronic Products - 1996

Shipments are shown in thousands of units for 1996.

TVs, LCD color	350
C-band Home Satellite Earth stations . .	335
Laserdisc players	260

Source: *Appliance Manufacturer*, January 1996, p. 106, from EIA Market Research Development.

★ 1052 ★
Consumer Electronics (SIC 3651)

Leading AM/FM Receivers

The top three suppliers of AM/FM receivers are ranked by market share.

Sony	22.0%
JVC	11.0
Pioneer	11.0
Other	56.0

Source: *Dealerscope*, July 1995, p. 38.

★ 1053 ★
Consumer Electronics (SIC 3651)

Leading Speaker Suppliers

Market shares of the top three suppliers are shown in percent.

Bose	22.0%
Pioneer	10.0
Sony	9.0
Other	59.0

Source: *Dealerscope*, July 1995, p. 38.

★ 1054 ★
Consumer Electronics (SIC 3651)

Mini System Market

Shares refer to systems costing less than $200. In 1995, 70% of all mini systems sold cost less than $300. Aiwa lead the $200-$299 segment with a 56.2% share.

RCA	26.2%
Sharp	22.3
Emerson	10.6
Soundesign	6.4
Aiwa	3.7
Magnavox	3.3
Sanyo	2.7
Gran Prix	2.2
Others	22.6

Source: *Dealerscope*, May 1996, p. 62, from Intellect.

★ 1055 ★
Consumer Electronics (SIC 3651)

Minicomponent Stereo Systems Market

The market leader shown has combined the components of stereo systems, such as amplifiers, cassette decks, tuners, and speakers, in a compact package to excell in the mini stereo market.

Aiwa	50.0%
Others	50.0

Source: *Forbes*, January 1, 1996.

★ 1056 ★

Consumer Electronics (SIC 3651)

TV Set Sales by Size

The table compares the sales of television receivers by size of cathode ray tubes for the first six months of each year.

	1994	1995
25" to 27"	34.5%	38.9%
19" to 20"	33.5	31.2
Less than 18"	22.7	18.1
30" to 35"	6.6	8.5
Greater than 39"	2.6	3.2

Source: *Electronic Business Today*, January 1996, p. 30, from *Twice*.

★ 1057 ★

Consumer Electronics (SIC 3651)

VCR Market Leaders

Shares are shown based on 18.35 million units shipped in 1995.

Thomson	16.0%
NAP	10.0
Matsushita	8.0
Emerson	7.0
JVC	5.0
Mitsubishi	5.0
Sanyo Fisher	5.0
Sony	5.0
Zenith	5.0
Goldstar	4.0
Samsung	4.0
Sharp	4.0
Hitachi	3.0
Toshiba	3.0
Daewoo	2.0
Other	14.0

Source: *Appliance Manufacturer*, April 1996, p. 32, from industry reports.

★ 1058 ★

Prerecorded Music (SIC 3652)

Best-Selling Albums - 1995

Data are in millions of units for the first nine months of 1995.

Cracked Rear View by Hootie & the Blowfish	4.4
The Hits by Garth Brooks	3.1
CrazySexyCool by TLC	3.1
II by Boyz II Men	2.9
Throwing Copper by Live	2.9

Source: *U.S. News & World Report*, September 25, 1995, p. 68, from *SoundScan*.

★ 1059 ★

Prerecorded Music (SIC 3652)

Country Music Distributors - 1996

Data are for the first three months of 1996.

WEA	20.0%
UNI	19.3
BMG	17.7
Sony	12.4
PGD	10.8
CEMA	10.6
Indies	9.3

Source: *Billboard*, April 27, 1996, p. 63, from *Soundscan*.

★ 1060 ★
Prerecorded Music (SIC 3652)

Leading Music Formats - 1995

Shares of the $12 billion market are shown by type.

CD album	65.0%
Cassette album	25.0
Cassette single	5.0
CD single	3.0
LP-album, 7-12 in. single	1.0
Music video	1.0

Source: *USA TODAY*, June 28, 1996, p. D1, from Recording Industry Association of America.

★ 1061 ★
Prerecorded Music (SIC 3652)

Music Distribution - 1996

Data are for the first three months of 1996.

WEA	22.3%
Indies	21.6
Sony	14.6
PGD	13.7
BMG	10.5
CEMA	9.9
UNI	7.5

Source: *Billboard*, April 27, 1996, p. 63, from *Soundscan*.

★ 1062 ★
Prerecorded Music (SIC 3652)

Music Producers

Data are current as of November 26, 1995.

Warner, Elektra, Atlantic	22.1%
Polygram	13.8
Sony	13.6
Bertelsmann	12.0
MCA	10.1
Capital/EMI	9.2
Independents	19.1

Source: *New York Times*, December 6, 1995, p. C4, from *Soundscan*, Nielsen Media Research, and Exhibitor Relations Company.

★ 1063 ★
Prerecorded Music (SIC 3652)

Music Sales by Genre

Data are for 1994.

Rock	35.0%
Country	16.0
Pop	10.0
Urban contemporary	10.0
Rap	8.0
Classical	4.0
Gospel	3.0
Jazz	3.0
Other	11.0

Source: *U.S. News & World Report*, September 25, 1995, p. 67, from Recording Industry Association of America and International Federation of the Phonographic Industry.

★ 1064 ★

Prerecorded Music (SIC 3652)

Music Sales by Type

Shipments are shown in millions of units for the first six months of 1994 and 1995. Twelve inch singles are included under LPs.

	1994	1995	Share
CDs	276.8	311.8	63.9%
Cassettes	148.2	126.5	25.9
Cassette singles	39.1	32.9	6.7
CD singles	4.1	5.9	1.2
Vinyl singles	6.1	5.7	1.2
Music videos	4.3	4.5	0.9
Vinyl LP/EPs	0.9	1.0	0.2

Source: *Billboard*, August 19, 1995, p. 96, from Recording Industry Association of America.

★ 1065 ★

Prerecorded Music (SIC 3652)

Popular Musicians

Artists are ranked by millions of records sold from 1985 - April 1996.

Michael Jackson	62.0
Whitney Houston	51.0
Mariah Carey	39.5
Prince	33.5
Janet Jackson	28.5

Source: *Ebony*, June 1996, p. 117, from Recording Industry Association of America.

★ 1066 ★

Prerecorded Music (SIC 3652)

R&B Music Distributors - 1996

Shares are shown for the first three months of 1996.

BMG	25.9%
Sony	19.5
PGD	17.3
WEA	12.9
Indies	12.1
CEMA	7.1
Uni	5.3

Source: *Billboard*, April 27, 1996, p. 63, from *Soundscan*.

★ 1067 ★

Prerecorded Music (SIC 3652)

U.S. Music Producers

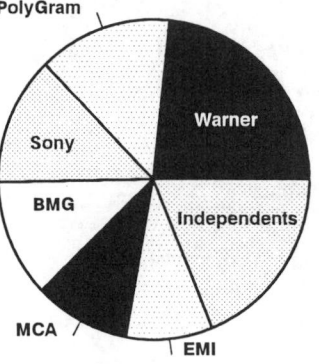

The $11 billion music industry is shown by company for 1995.

Warner (Time Warner)	22.65%
PolyGram (Philips)	14.37
Sony (Sony)	13.19
BMG (Bertelsmann)	12.12
MCA (Seagrams)	10.42
EMI (Thorn-EMI)	8.61
Independents	18.64

Source: *Financial Times*, June 26, 1995, p. 28, from *Soundscan*.

★ 1068 ★

Telecommunications Equipment (SIC 3661)

Ethernet Switch Market

Shares of the $429.6 million ethernet switch market are shown for the first six months of 1995.

Cisco Systems	22.0%
3Com	16.6
Bay Networks	8.6
Cabletron Systems	8.2
Standard Microsystems	5.8
Other	38.8

Source: *Computerworld*, September 18, 1995, p. 20, from Dell'Oro Group.

★ 1069 ★

Telecommunications Equipment (SIC 3661)

Fiber-optic Optoelectronic Subsystems

Sales are estimated in North America for 1999.

Telecommunications	38.0%
Premises data networks	24.0
Cable TV and broadcasting	16.0
Military/aerospace	5.0
Specialty applications	17.0

Source: *Lightwave*, March 1996, p. 45.

★ 1070 ★

Telecommunications Equipment (SIC 3661)

ISDN Penetration

Percentage of lines that have ISDN (integrated services digital network) service among regional bell operating companies.

Pacific Telesis	83.0%
Ameritech	81.0
Bell Atlantic	77.0
BellSouth	71.0
Southwestern Bell	66.0
US West	51.0
NYNEX	50.0

Source: *Telecommunications*, March 1996, p. 22, from Bellcore.

★ 1071 ★

Telecommunications Equipment (SIC 3661)

Leading Modem Makers

Shares of the North American market are shown in percent for 1995.

U.S. Robotics/Megahertz	21.9%
Maxtech/GVC Technologies Inc.	18.4
Hayes	8.6
Boca Research	5.8
Compaq	5.1
Global Village	5.1
Zoom	5.1

AT&T	2.1%
Motorola	2.0
Cardinal	1.9
Others	24.0

Source: *Computer Reseller News*, April 1, 1996, p. 87, from Dataquest Inc.

★ 1072 ★

Telecommunications Equipment (SIC 3661)

Optical Fiber Amplifiers

The table shows optical fiber amplifier consumption in North America.

	1994	1999
Telecommunications	89.8%	68.7%
Cable television	4.8	13.7
Military/aerospace	1.3	9.5
Specialty applications	3.9	7.0
Premises data networks	0.1	1.1

Source: *Lightwave*, December 1995, p. 46, from Electronicast Corp.

★ 1073 ★

Telecommunications Equipment (SIC 3661)

RBOCs by Access Lines

Regional bell operating companies (RBOCs) are ranked by millions of local access lines.

BellSouth	$ 20.9
Bell Atlantic	19.7
Ameritech	18.8
Nynex	17.0
PacTel	15.8
US West	14.7
SBC	14.1

Source: *Fortune*, April 29, 1996, p. 42.

★ 1074 ★

Telecommunications Equipment (SIC 3661)

Telecom Equipment Consumption

Consumption of telephone and telecommunications equipment is shown in millions of dollars for 1995.

	($ mil.)	Share
Switching equipment	$ 6,646.0	30.5%
Other telecom accessories . . .	4,493.0	20.6
Transmission equipment	3,614.0	16.6
Telephone sets	2,112.0	9.7
Accessories & parts	1,867.0	8.6
Other data & text terminal equip.	1,724.0	7.9
Fax machines	1,350.0	6.2

Source: *Electronic Business Today*, January 1996, p. 36, from Elsevier Advanced Technology.

★ 1075 ★

Wireless Communications (SIC 3663)

Cellular Phone Makers

Motorola	32.0%
Nokia	15.0
Audiovox	11.0
NEC	11.0
OKI	11.0
AT&T	6.0
Ericsson	6.0
Other	8.0

Source: *USA TODAY*, November 8, 1995, p. B1, from Cellular Telecommunications Industry Association and Cellular Marketing.

★ 1076 ★

Wireless Communications (SIC 3663)

Cellular Phone Makers - Canada

Other companies in the market include GE/ Ericcson, AT&T, Radio Shack, Toshiba, and Mitsubishi.

Motorola	55.0%
Nokia-Mobira	20.0
Other	25.0

Source: *National Trade Data Bank*, March 2, 1996, p. 111089976.

★ 1077 ★

Wireless Communications (SIC 3663)

Pager Manufacturers

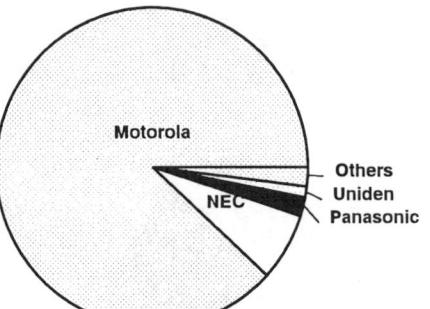

Shares are shown in percent based on all pagers in service.

Motorola	88.0%
NEC	7.0
Panasonic	2.0
Uniden	1.0
Others	2.0

Source: *Financial Times*, November 27, 1995, p. 5, from EMCI.

★ 1078 ★

Wireless Communications (SIC 3663)

Pager Usage by Type

Data show pagers currently in service by type. Data are for 1994. Average rental fees for digital display pagers has dropped from $18.20 in 1989 to $13.10 per month in 1994.

Digital display	87.0%
Alphanumeric	7.0
Tone voice	3.0
Tone only	2.0

Source: *Communications*, October 1995, p. 10, from MTA-EMCI.

★ 1079 ★

Wireless Communications (SIC 3663)

Wireless Equipment Makers

Data are for 1995.

AT&T Network Systems	36.7%
Ericcson	27.3
Motorola	19.2
Northern Telecom	15.6
Other	1.2

Source: *Investor's Business Daily*, March 27, 1996, p. A6, from Dataquest Inc.

★ 1080 ★

Wireless Communications (SIC 3663)

Wireless LAN Market

Shares of the 1995 wireless LAN (local area network) market are shown based on revenues of $159 million. "Others" include Photonics, InfraLAN, and Windata with shares of 1%.

AT&T	36.0%
Motorola	21.0
Proxim	12.0
Aironet/Telxon	11.0
Symbol	10.0
Others	10.0

Source: *Informationweek*, February 26, 1996, p. 56, from Business Research Group.

★ 1081 ★

Data Communications (SIC 3669)

Access Products

Shares are for 1994.

AT&T	29.0%
DSC	21.0
Nortel	12.0
Reliance Comm-Tech	11.0
Fujitsu	8.0
ADC	3.0
Othr	15.0

Source: *Investext,* Thomson Financial Services, November 17, 1995, p. 7.

★ 1082 ★

Data Communications (SIC 3669)

Backbone Equipment Market

Data are for 1995.

StrataCom	24.9%
Cascade Communications	17.5
Northern Telecom	12.4
Newbridge Networks	10.6
Alcatel Data Networks	5.4
Ascom Timeplex	5.0
Telematics International	4.2
Other	20.0

Source: *Telephony*, April 29, 1996, p. 10, from Dataquest Inc.

★ 1083 ★

Data Communications (SIC 3669)

Data Communications Products

The data communications market is shown by segment. The total market reached $25.643 billion. PBX stands for private branch exchange.

	Rev. ($ mil.)	Share
Servers	$ 8,100.0	31.6%
Modems	2,120.0	8.3
Low-speed LAN cards	1,975.0	7.7
Shared-media hubs	1,757.0	6.9
PBXs	1,625.0	6.3
Wiring	1,427.0	5.6
Routers	1,356.0	5.3
Network operating systems . . .	1,125.0	4.4
Network management	527.0	2.1

Continued on next page.

★ 1083 ★ *Continued*
Data Communications (SIC 3669)

Data Communications Products

The data communications market is shown by segment. The total market reached $25.643 billion. PBX stands for private branch exchange.

	Rev. ($ mil.)	Share
Packet-switching equipment . . .	$ 488.0	1.9%
Others	5,143.0	20.1

Source: *Data Communications*, December 1995, p. 71.

★ 1084 ★
Data Communications (SIC 3669)

Ethernet NIC Market - Canada

Shares of the market are shown in percent.

3Com	19.0%
Standard Microsystems	17.0
Artisoft/Eagle	12.0
Intel	10.0
Other	42.0

Source: *National Trade Data Bank*, September 13, 1995, p. IS9507.420.

★ 1085 ★
Data Communications (SIC 3669)

Leading UPS Vendors

Firms are ranked by 1995 sales in millions of dollars. Shares of the group are shown in percent. UPS stands for uninterruptible power supply.

	Sales ($ mil.)	% of Group
American Power Conversion . .	$ 515.3	33.1%
Exide Electronics	391.0	25.1
Liebert	305.7	19.6
Best Power/Sola	211.0	13.5
Daltec	135.0	8.7

Source: *Informationweek*, May 13, 1996, p. 74.

★ 1086 ★
Data Communications (SIC 3669)

Prepaid Phone Card Market

An estimated 40-50 million cards were issued in 1995.

Promotional	50.0%
Retail	30.0
Fund raising	15.0
Collectibles	5.0

Source: *Incentive*, November 1995, p. 5, from Prepaid Communications Association.

★ 1087 ★
Data Communications (SIC 3669)

Remote Access Servers

Shares are shown as based on $153.1 million in revenues generated for the first six months of 1995. Data refer only to small and midsize access servers.

Shiva	21.9%
Cisco	20.9
Xylogics	12.0
Livingston	9.6
Microcom	8.1
Motorola	3.5
Others	24.0

Source: *Business Communications Review*, December 1995, p. 29, from Dell'Oro Group.

★ 1088 ★
Data Communications (SIC 3669)

Router Market - 1995

Cisco	51.0%
Bay Networks	18.0
3Com	7.0
Other	24.0

Source: *Manufacturing Systems*, May 1996, p. S7, from Gartner Group.

★ 1089 ★

Data Communications (SIC 3669)

Security System Market

The market for wireless security systems is shown by company.

ITI 45.0%
Linear Corp. 33.0
Other 22.0

Source: *Investor's Business Daily*, August 9, 1996, p. A3, from industry estimates.

★ 1090 ★

Electronics (SIC 3670)

ATM Adapter Makers

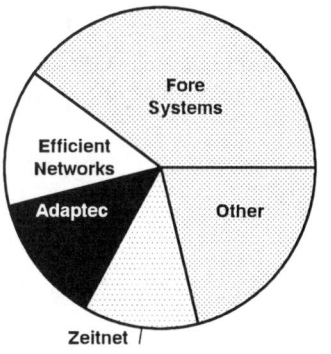

Shares are shown for 1995 based on 38,000 units shipped.

Fore Systems 40.0%
Efficient Networks 14.4
Adaptec 12.5
Zeitnet 11.9
Other 21.2

Source: *PC Week*, June 24, 1996, p. 1, from International Data Corp.

★ 1091 ★

Electronics (SIC 3670)

Automotive Systems

The market for electronic automotive systems is estimated to reach $6.6 billion in 1995.

Power trains 51.0%
Body controllers 26.0
Driver info/entertainment 14.0
Chassis and safety 9.0

Source: *Computer Design*, January 1996, p. 98, from Motorola Semiconductor.

★ 1092 ★

Electronics (SIC 3670)

Opto-Electronic Products Market

This table shows the opto-electronic components demand in the United States for 1994. Market potential is projected for the year 2000.

	1994 ($ mil.)	2000 ($ mil.)	Share
Flat panel displays . .	$ 2,540.0	$ 5,700.0	77.0%
Light-emitting diodes .	365.0	600.0	8.1
Optocouplers	150.0	235.0	3.2
Laser diodes	90.0	140.0	1.9
Solar cells	65.0	125.0	1.7
Other	380.0	600.0	8.1

Source: *Solid State Technology*, December 1995, p. 24, from Freedonia Group Inc.

★ 1093 ★

Electronics (SIC 3670)

Surge Protector Devices

Shares shown reflect the $43.8 million market in 1994 and the estimated $775.5 million market in 1999.

	1994	1999
Line cord	47.7%	43.1%
Hardwire	34.1	38.5
Wall plug	18.2	18.4

Source: *Electronic Design*, March 20, 1995, p. 103, from Venture Development Corp.

★ 1094 ★
Circuit Boards (SIC 3672)

Circuit Board Market - Canada

The market for printed circuit boards is shown in percent by end user for 1994.

Computer firms	35.0%
Telecommunications	28.0
Military/government	15.0
Consumer products	8.0
Instrumentation	6.0
Business/education	4.0
Industrial/electrical	4.0

Source: *National Trade Data Bank*, March 2, 1996, p. IS9505.608.

★ 1095 ★
Semiconductors (SIC 3674)

Chip Market Revenues - 1995

	1990	1995
Data processing	38.0%	47.0%
Consumer electronics	23.9	19.2
Communications	15.4	17.9
Industrial	11.7	9.2
Transportation	5.9	4.8
Aerospace	5.1	1.9

Source: *U.S. News & World Report*, March 25, 1996, p. 56, from VLSI Research, Computer Economics Inc., Semiconductor Industry Association, Merrill Lynch, Dataquest Inc., Nuala Beck & Associates, and United States Department of Commerce.

★ 1096 ★
Semiconductors (SIC 3674)

Compound Semiconductor Market

Shares of the $4.4 billion market are shown by segment. LED stands for light-emitting diodes.

Visible-wavelength LEDs	33.0%
Business & infrared LEDs	26.0
Other	41.0

Source: *Photonics Spectra*, February 1996, p. 19, from Hewlett-Packard Optoelectronics Division.

★ 1097 ★
Semiconductors (SIC 3674)

Memory Chip Makers

Shares are shown based on $26.0 billion in revenues in 1995.

Samsung	13.2%
NEC	9.7
Hitachi	9.6
Toshiba	7.2
Hyundai	7.2
Texas Instruments	6.8
L.G. Semicon	6.2
Fujitsu	4.7
Mitsubishi	4.6
Micron Technology	4.2
Others	26.0

Source: *Purchasing*, March 7, 1996, p. 64, from Dataquest Inc.

★ 1098 ★
Semiconductors (SIC 3674)

Merchant Photomask Market

Shares are shown for the North American market in 1995.

Photronics	54.6%
DuPont	31.8
Align-Rite	9.3
Diamon	2.2
Other	2.2

Source: *Investext*, Thomson Financial Services, April 24, 1996, p. 11, from EVEREN estimates.

★ 1099 ★
Semiconductors (SIC 3674)

Microcontroller Market by Segment

The 8-bit microcontroller market is shown by segment.

Consumer	27.6%
Communications	22.3
Transportation	20.5
Data processing	17.1
Industrial	10.9
Other	1.6

Source: *Computer Design*, February 1996, p. 127, from Dataquest Inc.

★ 1100 ★

Semiconductors (SIC 3674)

Microprocessor Makers

Shares are shown based on the $12.6 billion industry.

Intel	85.6%
AMD	8.7
Cyrix	1.8
Others	3.8

Source: *Business Week*, November 6, 1995, p. 40, from Mercury Research Inc.

★ 1101 ★

Semiconductors (SIC 3674)

Top 10 GaAs Manufacturers

Gallium arsenide (GaAs) semiconductor shares are shown based on total sales of $430 million in 1994 and $535 million in 1995.

	1994	1995
Fujitsu	18.1%	17.9%
Anadigics	8.1	9.3
Vitesse	8.4	9.2
Thomson-CSF	8.4	8.2
TI	6.7	6.5
TriQuint	7.0	6.2
Philips	5.8	6.0
Oki	6.0	5.8
Rockwell	5.3	5.0
NEC	4.2	4.7
Others	21.9	21.1

Source: *Solid State Technology*, November 1995, p. 60.

★ 1102 ★

Capacitors (SIC 3675)

Ceramic Capacitors Market

Shares of the $2.8 billion market are shown in percent.

Murata	30.0%
Kyovera/AVX	25.0
TDK	19.0
Kemet	7.0
Vishay	7.0
Philips	3.0
Others	9.0

Source: *Investor's Business Daily*, October 25, 1995, p. A6, from Lehman Brothers.

★ 1103 ★

FPD Equipment (SIC 3679)

Flat Panel Market

Data are estimated for 2001. LCD stands for liquid crystal display.

LCD	83.3%
Plasma	7.2
Vacuum fluorescent	4.0
Light-emiting diode	3.0
Others	3.0

Source: *Computer Reseller News*, April 1, 1996, p. 155, from Stanford Resources Inc.

★ 1104 ★
Switches (SIC 3679)
Photonic Switch Market

Consumption of fiber-optic switches and switch matrices is estimated to grow from $33.26 million in 1994 to $206.33 million in 1999.

	1994	1999
Telecommunications	20.0%	31.0%
Premise data networks	34.0	24.0
Military/aerospace	18.0	17.0
Specialty applications	14.0	12.0
Cable television	1.0	2.0

Source: *Telecommunications*, January 1996, p. 14, from ElectroniCast.

★ 1105 ★
Batteries (SIC 3691)
Battery Market

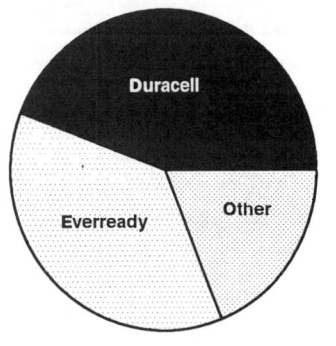

Shares of the $1.8 billion market are shown in percent.

Duracell	44.0%
Everready	37.0
Other	19.0

Source: *Advertising Age*, June 10, 1996, p. 38.

★ 1106 ★
Batteries (SIC 3691)
Replacement Battery Shipments

Shipments are shown in millions of units.

	1993	1994	Share
Cars and light commercial .	55.23	62.36	78.1%
Heavy-duty commercial . .	5.55	6.11	7.6
Other	10.13	11.42	14.3

Source: *Battery Man*, January 1996, p. 12, from Battery Council International.

★ 1107 ★
Batteries (SIC 3691)
U.S. Battery Market

Shares are shown for the second quarter of 1996.

Duracell	47.7%
Energizer	36.5
Ray-O-Vac	9.4
Kodak	0.3
Private label	5.5
Other	0.6

Source: *Investext*, Thomson Financial Services, February 5, 1996, p. 9.

★ 1108 ★
Recording Media (SIC 3695)
Computer Tape Makers - Half-Inch Cartridge

Data show the leading makers of half-inch cartridge computer tape.

Storage Tech	45.0%
IBM	27.0
Fujitsu	12.0
Philips LMS	7.0
Hitachi	5.0
NEC	3.0
Overland	1.0

Source: *Investor's Business Daily*, January 23, 1996, p. A8, from Freeman Associates Inc.

★ 1109 ★
Recording Media (SIC 3695)

Digital Audio Tape Makers

Shares refer to digital audio tape, 8.0 milimeter, half inch.

Exabyte	31.0%
Hewlett-Packard	25.0
Conner	20.0
DEC	7.0
Rexon	6.0
Sony	5.0
Quantum	3.0
4 others	3.0

Source: *Investor's Business Daily*, January 9, 1996, p. A8, from Freeman Associates Inc.

★ 1110 ★
Recording Media (SIC 3695)

Optical Disk Libraries

Optical disk makers generated $380 million in revenues in 1994. Shares are shown in percent.

Hewlett-Packard	34.0%
Philips LMS	9.0
Pioneer	7.0
Sony	7.0
Eastman Kodak	6.0
NKK	6.0
Plasmon	4.0
ATG Cygnet	4.0
Filenet	4.0
Matsushita	3.0
Hitachi	3.0
Others	12.0

Source: *Investor's Business Daily*, December 28, 1995, p. A8, from Freeman Associates Inc.

★ 1111 ★
Robots (SIC 3699)

Robots by Application

Distribution of industrial robots is shown in percent. Approximately 53,000 robots are currently in use. Dispensing includes painting and sealing; loading/unloading includes materials handling.

Welding	53.0%
Loading/unloading	24.0
Assembly	10.0
Dispensing	8.5
Measuring/testing/inspecting	1.0
Other	3.5

Source: *Manufacturing Systems*, March 1995, p. 44, from Robotic Industries Association.

★ 1112 ★
Robots (SIC 3699)

Robots in the Auto Industry - Mexico

The table shows the percentage of robots installed in automotive and auto parts industries in Mexico.

Kawasaki	55.85%
Fanuc	26.60
ABB	5.67
NACHI	3.72
Motoman	3.37
Cincinnati	1.24
Miller	0.18
Unspecified	3.37

Source: *National Trade Data Bank*, March 2, 1996, p. 111089959.

SIC 37 - Transportation Equipment

★ 1113 ★
Autos & Trucks (SIC 3710)

Autos & Trucks - Top Brands

The top selling models for 1995 are ranked by vehicle sales.

Ford F-Series pickup	669,127
Chevrolet C/K pickup	510,982
Ford Taurus	397,763
Honda Accord	345,845
Ford Explorer	345,427
Toyota Camry	319,800
Ford Ranger pickup	315,201
Ford Escort	301,617
Saturn	286,926
Honda Civic	273,441

Source: *Detroit News*, November 12, 1995, p. 1D, from WARD's Automotive Reports.

★ 1114 ★
Autos & Trucks (SIC 3710)

Light-Vehicle Unit Sales

Company sales are shown in millions of cars and trucks for 1995 with projected sales for 1996.

	1995	1996
Dupont	14.8	15.1
DRI/McGraw-Hill	14.8	15.0
Dean Witter Reynolds	14.6	15.0
Ford Motor Co.	14.7	15.0
General Motors	14.8	15.0
WEFA Group	14.8	14.7

Source: *Automotive News*, December 18, 1995, p. 34.

★ 1115 ★
Autos & Trucks (SIC 3710)

U.S. Vehicle Producers

Shares are shown based on 1996 model capacity. Trans. stands for transplant manufacturers.

GM	36.6%
Ford	28.0
Chrysler	14.5
Trans.	19.4
Other	1.5

Source: *WARD's Auto World*, October 1995, p. 77, from *WARD's Automotive Reports*.

★ 1116 ★
Autos & Trucks (SIC 3710)

Vehicle Producers - Mexico

Shares are shown based on 1996 model capacity. Trans. stands for transplant manufacturers.

Ford	24.5%
GM	21.0
Chrysler	20.3
Trans.	33.0
Other	1.2

Source: *WARD's Auto World*, October 1995, p. 77, from *WARD's Automotive Reports*.

★ 1117 ★
Autos (SIC 3711)

Auto Makers

Shares are for 1995.

General Motors	33.0%
Ford Motor Company	26.0
Chrysler	14.0
Other	27.0

Source: *Brandweek*, January 1, 1996, p. 24, from J.D. Power & Associates.

★ 1118 ★
Autos (SIC 3711)

Auto Production - North America

Shares of 1996 model production are shown in percent.

United States	74.5%
Canada	15.1
Mexico	10.4

Source: *WARD's Auto World*, October 1995, p. 77, from *WARD's Automotive Reports*.

★ 1119 ★
Autos (SIC 3711)

Auto Salvaging Market

The companies shown process and sell junk cars through auctions. Shares of the market are shown based on total vehicles processed. No other company has more than 2% of the market.

Insurance Auto Auctions Inc.	15.0%
Copart	13.0
SADISCO	8.0
Others	64.0

Source: *Investor's Business Daily*, February 9, 1996, p. A4, from Copart and Merrill Lynch Small Co. Group.

★ 1120 ★
Autos (SIC 3711)

California Auto Market

The top 10 sellers are ranked by unit sales for 1995.

Civic Honda	55,949
Honda Accord	49,521
Toyota Camry	47,826
Ford F-series	43,378

Ford Explorer	41,242
Ford Taurus	36,064
Chevrolet C/K	34,181
Ford Escort	31,867
Ford Ranger	31,226
Toyota Corolla	30,985

Source: *Automotive News*, June 24, 1996, p. 3, from Automotive News Data Center.

★ 1121 ★
Autos (SIC 3711)

Car Sales - 1996

Data are for the first seven months of 1996.

Ford Taurus	224,642
Honda Accord	215,750
Ford Escort	181,404
Toyota Camry	171,311
Honda Civic	167,907

Source: *Detroit News*, August 6, 1996, p. B1, from WARD's Automotive Reports.

★ 1122 ★
Autos (SIC 3711)

Car Sales - Canada

Canadian automobile sales are shown through December 6, 1995.

	No.	Share
GM	215,249	34.1%
Ford	105,077	16.6
Chrysler	91,313	14.5
Honda	62,546	9.9
Toyota	53,144	8.4
Volkswagen	20,742	3.3
Nissan	20,005	3.2
Mazda	19,304	3.1
Hyundai	17,611	2.8
Volvo	7,531	1.2
BMW	4,735	0.8
Mercedes	3,946	0.6
Suzuki	3,829	0.6
Subaru	3,792	0.6
Lada	1,186	0.2
Jaguar	878	0.1
Porsche	283	0.0

Source: *Globe and Mail*, December 6, 1995, p. B7.

★ 1123 ★
Autos (SIC 3711)

Car Sales by Size

Auto sales by size are shown for the period October 1, 1994 through September 30, 1995. Domestic auto production reached 6.5 million units in 1995.

Middle 48.7%
Small 26.7
Luxury 13.6
Large 11.0

Source: *Survey of Current Business*, January 1995, p. 43, from *WARD's Automotive Reports*.

★ 1124 ★
Autos (SIC 3711)

Japanese Auto Makers in North America

Production is shown for 1995.

Toyota 1,200,000
Honda 840,000
Nissan 650,000
Mazda 150,000
Subaru 150,000
Suzuki 150,000
Mitsubishi 100,000

Source: *Detroit News*, June 26, 1996, p. E1.

★ 1125 ★
Autos (SIC 3711)

Luxury Minivans

Sales of luxury minivans are shown for 1994 and 1995.

	1994	1995
Mercury Villager	76,844	75,052
Nissan Quest	49,651	54,050
Chrysler Town & Country	33,656	50,733
Honda Odyssey	230	25,911
Toyota Previa	18,005	18,234
Oldsmobile Silhouette	14,508	11,874

Source: *Detroit News*, February 6, 1996, p. B1, from *WARD's Automotive Reports*.

★ 1126 ★
Autos (SIC 3711)

Minivan Makers

Chrysler 46.8%
Ford 27.6
GM 16.3
Other 9.3

Source: *Business Week*, March 11, 1996, p. 30.

★ 1127 ★
Autos (SIC 3711)

Top 1995 Models - U.S.

The top 25 models are ranked by unit sales.

Ford Taurus 366,266
Honda Accord 341,384
Toyota Camry 328,602
Honda Civic 289,435
Saturn 285,674
Ford Escort 285,570
Dodge/Plymouth Neon 240,189
Pontiac Grand Am 234,226
Chevrolet Lumina 214,595
Toyota Corolla 213,640
Chevrolet Cavalier 199,001
Chev. Corsica-Beretta 192,361
Ford Contour 174,214
Nissan Altima 148,171
Dodge Intrepid 147,576
Buick LeSabre 141,410
Ford Mustang 136,962
Nissan Sentra 134,691
Continued on next page.

★ 1127 ★ *Continued*
Autos (SIC 3711)

Top 1995 Models - U.S.

The top 25 models are ranked by unit sales.

Pontiac Grand Prix	131,747
Olds. Cutlass Ciera	128,860
Chevrolet Camero	111,771
Cadillac DeVille	106,581
Ford Thunderbird	104,254
Mercury Sable	102,565
Ford Crown Victoria	98,163

Source: *Automotive News*, April 24, 1996, p. 145.

★ 1128 ★
Autos (SIC 3711)

Top Car Makers

Market shares are shown in percent.

	1994	1995
GM	33.1%	32.6%
Ford	25.3	25.8
Chrysler	14.6	14.7
Other	27.0	26.9

Source: *Automotive Industry*, April 1996, p. 49.

★ 1129 ★
Autos (SIC 3711)

Top Car Makers - Canada

Shares are shown for the first nine months of each year.

	1994	1995
General Motors	33.0%	34.5%
Ford	17.0	16.6
Chrysler	15.4	14.6
Honda	9.1	9.4
Toyota	7.7	8.5
Nissan	3.2	3.1
Other	14.5	13.3

Source: *Investext,* Thomson Financial Services, October 30, 1995, p. 8, from Annual Canada Retail Sales estimates.

★ 1130 ★
Autos (SIC 3711)

U.S. Auto Sales

Market shares are shown for 1995.

GM	33.9%
Ford	20.7
Toyota/Lexus	9.2
Chrysler	9.1
Honda/Acura	8.6
Nissan/Infiniti	6.0
VW/Audi	1.5
Other	11.0

Source: *Automotive News*, April 24, 1996, p. 139.

★ 1131 ★
Autos (SIC 3711)

U.S. Car Registrations by Region

Distribution is shown based on 8,706,970 automobiles registered in 1995.

South Atlantic	22.7%
Northeast Central	18.2
Mid-Atlantic	14.6
Pacific	13.5
Southwest Central	9.7
Northwest Central	5.6
Mountain	5.3
New England	5.3
Southeast Central	5.1

Source: *Automotive News*, April 24, 1996, p. 179.

★ 1132 ★
Buses (SIC 3713)
Transit Bus Makers

Shares are for 1991-93.

TMC	30.5%
Flxible	26.7
BIA	18.2
Gillig	10.2
New Flyer	5.3
Ikarus	4.3
MCI	3.4
Neoplan USA	1.6
Others	0.1

Source: *Metro Magazine Fact Book*, 1995, p. 22, from American Public Transit Authority.

★ 1133 ★
Trucks (SIC 3713)
Class 8 Truck Market

Shares are shown for the first five months of 1996.

Freightliner	29.7%
Navistar	17.0
Mack Trucks	11.3
Peterbilt Motors	11.1
Kenworth Trucks	10.9
Volvo GM	9.5
Ford Motor	8.7
Other	1.8

Source: *Wall Street Journal*, July 22, 1996, p. B4, from American Automobile Manufacturers Association.

★ 1134 ★
Trucks (SIC 3713)
Construction Truck Market - Mexico

Data are for the first nine months of 1995.

Dina	69.62%
Kenworth	15.19
Mercedes Benz	12.66
Ford	2.53

Source: *National Trade Data Bank*, March 2, 1996, p. IM60213.008.

★ 1135 ★
Trucks (SIC 3713)
Full-Size Pickup Makers

Shares of the 1.7 million unit market are shown in percent.

Ford	40.6%
GM	37.2
Chrysler	20.6
Other	1.6

Source: *Advertising Age*, June 24, 1996, p. 20.

★ 1136 ★
Trucks (SIC 3713)
Heavy Truck Manufacturers

Class 8 truck sales reached 201,700 units in 1995. Market shares are shown in percent.

Freightliner	25.0%
Paccar	22.0
Navistar	19.0
Volvo GM	12.0
Mack Trucks	12.0
Ford	10.0

Source: *Wall Street Journal*, January 18, 1996, p. B4, from American Trucking Association and industry sources.

★ 1137 ★

Trucks (SIC 3713)

Top Light Truck Makers - Canada

	1994	1995
General Motors	32.5%	31.8%
Ford	28.6	30.3
Chrysler	26.5	25.4
Nissan	2.8	2.2
Toyota	2.6	2.0
Honda	--	0.6
Other	7.0	7.6

Source: *Investext*, Thomson Financial Services, October 30, 1995, p. 8, from Annual Canada Retail Sales estimates.

★ 1138 ★

Trucks (SIC 3713)

Truck Production - North America

Shares of 1996 model production are shown in percent.

United States	77.6%
Canada	16.8
Mexico	5.6

Source: *WARD's Auto World*, October 1995, p. 77, from *WARD's Automotive Reports*.

★ 1139 ★

Trucks (SIC 3713)

Truck Sales - 1996

Data are for the first seven months of 1996.

Ford F-Series	476,837
Chevrolet C/K	309,988
Dodge Caravan	254,356
Ford Explorer	237,381
Dodge Ram	232,552

Source: *Detroit News*, August 6, 1996, p. B1, from WARD's Automotive Reports.

★ 1140 ★

Trucks (SIC 3713)

Truck Sales - Canada

Truck manufacturer sales are shown through December 6, 1995.

	No.	Share
GM	144,641	33.7%
Ford	137,494	32.0
Chrysler	116,915	27.2
Nissan	10,477	2.4
Toyota	8,584	2.0
Mazda	5,141	1.2
Suzuki	3,584	0.8
Volkswagen	1,007	0.2
Land Rover	722	0.2
Lada	527	0.1

Source: *Globe and Mail*, December 6, 1995, p. B7.

★ 1141 ★

Trucks (SIC 3713)

Truck Sales - U.S.

Market shares are shown for 1995.

Ford	32.8%
GM	31.2
Chrysler	22.5
Toyota/Lexus	4.7
Nissan/Infiniti	4.1
Honda/Acura	0.9
Other	3.8

Source: *Automotive News*, April 24, 1996, p. 139.

★ 1142 ★

Trucks (SIC 3713)

Van Conversion Market

Full-sized conversion van registrations are shown for 1995. Shares of the market are shown in percent.

	Vans	Share
Ford	41,286	33.5%
Chevy	41,243	33.5
Dodge	25,001	20.3
GMC	15,754	12.8

Source: *Automotive News*, March 11, 1996, p. 26, from R.L. Polk & Co.

★ 1143 ★
Auto Parts (SIC 3714)

Auto Seating Market

Shares are estimated in percent.

Johnson Controls	40.0%
Lear Seating	30.0
Others	30.0

Source: *Investext,* Thomson Financial Services, March 19, 1996, p. 9.

★ 1144 ★
Auto Parts (SIC 3714)

Automotive Brake Producers

Brake systems suppliers to North American automakers are shown based on 1994 sales. Data are in millions of dollars. Delphi Chasiss Systems is ranked first, and Robert Borsch Corp., Nippondenso America Inc., and Dana Corp. are ranked 5th, 7th, and 8th respectively but their sales figures were not available.

Kelsey-Hayes Co.	$ 1,154.0
ITT Automotive	883.0
AlliedSignal Automotive	794.0
Lucas Automotive	86.0
Amcast Automotive	32.0
Continental Hose	12.0

Source: *Automotive News,* July 24, 1995, p. 6, from company reports.

★ 1145 ★
Auto Parts (SIC 3714)

Convertible Top Makers

Shares are for North America.

Dura Convertible Systems	76.0%
ASC Inc.	23.0
Other	1.0

Source: *Crain's Detroit Business,* June 10, 1996, p. 37.

★ 1146 ★
Auto Parts (SIC 3714)

Four Wheel ABS Market

Shares of the North American market are shown in percent.

	1994	1997
Kelsey-Hayes	24.0%	31.0%
Teves	29.0	27.0
Delco	30.0	23.0
Bosch	9.0	11.0
Bendix	4.0	5.0
Other	4.0	3.0

Source: *Investext,* Thomson Financial Services, April 27, 1995, p. 6, from Tier One.

★ 1147 ★
Auto Parts (SIC 3714)

Leading Auto Parts Makers

Firms are ranked by 1995 revenues in billions of dollars.

GM Delphi	$ 26.4
AlliedSignal	14.3
TRW	10.2
Johnson Controls	8.3
Dana	7.6
Eaton	6.8
Cummins Engine	5.2
Lear	4.7
Magna International	4.5

Source: *USA TODAY,* July 25, 1996, p. 3B, from Bloomberg Business News.

★ 1148 ★
Auto Parts (SIC 3714)

OEM Suppliers of the Auto Industry

The leading component suppliers to the automotive industry are shown based on 1995 sales. OEM stands for original equipment manufacturers.

Delphi Automotive Systems	$ 21,800.0
Ford Automotive Components Div. . . .	8,140.0
Delco Electronics Corp.	4,700.0
Dana Corp.	4,205.0
Bridgestone/Firestone Inc.	4,200.0
Lear Corp.	3,373.0
TRW Inc.	3,300.0
Johnson Controls Automotive Sys. Grp. .	3,257.0
ITT Automotive	2,600.0
Chrysler Component Operation	2,600.0

Source: *Automotive News*, April 24, 1996, p. 188.

★ 1149 ★
Auto Parts (SIC 3714)

Top Anti-lock Brake Producers

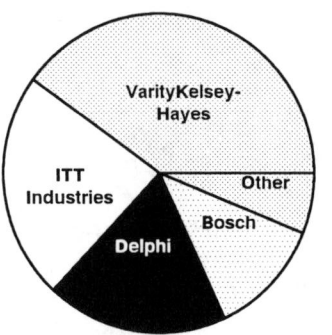

Producer shares are shown in percent.

VarityKelsey-Hayes	40.0%
ITT Industries	23.0
Delphi	19.0
Bosch	12.0
Other	6.0

Source: *Wall Street Journal*, March 26, 1996, p. B1.

★ 1150 ★
Auto Parts (SIC 3714)

Truck Engine Makers - North America

The table shows who manufactures heavy-duty truck engines.

	1993	1994
Cummins Engine	35.1%	34.3%
Caterpillar	27.7	27.6
Detroit Diesel	25.6	24.8
Mack	11.2	12.5
Volvo	0.4	0.8

Source: *Investext*, Thomson Financial Services, May 5, 1995, p. 5, from American Automobile Manufacturers Association.

★ 1151 ★
Truck Trailers (SIC 3715)

Transportation Fleet Trailers

This table shows the 234,287 trailers purchased by the trucking industry in 1994.

	No.	Share
Vans	174,237	74.4%
Platforms	21,459	9.2
Tanks	4,758	2.0
Other	33,833	14.4

Source: *Traffic Management*, November 1995, p. 18, from United States Bureau of the Census.

★ 1152 ★
Truck Trailers (SIC 3715)

Truck Trailer Makers - Mexico

Remolques de Occidente	30.0%
Fruehauf de Mexico	20.0
Sycsa	18.0
Grupo Exa	9.0
Cytsa	5.0
Others	18.0

Source: *National Trade Data Bank*, March 2, 1996, p. IS9501.852.

★ 1153 ★

Motorhomes (SIC 3716)

Motorhome Market - 1995

Fleetwood	
Winnebago	
Coachmen	
Thor	
Gulf Stream	
Damon	
Holiday Rambler	
National RV	
Newmar	
Tiffin	
Other	

Fleetwood	27.4%
Winnebago	16.5
Coachmen	11.6
Thor	7.9
Gulf Stream	4.9
Damon	4.6
Holiday Rambler	4.3
National RV	2.9
Newmar	2.9
Tiffin	2.8
Other	14.2

Source: *RV Business*, April 1996, p. 7, from Statistical Surveys Inc.

★ 1154 ★

Recreational Vehicles (SIC 3716)

Recreational Vehicle Shipments - 1995

Market shares are shown for 1995.

Conversions	45.56%
Travel trailers	26.31
Conventional	16.48
Fifth-wheels	9.83
Folding trailers	14.50
Truck campers	2.58
Motorhomes	11.07
Class A	6.81
Class B	0.81
Class C	3.46

Source: *RVBusiness*, October 1995, p. 47, from Indiana Business Research Center.

★ 1155 ★

Aircraft (SIC 3721)

Air Transport Market

Shares are for 1994.

Honeywell	51.0%
Collins (Rockwell)	28.0
Sextant	11.0
Bendix/King (Allied Signal)	8.0
Sundstrand Avionics	2.0

Source: *Investext,* Thomson Financial Services, March 3, 1995, p. 13, from Honeywell, company reports, industry reports, and Smith Barney estimates.

★ 1156 ★

Aircraft (SIC 3721)

Civil Airplane Makers

The table shows the 1994 civil airplane billings of the five largest manufacturers. Figures are in millions of dollars.

Cessna Aircraft Co.	$ 634.5
Beech Aircraft Corp.	570.9
Gulfstream Aerospace Corp.	518.1
Learjet Inc.	268.6
Fairchild Aircraft Inc.	62.3

Source: *World Trade*, May 1995, p. 74, from General Aviation Manufacturers Association.

★ 1157 ★

Aircraft (SIC 3721)

Commercial Jet Suppliers

Airplane orders have increased from $18.8 billion in 1994 to $48.8 billion in 1995.

	1994	1995
Boeing	41.0%	70.0%
Airbus Industries	41.0	20.0
McDonnell Douglas	8.0	10.0

Source: *Purchasing*, March 7, 1996, p. 7.

★ 1158 ★
Aircraft (SIC 3721)

Federal Helicopter Production

	1994	1995	1996
Army	161	114	51
Navy	48	12	-
Air Force	5	-	-

Source: *Aerospace America*, April 1996, p. 42, from United States Department of Defense.

★ 1159 ★
Aircraft (SIC 3721)

Large-Cabin Business Jets

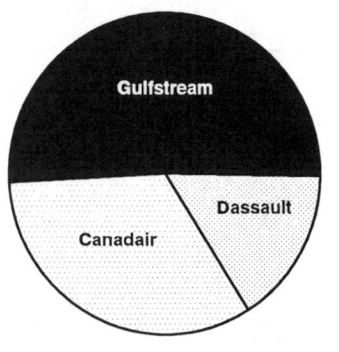

The table shows the large-cabin business jet market by company. Data are for 1980-94.

Gulfstream	51.0%
Canadair	33.0
Dassault	16.0

Source: *Aviation Week & Space Technology*, January 15, 1996, p. S2.

★ 1160 ★
Aircraft (SIC 3721)

Military Aircraft Orders

Share of pentagon orders is shown in percent for 1994.

Lockheed Martin	8.2%
McDonnell Douglas	7.8
Northrop Grumman	4.4
Boeing	1.0
Other	78.6

Source: *Business Week*, December 4, 1995, p. 36, from Cowen & Co. and United States Department of Defense.

★ 1161 ★
Aircraft (SIC 3721)

Passenger Jet Producers

Shares are shown based on new passenger jet orders.

Boeing	70.0%
Airbus Industrie	15.0
McDonnell Douglas	10.0
Other	5.0

Source: *Financial Times*, May 31, 1996, p. 12.

★ 1162 ★
Aircraft Parts (SIC 3724)

Aircraft Engine Makers

Data are shown based on 346 total 747-400 engines delivered at the end of 1995.

General Electric	43.0%
Pratt & Whitney	34.0
Rolls Royce	23.0

Source: *Wall Street Journal*, May 9, 1996, p. A3, from Boeing Co.

★ 1163 ★
Aircraft Parts (SIC 3724)

Jet Engine Producers

Shares are shown based on net orders in 1994.

CFM Intl.	63.0%
P&W	18.0
Rolls Royce	7.0
GEAE	6.0
IAE	6.0

Source: *Air Transport World*, November 1995, p. 59, from Pratt & Whitney.

★ 1164 ★
Aircraft Parts (SIC 3728)

Aircraft Brake Suppliers

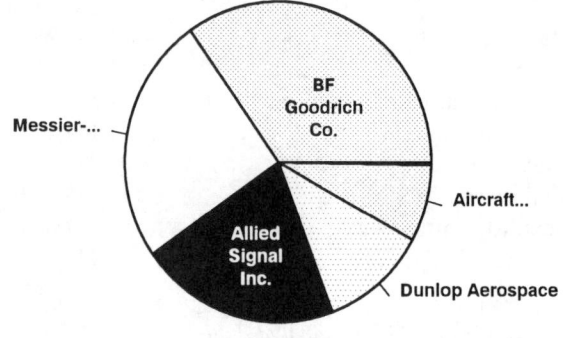

Shares of the carbon-carbon brake market are shown in percent.

BF Goodrich Co. 35.0%
Messier-Bugatti/SEP/Carbone 25.0
Allied Signal Inc. 21.0
Dunlop Aerospace 11.0
Aircraft Braking Systems Corp. 8.0

Source: *Plastics News*, December 11, 1995, p. 4, from industry sources.

★ 1165 ★
Ships (SIC 3731)

Largest U.S. Shipowners

Major U.S. based shipowners are ranked by GRT (gross registered tons).

Overseas Shipholding Group 4,324,111
U.S. Government 2,448,642
Exxon Corp. 2,324,286
Mobil Corporation 2,148,889
Chevron Corp. 1,834,758
Sea-Land Service Inc. 1,795,517
Carnival Corp. 1,454,586
OMI Corporation 1,357,779
Wilmington Trust Co. 940,410
American President Cos. 855,556
Lygnos Brothers 742,953
National Bulk Carriers Inc. 660,740
International Shipholding Corp. 639,333
Marine Transport Lines Inc. 597,192
Atlantic Richfield Co. 570,811
Bank of California 506,892
Shawmut Bank 449,406

Lasco Shipping Co. 443,806
Texaco Inc. 403,445
Matson Navigation Company 403,445

Source: *Marine Log*, June 1996, p. 19, from Colton & Co.

★ 1166 ★
Ships (SIC 3731)

Top U.S. Shipbuilders

Shares are shown based on a total of 473 ships and boats to be built at 40 shipyards. Total published contract values were $23.49 billion.

Newport News Shipbuilding 22.0%
Ingalls Shipbuilding 19.3
GD/Electric Boat 18.9
Bath Iron Works 11.8
NASSCO 9.9
Avondale Industries 8.7
Trinity Marine Group 3.0
Bollinger Shipyards 1.6
Intermarine USA 1.0
Marinette Marine 1.0
Other 2.8

Source: *Marine Log*, June 1996, p. 39, from Colton & Co.

★ 1167 ★
Boats (SIC 3732)

Boat Ownership - Cleveland

Ownership is shown by county for 1995.

Cuyahoga 27,799
Summit 19,871
Lorain 9,394
Lake 8,768
Portage 6,849
Medina 5,238
Geauga 4,243

Source: *Crain's Cleveland Business*, July 1, 1996, p. M7, from Ohio Department of Natural Resources Watercraft Division.

★ 1168 ★
Boats (SIC 3732)

Boat Registrations by State

Michigan
California
Minnesota
Florida
Texas
Wisconsin
New York
Ohio
Illinois
South Carolina

Data are in thousands of boats.

Michigan	898.3
California	838.5
Minnesota	738.0
Florida	698.8
Texas	602.4
Wisconsin	527.0
New York	441.9
Ohio	385.2
Illinois	361.0
South Carolina	333.2

Source: *Detroit Free Press*, January 31, 1996, p. B1, from National Maritime Manufacturers Association.

★ 1169 ★
Boats (SIC 3732)

Boat Spending by State

States are ranked by millions of dollars spent on boats, outboard motors, trailers, and accessories.

Florida	$ 911.5
Michigan	461.0
Texas	381.1
California	368.6
New York	300.8
Washington	284.2
Wisconsin	252.0
Minnesota	229.3
Ohio	217.7
North Carolina	206.4

Source: *Boating Business Annual Industry Review*, 1995, p. 9, from National Marine Manufacturers Association.

★ 1170 ★
Boats (SIC 3732)

Boating Sales - 1995

Sales are shown in thousands of dollars.

Outboard motors	$ 1,793,260
Sterndrive boats	1,791,310
Inboard cruisers	1,169,500
Personal watercraft	1,144,400
Sailboats	287,520
Trailers	195,559
Inboard sportsboats	147,660
Jet boats	141,796
Canoes	55,941

Source: *Boating Business Annual Industry Review*, 1995, p. 3, from National Marine Manufacturers Association.

★ 1171 ★
Boats (SIC 3732)

Pleasure Boat Market - Canada

"Other" includes rowboats, dinghies, skiffs, and similar crafts. The market for boating equipment and accessories reached $295.4 million in 1992 and is expected to grow annually by 5% between 1993-1995.

Outboards	45.0%
Canoes	29.0
Sailboats	9.0
Inboard/outboard	5.0
Other	12.0

Source: *National Trade Data Bank*, May 27, 1996, p. 111097491.

★ 1172 ★
Railroad Equipment (SIC 3743)

Braking Systems Market

The market for electro-pneumatic braking systems for locomotives is shown by company. "Other" includes New York Air Brake.

WAB	75.0%
Other	25.0

Source: *Investext*, Thomson Financial Services, July 24, 1995, p. 5, from company data.

★ 1173 ★
Railroad Equipment (SIC 3743)

Freight Car Fleet - Mexico

The 45,560 car fleet is shown by type. Data include FNM- and privately owned cars.

Box car	49.4%
Gondola	29.1
Covered hopper	8.1
Tank	5.0
Flat car	4.0
Hopper	2.7
Refrigerator	0.3
Other	1.3

Source: *Railway Age*, November 1995, p. 50, from Universal Machine Language Equipment Register and Association of American Railroads.

★ 1174 ★
Railroad Equipment (SIC 3743)

Freight Car Market

	1995	1996	Share
Covered hoppers	17,700	16,500	37.0%
Tank	11,300	9,000	20.2
Gondola	9,800	6,600	14.8
Open hopper	6,300	5,500	12.3
Flat	13,500	5,000	11.2
Box car	1,750	2,000	4.5

Source: *Railway Age*, January 1, 1996, p. 8, from American Railway Car Institute and Economic Planning Associates Inc.

★ 1175 ★
Railroad Equipment (SIC 3743)

Passenger Rail Cars - Mexico

Data show the percentage of passenger rail equipment in Mexico.

First class cars	23.5%
Express cars	20.7
First class special	16.9
Second class	13.0
Coaches	9.8

Mail cars	7.6%
Mail/express	3.1
Autocars	2.2
Mixed cars	0.2

Source: *National Trade Data Bank*, March 2, 1996, p. 111090143.

★ 1176 ★
Railroad Equipment (SIC 3743)

Railcar Fleet - North America

Shares are shown based on 1,485,583 cars in 1995.

Covered hopper	26.0%
Boxcar	16.0
Tank car	15.0
Hopper	14.6
Gondola	13.5
Flat cart	11.3
Refrigerator	2.8
Other	0.9

Source: *Traffic World*, May 27, 1996, p. 28, from Association of American Railroads.

★ 1177 ★
Railroad Equipment (SIC 3743)

U.S. Railcar Fleet

Shares are shown based on 1,310,253 cars in 1995.

Covered hopper	27.1%
Tank car	16.3
Hopper	14.3
Gondola	14.1
Box car	13.8
Flat car	10.7
Refrigerator	2.9
Other	0.8

Source: *Traffic World*, May 27, 1996, p. 28, from Association of American Railroads.

★ 1178 ★
Bicycles (SIC 3751)

Bicycle Ownership in Canada

The table shows the percentage of households in each province that have at least one bicycle. Popular brands in the market include Giant, Krane Rand, Taiwan Hodaka, Kozaki, and Norco.

Alberta	59.0%
Quebec	56.0
Manitoba	54.0
Saskatchewan	54.0
Ontario	51.0
British Columbia	50.0
New Brunswick	47.0
Nova Scotia	39.0

Source: *National Trade Data Bank*, March 21, 1995, p. 1110926966.

★ 1179 ★
Bicycles (SIC 3751)

Bike Trailer Market

Shares are shown in percent. Burley Design Cooperative also has a 30% share of the high-priced tandem market.

Burley Design	50.0%
Other	50.0

Source: *Forbes*, April 22, 1996, p. 149.

★ 1180 ★
Motorcycles (SIC 3751)

Motorcycle Manufacturers

This table shows the motorcycle industry by company. Harley is expected to produce 115,000 motorcycles in 1996.

Harley	54.0%
Others	46.0

Source: *Financial World*, September 26, 1995, p. 27.

★ 1181 ★
Motorcycles (SIC 3751)

Motorcycle Market - 1995

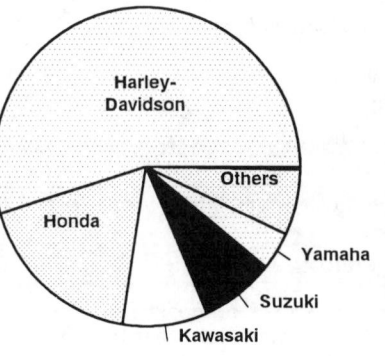

Shares are shown in percent.

Harley-Davidson	55.8%
Honda	17.6
Kawasaki	8.5
Suzuki	7.9
Yamaha	3.6
Others	6.6

Source: *Chicago Tribune*, April 28, 1996, p. C1, from company reports.

★ 1182 ★
Motorcycles (SIC 3751)

Motorcycle Registrations - Bay Area

Registrations are shown by county.

Santa Clara	32,036
Alameda	25,790
Contra Costa	17,782
San Francisco	17,699
San Mateo	14,002
Sonoma	9,987
Solano	7,725
Marin	6,196
Napa	2,954

Source: *Aftermarket Business*, March 1996, p. 26, from *Sales & Marketing Management*.

★ 1183 ★
Aerospace (SIC 3761)

Aerospace Industry by Segment

Sales are estimated for 1996.

	No.	Share
Military aircraft	30,920	31.0%
Space	27,074	27.1
Civil aircraft	23,581	23.6
Related products & services	18,210	18.2

Source: *American Metal Market*, April 26, 1996, p. A12, from Aerospace Industries Association.

★ 1184 ★
Aerospace (SIC 3761)

Leading Aerospace Firms - Canada

Bombardier Inc.

Pratt & Whitney Canada

CAE Electronics Ltd.

Bell Helicopter Textron

Spar Aerospace Limited

Hughes Aircraft of Canada

McDonnell Douglas Canada

Boeing Co.

Sales are shown in millions of dollars for 1994.

Bombardier Inc.	$ 2,100
Pratt & Whitney Canada	1,100
CAE Electronics Ltd.	750
Bell Helicopter Textron	700
Spar Aerospace Limited	430
Hughes Aircraft of Canada	180
McDonnell Douglas Canada	170
Boeing Co.	25

Source: *National Trade Data Bank*, May 27, 1996, p. IMI960306.

★ 1185 ★
Aerospace (SIC 3761)

Top 10 Aerospace Firms

The leading defense contractors are ranked by 1994 sales in billions of dollars. United Technologies, Rockwell, and Allied Signal Aero's figures include aerospace and defense sales only.

Lockheed Martin	$ 22.9
Boeing	21.9
GM Hughes	14.1
McDonnell Douglas	13.2
Raytheon/Beech	12.0
United Technologies	9.0
Northrop Grumman	6.7
GE Aero Engines	5.7
AlliedSignal Aero	4.6
Rockwell	4.3

Source: *Interavia*, September 1995, p. 32.

★ 1186 ★
Aerospace (SIC 3761)

Top U.S. Defense Firms - 1995

Firms are ranked by defense industry sales in billions of dollars.

Lockheed Martin	$ 19.39
McDonnell Douglas	10.08
Boeing/Rockwell	7.82
Hughes Electronics	5.95
Northrop Grumman	5.70
Raytheon	4.00
United Technologies	3.65
General Dynamics	2.90
Litton Industries	2.40
General Electric	2.15
Teneco	1.80

Source: *Economist*, August 10, 1996, p. 46, from *Defense News*.

★ 1187 ★
Trailers (SIC 3792)

Top Trailer Builders

Shares are shown based on registrations for 1994.

Wabash	10.4%
Great Dane	10.0
Strick	9.2
Monon	6.5

Continued on next page.

★ 1187 ★ *Continued*
Trailers (SIC 3792)

Top Trailer Builders

Shares are shown based on registrations for 1994.

Utility	5.5%
Hyundai	5.1
Trailmobile	4.9
Stoughton	4.5
Fruehauf	4.2
Other	39.7

Source: *Commercial Carrier Journal*, July 1995, p. 56, from R.L. Polk.

★ 1188 ★
Trailers (SIC 3792)

Trailer Market - 1995

Fleetwood	27.2%
Thor	13.4
Jayco	11.6
Cobra	8.6
Coachmen	5.7
Skyline	5.2
Starcraft	3.8
Kit	2.7
Gulf Stream	1.9
Vanguard	1.9
Other	18.0

Source: *RV Business*, April 1996, p. 7, from Statistical Surveys Inc.

★ 1189 ★
Trailers (SIC 3792)

Trailer Registrations - Bay Area

Registrations are shown by county.

Alameda	85,861
Santa Clara	74,695
Contra Costa	57,649
San Mateo	53,167
Sonoma	41,398
Solano	26,096
San Francisco	24,615

Source: *Aftermarket Business*, March 1996, p. 26, from *Sales & Marketing Management*.

★ 1190 ★
Trailers (SIC 3792)

Trailer Shipments

	1995	1996	Share
Vans	35,737	31,007	70.6%
Containers/chassis . . .	6,084	4,003	9.1
Platform	3,704	2,856	6.5
Lowbed heavy haulers . .	1,563	1,565	3.6
Dumps	1,342	1,316	3.0
Tanks	798	735	1.7
Pole and logging	228	287	0.7
Dollies and convertor gear	376	186	0.4
Auto transporters	154	128	0.3
Bulk	82	108	0.2
Other	1,291	1,709	3.9

Source: *Transport Topics*, April 22, 1996, p. 15, from United States Bureau of the Census.

SIC 38 - Instruments and Related Products

★ 1191 ★
Control Equipment (SIC 3822)
Air-Control Equipment Imports - Mexico

U.S.	72.0%
Germany	10.0
Japan	6.0
Canada	3.0
Other	9.0

Source: *Business Mexico*, March 1996, p. 53.

★ 1192 ★
Control Equipment (SIC 3822)
Military Control Systems

Bendix/King	
Collins	
Honeywell	

Shares are for 1994.

Bendix/King (Allied Signal)	42.0%
Collins (Rockwell)	38.0
Honeywell	20.0

Source: *Investext*, Thomson Financial Services, March 3, 1995, p. 13, from Honeywell, company reports, industry reports, and Smith Barney estimates.

★ 1193 ★
Thermostats (SIC 3822)
Thermostat Market by Type

Data are for 1992-97. The market was lead in 1992 by White Rogers with a 59.0% share.

Digital	61.0%
Mechanical	36.0
Clock	3.0

Source: *Investext*, Thomson Financial Services, April 21, 1995, p. 6, from Emerson Electric.

★ 1194 ★
Measuring Instruments (SIC 3824)
Automatic Meter Reader Devices

Shares are shown based on an installed market.

Itron	80.0%
Other	20.0

Source: *Investext*, Thomson Financial Services, March 28, 1996, p. 5.

★ 1195 ★
Measuring Instruments (SIC 3825)
Electronic Measurement Equipment

The table shows the leading producers of electronic level measurement equipment in 1995. The total market reached $918.2 million.

Endress & Hauser	27.0%
Rosemount	10.0
Vega	10.0
Milltronics	8.0
Drexelbrook	5.0
Other	41.0

Source: *Investext*, Thomson Financial Services, April 23, 1996, p. 6, from Milltronics.

★ 1196 ★
Optical Instruments (SIC 3827)
Interocular Lenses Makers

	1994	1995
Allergan	43.0%	33.0%
STAAR	31.0	27.0
Chiron	25.0	22.0
Alcon	-	18.0

Source: *Investext*, Thomson Financial Services, May 9, 1996, p. 3, from company estimates.

★ 1197 ★

Optical Instruments (SIC 3827)

Leading Optometry Advertisers

Data are for 1995, based on total advertising expenditures.

Sola Optical USA	4.70%
Marchon Eyewear	2.81
Brain Power Inc.	2.56
Hart Specialties	2.19
Rodenstock USA Inc. Medical Division . .	2.04
Ciba Vision Ophthalmics	1.99
Safilo Group	1.75
Varilux Corporation	1.65
Alcon Laboratories Inc.	1.62
Luxottica Group	1.62
Other	77.07

Source: *Medical Marketing & Media*, April 1996, p. 85, from HCI Medical Promotion Audit, 1995.

★ 1198 ★

Optical Instruments (SIC 3827)

Proximity/Photoelectric Sensor Market

U.S. sensor consumption is shown by type based on the projected 1999 market of $548 million.

Photoelectric	46.9%
Inductive	42.2
Magnetic-actuated	4.7
Capacitive	3.1
Ultrasonic	1.9
Magnetic	1.2

Source: *Electronic Design*, November 6, 1995, p. 80G, from Venture Development Corp.

★ 1199 ★

Medical Equipment (SIC 3840)

Hi-Tech Medical Products

Total revenues are expected to grow from $13.190 billion in 1993 to $23.5 billion in 1998. The market is shown by segment.

	1993	1998
Hospitals	48.8%	45.1%
Home market	20.8	22.6
Physicians' office	16.5	17.1
Ambulatory care facilities	10.5	11.4
Nursing homes/other	3.4	3.8

Source: *Assembly*, January 1996, p. 40, from Freedonia Group.

★ 1200 ★

Medical Appliances (SIC 3841)

Diabetes Pump Makers

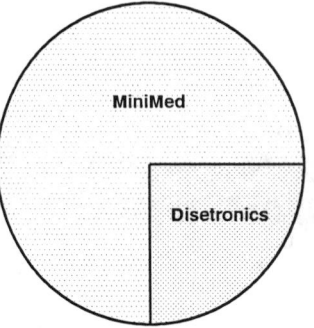

External diabetes pumps are devices that inject microdoses of insulin through a tiny tube inserted into the abdomen. The device allows diabetics to decrease their number of shots taken a month from 120 to 10. Approximately 22,000 patients take this form of therapy. The table shows the shares of the estimated $70.0 million market. Disetronics is a Swiss firm.

MiniMed	75.0%
Disetronics	25.0

Source: *Investor's Business Daily*, April 29, 1996, p. A4, from UBS Securities.

★ 1201 ★
Medical Appliances (SIC 3841)
Mechanical Heart Valve Market

Shares of the $148.7 million market are shown in percent.

St. Jude Medical 78.0%
Medtronic Inc. 11.0
CarboMedics 7.0
Baxter International Inc. 1.0
Others 3.0

Source: *Investext,* Thomson Financial Services, October 24, 1995, p. 106, from Raymond James & Associates and industry sources.

★ 1202 ★
Medical Instruments (SIC 3841)
Blood-Monitoring Device Makers

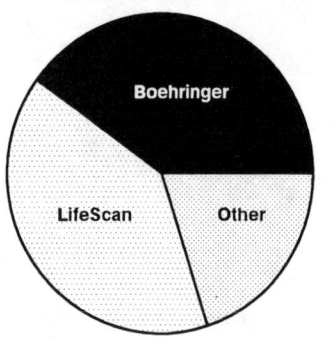

Shares of the $1.75 billion market for blood monitoring equipment for diabetics are shown in percent.

Boehringer 40.0%
LifeScan 40.0
Other 20.0

Source: *Business Week*, July 8, 1996, p. 34.

★ 1203 ★
Medical Instruments (SIC 3841)
DPT Market Shares

The disposable pressure transducer market (DPT) is valued at $115 million, nearly half of the $250 million blood pressure marketing equipment market.

Abbott Laboratories 45.0%
Baxter International 28.0
Ohmeda Corp. (Spectromed) 15.0
Utah Medical Products Inc. 5.0
Argon Corp. 4.0
Healthdyne Inc. 2.0
Medex Inc. 1.0

Source: *Investext,* Thomson Financial Services, May 23, 1995, p. 3.

★ 1204 ★
Medical Instruments (SIC 3841)
Intrauterine Fetal Monitor Market

Utah Medical Products Inc. 65.0%
Marquette Electronics Inc. (Corometrics) . . 13.0
Hewlett-Packard Inc. 7.0
Quest Medical Inc. (Healthdyne) 6.0
Others 9.0

Source: *Investext,* Thomson Financial Services, May 23, 1995, p. 5.

★ 1205 ★
Medical Instruments (SIC 3841)
Vascular Access Devices

The market is expected to grow from $541 million in 1995 to $810 million in 2001.

	1995	2001
Central vascular devices	57.0%	64.0%
Peripheral vascular devices	43.0	36.0

Source: *Health Care Strategic Management*, May 1996, p. 9, from Frost & Sullivan.

★ 1206 ★
Medical Supplies (SIC 3842)
Exam Glove Market

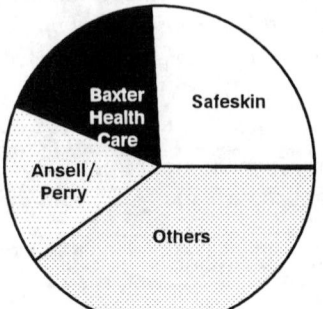

Shares are for the fourth quarter of 1995. Safeskin also has a 50% share of the powder-free exam glove market, which commands a 39% share of the $400 million exam glove market.

Safeskin	26.0%
Baxter Health Care	18.0
Ansell/Perry	16.0
Others	40.0

Source: *Investor's Business Daily*, April 4, 1996, p. A6, from IMS America.

★ 1207 ★
Medical Supplies (SIC 3842)
Orthopedic Soft Goods Market

Data are for 1996.

Smith & Nephew	14.0%
Zimmer	12.0
DePuy/Orthopedic Technology	9.0
DeRoyal Industries	6.0
Professional Products	4.0
Biomet	4.0
Other	47.0

Source: *Investor's Business Daily*, February 7, 1996, p. A4, from First Albany Corp.

★ 1208 ★
Medical Supplies (SIC 3842)
Powder-Free Exam Glove Market

Shares are shown for 1994.

Safeskin	57.5%
Ansell Medical	15.0
Aladan	13.5
Baxtrer Healthcare	10.0
Other	4.0

Source: *Investext,* Thomson Financial Services, May 16, 1996, p. 3, from Frost & Sullivan.

★ 1209 ★
Medical Supplies (SIC 3842)
Top Adhesive Bandages

The top brands are ranked by volume of sales in thousands of dollars for the 52 weeks ended December 9, 1996.

Johnson & Johnson Band-Aid	$ 48,697
Curad	16,998
Private label	15,983
3M Adhesive Strips	7,519
3M Active Strips Brights	1,726
Mickey & Pals	1,693
Kid Care	1,576
Curity Talia	1,008

Source: *Nonfoods Merchandising*, August 1996, p. 28, from A.C. Nielsen.

★ 1210 ★
Orthopedic Appliances (SIC 3842)
Bone Growth Stimulators Market

Shares are shown based on the estimated $129 million market in 1995 and the $155 million market in 1996.

	1995	1996
Biomet Inc.	51.0%	47.0%
OrthoFix Inc.	25.0	22.0
OrthoLogic Corp.	13.0	19.0
Bioelectron Inc.	9.0	9.0
Exogen Inc.	2.0	3.0

Source: *Investor's Business Daily*, January 26, 1996, p. A4, from First Albany Corp.

★ 1211 ★
Orthopedic Appliances (SIC 3842)

Hip Implant Market

Shares are for 1995.

Zimmer 23.1%
DePuy 21.7
Howmedica 14.8
Stryker 12.8
Biomet 11.3
Sulzer 5.4
J&J 4.5
Smith & Nephew 4.0
Wright Medical 1.1
Others 1.3

Source: *Investext,* Thomson Financial Services, October 23, 1995, p. 7.

★ 1212 ★
Orthopedic Appliances (SIC 3842)

Knee Implant Market

Shares are for 1995.

Zimmer 22.0%
J&J 15.3
Howmedica 14.3
DePuy 12.3
Sulzer 10.6
Biomet 8.8
Smith & Nephew 6.3
Wright Medical 5.5
Stryker 4.5
Others 0.4

Source: *Investext,* Thomson Financial Services, October 23, 1995, p. 7.

★ 1213 ★
X-Ray Equipment (SIC 3844)

X-Ray Equipment Market - Canada

The public sector has a 90% share of the x-ray and equipment market for Canada; the rest of the market is devoted to the private sector. Leading producers include Raymax, Electromed, and Varian Canada.

Long term care centers 1,481
Public hospitals 1,211
Federal hospitals 33

Source: *National Trade Data Bank,* March 2, 1996, p. ISA9406.

★ 1214 ★
Electromedical Apparatus (SIC 3845)

ECD Producers

The $215 million market for external cardiac defibrillators (ECDs) is shown by company. ECDs are the round paddles that provide electric shocks to revive patients after heart attacks.

Physio-Control Corp. 55.0%
Other 45.0

Source: *Investor's Business Daily,* March 13, 1996, p. A6.

★ 1215 ★
Electromedical Apparatus (SIC 3845)

Electromedical Equipment Market

Distribution of the market is shown based on revenues of $9.576 billion in 1994 and $13.742 billion in 1999.

	1994	1999
Diagnostics	26.2%	28.7%
Therapeutic	21.3	23.8
Irradiation	20.8	15.8
Patient monitoring	11.6	10.6
Other	20.1	21.1

Source: *Electronic Business Today,* October 1995, p. 30, from Henderson Electronic Market Forecast.

★ 1216 ★
Electromedical Apparatus (SIC 3845)

Implantable Defibrillator Makers

Shares are for 1995.

Medtronic Inc. 45.0%
Guidant Corp. 40.0
Ventritex Inc. 15.0

Source: *Investor's Business Daily,* May 20, 1996, p. A4.

★ 1217 ★
Contact Lenses (SIC 3851)

Contact Lens Market

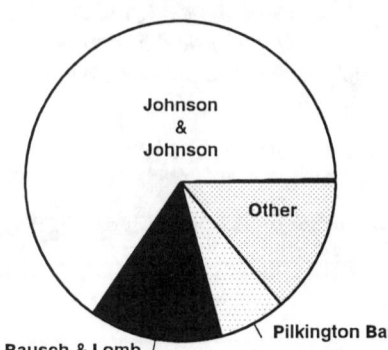

Shares of the $500 million disposable contact lens market are shown in percent.

Johnson & Johnson 65.0%
Bausch & Lomb 14.0
Pilkington Barnes 7.0
Other 14.0

Source: *Chicago Tribune*, June 24, 1996, p. D4.

★ 1218 ★
Opthalamic Goods (SIC 3851)

Sport Optics Market

The category includes ski goggles, driving shields, and a wide array of lenses and frames. Category leaders are ranked by 1995 sales in millions of dollars. The market has been estimated at $250 - $390 million.

Oakley . . . . $ 173.0
Ray Ban 37.5
Bolle 30.0
Smith Optics 30.0
Gargoyles 5.0

Source: *Sportstyle*, May 1996, p. 48.

★ 1219 ★
Opthalamic Goods (SIC 3851)

Sunglasses Market

Data show the market leaders for sunglasses priced $30 and above. Oakley's figure is estimated.

Ray-Ban 40.0%
Oakley Inc. 20.0
Other 40.0

Source: *Wall Street Journal*, August 9, 1996, p. B4.

★ 1220 ★
Movie Projectors (SIC 3861)

Movie Projector Makers

The table shows Ballantyne of Omaha Inc.'s share of the movie projector market. It produces the Simplex projector system, one of the most popular types of projectors in the industry.

Ballantyne of Omaha Inc. 65.0%
Other 35.0

Source: *Forbes*, May 6, 1995, p. 64.

★ 1221 ★
Photocopy Equipment (SIC 3861)

Copy Machine Market

Copier brand shares are shown for 1994.

Canon 63.4%
Xerox 18.4
Kodak 7.8
Ricoh 6.8
Minolta 2.1
Konica 1.4

Source: *Business Week*, October 16, 1995, p. 59, from Dataquest Inc.

★ 1222 ★
Photocopy Equipment (SIC 3861)
Inkjet Cartridge Market

	1994	1995	1996
Black cartridges	62.3%	62.8%	62.4%
Color cartridges	34.7	34.1	34.5
Black ink liters	2.2	2.3	2.3
Color ink liters	0.8	0.8	0.8

Source: *American Ink Maker*, October 1995, p. 18.

★ 1223 ★
Photographic Film (SIC 3861)
Film Market Leaders

Shares of the market are shown in percent.

Kodak	70.0%
Fuji	15.0
Other	15.0

Source: *Washington Post National Weekly Edition*, April 15, 1996, p. 23, from Donaldson, Lufkin & Jenrette Securities.

★ 1224 ★
Photographic Film (SIC 3861)
Film Market by Type

Market shares are shown by type.

35mm print	80.5%
One-time use camera	6.9
110	6.5
Instant	2.7
35mm slide	2.6
Disc	0.8

Source: *Photo Marketing*, July 1996, p. 21, from *PMA Quarterly Consumer Survey, 1995*.

★ 1225 ★
Photographic Film (SIC 3861)
U.S. Film Market Leaders

Kodak	70.0%
Fuji	10.0
Other	20.0

Source: *Asiaweek*, July 5, 1996, p. 64.

★ 1226 ★
Theatrical Equipment (SIC 3861)
Digital Sound in Movie Theaters

Systems are ranked by use on total screens in North America.

Digital theater sound	3,305
Sony dynamic digital sound	1,502
Dolby digital sound	1,004

Source: *New York Times*, February 5, 1990, p. C5.

★ 1227 ★
Theatrical Equipment (SIC 3861)
Theatrical Equipment Sales - Mexico

Sales are estimated in millions of dollars for 1995.

Loudspeakers	$ 20.0
Projectors for 35mm film	6.0
Seats for theaters	3.0
Screens	3.0
Movie projector parts	2.0

Source: *National Trade Data Bank*, March 2, 1996, p. IS9410.026.

★ 1228 ★

Theatrical Equipment (SIC 3861)

Who Purchased Movie Equipment in Mexico

Demand is shown in percent. The market is expected to increase slightly over the next three years.

Theater Operating Company - COTSA . . . 30.0%
RamArez Circuit 20.0
Hollywood Organization 11.0
Carlos Amador 6.0
Other 34.0

Source: *National Trade Data Bank*, March 2, 1996, p. IS9410.026.

SIC 39 - Miscellaneous Manufacturing Industries

★ 1229 ★
Flatware (SIC 3914)

Flatware Makers

The table shows Oneida's share of the stainless steel flatware market in houseware departments.

Oneida	70.0%
Other	30.0

Source: *HFN*, August 28, 1995, p. 12.

★ 1230 ★
Flatware (SIC 3914)

Flatware Market by Segment

Shares of the $683 million market are shown by segment.

Stainless steel	66.0%
Sterling silver	24.0
Silverplate	10.0

Source: *HFN*, September 18, 1995, p. A8.

★ 1231 ★
Musical Instruments (SIC 3931)

Reed Market in North America

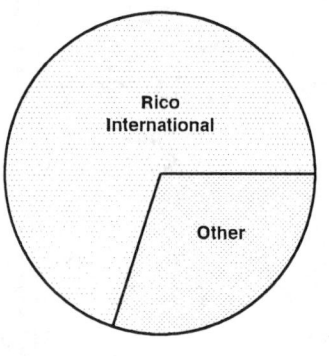

Tha market for saxophone and clarinet reeds in North America is shown by company. Rico International produces 26 million reeds a year.

Rico International	70.0%
Other	30.0

Source: *Financial Times*, August 7, 1996, p. 14.

★ 1232 ★
Musical Instruments (SIC 3931)

U.S. Guitar Sales

Shares of the estimated $300 million market are shown in percent.

Fender Musical Instruments	50.0%
Other	50.0

Source: *Forbes*, March 25, 1996, p. 81.

Toys and Games (SIC 3940)

Infant Toy Brands

Brand shares of the infant/preschool toy market are shown in percent. Company names are shown in parentheses.

Fisher-Price (Mattel) 30.0%
Playskool (Hasbro) 15.0
Others 55.0

Source: *Christian Science Monitor*, January 29, 1996, p. 9.

★ 1234 ★

Toys and Games (SIC 3940)

Toy Shipments by Category

Shipments are estimated in millions of dollars. Retail sales grew from $18.7 billion in 1994 to $20 billion in 1995.

	1994 ($ mil.)	1995 ($ mil.)	Share
Video games . . .	$ 3,148.0	$ 2,533.0	11.3%
Games/puzzles . . .	1,220.0	1,312.0	5.8
Plush	921.0	914.0	4.1
Trading cards & accessories . . .	954.0	887.0	3.9
Male action toys . . .	926.0	795.0	3.5
Water/pool/sand toys	296.0	323.0	1.4
Crayons/markers/ chalk, etc.	255.0	270.0	1.2
Other	10,980	15,449.0	68.7

Source: *Nonfoods Merchandising*, April 1996, p. 7, from Toy Manufacturers of America National Statistics Program.

★ 1235 ★

Toys and Games (SIC 3942)

Doll Market - 1995

Shipments are shown in millions of dollars.

	($ mil.)	Share
Fashion dolls/clothes/ accessories	$ 855.0	48.7%
Large dolls	341.0	19.4
Mini dolls	273.0	15.5
Doll houses and furniture	108.0	6.2
Mini doll accessories	70.0	4.0
Large doll accessories	$ 49.0	2.8%
Soft dolls	30.0	1.7
Other dolls and accessories . . .	30.0	1.7

Source: *Playthings*, April 1996, p. 30, from NPD Group/Toy Manufacturers of America.

★ 1236 ★

Toys and Games (SIC 3942)

Male Action Toy Makers

The table compares the 1995 sales of action figures of the leading manufacturers. Figures are in millions of dollars. Mattel makes Street Sharks; Hasbro makes Batman, Star Wars, G.I. Joe, Mask, Mortal, Kombat, Transformers, Starting Lineup, and Gargoyles.

Hasbro . . . . $ 244
Mattel 40

Source: *Plastics News*, February 5, 1996, p. 8, from William Blair & Co.

★ 1237 ★

Toys and Games (SIC 3944)

Top Sports Video Game Producers

EA Sports 53.0%
Sega 15.0
Acclaim 6.0
Sony 5.0
Tecmo 4.0
Nintendo 3.0
Other 14.0

Source: *Brandweek*, July 15, 1996, p. 18, from EA Sports and NPD Group.

★ 1238 ★

Toys and Games (SIC 3944)

Toys and Games Producers - Mexico

Industrias Salver 85.0%
Other 15.0

Source: *Mexico Business*, May 1996, p. 42.

★ 1239 ★
Toys and Games (SIC 3944)
Video Game Market - 1996

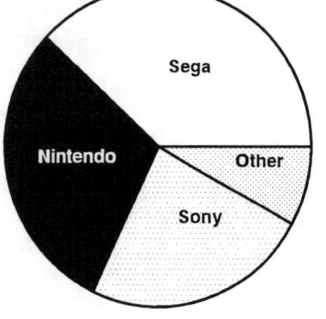

Shares are estimated for 1996. Sales include software and older, 16-bit hardware.

Sega	38.0%
Nintendo	30.0
Sony	24.0
Other	8.0

Source: *Wall Street Journal*, May 31, 1996, p. B3, from Gerard Klauer Mattison & Co.

★ 1240 ★
Toys and Games (SIC 3944)
Video Game Platform Leaders

Shares are shown based on retail hardware sales of $1.57 billion in 1994.

Sega	56.5%
Nintendo	35.1
3DO	5.3
Atari	2.2
Other	0.9

Source: *Advertising Age*, September 27, 1995, p. 8, from Jeffries & Co.

★ 1241 ★
Sporting Goods (SIC 3949)
Golf Club Makers

Shares are shown in percent. Figures are for the first six months of 1995.

	Dol. Share	Unit Share
Cobra	16.0%	12.0%
Callaway	17.0	9.0
Other	67.0	79.0

Source: *New York Times*, December 19, 1995, p. C4.

★ 1242 ★
Sporting Goods (SIC 3949)
Golf Equipment Market

Data are for the 12 months ended August 1994. Golf club leaders include Calloway and Cobra; the men's apparel segment was lead by Ashworth Inc. with a 10% share, followed by Izod.

Golf clubs	44.8%
Apparel	15.6
Other equipment	30.3
Other	9.3

Source: *Investor's Business Daily*, June 17, 1996, p. A4, from National Golf Foundation and company reports.

★ 1243 ★
Sporting Goods (SIC 3949)
Golf Equipment Market - Canada

Data are for 1992.

Golf clubs	53.0%
Balls	22.0
Bags	12.0
Shoes	7.0
Gloves	5.0
Pull carts	1.0

Source: *National Trade Data Bank*, March 2, 1996, p. 111097459.

★ 1244 ★
Sporting Goods (SIC 3949)

In-line Skate Makers

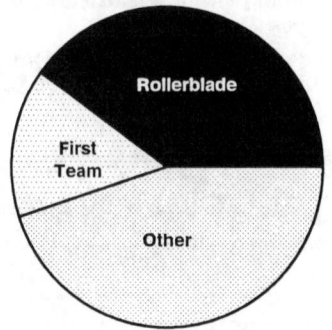

Rollerblade	40.0%
First Team	15.0
Other	45.0

Source: *U.S. News & World Report*, October 30, 1995, p. 62.

★ 1245 ★
Sporting Goods (SIC 3949)

Popular Sports - 1995

Sales are shown in millions of dollars.

Golf	$ 2,130
Exercise equipment	1,770
Firearms/hunting	1,680
Camping	1,510
Fishing	1,500
In-line skating	725

Source: *Oakland Press*, June 16, 1996, p. D1, from Sporting Goods Manufacturers Association.

★ 1246 ★
Sporting Goods (SIC 3949)

Skis & Snowboards Market

The ski and snowboard market is shown based on unit sales from August 1 to December 31, 1995.

	Units	Share
Skis	577,539	81.5%
Snowboards	131,343	18.5

Source: *STN/Skiing Trade News*, March 1996, p. 1, from Ski Industries America Retail Audit.

★ 1247 ★
Sporting Goods (SIC 3949)

Snow Sport Equipment Market

Sports equipment retail sales are shown in millions of dollars.

	($ mil.)	Share
Skiing	$ 214.0	74.0%
Snowboarding	64.0	22.1
Snowshoeing	11.0	3.8

Source: *Time*, January 15, 1996, p. 18, from Ski Industries America.

★ 1248 ★
Sporting Goods (SIC 3949)

Sporting Goods Sales by City

Sales are shown in millions of dollars for 1995.

San Francisco	$ 761.6
Chicago	655.4
Philadelphia	539.9
Washington D.C.	496.4
Seattle-Tacoma	459.6
Boston	458.1
Dallas-Fort Worth	409.4
Detroit	373.4
Denver	360.4

Source: *Detroit News*, August 23, 1996, p. B1.

★ 1249 ★
Sporting Goods (SIC 3949)

Sports Medicine Market

The sports medicine market includes such varied products as braces, neoprenes, and medicines. The leading companies are ranked by 1995 sales in millions of dollars.

Spenco	$ 25.0
Bike Athletic	24.0
Mueller Sports Medicine	18.0
Cramer Products	15.0
McDavid	10.0
Body Glove	7.9
Bollinger	5.0
NDL/Grid	5.0

Source: *Sportstyle*, May 1996, p. 42.

★ 1250 ★
Sporting Goods (SIC 3949)
TV-Shopping for Exercise Equipment

Consumers purchased $160 million in workout equipment over the airwaves in 1994. The table shows the top items purchased.

Stair climbers	10.1%
Fitness videos	9.8
Treadmills	6.8
Stationary bikes	6.0
Other	67.3

Source: *Sporting Goods Business*, December 1995, p. 22, from National Sporting Goods Association.

★ 1251 ★
Sporting Goods (SIC 3949)
Tennis Racket Manufacturers

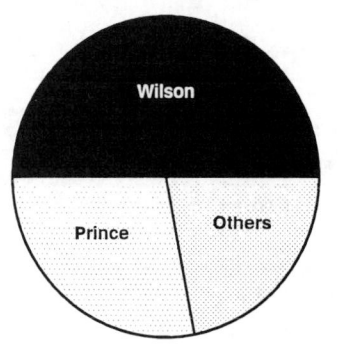

Market shares are shown in percent for 1995. Figures refer to rackets over $100.

Wilson	50.0%
Prince	28.0
Others	22.0

Source: *Forbes*, March 11, 1996, p. 62.

★ 1252 ★
Sporting Goods (SIC 3949)
Tennis Racket Market

The longer racket market is shown in percent.

Prince	57.0%
Wilson	41.0
Dunlop	2.0

Source: *Sporting Goods Dealer*, June 1996, p. 27.

★ 1253 ★
Sporting Goods (SIC 3949)
Top Outdoor Equipment Makers

Firms are ranked by 1995 sales in millions of dollars.

Coleman	$ 449.0
American Recreation	123.0
JanSport	100.0
Nelson/Weather-Rite	100.0
Johnson Camping	98.9
Eastpak	47.0
Outdoor Products	44.0
The North Face	40.0
Henderson Camp	35.0
Avid Outdoors	25.0

Source: *Sportstyle*, May 1996, p. 40.

★ 1254 ★
Sporting Goods (SIC 3949)
Top Sporting Goods Companies - 1995

Companies are ranked by 1995 sales in millions of dollars.

Nike	$ 2,733
Reebok	2,087
Russell	1,153
Spalding	794
VF Corp.	654
Tultex	585
Fila	530
Adidas	520
Benetton	490
Timberland	460
Coleman	449
Wilson	440
Champion	387
Starter	340
Columbia	255

Source: *Sportstyle*, May 1996, p. 16.

★ 1255 ★

Art Supplies (SIC 3950)

Leading Art/Hobby Supplies

The top five brands are ranked by sales in thousands of dollars for the 52 weeks ended September 9, 1995. Shares of the group are shown in percent.

	($000)	% of Group
Brayola	. $ 3,702	24.4%
Mead Academie	. . 3,685	24.3
Mead	. . 3,548	23.4
Pen-Tab	. . 2,468	16.3
Stuart Hall	. . 1,783	11.7

Source: *Nonfoods Merchandising*, May 1996, p. 40, from A.C. Nielsen.

★ 1256 ★

Office Supplies (SIC 3950)

Leading School/Office Supply Brands

Brands are ranked by sales for the 52 weeks ended September 9, 1995. Shares of the group are shown in percent. The top 10 brands generated sales of $122.3 million.

	($000)	% of Group
Mead	. $ 55,359	45.3%
Stuart Hall	. 16,266	13.3
Top Flight	. 11,183	9.1
Pen-Tab	. 8,553	7.0
Ambassador	. 6,988	5.7
K&M	. 5,925	4.8
Norcom	. 5,572	4.6
Private label	. 4,359	3.6
Empire	. 4,314	3.5
Mead the Spiral	. 3,799	3.1

Source: *Nonfoods Merchandising*, May 1996, p. 40, from A.C. Nielsen.

★ 1257 ★

Office Supplies (SIC 3950)

Office Products Market - Canada

The table shows the office products market in Canada in 1992. The leading brands of paper products include Avery Dennison, 3M, Esselte Pendaflex, Hilroy, Maco, Mactac, and Rotex; leading brands of writing instruments include Berol, Bic, Cross, Faber Castell, Papermate, Parket and Scripto, and Waterman; the leading brands of staples, letter corners, and fasteners include Acco, Stanley Bostitch, and Dominion Blueline.

Office products	.93.6%
Writing instruments	. 5.6
Misc. fasteners & letter corners	. 0.8

Source: *National Trade Data Bank*, March 2, 1996, p. 111096779.

★ 1258 ★

Writing Instruments (SIC 3950)

Writing Instrument Market

Distribution is shown based on 5.41 billion units shipped in 1994.

Ballpoint pens	.60.0%
Markers/highlighters	.13.1
Coloring markers	. 8.9
Roller pens	. 8.0
Mechanical pens	. 5.6
Porous point pens	. 4.1
Fountain pens	. 0.3

Source: *Jewelers Circular-Keystone*, January 1996, p. 32, from Writing Instrument Manufacturers Association.

★ 1259 ★
Writing Instruments (SIC 3951)

Top Pens and Pencils Brands

The leading brands are ranked by sales in thousands of dollars for the 52 weeks ended September 9, 1995. Shares of the group are shown in percent.

	($000)	% of Group
Bic	$ 22,752	33.7%
Paper Mate	16,418	24.3
Pentel	8,722	12.9
Empire	5,383	8.0
Pilot	3,826	5.7
Pentech	2,493	3.7
Scripto	2,403	3.6
Faber Castell	2,126	3.1
Parker	2,004	3.0
Sanfords	1,484	2.2

Source: *Nonfoods Merchandising*, May 1996, p. 40, from A.C. Nielsen.

★ 1260 ★
Markers (SIC 3953)

Leading Markers

Brands are ranked by sales for the the 52 weeks ended September 9, 1995. Shares of the group are shown in percent.

	($000)	% of Group
Crayola (Binney & Smith) . .	$ 13,185	43.7%
Sanfords (Newell)	7,823	25.9
Paper Mate (Gillette)	3,611	12.0
Dennison (Avery Dennison) . . .	3,603	11.9
Pentech (Pentech)	1,955	6.5

Source: *Nonfoods Merchandising*, May 1996, p. 40, from A.C. Nielsen.

★ 1261 ★
Brushes (SIC 3991)

Hair Accessories Market

Unit shares are shown for the year ended December 25, 1995.

Goody	54.2%
Wilhold	7.5
L&N	4.4
Helen of Troy	4.3
Fantasia	3.8
Conair	1.6
Other	24.2

Source: *Nonfoods Merchandising*, August 1996, p. 14, from Information Resources Inc. and Goody's.

★ 1262 ★
Toothbrushes (SIC 3991)

Toothbrush Brand Leaders

Shares are shown for the 52 weeks ended December 9, 1995.

Oral-B	23.0%
Reach	16.8
Colgate Plus	15.5
Crest Complete	14.4
Private label	7.5
Colgate Total	6.5
Aqua-Fresh Flex	4.2
Aqua-Fresh Flex Direct	2.8
Butler G-U-M	2.1
Colgate	1.8
Dentrust	1.0
TEK	0.6
Other	3.8

Source: *Supermarket Business*, July 1996, p. 79, from A.C. Nielsen.

★ 1263 ★
Toothbrushes (SIC 3991)

Toothbrush Leaders

Shares of the $519.6 million market are shown for the year ended June 30, 1996.

Colgate 21.6%
Crest 11.3
Other 67.1

Source: *Advertising Age*, August 5, 1996, p. 36.

★ 1264 ★
Toothbrushes (SIC 3991)

Top Toothbrush Brands

Brand shares of the $490.8 million market are shown in percent for the 52 weeks ended June 18, 1995.

Colgate 23.1%
Oral B 22.1
J&J/Reach 16.3
Crest Complete 14.3
Aquafresh 5.8
Butler 3.4
Pepsodent 1.1
Tek 0.8
Dentax 0.6
Private label 7.5
Other 5.0

Source: *Nonfoods Merchandising*, December 1995, p. 57, from Information Resources Inc. InfoScan.

★ 1265 ★
Flooring (SIC 3996)

Flooring Shipments by Type

Data are for 1994.

Carpet 74.6%
Resilient 13.1
Hardwood 6.5
Ceramic 5.9

Source: *Investext,* Thomson Financial Services, September 1, 1995, p. 4, from Floor Focus and WFBS estimates.

★ 1266 ★
Candles (SIC 3999)

Candle Makers

Firms are ranked by estimated 1995 sales in millions of dollars. The market has been estimated at $1.0 billion, but some estimates put the market even higher or as low as $800 million.

Blyth Industries Inc. . . . . $ 470.0
Candle Lite 100.0
Yankee Candle Co. 40.0

Source: *Investor's Business Daily*, June 19, 1996, p. A4.

★ 1267 ★
Candles (SIC 3999)

Candle Market

The market is shown by company. Blyth Industries had sales of $331 million and is by far the dominant player in the industry.

Blyth Industries 25.0%
Other 75.0

Source: *Forbes*, May 20, 1996, p. 278.

★ 1268 ★
Kitty Litter (SIC 3999)

Popular Kitty Litters

Shares are for October - December 1995.

Golden Cat 28.8%
First Brands 22.1
Clorox 18.1
Other 31.0

Source: *Investext,* Thomson Financial Services, February 7, 1996, p. 2, from First Brands and A.C. Nielsen.

★ 1269 ★
Pet Products (SIC 3999)

Cat Product Sales

Sales are shown in millions of dollars by product for 1995. Data refer to pet specialty stores sales.

	($ mil.)	Share
Food	$ 166.70	41.4%
Toys	37.17	9.2
Litter	36.28	9.0

Continued on next page.

★ 1269 ★ *Continued*
Pet Products (SIC 3999)
Cat Product Sales

Sales are shown in millions of dollars by product for 1995. Data refer to pet specialty stores sales.

	($ mil.)	Share
Furniture/scratchers	$ 35.75	8.9%
Livestock	32.28	8.0
Flea/tick products	31.11	7.7
Beds/enclosures/carriers	25.28	6.3
Collars/leashes	23.08	5.7
Other products	15.21	3.8

Source: *Pet Product News*, January 1996, p. 45, from *Pet Supplies Marketing Directory*.

★ 1270 ★
Pet Products (SIC 3999)
Pet Product Sales

The $1.24 billion market is shown by segment.

Kitty litter	20.38%
Food/treats	18.72
Flea/tick products	16.49
Accessories	16.49
Toys	11.96
Grooming products	8.86
Other	10.27

Source: *DM*, June 1996, p. 50.

★ 1271 ★
Slot Machines (SIC 3999)
Slot Machine Makers

International Game Technology	70.0%
Other	30.0

Source: *Wall Street Journal*, February 6, 1996, p. B4.

SIC 40 - Railroad Transportation

Railroads (SIC 4011)

Leading U.S. Railroads

Firms are ranked by 1995 revenues in millions of dollars.

Burlington Northern	$ 8,170.0
Union Pacific	. 6,328.0
CSX Transportation	. 4,819.0
Norfolk Southern	. 4,011.8
Conrail	. 3,686.0
Southern Pacific	. 3,060.5
Kansas City Southern	502.1
Wisconsin Central	263.4

Source: *Traffic World*, February 12, 1996, p. 34, from Railroad news releases.

Railroads (SIC 4011)

Top Chemical Transporters

Shares are shown based on a total of 1,622,069 originated carloads in 1995.

Union Pacific	31.1%
CSX	20.2
Southern Pacific	10.0
Norfolk Southern	7.6
Burlington Northern	6.6
Illinois Central	5.5
Conrail	5.3
Kansas City Southern	3.7
Others	3.4

Source: *Chemicalweek*, March 13, 1996, p. 28, from American Association of Railroads.

Railroads (SIC 4011)

Top Railroad Companies

Firms are ranked by estimated 1995 sales in millions of dollars.

CSX	$ 10,410.0
Union Pacific	. 7,814.0
Burlington Northern Santa Fe	6,232.0
Norfolk Southern	. 4,729.0
Conrail	. 3,700.0
Kansas City Southern	1,254.0
Illinois Central	650.0

Source: *Forbes*, December 18, 1995, p. 64, from OneSource Information Services, Value Line, and IBES Inc.

Railroads (SIC 4011)

Top Railroads

The table shows the leading railroads after the planned merger of Union Pacific and Southern Pacific. Figures show the volume of freight transported in billions of ton-miles.

Union Pacific/Southern Pacific	405.9
Burlington Northern Santa Fe	360.6
CSX Transportation	153.7
Norfolk Southern	122.3
Conrail	94.4
Illinois Central	21.2
Soo Line	20.6
Kansas City Southern	15.6
Gran Trunk Western	6.5

Source: *New York Times*, June 28, 1996, p. C3, from Kansas City Southern Railroad Company and Association of American Railroads.

★ 1276 ★
Railroads (SIC 4011)

U.S./Mexico Railroad Traffic

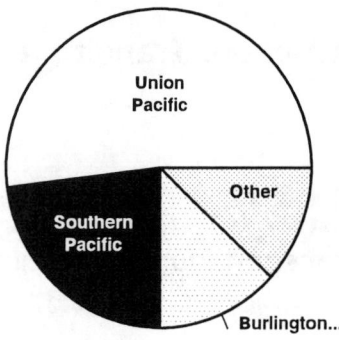

Share of traffic between the United States and Mexico.

Union Pacific	52.0%
Southern Pacific	23.0
Burlington Northern Santa Fe	13.0
Other	12.0

Source: *New York Times*, June 28, 1996, p. C3, from Kansas City Southern Railroad Company and Association of American Railroads.

SIC 41 - Local and Interurban Passenger Transit

★ 1277 ★
Mass Transit (SIC 4111)

Bus Transportation - Chicago

Data show the millions of users for each line in 1994.

Metra
Burlington Northern	13.2
Chicago & North Western	25.2
Chicago South Shore	3.5
Electric Mainline	9.4
Electric Blue Line	0.4
Electric South Chicago	1.7
Heritage	0.4
Milwaukee District	11.4
Southwest Service	1.5
Rock Island	8.2
Pace	38.6

Source: *Chicago Crain's Business - Crain's Market Facts*, July 1995, p. F28, from Metra, Pace, and Chicago Transit Authority.

★ 1278 ★
Mass Transit (SIC 4111)

Rail Fleet by Type

The table shows the types of rail cars in the U.S. and Canadian passenger rail fleet.

Heavy rail	61.0%
Commuter rail	23.0
Light rail	8.0
Locomotives	5.0
Other	3.0

Source: *Metro Magazine*, May/June 1996, p. 36.

★ 1279 ★
Mass Transit (SIC 4111)

Rail Transportation - Chicago

Data show millions of users for 1994.

Howard	27.3
Dan Ryan	17.4
O'Hare	16.5
State subway	12.5
Dearborn subway	10.2
Loop elevated	9.7
Ravenswood	9.4
Congress	6.4
Midway	5.6
Douglas	4.0
Evanston	3.2

Source: *Chicago Crain's Business - Crain's Market Facts*, July 1995, p. F28, from Metra, Pace, and Chicago Transit Authority.

★ 1280 ★
Mass Transit (SIC 4111)

Top Motorcoach Companies

The leading companies in the United States and Canada are ranked by number of motorcoaches. According to a survey, there are an estimated 13,420 private coaches.

Greyhound Lines Inc.	2,000
Ryder-ATE	1,280
ATC/Vancom Inc.	1,241
Laidlaw Transit Services	955
Academy Bus Tours Inc.	559
Liberty Lines Transit	419
Greyhound Lines of Canada Ltd.	403
Diversified Transportation Ltd.	350
Suburban Transit Corp.	333
Holland America Line-Westours Inc.	290
Queens Surface Corp.	272
Robert's Tours & Transportation	261
Gray Line of Fort Lauderdale	223

Continued on next page.

★ 1280 ★ *Continued*

Mass Transit (SIC 4111)

Top Motorcoach Companies

The leading companies in the United States and Canada are ranked by number of motorcoaches. According to a survey, there are an estimated 13,420 private coaches.

Triboro Coach Corp.	208
Peter Pan Bus Lines Inc.	206

Source: *Metro Magazine*, January/February 1996, p. 28.

★ 1281 ★

Mass Transit (SIC 4111)

Top Rail Transit Fleets

The top 10 firms in the United States and Canada have 16,053 rail cars, or 84% of the total fleet of 19,474 cars.

MTA New York City Transit	5,840
Amtrak	2,030
Chicago Transit Authority	1,239
MTA Long Island Rail Road	1,192
Mass. Bay Transp. Auth.	1,042
Metropolitan Rail	1,001
Southeastern PA Transp. Auth.	942
Toronto Transit Comm.	927
Montreal Urban Comm. Trust	918
NJ Transit	872

Source: *Metro Magazine Fact Book*, 1995, p. 16, from American Public Transit Authority.

★ 1282 ★

Mass Transit (SIC 4111)

Top Transit Bus Fleets

Agencies are ranked by fleet size. The top 10 companies in the United States and Canada have 39% of the 70,000 buses held by the two nations.

MTA New York Transit	3,671
New Jersey Transit Corp.	2,922
Los Angeles County MTA	2,508
Chicago Transit Authority	2,098
Washington Metropolitan Area Transit	1,690
Toronto Transit Commission	1,679
Montreal Urban Community Transit	1,670
Southeastern Pennsylvania Transportation	1,551

Metropolitan Transit Authority of Harris County (TX)	1,240
Seattle Metro	1,141

Source: *Metro Magazine Fact Book*, 1995, p. 14.

★ 1283 ★

Ambulance Services (SIC 4119)

EMS Delivery Agencies

Fire departments	45.3%
Ambulance services, non-profit	17.1
City-operated services	9.3
For-profit agencies	6.1
Hospital-based services	5.0
Other	18.0

Source: *JEMS - Journal of Emergency Medical Services*, March 1996, p. 53, from *EMS Market Report*.

★ 1284 ★

Taxicabs (SIC 4121)

Taxi Fleet - New York

This table shows the number of taxicabs in New York by model year. There are 11,799 taxis in New York as of December 20, 1995.

1991-93	4,053
1990 and earlier	4,026
1994-96	3,700

Source: *New York Times*, December 22, 1995, p. A13, from Taxi and Limousine Commission.

★ 1285 ★

Taxicabs (SIC 4121)

Taxicab Licenses by City

Cities are ranked by taxicab licenses.

New York City	11,787
Chicago	5,500
Houston	2,049
Los Angeles	1,850
Philadelphia	1,500

Source: *USA TODAY*, May 20, 1996, p. A2, from International Taxicab and Livery Association.

SIC 42 - Trucking and Warehousing

★ 1286 ★
Trucking (SIC 4210)

Largest Trucking Companies

The top trucking companies in the United States are ranked by 1994 revenues in millions of dollars.

United Parcel Service	$ 14,697.7
Yellow Freight Service	2,196.8
Roadway Express	2,137.3
CF Motor Freight	1,846.6
Schneider National Transportation	1,324.7
Roadway Package System	1,210.7
J.B. Hunt Transport	1,068.9
Overnite Transportation Co.	1,037.2
Con-Way Express Carriers	916.5
ABF Freight System	903.4
Ryder Dedicated Logistics	629.7
North American Van Lines	626.2
Carolina Freight Carriers Corp.	624.0
United Van Lines	562.7
Werner Enterprises	516.0
Commercial Carriers	507.7
Watkins Motor Lines	487.9
American Freightways	465.5
TNT Holland Motor Express	448.0
NationsWay Transport Service	432.3

Source: *Transport Topics*, August 14, 1995, p. 29.

★ 1287 ★
Trucking (SIC 4210)

Major Trucking Companies

Firms are ranked by 1995 revenues in millions of dollars.

Yellow Freight	$ 2,339.0
Roadway Express	2,255.0
Consolidated Freightways	2,014.4
Con-Way Trans.	1,049.2
Overnite Transp.	975.9
American Freightways	572.1

TNT Holland Motor Express	$ 527.3
Watkins Motor	475.3
Viking Freight System	368.5
AAA Cooper Transp.	269.5
Southern Freight Lines	263.4
Estes Express Lines	259.1
Old Dominion Freight	248.0
Central Freight Line	240.8
New Penn Motor Express	167.0

Source: *Traffic World*, April 8, 1996, p. 46, from Eastern Central Motor Carriers Association and Middle Atlantic Conference.

★ 1288 ★
Trucking (SIC 4210)

Refrigerated Trucking Market

The largest providers of refrigerated trucking services are ranked by revenues for the first nine months of 1995. Data are in millions of dollars. Shares of the group are shown in percent.

	($ mil.)	% of Group
Frozen Food Express	$ 216.593	42.8%
KLLM Transport	186.236	36.8
Marten Transport	102.677	20.3

Source: *Transport Topics*, November 13, 1995, p. 55.

★ 1289 ★
Trucking (SIC 4210)

Top General Freight Carriers

The top five carriers of general freight are ranked by revenues for the first nine months of 1995.

Yellow Freight	$ 1,765,494
Roadway Express	1,546,758
Consolidated Fitways	1,537,716
Overnite	731,149
ABF Freight	720,700

Source: *Traffic World*, January 1, 1996, p. 24, from ICC.

★ 1290 ★
Trucking (SIC 4210)

Top Household Goods Movers

Firms are ranked by 1994 revenues in millions of dollars.

North American Van Lines	$ 626.2
United Van Lines	562.7
Allied Van Lines	420.2
Mayflower Transit	317.4
Atlas Van Lines	244.0
Bekins Van Lines Co.	189.8
Graebel Van Lines	136.8
Burnham Service Co.	100.2

Source: *Transport Topics*, August 14, 1995, p. 33.

★ 1291 ★
Trucking (SIC 4210)

Top Trucking Groups

The top groups are ranked by 1994 revenues in millions of dollars.

Consolidated Freightways Inc.	$ 4,680.4
Roadway Services	4,572.0
Yellow Corp.	2,867.4
Ryder System	1,275.2
NFC	1,221.1
J.B. Hunt Transport Services	1,207.6
TNT Freightways Corp.	1,016.4
Landstar System	984.3
WorldWay Corp.	935.9
Leaseway Transportation Corp.	630.6

Source: *Transport Topics*, August 14, 1995, p. 29.

★ 1292 ★
Trucking (SIC 4212)

Self-Move Market

The consumer self-move market is shown by company.

Amerco Inc. (U-Haul)	60.0%
Other	40.0

Source: *Investor's Business Daily*, August 21, 1996, p. A4.

★ 1293 ★
Courier Services (SIC 4215)

Package Delivery Market

Shares of the second-day parcel delivery market are shown in percent for 1995. The Postal Service figure refers to priority mail. Data refer to shipments of 70 lbs. or less.

U.S. Postal Service	68.63%
UPS	12.28
Federal Express	11.49
Airborne Express	7.20
Others	39.00

Source: *Washington Post*, January 22, 1996, p. A17, from Colography Group.

SIC 43 - U.S. Postal Service

★ 1294 ★

Postal Service (SIC 4311)

Best-Selling Stamp Sets

| The Civil War |
| Legends of the West |
| World War II |
| Jazz Musicians |
| Great Lakes Lighthouses |

Sales are shown in millions of sets in 1995.

The Civil War	46.6
Legends of the West	46.5
World War II	32.5
Jazz Musicians	30.0
Great Lakes Lighthouses	26.2

Source: *USA TODAY*, January 3, 1996, p. A1, from Associated Press.

★ 1295 ★

Postal Service (SIC 4311)

Mexican Postal Service

The table compares postal traffic in millions of pieces.

	1992	1993	1994
Domestic	525	557	579
International	365	378	390

Source: *National Trade Data Bank*, March 2, 1996, p. 111089957.

SIC 44 - Water Transportation

★ 1296 ★

Shipping (SIC 4412)

Cargo Handling in Mexico

The table shows the type of cargo handled at sea ports in Mexico. Total cargo fell from 29.85 million tons in 1992 to 28.74 million tons in 1993.

	1992	1993
Bulk minerals	31.8%	33.7%
General cargo	20.5	21.7
Containerized cargo	14.5	15.7
Bulk agricultural prods.	20.6	15.3
Liquids	12.6	13.6

Source: *National Trade Data Bank*, March 2, 1996, p. 111086553.

★ 1297 ★

Shipping (SIC 4412)

Cargo Market - Pacific Coast

The table shows the type of cargo transported in 1994, based on total tonnage of 198.98 million tons.

Containers	62.5%
Bulk cargo	25.7
Cars & trucks	7.6
General cargo	4.2

Source: *Journal of Commerce*, October 30, 1995, p. 1, from Pacific Maritime Association.

★ 1298 ★

Shipping (SIC 4412)

Container Shipping - Mexico

Mexico's dry cargo container shipping market is shown by company.

Transportacion Maritima Mexicana (TMM)	50.0%
Others	50.0

Source: *Mexico Business*, February 1996, p. 62.

★ 1299 ★

Shipping (SIC 4412)

Top North American Ports

Container ports are ranked by capacity in 20 foot equivalent units.

Long Beach	2,842,502
Los Angeles	2,555,344
New York/New Jersey	2,262,792
Oakland	1,549,886
San Juan	1,539,000
Seattle	1,479,076
Tacoma	1,092,087
Hampton Roads	1,077,848
Charleston	1,023,003
Honolulu	805,035

Source: *Purchasing*, June 6, 1996, p. 49, from American Association of Port Authorities.

★ 1300 ★

Shipping (SIC 4424)

Chemical Merchant Fleet Operators

The size of the fleet is shown as of March 1996.

Kirby Corp.	520
Hollywood Marine	248
American Commercial	235
National Marine	223
Ingram Barge	97

Source: *Chemicalweek*, June 12, 1996, p. 40, from Phalanx Publishing.

★ 1301 ★

Shipping (SIC 4424)

Proprietary Fleet Operators

The size of the fleet is shown as of March 1996.

Ashland 160
Union Carbide 101
Occidental Petroleum 82
PPG Industries 56
DuPont 47

Source: *Chemicalweek*, June 12, 1996, p. 40, from Phalanx Publishing.

★ 1302 ★

Shipping (SIC 4449)

Tank Barge Owners on the Mississippi

Leading companies operating on the Mississippi are ranked by total tank barges owned.

Kirby Corp. 521
Hollywood Marine Inc. 249
American Commercial Barge Lines 242
National Marine Inc. 230
Coastal Towing Co. 133
Ingram Barge Co. 115

Source: *Times Picayune*, May 19, 1996, p. F1, from various companies.

★ 1303 ★

Cruise Lines (SIC 4481)

Cruise Line Market

Shares are shown based on total industry capacity in 1995.

Carnival Corp. 23.5%
Royal Caribbean 13.5
Princess Cruises 11.3
Kloster Cruise Limited 8.8
Costa Cruise Line 6.7
Cunard 5.2
Other 31.0

Source: *New York Times*, August 6, 1996, p. C1, from *Cruise Lines International Association Manual, 1996* and company brochures.

★ 1304 ★

Cruise Lines (SIC 4481)

Leading Cruise Lines - 1995

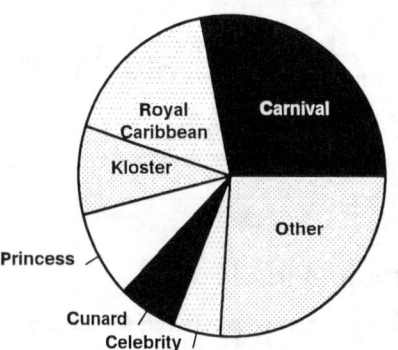

Shares are estimated for the United States and Canada.

Carnival 28.0%
Royal Caribbean 17.0
Kloster 9.0
Princess 9.0
Cunard 6.0
Celebrity 5.0
Other 26.0

Source: *Corporate Growth Weekly Report*, November 13, 1995, p. 8143, from Cruise Lines International Association and Strategic Decisions, Inc.

★ 1305 ★

Tugboats (SIC 4492)

Tugboat Operators on the Missisippi

Leading operators are ranked by number of towboats.

Kirby Corp. 120
American Commercial Barge Lines 115
Hollywood Marine Inc. 100
Ingram Barge Co. 60
National Marine Inc. 55
Cenac Towing Co. 47
Coastal Towing Co. 34
Canal Barge Co. 27
Blessey Marine Services Inc. 17

Source: *Times Picayune*, May 19, 1996, p. F1, from various companies.

★ 1306 ★

Marinas (SIC 4493)

Largest Marinas - South Florida

Marinas are ranked by number of slips.

Black Point Marina	527
Keystone Point Marina	515
Harbour Towne Marina	505
Seagate Marina	465
Rickenbecker Marina Inc.	455
Thunderbolt Marina	430
Dry Marina	403
Miami Beach Marina	400
Johnathan's Landing Marina	381
Crandon Park Marina	352

Source: *South Florida Business Journal*, April 19, 1996, p. 18A.

SIC 45 - Transportation by Air

★ 1307 ★

Airlines (SIC 4512)

Airline Market - St. Louis

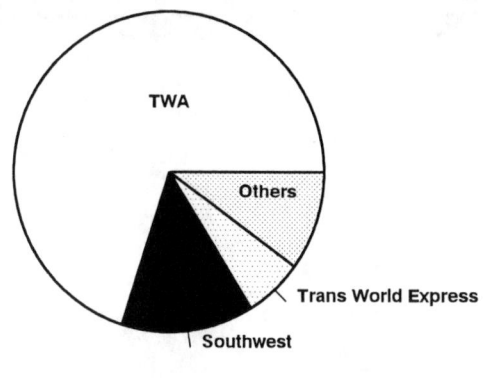

Market shares are shown based on departures.

TWA 70.0%
Southwest 14.0
Trans World Express 6.0
Others 10.0

Source: *Air Transport World*, March 1996, p. 38, from company reports.

★ 1308 ★

Airlines (SIC 4512)

Airline Market by City

The table shows the passenger shares in selected cities for 1994. Data are for USAir, American Airlines, and United Airlines.

	USAir	Amer.	United
Baltimore	47.0%	11.0%	7.0%
Charlotte	85.0	1.0	1.0
Chicago	2.0	34.0	48.0
Los Angeles	6.0	11.0	24.0
New York City (La Guardia)	24.0	17.0	8.0
Philadelphia	56.0	10.0	7.0
Pittsburgh	82.0	2.0	1.0

	USAir	Amer.	United
San Francisco	6.0%	7.0%	57.0%
Washington (National Airport)	25.0	13.0	8.0

Source: *Wirtschaftwoche*, October 12, 1995, p. 65, from United States Department of Transportation.

★ 1309 ★

Airlines (SIC 4512)

Airlines by RPMs

Market shares are shown based on 27,948 million revenue passenger miles (RPMs) generated in the first nine months of 1995.

United 20.1%
American Airlines 19.5
Delta 17.7
Northwest 10.2
USAir 9.3
Continental 7.9
Southwest 6.6
TWA 5.0
America West 3.7

Source: *Interavia*, February 1996, p. 39.

★ 1310 ★

Airlines (SIC 4512)

Business Travel Leaders

The major airlines shown are ranked by share of the business travel industry in 1994 and 1995.

	1994	1995
Delta	18.9%	19.9%
USAir	17.7	16.6
United	16.8	16.2
American	15.3	15.9
Northwest	8.9	9.9
Southwest	8.8	9.0
Continental	7.3	6.2

Continued on next page.

★ 1310 ★ *Continued*
Airlines (SIC 4512)

Business Travel Leaders

The major airlines shown are ranked by share of the business travel industry in 1994 and 1995.

	1994	1995
TWA	3.9%	3.5%
America West	2.4	2.7

Source: *USA TODAY*, April 9, 1996, p. 8B, from D.K. Schifflet & Associates.

★ 1311 ★
Airlines (SIC 4512)

Executive Transportation Fleet - Mexico

Airlines are ranked by number of units.

	No.	Share
Citation	1,028	22.3%
King Air	855	18.6
Gulfstream	755	16.4
Learjet	716	15.5
Beechcraft	442	9.6
Falcon	360	7.8
Sabreliner	137	3.0
Commander	71	1.5
De Haviland	32	0.7
Conquest	26	0.6
Cheyenne	23	0.5
Challanger	14	0.3
Fairchild	14	0.3
Hawker	8	0.2
Mooney	4	0.1
Caravan	2	0.0
Other	120	2.6

Source: *National Trade Data Bank*, March 2, 1996, p. 111089957, from industry specialists.

★ 1312 ★
Airlines (SIC 4512)

Flight Hubs - Phoenix

The table shows the airline market in Phoenix, Arizona.

America West	42.3%
Southwest	32.3
Other	25.4

Source: *USA TODAY*, December 18, 1995, p. 5B, from Back Information Services.

★ 1313 ★
Airlines (SIC 4512)

Frequent Flyer Market

Data show the thousands of free flights redeemed for each frequent flyer organization. Data are for 1994.

Delta Frequent Flyer	5,700
American AAdvantage	2,198
United Mileage Plus	1,900
Northwest WorldPerks	1,255
USAir Frequent Traveler	927
Continental OnePass	590
TWA Frequent Flight Bonus	502
Southwest Company Club	279
America West FlightFund	109

Source: *Washington Post National Weekly Edition*, April 29, 1996, p. 20, from *InsideFlyer*.

★ 1314 ★
Airlines (SIC 4512)

Frequent Flyer Programs

Frequent flyer programs are ranked by membership in millions. Data are current as of October 1995.

American	28.0
United	22.1
Delta	18.1
Continental	15.1
Northwest	14.8
USAir	13.8
TWA	9.4
America West	2.1

Source: *New York Times*, November 1, 1995, p. C5, from *Inside Flyer*.

★ 1315 ★

Airlines (SIC 4512)

Largest Regional Air Markets

Data show regional airline passenger traffic in 1994. Figures are for traffic in both directions.

Seattle/Tacoma-Spokane	520,264
Seattle/Tacoma-Portland	479,002
Chicago O'Hare-Milwaukee	477,780
Denver-Aspen	433,465
Las Vegas McCarran-Grand Canyon . .	423,721
Las Vegas-San Diego	412,342
Chicago O'Hare-Madison	360,508
Chicago O'Hare-South Bend	356,982
Miami-Nassau International	342,848
Miami-Key West	296,406

Source: *Business & Commercial Aviation*, December 1995, p. C14.

★ 1316 ★

Airlines (SIC 4512)

Leading Airlines - Canada

Shares are for 1993.

Canada 3000	73.7%
Air Transat	11.8
Royal Airlines	11.7
Bradley Air	1.6
Nationair	1.1
Others	0.1

Source: *Investext,* Thomson Financial Services, December 15, 1994, p. 28, from Statistics Canada.

★ 1317 ★

Airlines (SIC 4512)

Leading U.S. Airlines

AMR
UAL
Delta
Northwest
USAir
Continental
Trans World
Southwest
America West

Airlines are ranked by first quarter revenues for 1995 and 1996.

	1995 ($ bil.)	1996 ($ bil.)
AMR (American)	$ 4.0	$ 4.3
UAL (United)	3.3	3.7
Delta	2.9	3.0
Northwest	2.0	2.3
USAir	1.8	1.9
Continental	1.4	1.5
Trans World	0.7	0.8
Southwest	0.6	0.8
America West	0.3	0.4

Source: *Financial Times*, April 26, 1996, p. 20, from companies.

★ 1318 ★

Airlines (SIC 4512)

Leading U.S. Airlines by RPMs

Airlines market shares are shown based on revenue passenger miles (RPMs). American does not include AMR Eagle; figures for AMR Corp., USAir Express, and USAir Shuttle figures are not included.

United	21.0%
American	20.0
USAir	7.0
Others	52.0

Source: *Air Transport World*, November 1995, p. 9, from airlines.

★ 1319 ★
Airlines (SIC 4512)
Regional Air Carrier Traffic

Traffic is shown for the first six months of 1995.

Mesa	2,987,794
ValuJet	2,151,348
Comair	1,796,042
SkyWest	1,206,791
Executive	781,000
Mesaba	692,757
Atlantic Coast	661,056
Rich	458,000
Commutair	394,319
CCAir	387,383
Air South	371,000
UFS	323,000
Spirit	317,000
Viscount	266,000
Frontier	253,355

Source: *Air Transport World*, November 1995, p. 112, from United States Department of Transportation and direct airline reports.

★ 1320 ★
Airlines (SIC 4512)
Top 10 Airlines

Data are for 1994.

	Rev. ($ mil.)	% of Group
American	$ 16,137	23.3%
United	12,295	17.7
Delta	12,062	17.4
Northwest	9,200	13.3
USAir	6,578	9.5
Continental	5,700	8.2
TWA	3,407	4.9
Southwest	2,497	3.6
America West	1,400	2.0

Source: *Brandweek*, August 21, 1995, p. 43, from *Business Travel News*.

★ 1321 ★
Airlines (SIC 4512)
Top Airlines - New York

Airlines are ranked by passenger arrivals and departures at JFK, La Guardia, and Newark for the 12 months ended June 30, 1995.

Continental	13.84
American	11.85
Delta	8.20
USAir	6.17
United	5.96
TWA	5.33
Northwest	2.18
Delta Shuttle	1.88
Continental Express	1.49
USAir Shuttle	1.35
British Airways	1.31
Tower Air	1.06
Air Canada	1.02
America West	0.89
Flagship/AA Eagle	0.86

Source: *Crain's New York Business*, September 18, 1995, p. 32.

★ 1322 ★
Airlines (SIC 4512)
Top Airlines by Capacity

Shares of total industry capacity are shown for the first eight months of 1995.

United	20.06%
American	19.88
Delta	16.62
Northwest	11.07
Continental	7.96

Continued on next page.

★ 1322 ★ *Continued*
Airlines (SIC 4512)

Top Airlines by Capacity

Shares of total industry capacity are shown for the first eight months of 1995.

USAir	7.63%
TWA	4.80
Southwest	4.51
America West	2.45
Alaska	1.79
Other	3.23

Source: *New York Times*, October 20, 1995, p. C2, from Avitas.

★ 1323 ★
Airlines (SIC 4512)

Top Airlines by RPMs

Shares are shown for the first nine months of 1995, based on revenue passenger miles (RPMs).

United	22.0%
American	21.0
Delta	17.0
Northwest	13.0
Continental	8.0
USAir	8.0
Southwest	5.0
TWA	5.0
Other	1.0

Source: *Wall Street Journal*, November 15, 1995, p. A6, from company reports, *Air Watch Report*, and United States Department of Transportation.

★ 1324 ★
Airlines (SIC 4512)

Top Airlines by RPMs - 1995

Airlines are ranked by billions of revenue passenger miles generated in 1995.

United	111.5
American	102.9
Delta	85.2
Northwest	62.5
Continental	40.0
USAir	38.1
TWA	24.9
Southwest	23.3
America West	13.3

American Trans Air	8.9
Alaska	8.6
Tower	3.6
ValuJet	2.6
Kiwi	1.2

Source: *Wall Street Journal*, May 14, 1996, p. B1, from *Aviation Daily* and Avitas Aviation.

★ 1325 ★
Airlines (SIC 4512)

U.S./Canada Air Travel Market

An estimated 11.5 million passengers traveled between Canada and the United States in 1995. Data show airlines' share by location.

U.S.	63.0%
Canadian	37.0

Source: *Air Transport World*, April 1996, p. 7, from United States Department of Transportation.

★ 1326 ★
Air Cargo (SIC 4513)

Air Cargo Revenues by Airline

Airlines are ranked by air cargo revenues in millions of dollars for the first nine months of 1995.

Northwest	$ 558.0
United	557.0
American	503.0
Delta	401.0

Source: *Traffic World*, December 18, 1995, p. 34.

★ 1327 ★
Air Cargo (SIC 4513)

Air Export Market

The table shows the growing share of the air export market represented by integrated air carriers, such as Federal Express, UPS, and DHL.

	1995	2000	Share
Integrators	1.7	2.7	67.5%
Non-Integrators	1.5	1.3	32.5

Source: *Journal of Commerce*, June 14, 1996, p. B1, from Colography Group.

★ 1328 ★
Air Cargo (SIC 4513)

Domestic Air Freight Market

Shippers spent $20.4 billion on domestic air freight in 1994. Shares of the market are shown in percent.

Federal Express	35.6%
United Parcel Service	23.8
Airborne	8.1
CF/Emery	4.4
U.S. Postal Service (express mail)	3.3
BAX/WTC	2.8
DHL	2.1
Air Express International	0.2
Others	19.9

Source: *Traffic Management*, September 1995, p. 14, from Colography Group.

★ 1329 ★
Air Cargo (SIC 4513)

U.S. Air Cargo - 1995

Airports are ranked by cargo transported in 1995.

Memphis, TN	1,712,006
Los Angeles, CA	1,597,219
Miami, FL	1,584,680
New York, NY	1,572,840
Louisville, KY	1,351,147
Chicago, IL	1,235,806
Anchorage, AK	987,484
Newark, NJ	905,966
Dallas/Ft. Worth, TX	777,698
Atlanta, GA	771,389
San Francisco, CA	697,802
Dayton, OH	632,658
Oakland, CA	541,776
Indianapolis, IN	520,955
Philadelphia, PA	492,268

Source: *International Business*, April 1996, p. 24, from Air Cargo Institute.

★ 1330 ★
Airports (SIC 4581)

Airport Traffic - Washington D.C.

Data are for the first six months of 1995.

National (DCA)	616,809
Baltimore (BWI)	443,945
Dulles (TAD)	277,362

Source: *Aviation Week & Space Technology*, January 22, 1996, p. 45, from Avitas Inc.

★ 1331 ★
Airports (SIC 4581)

Busiest U.S. Airports - 1995

Data show the millions of passengers for each airport.

O'Hare Intl., Chicago	67.2
Hartsfield Intl., Atlanta	57.7
Dallas-Ft. Worth regional	54.3
Los Angeles Intl.	53.9
San Francisco Intl.	36.2
Miami Intl.	33.2
Denver Intl.	31.0
John F. Kennedy Intl.	30.3
Detroit Metro	29.0
McCarran Intl., Las Vegas	28.0

Source: *Detroit Free Press*, May 1, 1996, p. B1, from Airports Council International.

SIC 46 - Pipelines, Except Natural Gas

★ 1332 ★
Pipelines (SIC 4610)

Leading Pipeline Firms

*Firms are ranked by 1995 revenues in millions of
dollars. Shares of the group are shown in percent.*

	($ mil.)	% of Group
Enron	$ 9,189	29.6%
Panenergy	4,968	16.0
NGC	3,666	11.8
Noram Energy	2,862	9.2
Williams	2,856	9.2
Sonat	1,990	6.4
Enserch	1,931	6.2
Equitable Resources	1,426	4.6
KN Energy	1,103	3.6
Tejas Gas	1,044	3.4

Source: *Fortune*, April 29, 1996, p. F59.

★ 1333 ★
Pipelines (SIC 4610)

Pipelines in Mexico

*Pipelines are shown in kilometers as of December
31, 1994.*

Collection	28,651.0
Gas	12,582.4
Refined products	11,755.0
Crude oil	5,648.6
Petrochemicals	1,569.5
Fuel oil	246.5

Source: *National Trade Data Bank*, May 27, 1996, p.
IS960429.149, from Pemex.

★ 1334 ★
Pipelines (SIC 4619)

Top 10 Oil Pipelines

*The top managers of liquid interstate pipelines are
ranked by miles of pipe in 1994. Total pipeline
mileage decreased from 76,373 miles in 1993 to
76,371 miles in 1994. The top 10 companies
managed 47.02% of all pipelines.*

Amoco Pipeline Co.	11,006
Exxon Pipeline Co.	8,872
Chevron Pipe Line Co.	8,282
Mobil Pipe Line Co.	7,428
Williams Pipe Line Co.	7,389
Mid-America Pipeline Co.	7,204
Texaco Pipeline Co.	6,683
Conoco Pipe Line Co.	6,485
Koch Pipeline Inc.	5,607
Colonial Pipeline Co.	5,317

Source: *Oil & Gas Journal*, November 27, 1995, p. 42,
from United States Federal Energy Regulatory
Commission.

SIC 47 - Transportation Services

★ 1335 ★
Tourism (SIC 4720)
Popular Touring Packages

The table shows the most popular types of tour packages booked. FITs are individual tour packages that can be sold by travel agents usually offered by tour operators. Independent tours by travel agents are custom packages.

FITs	43.3%
Independent tours	30.2
Escorted tours	26.4

Source: *Travel Weekly*, January 22, 1996, p. 7, from Institute of Certified Travel Agencies Survey.

★ 1336 ★
Tourism (SIC 4720)
Top Cities for Travel

The top destinations for tourists are ranked by market share.

Los Angeles	3.6%
New York	2.8
San Francisco	2.3
Orlando, FL	1.6
Chicago	1.5
Las Vegas	1.4
Atlantic City, NJ	1.4
Philadelphia	1.2
Washington	1.2
San Diego	1.2
Other	81.8

Source: *Wall Street Journal*, May 24, 1996, p. A2, from D.K. Shifflet & Associates, California Tourism Office, and CIC Research Inc.

★ 1337 ★
Tourism (SIC 4720)
Top States For Overseas Visitors

Data are in thousands.

	1994	1995
Florida	4,910	5,346
California	4,984	5,304
New York	4,190	4,479
Hawaii	2,639	2,910
Nevada	1,790	1,858
Guam	941	1,238
Illinois	960	1,115
Massachusetts	960	1,053
Arizona	904	887
Texas	923	867

Source: *USA TODAY*, August 12, 1996, p. D1, from United States Department of Commerce.

★ 1338 ★
Tourism (SIC 4720)
Tourism Spending by State

States are ranked by tourism spending in 1995-96. Data are in millions of dollars.

Illinois	$ 31.5
Hawaii	24.5
Texas	21.0
South Carolina	19.2
Florida	15.9
Pennsylvania	15.2
New York	15.0
Massachusetts	14.5
Louisiana	13.0
Virginia	13.0

Source: *Chicago Tribune*, April 7, 1996, p. C2, from Travel Industry Association of America.

★ 1339 ★

Tourism (SIC 4720)

Tourism in California

The table shows the millions of visitors to selected cities in California and the billions of dollars they spent in 1994.

	($ mil.)	(mil.)
Los Angeles	$ 9.3	22.2
San Diego	3.6	13.4
San Francisco	4.1	4.3

Source: *Black Issues in Higher Education*, August 24, 1995, p. 16, from San Diego Convention & Visitors Bureau, San Francisco Convention & Visitors Bureau, and Los Angeles Convention & Visitors Bureau.

★ 1340 ★

Tourism (SIC 4720)

U.S. Visitors by Region

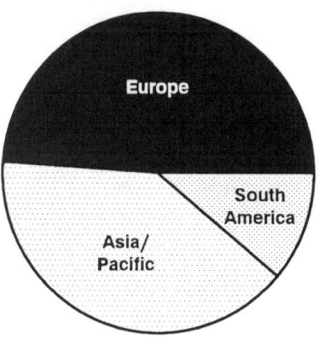

The table shows the 15.05 million visitors to the United States in 1995, by region.

Europe	48.7%
Asia/Pacific	40.0
South America	11.3

Source: *Financial Times*, August 9, 1996, p. 5, from International Trade Administration and Tourism Industries.

★ 1341 ★

Tourism (SIC 4720)

Who Visited Washington D.C.

The table shows the country of origin of visitors in 1994.

United Kingdom	187,000
Germany	174,000

France	105,000
Canada	104,000
Japan	102,000
Italy	60,000
Mexico	52,000
Australia	35,000
Brazil	35,000
Argentina	32,000
Central America	21,000
Spain	21,000
Caribbean	19,000
Venezuela	13,000
Other	464,000

Source: *Washington Post*, April 29, 1996, p. 13, from United States Travel and Tourism Administration.

★ 1342 ★

Travel (SIC 4720)

Top City Destinations

The top cities for international tourists are ranked by millions of visitors. Shares are estimated and exceed 100% due to multiple responses.

	(mil.)	Share
New York City	4.1	21.5%
Los Angeles	3.3	17.3
Miami	2.8	14.5
San Francisco	2.5	13.0
Orlando	2.3	12.2
Honolulu	2.3	11.9
Las Vegas	1.8	9.2
Washington D.C.	1.2	6.0
Chicago	1.0	5.0
Boston	0.9	4.8

Source: *Travel Weekly*, November 27, 1995, p. 51, from United States Travel and Tourism Administration.

★ 1343 ★

Travel (SIC 4720)

Travel Market by State

State governments plan to spend $413 million on travel and tourism in fiscal year 1996. Budgets are in millions of dollars.

Illinois	$ 31.5
Hawaii	24.5
Texas	21.0
South Carolina	19.2

Continued on next page.

★ 1343 ★ *Continued*
Travel (SIC 4720)

Travel Market by State

State governments plan to spend $413 million on travel and tourism in fiscal year 1996. Budgets are in millions of dollars.

Florida	$ 15.9
Pennsylvania	15.2
New York	15.0
Massachusetts	14.5
Louisiana	13.0
Virginia	13.0

Source: *Lodging Hospitality*, May 1996, p. 10, from Travel Industry Association of America.

★ 1344 ★
Travel Agencies (SIC 4724)

Business Travel Services - Chicago

Corporate travel agents are ranked by 1994 ticket revenues in millions of dollars.

Carlson Wagonlift Travel	$ 351.0
Am. Express Travel Related Serv. Co.	258.6
BTI Americas Inc.	218.6
Arrington Travel Center	133.1
McCord Travel Management	120.7
Corporate Travel Consultants	104.0
Uniglobe Travel (Midwest) Inc.	58.4
Best/Easy Travel-Woodside	57.1
Travelmasters Inc.	48.0
Caravelle Travel Management Inc.	42.0

Source: *Crain's Chicago Business*, September 18, 1995, p. SR6.

★ 1345 ★
Travel Agencies (SIC 4724)

Largest U.S. Travel Agencies - 1995

Firms are ranked by gross sales in millions of dollars.

American Express	$ 8,700.0
Carlson Wagonlit Travel	4,500.0
RTI Americas	3,500.0
Rosenbluth International	2,500.0
Maritz Travel Co.	1,400.0
Liberty Travel	1,236.0
Sato Travel	942.2
Japan Travel Bureau Intl.	796.0

WorldTravel Partners	$ 530.0
Travel One	435.0
Omega World Travel	428.0
Travel and Transport	424.0
Total Travel Management	398.0
VTS Travel Enterprises	375.2
Northwesterb Business Travel	347.2

Source: *Travel Weekly*, June 27, 1996, p. 14.

★ 1346 ★
Travel Agencies (SIC 4724)

Top Travel Agencies - 1994

Firms are ranked by 1994 revenues in millions of dollars. Shares of the group are shown in percent.

	Sales ($ mil.)	% of Group
American Express	$ 6,440	47.3%
Carlson Wagonlit	2,350	17.3
Rosenbluth International	1,000	7.4
Maritz Travel	896	6.6
US Travel	812	6.0
M Business Travel	718	5.3
World Travel Partners	452	3.3
Omega World Travel	382	2.8
Travel and Transport	282	2.1
Travel One	273	2.0

Source: *Brandweek*, August 21, 1995, p. 43, from *Business Travel News*.

★ 1347 ★
Travel Agencies (SIC 4724)

Travel Agencies by State

California	6,864
New York	4,076
Florida	3,251
Texas	3,195
Illinois	2,768
New Jersey	2,022
Pennsylvania	1,855
Massachusetts	1,677
Ohio	1,617
Georgia	1,439

Source: *Travel Weekly*, April 22, 1996, p. 45, from Airlines Reporting Co.

★ 1348 ★

Travel Agencies (SIC 4724)

Travel Agency Locations

The table shows U.S. travel agencies by location. Independents are also known as single-office agencies.

	No.	Share
Independents	21,442	45.9%
Satellite ticket printers	13,172	28.2
Branches	9,915	21.2
Home office	2,236	4.8

Source: *Travel Weekly*, March 11, 1996, p. 47, from Airline Reporting Co.

★ 1349 ★

Tour Operators (SIC 4725)

Leading Tour Operators - Canada

Air Transat	20.0%
Holidays Signature	15.0
Sunquest	14.0
Canadian Holidays	10.0
Regent Holidays	5.0
Albatours	4.0
Conquest Tours	4.0
Air Canada	3.0
Globespan Group	3.0
Mont Royal	3.0
Nolitour	3.0
Nouvelles Frontieres	2.0
Royal Vacations	2.0
Exosol	1.0
Others	7.0

Source: *Investext,* Thomson Financial Services, April 11, 1996, p. 4, from Transat and CIBC Wood Gundy.

★ 1350 ★

Forwarding Services (SIC 4731)

Freight Forwarding Market - Canada

The market in Canada is shown by segment.

Sea freight	30.0%
Air freight	26.0
Rail freight	26.0
Truck freight	18.0

Source: *National Trade Data Bank*, March 2, 1996, p. ISA9307.

★ 1351 ★

Freight Car Leasing (SIC 4741)

Freight Car Leasing Companies

GE Rail Service Corp.		
	USL Capital Services	
	CitiRail	
	First Union Rail	
	Chicago Freight Car Co.	

Companies shown are the leaders in the freight car leasing industry. Ranking is based on total cars leased. First Union Rail's figures are shown following the acquisition of Northbrook Rail.

GE Rail Service Corp.	147,000
USL Capital Services	26,000
CitiRail	18,000
First Union Rail	13,000
Chicago Freight Car Co.	5,000

Source: *American Banker*, February 1, 1996, p. 1, from First Union Corp.

SIC 48 - Communications

★ 1352 ★
Wireless Communications (SIC 4812)

Cellular Services Market

Shares of the $14.0 billion market are shown in percent.

AT&T	15.0%
Bell Atlantic/Nynex	15.0
SBC Communications	15.0
Other	55.0

Source: *Economist*, January 20, 1996, p. 62, from Forrester Research.

★ 1353 ★
Wireless Communications (SIC 4812)

Mobile Telephony Services

Shares of the mobile telephony market are shown by type of license for 2005. PCS stands for personal communications services. ESMR stands for enhanced specialized mobile radio.

Cellular	65.0%
PCS	28.0
ESMR	7.0

Source: *Communications*, August 1995, p. 8, from EMCI.

★ 1354 ★
Wireless Communications (SIC 4812)

PCS Installed Market

The installed base for personal communications services is estimated for 2000.

CDMA	49.0%
PCS 1900	23.0
TDMA	16.0
Omnipoint	3.0
Other	9.0

Source: *Telephony*, April 1, 1996, p. 6, from Dataquest Inc.

★ 1355 ★
Wireless Communications (SIC 4812)

PCS Market - North America

The market for personal communications services is estimated by company.

AT&T	39.0%
Nortel	24.0
Ericsson	23.0
Motorola	14.0

Source: *RCR*, February 26, 1996, p. 1, from Yankee Group.

★ 1356 ★
Wireless Communications (SIC 4812)

Pager Market - 1995

Shares are shown based on installed subscriber base.

Paging Network	25.2%
MobileMedia	13.6
Arch Comm.	7.7
AirTouch	7.1
PageMart	4.3
AT&T Wireless	3.4
Metrocall	3.3

Continued on next page.

★ 1356 ★ *Continued*
Wireless Communications (SIC 4812)

Pager Market - 1995

Shares are shown based on installed subscriber base.

Mtel(Skytel) 3.3%
Other 32.1

Source: *Wall Street Journal*, August 22, 1996, p. B3, from
International Data Corp.

★ 1357 ★
Wireless Communications (SIC 4812)

U.S. International Voice Traffic

*Traffic is shown by type. PSTN stands for Public
Switched Telephone Network. VPN stands for virtual
private network.*

PSTN 68.0%
Private network 16.0
IVPN 15.0
ICB 1.0

Source: *Business Communications Review*, April 1996, p.
31, from Yankee Group.

★ 1358 ★
Wireless Communications (SIC 4812)

Wireless Service - Canada

*Distribution is shown based on 2,733,000 bases
installed in 1994 and an estimated 11,817,000 bases
installed in 2000.*

	1994	2000
Cellular	69.5%	55.4%
Paging	29.3	39.1
Wireless data	1.2	5.5

Source: *Telecommunications*, November 1995, p. 18,
from BIS Strategic Decisions.

★ 1359 ★
Wireless Communications (SIC 4812)

Wireless Services Leaders

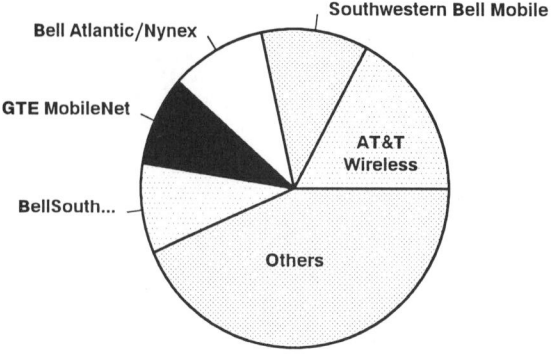

AT&T Wireless 16.6%
Southwestern Bell Mobile 11.4
Bell Atlantic/Nynex 10.4
GTE MobileNet 9.4
BellSouth Cellular 8.9
Others 43.3

Source: *Investor's Business Daily*, March 27, 1996, p. A6,
from Dataquest Inc.

★ 1360 ★
Telephone Services (SIC 4813)

Canada's Long-Distance Market

The $6.4 billion market is shown by segment.

Consumer 55.0%
Business outbound 35.0
1-800 and 1-888 . . . . 8.0
Private network 2.0

Source: *Toronto Star*, July 26, 1996, p. B1, from Yankee
Group.

★ 1361 ★
Telephone Services (SIC 4813)

Largest Telephone System Firms - South Florida

*Firms are ranked by number of stations in the South
Florida area. Switches refer to individual telephones.
Data are in thousands of units.*

AT&T Global Business Communications
    Systems 1,800.0
BellSouth 1,400.0
Continued on next page.

★ 1361 ★ *Continued*
Telephone Services (SIC 4813)

Largest Telephone System Firms - South Florida

Firms are ranked by number of stations in the South Florida area. Switches refer to individual telephones. Data are in thousands of units.

Wiltel Communications Systems Inc. . . .	286.9
TIE/Communications Inc.	199.3
Advanced Telephone	194.1
Unique Communications Inc.	184.9
United States Telephone Co.	173.6
Pavarini Business Communications Inc. . .	169.2
Telcorp Communications Inc.	158.2
ABC Telephone Systems	140.0

Source: *South Florida Business Journal*, December 26, 1995, p. 5.

★ 1362 ★
Telephone Services (SIC 4813)

Leading RBOCs

Leading regional bell operating companies (RBOCs) are ranked by 1995 revenues in billions of dollars. Shares of the group are shown in percent.

	Rev. ($ bil.)	% of Group
BellSouth	$ 14.5	16.5%
Ameritech	13.4	15.2
Bell Atlantic	13.4	15.2
Nynex	13.4	15.2
SBC Communications	12.7	14.4
US West Communications . . .	11.7	13.3
Pacific Telesis Group	9.0	10.2

Source: *Computerworld*, February 26, 1996, p. 122.

★ 1363 ★
Telephone Services (SIC 4813)

Local Phone Market by Segment

The market is shown by segment based on $94 billion in revenues in 1995.

Basic local service	42.6%
Access	29.8
Toll	18.1
Directories & other	9.6

Source: *Financial Times*, August 5, 1996, p. 15, from Salomon Brothers estimates.

★ 1364 ★
Telephone Services (SIC 4813)

Long-Distance Carriers - British Columbia

The table shows the leading carriers based on a survey of 1,000 respondents.

BC Tel	57.0%
Sprint	13.0
Unitel	13.0
CamNet	3.0
Fonorola	3.0
ProvNet	3.0
ACC	2.0
Westel	2.0
Unknown	2.0
Other	2.0

Source: *BC Business*, March 1996, p. 14, from *Telecom Advisor*.

★ 1365 ★
Telephone Services (SIC 4813)

Long-Distance Leaders

Shares of the market are shown in percent.

AT&T	60.0%
MCI	20.0
Sprint	10.0
Other	10.0

Source: *Kiplinger's Personal Finance*, April 1996, p. 30.

★ 1366 ★

Telephone Services (SIC 4813)

Long-Distance Market

Shares of the $76.0 billion market are shown in percent.

AT&T 58.0%
MCI 20.0
Sprint 9.0
Other 13.0

Source: *Economist*, January 20, 1996, p. 62, from Forrester Research.

★ 1367 ★

Telephone Services (SIC 4813)

Long-Distance Market - Canada

Stentor 76.0%
Unitel Communications 9.5
Sprint Canada 7.0
Other 7.5

Source: *Marketing Magazine*, May 6, 1996, p. 4, from James Capel Canada.

★ 1368 ★

Telephone Services (SIC 4813)

Long-Distance Service Providers

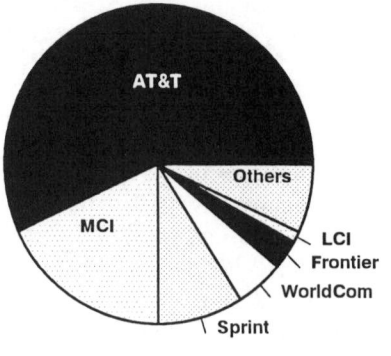

Shares of the long-distance market are shown in percent.

AT&T 57.0%
MCI 18.0
Sprint 9.0
WorldCom 5.0
Frontier 3.0
LCI 1.0
Others 7.0

Source: *USA TODAY*, April 5, 1996, p. 3B, from FCC and Kagan Telecom Association.

★ 1369 ★

Telephone Services (SIC 4813)

Mexican Phone Market

Avantel and Alestra each hope to obtain 20% of the Mexican long-distance market with the end of Telemex's market monopoly.

Telemex 60.0%
Other 40.0

Source: *New York Times*, August 13, 1996, p. C2.

★ **1370** ★
Telephone Services (SIC 4813)

Preferred Phone Services - Dallas

The table shows the preferred carriers based on a survey. Data are for respondents in the Dallas area in the Southwestern Bell territory.

AT&T	44.6%
Southwestern Bell	20.6
MCI	6.9
Sprint	4.4
GTE	3.4
Other	20.1

Source: *Dallas Business Journal*, March 8, 1996, p. 12, from Yankee Group.

★ **1371** ★
Telephone Services (SIC 4813)

Top Regional Bells - 1995

The regional bell operating companies are ranked by long-distance business in billions of dollars.

SBC-Pactel	$ 21.0
BellSouth	17.9
Ameritech	13.4
NYNEX	13.4
Bell Atlantic	12.8
US West	11.7

Source: *Wall Street Journal*, April 2, 1996, p. B1.

★ **1372** ★
Telephone Services (SIC 4813)

U.S. Long-Distance Market by Segment

The market is shown by segment based on $70 billion in revenues in 1995.

Domestic business	40.1%
Domestic residential	36.3
Wholesale	6.7
International residential	6.1
Other & private line	10.9

Source: *Financial Times*, August 5, 1996, p. 15, from Salomon Brothers estimates.

★ **1373** ★
Telephone Services (SIC 4813)

U.S. Telephone Companies

Telephone service providers are ranked by 1994 revenues in billions of dollars.

AT&T	$ 75.1
GTE	19.9
Bell South	16.8
Bell Atlantic	13.8
Nynex	13.3
MCI	13.3
Sprint	12.7
Ameritech	12.6
SBC Communications	11.6
U.S. West	11.0
Pacific Telesis	9.2

Source: *New York Times*, September 21, 1995, p. C5, from *Bloomberg Business News*.

★ **1374** ★
Telephone Services (SIC 4813)

Who Owns Public Pay Phones

The installed base is shown in thousands of units. Data are estimated for 1999.

	1994	1999
Bell operating companies	1,939	2,028
Independent pay phone providers . .	331	402
Independent telephone companies .	233	267

Source: *Investor's Business Daily*, June 3, 1996, p. A4, from MultiMedia Telecommunications Association.

★ 1375 ★

Data Communications (SIC 4822)

Frame Relay Market - 1995

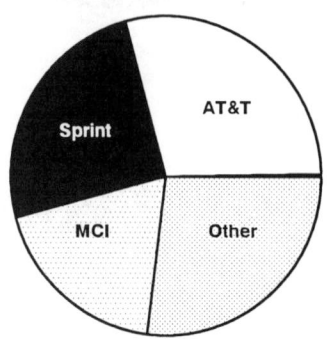

The market was valued at $630 million in 1995.

AT&T	29.0%
Sprint	25.0
MCI	19.0
Other	27.0

Source: *Network World*, April 1, 1996, p. 28, from International Data Corp.

★ 1376 ★

Data Communications (SIC 4822)

Internet Domains

There are more than 400,000 nonmilitary domain addresses on the Internet. The table shows the distribution by domain.

.COM	87.1%
.EDU	6.8
.NET	4.7
.ORD	1.0
Others	0.4

Source: *Washington Post*, June 22, 1996, p. C1, from Network Solutions.

★ 1377 ★

Data Communications (SIC 4822)

Popular E-Zines

The table shows the estimated readership of magazines on the World Wide Web, referred to as E-Zines. Mr. Showbiz and Suck are by day; Hotwired is by year; Word and Feed is by day; Salon is by month.

WWW.hotwired.com	3,000,000
WWW.word.com	80,000
WWW.salon.com	50,000
WWW.feedmag.com	25,000
WWW.mrshowbiz.com	23,000
WWW.suck.com	11,000

Source: *U.S. News & World Report*, June 24, 1996, p. 18.

★ 1378 ★

Data Communications (SIC 4822)

Voice Mail Leaders

Firms are ranked by revenues in millions of dollars.

	($ mil.)	Share
Octel	$ 396.0	20.0%
AT&T	332.0	16.5
Northern Telecom	274.0	14.0
Siemens-Rolm	141.0	7.0
Boston Technologies	106.0	5.0
Centigram	90.0	4.5

Source: *Wall Street Journal*, October 26, 1995, p. B1, from Yankee Group.

★ 1379 ★

Data Communications (SIC 4822)

Web Registrations

.COM	364,677
.ORG	25,778
.NET	3,473
.EDU	2,585
.GOV	401
.MIL	54

Source: *San Jose Mercury News*, June 17, 1996, p. E1, from InterNIC.

★ 1380 ★

Radio Broadcasting (SIC 4832)

Leading Radio Companies

Firms are ranked by 1995 radio revenues in millions of dollars.

Westinghouse	$ 1,000
Evergreen Media	275
Chancellor Broadcasting	178
Clear Channel Communications	137
Jacor Communications	124
American Radio Systems	119
SFX Broadcasting	117
Emmis Broadcasting	113
EZ Communication	99

Source: *Wall Street Journal*, June 21, 1996, p. A3, from Washington Research Group.

★ 1381 ★

Radio Broadcasting (SIC 4832)

Leading Radio Groups

America's leading radio companies are ranked by stations owned in 1996. The 10,200 stations in the United States are expected to generate advertising revenues of $12 billion.

Clear Channel	104
Westinghouse/Infinity	83
SFX	67
American Radio Systems	63
Jacor	57
Chancellor	41

Cox	38
Evergreen	35
Disney/ABC	21
Bonneville	20

Source: *Economist*, June 29, 1996, p. 70, from Duncan's American Radio.

★ 1382 ★

Radio Broadcasting (SIC 4832)

Radio Audience by Network

Data refer to listeners at least 12 years of age.

ABC	45.7%
Westwood One	34.9
CBS	15.1
American Urban Radio Networks	4.3

Source: *Broadcasting & Cable*, March 11, 1995, p. 38, from American Urban Radio Networks.

★ 1383 ★

Radio Broadcasting (SIC 4832)

Radio Format Shares

Radio broadcasting format shares are shown for Spring and Winter 1995. Data are for persons at least 12 years of age.

	Spring	Winter
News/Talk	15.8%	16.2%
Adult contemporary	14.9	15.0
Country	12.1	12.4
R&B	9.1	9.2
Top 40	9.1	9.2
Album rock	8.3	8.1
Oldies	7.5	7.2
Spanish	5.2	5.2
Classic rock	3.7	3.5
Modern rock	3.6	3.2
Adult standards	3.3	3.2
Jazz/AC	2.6	2.4
Religious	2.2	2.3
Classical	1.7	2.0
Easy listening	0.4	0.5
Rem. formats	0.3	0.3

Source: *Billboard*, October 14, 1995, p. 77, from Arbitron.

★ 1384 ★

Radio Broadcasting (SIC 4832)

Radio Stations by Format

The number of stations following each format is shown for 1995 and 1996. Shares are for 1996.

	1995	1996	Share
Country	2,587	2,570	27.1%
Adult contemporary	1,414	1,383	14.6
News/talk	1,132	1,205	12.7
Religious	844	865	9.1
Other	3,481	3,468	36.5

Source: *Adweek*, May 13, 1996, p. 24, from Center for Radio Information and *M Street Journal*.

★ 1385 ★

Radio Broadcasting (SIC 4832)

Radio Stations by State - Mexico

Aguascalientes	13
Baja California	54
Baja California (Sur)	7
Campeche	12
Coahuila	54
Colima	9
Chiapas	30
Chihuahua	63
Durango	20
Guanajuanto	51
Guerrero	28
Hidalgo	11
Jalisco	68
Mexico City	14
Michoacan	39
Morelos	13
Nayarit	16
Nuevo Leon	49
Oaxaca	25
Puebla	29
Queretaro	17
Quintana Roo	14
Sonora	61
Tamaulipas	67
Veracruz	78
Zacatecas	15

Source: *National Trade Data Bank*, September 1, 1995, p. IS9410.811, from Secreteria de Comunicaciones y Transportes.

★ 1386 ★

Radio Broadcasting (SIC 4832)

Religious Broadcasting by State

Data show the number of religious broadcasting stations by state. Data include both full and part-time broadcasting and AM/FM stations.

	No.	Share
Alabama	42	3.0%
Arkansas	28	2.0
Florida	80	5.8
Georgia	71	5.1
Kentucky	44	3.2
Louisiana	26	1.9
Mississippi	37	2.7
North Carolina	78	5.7
South Carolina	34	2.5
Tennessee	54	3.9
Texas	91	6.6
Virginia	59	4.3
West Virginia	14	1.0
Other	721	52.3

Source: *Southern Exposure*, Summer 1995, p. 7, from *National Religious Broadcaster's Directory of Religious Media*.

★ 1387 ★

Radio Broadcasting (SIC 4832)

Top 10 Radio Groups - 1996

Westinghouse/CBS/Infinity	
Jacor	
Clear Channel	
Evergreen	
Disney/ABC	
	American Radio System
SFX	
Cox	
Chancellor	
	Bonneville

The largest groups are ranked by estimated 1996 revenues in millions of dollars.

Westinghouse/CBS/Infinity	$ 1,050
Jacor	321
Clear Channel	319
Evergreen	290
Disney/ABC	284

Continued on next page.

★ 1387 ★ *Continued*
Radio Broadcasting (SIC 4832)

Top 10 Radio Groups - 1996

The largest groups are ranked by estimated 1996 revenues in millions of dollars.

American Radio System	$ 229
SFX	224
Cox	214
Chancellor	208
Bonneville	132

Source: *New York Times*, June 23, 1996, p. 2, from *Duncan's Radio Market Group*.

★ 1388 ★
Radio Broadcasting (SIC 4832)

Top Radio Broadcasters

The radio groups shown are ranked by listing audience. Listeners are those who tuned in for a minimum of five minutes between 6 a.m. and midnight and who are 12 years of age or older.

CBS/Group W/Infinity	2,568,050
Clear Channel Comm. Inc./Radio Equity Partners/U.S. Radio/Heftel	1,011,400
Evergreen Media Corp.	815,500
Disney/ABC	734,400
Chancellor Broadcasting Co.	618,000
Jacor/Noble/Citicasters	556,300
American Radio Systems Corp.	546,700
Emmis Broadcasting Corp.	527,400
Cox Communications Inc.	519,500
SFX Broadcasting Inc./Multi-Market Radio	480,000
Viacom	423,400
EZ Communications Inc.	340,000
Bonneville International Corp.	339,500
Spanish Broadcasting Systems Inc.	316,600
Gannett Co. Inc.	274,800

Source: *Broadcasting & Cable*, July 1, 1996, p. 27, from Arbitron survey.

★ 1389 ★
Radio Broadcasting (SIC 4832)

Top Stations - San Francisco

Shares indicate the average quarter-hour listenership of people 12 years or older, weekdays from 6 a.m. to midnight during the winter of 1995-96.

KGO-AM	6.8%
KCBS-AM	4.8
KMEL-FM	4.1
KOIT-FM	3.8
KYLD-FM	3.7
KNBR-AM	3.6
KKSF-FM	3.5
KIOI-FM	3.3
KBLX-FM	3.0
KITS-FM	2.8

Source: *New York Times*, June 21, 1996, p. C1, from Arbitron.

★ 1390 ★
Radio Broadcasting (SIC 4832)

Top Stations - Washington D.C.

Shares indicate the average quarter-hour listenership of people 12 years or older, weekdays from 6 a.m. to midnight during the winter of 1995-96.

WPGC-FM	6.5%
WHUR-FM	5.4
WMZQ-FM	5.3
WMMJ-FM	4.9
WASH-FM	4.8
WGMS-FM	4.5
WRQX-FM	4.5
WBIG-FM	4.4
WKYS-FM	4.1
WMAL-AM	4.0

Source: *Washington Post*, July 1, 1996, p. 5, from Arbitron and BIA Publications.

★ 1391 ★
Television Broadcasting (SIC 4833)

Leading TV Shows - Mexico

Leading television shows are ranked by household rating as of January 1996. All the shows are aired during prime time hours.

Maria la del Barrio	39.8%
El Premio Mayor	35.1

Continued on next page.

★ 1391 ★ *Continued*

Television Broadcasting (SIC 4833)

Leading TV Shows - Mexico

Leading television shows are ranked by household rating as of January 1996. All the shows are aired during prime time hours.

A Traves del Video	33.1%
Lazos de Amor	29.9
Marisol	29.7
Acapulco, Cuerpo y Alma	29.6
Morelia	28.5
Camara Infraganti	23.3
Siempre en Domingo	23.1
Accion	22.6

Source: *Variety*, March 31, 1996, p. 42, from IBOPE Mexico.

★ 1392 ★

Television Broadcasting (SIC 4833)

Prime-Time Leaders

Warner Bros.	
Columbia-TriStar	
Paramount-Viacom	
Disney	
20th Century Fox	
Universal	
CBS Entertainment	
	NBC Productions

Firms are ranked by number of shows in prime time.

Warner Bros.	20
Columbia-TriStar	11
Paramount-Viacom	10
Disney	9
20th Century Fox	8
Universal	7
CBS Entertainment	7
NBC Productions	5

Source: *Fortune*, April 15, 1996, p. 102, from Warner Bros. Television.

★ 1393 ★

Television Broadcasting (SIC 4833)

Regional TV Networks - New York

Networks are ranked by households reached.

Madison Square Garden Network . . .	5,280,000
SportsChannel New York	2,700,000
NY1 News	1,400,000
News 12 Long Island	700,000
News 12 Westchester	200,000

Source: *Crain's New York Business*, September 25, 1995, p. 26.

★ 1394 ★

Television Broadcasting (SIC 4833)

TV Network Leaders

The table shows the household ratings (percentage of nation's 95 million viewing households) for each network for each television season. Data are for the season to date.

	94-95	95-96
NBC	11.6%	11.7%
ABC	10.9	10.6
CBS	10.9	9.6
Fox	7.5	7.3

Source: *Wall Street Journal*, May 17, 1996, p. B4, from Nielsen Media Research.

★ 1395 ★

Television Broadcasting (SIC 4833)

Top 5 TV Companies

This table shows the percent of viewers the companies reach in the U.S. market.

Fox Television Stations Inc.	40.0%
Tribune Broadcasting Co.	33.4
CBS Station Group	32.5
Walt Disney Co.	25.0
NBC/GE	25.0

Source: *Chicago Tribune*, July 18, 1996, p. 1, from BIA Cos.

★ 1396 ★

Cable Broadcasting (SIC 4841)

Audio Network Services

The table shows the providers of specialized audio services ranked by thousands of subscribers.

Cable Radio Network	8,225
Superaudio	7,500
C-SPAN Audio Network	6,600
AEI Spectra Network	5,000
C-SPAN Audio Network II	3,200
KJAZ Cable Radio Network	2,000
Music Choice	1,000
WFMT	900
KLON	800
Moody Bible Institute	750

Source: *Cablevision*, April 29, 1996, p. 134.

★ 1397 ★

Cable Broadcasting (SIC 4841)

Basic Cable Stations - Ratings

Stations are ranked by thousands of viewing households during weekdays at prime-time (8-11 p.m.).

USA	1,524
TNT	1,294
TBS	1,284
ESPN	1,098
NICK	1,038
LIFE	905
CNN	771
DISC	737
A&E	633
TNN	610
FAM	582
MTV	409
WGN	393
TOON	255
CNBC	245

Source: *Broadcasting & Cable*, January 1, 1996, p. 39, from A.C. Nielsen and Turner Broadcasting System.

★ 1398 ★

Cable Broadcasting (SIC 4841)

Cable Companies - New York

Cable broadcasting networks are ranked based on household subscribers in 1995.

Cablevision of NYC/Bronx	375,000
Cablevision of NYC/Brooklyn	375,000
Time Warner Cable of NYC/Brooklyn-	
Queens	373,500
Time Warner Cable of NYC/Manhattan .	294,600
Paragon Cable Manhattan	200,000
Staten Island Cable	91,300
QUICS Cable Systems	90,600
Liberty Cable Television	25,000

Source: *Crain's New York Business*, September 25, 1995, p. 25.

★ 1399 ★

Cable Broadcasting (SIC 4841)

Cable Leaders - Washington

Systems are ranked by number of subscribers. System owners include Jones Communications, Tele-Communications Inc., Great Southern Printing and Manufacturing, and Goldman Sachs Partnership.

Fairfax	223,600
Montgomery County	200,117
District	101,000
Prince George's County (north)	85,000
Prince George's County (south)	72,359
Arlington County	56,661
Howard County (east)	51,000
Prince William County (east)	50,000
Frederick County	48,860
Alexandria	40,065

Source: *Washington Post*, May 18, 1996, p. A9, from cable companies.

★ 1400 ★

Cable Broadcasting (SIC 4841)

Cable Market Shares

TCI	20.1%
Time Warner	19.8
Comcast	5.9
Cox	5.4
Continental	5.3
Cablevision	4.4
Other	39.1

Source: *Investext,* Thomson Financial Services, March 27, 1995, p. 14, from Baseline, *Variety,* Cabletelevision Advertising Bureau, and company reports.

★ 1401 ★

Cable Broadcasting (SIC 4841)

Cable Network Penetration

The table shows the thousands of subscribers as of November 1995.

ESPN	67,248.0
TBS	67,029.0
CNN	67,077.0
USA	66,345.0
Discovery	66,251.0
TNT	65,713.0
Wired Cable	65,058.0
Nickelodeon	64,691.0
Nashville Network	64,063.0
Family Channel	63,570.0
Lifetime	63,487.0
A&E	62,838.0
MTV	62,661.0
Weather Channel	60,689.0
CNN Headline	58,920.0
CNBC	56,021.0
VH1	52,787.0

BET	43,420.0
Learning Channel	42,389.0
WGN	39,399.0
Prevue	38,562.0
Comedy Central	36,247.0
E!	34,662.0
Pay Cable	33,138.0
CMT	31,375.0
ESPN2	26,180.0
Sci-Fi	25,871.0
Faith & Value	24,051.0
f/X	24,029.0
HBO	24,018.0
Court TV	23,635.0
Cartoon Network	21,963.0
Travel Channel	17,826.0
Food Channel	13,901.0
Showtime	12,164.0
Nostalgia	7,357.0

Source: *Broadcasting & Cable,* November 27, 1995, p. 70, from Nielsen Media Research.

★ 1402 ★

Cable Broadcasting (SIC 4841)

Cable Service Leaders - Chicago

Data are for 1995.

Continental Cablevision	350,000
TCI of Illinois Inc.	280,000
Chicago Cable TV	210,000
Prime Cable of Chicago Inc.	128,404

Source: *Crain's Chicago Business,* July 1996, p. F24, from company reports.

★ 1403 ★

Cable Broadcasting (SIC 4841)

Largest Cable Markets

The table shows cable penetration in the largest markets. Figures show the millions of cable households.

	Ho.	%
New York City	6.69	68.0%
Los Angeles	4.91	61.0
Chicago	3.08	58.0
Philadelphia	2.64	74.0
San Francisco	2.25	70.0
Boston	2.12	77.0

Continued on next page.

★ 1403 ★　*Continued*

Cable Broadcasting (SIC 4841)

Largest Cable Markets

The table shows cable penetration in the largest markets. Figures show the millions of cable households.

	Ho.	%
Washington D.C.	1.88	66.0%
Dallas/Ft. Worth	1.82	51.0
Detroit	1.73	65.0
Atlanta	1.58	64.0
Houston	1.57	55.0
Seattle/Tacoma	1.46	71.0
Cleveland	1.45	67.0
Minneapolis/St. Paul	1.41	50.0
Tampa/St. Petersburg	1.41	70.0

Source: *Cablevision*, April 29, 1996, p. 131, from Nielsen Media Research.

★ 1404 ★

Cable Broadcasting (SIC 4841)

New Cable Network Launches

The table shows the millions of subscribers to channels scheduled to be launched in 1996.

MSNBC	20.0
Nick at Nite's TV Land	6.0
Animal Planet	4.0
Ovation	3.0

Source: *Mediaweek*, May 13, 1996, p. 6.

★ 1405 ★

Cable Broadcasting (SIC 4841)

Pay Cable Channels

The table shows the millions of subscribers to specialty cable television channels for 1995. Figures for the Disney Channel include 6.0 million households who carry Disney as a basic home service.

Home Box Office	20.8
Disney Channel	16.5
Showtime	9.3
Cinemax	8.9
Movie Channel	4.2
Star Television	3.6
Playboy Channel	0.4

Source: *New York Times*, April 8, 1996, p. C9, from Paul Kagan Associates.

★ 1406 ★

Cable Broadcasting (SIC 4841)

Top Cable Operators

Operators are ranked by thousands of subscribers.

Tele-Communications Inc.	12,700.0
Time Warner Cable	10,000.0
Continental Cablevision Inc.	4,100.0
Comcast	3,361.0
Cox Communications Inc.	3,216.1
Cablevision Systems Corp.	2,674.4
Adelphia Communications Inc.	1,642.0
Cablevision Industries Inc.	1,402.5
Jones Intercable Inc.	1,362.7
Marcus Cable	1,160.8
Viacom Cable	1,088.9
Falcon Cable TV	1,088.4
Century Communications Corp.	1,034.2
Charter Communications Inc.	811.3
E.W. Scripps Inc.	752.2

Source: *TV Digest*, November 27, 1995, p. 2.

★ 1407 ★

Cable Broadcasting (SIC 4841)

Top Systems Operators

Multiple systems operators are ranked by thousands of subscribers.

Tele-Communications Inc.	13,319
Time Warner Cable	10,058
Comcast	3,375
Cox Communiations Inc.	3,204
Continental Cablevision Inc.	3,133
Cablevision Systems Corporation	2,830
Adelphia Communications	1,635
Cablevision Industries	1,434
Jones Intercable Inc.	1,352
Viacom Cable	1,158

Source: *Telecommunications*, March 1996, p. 25, from National Cable Television Association.

★ 1408 ★

Cable Broadcasting (SIC 4841)

Top Wireless Cable Firms

Companies are ranked by number of subscribers.

American Telecasting	173,700
Heartland Wireless	121,500
People's Choice TV	89,700
CAI Wireless Systems	86,700
Pacific Telesis Group	59,300

Source: *Investor's Business Daily*, June 6, 1996, p. A10, from Alex. Brown & Sons Inc.

★ 1409 ★

Satellite Broadcasting (SIC 4841)

Satellite Broadcasting

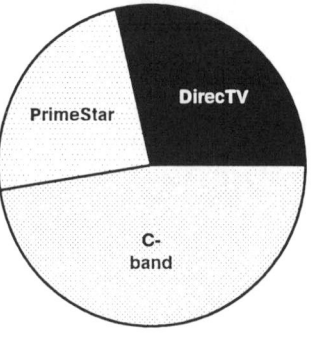

DirecTV	28.5%
PrimeStar	23.5
C-band	48.0

Source: *Investor's Business Daily*, May 15, 1996, p. A6, from *SkyReport*.

★ 1410 ★

Satellite Broadcasting (SIC 4841)

Satellite TV Broadcasters

Leading broadcasters are ranked by number of subscribers. The three companies have a combined total of 295 channels; an additional 370 are in the works for 1996 as three new companies join the market.

DirectTV	1,300,000
Primestar Partners	1,100,000
U.S.S.B.	628,000

Source: *Wall Street Journal*, March 11, 1996, p. B2, from UBS Securities Inc.

★ 1411 ★

Satellite Broadcasting (SIC 4841)

Satellite TV Market

The satellite television market is estimated for the year 2000.

DirecTV	50.0%
Primestar	30.0
AlphaStar	15.0
EchoStar	5.0

Source: *Forbes*, October 9, 1995, p. 12.

SIC 49 - Electric, Gas, and Sanitary Services

★ 1412 ★
Energy (SIC 4900)

Fuel Sources - Canada

Gas	45.9%
Electricity	34.1
Oil	14.5
Other	5.5

Source: *National Trade Data Bank*, March 2, 1996, p. 111091168.

★ 1413 ★
Energy (SIC 4900)

Household Energy Consumption

Consumption is shown by appliance.

Refrigerators	34.0%
Water heaters	29.0
Space heaters	24.0
Water pump	2.0
Other	1.0

Source: *Epri Journal*, March/April 1996, p. 27.

★ 1414 ★
Electric Services (SIC 4911)

Electric Power Production

Southern Company
American Elect. Power
Entergy
Texas Utilities
Commonwealth Edison
Florida Power & Light
Enron/Portland General
S. Calif. Edison
Pacific Gas & Electric
Duke Power
Houston Lighting & Power

The top firms are ranked by power generation shown in millions of megawatt hours.

Southern Company	121.1
American Elect. Power	95.1
Entergy	89.8
Texas Utilities	84.8
Commonwealth Edison	76.4
Florida Power & Light	73.6
Enron/Portland General	72.0
S. Calif. Edison	71.7
Pacific Gas & Electric	71.5
Duke Power	66.4
Houston Lighting & Power	60.4

Source: *Wall Street Journal*, July 22, 1996, p. A11, from Utility Data Institute; McKinsey & Co. and Federal Information Agency.

★ 1415 ★
Electric Services (SIC 4911)
Electric Power Sales

Sales are shown in gigawatt hour.

	1995	1996	1997
Medium cos.	34,469	36,876	39,172
Residential	26,854	28,437	30,124
Large cos.	24,104	25,936	27,359
Commercial	9,840	10,295	10,803
Agriculture	6,068	6,220	6,377
Services	5,425	5,571	5,703
Exports	1,947	1,947	1,952

Source: *National Trade Data Bank*, January 1, 1996, p. IS9509.638, from Federal Electricity Commission.

★ 1416 ★
Electric Services (SIC 4911)
Largest Electric/Gas Utilities

Uilities are ranked by revenues in millions of dollars. Shares of the group are shown in percent.

	($ mil.)	% of Group
Pacific Gas & Electric	$ 9,622	7.6%
Southern	9,180	7.3
Edison International	8,405	6.7
Unicom	6,910	5.5
Con. Edison of New York	6,402	5.1
Entergy	6,274	5.0
Public Svc. Entr. Group	6,164	4.9
American Electric Power	5,670	4.5
Texas Utilities	5,639	4.5
FPL Group	5,592	4.4
Duke Power	4,677	3.7
Dominion Resources	4,652	3.7
Houston Industries	4,388	3.5
Peco Energy	4,186	3.3
Niagara Mohawk Power	3,917	3.1
CMS Energy	3,890	3.1
General Public Utilities	3,805	3.0
Northeast Utilities	3,749	3.0
Central & South West	3,735	3.0
DTE Energy	3,636	2.9
Pacificorp	3,401	2.7
Consol. Natural Gas	3,307	2.6
Long Island Lighting	3,075	2.4
Florida Progress	3,056	2.4
Cinergy	3,031	2.4

Source: *Fortune*, April 29, 1996, p. F48.

★ 1417 ★
Electric Services (SIC 4911)
Rural Electric Cooperatives

Co-ops are ranked by revenues in millions of dollars. Locations are shown in parentheses.

Oglethorpe Power Corp. (Ga.)	$ 1,065.0
North Carolina EMC	672.0
Associated Electric Cooperative (Mo.)	486.0
Seminole Electric Cooperative (Fla.)	481.0
Tri-State G&T Association (Colo.)	438.0
Basin Electric Power Co-op (N.D.)	431.0
Cajun Electric Power Co-op (La.)	380.0
Old Dominion Elec. Cooperative (Va.)	337.0
East Kentucky Power Cooperative	330.0
Big Rivers Electric Corp. (Ky.)	316.0
Central Electric Power Coop. (S.C.)	297.0
Arkansas Electric Coperative	293.0

Source: *Rural Electrification*, March 1996, p. 13.

★ 1418 ★
Electric Services (SIC 4922)
Independent Power Producers

The table shows the energy generated by independent power producers in 1994, including independent power's share of total state capacity.

	Watts	Share
California	11,030	20.0%
Texas	7,528	10.0
New York	5,367	14.0
Florida	3,383	8.0
New Jersey	3,108	21.0

Source: *New York Times*, April 25, 1996, p. C4, from Energy Information Administration and Electric Generation Association.

★ 1419 ★
Electric Services (SIC 4922)
Top Utilities - Louisiana

Companies are ranked by 1995 revenues in millions of dollars.

Entergy Corp.	$ 6,274.4
Century Telephone Enterprises	644.8
Central Louisiana Electric Co.	394.2
Network Long Distance Inc.	28.7

Source: *Times Picayune*, May 19, 1996, p. I20, from TopBiz Network Inc.

★ 1420 ★

Gas Distribution (SIC 4923)

Leading Gas Distributors

The leading gas distributors are ranked by 1995 revenues in millions of dollars.

Utilicorp United	$ 1,524
MCN	1,456
Nicor	1,409
Brooklyn Union Gas	1,216
Atlanta Gas Light	1,063
Peoples Energy	1,033
Eastern Enterprises	921
Washington Gas Light	829
Wicor	821
UGI	776

Source: *Forbes*, January 1, 1996, p. 124, from Value Line Data Base Service and OneSource Information Services.

★ 1421 ★

Pipelines (SIC 4923)

Gas Pipeline Companies' Sales

Leading gas pipelines companies are ranked by sales shown in millions of cubic feet (MMcf) in 1994. Total sales fell from 2,003,941 MMcf in 1993 to 1,372,766 MMcf in 1994. The top 10 companies had 81.71% of the market.

Northwest Alaskan Pipeline Co.	367,461
Transcontinental Gas Pipe Line Corp. . .	322,264
Natural Gas Pipeline of America	144,515
Tennessee Gas Pipeline Co.	127,699
Southern Natural Gas Co.	105,670
Trunkline Gas Co.	89,122
Pacific Interstate Transmission Co. . . .	84,896
Texas Gas Transmission Corp.	54,743
NorAm Gas Transmission Co.	39,947
Distrigas of Massachusetts Corp.	36,449

Source: *Oil & Gas Journal*, November 27, 1995, p. 42, from United States Federal Energy Regulatory Commission.

★ 1422 ★

Water Services (SIC 4941)

Largest Pumped Storage Projects

Output is shown in megawatts. Locations are shown in parentheses.

Bath County (Virginia)	2,100
Ludington (Minnesota)	2,060
Castaic (California)	1,560
Raccoon Mountain (Tennessee)	1,540
Blenheim-Gilboa (New York)	1,200
Bad Creek (South Carolina)	1,065
Northfield Mountain (Massachusetts) . .	1,000
Rocky Mountain (Georgia)	900

Source: *International Water Power & Dam Construction*, June 1995, p. 34.

★ 1423 ★

Water Services (SIC 4941)

Water Companies - Minnesota

Revenues are shown in thousands of dollars for the 12 months ended June 30, 1995.

Osmonics Inc.	$ 101,469
Recovery Engineering Inc.	17,917
Harmony Brook Inc.	6,766
WTC Industries Inc.	1,673

Source: *Corporate Report Minnesota*, November 1995, p. 88.

★ 1424 ★

Sewage Systems (SIC 4952)

Drainage Systems by State - Mexico

The table shows the number of dwellings with drainage systems in each state. Figures are for 1990, the latest available.

Aguascalientes	111,787
Baja California	242,251
Baja California Sur	44,249
Campeche	50,860
Coahuila	275,989
Colima	72,292
Chiapas	244,444
Chuhuahua	352,355
Distrito Federal	1,677,692
Durango	142,569
Guanajuanto	403,210
Guerrero	188,596

Continued on next page.

★ 1424 ★ *Continued*

Sewage Systems (SIC 4952)

Drainage Systems by State - Mexico

The table shows the number of dwellings with drainage systems in each state. Figures are for 1990, the latest available.

Hidalgo	157,994
Jalisco	835,419
Mexico	1,387,934
Michoacan	378,653
Morelos	169,500
Nayarit	101,205
Nuevo Leon	519,751
Oaxaca	175,542
Puebla	373,699
Queretaro	110,033
Quintana Roo	58,906
Sain Luis	184,809
Tabasco	180,379
Tamaulipas	291,901
Veracruz	671,030
Yucatan	671,030

Source: *National Trade Data Bank*, January 2, 1996, p. IS9508.641, from National Institute of Geography, Statistics, and Data Processing.

★ 1425 ★

Sewage Systems (SIC 4952)

Water Sewage Plants - Mexico

Stabilization plants	48.20%
Aeration lagoons	23.54
Extended aeration	5.98
Imhoff tank	5.71
Other	16.57

Source: *National Trade Data Bank*, January 2, 1996, p. IS9508.641, from National Institute of Geography, Statistics, and Data Processing.

★ 1426 ★

Refuse Services (SIC 4953)

Hazardous Waste Managers - Mexico

The table shows the leading companies involved in recycling, transporting, collecting, processing, and incinerating useful secondary products from hazardous waste.

Residuos Industriales Multiqum (RIMSA)	40.0%
Omega (Metalclad)	15.0
Solver	10.0
Laidlaw Environmental	5.0
Other	30.0

Source: *National Trade Data Bank*, January 2, 1996, p. IS9506.647.

★ 1427 ★

Refuse Services (SIC 4953)

Waste Management Firms - Detroit

Companies in the metro Detroit area are ranked by revenues in millions of dollars. Activities include consulting, engineering, and waste hauling.

City Management Corp.	$ 222.9
Browning-Ferris Industries	200.0
EQ-The Environmental Quality Co.	94.5
McClain Industries Inc.	82.0
Durr Environmental	60.0
Clayton Environmental Consultants Inc.	32.3
McNamee, Porter & Seely Inc.	30.0
Laidlaw Waste Systems Inc.	19.8
NTH Consultants Ltd.	17.3
Soil and Materials Engineers Inc.	13.4

Source: *Crain's Detroit Business*, April 1, 1996, p. 22.

★ 1428 ★

Refuse Services (SIC 4953)

Waste Managers

Firms are ranked by 1995 revenues in millions of dollars.

WMX Technologies	$ 10,979
Browning-Ferris	5,779
Ogden	2,185

Source: *Fortune*, April 29, 1996, p. F63.

★ 1429 ★
Irrigation (SIC 4971)

Crop Irrigation

Data show the percentage of crops irrigated in the United States.

Rice	100%
Orchards	76
Potatoes	71
Vegetables	65
Sugarcane	50
Dry edible beans	42
Popcorn	42
Cotton	34
Feed grains	14
Wheat	7

Source: *Quick Facts from the Census of Agriculture*, December 5, 1995, p. 2, from United States Department of Commerce.

SIC 50 - Wholesale Trade - Durable Goods

★ 1430 ★
Wholesale Trade (SIC 5000)

Leading Industrial Distributors

Firms are ranked by 1995 sales in millions of dollars.

W.W. Grainger Inc.	$ 3,270
Graybar Electric Co.	2,700
WESCO Distribution Inc.	1,850
G.E. Supply	1,650
Motion Industries Inc.	1,500
Bearings Inc.	1,050
Airgas Inc.	840
Premier Industrial Corp.	818
McJunkin Corp.	667
Sun Distributors	601

Source: *Industrial Distribution*, June 1996, p. 52.

★ 1431 ★
Wholesale Trade - Auto Supplies (SIC 5013)

Auto Parts Wholesalers

The leading auto supply chains are ranked by number of outlets.

Genuine Parts	738
General Parts	540
Fisher Auto Parts	202
APS	200
O'Reilly Auto	170
Parts Inc.	129
Mid-State Auto	123
Crow-Burlington Co.	106
STRAFCO	105
Mid-Atlantic Warehouse	102

Source: *Automotive Marketing*, July 1995, p. 42.

★ 1432 ★
Wholesale Trade - Computers (SIC 5045)

Computer Distributors

Companies are ranked by 1995 sales in billions of dollars.

Ingram Micro	$ 8.6
Merisel	6.0
Computer 2000	3.4
Tech Data	3.1
Intelligent Electronics	2.9
Inacom	2.0
Microage	1.8

Source: *Computer Reseller News*, June 3, 1996, p. 108, from industry analysts and company reports.

★ 1433 ★
Wholesale Trade - Computers (SIC 5045)

Leading Computer Wholesalers

Shares of the top five wholesalers are shown by year.

	1994	1995
Ingram Micro	31.0%	36.0%
Merisel	27.0	25.0
Intelligent Electronics	17.0	15.0
Tech Data	13.0	13.0
MicroAge	12.0	12.0

Source: *Investext,* Thomson Financial Services, January 17, 1996, p. 7, from company reports, J.C. Bradford & Co. estimates, and First Call estimates.

★ 1434 ★
Wholesale Trade - Computers (SIC 5045)

Video Game System/Software Distribution

Toy chains	35.0%
Software chains	16.8
Department stores	16.1

Continued on next page.

★ 1434 ★ *Continued*
Wholesale Trade - Computers (SIC 5045)

Video Game System/Software Distribution

Discounters	15.3%
Showrooms	5.8
Appliance stores	5.5
Warehouse club	2.5
Audio specialty stores	1.5
Drug stores	1.5

Source: *DM*, June 1996, p. 69, from International Data Corp. Link.

★ 1435 ★
Wholesale Trade - Software (SIC 5045)

Software Distribution in the Pacific

Distributors' market shares are shown for the Pacific area.

Technical	34.9%
Broad-line	33.3
Master resellers	11.1
Hardware & supplies	10.1
Other	10.6

Source: *Computer Reseller News*, May 13, 1996, p. 157, from MSI Consulting Group.

★ 1436 ★
Wholesale Trade - Electronics (SIC 5060)

Top Connector Distributors - 1994

Companies are ranked by revenues in millions of dollars.

	Rev. ($ mil.)	Share
Avnet	$ 324.8	27.1%
Arrow	170.0	14.2
Kent	97.1	8.1
Premier	91.4	7.6
Marshall	87.6	7.3
Future	64.7	5.4
DAC Group	60.1	5.0
Deanco	51.4	4.3
Powell	50.7	4.2
Sterling	50.2	4.2
Other	152.0	12.7

Source: *Electronic Business Today*, October 1995, p. 20, from Bishop & Associates.

★ 1437 ★
Wholesale Trade - Electronics (SIC 5060)

Top Electronics Distributors - North America

Leading companies are ranked by 1995 sales in millions of dollars.

Arrow Electronics Inc.	$ 4,000.0
Avnet Inc.	3,510.0
Pioneer-Standard Electronics Inc.	1,282.0
Future Electronics	1,150.0
Marshall Industries	1,116.0
Wyle Electronics	1,078.0
Premier Industrial, Electronic Group	594.0
Bell Industries	564.0
TTI Inc.	383.0
Bell Microproducts Inc.	347.0
Kent Electronics Corp.	341.9
EIS	332.0
Sterling Electronics Corp.	310.0
Milgray Electronics Inc.	281.0
Insight Electronics Corp.	255.0
Reptron Electronics Inc.	223.3
All American	220.0
Richey Electronics Inc.	217.0
Nu Horizons Electronics	200.0
Digi-Key Corp.	157.6

Source: *Purchasing*, April 25, 1996, p. 58.

★ 1438 ★
Wholesale Trade - Electronics (SIC 5064)

U.S. Factory Sales

Factory sales are shown for the first 9 months of 1995. Total sales were $173.718 billion.

Electronic components	28.0%
Computers & peripherals	18.5
Telecommunications	16.3
Industrial electronics	9.3
Defense communications	8.0
Electromedical equipment	2.6
Audio, video, blank media	2.4
Other	14.9

Source: *TV Digest*, November 20, 1995, p. 13, from United States Department of Commerce.

★ 1439 ★

Wholesale Trade - Electronics (SIC 5065)

Connector Distributors

Companies are ranked by passive connector sales in millions of dollars.

Avnet EMG	$ 855.0
Arrow Electronics	592.4
TTI	383.0
Kent Electronics	314.6
Pioneer-Standard Electronics	217.9
Bell Industries	168.6
Sterling Electronics	149.5
Sager Electronics	136.2
Digi-Key	117.8
RicheyCypress Electronics	117.5

Source: *Electronic Business Today*, April 1996, p. 64.

★ 1440 ★

Wholesale Trade - Building Materials (SIC 5072)

Top Hardware Co-ops

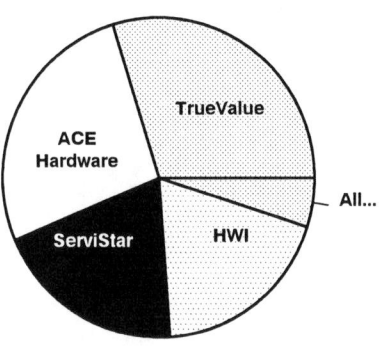

The top four hardware co-ops are ranked by share of $8.711 billion in wholesale sales in 1994.

TrueValue	30.0%
ACE Hardware	26.7
ServiStar	19.9
HWI	18.7
All remaining co-op members	4.7

Source: *Hardware Age*, October 1995, p. 40, from *Hardware Age Survey of Hardware Wholesalers*.

★ 1441 ★

Wholesale Trade - Exercise Equipment (SIC 5091)

Wholesale Work Out Equipment Sales

Sales to retailers grew from $1.57 billion in 1993 to $1.66 billion in 1994.

	1993	1994
Treadmills	28.4%	33.0%
Ski machines, cross-country	21.6	18.0
Home gyms	11.1	12.6
Stationary cycles	12.3	12.0
Stair-climbing machines	11.7	9.9
Benches	4.9	5.1
Rowing machines	0.6	0.3
Other	9.3	9.0

Source: *Sporting Goods Business*, July 1995, p. 32, from Fitness Products Council and Sporting Goods Manufacturers Association.

★ 1442 ★

Wholesale Trade - Sporting Goods (SIC 5091)

Wholesale Sporting Goods Sales

Wholesale sales are shown in millions of dollars. "Other" includes snow skiing, fishing, firearms, and team sports.

	($ mil.)	Share
Sports apparel	$ 16,950	40.7%
Athletic footwear	8,150	19.6
Exercise equipment	2,430	5.8
Golf equipment	2,250	5.4
Camping	1,660	4.0
In-line skating	1,040	2.5
Bowling/billiards	455	1.1
Water sports	390	0.9
Baseball/softball	350	0.8
Tennis	265	0.6
Archery	260	0.6
Soccer	212	0.5
Other	7,220	17.3

Source: *Swimming Pool/Spa Age*, May 1996, p. 18, from *Sporting Goods Manufacturers Association Participation Trends Report*.

SIC 51 - Wholesale Trade - Nondurable Goods

★ 1443 ★
Wholesale Clubs (SIC 5100)

Top Wholesale Club Chains

The top clubs shown are ranked by total sales in 1994 and 1995. The companies had 738 locations in 1995.

	1994 ($ bil.)	1995 ($ bil.)
Sam's Club	$ 19.0	$ 20.1
PriceCostco	16.2	17.9
BJ's	2.3	2.5

Source: *DM*, December 1995, p. 56, from Management Ventures Inc.

★ 1444 ★
Wholesale Trade (SIC 5100)

Leading Wholesalers

Firms are ranked by 1995 revenues in millions of dollars.

Fleming	$ 17,502
Supervalu	16,564
McKesson	13,326
Sysco	12,118
Alco Standard	9,892
Bergen Brunswig	8,448
Cardinal Health	7,806
Arrow Electronics	5,919
Merisel	5,802
Genuine Parts	5,282
Foxmeyer Health	5,177
Nike	4,761

Source: *Fortune*, April 29, 1996, p. F63.

★ 1445 ★
Wholesale Trade (SIC 5100)

Top Distributors - Candy & Tobacco

Candy and tobacco distributors are ranked by revenues for the latest fiscal year in millions of dollars. Data refer to sales to convenience stores.

McLane Co. Inc.	$ 7,147.0
Core-Mark International Inc.	1,900.0
EBY-Brown Co. L.P.	1,530.0
Eli Witt Co.	1,522.0
GSC Enterprises Inc.	789.0
S. Abraham & Sons Inc.	647.0
Jos. H. Stomel & Sons	450.0
Minter-Weisman Co.	361.0
J.F. Walker Co. Inc.	357.0
Thomas & Howard Co. of Hickory Inc. . . .	319.0

Source: *U.S. Distribution Journal*, August 15, 1995, p. 16.

★ 1446 ★
Wholesale Trade - Office Supplies (SIC 5112)

Leading Contract Stationers

Shares of the $30 billion market are shown in percent.

Boise Cascade Office Products	3.8%
Corporate Express	3.5
Office Depot	3.2
BT Office Products International	2.5
U.S. Office Products	1.4
Staples	1.3
Other	84.3

Source: *Investext*, Thomson Financial Services, October 20, 1995, p. 10, from company reports and Lehman Brothers estimates.

★ 1447 ★

Wholesale Trade - Office Supplies (SIC 5112)

Office Supply Shipments

Percentages are shown based on dollar volume of shipments to retailers. Data are for 1994.

Large dealers	23.4%
Superstores	18.7
National wholeslaers	15.6
Small/med. dealers	10.2
Mass market	10.1
Warehouse clubs	4.3
Regional wholesalers	4.0
Direct & government	3.5
Mail order	3.4
Other	6.8

Source: *Purchasing*, April 25, 1996, p. 86, from Business Products Industry Association.

★ 1448 ★

Wholesale Trade - Groceries (SIC 5141)

Food Distribution in Canada

Firms are ranked by revenues in millions of dollars.

George Weston Ltd.	$ 12,966.0
Loblaw Cos.	9,901.5
Oshawa Group	6,180.3
Provigo	5,704.3
Canada Safeway	4,795.9

Source: *Globe and Mail's Report on Business*, July 1996, p. 164.

★ 1449 ★

Wholesale Trade - Groceries (SIC 5141)

Major Wholesale Grocers - 1995

The wholesale grocers shown are ranked by revenues in millions of dollars for the latest fiscal year. Supervalu Inc. and Giant Eagle Co. figures are estimated.

Fleming Cos.	$ 19,000.0
Supervalu Inc.	16,564.0
Wakefern Food Corp.	3,516.0
Penn Traffic Co.	3,300.0
C&S Wholesale Grocers Inc.	2,650.0
Associated Wholesale Grocers Inc. . . .	2,611.0
Spartan Stores Inc.	2,512.0
Roundy's Inc.	2,462.0
Giant Eagle Co.	2,000.0

Certified Grocers of California Ltd. . . .	$ 1,874.0
Nash Finch Co.	1,855.0
Richfood Inc.	1,520.0

Source: *U.S. Distribution Journal*, September 15, 1995, p. 18.

★ 1450 ★

Beverage Bottling (SIC 5149)

Leading Bottlers

Firms are ranked by number of outlets in 1995.

CCE	210
Pepsi COBO	190
Pepsi General	55
Chicago Coke	27
Pepsi Northern CA	26
New York Coke	21

Source: *Beverage World*, March 1996, p. 83, from Beverage Marketing Corp.

★ 1451 ★

Wholesale Trade - Beverages (SIC 5149)

Bottled Water Distribution

Distribution of the bottled water market is shown by channel.

Grocery/off-premise	44.0%
Home	20.7
Commercial	18.6
Restaurants	8.5
Vending	8.2

Source: *Beverage World's Periscope*, September 30, 1995, p. 1, from Beverage Marketing Corp.

★ 1452 ★

Wholesale Trade - Nurseries (SIC 5193)

Where Landscapers Buy Materials

Landscapers spent an average of $26,340 on trees and ornamentals, and an average of $10,450 on bedding plants in 1995.

Wholesale growers	66.9%
Nursery retailers	22.5
Nursery brokers	14.7
Company-owned nurseries	9.2
Other	3.8

Source: *American Nurseryman*, June 1, 1996, p. 12, from *Lawn & Landscape* and Research USA.

SIC 52 - Building Materials and Garden Supplies

★ 1453 ★
Retailing - Building Materials (SIC 5211)

Home Improvement Market - Minneapolis

Shares are for 1995.

Menards	22.82%
Scherer Bros.	12.96
Knox	8.99
Builders Square	6.48
Mills	2.42
Budget Power	2.16
Other	44.17

Source: *Hardware Age*, February 1996, p. 26, from Business Dimensions.

★ 1454 ★
Retailing - Building Materials (SIC 5211)

Top Building Supply Retailers

Building and home improvement leaders are ranked by 1994 sales in millions of dollars.

Home Depot	$ 12,477.0
Lowe's Cos	6,111.0
Builders Square	2,952.0
Payless Cashways	2,723.0
Hechinger	2,450.0
Menard's	2,300.0
HomeBase	1,357.0
84 Lumber	1,275.0
Wickes Lumber	987.0
Sutherland Lumber	900.0

Source: *Forbes*, December 18, 1995, p. 116, from *National Home Center News*.

★ 1455 ★
Retailing - Building Materials (SIC 5211)

Top Home Supply Stores - 1996

Home Depot

Lowe's Cos.

Menard Inc.

Payless Cashways

Builders Square

Hechinger

HomeBase

84 Lumber Co.

Wickes Lumber

Carolina Holdings

Companies are ranked by sales in millions of dollars.

Home Depot	$ 15,470
Lowe's Cos.	7,075
Menard Inc.	2,700
Payless Cashways	2,680
Builders Square	2,639
Hechinger	2,250
HomeBase	1,449
84 Lumber Co.	1,250
Wickes Lumber	973
Carolina Holdings	900

Source: *Building Supply Business*, April 1996, p. 21.

★ 1456 ★

Retailing - Home Supplies (SIC 5231)

Paint, Glass & Wallpaper Sales by Outlet

Total sales are shown by outlet.

Paint, glass, and wallpaper stores	45.6%
Home centers	24.7
Discount stores	14.4
Hardware stores	14.2
Misc. general merchandise stores	0.8
Variety stores	0.2

Source: *DM*, July 1995, p. 68.

★ 1457 ★

Retailing - Paint (SIC 5231)

Paint Sales by Outlet

Sales are shown by outlet in percent. The paints and coatings market is expected to reach the $26.2 billion mark by 2004.

Paint, glass, and wallpaper stores	40.5%
Lumber and building material dealers	31.4
Hardware stores	13.6
Department stores	9.8
Other outlets	4.7

Source: *Modern Paint and Coatings*, September 1995, p. 6, from Business Trend Analysts Inc.

SIC 53 - General Merchandise Stores

★ 1458 ★
Retailing (SIC 5300)

Leading Retailers

Retailers are ranked by sales in millions of dollars for 1995.

Wal-Mart Stores	$ 93,627.0
Sears	34,925.0
Kmart	34,389.0
Dayton Hudson	23,516.0
J.C. Penney	20,562.0
Federated	15,048.5
May Dept.	10,952.0
Woolworth	8,224.0
Limited	7,881.4
Dillard	5,918.0
TJX Cos.	4,447.5
Gap	4,400.0
Nordstrom	4,113.5
Mercantile Stores	2,944.3
Spiegel	2,900.0

Source: *Women's Wear Daily*, April 2, 1996, p. 10.

★ 1459 ★
Retailing (SIC 5300)

Major Retail Channel Sales

The table shows the estimated sales through major channels. Data are in billions of dollars. Non-store retailing includes mail order, home shopping, and automatic vending machines.

	Vol. ($000)	Share
Supermarkets	$ 330.34	26.29%
Discount stores	161.9	12.89
Department stores	86.16	6.86
Drug/proprietary stores	85.74	6.82
Grocery stores	65.58	5.22
TV, radio, computer stores	49.75	3.96
Auto/home supply stores	40.89	3.25
Wholesale club	$ 39.54	3.15%
Home centers	38.95	3.10
Furniture stores	37.63	3.00
Non-store retailing	36.78	2.92
Women's ready-to-wear stores	30.38	2.41
Sporting goods/bicycle stores	23.35	1.86
Family apparel stores	22.92	1.83
Shoe stores	17.07	1.36

Source: *DM*, June 1996, p. 62.

★ 1460 ★
Retailing (SIC 5300)

Top Supercenters

Centers are ranked by sales in billions of dollars.

Wal-Mart Supercenter	$ 17.622
Meijer	7.490
SuperKmart	4.592
Fred Meyer	3.850
Target	0.395

Source: *DM*, March 1996, p. 50, from Management Ventures Inc.

★ 1461 ★
Department Stores (SIC 5311)

Leading Department Stores

Stores are ranked by millions of dollars in furniture and bedding sales in millions of dollars. Figures are estimated for 1995. Shares of the group are shown based on $2.16 billion generated by the top 25 stores.

	Sales ($ mil.)	% of Group
J.C. Penney	$ 696.0	32.2%
Rich's Lazarus Goldsmith's	161.4	7.5
Macy's East	142.4	6.6

Continued on next page.

348

★ 1461 ★ *Continued*

Department Stores (SIC 5311)

Leading Department Stores

Stores are ranked by millions of dollars in furniture and bedding sales in millions of dollars. Figures are estimated for 1995. Shares of the group are shown based on $2.16 billion generated by the top 25 stores.

	Sales ($ mil.)	% of Group
Dayton's Hudson's Marshall Field's	$ 128.0	5.9%
Dillard's	100.6	4.7
Burdines	85.7	4.0
Broadway Stores	83.0	3.8
Macy's West	81.5	3.8
The Bon Marche	75.3	3.5
Robinsons-May	73.0	3.4
Other	533.1	24.7

Source: *Furniture Today*, July 29, 1996, p. 21.

★ 1462 ★

Department Stores (SIC 5311)

Leading Department Stores - Mexico

Stores are ranked by number of outlets.

Sears Roebuck de Mexico	41
Almacenes GarcAa	22
Distribuidora Liverpool	10
El Palacio de Hierro	5

Source: *National Trade Data Bank*, March 2, 1996, p. IS9506.282, from Industriadata and Mercamtrica Ediciones.

★ 1463 ★

Department Stores (SIC 5311)

Leading Stores - Birmingham, AL

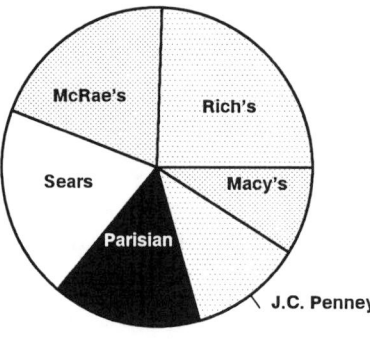

Department store market shares are shown for 1995.

Rich's	24.7%
McRae's	19.6
Sears	19.6
Parisian	15.9
J.C. Penney	11.6
Macy's	8.6

Source: *Investext*, Thomson Financial Services, February 9, 1996, p. 13.

★ 1464 ★

Department Stores (SIC 5311)

Top Department Stores

Companies are ranked by 1995 volume of sales in millions of dollars.

Sears	$ 28,020.0
Federated	15,048.5
J.C. Penney	14,973.0
May	10,507.0
Dillard	5,918.0
Mervyn's	4,516.0
Nordstrom	4,113.5
Dayton Hudson	3,193.0
Mercantile	2,944.3
Kohl's	1,925.7
Neiman Marcus	1,888.2
Belk	1,750.0
Saks Fifth Avenue	1,690.0
Proffitt's	1,333.4
Carson Pirie Scott	1,083.8

Source: *Stores*, July 1996, p. S22, from *American Express Survey of Top 100 Retailers*.

★ 1465 ★
Department Stores (SIC 5311)

Top Department Stores - Canada

Firms are ranked by revenues in billions of dollars.

Hudson's Bay Co.	$ 5.984
Sears Canada	3.925
Zellers Inc.	3.536
Price Costco Canada	2.372
Jean Coutu Group	1.273
Kmart Canada	1.262

Source: *Globe and Mail's Report on Business*, July 1996, p. 166.

★ 1466 ★
Discount Merchandising (SIC 5331)

Discount Market - Canada

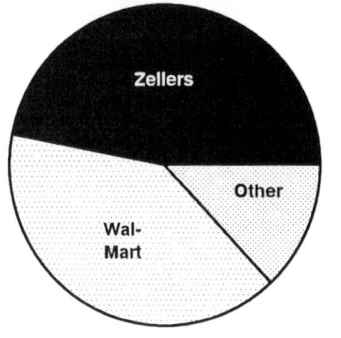

Market shares are shown in percent.

Zellers	47.0%
Wal-Mart	40.0
Other	13.0

Source: *Wall Street Journal*, May 24, 1996, p. B4.

★ 1467 ★
Discount Merchandising (SIC 5331)

Discount Merchandisers

Market leaders are shown for 1994.

Wal-Mart	38.6%
Kmart	19.5
Target	9.8
Other	32.1

Source: *Investext,* Thomson Financial Services, October 25, 1995, p. 11, from ABS estimates and company reports.

★ 1468 ★
Discount Merchandising (SIC 5331)

Discount Store Leaders

Companies are ranked by 1994 sales in millions of dollars.

Wal-Mart	$ 58,000
Kmart	28,386
Target (Dayton Hudson)	13,600
Meijer	6,000
Fred Meyer	3,128
Caldor	2,749
Ames	2,143
Venture	2,017
Bradlees	1,917
Hills	1,872

Source: *Chain Store Age*, August 1995, p. 22A.

★ 1469 ★
Discount Merchandising (SIC 5331)

Leading Discount Supercenters

Market shares are shown for 1994 and 1995.

	1994	1995
Wal-Mart	28.5%	43.7%
Meijer	36.8	25.1
Super Kmart	8.6	13.9
Fred Meyer	16.1	11.0
Smitty's	4.1	2.6
Bigg's	2.1	1.4
Big Bear	1.9	1.2
Other	1.9	1.1

Source: *Discount Store News*, March 4, 1996, p. 4.

★ 1470 ★

General Merchandising (SIC 5399)

Farm Equipment Suppliers

The top retailers of specialty farm equipment are ranked by 1995 sales in millions of dollars. Tractor Supply Co. has 195 stores; Country General has 125 stores; Quality Farm and Fleet has 90 stores; Central Tractor has 71 stores.

Tractor Supply Co.	$ 384
Quality Farm and Fleet	297
Country General	275
Central Tractor Farm & Country Inc.	252

Source: *Investor's Business Daily*, March 29, 1996, p. A3, from company reports.

SIC 54 - Food Stores

Convenience Stores (SIC 5411)

Convenience Stores in Detroit

Data show the number of outlets.

Mobil	175
Unocal	98
Amoco	96
Total	82
Shell	69
Speedway	68
Clark	60

Source: *National Petroleum News*, February 1996, p. 64.

Convenience Stores (SIC 5411)

Leading Convenience Stores

Firms are ranked by 1994 sales in millions of dollars.

Southland Corp.	$ 6,684
Circle K Corp.	2,684
Cumberland Farms Inc.	1,110
Dillon Cos. (Kroger)	898
National Convenience Stores Inc.	881
Dairy Mart Convenience Stores Inc.	753
Casey's General Stores Inc.	731
Lil' Champ Food Stores Inc.	476
E-Z Serve Corp.	411
Uni-Marts Inc.	314

Source: *Chain Store Age*, August 1995, p. 24A.

Grocery Stores (SIC 5411)

Leading Grocery Stores - Greensboro, NC

Shares are for 1994.

Food Lion	28.6%
Harris-Teeter	12.0
Winn-Dixie	11.0
Kroger	10.2
Food Fair	5.9
Lowe's	5.5
Other	26.8

Source: *Investext,* Thomson Financial Services, August 25, 1995, p. 13, from *Grocery Distribution Guide*.

★ 1474 ★
Grocery Stores (SIC 5411)

Leading Grocery Stores - Little Rock, AK

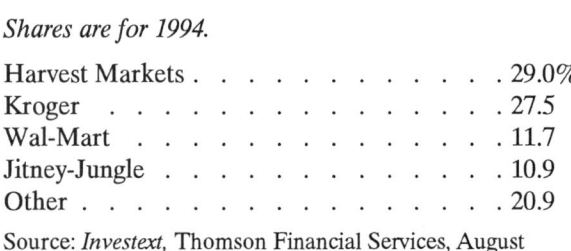

Shares are for 1994.

Harvest Markets	29.0%
Kroger	27.5
Wal-Mart	11.7
Jitney-Jungle	10.9
Other	20.9

Source: *Investext,* Thomson Financial Services, August 25, 1995, p. 12, from *Grocery Distribution Guide.*

★ 1475 ★
Grocery Stores (SIC 5411)

Leading Grocery Stores - Peoria, IL

Shares are for 1994.

Kroger	36.0%
Thompson Foods	12.4
Eagle Foods	8.7
Randall Foods	6.5
Other	36.4

Source: *Investext,* Thomson Financial Services, August 25, 1995, p. 12, from *Grocery Distribution Guide.*

★ 1476 ★
Grocery Stores (SIC 5411)

Leading Grocery Stores - Phoenix, AZ

Shares are for 1994.

Fry's (Kroger)	22.2%
ABCO	12.8
Smitty's	12.5

Safeway	8.1%
Basha's	8.0
Albertson's	6.4
Smith's Food	6.3
Other	23.7

Source: *Investext,* Thomson Financial Services, August 25, 1995, p. 12, from *Grocery Distribution Guide.*

★ 1477 ★
Grocery Stores (SIC 5411)

Leading Supermarket Stores - Mexico

Stores are ranked by number of outlets.

Gigante	183
Aurrera	109
Comerical Mexicana	88
Casa Ley	55
Almacenes 5-10-15	31
Tiendas de Descuento Sultana	28
Tiendas Chedraui	27
Supermercados	17
Tiendas de Descuento del Nazas	16

Source: *National Trade Data Bank,* March 2, 1996, p. IS9506.282, from Industriadata and Mercamtrica Ediciones.

★ 1478 ★
Grocery Stores (SIC 5411)

Top Supermarket Companies

Firms are ranked by 1995 sales in millions of dollars.

Kroger	$ 23.7
American Stores	18.2
Safeway	16.3
Wal-Mart Supercenters	13.5
Ahol and Stop & Shop	12.4
Albertson's	12.0
Winn-Dixie Stores	11.8
A&P	10.3
Publix Supermarkets	9.4
Food Lion	8.2

Source: *Financial Times,* April 3, 1996, p. 18, from Ahold.

★ 1479 ★
Grocery Stores (SIC 5411)

Top Supermarkets

Companies are ranked by 1995 volume of sales in billions of dollars.

Kroger	$ 23.93
Safeway	16.39
American Stores	13.30
Albertsons	12.58
Winn-Dixie	11.78
A&P	10.10
Publix	9.40
Ahold USA	8.33
Food Lion	8.21
Ralphs	5.50
Fleming Retail	5.20
H.E.B.	5.15
Vons	5.07
Pathmark	4.37
Stop & Shop	4.11
Super Value Retail	4.00
Giant Food	3.86
Penn Traffic	3.10
Smith's Food & Drug	3.08
Bruno's	2.86

Source: *Stores*, July 1996, p. S18, from *American Express Survey of Top 100 Retailers*.

★ 1480 ★
Grocery Stores (SIC 5411)

Top Supermarkets - Philadelphia

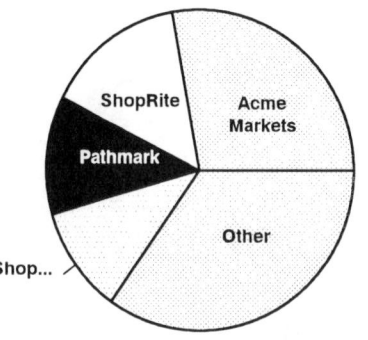

Shares are shown based on $8.9 billion in sales for the year ended March 31, 1996.

Acme Markets	27.5%
ShopRite	14.8
Pathmark	11.8
Shop n Bar/Thriftway	11.0
Other	34.9

Source: *Philadelphia Inquirer*, July 8, 1996, p. E6, from *Food Trade News*, Bloomberg Business News, and Acme Markets Inc.

★ 1481 ★
Grocery Stores (SIC 5411)

Top Supermarkets - Quebec

Shares of the $13.5 billion market are shown in percent.

Metro Richelieu Inc.	30.0%
Provigo	30.0
IGA/Oshawa Group	15.0
Other	25.0

Source: *Marketing Magazine*, July 15, 1996, p. 4.

★ 1482 ★

Candy Stores (SIC 5441)

Candy Sales by Outlet

Food stores	. 30.7%
Convenience stores	. 25.6
Mass merchants	. 18.8
Drug stores	. 16.3
Club stores	. 8.5

Source: *DM*, July 1996, p. 62, from Information Resources Inc.

★ 1483 ★

Bakeries (SIC 5461)

Leading Bagel Stores

Bruegger's

Manhattan Bagel

Chesapeake Bagel

Einstein Bros.

Big Apple Bagel

Firms are ranked by number of outlets at the end of 1995.

Bruegger's	. 250
Manhattan Bagel	. 160
Chesapeake Bagel	. 130
Einstein Bros.	. 117
Big Apple Bagel	. 77

Source: *Restaurant Business*, May 1, 1996, p. 162.

★ 1484 ★

Bakeries (SIC 5461)

New York Baking Industry

This table shows the location of bakeries in New York by borough.

Brooklyn	. 80
Queens (L.I. City 25)	. 49
Manhattan	. 34
Staten Island	. 18
Bronx	. 16

Source: *New York Times*, March 1, 1996, p. C16, from *Bakery Industry Study, 1995*.

SIC 55 - Automotive Dealers and Service Stations

★ 1485 ★

Auto Dealerships (SIC 5511)

Auto Dealer Franchises

Dealerships are ranked by number of franchise outlets.

Ford	4,424
Chevrolet	4,420
Oldmobile	2,960
Chrysler	2,949
Plymouth	2,938
Dodge	2,911
Pontiac	2,875
Buick	2,845
Mercury	2,642
Eagle	2,206
Lincoln	1,628
Cadillac	1,575
Toyota	1,190
Nissan	1,090
Honda	995
Mazda	896
Volkswagen	613
Saturn	349

Source: *Automotive News*, April 24, 1996, p. 128.

★ 1486 ★

Auto Dealerships (SIC 5511)

Canadian Auto Dealers

Data show the number of outlets.

	1995	1996
GM	864	834
Ford	640	616
Chrysler/Jeep/Eagle	607	608
Toyota	231	229
Honda	212	205
Mazda	180	175
Volkswagen/Audi	166	162
Nissan	152	147

	1995	1996
Hyundai	161	140
Suzuki	106	105
Subaru	92	97
Lada	86	82
Saturn/Saab/Isuzu	63	63
Mercedes-Benz	57	57
Volvo	50	48
Acura	40	37
BMW	36	33
Lexus	22	22
Infinity	22	21
Jaguar	21	20
Land Rover	11	13

Source: *Automotive News*, June 14, 1996, p. 28, from Canadian Automobile Dealer Association.

★ 1487 ★

Auto Dealerships (SIC 5511)

U.S. Auto Dealer Groups

The top auto dealerships are shown ranked by unit sales in 1995.

Hendrick Automotive Group	58,739
Potamkin Cos.	43,303
V.T. Inc.	42,588
United Auto Group Inc.	33,360
Bill Heard Enterprises Inc.	27,469
Ed Morse Automotive Group	26,288
McCombs Enterprises	24,024
Dobbs Brothers Management	23,032
Penske Automotive Group	23,030
Rosenthal Automotive Group	21,219
Mullinax Management	20,374
Holman Enterprises	18,304

Source: *Automotive News*, April 24, 1996, p. 182.

★ 1488 ★
Retailing - Auto Parts (SIC 5531)

DIY Auto Repair Parts

Data show do-it-yourselfer's (DIY) car part purchases by outlet. The four largest retail chains are expected to capture 40% of the market by the year 2000.

Retail auto parts stores 35.0%
Mass merchandisers/discounters 28.0
Jobbers 22.0
Other 15.0

Source: *Automotive Marketing*, December 1995, p. 24, from Salomon Brothers.

★ 1489 ★
Retailing - Auto Parts (SIC 5531)

Replacement Brake Sales by Outlet

Jobber 58.0%
Warehouse distributor 25.0
Undercar specialist 6.0
Car dealer 4.0
Manufacturer direct 4.0
Rebuilder direct 2.0
Other 1.0

Source: *Brake & Front End*, October 1995, p. 86.

★ 1490 ★
Retailing - Auto Parts (SIC 5531)

Top Auto Parts Chains

Leading auto parts retailers are ranked by annual sales shown in millions of dollars. The top 10 firms account for 8% of the $93 billion market.

AutoZone . . . . $ 1,800.0
Western Auto 1,800.0
PepBoys 1,471.0
Northern Automotive 690.0
Advance Auto Parts 593.0
Chief Auto Parts 383.0
Trak Auto 337.0
Discount Auto Parts 267.0
Hi-Lo 257.0
WSR 135.0

Source: *Automotive Marketing*, April 1996, p. 24, from Schroder-Wertheim.

★ 1491 ★
Retailing - Auto Supplies (SIC 5531)

Auto Cleaner Purchases by Outlet

Data show where all-purpose cleaners were purchased in 1995. National brands generated a 91.7% share of total sales; private label had the rest of the market.

Discount store chains 46.0%
Automotive chains 30.0
Non-automotive chains 22.0
Department stores 2.0

Source: *Aftermarket Business*, April 1, 1996, p. 24.

★ 1492 ★

Retailing - Auto Supplies (SIC 5531)

Auto Freshener Purchases by Outlet

The auto air freshener market reached $185 million in 1995.

Automotive chains	45.0%
Discount stores	20.0
Non-automotive chains	20.0
Department stores	15.0

Source: *Aftermarket Business*, April 1, 1996, p. 22.

★ 1493 ★

Retailing - Auto Supplies (SIC 5531)

Touch-Up Purchases by Outlet

Total aftermarket sales reached $362 million in 1995.

Automotive chains	56.0%
Discount stores	30.0
Department stores	8.0
Non-automotive chains	6.0

Source: *Aftermarket Business*, April 1, 1996, p. 74.

★ 1494 ★

Retailing - Tires (SIC 5531)

Independent Tire Dealerships

The top independent dealers are ranked by retail sales shown in millions of dollars.

Discount Tire Co. Inc.	$ 590.0
Les Schwab Tire Centers Inc.	450.5
Tire Kingdom Inc.	188.0
Winston Tire Co.	140.0
Merchant's Inc.	129.0
Tire Centers Inc.	100.0
AKH Co. Inc./Discount Tire Centers . . .	88.0
Don Olson Tire & Auto Centers	77.0
Kal Tire	67.5
Somerset Tire Service Inc.	62.0

Source: *Tire Business*, December 11, 1995, p. 19.

★ 1495 ★

Retailing - Tires (SIC 5531)

North American Tire Dealerships

Leading tire dealerships are ranked by 1994 commercial sales in millions of dollars. Shares of the group are shown in percent.

	Sales ($ mil.)	% of Group
Tire Center's Inc.	$ 175.0	14.7%
Treadco Inc.	158.0	13.3
Kal Tire	132.0	11.1
Fletcher's Cobre Tire	130.0	11.0
Purcell Tire & Rubber Co. . . .	96.0	8.1
Les Schwab Tire Centers Inc. . .	91.7	7.7
J.W. Brewer Tire Co.	82.5	7.0
Pomp's Tire Service Inc.	55.4	4.7
Southern Tire Mart Inc.	53.0	4.5
Bauer Built Inc.	52.5	4.4
Universal Tire Inc.	42.0	3.5
Parkhouse Tire Inc.	40.0	3.4
Talin Tire Inc.	40.0	3.4
Snider Tire Inc.	38.5	3.2

Source: *Tire Business*, December 11, 1995, p. 20.

★ 1496 ★

Retailing - Tires (SIC 5531)

Tire Sales by Outlet

There are 22,000 independent dealerships nationwide.

Small independent dealerships	30.0%
Stong regional dealerships	29.0
Major national dealerships	16.0
Mass merchandisers	10.0
Manufacturer owned stores	8.0
Warehouse clubs	7.0

Source: *Tire Business*, November 27, 1995, p. 2, from Michelin Americas Small Tires.

★ 1497 ★

Retailing - Tires (SIC 5531)

Top Tire Dealerships - 1995

The largest firms in North America are ranked by sales in millions of dollars.

Tire Centers Inc.	$ 204.0
Fletcher's Cobre Tire	185.0
Treadco Inc.	172.0

Continued on next page.

★ 1497 ★ *Continued*
Retailing - Tires (SIC 5531)

Top Tire Dealerships - 1995

The largest firms in North America are ranked by sales in millions of dollars.

Brad Ragan Inc.	$ 151.0
Kal Tire	145.2
Purcell Tire & Rubber Co.	103.0
Les Schwab Tire Centers Inc.	100.7
J.W. Brewer Tire Co.	90.0
Southern Tire Mart Inc.	83.0
Pomp's Tire Service Inc.	59.8
Bauer Built Inc.	52.5
Parkhouse Tire Inc.	45.0
Snider Tire Co.	45.0
Universal Tire Co.	45.0
Talin Tire Inc.	43.2

Source: *Tire Business*, May 27, 1996, p. 12, from survey reports.

★ 1498 ★
Gas Stations (SIC 5541)

Gasoline Retailers - Detroit

There were 1,527 gasoline outlets in the Detroit area as of June 1995.

Mobil	17.0%
Shell	14.4
Amoco	11.9
Unocal/Uno-Ven	9.7
Marathon	9.3
Sunoco	8.3
Total	5.8
Citgo	5.4

Speedway	5.1%
Clark	4.1
BP	2.8
Others	6.2

Source: *National Petroleum News*, February 1996, p. 62.

★ 1499 ★
Retailing - Boats (SIC 5551)

Marine Retailers by Type

Distribution is shown based on 10,000 marine retailers.

Boat, motor & equipment	50.0%
Boat, motor, equipment & marine facilities	30.0
Equipment only	10.0
Service only	10.0

Source: *Boating Business Annual Industry Review*, 1995, p. 7.

SIC 56 - Apparel and Accessory Stores

★ 1500 ★
Retailing - Apparel (SIC 5611)

Men's Apparel Industry

Data are for 1994.

Department stores	29.2%
Discount dept. stores	22.4
Specialty apparel stores	14.8
Off-price stores	14.0
Sears/Wards	5.1
Catalog/mail order	4.0
Other	10.5

Source: *Investext,* Thomson Financial Services, February 20, 1996, p. 8, from MRCA Information Services.

★ 1501 ★
Retailing - Apparel (SIC 5611)

Men's Sport Shirt Sales

Sales of woven and knit shirts are shown for the year ended February 1996. Chains refers to Sears, Montgomery Ward, and J.C. Penney.

	Woven	Knit
Department stores	31.7%	30.3%
Discount stores	22.1	21.4
Chains	19.9	18.1
Price/factory outlets	12.5	13.2
Other	13.8	17.0

Source: *Discount Store News*, May 6, 1996, p. A16, from NPD Consumer Purchase Panel.

★ 1502 ★
Retailing - Apparel (SIC 5621)

Where Women Purchased Dress Clothes

The top stores are shown based on a survey of 6,525 households.

J.C. Penney	12.9%
Wal-Mart	7.2
Sears	5.7
Kmart	3.8
Target	1.2

Source: *Women's Wear Daily*, February 7, 1996, p. 17, from Management Horizons.

★ 1503 ★
Retailing - Apparel (SIC 5621)

Women's Clothing Retailers

Melville Corp.
The Limited
The Gap
Charming Shoppes
Ann Taylor
Dress Barn
Claire's
Designs Inc.

Leading retailers of women's apparel are ranked by annual revenues in millions of dollars.

Melville Corp.	$ 11,885.0
The Limited	7,950.0
The Gap	4,300.0
Charming Shoppes	1,273.0

Continued on next page.

★ 1503 ★ *Continued*
Retailing - Apparel (SIC 5621)

Women's Clothing Retailers

Leading retailers of women's apparel are ranked by annual revenues in millions of dollars.

Ann Taylor	$ 740.0
Dress Barn	501.0
Claire's	301.0
Designs Inc.	300.0

Source: *Corporate Growth Weekly Report*, December 26, 1995, p. 8220, from company reports.

★ 1504 ★
Retailing - Apparel (SIC 5632)

Legging Sales by Outlet

	1995	1996
Mass	27.9%	29.1%
Dept./specialty	21.1	20.9
Food/drug	17.3	16.5
Other	34.3	33.6

Source: *Discount Store News*, May 6, 1996, p. A22, from Information Resources Inc. and NPD Group.

★ 1505 ★
Retailing - Apparel (SIC 5632)

Legwear Sales by Outlet

Sales are shown by outlet.

Grocery stores	29.0%
Discount stores	25.0
Other	46.0

Source: *Body Fashions/Intimate Apparel*, November 1995, p. 13.

★ 1506 ★
Retailing - Apparel (SIC 5632)

Lingerie Sales by Outlet - Canada

Sales are shown by outlet. An estimated 80% of intimate apparel retailers are located in Ontario. Some popular companies are Lingerie Arianne, Linda Lingerie, Hanna, Lou Batten, Romantic Night, Papillon Blanc, and French Maid.

Specialized lingerie stores	46.0%
Department stores	31.0
Discount stores	23.0

Source: *National Trade Data Bank*, September 1, 1995, p. ISA9503.

★ 1507 ★
Retailing - Apparel (SIC 5641)

Children's Apparel Retailers

Shares are estimated for 1994 based on total sales of $23.85 billion.

J.C. Penney	13.7%
Wal-Mart	11.0
Kmart	8.2
Sears	5.7
Target	4.5
Mervyn's	3.3
Toys R Us	3.1
May	2.6
GapKids	2.5
Federated	2.1
Montgomery Ward	1.8
Gymboree	0.8
Limited Too	0.7
OshKosh B'Gosh	0.4
Baby Superstore	0.1
Talbot's Kids	0.1
Other	39.0

Source: *Investext*, Thomson Financial Services, December 19, 1995, p. 4, from NPD Group, PaineWebber estimates, and company reports.

★ 1508 ★
Retailing - Apparel (SIC 5641)

Infant Wear Sales by Outlet

Sales in 1994 reached $9.6 billion.

Discount stores	36.5%
Department stores	35.9
Children's /infant's wear stores	13.8
Family apparel stores	8.7
Women's ready to wear stores	5.1

Source: *DM*, July 1995, p. 64.

★ 1509 ★
Retailing - Apparel (SIC 5651)

Top Apparel Stores

Companies are ranked by 1995 volume of sales in millions of dollars.

Limited	$ 7,881.4
TJX	4,447.5
The Gap	4,395.2
Woolworth	3,600.0
Melville Apparel	3,055.6
Burlington Coat	1,584.9
Ross Stores	1,426.3
American Retail Group	1,250.0
Eddie Bauer	1,134.6
Charming Shoppes	1,102.3
Petrie Stores	1,050.0
Talbot's	981.0
Ann Taylor	731.1
Goody's	696.8
Country Seat	625.0

Source: *Stores*, July 1996, p. S22, from *American Express Survey of Top 100 Retailers*.

★ 1510 ★
Retailing - Apparel (SIC 5651)

Top Clothing Stores - Canada

Firms are ranked by revenues in millions of dollars.

Dylex Ltd.	$ 1,692.3
Reitmans (Canada)	360.4
Suzy Shier	267.4
Mark's Work Wearhouse	185.9
Chateau Stores of Canada	159.7
Pantorama Industries	147.7

Source: *Globe and Mail's Report on Business*, July 1996, p. 166.

★ 1511 ★
Retailing - Footwear (SIC 5661)

Athletic Shoe Sales by Outlet

Sales are shown by outlet.

Discount stores	28.0%
Athletic shoe stores	11.0
Traditional shoe stores	9.0
Sporting goods/pro shops	8.6
Department stores	8.5
Other	34.9

Source: *Discount Store News*, January 15, 1996, p. 63, from Sporting Goods Manufacturers Association/ Footwear Market Insights.

★ 1512 ★
Retailing - Footwear (SIC 5661)

Footwear Sales by Outlet

	1991	1994
Discount stores	24.3%	24.6%
Self-service shoe stores	12.7	15.6
Shoe stores	15.3	14.5
Department stores	13.3	11.5
Other	46.4	33.8

Source: *Footwear News*, November 13, 1995, p. 4, from Footwear Market Insights.

★ 1513 ★

Retailing - Footwear (SIC 5661)

Men's Shoe Market by Outlet

Athletic stores

Shoe stores

Dept. stores

Mass discounters

Discount shoe stores

Mail order

Off-pricers

Athletic stores	27.0%
Shoe stores	20.0
Dept. stores	20.0
Mass discounters	14.0
Discount shoe stores	10.0
Mail order	5.0
Off-pricers	4.0

Source: *Footwear News*, April 29, 1996, p. 13, from Tactical Retail Solutions Inc.

SIC 57 - Furniture and Homefurnishings Stores

★ 1514 ★

Retailing - Furniture (SIC 5712)

Retail Furniture Leaders

The top 10 companies are ranked by 1994 sales in millions of dollars. Shares of the group are shown in percent.

	Sales ($ mil.)	% of Group
Levitz	$ 1,036.3	15.2%
Sears	875.0	12.9
Montgomery Ward	798.0	11.7
Ethan Allen	710.0	10.4
Heilig-Meyers	697.2	10.2
J.C. Penney	691.0	10.2
Wal-Mart	592.0	8.7
Office Depot	550.3	8.1
Pier 1 Imports	442.5	6.5
La-Z-Boy	412.5	6.1

Source: *Furniture Today*, September 11, 1995, p. 9.

★ 1515 ★

Retailing - Furniture (SIC 5712)

Top Furniture Stores

Companies are ranked by 1994 sales in millions of dollars.

Levitz	$ 1,036.3
Heiling-Meyers	697.2
Pier 1 Imports	442.5
The Bombay Company	323.3
Wickes Furniture	247.0
Mattress Discounters	191.0
Jennifer Convertibles	152.0
This End Up	123.6
Ethan Allen	123.5
Krause's Furniture	116.5
Crate & Barrel	69.0
Aaron Rents	68.4
Leather Center	55.8

Expressions Custom Furniture	$ 54.6
US Baby	49.2

Source: *Furniture Today*, December 25, 1995, p. 40.

★ 1516 ★

Retailing - Floor Coverings (SIC 5713)

Floor Covering Retailers

The table shows the top stores ranked by sales in millions of dollars. Shares are shown based on sales by the top 24 companies.

	($ mil.)	Share
Carpet One	$ 1,900	33.3%
Maxim	1,400	24.6
Abbey Carpet	900	15.8
America's Flooring Partnership .	300	5.3
Pro Flooring Association	300	5.3
Carpetland USA	200	3.5
Other	700	12.3

Source: *Investext,* Thomson Financial Services, February 5, 1996, p. 4, from *Floor Covering Weekly*.

★ 1517 ★
Retailing - Floor Coverings (SIC 5713)

Rug Sales by Outlet

National chains

Department stores

Home centers

Mass merchants

Specialty stores

Furniture stores

Catalogs

Warehouse clubs

National chains	19.0%
Department stores	18.0
Home centers	17.0
Mass merchants	16.0
Specialty stores	13.0
Furniture stores	7.0
Catalogs	6.0
Warehouse clubs	4.0

Source: *HFN*, March 11, 1996, p. 16.

★ 1518 ★
Retailing - Homefurnishings (SIC 5719)

Bedding Sales by Outlet

Leading suppliers in 1995 include Sealy, Serta, Simmons, and Spring Air. National chains include J.C. Penney, Montgomery Ward, and Sears.

Furniture stores	40.0%
Specialty stores	23.0
National chains	14.0
Department stores	12.0
Other	11.0

Source: *HFN*, March 11, 1996, p. 14.

★ 1519 ★
Retailing - Homefurnishings (SIC 5719)

Blanket Sales by Outlet

Sales reached $425 million in 1995.

Mass merchants	53.0%
Specialty stores	20.0
Department stores	19.0
Catalogs	6.0
Other	2.0

Source: *HFN*, March 11, 1996, p. 32.

★ 1520 ★
Retailing - Homefurnishings (SIC 5719)

Cookware Sales by Outlet

Wal-Mart	15.0%
Department stores	13.0
Kmart	10.0
Gourmet/specialty	7.0
Direct mail	6.0
Catalog/showroom	5.0
Sears/Montgomery Ward/J.C. Penney . . .	5.0
Supermarkets	5.0
Wholesale clubs	5.0
Drug/variety	3.0
Home center/hardware	3.0
TV shopping	3.0
Other discount	14.0
Other	6.0

Source: *HFN*, May 6, 1996, p. 46.

★ 1521 ★
Retailing - Homefurnishings (SIC 5719)

Dinnerware Retailers

The top 75 retailers sold $1.425 billion in 1993 and $1.519 billion in 1994.

	1993 ($ mil.)	1994 ($ mil.)
Service Merchandise	$ 114.4	$ 121.5
Ross-Simons	70.0	80.0
Macy's East	72.5	78.6
Dayton's/Hudson's/Marshall Field's	67.0	73.0
Dillard's	61.6	66.0
Macy's West/Bullock's	61.8	65.3
Broadway	54.0	53.3
Fortunoff's	49.9	49.9

Continued on next page.

★ 1521 ★ *Continued*
Retailing - Homefurnishings (SIC 5719)

Dinnerware Retailers

The top 75 retailers sold $1.425 billion in 1993 and $1.519 billion in 1994.

	1993 ($ mil.)	1994 ($ mil.)
Robinson's/May	$ 43.6	$ 49.3
Neiman Marcus/Neiman Marcus Direct	42.0	45.2
Hecht's	35.8	38.4
Foley's	36.6	37.6
Luria's	34.0	36.0
Rich's/Goldsmith's	28.8	36.0
Belk Stores	35.6	35.1

Source: *HFN*, October 16, 1995, p. 65.

★ 1522 ★
Retailing - Homefurnishings (SIC 5719)

Home Textile Retailers

Shares of retail sales are shown for 1994.

J.C. Penney	15.3%
Wal-Mart	10.3
Kmart	8.3
Target	6.4
Sears	4.3
Spiegel	3.1
Mervyns	3.0
Montgomery Ward	2.6
Linens 'N Things	2.4
Domestications	2.2
Other	42.1

Source: *Investext,* Thomson Financial Services, October 18, 1995, p. 6, from *Home Textiles Today.*

★ 1523 ★
Retailing - Homefurnishings (SIC 5719)

Metal Bed Sales by Outlet

Specialty stores

National chains

Department stores

Other

Sales reached $215 million in 1995. Leading suppliers include Elliott's, Fashion Bed Group, Powell, Rosalco, and Wesley Allen. National chains include J.C. Penney, Montgomery Ward, and Sears.

Specialty stores	32.0%
National chains	25.0
Department stores	12.0
Other	31.0

Source: *HFN*, March 11, 1996, p. 14.

★ 1524 ★
Retailing - Appliances (SIC 5722)

Electrical Appliance Retailers - Canada

The market for small appliance retailing is shown in percent. Canadian stores include Canadian Tire, Consumers Distributing, Zellers, and Eaton's; U.S. stores include Sears, Kmart, and Woolco.

Canadian stores	50.0%
U.S. stores	30.0
Other	20.0

Source: *National Trade Data Bank*, March 2, 1996, p. 111092698.

★ 1525 ★
Retailing - Appliances (SIC 5722)

Refrigerator Sales by Outlet

Sales are shown by outlet. The leading market share by price range was between $600-$799 with a 28.75% share; the most popular size was 18-19 cubic feet with a 26.7 % share. Consumers purchased 35.5% of refrigerators with ice makers. CE stands for consumer electronics.

CE Superstore	42.50%
Appliance store	30.75
Home builder	4.80
Discount department store	4.50

Continued on next page.

★ 1525 ★ *Continued*
Retailing - Appliances (SIC 5722)

Refrigerator Sales by Outlet

Sales are shown by outlet. The leading market share by price range was between $600-$799 with a 28.75% share; the most popular size was 18-19 cubic feet with a 26.7 % share. Consumers purchased 35.5% of refrigerators with ice makers. CE stands for consumer electronics.

Department store	3.85%
Home center	2.50
Landlord	1.40
Hardware store	1.20
Warehouse club	1.00
Mass merchandiser	0.80

Source: *Dealerscope*, May 1996, p. 57, from Hudson Valley Editorial Services.

★ 1526 ★
Retailing - Electronics (SIC 5731)

Cellular Sales by Outlet

Consumer electronics superstore	47.0%
Office superstore	16.0
Specialty store	12.0
Mass merchant	9.0
Warehouse club	7.0
Department store	4.0
Other	5.0

Source: *RCR*, August 21, 1995, p. 1, from BIS Strategic Decisions.

★ 1527 ★
Retailing - Electronics (SIC 5731)

Popular Electronics Stores

Retailers are ranked by 1994 electronics sales in millions of dollars.

Circuit City	$ 4,378.0
Best Buy.	4,317.0
Radio Shack	2,853.0
Sears	2,850.0
Wal-Mart	2,574.0

Source: *Brandweek*, September 11, 1995, p. 24, from *Twice*.

★ 1528 ★
Retailing - Electronics (SIC 5731)

Satellite System Sales

Sales reached $1.3 billion in 1995.

Software specialty	27.0%
Satellite dealers	26.0
Electronics/appliance stores	25.0
Department stores	3.0
Other	8.0

Source: *HFN*, March 11, 1996, p. 79.

★ 1529 ★
Retailing - Electronics (SIC 5731)

Top Electronics Dealers

Electronics dealers are ranked by 1994 sales in millions of dollars.

Tandy Corp.	$ 4,780.0
Circuit City Stores Inc.	4,070.0
Wal-Mart Stores	2,641.0
Search Merchandise Group	1,854.0
Best Buy.	1,700.0
Service Merchandise	1,615.0
Kmart	1,410.0
Target	1,250.0
Price/Costco	1,100.0
Montgomery Ward	1,024.0

Source: *HFN*, September 18, 1995, p. 70.

★ 1530 ★
Retailing - Electronics (SIC 5731)

Where We Purchased Camcorders

Data show the market share by retailer for camcorder sales.

Sears/Brand Central	11.0%
Circuit City	10.0
Best Buy.	6.3
Montgomery Ward/Electric Ave./ Lechmere	6.2
Nobody Beats the Wiz	4.4

Continued on next page.

★ **1530** ★ *Continued*

Retailing - Electronics (SIC 5731)

Where We Purchased Camcorders

Data show the market share by retailer for camcorder sales.

YES/Fretter/Solo	3.1%
Kmart	2.9
Wal-Mart	2.5
Radio Shack	2.5
The Good Guys	2.2
J.C. Penney	1.3
Caldor	0.8
QVC	0.8
Other	46.0

Source: *Dealerscope*, July 1995, p. 36.

★ **1531** ★

Retailing - Electronics (SIC 5731)

Where We Purchased TVs

Data show the market share by retailer for direct view color televisions (up to 27 inches).

Circuit City	10.0%
Sears/Brand Central	9.7
Wal-Mart	8.5
Montgomery Ward/Electric Ave./	
Lechmere	8.0
Best Buy	5.5
Nobody Beats the Wiz	5.0
Kmart	3.7
YES/Fretter/Solo	2.5
Target	1.4
The Good Guys	1.0
Radio Shack	1.0
P.C. Richard	0.9
J.C. Penney	0.8
Other	42.0

Source: *Dealerscope*, July 1995, p. 36.

★ **1532** ★

Retailing - Computers (SIC 5734)

Largest Computer Stores - Bay Area

Firms are ranked by number of employees.

CompUSA	600
Computer Attic	170
ComputerWare	165

Computown	89
The Good Guys	70
ComputerLand of Serramonte	50
Inacom Oakland	50
PC Professional Inc.	42
Basis Inc.	40
InfoTech	35

Source: *San Francisco Business Times*, September 15, 1995, p. 21.

★ **1533** ★

Retailing - Computers (SIC 5734)

Microcomputer Sales by Channel

Data are for 1995. VAR stands for value added reseller. OEM stands for original equipment manufacturer.

Retail	50.8%
Direct	18.5
VAR/SI	15.0
Dealer	12.5
OEM	3.2

Source: *Purchasing*, October 19, 1995, p. 80, from Frost & Sullivan.

★ **1534** ★

Retailing - Computers (SIC 5734)

Popular Computer Stores - St. Louis

The retailers shown are the leading sources for computer hardware and software in the St. Louis area. Data are based on a 1995 survey.

Best Buy	19.5%
Circuit City	14.9
Office Depot	9.4
Computer City	7.4
CompUSA	6.8
Mail Order	6.3
Babbage's	6.0
OfficeMax	5.2
Radio Shack	4.1
Software Plus	3.7

Source: *St. Louis Post-Dispatch*, July 1, 1996, p. 12BP, from Scarborough Research Corp.

★ 1535 ★
Retailing - Software (SIC 5734)

Software Distribution by Outlet

	1992	1996
Full-line	76.0%	77.7%
Master resellers	7.4	20.7
Local	0.6	1.5
Other	16.0	0.1

Source: *Computer Reseller News*, January 22, 1996, p. 105, from MSI Consulting Group.

★ 1536 ★
Retailing - Software (SIC 5734)

Software Distributors - Mexico

Shares are shown in percent.

Distribuidor de Computo	27.0%
Central del Software	22.0
Megaplan	11.0
MPS Mayorista	11.0
Merisel de Mexico	7.0
Intertec	5.0
Other	17.0

Source: *National Trade Data Bank*, September 1, 1995, p. IS9504.231.

★ 1537 ★
Retailing - Music (SIC 5735)

Leading Music Retailers

Companies are ranked by 1994 music sales in millions of dollars. Music retailers had a 53.3% share of the $12.1 billion industry; music clubs had a 15.1% share, mail order had a 3.4% share and other retailers accounted for 26.7% of the market. Trans World Entertainment owns Coconuts, Record Town, and Music World.

Musicland Stores	$ 849
MTS/Tower Records	600
Blockbuster	559
Best Buy	550
Trans World Entertainment	403
Camelot Music	370
Wherehouse Entertainment	334
Circuit City Stores	225

Source: *Forbes*, December 4, 1995, p. 167, from company reports.

SIC 58 - Eating and Drinking Places

★ 1538 ★

Catering (SIC 5812)

Top Caterers - Dallas

The companies shown are ranked by functions catered in 1995 in Dallas.

Goodies from Goodman Inc.	13,500
Culinaire International	9,144
Omni Mandolay Hotel at Las Colinas	5,000
Southern Methodist University Catering	3,500
Eddia Doan & Co. Inc.	3,000
Bagelstein's Restaurant & Catering	2,500
Ellis Castle Catering	2,500
Two Sisters Catering	2,225
Hyatt Regency-Dallas	2,200
Marty's	2,100

Source: *Dallas Business Journal*, January 4, 1996, p. 4, from caterers.

★ 1539 ★

Foodservice (SIC 5812)

Foodservice Market - 1996

Sales are shown by segment.

	($ bil.)	Share
Quick service	$ 105.003	33.4%
Full service	96.073	30.6
Business and industry	19.365	6.2
Schools	16.972	5.4
Lodging	14.457	4.6
Hospitals	11.993	3.8
Colleges	8.533	2.7
Corrections	5.457	1.7
Nursing homes	4.998	1.6
Supermarkets	4.934	1.6
Military	4.726	1.5
Transportation	3.696	1.2
Recreation	3.428	1.1
Caterers	3.165	1.0
Convenience stores	3.093	1.0
Child care	2.494	0.8

	($ bil.)	Share
Life care/elder care	$ 2.214	0.7%
Department/discount stores	1.151	0.4
Other commercial	2.354	0.7
Other institutional	0.236	0.1

Source: *Nation's Restaurant News*, January 1996, p. 19, from Cahners Bureau of Foodservice Research.

★ 1540 ★

Foodservice (SIC 5812)

Foodservice Market - Canada

The foodservice and hospitality market is shown by segment for 1993.

	($ mil.)	Share
Restaurants, licensed	$ 6,918	32.9%
Restaurants, unlicensed	4,127	19.6
Accomodation foodservice	2,374	11.3
Take-out and delivery	1,911	9.1
Institutional foodservice	1,838	8.7
Social/contract caterers	1,241	5.9
Pubs/taverns/lounges	1,014	4.8
Leisure activities	883	4.2
Vending	271	1.3
Department stores	213	1.0
Other retail foodservice	231	1.1

Source: *National Trade Data Bank*, March 2, 1996, p. 111089979, from Canadian Restaurant and Foodservice Association.

★ 1541 ★
Foodservice (SIC 5812)

Healthcare Foodservice Market

Marriott

Aramark Corp.

Sodexho

Morrison

Wood Co.

Canteen

Other

Shares are shown based on 2,303 accounts in 1994.

Marriott	26.2%
Aramark Corp.	16.1
Sodexho	12.3
Morrison	11.8
Wood Co.	7.3
Canteen	6.7
Other	19.7

Source: *Investext,* Thomson Financial Services, September 18, 1995, p. 11, from Foodservice Director.

★ 1542 ★
Foodservice (SIC 5812)

Institutional Foodservice Industry

The noncommercial foodservice market is shown in percent.

Business & industry	24.0%
Vending	23.0
Schools	13.0
Colleges	10.0
Hospitals	10.0
Transportation	6.0
Nursing homes	6.0
Military	4.0
Other	4.0

Source: *School Foodservice & Nutrition,* October 1995, p. 32, from International Foodservice Manufacturers Association and Technomic Inc.

★ 1543 ★
Foodservice (SIC 5812)

Top Concession Companies

Firms are ranked by sales in millions of dollars. Leading companies include Fine Host Corporation and the Swanson Corp. who did not release revenues figures.

Aramark	$ 5,000
Ogden Entertainment Services	2,200
Host Marriott Services Corp.	1,160
Service America Corp.	750
Elias Brothers	670
Volume Services	200
Sportservice Corp.	180
The Levy Restaurants	100
Premier Food Services	16

Source: *Amusement Business,* May 13, 1996, p. 24.

★ 1544 ★
Foodservice (SIC 5812)

Top Contract Chains

Shares are shown based on total sales of contract chains in the top 100 restaurants.

Marriott Management Services	25.22%
Aramark	22.23
Canteen Corp.	9.87
Service America Corp.	6.28
Dobbs International Services	6.27
LSG Lufthansa Services/Sky Chef	3.98
Sodexho U.S.A.	3.76
Caterair International	3.25
Gardner Merchant Food Service	3.08
Daka Inc.	2.92
Other	13.14

Source: *Nation's Restaurant News,* August 7, 1995, p. 112.

★ 1545 ★
Foodservice (SIC 5812)

U.S. Foodservice Leaders

Data are for 1994.

Sysco	9.0%
Kraft Foodservice	4.0
ProSource	4.0
Gordon Food Service	1.0
JP Foodservice	1.0

Continued on next page.

★ 1545 ★ *Continued*
Foodservice (SIC 5812)

U.S. Foodservice Leaders

Data are for 1994.

PYA/Monarch	1.0%
Rykoff-Sexton	1.0
U.S. Foodservice	1.0
Other	78.0

Source: *Investext,* Thomson Financial Services, May 11, 1995, p. 7, from Sysco, Food Institute, and Morgan Stanley Equity Research.

★ 1546 ★
Restaurants (SIC 5812)

Family Dining Market

Shares are shown for 1994 based on total sales of $29.5 million.

Denny's	5.8%
Shoney's	4.6
Big Boy	3.5
Cracker Barrel	2.4
Perkins Family Restaurants	2.1
IHOP	2.0
Friendly's	2.0
Bob Evans	1.8
Carrow's/Coco's	1.7
Waffle House	1.0
Other	73.1

Source: *Investext,* Thomson Financial Services, September 11, 1995, p. 16, from Technomic.

★ 1547 ★
Restaurants (SIC 5812)

Hamburger Chains

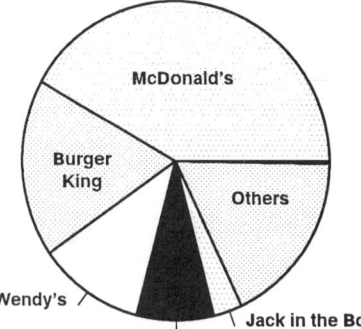

Shares are shown for 1995 based on the $37.6 billion market.

McDonald's	42.3%
Burger King	18.2
Wendy's	10.7
Hardee's	8.3
Jack in the Box	2.9
Others	17.6

Source: *Economist,* June 29, 1996, p. 62, from McDonald's and Technomic.

★ 1548 ★
Restaurants (SIC 5812)

Italian Restaurant Market

The table shows the growing share of Italian dinner house chains in the Italian restaurant market.

	1993	1994	1995
Independents	85.5%	84.1%	82.8%
Chains	14.5	15.9	17.2

Source: *Restaurant Business,* March 1, 1996, p. 192.

★ 1549 ★
Restaurants (SIC 5812)

Leading Dinner-House Chains

Shares are shown for 1995 based on sales of dinner-house chains in the top 100 restaurants.

Red Lobster	18.95%
Olive Garden	12.80
Applebee's	10.37
Chili's	9.73

Continued on next page.

★ 1549 ★ *Continued*
Restaurants (SIC 5812)

Leading Dinner-House Chains

Shares are shown for 1995 based on sales of dinner-house chains in the top 100 restaurants.

T.G.I. Friday's	8.91%
Outback Steakhouse	8.41
Ruby Tuesday	5.58
Bennigan's	4.66
Chi-Chi's	3.48
Ground Round	3.12
Lone Star Steakhouse	3.09
Fuddruckers	2.81
Hooters	2.76
Red Rodin Burger & Spirits Emporium	2.67
Stuart Anderson's Black Angus	2.65
Other	3.01

Source: *Nation's Restaurant News*, August 7, 1995, p. 122.

★ 1550 ★
Restaurants (SIC 5812)

Leading Pizza Chains

Shares are shown based on aggregate sales of the pizza chains of the top 100 restaurants.

Pizza Hut	48.07%
Little Caesar's Pizza	18.25
Domino's Pizza	17.56
Papa John's Pizza	4.01
Sbarro, The Italian Eatery	3.74
Round Table Pizza	3.33
Chuck E. Cheese's	2.73
Godfather's Pizza	2.31

Source: *Nation's Restaurant News*, August 7, 1995, p. 116.

★ 1551 ★
Restaurants (SIC 5812)

Restaurant Chains - Milwaukee

Chains are ranked by number of locations.

McDonald's Restaurants	105
Pizza Hut	51
Subway Sandwiches & Salads	50
George Webb Restaurants	45
Cousins Submarines	44
Burger King Restaurants	43

Dairy Queen	38
Hardee's Restaurants	34
Taco Bell Restaurants	33
Kentucky Fried Chicken	32

Source: *Business Journal*, September 2, 1995, p. 11.

★ 1552 ★
Restaurants (SIC 5812)

Steak Restaurant Chains

Market shares are shown based on the grill-buffet restaurants in the top 100 restaurants.

Ponderosa Steakhouse	23.21%
Golden Corral	19.71
Sizzler	19.57
Ryan's Family Steak House	17.60
Western Sizzlin	10.93
Quincy's Family Steakhouse	8.99

Source: *Nations Restaurant News*, August 7, 1995, p. 142.

★ 1553 ★
Restaurants (SIC 5812)

Take-Out Market

	1990	1994
QSRs	45.5%	49.0%
Full-service	40.6	34.0
Supermarkets	13.9	17.0

Source: *Restaurant Business*, July 1, 1996, p. 172, from Food Marketing Institute.

★ 1554 ★
Restaurants (SIC 5812)

Top Chicken Restaurants

Companies are ranked by 1994 sales in millions of dollars.

KFC	$ 7,100
Popeye's/Church's	1,240
Chick-fil-A	451
Kenny Rogers Roasters	300
El Pollo Loco	223
Bojangles Chicken	186
Grandy's	170
Lee's Famous Recipe	156

Continued on next page.

★ 1554 ★ *Continued*
Restaurants (SIC 5812)

Top Chicken Restaurants

Companies are ranked by 1994 sales in millions of dollars.

Mrs. Winner's	$ 85
Pudgie's	58

Source: *New York Times*, April 3, 1996, p. C3, from *Restaurants & Institutions*.

★ 1555 ★
Restaurants (SIC 5812)

Top Hamburger Chains

This table shows the top hamburger chains and share of the $36 billion industry.

McDonald's	41.5%
Burger King	16.9
Wendy's	10.8
Other	30.8

Source: *Wall Street Journal*, December 4, 1995, p. B4, from Burger King and Technomic Inc.

★ 1556 ★
Restaurants (SIC 5812)

Top Parent Companies

The parent companies of theme restaurants are ranked by combined 1995 sales in millions of dollars. PepsiCo. includes Pizza Hut, KFC, Taco Bell, California Pizza Kitchen, and Chevys Mexican Restaurants.

PepsiCo. Restaurants Intl.	$ 20,603.2
Grand Metropolitan	8,612.5
Darden Restaurants	3,190.0
Intl. Dairy Queen	2,560.9
Allied Domecq	2,477.2
Carlson Cos.	2,034.9
Flagstar Corp. Inc.	1,984.0
Shoney's Inc.	1,788.2
Metromedia Restaurant Group	1,485.0
America's Favorite Chicken	1,447.0

Source: *Restaurants & Institutions*, July 1, 1996, p. 56, from company reports.

★ 1557 ★
Restaurants (SIC 5812)

Top Pizza Firms

Firms are ranked by sales in millions of dollars.

Pizza Hut	$ 6,300
Domino's	2,500
Little Caesar's	2,000
Sbarro	346
Papa John's	161

Source: *Investor's Business Daily*, October 26, 1995, p. A6.

★ 1558 ★
Restaurants (SIC 5812)

Top U.S. Restaurants

The top 100 independent restaurants in 1995 had $912.765 billion in sales. This table shows the leading 15 ranked by total sales in thousands of dollars.

Tavern on the Green	$ 30,500.0
Rainbow Room	30,003.0
Smith & Wollensky	21,371.0
Bob Chinn's Crabhouse	20,341.0
Sparks Steakhouse	19,600.0
Joe's Stone Club	15,050.0
Manor	14,000.0
Scoma's Restaurant	13,122.0
"21" Club	13,067.0
Spenger's Fish Grotto	11,883.0
Gladstone's 4 Fish	11,694.0
Del Frisco's Double Eagle Steak House	11,630.0
Four Seasons	11,600.0
Trattoria Dell' Arte	11,572.0
Sequoia	11,392.0

Source: *Restaurants & Institutions*, May 15, 1996, p. 48.

★ 1559 ★

Coffee Shops (SIC 5813)

Coffee Shops in North America

| Starbucks |
| Second Cup |
| The Coffee Beanery |
| Barnie's Coffee & Tea |
| Timothy's World Coffee |

Chains are ranked by number of outlets in North America.

Starbucks	682
Second Cup	444
The Coffee Beanery	157
Barnie's Coffee & Tea	86
Timothy's World Coffee	70

Source: *Fortune*, November 27, 1995, p. 44.

SIC 59 - Miscellaneous Retail

★ 1560 ★
Drug Stores (SIC 5912)

Leading Drug Stores in Florida

Figures indicate where 345,800 people shopped in Florida's Volusia and Flagler counties over a 30-day period. Eckerd leads Walgreens in most major markets in Florida.

Eckerd	51.0%
Walgreen's	43.0
Wal-Mart	25.0
Kmart	13.0

Source: *Daytona Beach Sunday News Journal*, June 23, 1996, p. 2E, from Minnesota Opinion Research Inc.

★ 1561 ★
Drug Stores (SIC 5912)

Top Drug Store Chains

Firms are ranked by 1994 sales in millions of dollars.

Walgreen	$ 9,235
Eckerd	4,549
American Drug	4,544
Rite Aid	4,534
CVS (Melville)	4,330
Revco	4,320
Thrifty Payless	3,163
Longs	2,558
Phar-Mor	1,852
Thrift (J.C. Penney)	1,540

Source: *Chain Store Age*, August 1995, p. 16A.

★ 1562 ★
Drug Stores (SIC 5912)

Top Drug Stores

Companies are ranked by revenues in millions of dollars.

Walgreen	$ 11,600
Rite Aid	6,200
Revco D.S.	5,100
Eckerd	4,495
Longs Drug	2,770
Fay S.	1,180
Arbor	815
Big B	800
Drug Emporium	695
Genovese Drug	680

Source: *Corporate Growth Weekly Report*, March 25, 1996, p. 8359.

★ 1563 ★
Retailing - Drugs (SIC 5912)

Pharmaceutical Diagnostics Distribution

Data are for 1995.

Chains	27.2%
Independents	17.8

Continued on next page.

★ 1563 ★ *Continued*
Retailing - Drugs (SIC 5912)

Pharmaceutical Diagnostics Distribution

Data are for 1995.

Non-federal hospitals	11.7%
Mass merchandisers	10.7
Foodstores/with pharmacy	7.7
Mail order	6.4
Clinics	4.1
Foodstores w/o pharmacy	3.8
Long term care	2.4
HMOs	1.5
Home health	0.8
Others	3.9

Source: *Medical Marketing & Media*, May 1996, p. 58, from NPA Plus.

★ 1564 ★
Retailing - Sporting Goods (SIC 5941)

NFL Sports Merchandise Sales

This table shows the shares of the licensed merchandise market for the first six months of 1995.

Dallas Cowboys	20.8%
San Francisco 49ers	11.3
Miami Dolphins	6.6
Green Bay Packers	5.1
Carolina Panthers	5.0
Kansas City Chiefs	4.8
Pittsburgh Steelers	4.7
Oklahoma Raiders	4.7
New England Patriots	3.6
New York Giants	3.2
Other	30.2

Source: *Advertising Age*, September 25, 1995, p. 3, from NFL Properties.

★ 1565 ★
Retailing - Sporting Goods (SIC 5941)

Racquet Sales by Outlet

Data are for 1995.

Sporting goods stores	40.6%
Specialty sport shops	22.8
Discount stores	13.7
Pro shops	8.2
Department stores	3.7
Mail order	3.1
Other	7.9

Source: *Sporting Goods Dealer*, June 1996, p. 29, from National Sporting Goods Association.

★ 1566 ★
Retailing - Sporting Goods (SIC 5941)

Sporting Goods Retailers

Market leaders are shown for 1994.

Sports Authority	2.4%
Sportmart	1.2
Sports and Recreation	1.1
Other	95.3

Source: *Investext*, Thomson Financial Services, October 25, 1995, p. 11, from ABS estimates and company reports.

★ 1567 ★
Retailing - Sporting Goods (SIC 5941)

Top Sporting Goods Retailers

Companies are ranked by retail sporting goods sales in millions of dollars for 1995.

Foot Locker	$ 1,905
The Sports Authority	1,100
L.L. Bean	1,078
J.C. Penney Simply for Sports	950
Champs	550
Sports & Recreation	526
Sportmart	492
The Athlete's Foot	450
REI	448
Footaction USA	424
Big 5	400

Continued on next page.

★ 1567 ★ *Continued*
Retailing - Sporting Goods (SIC 5941)

Top Sporting Goods Retailers

Companies are ranked by retail sporting goods sales in millions of dollars for 1995.

Lady Foot Locker	$ 370
Oshman's	343
Academy	327
Herman's	327

Source: *Sportstyle*, May 1996, p. 18.

★ 1568 ★
Retailing - Western Equipment (SIC 5941)

Where Horsemen Shop - Canada

Tack shop	95.0%
Department stores	59.0
Co-op stores	42.0
Direct mail catalogs	16.0
Specialty stores	12.0

Source: *National Trade Data Bank*, September 1, 1995, p. 111096781, from *Saddle and Harnesses Market in Canada Report*.

★ 1569 ★
Retailing - Books (SIC 5942)

Book Sales by Outlet

Book sales by outlet are shown for 1994. Adults purchased 986 million books in 1993 and 1.01 billion in 1994; Juveniles purchased 532 million in 1993 and 526 million in 1994.

Chain bookstores	25.0%
Independent bookstores	21.0
Book clubs	18.0
Discount stores	8.0
Warehouse clubs	6.0
Food/drug stores	4.0
Mail order	4.0
Used bookstores	4.0
Other	10.0

Source: *Investor's Business Daily*, October 30, 1995, p. A4, from *Consumer Research Study on Book Purchasing, 1994*.

★ 1570 ★
Retailing - Books (SIC 5942)

Children's Book Sales by Outlet

The children's retail book market was valued at $1.17 billion in 1994. Hardcover book sales are expected to reach $856.4 million by 1999 with paperback book sales rising to $612.6 million.

General retailers	70.2%
Libraries & institutions	12.2
School	9.8
Export	3.2
College	1.2
Direct to consumer	0.5
Other	2.9

Source: *Publishers Weekly*, August 21, 1995, p. 24, from *Book Industry Study Book Trends, 1995*.

★ 1571 ★
Retailing - Books (SIC 5942)

Juvenile Book Sales by Outlet

Discount stores	29.8%
Book clubs	17.0
Chains	10.4
Food/drug stores	8.5
Mail order	5.5
Toy stores	5.2
Independents	5.2
Variety stores	3.2
Price clubs	2.8
Other	12.4

Source: *Playthings*, June 1996, p. 23, from American Booksellers Association.

★ 1572 ★
Retailing - Books (SIC 5942)

Leading Book Chains - 1996

Shares are estimated for 1996.

Barnes & Noble	13.1%
Borders Group	10.1
Books-A-Million	1.8
Media Play (books only)	1.5
Other	73.5

Source: *Investext*, Thomson Financial Services, February 16, 1996, p. 8, from Book Industry Study Group, United States Department of Commerce, and PaineWebber.

★ 1573 ★

Retailing - Books (SIC 5942)

Magazine Sales by Outlet

	Sales ($ mil.)	Market Share
Supermarkets	$ 1,622.1	41.5%
Convenience stores	598.0	15.3
Discount stores	418.2	10.7
Drug stores	308.8	7.9
Book stores	222.8	5.7
Terminals	191.5	4.9
Newsstands	179.8	4.6
Other	367.4	9.4

Source: *Nonfoods Merchandising*, December 1995, p. 52, from Council for Periodical Distributors Association.

★ 1574 ★

Retailing - Jewelry (SIC 5944)

Jewelry/Watch Sales by Outlet

| Jewelry stores |
| **Department stores** |
| **Discount stores** |
| **Catalog showrooms** |
| **Misc. general merchandise stores** |
| **Non-store retailers** |
| **Gift, novelty, & souvenir shops** |
| **Variety stores** |

Total sales reached $24.8 billion.

Jewelry stores 60.0%
Department stores 12.6
Discount stores 10.9
Catalog showrooms 7.2
Misc. general merchandise stores 3.7
Non-store retailers 3.5
Gift, novelty, & souvenir shops 1.6
Variety stores 0.5

Source: *DM*, July 1995, p. 67.

★ 1575 ★

Retailing - Toys (SIC 5945)

Action Figure Sales by Outlet

Distribution is shown based on 147.2 million action figures sold in 1995.

Discount stores 53.0%
Toys R Us 21.0
Other toy stores 13.0
Food/drug stores 3.0
Variety 3.0
Catalog showrooms 1.0
Department stores 1.0
Other 5.0

Source: *Playthings*, May 1996, p. 29, from NPD Group Inc. Toy Market Index.

★ 1576 ★

Retailing - Toys (SIC 5945)

Crayon Sales by Outlet

Data are for 1994.

Discount stores 54.0%
Grocery 17.0
Drug stores 12.0
Warehouse clubs 2.0
Other 15.0

Source: *American Demographics*, June 1996, p. 8, from A.C. Nielsen.

★ 1577 ★

Retailing - Toys (SIC 5945)

Plush Toy Market Shares

Shares are shown based on total sales of $1.149 billion in 1995.

Discount stores 37.0%
Food/drug stores 12.0
Other toy stores 8.0
Department stores 7.0
Toys R Us 7.0
Variety 2.0
Other outlets 27.0

Source: *Playthings*, May 1996, p. 27, from NPD Group, Inc. Toy Market Index.

★ 1578 ★
Retailing - Toys (SIC 5945)

Top Toy Retailers - 1996

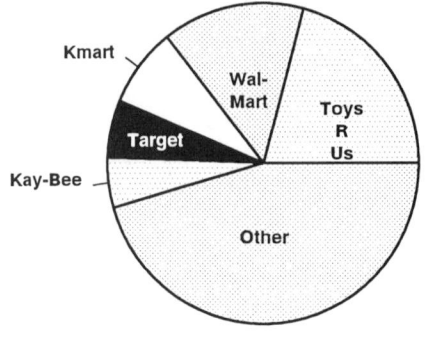

Toys R Us	20.5%
Wal-Mart	15.0
Kmart	7.5
Target	6.0
Kay-Bee	5.0
Other	46.0

Source: *Wall Street Journal*, May 23, 1996, p. A3, from Tactical Retail Solutions Inc.

★ 1579 ★
Retailing - Toys (SIC 5945)

U.S. Toy Market

Share of the market are shown in percent for 1994.

Toys R Us	20.7%
Wal-Mart	13.6
Kmart	7.1
Target	5.7
Kay-Bee	4.7
J.C. Penney	1.9
Service Merchandise	1.8
Hills	1.3
Bradless	1.1
Caldor	1.1
Ames	1.0
Meijer	1.0
Venture	0.8
Radio Shack	0.6
Shopko	0.6
Others	37.0

Source: *Playthings*, March 1996, p. 38, from NPD Group, Inc./ Toy Makers Index.

★ 1580 ★
Photography Stores (SIC 5946)

Camera Sales by Outlet

The table shows where cameras were purchased in 1995. Data show that 55.6% of cameras were purchased for personal use while 37.1% were purchased as gifts.

Discount department stores	45.4%
Camera store/one-hour lab	12.2
Catalog showroom	8.4
Drugstore/pharmacy	7.9
Mail order	6.3
Electronics/video store	5.4
Department store (not discount)	3.5
Wholesale club	3.2
Combination/hypermarket/supermarket . .	3.0
Other	4.7

Source: *Photomarketing*, August 1995, p. 27, from *PMA Camera and Camcorder Survey*.

★ 1581 ★
Mail Order (SIC 5961)

Popular Consumer Catalogs

Catalogers are ranked by sales in millions of dollars for the second quarter of 1995.

J.C. Penney	$ 4,435.0
Talbots	226.9
Williams-Sonoma	127.7
CML Group	124.8
The Sharper Image	45.7
E&B Marine	42.7
Joseph A. Brooks	41.2
Trend-Lines	37.3
Brookstone	34.7
Frederick's of Hollywood	33.3

Source: *Catalog Age*, November 1995, p. 8, from Ulin & Holland Inc.

★ 1582 ★
Mail Order (SIC 5961)

Top Consumer Catalogs

Companies are ranked by 1994 sales in millions of dollars.

J.C. Penney	$ 3,817
Dell Computer	3,420
Gateway 2000	2,600

Continued on next page.

★ 1582 ★ *Continued*
Mail Order (SIC 5961)

Top Consumer Catalogs

Companies are ranked by 1994 sales in millions of dollars.

DEC Direct	$ 2,000
Spiegel	1,742
Fingerhut	1,719
Lands' End	990
IBM Direct	950
L.L. Bean	848
Micro Warehouse	776

Source: *Philadelphia Inquirer*, December 4, 1995, p. E1, from Direct Marketing Association.

★ 1583 ★
Vending Machines (SIC 5962)

Snack Sales - Vending Machines

The table shows the share of columns in vending machines represented by company.

Frito-Lay Inc.	18.8%
M&M/Mars	12.3
Nabisco Inc.	11.3
Hershey Foods Corp.	8.3
Wm. Wrigley Jr. Co.	4.6
Lance Inc.	4.0
Nestle Food Co.	3.9
Continental Baking Co.	2.0
Snyder's of Hanover Inc.	2.0
Sunshine Biscuits Inc.	1.8
Other	31.0

Source: *Snack Food*, December 1995, p. 20, from VENDtrack On-Site Intelligence and Audits & Surveys Worldwide Inc.

★ 1584 ★
Vending Machines (SIC 5962)

Vending Machine Food Sales

Data are for 1994.

Sandwiches	49.0%
Ethnic specialties	11.0
Salads	11.0
Canned/bottled juices	10.0
Desserts/pastries	4.0
Fresh fruit/vegetables	2.0
Platters, entrees	2.0

Yogurt, cottage cheese	2.0%
Canned fruit, puddings	1.0
Milk shakes	1.0
Other	7.0

Source: *Vending Times*, May 1996, p. 27, from *Vending Times Census of the Industry Report*.

★ 1585 ★
Retailing - Tobacco (SIC 5993)

Where Teenagers Buy Tobacco

Convenience stores	43.0%
Gas stations	29.0
Grocery stores	11.0
Vending machines	9.0
Drug stores	6.0
Other	2.0

Source: *New York Times*, May 16, 1996, p. A8, from National Automatic Merchandising Association.

★ 1586 ★
Retailing - Optical Goods (SIC 5995)

Where We Purchased Sunglasses

The table shows sales of sunglasses in 1990 and 1994. Sunglasses priced $30 and over had 45% of the $2.5 billion market in 1994. The largest U.S. retailer in 1995 was Sunglass Hut.

	1990	1994
Sunglass specialty store	17.2%	32.9%
Optical stores	19.0	16.7
Department stores	13.5	11.5
Sporting goods specialty store	9.1	9.5
Other	41.2	29.4

Source: *Investor's Business Daily*, November 7, 1995, p. A6, from Robertson, Stephens & Co.

★ 1587 ★
Religious Bookstores (SIC 5999)

What Sells in Christian Bookstores

The Christian retailing industry is estimated to have annual sales of $3.0 billion. The table shows sales by product.

Books	28.0%
Music	15.0
Bibles	14.0

Continued on next page.

★ 1587 ★ *Continued*
Religious Bookstores (SIC 5999)

What Sells in Christian Bookstores

The Christian retailing industry is estimated to have annual sales of $3.0 billion. The table shows sales by product.

Gifts/jewelry	14.0%
Greeting cards	8.0
Curriculum	7.0
Children's items	3.0
Church supplies	2.0
Clothing/T-shirts	2.0
Video	2.0
Art/collectibles	1.0
Other	4.0

Source: *Atlanta Constitution*, August 6, 1995, p. D1, from Christian Booksellers Association.

★ 1588 ★
Retailing - Mailing Supplies (SIC 5999)

Where We Purchased Mailing Needs

The table shows where we purchased mailing supplies and accessories in the four main channels of trade. Shares are estimated for the fourth quarter of 1995.

Drug stores	41.0%
Mass merchandisers	29.1
Food stores	26.3
Food/drug stores	3.5

Source: *Supermarket News*, April 22, 1996, p. 98, from A.C. Nielsen.

★ 1589 ★
Retailing - Pet Products (SIC 5999)

Pet Food Sales by Outlet

The table shows the top sellers of pet food in America.

Wal-Mart	8.0%
Petsmart	7.0
Other	85.0

Source: *Investor's Business Daily*, June 6, 1996, p. A6.

★ 1590 ★
Retailing - Pet Products (SIC 5999)

Pet Food/Supply Retailing

Petsmart/Petstuff	6.0%
Petco	1.6
Pet Supplies "Plus"	1.2
Pet Care Superstore	0.6
Pet Supermarket	0.4
Pet Food Warehouse	0.3
Other	88.9

Source: *Investext,* Thomson Financial Services, May 8, 1995, p. 3, from *Pet Product News* and PaineWebber estimates.

★ 1591 ★
Retailing - Pet Products (SIC 5999)

Pet Product Sales by Outlet

Grocery stores	55.0%
Pet superstores	13.0
Mass merchandisers	11.0
Other	21.0

Source: *Supermarket Business*, June 1996, p. 77, from Hartz Mountain.

SIC 60 - Depository Institutions

★ 1592 ★

Banking (SIC 6020)

Atlanta's Largest Banks

Shares are shown based on deposits.

NationsBank	28.8%
Suntrust	16.0
Wachovia	15.1
First Union	13.7
Southtrust	7.1
Other	19.3

Source: *New York Times*, September 6, 1995, p. C8, from SNL Securities.

★ 1593 ★

Banking (SIC 6020)

Banking Leaders - New York City

Share of deposits is current as of June 1994.

Chase Manhattan	30.4%
Citicorp.	14.9
Republic New York/Crossland	5.4
Bank of New York	5.4
Bankers Trust	3.9
Other	40.0

Source: *New York Times*, March 29, 1996, p. C4, from Republic New York Corp.

★ 1594 ★

Banking (SIC 6020)

Banking Market - North Carolina

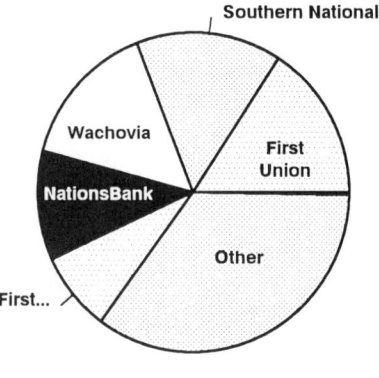

Shares are shown based on deposits.

First Union	15.7%
Southern National	15.2
Wachovia	15.0
NationsBank	10.7
First Citizens BancShares	8.4
Other	35.0

Source: *Wall Street Journal*, June 13, 1996, p. B4, from company reports and SNL Securities.

★ 1595 ★

Banking (SIC 6020)

Depository Institutions - Cincinnati

Leading depository institutions are shown for the tri-state area. Figures are for an eight-county area as of June 30, 1996. Total deposits reached $14.33 billion as of June 30, 1995.

Fifth Third	21.0%
Provident	14.4
Star	12.3
PNC	10.6
Others	41.7

Source: *Cincinnati Business Courier*, March 24, 1996, p. 1, from Sheshunoff Information Services Inc.

★ 1596 ★

Banking (SIC 6020)

Largest Banks

Banks are ranked by assets in billions of dollars.

Chase Manhattan	$ 297.3
Citicorp	257.0
BankAmerica	226.6
NationsBank	184.2
J.P. Morgan	166.6

Source: *Washington Post*, August 29, 1995, p. 1, from *Bloomberg Business News*.

★ 1597 ★

Banking (SIC 6020)

Largest Banks in Chicago

Banks are ranked by number of branches. Data for First National Bank of Chicago includes the merger with NBD Bank in July 1996.

Harris Trust & Savings Bank	140
First National Bank of Chicago	130
First of America, Illinois	129
LaSalle National Corp. and LaSalle Bank	125
Magna Bank of Illinois	72
St. Paul Federal Bank for Savings	52

Source: *Chicago Tribune*, April 17, 1996, p. C1, from bank reports.

★ 1598 ★

Banking (SIC 6020)

Largest New York Thrifts

Banks are ranked by assets in millions of dollars.

Dime Banccorp Inc./Dime Savings Bank of NY	$ 20,236.6
Greenpoint Financial Corp./ GreenPoint Bank	14,670.5
Astoria Financial Corp./Astoria Federal	6,620.1
Emigrant Bancorp./Emigrant Savings Bank	6,080.9
Long Island Bancorp. Inc.	4,901.6
Apple Bank for Savings	4,106.9
T R Financial Corp./Roosevelt Savings Bank	2,904.6
Independence Community Bank Corp.	2,762.0
New York Bancorp Inc.	2,731.6
Greater New York Savings Bank	2,583.0

Source: *Crain's New York Business*, April 15, 1996, p. 32.

★ 1599 ★

Banking (SIC 6020)

Largest Thrifts - Detroit

Firms are ranked by 1995 assets in millions of dollars.

Standard Federal Bancorp Inc.	$ 13,275.6
First Federal of Michigan	6,755.0
Great Lakes Bancorp.	2,516.0
Sterling Bancorp	878.8
Flagstar Bank	842.5
Dearborn Federal Savings Bank	209.3
D&N Bank	201.6
Home Federal Savings Bank	24.9

Source: *Crain's Detroit Business*, May 13, 1996, p. 18.

★ 1600 ★

Banking (SIC 6020)

Largest U.S. Banks

Assets of the largest U.S. banks are shown in billions of dollars.

Chase/Chemical	$ 304.0
Citicorp	257.0
BankAmerica	232.0
NationsBank	187.0
J.P. Morgan	185.0

Continued on next page.

★ 1600 ★ *Continued*
Banking (SIC 6020)

Largest U.S. Banks

Assets of the largest U.S. banks are shown in billions of dollars.

First Union	$ 132.0
First Chicago NBD	122.0
Wells Fargo/First Interstate	108.0

Source: *American Banker*, January 25, 1996, p. 1.

★ 1601 ★
Banking (SIC 6020)

Leading Banks - Fairfield County

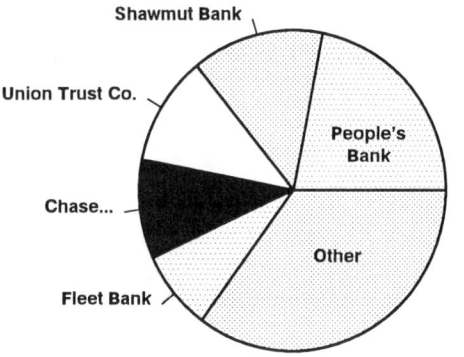

The leading banks are shown for Fairfield County, New York.

People's Bank	22.27%
Shawmut Bank	14.12
Union Trust Co.	10.84
Chase Manhattan Bank	9.59
Fleet Bank	7.87
Other	35.31

Source: *Crain's New York Business*, August 21, 1995, p. 24, from Sheshunoff Information Services.

★ 1602 ★
Banking (SIC 6020)

Leading Banks - South Bay

The largest banks in the South Bay, California area are ranked by assets in millions of dollars.

Silicon Valley Bank	$ 1,100
Greater Bay Bancorp.	500
San Jose National Bank	255
Bank of Santa Clara	230
South Valley National Bank	180

Source: *American Banker*, June 17, 1996, p. 25.

★ 1603 ★
Banking (SIC 6020)

Leading Financial Service Providers - Mexico

Firms are ranked by assets in millions of dollars.

Grupo Financiero Citibank	$ 1,500.0
J.P. Morgan	1,100.0
Grupo Financiero Santander Mexico	610.9
Chase Manhattan/Chemical	416.4
Bank of America Mexico	145.0
Societe Generale Mexico	50.6
ING-Baring Grupo Financiero	29.8

Source: *Mexico Business*, May 1996, p. 54.

★ 1604 ★
Banking (SIC 6020)

Mexican Banking Market

This table shows the leading Mexican banks ranked by market share.

Banacci	20.0%
Bancomer	20.0
Others	60.0

Source: *New York Times*, February 11, 1996, p. F8, from Morgan Stanley.

★ 1605 ★
Banking (SIC 6020)

Popular Banking Methods

The table shows the percentage of total banking transactions, based on 12 billion in 1993 and 16 billion in 2000. POS stands for point-of-service.

	1993	2000
Telephone	24.0%	35.0%
ATMs	31.0	30.0
Branches	43.0	23.0
POS/other	2.0	13.0

Source: *Bank Management*, March/April 1996, p. 24, from Bank Administration Institute and FMCG.

★ 1606 ★
Banking (SIC 6020)

Supermarket Bank Branches

Banc One

Fifth Third

TCF Financial

First Chicago

Comerica

BankAmerica

This table shows the banks with the most branches in supermarkets.

Banc One	150
Fifth Third	90
TCF Financial	37
First Chicago	31
Comerica	27
BankAmerica	4

Source: *American Banker*, February 22, 1996, p. 5, from National Commerce Bank Services Inc.

★ 1607 ★
Banking (SIC 6020)

Top Banks

Banks are ranked by tier one capital shown in millions of dollars as of June 30, 1994.

Citicorp	$ 17,216.0
BankAmerica Corp.	13,865.0
Chemical Banking Corp.	10,002.0
NationsBank	9,761.0
JP Morgan & Co.	8,863.0

Chase Manhattan Corp.	$ 8,162.0
Banc One Corp.	7,152.0
Bankers Trust New York Corp.	5,010.0
First Union Corp.	4,514.0
First Chicago Corporation	4,452.0
KeyCorp	4,255.0
PNC Bank Corp.	4,144.0
Bank of New York	4,025.0
Norwest Crop.	4,004.0
Fleet Financial	3,615.0

Source: *Banker*, June 1995, p. 28.

★ 1608 ★
Banking (SIC 6020)

Top Banks - California

Market shares are shown based on deposits.

Bank of America	20.9%
Wells Fargo	15.0
H.F. Ahmanson	8.0
Great Western	6.0
Bank of Tokyo/Union Bank	4.2
First Nationwide/Cal Fed	4.2
Washington Mutual/American Savings	3.6
Golden West	3.1
Glendale Federal	2.4
Other	32.6

Source: *Wall Street Journal*, July 30, 1996, p. A3, from SNL Securities.

★ 1609 ★
Banking (SIC 6020)

Top Banks - Canada

Assets are shown in millions of dollars.

Royal Bank	$ 123,382
CIBC	106,302
Bank of Montreal	99,627
Scotiabank	94,737
TD Bank	70,203
National Bank	32,177

Source: *Canadian Banker*, September 1995, p. 38, from *Banker* and *Financial Times*.

★ 1610 ★

Banking (SIC 6020)

Top Banks - Denver

Shares are shown based on total deposits of $21.73 billion.

Colorado NB	19.61%
Norwest BK Colorado	13.39
World S&LA, A FS&LA	8.02
Commercial Federal	4.48
Bank One-Denver NA	4.24
First FSB of Colorado	3.68
First Interstate BK	3.62
First TC	3.26
Colorado Corporate	2.36
Bellco First FCU	2.19
Other	35.15

Source: *Investext,* Thomson Financial Services, October 3, 1995, p. 6.

★ 1611 ★

Banking (SIC 6020)

Top Banks - Los Angeles

Banks are ranked by assets in millions of dollars.

City National	$ 4,158.0
Imperial Baorp	2,780.0
Farmers & Merchants	1,521.0
Southern Pacific T&LA	1,329.0
GBC Bancorp	1,149.0
Cathay Bancorp	1,047.0
1st Business	870.0
California Commerce	744.0
Community Bank	692.0
Santa Monica Bank	616.0

Source: *New York Times,* February 10, 1996, p. 17, from SNL Securities.

★ 1612 ★

Banking (SIC 6020)

Top Banks - North Carolina

Banks are ranked by assets in millions of dollars. Figures are current as of March 31, 1995.

NationsBank	$ 51,144.0
First Union	24,189.0
Wachovia	23,375.0
BB&T	9,324.0
First Citizens	6,379.0
Southern National	5,653.0
Centura	4,414.0
Central Carolina	3,448.0
United Carolina	3,081.0
Security Capital	684.0
Southtrust Bank of Central Carolina	595.0
First Union Home Equity	515.0

Source: *Business North Carolina*, November 1995, p. 39, from Sheshunoff Information Services and North Carolina Banking Commission.

★ 1613 ★

Banking (SIC 6020)

Top Banks - Omaha

Shares are shown based on total deposits of $8.83 billion.

First NB of Omaha	20.93%
Norwest Bank of Nebraska	18.00
Commercial Federal	8.32
Metropolitan Federal	3.42
Douglas County B&TC	2.42
Firstar BK	2.26
First BK	2.00
American NB	1.95
Bell FCU	1.86
Southwest B&TC of Omaha	1.73
Other	37.11

Source: *Investext,* Thomson Financial Services, October 3, 1995, p. 6.

★ 1614 ★

Banking (SIC 6020)

Top Banks - Virginia

Shares are shown based on core deposits.

Crestar	17.9%
NationsBank	14.5
First Union	11.2
Central Fidelity	11.1
First Virginia	8.9
Signet	7.1
Other	29.3

Source: *Investext,* Thomson Financial Services, August 8, 1995, p. 4.

★ 1615 ★

Banking (SIC 6020)

Top Banks - Washington D.C.

Shares are shown based on deposits as of March 31, 1995.

NationsBank	17.3%
First Union	12.5
Crestar Financial	12.3
Other	57.9

Source: *Investext,* Thomson Financial Services, September 20, 1995, p. 2, from company data.

★ 1616 ★

Banking (SIC 6020)

Top U.S. Banks

Firms are ranked by assets in millions of dollars.

Citicorp	$ 256,853
BankAmerica Corporation	232,446
NationsBank	187,298
J.P. Morgan & Co. Inc.	184,879
Chemical Banking Corp.	182,296
First Union Corp.	131,880
First Chicago NBD Corp.	122,002
Chase Manhattan Corp.	121,173
Bankers Trust New York Corp.	104,002
Banc One Corp.	90,454
Fleet Financial Group	84,432
PNC Bank Corp.	73,404
Norwest Corp.	72,134
KeyCorp	66,339
First Interstate Bancorp.	58,071
Bank of New York Co. Inc.	53,700

Wells Fargo & Co.	$ 50,316
Bank of Boston Corp.	47,397
SunTrust Banks Inc.	46,474
Wachovia Corp.	44,981

Source: *USBanker,* April 1996, p. 50.

★ 1617 ★

Banking (SIC 6020)

Top U.S. Thrifts

Assets of the top thrifts are shown in billions of dollars.

H.F. Abmanson	$ 49.5
Great Wester	43.7
Washington Mutual/American Savings	42.0
Golden West	35.7
Dime Bancorp	19.0
First Nationwide	19.0
Glendale Federal	14.7
California Federal	14.2

Source: *Wall Street Journal,* July 22, 1996, p. A3, from company reports.

★ 1618 ★

Community Banks (SIC 6029)

Leading Community Banks

Leading banks are ranked by assets in millions of dollars.

Bank of Canton of California	$ 817.51
Putnam Trust Company	661.03
Associated Bank North (Wisconsin)	438.02
Drovers Bancshares Corp.	375.98
Palmetto Bank (South Carolina)	343.48

Continued on next page.

★ 1618 ★ *Continued*
Community Banks (SIC 6029)

Leading Community Banks

Leading banks are ranked by assets in millions of dollars.

First National Bank of Dona Ana County	$ 333.90
Hawaii National Bank	291.94
First National Iowa	279.70
Citizens National Bank	194.27

Source: *ABA Banking Journal*, September 1995, p. 24.

★ 1619 ★
Savings Banks (SIC 6035)

Savings Banks - Cleveland

The top banks are ranked by assets in millions of dollars as of December 31, 1994.

Charter One Bank, SSB	$ 6,116.1
Third Federal Savings & Loan Assn.	4,537.7
Ohio Savings Bank	2,037.1
First Federal Savings & Loan of Lakewood	621.0
Metropolitan Savings Bank	479.6
Strongsville Savings Bank	419.4
Republic Savings Bank	406.9
Security Federal S&L Assn. of Cleveland	406.0
Home Bank, FSB	316.0
Cuyahoga Savings Association	310.3

Source: *Crain's Cleveland Business*, August 28, 1995, p. 24, from Sheshunoff Information Services Inc. and Federal Deposit Insurance Corp.

★ 1620 ★
Credit Unions (SIC 6060)

Credit Union Market - Washington D.C.

Banks are ranked by assets in millions of dollars.

Navy	$ 8,723
Pentagon	2,284
Bank Fund Staff	755
Northwest	560
Andrews	489

Source: *Washington Post*, March 18, 1996, p. 12, from National Association of Federal Credit Unions.

★ 1621 ★
International Banking (SIC 6081)

Foreign Bank Offices in America

This table shows the home country of foreign banks that have more than $10 billion in assets in the United States. Countries are ranked by total assets in millions of dollars.

Japan	$ 363,896.0
France	106,520.0
United Kingdom	61,857.0
Canada	59,253.0
Germany	56,573.0
Switzerland	47,525.0
Netherlands	41,280.0
Spain	39,310.0
Italy	28,509.0
Korea	10,690.0

Source: *Banker*, March 1996, p. 47, from *US Federal Reserve Bank: Structure Data and Call Reports*.

★ 1622 ★
Bank Services (SIC 6099)

Largest ATM Networks - Chicago

Banks are ranked by number of cash machines.

First National Bank	500
Citibank	200
St. Paul Federal Bank for Savings	178
Bank of America Illinois	172
LaSalle Banks	137

Source: *Crain's Chicago Business*, July 3, 1995, p. 3.

★ 1623 ★
Bank Services (SIC 6099)

Merchant Processors

The table shows the leading card processors ranked by volume of transactions in billions of dollars. Data are for 1993.

NaBANCO	17.0%
National Processing	15.0
Card Establishment	14.0
Bank of America	5.0
National Data	4.0
Other	45.0

Source: *Investext*, Thomson Financial Services, February 23, 1995, p. 6, from Nilson Report.

★ 1624 ★

Bank Services (SIC 6099)

Money Order Vendors

Travelers Express	
Global Express	
FDC	
U.S. Postal Service	
Mid America/Western Union	
Other	

Shares are for 1993.

Travelers Express	30.0%
Global Express	24.0
FDC	23.0
U.S. Postal Service	19.0
Mid America/Western Union	2.0
Other	2.0

Source: *Investext,* Thomson Financial Services, February 23, 1995, p. 8, from Nilson Report and Morgan Stanley Research.

★ 1625 ★

Bank Services (SIC 6099)

Remote Payment Market

The remote bill payment market allows consumers to electronically conduct banking and bill payment activities. The table shows who leads the market by volume of transactions.

	($ mil.)	Share
Checkfree	$ 6,050	43.0%
In-house bank systems	4,838	34.0
Amresco	1,550	11.0
Paymate	850	6.0
Intuit	395	3.0
Online	175	1.0
Visa Interactive	150	1.0
Other	91	1.0

Source: *Investext,* Thomson Financial Services, October 31, 1995, p. 3, from Nilson Report.

SIC 61 - Nondepository Institutions

★ 1626 ★
Auto Loans (SIC 6141)

Auto Loans - Shelby County

Shares are shown based on the 22,369 cars sold and registered in Shelby County, Tennessee.

Ford Motor Credit	11.3%
NationsBank	9.0
Boatmen's Bank	5.6
NBC	5.0
Chrysler Credit	4.5
GMAC	4.4
First Tennessee	2.3
Citibank	1.8
Mitsubishi Motor Credit	1.6
First American	1.5
First Commercial	1.5
American Honda Finance	1.4
Memphis Teachers Credit Union	1.4
Nissan Motors Acceptance	1.4
Mazda American Credit	0.7
Other	46.6

Source: *Commercial Appeal*, July 28, 1996, p. C1, from Cross Seil Report.

★ 1627 ★
Auto Loans (SIC 6141)

Automobile Loans

Outstanding auto loans are shown by source, based on a $337 million market in July 1995.

Commercial banks	43.0%
Finance companies	20.0
Securitized asset pools	11.0
Other	26.0

Source: *Journal of Retail Banking Services*, Spring 1996, p. 55, from Federal Reserve Bulletin.

★ 1628 ★
Credit Cards (SIC 6141)

Credit Card Market - 1995

Brands are ranked by point-of-sale volume in billions of dollars.

	($ bil.)	Share
Visa	$ 288.86	47.3%
MasterCard	162.14	26.5
American Express	112.28	18.4
Discover	38.86	6.4
Diners Club	8.83	1.4

Source: *Wall Street Journal*, May 3, 1996, p. B1, from Nilson Report.

★ 1629 ★
Credit Cards (SIC 6141)

Credit Card Market - Grocery Stores

The table shows the credit cards used in supermarkets.

Visa	51.0%
MasterCard	32.0
Novus/Discover	15.0
American Express	2.0

Source: *Nonfoods Merchandising*, February 1996, p. 24, from Information Resources Inc.

★ 1630 ★
Credit Cards (SIC 6141)

Leading Credit Cards

Data are for 1995.

Visa	49.4%
MasterCard	27.3
Diner's Club	16.1
Discover Card	6.0
Other	1.2

Source: *Fortune*, October 30, 1995, p. 72, from Nilson Report.

★ 1631 ★
Credit Cards (SIC 6141)

Popular Credit Cards

Shares are shown based on $746 billion in spending.

Visa	49.9%
MasterCard	27.1
American Express	15.4
Discover	6.4
Diners Club	1.2

Source: *Forbes*, July 1, 1996, p. 64, from Nilson Report.

★ 1632 ★
Credit Cards (SIC 6141)

Top Co-Branded Card Issuers

Firms are ranked by millions of co-branded cards in use in 1995.

AT&T	24.0
General Motors	12.5
Ford	8.2
AAA	5.7
Shell MasterCard	3.5
GE Capital Consumer Card	3.0
AFL-CIO	2.2
American Airlines	2.1
United Airlines	1.8
National Education Association	1.7

Source: *Detroit Free Press*, April 24, 1996, p. 9A, from RAM Research Group.

★ 1633 ★
Credit Cards (SIC 6141)

Top Credit Card Issuers

Firms are ranked by receivables in billions of dollars as of September 30, 1995.

Citibank	$ 42.1
Discover	28.2
MBNA America	23.3
First USA	15.0
First Chicago	14.6
AT&T Universal	12.9
Chase Manhattan	11.9
Household Bank	11.2
Chemical Bank	10.4
Capital One	10.2

Source: *US Banker*, January 1996, p. 31, from RAM Research.

★ 1634 ★
Business Loans (SIC 6150)

Banking Leaders - Small Business Funding

Banks are ranked by small business loans in millions of dollars as of June 30, 1994.

NationsBank	$ 8,297.0
Banc One	6,197.0
Keycorp	5,806.0
First Union	5,192.0
BankAmerica	4,637.0
Norwest	4,480.0
Fleet Financial	3,805.0
SunTrust Banks	3,368.0

Continued on next page.

★ 1634 ★ *Continued*
Business Loans (SIC 6150)

Banking Leaders - Small Business Funding

Banks are ranked by small business loans in millions of dollars as of June 30, 1994.

NBD	$ 3,216.0
Comerica	2,871.0
Wells Fargo	2,789.0
National City	2,706.0

Source: *US Banker*, August 1995, p. 9, from Bauer Financial Reports.

★ 1635 ★
Agricultural Banking (SIC 6159)

Agricultural Banking Leaders

Banks are ranked by total value of farm loans in millions of dollars.

Bank of America National Trust & Savings	$ 1,272.0
Wells Fargo Bank, N.A.	976.7
Sanwa Bank California	586.2
U.S. Bank of Washington, N.A.	313.2
Norwest Bank South Dakota, N.A. . . .	290.7
Seattle-First National Bank	289.0
West One Bank-Idaho	270.9
NationsBank, N.A. Carolinas	256.4
Key Bank of Washington	246.8
Bank IV Kansas, N.A.	233.8
First Union National Bank of Florida . . .	225.6
Bank One-Arizona, N.A.	207.3
Key Bank of Idaho	184.7
Bank of California, N.A.	183.3
United States Natl. Bank of Oregon . . .	183.0

Source: *Agri Finance*, November 1995, p. 34, from Federal Reserve system reports.

★ 1636 ★
Agricultural Banking (SIC 6159)

Agricultural Loans

Data are for 1995.

Commercial banks	41.4%
Farm Credit System	24.1
Consolidated Farm Service Agency	6.9
Life insurance companies	5.5
Individuals and others	22.1

Source: *Farm Journal*, November 1995, p. 8, from Economic Research Service, United States Dept. of Agriculture.

★ 1637 ★
Mortgage Loans (SIC 6162)

Commercial Mortgage Firms

Firms are ranked by volume of mortgages serviced in millions of dollars.

AMRESCO Inc.	$ 11.34
Dornan & Wilson Inc.	10.56
Midland Loan Services	10.50
GMAC Mortgage Corporation	10.14
Bankers Trust Company	8.49
GE Capital Asset Management	8.38
Reilly Mortgage Group Inc.	7.96
Mellon Mortgage Company	6.37
Banc One Management & Consulting Corp.	4.34
Washington Mortgage Financial Group . .	4.11

Source: *National Real Estate Investor*, April 1996, p. 6, from Mortgage Bankers Association.

★ 1638 ★
Mortgage Loans (SIC 6162)

Mortgage Loans by County - Chicago

Counties are ranked by number of loans to moderate-to-low income households in 1994.

Suburban Cook	11,935
Chicago	8,855
DuPage Co.	3,463
Lake Co.	2,431
Will Co.	2,227
Kane Co.	1,946
McHenry Co.	1,228

Source: *Chicago Tribune*, May 8, 1996, p. C1, from Woodstock Institute.

★ 1639 ★

Mortgage Loans (SIC 6162)

Mortgage Securization

The leaders in the loan securization market are ranked by market share for the first quarter of 1996.

Norwest Mortgage Inc.	11.5%
Countrywide Home Loans	9.6
Chase Manhattan Mortgage	4.7
Fleet Mortgage Corp.	4.5
Resource Bancshares	2.9
Prudential Home Mortgage	2.5
BancBoston Mortgage Corp.	2.4
North American Mortgage	2.0
Flagstar Bank FSB	1.8
Standard Federal Bank	1.8
Other	56.3

Source: *American Banker*, April 30, 1996, p. 14, from *Mortgage Marketplace*.

★ 1640 ★

Mortgage Loans (SIC 6162)

Top Closed Loan Providers

The top closed loan providers are ranked by volume of leases in millions of dollars. Data are for 1995.

Countrywide Funding	$ 16,777
Norwest Funding	12,860
Fleet Mortgage Group	9,213
Prudential Home Mortgage	7,701
BancBoston Mortgage	6,879
Resource Bancshares Mortgage	5,267
NationsBanc Mortgage	4,538
Independent National Mortgage	4,265
InterFirst FSB	3,153
Residential Funding	3,101

Source: *Mortgage Banking*, January 1996, p. 43, from Wholesale Access.

★ 1641 ★

Mortgage Loans (SIC 6162)

Who Provides Mortgage Loans

Data for 1995 are for the first quarter of the year.

	1994	1995
Mortgage banks	46.0%	51.0%
Commercial banks	31.0	29.0
Thrifts	23.0	20.0
Other	1.0	1.0

Source: *Secondary Mortgage Market*, Summer 1995, p. 43, from HUD Survey of Gross Flows.

★ 1642 ★

Loan Arrangers (SIC 6163)

Commercial Lenders - Michigan

NBD Bancorp

Comerica Bank

Mich. National

First of America

Old Kent

Leaders in the commercial loan market are ranked by loan values in billions of dollars.

NBD Bancorp	$ 17.2
Comerica Bank	12.2
Mich. National	4.6
First of America	2.3
Old Kent	2.0

Source: *Detroit News*, February 14, 1996, p. 1B, from Michigan banks.

SIC 62 - Security and Commodity Brokers

★ 1643 ★

Investment Banking (SIC 6211)

High-Tech IPO Underwriters

High-tech deals include biotech, communications, computer equipment, and electronics. IPO stands for initial public offerings. Managers are ranked by deal values shown in millions of dollars. The market share for New York firms is approximately 50%; the market share for specialty firms is approximately 40%.

Robertson Stephens	$ 1,091.0
Morgan Stanley	1,043.0
Alex. Brown & Sons	748.0
Goldman Sachs	728.0
Hambrecht & Quist	662.0
Merrill Lynch	589.0
Lehman Brothers	381.0
Montgomery Securities	337.0
J.P. Morgan	326.0
Donaldson, Lufkin & Jenrette	252.0

Source: *Business Week*, March 11, 1996, p. 75, from Securities Data Co.

★ 1644 ★

Investment Banking (SIC 6211)

Investment Firms - San Francisco

Firms are ranked by 1995 capital investments shown in millions of dollars.

Summit Partners	$ 156.4
Kleiner Perkins Caufield & Byers	107.0
Burr, Egan, Deleage & Co.	86.5
New Enterprise Assoc.	75.7
McCown De Leeuw & Co.	65.0
Mayfield Fund	63.4

Institutional Venture Partners	$ 58.8
InterWest Partners	56.3
Patricof & Co. Ventures Inc.	52.0
Weiss, Peck & Greer Venture Partners L.P.	47.0

Source: *San Francisco Business Times*, February 29, 1996, p. 12A.

★ 1645 ★

Investment Banking (SIC 6211)

Investment Managers - Denver

Denver area managers are ranked by total assets under management in millions of dollars. Data are as of December 31, 1995.

OppenheimerFunds Services	$ 41,000.0
Janus Capital Corp.	31,000.0
First Asset Management	29,000.0
Invesco Trust Co.	15,462.0
Denver Investment Advisors Inc.	9,550.0
Voyageur Asset Management	6,124.0
Berger Associates Inc.	3,320.0
Founders Asset Management Inc.	3,130.0
Trinity Investment Management Corp.	2,699.0
American Money Mgmt. Assoc. Inc.	1,121.0

Source: *Denver Business Journal*, January 25, 1996, p. 26A.

★ 1646 ★

Investment Banking (SIC 6211)

Largest Mutual Fund Companies

Companies are ranked by assets in billions of dollars.

Fidelity Investments	$ 324.0
Vanguard Group	160.0
Merrill Lynch Asset Management	135.8
Capital Research & Management	129.5
Franklin/Templeton Group	95.7

Continued on next page.

★ 1646 ★ *Continued*
Investment Banking (SIC 6211)

Largest Mutual Fund Companies

Companies are ranked by assets in billions of dollars.

Putnam Funds	$ 72.8
Dreyfus Corporation	71.8
Dean Witter Intercapital Inc.	61.5
Smith Barney Inc.	59.9
Federated Investors	59.7

Source: *New York Times*, September 19, 1995, p. C4, from Investment Company Institute.

★ 1647 ★
Investment Banking (SIC 6211)

Largest Mutual Funds - 1995

Funds are ranked by net assets in millions of dollars.

Fidelity Magellan	$ 53,702
Investment Co. of America	25,678
Washington Mutual Inv	18,876
Vanguard Index: 500 Port	17,372
Fidelity Puritan	15,628
Fidelity Contrafund	14,832
Fidelity Growth & Growth	14,819
Twentieth Century Ultra	14,551
Income Fund of America	13,778
Vanguard Windsor	13,646

Source: *Black Enterprise*, April 1996, p. 89, from Lipper Analytical Services Inc.

★ 1648 ★
Investment Banking (SIC 6211)

Leading Mutual Fund Groups

Fund families are ranked by assets in billions of dollars as of May 31, 1996.

Fidelity	$ 302.6
Vanguard	172.5
American Funds	151.6
Franklin/Templeton	103.7
Putnam	89.5
Merrill Lynch	64.3

T. Rowe Price	$ 53.3
IDS	49.6
Dean Witter Funds	41.9
Twentieth Century/Benham	41.8

Source: *Christian Science Monitor*, July 12, 1996, p. B5, from *Morningstar*.

★ 1649 ★
Investment Banking (SIC 6211)

Major Underwriters

This table shows the top underwriters by market share.

Drexel Burnham	46.8%
Morgan Stanley	9.8
Merrill Lynch	9.6
First Boston	8.1
Salomon Brothers	6.1
Goldman Sachs	4.9
Prudential Bache	2.8
DLJ	2.4
Leyman Brothers	2.1
Bear Sterns	2.1
Kidder Peabody	2.0
Other	3.3

Source: *Journal of Applied Corporate Finance*, Spring 1995, p. 92.

★ 1650 ★
Investment Banking (SIC 6211)

Municipal Bond Issuers

Shares are shown for 1995. MBIA stands for Municipal Bond Insurance Agency, AMBAC stands for American Municipal Bond Assurance Corp.; FGIC stands for Financial Guaranty Insurance Corp.

MBIA	42.0%
AMBAC	26.0
FGIC	19.0
Other	13.0

Source: *Financial World*, May 20, 1996, p. 72.

★ 1651 ★

Investment Banking (SIC 6211)

Municipal Underwriters - 1995

Shares are shown based on the industry total of $154.9 billion.

Goldman Sachs	12.8%
Merrill Lynch	11.0
Smith Barney	8.4
PaineWebber	8.2
Lehman Brothers	6.3
J.P. Morgan Securities	4.7
Morgan Stanley	4.5
Prudential Securities	4.2
Bear, Stearns	4.0
A.G. Edwards	1.5
Other	34.4

Source: *Wall Street Journal*, January 2, 1996, p. R38, from Securities Data Co. and *Bond Buyer*.

★ 1652 ★

Investment Banking (SIC 6211)

Mutual Fund Custodians

Firms are ranked by assets in billions of dollars as of March 31, 1996.

Bank of New York	$ 91.6
State Street	70.2
Chase Manhattan	37.3
PNC	31.3
NationsBank	16.7

Source: *American Banker*, June 26, 1996, p. 4A, from Lipper Analytical Services.

★ 1653 ★

Investment Banking (SIC 6211)

Mutual Fund Leaders

Market shares of the top U.S. mutual fund companies are shown in percent.

Fidelity Investments	12.70%
Vanguard Group	6.26
Merrill Lynch Asset Management	5.57
Capital Research & Management	5.09
Franklin Templeton Group	4.09
Dreyfus Corporation	2.90
Putnam Funds	2.88
Federated Investors	2.86
TIAA-CREF	2.78

Dean Witter InterCapital	2.59%
Smith Barney Inc.	2.48
Prudential Mutual Funds	2.34
IDS Mutual Fund Group	2.14
T. Rowe Price	1.79
Kemper Financial Service	1.77
Scudder	1.47
SEI Financial Services	1.43
Oppenheimer/Centennial	1.35
Twentieth Century	1.18
AIM Group	1.16
Others	35.17

Source: *Business India*, May 7, 1995, p. 15.

★ 1654 ★

Investment Banking (SIC 6211)

Mutual Fund Managers - Canada

Market shares are shown based on assets as of March 31, 1995.

Investors Group	14.0%
Royal Mutual Funds	8.8
Trimark	8.2
Mackenzie Financial	7.7
CIBC	4.7
Fidelity	4.5
TD Bank	4.0
Altamira	3.9
Templeton Management	3.8
Bank of Montreal	3.4
AGF	3.3
Canadian International	3.2
CT Fund Services	3.0
Global Strategy	2.5
Dynamic	2.1
Other	22.9

Source: *Investext*, Thomson Financial Services, May 15, 1995, p. 1, from IFIC and *Financial Post*.

★ 1655 ★

Investment Banking (SIC 6211)

Non-U.S. Securities Managers

Firms are ranked by non-U.S. security holdings in millions of dollars as of December 31, 1995.

BZW Barclays Global Investors	$ 69,521
Capital Group	62,873
J.P. Morgan	53,521

Continued on next page.

★ 1655 ★ *Continued*
Investment Banking (SIC 6211)

Non-U.S. Securities Managers

Firms are ranked by non-U.S. security holdings in millions of dollars as of December 31, 1995.

State Street Global Advisors	$ 48,032
Franklin Templeton Group	38,963
Bankers Trust Co.	36,403
Citibank Global Asset Mgmt.	28,921
Brinson Partners	24,458
Merrill Lynch Asset Mgmt.	24,420
Morgan Stanley Asset Mgmt.	23,356

Source: *Institutional Investor*, July 1996, p. 60.

★ 1656 ★
Investment Banking (SIC 6211)

Top Brokerages

The top brokerages are ranked by 1995 assets in billions of dollars.

Merrill Lynch	$ 703.0
Smith Barney	419.7
Dean Witter	221.3
PaineWebber	216.3
Charles Schwab	195.6
Fidelity Brokerage	181.0
Prudential Securities	168.0

Source: *Forbes*, April 22, 1996, p. 74.

★ 1657 ★
Investment Banking (SIC 6211)

Top Corporate Trustees

Shares are for the first 5 months of 1995.

Chase Manhattan	7.6%
Citicorp	5.9
Bank of New York	5.1
Chemical Banking Corp.	4.5

First Chicago Corp.	2.8%
Bankers Trust	2.3
First Trust	2.3
State Street Bank & Trust	1.9
Nesbitt Burns & Securities	1.4
United States Trust	1.2
Other	65.0

Source: *ABA Banking Journal*, June 1996, p. 48, from Securities Data.

★ 1658 ★
Investment Banking (SIC 6211)

Top Domestic Equity Holders - 1995

Firms are ranked by volume of domestic equity holdings in millions of dollars as of December 31, 1995.

Fidelity Investments	$ 265,037
BZW Barclays Global Investors	145,255
Capital Group	101,233
Bankers Trust Co.	91,192
State Street Global Advisors	90,379
Mellon Bank Corp.	88,908
United Asset Mgmt. Corp.	84,117
Equitable Cos.	74,478
TIAA-CREF	60,346
Wellington Mgmt. Co.	56,984

Source: *Institutional Investor*, July 1996, p. 58.

★ 1659 ★
Investment Banking (SIC 6211)

Top Investment Managers

Firms are ranked by billions of dollars in assets as of December 31, 1994.

Fidelity Mgmt. & Research	$ 314.54
Bankers Trust	186.80
Merrill Lynch Asset Mgmt.	163.82
Capital Group	162.63
Wells Fargo/BZW	158.39
State Street Global Advisors	140.41
Alliance Capital Mgmt.	121.29
Franklin/Templeton Group	114.10
J.P. Morgan Inv. Mgmt.	111.98
American Express Financial/IDS	102.13

Source: *Wall Street Journal*, November 16, 1995, p. C1, from Goldman Sachs & Co.

★ 1660 ★

Investment Banking (SIC 6211)

Top Money Managers - 1995

| Fidelity Investments |
| Prudential Ins. Co. of America |
| Mellon Bank Corp. |
| State Street Global Advisors |
| J.P. Morgan |
| Capital Group |
| Equitable Cos. |
| Bankers Trust Co. |
| Metropolitan Life |
| Travelers |

Firms are ranked by total assets under management in millions of dollars.

Fidelity Investments	$ 426,742
Prudential Ins. Co. of America	271,500
Mellon Bank Corp.	251,713
State Street Global Advisors	231,722
J.P. Morgan	227,416
Capital Group	216,909
Equitable Cos.	205,000
Bankers Trust Co.	202,168
Metropolitan Life	171,594
Travelers	166,346

Source: *Institutional Investor*, July 1996, p. 58.

★ 1661 ★

Investment Banking (SIC 6211)

Top Underwriters - 1996

Data are for the first six months of 1996.

Merrill Lynch	16.2%
Salomon Brothers	10.4
Lehman Brothers	10.3
Morgan Stanley	10.1
Goldman Sachs	8.9
J.P. Morgan	6.0
CS First Boston	5.6
Bear Stearns	4.9
Donaldson, L&J	4.0
Smith Barney	3.4
Other	20.2

Source: *Financial Times*, August 12, 1996, p. 19, from *Investment Dealer's Digest*.

★ 1662 ★

Investment Banking (SIC 6211)

Underwriters of New Securities

Shares are shown based on a total amount underwritten of $6,576.7 billion.

Goldman Sachs	16.3%
Merrill Lynch	14.9
Morgan Stanley	10.7
Donaldson, Lufkin & Jenrette	6.2
CS First Boston	5.7
Smith Barney	5.6
Lehman Brothers	5.5
Salomon Brothers	4.0
Alex, Brown & Sons	2.9
Montgomery Securities	2.5
Other	25.8

Source: *Wall Street Journal*, January 2, 1996, p. R38, from Securities Data Co.

★ 1663 ★

Investment Banking (SIC 6211)

Venture Capital Firms - Maryland

The Maryland companies shown are ranked by total capital under management in millions of dollars.

New Enterprise Associates	$ 760.0
Grotech Capital Group Inc.	212.0
Arete Ventures Inc.	95.0
Anthem Capital LP	40.0
New Venture Partners	40.0
Catalyst Ventures LP	26.0
Sterling Capital Ltd.	25.0
Triad Investors Corp.	25.0
Calvert Social Venture Partners LP	10.0
Delmag Inc.	6.0

Source: *Baltimore Business Journal*, March 28, 1996, p. 16, from company representatives.

★ 1664 ★

Securities Exchanges (SIC 6231)

Options Market - 1995

CBOE

AMEX

PSE

PHLX

NYSE

PSE stands for Pacific Stock Exchange; PHLX stands for Philadelphia Stock Exchange; CBOE stands for Chicago Board Options Exchange; NYSE stands for New York Stock Exchange; AMEX stands for American Stock Exchange.

CBOE	65.2%
AMEX	17.3
PSE	8.5
PHLX	8.1
NYSE	0.9

Source: *Investor's Business Daily*, March 12, 1996, p. A4, from Chicago Board Options Exchange.

SIC 63 - Insurance Carriers

★ 1665 ★

Insurance (SIC 6300)

Captive Managers - Cayman Islands

Captive managers shown are ranked by premium volume in millions of dollars.

	1994	1995
Johnson & Higgins Ltd.	$ 481.0	$ 533.1
International Risk Mgmt. Ltd. . . .	330.0	330.0
Midland Bank Trust Corp. Ltd. . . .	201.0	236.6
Cayside Insurance Mgmt. Ltd. . . .	135.0	107.3
Mutual Risk Management Ltd. . . .	70.0	64.0
Marsh & McLennan Mgmt. Serv. Ltd.	75.4	64.0
Crusader Intl. Management Ltd. . .	37.0	62.0
Willis Corroon Management Ltd. . .	25.0	52.0
Catledonian Bank & Trust Ltd. . . .	43.0	49.6
Chandler Insurance Mgmt. Ltd. . .	20.5	19.6

Source: *Business Insurance*, April 22, 1996, p. 36.

★ 1666 ★

Insurance (SIC 6300)

Fitness Facilities Underwriting

A total of $800 million in commercial insurance premiums was written for sports clubs and fitness facilities. There are an estimated 26,650 fitness facilities in the United States, carving out a 0.6% share of total commercial insurance premiums.

Northeast	$ 213.6
West	180.3
Southeast	166.1
Midwest	132.1
Southwest	106.4

Source: *Rough Notes*, May 1996, p. 63, from Insurance Market Research.

★ 1667 ★

Insurance (SIC 6300)

Hawaiian Captive Managers

Captive managers shown are ranked by premium volume in millions of dollars.

	1994	1995
M&M Ins. Management Serv. Inc. . .	$ 97.8	$ 94.7
Becher & Carlson Risk Mgmt. Inc. . .	29.3	51.1
Johnson & Higgins Services Inc. . . .	24.1	29.4
Sedgwick Mgmt. Serv. (U.S.) Ltd. . .	17.1	14.5
Willis Corroon Management Ltd. . .	14.7	13.7
Alexander Insurance Managers . . .	7.6	13.1
Hawaii Captive Ins. Mgmt. Inc./ USA Risk Grp.	1.6	1.5
IAS Ins. Management Inc.	1.1	1.1
50th State Risk Mgmt. Services Inc. .	0.5	0.9

Source: *Business Insurance*, April 22, 1996, p. 65.

★ 1668 ★

Insurance (SIC 6300)

Heavy Construction Insurance Market

The general contracting and heavy construction market accounts for $5.6 billion in premiums and has a 4.3% of the total commercial line market. Directly written premiums are shown by region in millions of dollars.

	($ mil.)	Share
Western U.S.	$ 1,435	33.5%
Southeast	1.242	0.0
Northeast	1,066	24.9
Southwest	991	23.1
Midwest	790	18.4

Source: *Rough Notes*, November 1995, p. 63, from Insurance Market Research.

★ 1669 ★

Insurance (SIC 6300)

Insurance Market - Mexico

Total sales for insurance services in Mexico was expected to grow from $5.104 billion in 1995 to $6.04 billion in 1996.

	1995	1996
Local firms	99.7%	95.4%
Foreign owned firms	0.3	2.4
U.S. owned firms		2.2

Source: *World Trade*, March 1996, p. 42, from United States Department of Commerce.

★ 1670 ★

Insurance (SIC 6300)

Laptop Insurance Claims

There were 585,000 incidents of laptop damage in 1995. Figures show the value of damage in millions of dollars.

	($ mil.)	Share
Theft/robbery	$ 639.74	70.7%
Accidental damage	190.87	21.1
Lost/damaged in transit	31.35	3.5
Power supply surge	27.63	3.1
Lightning surge via telephone pole	9.00	1.0
Fire damage	4.45	0.5
Water damage	1.94	0.2

Source: *Newsweek*, May 6, 1996, p. 12, from Safeware.

★ 1671 ★

Insurance (SIC 6300)

Largest Business Insurers - Detroit

Firms are ranked by number of employees in 1994.

Meadowbrook Insurance Group	254
Marsh & McLennan Cos.	167
Johnson & Higgins of Mich. Inc.	145
Alexander & Alexander of Mich.	107
Acordia of Michigan Inc.	106
Rollins Hudig Hall of Michigan	89
Willis Corroon Corp. of Michigan	84
Proctor Homer Warren Inc.	80
Abow Cos.	75
Allied Cos. Inc.	66

Source: *Crain's Detroit Business*, August 28, 1995, p. 24.

★ 1672 ★

Insurance (SIC 6300)

Largest U.S. Reinsurers - 1995

Firms are ranked by net insurance premiums written in 1995.

	($000)	Share
General Re	$ 2,964,374	15.8%
Employers Re	2,391,393	12.8
American Re	1,611,509	8.6
Transatlantic/Putnam	1,008,781	5.4
Swiss Re Group	919,312	4.9
Berkshire Hathaway	777,000	4.1
The St. Paul Cos.	713,474	3.8
Munich Re	713,371	3.8
Prudential Re	667,697	3.6
Zurich Re Centre	602,269	3.2
Constitution Re	558,610	3.0
Hartford Re Co.	552,032	2.9
TIG Re Co.	510,718	2.7
F&G Re	506,818	2.7
NAC Re	476,048	2.5
Kemper Re	441,833	2.4
National Re	334,392	1.8
Underwriters Re	275,728	1.5
SCOR U.S. Group	256,656	1.4
Signet Star Re	217,018	1.2
Other	2,228,715	11.9

Source: *Business Insurance*, April 1, 1996, p. 28, from Reinsurance Association of America.

★ 1673 ★

Insurance (SIC 6300)

Mexican Insurance Market

General accident	58.0%
Life	33.2
Health	8.8

Source: *Business Mexico*, November 1995, p. 8, from AMIS.

★ 1674 ★

Insurance (SIC 6300)

Retail Insurance Market by Region

The retail store insurance market is shown by region, based on directly written premiums in 1994.

	($ mil.)	Share
Northeast	$ 483.9	23.8%
West	471.3	23.2
Southeast	406.8	20.0
Mountain	354.8	17.5
Southwest	313.3	15.4

Source: *Rough Notes*, December 1995, p. 49, from Insurance Market Research.

★ 1675 ★

Life Insurance (SIC 6311)

Detroit's Life Insurance Companies

Firms are ranked by 1994 assets in millions of dollars.

Alexander Hamilton Life Ins. Co. . . .	$ 7,287.9
Ford Life Insurance Co.	2,856.7
Royal Maccabees Life Ins. Co.	1,995.3
American Community Mutual Ins. Co. . .	213.8
Hamilton National Life Ins. Co.	139.2
Auto Club Life Ins. Co.	84.2
Mutual of Detroit Ins. Co.	50.4
Chrysler Life Ins. Co.	35.8
Vista Life Insurance Co.	31.7
Lutheran Fraternities of Am. Life	20.1

Source: *Crain's Detroit Business*, September 11, 1995, p. 15.

★ 1676 ★

Life Insurance (SIC 6311)

Life Insurance Companies - Columbus Area

Life insurance leaders are ranked by 1995 assets in millions of dollars.

Nationwide Life Insurance Co.	$ 35,656.6
Columbus Life Insurance Co.	1,760.6
Midland Life Insurance Co.	1,218.7
Nationwide Life & Annuity Insurance . .	926.9
Ohio State Life Insurance Co.	798.9
Motorists Life Insurance Co.	139.2
Community National Assurance Co. . . .	114.6
Acceleration Life Insurance Co.	85.7

Orange Life Insurance Co.	$ 69.1
American Physicians Life Insurance Co. . .	61.8

Source: *Business First Columbus*, April 5, 1996, p. 15, from company representatives.

★ 1677 ★

Life Insurance (SIC 6311)

Life Insurers - Quebec

Shares are shown for 1993, based on the top 164 companies generating $5.95 billion in premiums.

Assurance-vie Desjardins	11.9%
Industrial-Alliance Life	8.3
Sun Life of Canada	6.8
Standard Life	5.4
SSQ-Vie	5.2
Prudential of America	4.2
Mutual Life of Canada	3.9
Manufacturers	3.6
Laurentian	3.5
London Life	3.4
Other	43.8

Source: *Forces*, No. 107, 1995, p. 18, from Inspecteur general des institutions financieres du Quebec.

★ 1678 ★

Life Insurance (SIC 6311)

Top U.S. Life Insurance Firms

Life insurance companies shown are ranked by 1994 assets in billions of dollars. Metropolitan Life/New England Mutual Life and Massachusetts Mutual Life/Connecticut Mutual Life's figures are a reflection of assets after the proposed mergers.

Prudential	$ 167.3
Metropolitan Life and New England Mutual Life	146.9
Teachers Insurance & Annuity	73.2
New York Life	55.3
Connecticut General Life	50.9
Northwestern Mutual Life	48.1
Aetna Life	47.4
Equitable Life	46.9
Massachusetts Mutual Life and Connecticut Mutual life	46.9
John Hancock Mutual Life	46.9

Source: *New York Times*, August 17, 1995, p. C6, from A.M. Best Company.

★ 1679 ★

Auto Insurance (SIC 6321)

Auto Insurance Market

State Farm

Allstate

Farmers

Nationwide

USAA

Geico

Liberty Mutual

Prudential of America

Progressive

American Family

Other

State Farm	22.2%
Allstate	12.1
Farmers	6.2
Nationwide	3.7
USAA	3.5
Geico	2.0
Liberty Mutual	2.0
Prudential of America	1.6
Progressive	1.6
American Family	1.6
Other	43.5

Source: *Financial Times*, May 2, 1996, p. 17, from A.M. Best Co.

★ 1680 ★

Auto Insurance (SIC 6321)

Commercial Auto Insurance Writers

Shares are shown based on $17.556 billion in premiums written in 1994.

CNA Ins. Companies	4.0%
Zurich Ins. Group - U.S.	3.8
State Farm Goup	3.6
American Inter. Group	3.4
Aetna Life & Casualty Group	3.1
ITT Hartford Insurance Group	2.8
Nationwide Group	2.6
Travelers Insurance Group	2.6
Allstate Insurance Group	2.6
Liberty Mutual Group	2.4
Other	69.1

Source: *Best's Review*, October 1995, p. 19.

★ 1681 ★

Auto Insurance (SIC 6321)

Top Auto Insurers

Shares are shown based on 116.43 billion in total premiums in 1994.

State Farm	19.2%
Allstate Insurance	10.4
Farmers Insurance	5.2
Nationwide	3.6
USAA	2.8
Progressive	2.2
Geico	2.0
Liberty Mutual	1.8
ITT Hartford Insurance	1.5
American Family	1.4
Other	49.9

Source: *Wall Street Journal*, August 28, 1995, p. A3, from A.M. Best Co.

★ 1682 ★

Health Insurance (SIC 6321)

Top Pharmacy Benefit Managers

Groups are ranked by millions of lives insured.

	1994	1996
PCS (Lilly)	50	60
Medco (Merck)	41	52
Value Rx (Value Health/ Diagnostek)	6	23
DPS (SmithKline Beecham)	14	22
Caremark	13	17
Express Scripts	6	10
WellPoint	6	10
Systemed	4	6
Walgreens	3	5
PacificCare	3	5

Source: *Business & Health*, March 1996, p. 54, from Sanford Bernstein.

★ 1683 ★
Health Plans (SIC 6324)

Eye Care Health Insurance

Eye Care Plan of America

Vision Service Plan

Davis Vision

Coast To Coast Vision Plan

Spectrum Vision Systems

Eye Health Network

Block Vision

Outlook Vision Services

*Membership of managed vision care companies is
shown in millions. Surveyed optometrists and
opticians reported that 40% of their patients are
covered by private plans.*

Eye Care Plan of America	22.0
Vision Service Plan	16.0
Davis Vision	8.0
Coast To Coast Vision Plan	6.0
Spectrum Vision Systems	4.0
Eye Health Network	1.4
Block Vision	1.0
Outlook Vision Services	1.0

Source: *Business & Health*, January 1996, p. 39, from
Business & Health Executive Opinion Poll.

★ 1684 ★
Health Plans (SIC 6324)

HMO Penetration

*States with the highest penetration of national
managed care firms as of July 1, 1995.*

California	31.0%
Maryland	22.5
Oregon	22.5
Delaware	20.7
Colorado	20.5

Source: *American Medical News*, June 10, 1996, p. 2,
from InterStudy Competitive Edge.

★ 1685 ★
Health Plans (SIC 6324)

Health Care Plans - Michigan

*Health insurance plans are ranked by 1994 revenues
in millions of dollars.*

Blue Cross	$ 5,900.0
Health Alliance Plan	785.8
Blue Care Network SE Mich.	265.8
Physicians Health Plan Inc.	245.5
Comprehensive Health Services	224.9
Care Choice	219.3
Blue Care Network Great Lakes	216.8
Omnicare Health Plan	159.5
Healthplus of Mich.	148.1
Select Care HMO	140.7

Source: *Detroit Free Press*, March 22, 1996, p. 1A, from
Michigan State Medical Society.

★ 1686 ★
Health Plans (SIC 6324)

Largest HMOs

*Organizations are ranked by millions of subscribers
enrolled at the end of 1995.*

Blue Cross	8.5
Kaiser Permanente	6.7
United Healthcare	6.7
Aetna/U.S. Healthcare	5.7
Prudential	4.7
Cigna Healthplan	3.9
Humana	2.1
FHP	1.8
Health Systems	1.8
Pacificare	1.8

Source: *New York Times*, April 2, 1996, p. C1, from
Sanford C. Bernstein & Co.

★ 1687 ★
Health Plans (SIC 6324)

Leading Dental Plans - Dallas

*Dental health maintenance organizations in the
Dallas-Fort Worth area are shown ranked by local
membership.*

American Dental Corp.	197,000
Prudential Dental Maintenance Organization Inc.	126,967
United Dental Care Inc.	118,000

Continued on next page.

★ 1687 ★ *Continued*
Health Plans (SIC 6324)

Leading Dental Plans - Dallas

Dental health maintenance organizations in the Dallas-Fort Worth area are shown ranked by local membership.

Sanus Dental Plan of Texas Inc.	63,834
Delta Care	60,000
Safeguard Health Plans	41,000
DentlCare	15,750
Southwest Dental Plan	2,923

Source: *Dallas Business Journal*, September 8, 1995, p. C18, from health and dental maintenance organizations.

★ 1688 ★
Health Plans (SIC 6324)

Leading PPOs - Chicago

Preferred provider organizations (PPOs) in the Chicago area are ranked by subscribers as of June 30, 1995.

Preferred Plan Inc.	782,187
Blue Cross Blue Shield of Illinois	687,805
HealthNetwork Inc.	641,989
CNA Managed Care	229,657
Private Healthcare Systems Inc.	228,208
Midwest Business Medical Assn.	181,700
HealthStat Inc. - Managed Care Div.	155,200
HFN Inc.	152,000
HealthCare Compare Corp.	148,000
Metra Health	136,400
Health Direct Inc.	125,200
Beech Street Corp.	92,174

Source: *Crain's Chicago Business*, September 11, 1995, p. 29.

★ 1689 ★
Health Plans (SIC 6324)

Leading PPOs - General Service

Preferred provider organizations are ranked by number of employees and dependents in employer payer groups as of June 30, 1995. Data are in millions of people.

MultiPlan Inc.	19.999
USA Health Network Co. Inc.	12.367
HealthCare COMPARE Corp./The Affordable Medical Networks	9.800

Beech Street Corp.	9.037
ADMAR Corp.'s Med Network	6.970
MedView Services Inc.	6.800
Private Healthcare Systems	4.843
CAPP CARE Inc.	3.500
Aetna Health Plans	3.400
Preferred Health Network	2.733

Source: *Business Insurance*, December 19, 1995, p. 1.

★ 1690 ★
Health Plans (SIC 6324)

Managed Care Leaders

Figures are for the 12 months ended June 30, 1996. Firms show the millions of members.

Aetna	5.23
United Healthcare	4.51
Wellpoint Health Networks	4.24
Humana	3.29
Foundation Health	3.07
Pacificare Health Systems	1.99
FHP International	1.90
Health Systems International	1.80
Oxford Health Plans	1.162

Source: *New York Times*, August 6, 1996, p. C1, from Sherlock Company.

★ 1691 ★
Health Plans (SIC 6324)

Top 10 HMOs

Approximately 25 large organizations will be formed by mergers and consolidations in the health maintenance organization (HMOs) industry. This table shows the top 10 HMOs that will emerge and their enrollment membership in millions.

Blue Cross	8.5
Kaiser Permanente	6.7
United Healthcare	6.1
Aetna/U.S. Healthcare	5.8
Prudential	4.6
CIGNA Healthplan	3.9

Continued on next page.

★ 1691 ★ *Continued*
Health Plans (SIC 6324)

Top 10 HMOs

Approximately 25 large organizations will be formed by mergers and consolidations in the health maintenance organization (HMOs) industry. This table shows the top 10 HMOs that will emerge and their enrollment membership in millions.

Humana	2.1
FHP	1.8
Health Systems	1.8
Pacificare	1.8

Source: *Business & Health*, May 1996, p. 16, from InterStudy, American Association of Health Plans, Stanford C. Bernstein & Co., and Conning & Co.

★ 1692 ★
Health Plans (SIC 6324)

Top Corporate Managed Care Plans

Plans are ranked by thousands of prescriptions dispensed in 1995.

Blue Cross/Blue Shield Association	29,171.0
Aetna Health Plans	5,673.4
United Healthcare Corp.	4,895.9
Cigna Healthcare	4,764.0
Humana Healthcare Plans	4,422.9
Prudential Healthcare Plans	4,119.5
Pacificare Health Systems	3,084.1
Health Systems Intl.	3,030.9
FHP/Takecare	2,317.0
U.S. Healthcare	2,302.3

Source: *Medical Marketing & Media*, April 1996, p. 56, from Walsh America/Prime Medical Services Inc.

★ 1693 ★
Health Plans (SIC 6324)

Top General Service HMOs

Groups are ranked by number of employees and dependents in employer groups as of June 30, 1995.

Kaiser Permanente	5,836,648
Prudential Health Care Plan Inc.	3,624,282
United HealthCare Corp.	3,339,541
Aetna Health Plans	3,339,541
CIGNA Corp./CIGNA HealthCare	3,288,171

Source: *Business Insurance*, December 19, 1995, p. 1.

★ 1694 ★
Casualty Insurance (SIC 6331)

Corporate Casualty Insurers

Firms are ranked by consolidated revenues in millions of dollars.

American International Group	$ 25.87
CIGNA Corp.	18.95
CNA Financial Corp.	14.70
Aetna Life & Casualty Co.	12.97
ITT Hartford Group Inc.	12.15
General Re/Cologne Re Group	7.21
Lincoln National Corp.	6.63
Chubb Corp.	6.08
SAFECO Corp.	3.86
USF&G Corp.	3.45

Source: *Business Insurance*, March 25, 1996, p. 15.

★ 1695 ★
Marine Insurance (SIC 6331)

Inland Marine Insurers

Shares are shown based on $6.36 billion in premiums written in 1994.

American Intern Group	9.6%
Americas Bank Insurance Group	8.9
State Farm Group	5.2
Chubb Group of Ins. Cos.	4.2
Allstate Ins. Group	3.5
ITT Hartford Ins. Group	2.8
Zurich Insurance Group - U.S.	2.7
Travelers Ins. Group	2.6
Fireman's Fund Cos.	2.6
Continental Ins. Cos.	2.4
Home Ins. Cos.	2.4
Aetna Life & Cas. Group	2.0
Talegen Ins. Groups	1.8
Allendale Group	1.7
Amer Financial Group	1.7
Other	43.5

Source: *Best's Review*, December 1995, p. 50.

★ 1696 ★

Marine Insurance (SIC 6331)

Inland Marine Insurers - 1995

Firms are ranked by net premiums written in thousands of dollars.

State Farm Fire & Casualty	$ 344,106
Allstate Ins Co	223,281
American Bankers Ins Co.	184,304
Federal Ins Co.	126,837
St. Paul Fire & Marine Ins. Co.	110,892
Great American Ins Co.	94,365
Firemans Fund Ins Co.	84,738
Aetna Casualty & Surety Co.	78,988
Hartford Fire Ins. Co.	66,368
Maryland Casualty Co.	63,559

Source: *National Underwriter*, April 29, 1996, p. 1, from Standard & Poor's.

★ 1697 ★

Property Insurance (SIC 6331)

Homeowners Insurance Leaders

Shares are shown based on total direct premiums of $24.214 billion in 1994.

State Farm Group	23.6%
Allstate Insurance Group	11.9
Famers Ins. Group	5.7
USAA Group	3.2
Nationwide Group	2.9
Chubb Grp. of Ins. Cos.	2.0
Prudential of Am. Group	1.9
Aetna Life & Cas. Grp.	1.9
Safeco Ins. Companies	1.7
ITT Hartford Ins. Grp.	1.6
Amer. Family Group	1.6
Liberty Mutual Group	1.3
Others	40.7

Source: *Best's Review*, December 1995, p. 10, from A.M. Best Company.

★ 1698 ★

Property Insurance (SIC 6331)

Property & Liability Insurers

State Farm
Allstate Insurance
Merged Travelers/Aetna
American Intl. Group
Farmers Insurance
Nationwide
C.N.A. Insurance
ITT Hartford Insurance
Liberty Mutual Insurance
Aetna Life & Casualty
U.S.A.A.
Continental Insurance
Travelers

Companies are ranked by property and liability premiums shown in billions of dollars. The 1994 data exclude accident and health premiums.

State Farm	$ 31.0
Allstate Insurance	16.3
Merged Travelers/Aetna	8.2
American Intl. Group	7.6
Farmers Insurance	7.6
Nationwide	7.4
C.N.A. Insurance	5.8
ITT Hartford Insurance	5.6
Liberty Mutual Insurance	4.5
Aetna Life & Casualty	4.5
U.S.A.A.	4.4
Continental Insurance	3.8
Travelers	3.7

Source: *Corporate Growth Weekly Report*, December 11, 1995, p. 1, from A.M. Best Company and company reports.

★ 1699 ★
Property Insurance (SIC 6331)

Property/Casualty Leaders - Silicon Valley

The major Silicon Valley property insurance companies are ranked by volume of premiums written in millions of dollars.

Alburger Basso deGrosz Inc.	$ 350.0
Johnson & Higgins of California	100.0
Willis Corroon Corp. of San Jose	98.0
Minet Insurance Services Inc.	86.0
Alexander & Alexander of CA Inc.	85.0
Rollins Hudig Hall of Northern California Inc.	75.0
Tholts Insurance Service Inc.	60.0
Barlocker Insurance Services	55.0
Atlantic-Pacific Insurance Brokers	19.5
Lawson-Hawks & Associates	18.0

Source: *San Jose and Silicon Valley Business Journal*, December 3, 1995, p. 12.

★ 1700 ★
Property Insurance (SIC 6331)

Surplus Lines Insurers

The leading insurers are ranked by non-admitted direct premiums in millions of dollars for 1994.

Lexington Insurance Co.	$ 1,030.7
American Intl. Specialty Lines Ins. Co.	606.1
Scottsdale Insurance Co.	579.9
United National Insurance Co.	260.7
Illinois Insurance Exchange	222.5
General Star Indemnity Co.	213.4
Reliance Insurance Co. of Illinois	179.5
Steadfast Insurance Co.	172.9
St. Paul Surplus Lines Ins. Co.	140.4
Evanston Insurance Co.	127.8

Source: *Business Insurance*, September 11, 1995, p. 3.

★ 1701 ★
Workers Compensation Insurance (SIC 6331)

Leading Workers' Comp Writers

Shares are shown based on $31.23 billion in premiums written in 1994.

Liberty Mutual Group	8.8%
American Intern Group	5.9

CNA Ins. Companies	4.5%
ITT Hartford Ins. Group	4.4
Kemper Nat. Ins. Cos.	4.1
Travelers Ins. Group	4.1
Nationwide Group	4.0
Continental Ins. Group	3.2
Aetna Life & Cas. Group	3.0
Cigna Group	2.7
Other	55.3

Source: *Best's Review*, November 1995, p. 50.

★ 1702 ★
Workers Compensation Insurance (SIC 6331)

Long-Term Disability Market

The market for in-force premium life insurance is shown by company. The industry was valued at $3.76 billion in 1994.

UNUM	25.0%
CIGNA	12.0
Metropolitan	8.0
Hartford	7.0
Standard of Oregon	6.0
Fortis	5.0
CNA	4.0
Prudential	4.0
Paul Revere	3.0
Travelers	2.0
Other	25.0

Source: *Investext*, Thomson Financial Services, January 4, 1996, p. 21, from Employee BenefitPlan Review, John Hewitt & Associates, and UNUM.

★ 1703 ★
Workers Compensation Insurance (SIC 6331)

Top PPOs - Workers Comp

Preferred provider organizations are ranked by millions of employees in employer/payer groups as of June 30, 1995.

MedView Sciences Inc.	22.5
FOCUS Healthcare Management	17.1
Community Care Network Inc.	13.0
Beech Street Corp.	11.2
USA Workers Injury Network	6.9
HealthCare COMPARE Corp./The Affordable Medical Networks	6.6
Kemper National Services	3.0

Continued on next page.

★ 1703 ★ *Continued*

Workers Compensation Insurance (SIC 6331)

Top PPOs - Workers Comp

Preferred provider organizations are ranked by millions of employees in employer/payer groups as of June 30, 1995.

HealthStar Managed Care Corp.	1.5
HFN Inc.	1.2
Midwest Business Medical	1.0

Source: *Business Insurance*, December 19, 1995, p. 1.

★ 1704 ★

Surety Insurance (SIC 6351)

General Liability Insurers

1994 liability insurance premiums reached $23.95 billion in the United States. Market shares are shown for the top 15 companies.

Amer Intern Group	18.7%
Chubb Grp. of Ins. Cos.	5.4
CNA Ins. Companies	4.8
Aetna Life & Casualty Grp.	3.7
Nationwide Group	3.4
Home Ins. Cos.	3.3
Reliance Ins. Grp.	3.0
Talegen Ins. Groups	2.9
St. Paul Group	2.7
Travelers Ins. Group	2.6
Zurich Ins. Group-US	2.5
Cigna Group	2.2
Continental Ins. Cos.	2.0
ITT Hartford Ins. Grp.	2.0
Fireman's Fund Cos.	1.8
Others	39.0

Source: *Best's Review*, January 1996, p. 18, from A.M. Best Company.

★ 1705 ★

Surety Insurance (SIC 6351)

Multiple-Peril Insurance Writers

Shares are shown based on $19.93 billion premiums written in 1994.

State Farm	5.1%
Continental Ins. Cos.	4.9
ITT Hartford Ins. Group	4.5
Aetna Life & Casualty Group	4.4
CNA Ins. Companies	4.1

Chubb Group of Ins. Cos.	3.5%
Fireman's Fund	3.5
United States F&G	3.2
Cigna Group	3.1
Farmers Ins Group	3.0
Zurich Insurance Group - U.S.	2.7
Nationwide Group	2.7
Allstate Ins. Group	2.4
Kemper National Ins. Cos.	2.3
Commercial Union Ins. Group	2.1
Other	48.5

Source: *Best's Review*, December 1995, p. 28.

★ 1706 ★

Pensions (SIC 6371)

Top Pension Fund Managers

Leading pension fund managers are ranked by assets shown in millions of dollars.

TIAA-CREF	$ 153,609.0
California Public Employees	92,620.0
General Motors	72,000.0
New York State & Local	71,456.0
California State Teachers	58,343.0
AT&T	57,097.0
New York State Teachers	49,463.0
Florida State Board	47,726.0
Texas Teachers	46,054.0
New York City Retirement	41,679.0
New Jersey	40,974.0
General Electric	40,000.0
IBM	39,159.0
Wisconsin Investment Board	35,586.0
Ohio Public Employees	34,986.0

Source: *Pensions & Investments*, January 22, 1996, p. 22.

★ 1707 ★

Pensions (SIC 6371)

Top Pension Managers - Canada

Managers are ranked by assets in billions of dollars as of June 1995.

Caisse de Depot	$ 20.3
TAL Investment Counsel	11.4
Philips Hager & North	10.4
RT Capital Management	9.9
Sceptre Investment	9.4

Continued on next page.

★ **1707** ★ *Continued*

Pensions (SIC 6371)

Top Pension Managers - Canada

Managers are ranked by assets in billions of dollars as of June 1995.

Beutel Goodman . . . .$ 8.6
Gryphon Investment 8.2
Jarislowsky, Fraser 7.9
Altamira Management 7.6
Connor Clark & Lunn 7.3

Source: *Globe and Mail*, June 4, 1996, p. B19, from Benefits Canada.

SIC 64 - Insurance Agents, Brokers, and Service

★ 1708 ★

Insurance Services (SIC 6411)

Environmental Risk Consultants

Leading environmental risk management consulting firms are ranked by 1994 revenues in millions of dollars. Shares of the group are shown in percent.

	Rev. ($ mil.)	% of Group
ERM Group	$ 229.6	19.2%
IT Corp.	212.0	17.8
Dames & Moore Inc.	148.4	12.4
Parsons Engineering Science Inc.	141.5	11.9
Groundwater Technology Inc. . .	127.3	10.7
Environmental Science & Engineering Inc.	119.5	10.0
Radian Corp.	64.2	5.4
Law Engineering & Environmental Services Inc. . .	59.5	5.0
GZA Environmental Inc. . . .	53.0	4.4
ENVIRON International Corp.	38.2	3.2

Source: *Business Insurance*, October 2, 1995, p. 21.

★ 1709 ★

Insurance Services (SIC 6411)

Insurance Claims Administrators

The top 10 administrators shown are ranked by claims paid for self insurers in billions of dollars.

First Health Strategies	$ 9.60
CoreSource Inc.	2.35
Crawford & Co.	2.09
Harrington Services Corp.	1.98
ESIS Inc.	1.95
Gallagher Bassett Services Inc.	1.74
Acordia Inc.	1.67
Sedgewick James Inc.	1.62

GAB Robins North America Inc.	$ 1.50
TPA, United HealthCare Admin. Inc. . . .	1.40

Source: *Business Insurance*, February 5, 1996, p. 3.

★ 1710 ★

Insurance Services (SIC 6411)

Top Insurance Brokers

Brokers are ranked by gross revenues in millions of dollars for the first six months of 1995.

Marsh & McLennan	$ 1,898.9
Rollins Hudig Hall	848.9
Alexander & Alexander	652.3
Acordia	266.2
Arthur J. Gallagher	182.8
Hilb, Rogal & Hamilton	76.0
Poe & Brown	53.0

Source: *Business Insurance*, July 7, 1995, p. 3, from company reports.

SIC 65 - Real Estate

★ 1711 ★
Commercial Real Estate (SIC 6510)

Housing Market - NYC

Rentals, not co-op or condo	62.7%
House, owner-occupied	19.2
Private co-op, owner-occupied	6.7
Private co-op, rental	6.3
Condo, owner-occupied	1.6
Condo, rental	1.6
Subsidized co-op owner-occupied	1.5
Subsidized co-op rental	0.4

Source: *New York Times*, November 1, 1995, p. B8, from Queens College, New York City Department of Finance, and *New York City Housing and Vacancy Survey*.

★ 1712 ★
Commercial Real Estate (SIC 6512)

Industrial Parks - Milwaukee

Milwaukee industrial parks are ranked by total acreage.

Northbranch Industrial Park	1,303
Milwaukee Industrial Park and Land Bank	1,074
New Berlin Industrial Park	640
Germantown Industrial Park, Phase I, II, & III	565
Dodge Industrial Park	540
Waukesha Industrial Park	500
Saukville Industrial Park	435
Renaissance	390
Moorland Industrial Park	370
RidgeView Corporate Park	230

Source: *Milwaukee Business Journal*, April 6, 1996, p. 33.

★ 1713 ★
Commercial Real Estate (SIC 6512)

Largest Leases in Manhattan - 1995

Companies are ranked by square feet leased in Manhattan in 1995.

CS First Boston	1,116,000
New York Life	830,000
Depository Trust Co.	575,000
Colgate-Palmolive Co.	520,000
Equitable Life	502,000
UN/UNICEF	200,000
Wilkie Farr & Gallagher	242,000
Avon Products Inc.	226,200
Sullivan & Cromwell	210,000
Viacom International Inc.	207,025

Source: *Crain's New York Business*, February 5, 1996, p. 28.

★ 1714 ★
Commercial Real Estate (SIC 6512)

Largest Shopping Centers - Buffalo

Data show the number of outlets.

Walden Galleria	206
Niagara Factory Outlet	150
McKinley Mall	108
Eastern Hills Mall	107
Boulevard Mall	106
Summit Park Mall	90
Main Place Mall	70
Rainbow Centre	65
Northtown Plaza	60
Southgate Plaza	60

Source: *Business First of Buffalo*, February 26, 1996, p. 14.

★ 1715 ★
Commercial Real Estate (SIC 6512)

Leasable Area - Top States

States are ranked by thousands of gross leasable square feet of outlet center space.

California	4,200
Florida	3,500
Pennsylvania	2,800
Texas	2,600
New York	2,500
Michigan	1,800
Tennessee	1,800
Georgia	1,600
Missouri	1,500
South Carolina	1,400

Source: *LandUse Digest*, September 1995, p. 3, from *Value Retail News*.

★ 1716 ★
Commercial Real Estate (SIC 6512)

Top Shopping Center Owners

The owners are ranked by gross leasable area owned as of December 31, 1995. Data are shown in thousands of square feet. Simon Property Group includes affiliated companies.

Equitable RE Investment Management Inc.	64,254.2
Simon Property Group	54,074.9
Heitman Advisory Corp.	43,769.7
Rouse Co.	41,991.0
General Growth Properties Inc.	39,254.8
DeBartolo Realty Corp.	39,066.8
Richard E. Jacobs Group	37,859.9
Westfield Corp. Inc.	35,861.8
Cafaro Co.	31,218.7

Kimco Realty Corp.	30,895.6
Corporate Property Investors	30,164.0
LaSalle Partners	21,333.9
RD Management Corp.	18,965.4
CBL & Associates Properties Inc. . . .	18,734.8

Source: *Shopping Center World*, January 1996, p. 49.

★ 1717 ★
Mobile Home Operators (SIC 6515)

Manufactured Home Communities

The largest manufactured home community managers are ranked by number of sites operated.

Manufactured Home	26,600
Chateau Properties Inc.	20,829
ROC	20,000

Source: *Detroit News*, August 20, 1996, p. 3B.

★ 1718 ★
Real Estate (SIC 6531)

Leading Real Estate Firms - Mexico

Firms are ranked by revenues in millions of dollars.

Cushman & Wakefield	$ 3.6
Mexico Real Estate Affiliates Inc.	2.5
CB Comercial de Mexico	1.7

Source: *Mexico Business*, May 1996, p. 52.

★ 1719 ★
Real Estate (SIC 6531)

Real Estate Brokerage Market

Agents handled the sale of 3.8 million existing homes in 1995. HFS is composed of Century 21, with a 10% share, Coldwell Banker with an 8% share and Electronic Realty Associates with a 3.5 % share.

HFS	21.5%
RE/MAX International	8.0
Better Homes & Gardens Real Estate Services	3.5
Prudential Real Estate	3.5
Indepedent brokers	64.0

Source: *New York Times*, August 9, 1996, p. C2, from REAL Trends.

★ 1720 ★
Real Estate (SIC 6531)

Top Owners - Senior Housing

Firms are ranked by units with ownership interest.

Holiday Retirement Corp./Colson & Colson	17,493
Forum Group Inc.	6,993
Marriott Senior Living Services	5,460
Adult Communities Total Services Inc. . .	5,351
Evangelical Lutheran Good Samaritan . .	5,172
Leisure Centers Inc.	4,550
ARV Assisted Living Inc.	4,221
Health and Retirement Properties Trust . .	4,051
Freedom Group Inc.	3,420
National Benevolent Association	3,378

Source: *LandUse Digest*, December 1995, p. 2, from American Seniors Housing Association.

★ 1721 ★
Real Estate (SIC 6531)

Top Real Estate Brokers - South Florida

Commercial real estate brokers are ranked based on square footage leased or sold as of December 1, 1995 in the South Florida area.

Trammel Crow Company	5,363,293
CB Commercial Real Estate Grp. Inc.	4,539,782
Cushman & Wakefield of Florida Inc. .	3,625,605
Grubb & Ellis of Florida Inc.	3,322,026
Keyes Company Realtors	3,195,000
Lehrer & Co./Colliers International . .	3,117,179
Easton Babcock & Associates Inc. . . .	3,099,900
Continental Real Estate Companies . .	3,006,000
Merin Hunter Codman	2,917,470
Steinbauer Associates Inc./Corfac Intl.	2,224,700

Source: *South Florida Business Journal*, January 26, 1996, p. 8B, from companies.

★ 1722 ★
Real Estate (SIC 6550)

Master Planned Communities - Arizona

The most active master planned communities are ranked based on housing starts in 1995.

Superstition Springs, Mesa	939
Sun City West	789
Arrowhead Ranch, Glendale	779
Fountain Hills	548
The Foothills, Phoenix	506
Terravita, Scottsdale	442
Desert Ridge, Phoenix	385
Tatum Ridge	380
Sun Lakes, Mesa	361
Amberlea, Phoenix	360

Source: *Arizona Republic*, May 5, 1996, p. AI8, from Landscor Aerial Information.

★ 1723 ★
Real Estate (SIC 6550)

Planned Communities - Home Sales

Major master planned communities are ranked by unit sales for 1994. Figures include the share of the local market. Summerlin, Las Vegas includes Sun City Las Vegas (at Summerlin).

	Units	Share
Summerlin, Las Vegas	2,306	12.3%
Highlands Ranch, Denver	1,619	14.5
Weston, Fort Lauderdale	1,320	--
Alia Viejo, Anaheim	1,205	14.0
Sun City, Phoenix	1,156	--
Green Valley, Las Vegas	1,150	10.0
Coral Ridge Comm., Fort Lauderdale	1,076	--
Mission Viejo, Anaheim	981	12.0
Woodlands, Houston	922	6.7
Silverlakes, Fort Lauderdale . . .	922	18.0

Source: *LandUse Digest*, November 1995, p. 1, from Arthur Andersen Real Estate Service Group.

★ 1724 ★

Real Estate (SIC 6550)

Top Residential Real-Estate Firms

Coldwell Banker	
Weichart Realtors	
	Long & Foster Real Estate
	Burnet Financial Group
	Prudential-Jon Douglas Co.
Edina Realty	
	Windemere Real Estate
	Prudential Florida Reality
	Realty Executives
	John L. Scott Real Estate

The top firms are ranked by number of closed transaction sides. A side is either the selling or buying side of a closed deal.

Coldwell Banker	100,465
Weichart Realtors	58,000
Long & Foster Real Estate	42,239
Burnet Financial Group	37,080
Prudential-Jon Douglas Co.	34,570
Edina Realty	27,754
Windemere Real Estate	25,541
Prudential Florida Reality	24,319
Realty Executives	19,469
John L. Scott Real Estate	19,467

Source: *Wall Street Journal*, June 7, 1996, p. B12, from *Real Trends Newsletter*.

SIC 67 - Holding and Other Investment Offices

★ 1725 ★

Bank Holding Companies (SIC 6712)

Automated Clearing House Leaders

The table shows the consolidated automated clearing house originators. Figures reflect completed and pending mergers in 1995. Data refer to millions of transactions.

Chase Manhattan	300.0
Norwest	182.0
Banc One	133.6
BankAmerica	110.6
Wachovia	107.7
Wells Fargo	82.5
NationsBank	74.1
First Union	69.1
Northern Trust	62.8
First Chicago NBD	59.3

Source: *American Banker*, April 15, 1996, p. 3.

★ 1726 ★

Bank Holding Companies (SIC 6712)

Leading Holding Companies - California

Market shares are shown based on deposits as of June 30, 1994.

BankAmerica	22.1%
Wells Fargo & Co.	10.9
H.F. Ahmanson & Co.	7.1
1st Bank System/1st Inter	6.2
Great Western Financial	6.0
Bank of Tokyo	4.1
NA Capital Holdings	3.5
Golden West Financial	2.6%
California Federal Bank	2.3
Glendale Federal Bank	2.0
Others	33.2

Source: *Investext*, Thomson Financial Services, January 24, 1996, p. 2, from regulatory data and SNL Securities.

★ 1727 ★

Bank Holding Companies (SIC 6712)

Top Bank Holding Companies

Banks are ranked by assets in billions of dollars as of June 30, 1995.

Chemical/Chase Manhattan	$ 297.0
Citicorp	257.0
BankAmerica	226.0
Nationsbank	184.1
J.P. Morgan & Company	166.0
First Union-First Fidelity	124.2
First Chicago-NBD Bancorp	123.3
Bankers Trust	102.9
Banc One	86.7
KeyCorp	67.4

Source: *New York Times*, August 29, 1995, p. C4, from Keefe, Bruyette & Woods and *American Banker*.

★ 1728 ★

Bank Holding Companies (SIC 6712)

Top Bank Holding Companies - Detroit

The leading companies are ranked by 1995 assets in thousands of dollars.

Comerica Inc.	$ 35,000.0
Michigan National Corp.	9,551.2
First of America Bank-Michigan N.A.	7,245.1
Huntington Bancshares Michigan Inc.	1,992.7
Republic Bancorp Inc.	1,472.7
Old Kent Financial Corp.	1,384.9

Continued on next page.

★ 1728 ★ *Continued*
Bank Holding Companies (SIC 6712)

Top Bank Holding Companies - Detroit

The leading companies are ranked by 1995 assets in thousands of dollars.

Society Bancorp of Mich. Inc.	$ 1,144.5
First State Financial Corp.	410.9
Capital Bancorp Ltd.	384.1
Charter National Bancorp Inc.	220.0

Source: *Crain's Detroit Business*, May 13, 1996, p. 14.

★ 1729 ★
Bank Holding Companies (SIC 6712)

Top Letters of Credit Holders

Bank holding companies are ranked by commercial letters of credit in millions of dollars. Data are for 1994.

Citicorp	$ 4,878
Bank of America	4,213
Chase Manhattan	2,946
Chemical Banking	2,860
Bank of New York	2,069
NationsBank	1,329
CoreStates Financial	1,244
Bank of Boston	1,174
First Chicago	842
Republic, New York	589
Bankers Trust	524
Comerica	509
Norwest	424
Natwest Holdings	294
Bancal Tri-State	291

Source: *World Trade*, August 1995, p. 34, from *American Banker*.

★ 1730 ★
Franchising (SIC 6794)

Franchisors - Soft Drinks

The leading soft drink franchisors' market shares are shown for 1993.

Coca-Cola	41.7%
Pepsi-Cola	30.6
Dr. Pepper/Seven-Up	11.2
Cadbury Beverages	3.2
Royal Crown	2.2
A&W Brands	1.8
Cott	1.7%
National Beverage	1.7
Monarch	1.6
Barq's	0.6
Other	3.7

Source: *Beverage World*, December 1995, p. 50, from Beverage Marketing Corp.

★ 1731 ★
Franchising (SIC 6794)

Top Business Service Companies

The top business service franchises are ranked by number of franchisee-owned units.

Jani-King International Inc.	4,950
ServiceMaster	4,408
H&R Block Tax Services Inc.	4,277
Coverall Cleaning Concepts	3,825
Mail Boxes Etc.	3,023
RoboClean	2,650
Jackson Hewitt Tax Service	1,289
Fantastic Sams	1,254
Tower Cleaning Systems Inc.	1,150
Uniglobe Travel International Inc.	1,140

Source: *Franchise Times*, June 1996, p. 14.

★ 1732 ★
Franchising (SIC 6794)

Top Education/Children's Service Centers

The top franchisors for education and children's services are ranked by number of outlets.

Futurekids Inc.	605
Sylvan Learning Systems Inc.	583
Gymboree Play Programs	373
Tutor Time Child Care Learning Ctr.	166
Computertots	145
Academy of Learning	140
New Horizons Computer Learning	140
United Studios of Self-Defense Inc.	123
Little Gym International Inc.	114
Fourth R Inc.	107

Source: *Franchise Times*, April 1996, p. 35.

SIC 70 - Hotels and Other Lodging Places

★ 1733 ★

Hotels (SIC 7011)

Hotel Programs for Frequent Stayers

| Marriott |
| Holiday Inn |
| Hilton |
| Hyatt |
| Sheraton |
| Best Western |
| Ramada |
| Westin |

Membership is shown in millions as of October 1995.

Marriott	6.1
Holiday Inn	4.5
Hilton	3.0
Hyatt	1.2
Sheraton	1.2
Best Western	0.8
Ramada	0.8
Westin	0.8

Source: *New York Times*, November 1, 1995, p. C5, from *Inside Flyer*.

★ 1734 ★

Hotels (SIC 7011)

Hotels by Region

Data are for 1995 and refer to hotels with at least 20 rooms.

South Atlantic	6,709
Pacific	5,170
East North Central	3,622
Mountain	3,179
West South Central	2,730
West North Central	2,561
Middle Atlantic	2,420

East South Central	1,994
New England	1,462

Source: *Cornell Hotel and Restaurant Administration Quarterly*, February 1996, p. 82, from Smith Travel Research.

★ 1735 ★

Hotels (SIC 7011)

Largest Hotels - Canada

Hotels are ranked by number of guestrooms. Locations are shown in parentheses.

Delta Chelsea Inn (Toronto)	1,587
Sheraton Centre (Toronto)	1,382
Royal York (Toronto)	1,365
Queen Elizabeth (Montreal)	1,020
Westin Harbour Castle (Toronto) . . .	980
Banff Spring Hotel (Banff, Alberta) . . .	828
Le Centre Sheraton (Montreal)	824
Toronto Colony Hotel	717
Regal Constellation (Toronto)	708
Hyatt Regency (Vancouver)	644

Source: *Globe & Mail*, October 11, 1995, p. B11, from KPMG and Hotel Association of Canada.

★ 1736 ★

Hotels (SIC 7011)

Largest Hotels - Dallas

Hotels are ranked by total rooms and suites available.

Wyndham Anatole Hotel	1,620
Hyatt Regency Dallas Hotel	939
Dallas Grand Hotel	710
Fairmont Hotel	550
Dallas Marriott Quorum Hotel	548
Sheraton Park Central Hotel	545
Stouffer Dallas Hotel	540
Grand Kempinski Dallas Hotel	528

Continued on next page.

★ 1736 ★ *Continued*
Hotels (SIC 7011)

Largest Hotels - Dallas

Hotels are ranked by total rooms and suites available.

Harvey Hotel-DFW Airport	506
Worthington Hotel	504

Source: *Dallas Business Journal*, June 16, 1995, p. 8, from hotels.

★ 1737 ★
Hotels (SIC 7011)

Largest Resorts - Arizona

Resorts are ranked by number of rooms.

Scottsdale Princess	650
Pointe Hilton on South Mountain	640
Arizona Biltmore	600
Pointe Hilton at Tapatio Cliffs	591
The Phoenician	580
Point Hilton at Squaw Peak	564
Hyatt Regency Scottdale	493
Marriott's Camelback Inn	424
Scottsdale Plaza	404
Doubletree Paradise Valley	387

Source: *Arizona Republic*, May 5, 1996, p. AI18.

★ 1738 ★
Hotels (SIC 7011)

Leading Hotel Chains

Shares are shown based on the top 100 hotel chains.

Hilton Hotels	22.48%
Marriott hotels, resorts, suites	21.16
Sheraton Hotels	17.56
Holiday Inns	10.41
Ramada Inn	7.97
Radisson/Colony/Country Inn	7.69
Hyatt Hotels	6.86
Westin Hotels & Resorts	5.87
Other	0.30

Source: *Nation's Restaurant News*, August 7, 1995, p. 132.

★ 1739 ★
Hotels (SIC 7011)

Popular Hotels in Mexico

Chains are ranked by number of outlets.

Best Western	39
Fiesta Americana	18
Calinda	16
Holiday Inn	16
Plaza Las Glorias	14
Mision	12
Camino Real	11
Howard Johnson	11
Days Inn	10
Club Mediterrane	9

Source: *National Trade Data Bank*, March 2, 1996, p. IS9506.633, from SECTUR.

★ 1740 ★
Hotels (SIC 7011)

Top 5 Hotels - Chicago

Chicago's largest hotels are ranked by number of rooms.

Hyatt Regency Chicago	2,019
Palmer House Hilton	1,639
Chicago Hilton & Towers	1,543
Sheraton Chicago Hotel & Towers	1,200
Chicago Marriott Downtown Hotel	1,172

Source: *Crain's Chicago Business*, March 4, 1996, p. 15.

★ 1741 ★
Hotels (SIC 7011)

Top Hotel Cities

The table shows the cities with the most hotel rooms.

Las Vegas	87,267
Orlando, Fla.	85,924
Los Angeles	78,984
Chicago	68,365
Washington D.C.	66,356
New York City	61,823
Atlanta	58,737
San Diego	46,453
Anaheim, Calif.	44,320
San Francisco	42,700

Source: *Travel Weekly*, April 4, 1996, p. 17, from SmithTravel Research.

★ 1742 ★

Resorts (SIC 7011)

Top Resort Markets

Occupany rates are for 1994.

Laughlin, NV	85.5%
Las Vegas, NV	84.6
Reno, NV	79.5
Hawaii	77.8
New Orleans	76.7

Source: *Lodging Hospitality*, July 1996, p. 8, from Kenneth Leventhal & Co.

★ 1743 ★

Resorts (SIC 7011)

Top Ski Resort Operators

The top four resort operators in North America are ranked by millions of skier visits in 1994-95. American Skiing Company is a company formed by the probable merger of LBO and S-K-I.

American Skiing Company	3.5
Ralcorp Holdings Inc.	2.5
Intrawest Corporation	2.5
Apollo Ski Partners	2.1

Source: *New York Times*, March 23, 1996, p. 21, from National Ski Areas Association.

★ 1744 ★

Trailer Parks (SIC 7033)

Trailer Parks in Arizona

The table shows the number of mobile home slots outside the Phoenix area. Data include the occupancy rate.

	No.	Rate
Yuma	3,500	98.0%
Tucson	17,000	95.0
Central region	5,000	91.0
Southeast region	3,000	89.0
Western region	2,500	88.0

Source: *Arizona Business*, July 1995, p. 2.

SIC 72 - Personal Services

★ 1745 ★

Laundromats (SIC 7215)

Dry-Cleaning Market - Mexico

Planchadurias	70.0%
Independents	15.0
Maquiladoras	2.0
Others	11.0

Source: *National Trade Data Bank*, March 2, 1996, p. IS9506.633.

★ 1746 ★

Laundromats (SIC 7215)

Laundromat Spending - 1996

The table shows what coin laundry operators are purchasing, based on a survey.

Top loaders	42.0%
Dryers	30.5
Double loaders	19.0
Triple loaders	19.0
Water heaters	14.0
Vendors	11.0
Changers	5.5

Source: *American Co-Op*, April 1996, p. 12, from *State of the Coin Laundry Business*.

★ 1747 ★

Funeral Services (SIC 7261)

Cremations by State

The table shows the states with the highest percentage of cremations in 1994.

Hawaii	60.6%
Washington	49.9
Nevada	49.8
Alaska	47.2
Montana	45.3

Source: *USA TODAY*, December 5, 1995, p. A1, from Cremation Association of North America.

★ 1748 ★

Textile Rental (SIC 7299)

Leading Textile Rental Firms

Firms are ranked by 1994 revenues in millions of dollars.

National Service	$ 1,880.0
Cintas Corp.	615.1
Angelica Corp.	472.8
UniFirst Corp.	318.0
G&K Services	262.5
Unitog Co.	189.1

Source: *Textile Rental*, October 1995, p. 38.

SIC 73 - Business Services

★ 1749 ★

Advertising (SIC 7310)

Canadian Ad Spending - 1994

Total media spending reached $9.214 billion in 1994. Distribution is shown in percent.

Daily newspapers	20.0%
Television	19.2
Yellow pages	9.2
Outdoor	8.6
Radio	8.0
Weeklies	6.1
Magazines	3.4
Business papers	1.7
Weekend supplements	0.2
Farm papers	0.1
Other print	22.6
Religious, school & other	0.7

Source: *Facts About Newspapers*, 1996, p. 10, from Canadian Daily Newspaper Association.

★ 1750 ★

Advertising (SIC 7310)

Top Ad Categories - 1995

Advertising expenditures are shown by category for 1995. Shares of the group are shown in percent.

	($ mil.)	% of Group
Automotive	$ 1,380.3	13.4%
Direct response companies . . .	1,319.7	12.8
Toiletries & cosmetics	898.2	8.7
Computers, office equipment . .	892.4	8.7
Business & consumer services . .	835.9	8.1
Foods & food products	725.7	7.0
Apparel, footwear & accessories	622.2	6.0
Drug & remedies	592.6	5.8
Travel, hotels & resorts	497.5	4.8
Cigarettes, tobacco	327.9	3.2
Retail	325.6	3.2

	($ mil.)	% of Group
Publishing & media	$ 297.2	2.9%
Sporting goods, toys & games . .	255.4	2.5
Jewelry, opticals & cameras . .	243.1	2.4
Liquor	199.9	1.9
Insurance & real estate	198.8	1.9
Household equipment & supplies	188.4	1.8
Household furnishings	179.7	1.7
Electronic entertainment equip.	171.9	1.7
Bldg. material & fixtures	143.6	1.4

Source: *Brandweek*, March 4, 1996, p. 27, from Competitive Media Reporting.

★ 1751 ★

Advertising (SIC 7310)

U.S. Advertising Spending - 1995

	($ mil.)	Share
Daily newspapers	$ 36,046	22.4%
Retail	18,076	11.2
Classified	13,724	8.5
National	4,245	2.6
Direct mail	32,900	20.4
Broadcast television	32,885	20.4
Radio	11,320	7.0
Yellow pages	10,275	6.4
Magazines	8,710	5.4
Cable television	3,595	2.2
Business publications	3,525	2.2
Outdoor advertising	1,260	0.8
Farm publications	290	0.2
Other	20,315	12.6

Source: *Facts About Newspapers*, 1996, p. 10, from Newspaper Advertising Association and McCann-Erickson Inc.

★ 1752 ★
Advertising (SIC 7311)

Leading Advertising Firms - Mexico

Firms are ranked by billings in millions of dollars.

McCann-Erickson Mexico	$ 88.0
J. Walter Thompson Mexico	65.0
Young & Rubicam Mexico	54.0
Leo Burnett Mexico	51.4
BBDO Mexico	42.9

Source: *Mexico Business*, May 1996, p. 54.

★ 1753 ★
Advertising (SIC 7311)

Top Ad Agencies - Canada

The top ad agencies are ranked by revenues in millions of dollars.

	1995 ($ mil.)	1996 ($ mil.)
BBDO Canada Inc.	$ 52.166	$ 54.742
Cossette Communication- Marketing	43.160	48.761
MacLaren McCann Canada Inc.	38.654	40.006
Young & Rubicam Group of Co's Ltd.	36.119	31.734
Leo Burnett Co. Ltd.	23.293	24.181
Oglivy & Mather (Canada) Ltd.	20.491	25.998
FCB Canada Ltd.	23.119	24.933
BCP Canada Inc.	16.842	27.697
Vickers & Benson Advertising Ltd.	16.020	16.784
Palmer Jarvis CommunicationsDDB	12.313	16.014
DDB Needham Worldwide	17.298	15.948
Grey Advertising Ltd.	15.193	15.262
Saatchi & Saatchi Advertising Inc.	11.056	12.937
TBWA Chiat/Day Inc. Advertising	12.927	12.494
SMW Advertising Ltd.	9.368	10.396

Source: *Marketing Magazine*, June 24, 1996, p. 13.

★ 1754 ★
Advertising (SIC 7311)

Top Ad Agencies - Milwaukee

Leading advertising agencies are ranked by 1995 billings in millions of dollars. Figures are for Milwaukee and Waukesha counties in Wisconsin.

Bader Rutter & Assoc.	$ 90.0
BVK/McDonald	83.0
Laughlin/Constable	75.0
Cramer-Krasselt	69.0
Hoffman York & Compton	55.0
William Eisner & Assoc.	38.0
AVA Advertising	34.0
TMP Worldwide	33.0
Sargent & Potratz	28.0
Nelson & Schmidt	26.0

Source: *Adweek*, February 5, 1996, p. 14, from agency reports.

★ 1755 ★
Advertising (SIC 7311)

Top Ad Agencies - Pittsburgh

Advertising agencies shown are ranked by 1995 billings in millions of dollars.

Marc Advertising	$ 154.0
Ketchum Advertising	94.0
St. George Group	41.0
Blattner/Brunner	35.0
Hallmark/Tassone	32.0
Elias/Savion	22.0
Dudreck DePaul Ficco & Morgan	20.0
Dymun/Nelson & Co.	20.0
Brabender Cos.	17.0
J.W. Messner	16.0

Source: *Adweek*, March 25, 1996, p. 18, from agencies.

★ 1756 ★
Advertising (SIC 7311)

Top Ad Agencies - San Diego

Leading advertising agencies are ranked by 1995 billings in millions of dollars. Data are for San Diego County, California.

Phillips-Ramsey	$ 49.0
Lambesis	35.0
Kenneth C. Smith	30.0
Franklin Stoorza	27.0

Continued on next page.

★ 1756 ★ *Continued*
Advertising (SIC 7311)

Top Ad Agencies - San Diego

Leading advertising agencies are ranked by 1995 billings in millions of dollars. Data are for San Diego County, California.

Capener, Matthews & Walcher	$ 22.0
Di Zinno Thompson	15.0
Chapman Warwick	14.0
VitroRobertson	13.0
McQuertergroup	10.0
Townsend Agency	7.0

Source: *Adweek*, January 22, 1996, p. 16, from agency reports.

★ 1757 ★
Advertising (SIC 7311)

Top Ad Agencies - San Francisco

Advertising agencies shown are ranked by billings in millions of dollars.

Foote, Cone & Belding	$ 548.0
Hal Riney & Partners	332.0
Goodby, Silverstein & Partners	316.0
J. Walter Thompson	300.0
Ketchum Advertising	162.0
Young & Rubicam	150.0
McCann-Erickson	147.0
Goldberg Moser O'Neill	145.0
FCB Healthcare	139.0
Cohn & Wells	119.0

Source: *Adweek*, September 4, 1995, p. 13, from agencies.

★ 1758 ★
Advertising (SIC 7311)

Top Ad Firms - Philadelphia

Advertising agencies are ranked by 1994 billings in millions of dollars.

Devon Direct Marketing	$ 139.0
Gillespie	120.0
Weightman Group	120.0
QLM Associates	116.0
Earle Palmer Brown	100.0
Thierney & Partners	100.0
Al Paul Lefton	70.0
Ted Thomas Associates	54.0
Elkman Advertising	43.0
McAdams, Rickman & Ong	40.0
Harris, Balo & McCullough	40.0
Dorland Sweeney Jones	40.0

Source: *Adweek*, October 5, 1995, p. 14, from agency reports.

★ 1759 ★
Advertising (SIC 7311)

Top Agency Networks

Firms are ranked by 1995 revenues in millions of dollars.

McCann-Erickson	$ 1,236.3
BBDO Worldwide	1,144.1
J. Walter Thompson	1,054.5
DDB Needham Worldwide	1,051.4
Ogilvy & Mather Worldwide	893.2
Young & Rubicam	817.5
Leo Burnett Worldwide	805.8
Grey Advertising	799.0
Ammirati Puris Lintas Worldwide	786.2
Saatchi & Saatchi Advertising	700.0

Source: *Adweek*, April 15, 1996, p. 72.

★ 1760 ★
Advertising (SIC 7312)

Outdoor Advertising Agencies - 1995

The top agencies are ranked by U.S. billings in millions of dollars.

Leo Burnett Co.	$ 140.7
Saatchi & Saatchi Advertising	100.2
Grey Advertising	91.3
BBDO Worldwide	57.9

Continued on next page.

★ 1760 ★ *Continued*
Advertising (SIC 7312)

Outdoor Advertising Agencies - 1995

The top agencies are ranked by U.S. billings in millions of dollars.

Bates Worldwide	.$ 48.7
DDB Needham Worldwide	43.0
Young & Rubicam	39.9
McCann-Erickson Worldwide	38.0
J. Walter Thompson Co.	29.4
Ogilvy & Mather Worldwide	28.5

Source: *Advertising Age*, April 15, 1996, p. S33.

★ 1761 ★
Advertising (SIC 7313)

Advertising Agencies - Network TV

The top agencies are ranked by U.S. billings in millions of dollars for 1995.

D'Arcy Masius Benton & Bowles	$ 1,190.0
Saatchi & Saatchi Advertising	838.3
Leo Burnett Co.	828.5
J. Walter Thompson Co.	813.0
McCann-Erickson Worldwide	794.0
Ogilvy & Mather Worldwide	767.2
BBDO Worldwide	751.4
Foote, Cone & Belding Communications	730.0
Grey Advertising	725.3
Bates Worldwide	514.8

Source: *Advertising Age*, April 15, 1996, p. S33.

★ 1762 ★
Advertising (SIC 7313)

Advertising Agencies - Radio

The top agencies are ranked by U.S. billings in millions of dollars for 1995.

DDB Needham Worldwide	$ 128.6
BBDO Worldwide	115.7
Foote, Cone & Belding Communications	115.0
J. Walter Thompson Co.	95.6
McCann-Erickson Worldwide	95.0
D'Arcy Masius Benton & Bowles	91.6

Bates Worldwide	.$ 86.4
Bozell Worldwide	78.8
Saatchi & Saatchi Advertising	77.7
Zimmerman & Partners Advertising	56.7

Source: *Advertising Age*, April 15, 1996, p. S33.

★ 1763 ★
Advertising (SIC 7313)

Newspaper Advertising Agencies - 1995

The top agencies are ranked by U.S. billings in millions of dollars.

Bernard Hoods Group	$ 294.3
Nationwide Advertising Services	230.3
TMP Worldwide	179.3
Allied Advertising	125.6
DDB Needham Worldwide	102.8
Grey Advertising	95.2
McCann-Erickson Worldwide	95.0
Ketchum Advertising	92.8
Foote, Cone & Belding Communications	90.0
Young & Rubicam	88.5

Source: *Advertising Age*, April 15, 1996, p. S33.

★ 1764 ★
Advertising (SIC 7313)

Top Radio Advertisers

This table shows the top companies advertising on radio nationwide. Figures are in millions of dollars.

Sear Roebuck	$ 100.03
AT&T Corp.	36.60
GM Corp. Dealer Assoc.	31.57
News Corp. (Fox TV)	28.67
Chrysler Corp. Dealer Assoc.	26.55
Tandy Corp. (Radio Shack)	25.24
Kmart	21.86
General Motors Corp.	21.50
U.S. Government	21.20
Warner-Lambert	18.70
Sunsource Health Products	18.04
American Home Products	17.07
Gateway Education Products	16.80
MCI Communications	16.43
Phillip Morris Corp.	16.20

Source: *Adweek*, September 4, 1995, p. 13, from Radio Advertising Bureau.

★ 1765 ★
Advertising (SIC 7319)

Interactive Media Spending by City

New York-Northern New Jersey-Long Island

Los Angeles-Riverside-Orange County

Chicago-Gary-Kenosha

Philadelphia-Wilmington-Atlantic City

Washington-Baltimore

Boston-Worchester-Lawrence

Detroit-Ann Arbor-Flint

Dallas-Ft. Worth

Houston-Galveston-Brazorin

Miami-Ft. Lauderdale

The table shows ad spending for 1995 in the top metro markets. Data are in millions of dollars.

New York-Northern New Jersey-Long Island	$ 89.2
Los Angeles-Riverside-Orange County	67.6
Chicago-Gary-Kenosha	42.2
Philadelphia-Wilmington-Atlantic City	30.1
Washington-Baltimore	36.8
Boston-Worchester-Lawrence	28.5
Detroit-Ann Arbor-Flint	28.0
Dallas-Ft. Worth	24.1
Houston-Galveston-Brazorin	20.0
Miami-Ft. Lauderdale	19.4

Source: *Web Week*, May 20, 1996, p. 23, from Ad Audit.

★ 1766 ★
Advertising (SIC 7319)

Internet Advertising

The table shows who received the $12.4 million spent on Internet advertising during the fourth quarter of 1995.

Netscape	14.0%
Lycos	10.4
InfoSeek	8.7
Yahoo	8.7
Pathfinder	6.5
HotWired	5.8
WebCrawler	5.3
ESPN SportZone	4.8
GNN	4.7

c/Net	4.3%
Other	26.8

Source: *Investor's Business Daily*, April 29, 1996, p. A6, from WebTrack Information Systems.

★ 1767 ★
Advertising (SIC 7319)

Leading Hospital Advertisers

Data show the top hospital advertisers in 1995, ranked by share of total advertising expenditures.

DuPont Pharma	1.46%
National Electric Information Corp.	1.16
Variable Annuity Life Insurance Co.	1.11
HBO & Company	1.08
Kodak	1.00
Siemens Medical Systems Inc.	0.95
Comphealth	0.93
Coastal Physician Services Inc.	0.89
Landis & Gyr Powers	0.89
IBM	0.85
Other	89.68

Source: *Medical Marketing & Media*, April 1996, p. 78, from HCI Medical Promotion Audit, 1995.

★ 1768 ★
Advertising (SIC 7319)

Leading Internet Advertisers

The firms are ranked by ad placement spending during the first month of 1996.

IBM	$ 460,900
Microsoft	248,200
AT&T	245,700
Netscape	227,400
NYNEX	198,500
MCI	187,300
c/Net	177,800
Internet Shopping Network	172,900
Excite	165,900
Saturn Corp.	158,400

Source: *Internet World*, July 1996, p. 52, from Webtrack.

★ 1769 ★
Advertising (SIC 7319)

Leading Laboratory Advertisers

Companies are ranked by share of total advertising expenditures in 1995.

Behring Diagnostics Inc.	8.43%
Boehringer Mannheim Diagnostics	5.94
DuPont Pharma	3.66
Olympus Coporation	3.44
Sigma Diagnostics	2.49
Becton Dickinson	2.33
Beckman Instruments Inc.	2.30
Johnson & Johnson Clinical Diagnostics	2.04
Bayer Diagnostic Division	1.97
Inova Diagnostics Incorporated	1.89
Other	65.51

Source: *Medical Marketing & Media*, April 1996, p. 80, from HCI Medical Promotion Audit, 1995.

★ 1770 ★
Advertising (SIC 7319)

Leading Medical Product Advertisers

Shares are shown based on total advertising expenditures.

	1994	1995
Glaxo Wellcome	5.01%	5.69%
Merck	0.82	5.20
Wyeth-Ayerst	5.82	5.14
Bayer Pharmaceuticals	3.64	4.37
Marion Merrell Dow	3.45	3.82
Pfizer Laboratories	3.45	3.63
SmithKline Beecham	4.37	3.47
Bristol-Myers Squibb	1.07	3.20
Astra/Merck Group	1.58	2.89
Janssen Pharmaceuticals	2.19	2.86
Upjohn Company	2.63	2.32
Roerig	3.75	2.31
Lederle Laboratories	3.20	2.07
CibaGeigy Corporation	1.33	2.04
Searle Pharmaceuticals	2.86	1.86
Other	54.83	49.13

Source: *Medical Marketing & Media*, March 1996, p. 56, from HCI Medical Promotion Audit (MPA).

★ 1771 ★
Advertising (SIC 7319)

Top 10 Internet Advertisers

Electronic advertisers 4th quarter placement spending is shown for 1995. Netscape had $1.77 million in ad revenues for the same period.

AT&T	$ 567,000
Netscape	556,000
Internet Shopping Network	329,000
NECX Direct	322,000
Mastercard	278,000
American Airlines	254,000
Microsoft	240,000
cinet	237,000
MCI	231,000
SportsLine	218,000

Source: *Sales and Marketing Management*, April 1996, p. 20, from WebTrack Information Services.

★ 1772 ★
Advertising (SIC 7319)

Web Advertising - 1996

Data are in thousands of dollars. Total spending reached $26 million in the first quarter of 1996.

IBM	$ 1,528.3
Microsoft	1,010.9
Netscape	929.0
C/Net	612.3
AT&T	606.7
Nynex	595.8
MCI	558.1
Internet Shopping Network	510.3
Saturn	415.9
Excite	415.3
Adobe Systems	396.1
NECX	390.0
Intel	337.6
Discovery Communications	331.7
Infoseek	313.2

Source: *Informationweek*, August 5, 1996, p. 41, from AdSpend.

★ 1773 ★
Advertising (SIC 7319)

Yellow Pages Advertising Agencies - 1995

The top agencies are ranked by U.S. billings in millions of dollars.

TMP Worldwide	$ 628.0
Berry Network	153.4
Ketchum Advertising	113.2
Foote, Cone & Belding Communications . .	98.6
D'Arcy Masius Benton & Bowles	57.1
Ruppman National Yellow Pages	53.5
Wunderman Cato Johnson	22.1
Bozell Worldwide	17.7
North Castle Partners	17.0
Ogilvy & Mather Direct	14.1

Source: *Advertising Age*, April 15, 1996, p. S33.

★ 1774 ★
Direct Marketing (SIC 7331)

Direct Advertising by Media

Data show the methods of advertising for direct response companies.

Magazines	58.2%
Sunday magazines	25.3
Newspapers	5.5
Syndicated TV	4.0
Cable television	2.2
Spot TV	2.2
Network TV	1.1
Network radio	0.8
National spot radio	0.6
Outdoor	0.2

Source: *Target Marketing*, April 1996, p. 12, from Magazine Publishers of America.

★ 1775 ★
Direct Marketing (SIC 7331)

Top Direct Response Agencies

Firms are ranked by 1995 revenues in thousands of dollars.

DIMAC Direct	$ 126,196
Wunderman Cato Johnson Worldwide . .	101,000
Rapp Collins Worldwide	80,088
Bronner Slosberg Humphrey	67,495

DraftDirect Worldwide	.$ 53,000
Ogilvy & Mather Direct	52,000
Barry Blau & Partners	49,873
Customer Development Corp.	32,543
Grey Direct	27,915
Devon Direct	25,100

Source: *Adweek*, April 15, 1996, p. 72.

★ 1776 ★
Direct Marketing (SIC 7331)

Top Insurance Mail Order Marketers

Firms are ranked by estimated new and renewal premiums in thousands of dollars.

USAA	$ 4,564.0
Prudential-AARP	.3,800.0
GEICO	2,476.0
American Family Ins. Group	2,300.0
American Bankers Insurance Group . . .	1,100.0
Hartford-AARP	1,000.0
CUNA Mutual	805.0
Providian Direct	779.7
20th Century	700.0
J.C. Penney Life Insurance Co.	507.8
Blue Cross	400.0
Physician's Mutual	380.1
AON	329.0
TIAA-CREF	324.2
National General	275.0

Source: *Direct Marketing*, October 1995, p. 15.

★ 1777 ★
Photocopying Services (SIC 7334)

Retail Copy Market

The table estimates Kinko's share of the $6.0 billion retail copy market.

Kinko	30.0%
Other	70.0

Source: *Business Week*, August 19, 1996, p. 58, from Prudential Services Inc.

★ 1778 ★

Janitorial Services (SIC 7349)

Largest Janitorial Services - Silicon Valley

Firms are ranked by number of employees.

ISS Building Maintenace Inc.	865
Pacific Maintenance Co.	750
Acme Building Maintenance Co. Inc.	725
American Building Maintenance	610
Service Performance Corp.	482
Service by Medallion	400
Continental Building Maintenance	196
First Pacific Maintenance Services Corp.	139
California Cleaning Systems	138
Tiger Contract Service Inc.	85

Source: *San Jose and Silicon Valley Business Journal,* February 26, 1996, p. 22.

★ 1779 ★

Leasing (SIC 7350)

Leading U.S. Lessors

Companies are ranked by annual volume of leasing in millions of dollars.

GE Capital	$ 16,800.0
GMAC	10,363.0
AT&T Capital Corp.	4,250.0
IBM Credit	2,800.0
D'Accord Financial	2,500.0
Newcourt Credit Group	2,468.0
Caterpillar Financial	2,183.0
USL Capital	2,145.0
Mercedes Benz Credit	1,876.0
Comdisco	1,582.0

Source: *Asset Finance & Leasing Digest,* April 1995, p. 19, from survey.

★ 1780 ★

Equipment Rental (SIC 7353)

Top Heavy Equipment Renters

The table shows the largest renters of heavy construction equipment, ranked by the value of fleet in millions of dollars.

Hertz Equipment Rental Corp.	$ 450.0
All Erection & Crane Rental	300.0
GE Capital	250.0

Carlisle Construction Co.	$ 200.0
Essex Crane Rental Corp.	200.0
Morrow Equipment Corp.	175.0
Bragg Crane & Rigging Co.	155.0
W.O. Grubb Steel Erection	105.0
Cashman Equipment Corp.	100.0
Laramie Crane & Equipment	85.0

Source: *Construction Equipment,* September 1995, p. 66.

★ 1781 ★

Employee Leasing (SIC 7363)

Top Employee Leasing Lenders

Firms are ranked by number of employees under lease in 1995.

Staff Leasing Co.	70,000
TTC Illinois	24,000
Administaff	20,000
Payroll Transfers Inc.	15,500
Employee Solutions Inc.	12,000
Vincam Human Resources	10,500
Express Personal Services	10,000
Staff Management Systems Inc.	9,800
Staffing Concepts International	7,500
Employers Resource Management	7,500
Altres	7,000

Source: *Investor's Business Daily,* August 16, 1996, p. A4, from Bankers Trust Co.

★ 1782 ★

Temp Agencies (SIC 7363)

Leading Temporary Service Firms

The top six companies in the staffing industry are ranked by revenues in millions of dollars in 1994.

Manpower	$ 4,296.0
Kelly Services	2,363.0
Olsten	2,260.0
CDI	1,098.0
Norrell	681.0
Interim Services	634.0

Source: *Forbes,* September 11, 1995, p. 43, from Robinson-Humphrey Co., Staffing Industry Reports, and company reports.

★ 1783 ★

Temp Agencies (SIC 7363)

Top Temp Agencies - Detroit

Firms are ranked by 1994 revenues in millions of dollars. Shares of the group are shown in percent.

	Rev. ($ mil.)	% of Group
Manpower of Detroit Inc. . . .	$ 85.7	25.6%
Bartech Inc.	57.7	17.2
Kelly Services Inc.	35.4	10.6
Arcadia Services Inc.	35.0	10.5
Entech Personnel Services Inc. .	33.2	9.9
Tech/Aid	29.8	8.9
Acro Service Corp.	15.0	4.5
Hollowell Engineering Inc. . . .	14.8	4.4
Accountemps	14.5	4.3
Software Services Corp.	13.5	4.0

Source: *Crain's Detroit Business*, August 14, 1995, p. 12.

★ 1784 ★

Temp Agencies (SIC 7363)

U.S. Staffing Industry - 1994

Shares are for 1994.

Manpower Inc.	15.0%
Kelly Services	8.0
Olsten Corp.	8.0
Interim Services	2.0
Norrell Corp.	2.0
Robert Half Intl..	2.0
Career Horizons	1.0
Other	62.0

Source: *Investext,* Thomson Financial Services, October 10, 1995, p. 5.

★ 1785 ★

Software (SIC 7372)

3-D Video Capture Tools

The table shows the 3-D and video capture tools used by video game developers. Data are based on a survey.

Autodesk 3D Studio	32.0%
Atlas	20.0
Adobe Premiere	15.0
Wavefront Gameware	12.0
Microsoft Softimage	10.0
Other	11.0

Source: *NewMedia*, October 1995, p. 29, from Computer Games Developers Association and 3Dfx Interactive Inc.

★ 1786 ★

Software (SIC 7372)

Anti-Virus Software

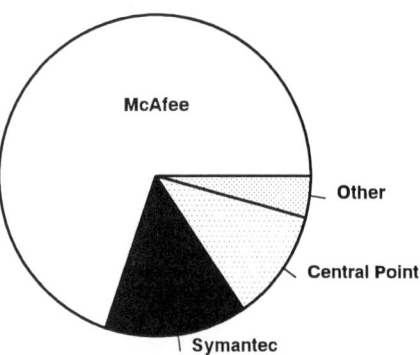

McAfee	67.0%
Symantec	14.0
Central Point	11.0
Other	4.0

Source: *Network Computing*, September 15, 1995, p. 92, from International Data Corp.

★ 1787 ★
Software (SIC 7372)

Backup Software Market

Shares of the backup software market are shown for 1995.

Cheyenne Software Inc. 59.0%
Arcada Software Inc. 18.0
Legato Systems Inc. 9.0
Palindrome Corp. 8.0
Others 6.0

Source: *Infoworld*, January 15, 1996, p. 41, from International Data Corp.

★ 1788 ★
Software (SIC 7372)

Business Intelligence Market

Shares are estimated for 1996.

Business Objects 36.0%
Cognos 22.0
Other 42.0

Source: *Informationweek*, December 4, 1995, p. 56, from Meta Group.

★ 1789 ★
Software (SIC 7372)

CAD Sales

The leaders in the CAD (computer-aided design) software market for Windows/DOS are shown for 1994. Total sales reached $709 million.

Autodesk 56.0%
CADAM Systems 8.0
Integraph/Bentley 8.0
Softdesk 3.0
Soft-Tech 3.0
Others 22.0

Source: *Informationweek*, November 20, 1995, p. 112, from Daratech.

★ 1790 ★
Software (SIC 7372)

CD-ROM Sales by Content

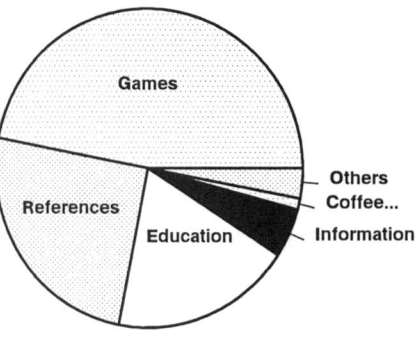

Sales are estimated for 1997.

Games 47.0%
References 25.0
Education 19.0
Information 5.0
Coffee table CD-ROMs 1.0
Others 3.0

Source: *CD-ROM Professional*, June 1995, p. 65, from Dataquest Inc.

★ 1791 ★
Software (SIC 7372)

CD-ROM Sales by Platform

This table shows the percentage of CD-ROM sales by operating system.

Windows 95 . . . . .75.0%
DOS 11.0
Windows 10.0
MAC 3.0
IBM OS/2 . . . . 1.0

Source: *CD-ROM Professional*, April 1996, p. 28, from 1995 SofTrends Report.

★ 1792 ★
Software (SIC 7372)

CD-ROM Titles by Subject - Canada

The table shows the number of CD-ROM and multimedia titles by category in 1993.

General interest 600
Arts & humanities 450
Continued on next page.

★ **1792** ★ *Continued*

Software (SIC 7372)

CD-ROM Titles by Subject - Canada

The table shows the number of CD-ROM and multimedia titles by category in 1993.

Education & training 420
Computers/computer programs 350
Crime/law & legislation 295
Advertising/design & marketing 275
Govt. information/census data 265
Maps/map data & geography 262
Languages & linguistics 260
Medical health & nursing 255

Source: *National Trade Data Bank*, March 2, 1996, p. 111093104, from Hitachi Canada.

★ **1793** ★

Software (SIC 7372)

Database Management Software

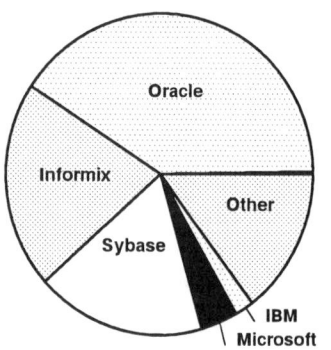

The database management system market for NT and Unix applications reached $1.85 billion in 1995.

Oracle 40.8%
Informix 20.7
Sybase 17.7
Microsoft 3.5
IBM 2.1
Other 15.2

Source: *Informationweek*, April 8, 1996, p. 14, from Gartner Group.

★ **1794** ★

Software (SIC 7372)

Desktop Database Market

Market shares are shown based on 3.1 million units shipped in 1994 and 4.4 million units shipped in 1995. Borland dBase is X-Base compatible.

	1994	1995
Microsoft Access	38.0%	57.0%
Lotus Approach	19.0	15.0
Microsoft FoxPro	12.0	9.0
Borland Paradox	17.0	7.0
Claris Filemaker	4.0	3.0
Borland dBase	4.0	2.0
Others	6.0	7.0

Source: *Informationweek*, February 19, 1996, p. 15, from Computer Intelligence Infocorp.

★ **1795** ★

Software (SIC 7372)

Document Management Software

This table reflects the $160 million document management software market in 1995.

PC Docs 18.0%
Documentum 13.0
Interleaf 12.0
Novell 8.0
Information Dimensions 7.0
Saros 7.0
Other 35.0

Source: *Informationweek*, June 24, 1996, p. 34, from Delphi Consulting Group.

★ **1796** ★

Software (SIC 7372)

ERP Market - 1995

Shares of the $3.8 billion market are shown in percent.

SAP 34.0%
Computer Associates 13.0
SSA 9.0
Bean 7.0
JBA 5.0
J.B. Edwards 5.0
Marcam 5.0
PeopleSoft 3.0

Continued on next page.

★ 1796 ★ *Continued*
Software (SIC 7372)

ERP Market - 1995

Shares of the $3.8 billion market are shown in percent.

QAD	3.0%
Other	11.0

Source: *Software Magazine*, May 1996, p. 70, from AMR.

★ 1797 ★
Software (SIC 7372)

Educational CD-ROM Sales

Units sales are shown by type.

Reading/storybooks	16.5%
Math	14.9
Early learning	9.6
Science	8.4
Creativity	7.8
Multiple educational	6.7
Typing	5.5
Languages	5.0
Geography	3.5
Standardized tests	3.4
Social studies	2.9
Writing/grammar	2.3
Computer training	2.1
Animals	2.0
Spelling	1.3
History	1.1
Music	0.7
Vocabulary	0.7
Sports instruction	0.3
Other	5.5

Source: *CD-ROM Professional*, June 1996, p. 28, from SofTrends.

★ 1798 ★
Software (SIC 7372)

Educational Software Producers

Shares are shown in percent.

Learning Co.	17.9%
Broderbund	5.6
M.E.C.C.	3.9
Softkey	2.8
Other	69.8

Source: *Corporate Growth Weekly Report*, December 18, 1995, p. 1, from PC Data and CompUSA.

★ 1799 ★
Software (SIC 7372)

Financial Software Market

Data are for 1995.

Intuit	81.51%
Block Financial	5.78
Microsoft	2.72
Peachtree	2.52
MECA	1.16
Best Software	1.04
NEBS	0.93
MySoftware	0.67
Market Arts	0.54
Cosmi	0.38
Others	2.75

Source: *Computer Reseller News*, April 1, 1996, p. 25, from PC Data.

★ 1800 ★
Software (SIC 7372)

Game Software Makers

Data are for 1995.

Sierra On-Line	11.6%
LucasArts	7.7
Electronic Arts	7.5
GT Interactive	6.6
Broderbund	5.6
Microsoft	5.3
Other	55.7

Source: *Investor's Business Daily*, March 13, 1996, p. A8, from PC Data.

★ 1801 ★
Software (SIC 7372)

Help Desk Market

Shares of the $210 million internal help desk market are shown for 1995. Applix is a subsidiary of Target Systems. Help desks refer to companies' internal clearinghouses. They provide salespeople or any employees in the field with information or aid.

Remedy Corp.	16.2%
Software Artisting Inc.	9.8
Magic Solutions	5.7
Applix Inc.	5.2
Astea International Inc.	4.6
Vantive Corp.	4.0
Clarify Inc.	2.0
Other	52.5

Source: *Investor's Business Daily*, July 31, 1996, p. A4, from Aberdeen Group.

★ 1802 ★
Software (SIC 7372)

Home Management Software

The market for personal productivity software is shown by category in 1994.

	Rev. ($ mil.)	Share
Word processing	$ 1,030.0	32.0%
Spreadsheets	830.0	25.8
Database	350.0	10.9
Presentation graphics	290.0	9.0
Desktop publishing	200.0	6.2
Personal organizer	150.0	4.7
Personal finance	140.0	4.3
Photo editing	90.0	2.8
Personal tax	80.0	2.5
Other home productivity	60.0	1.9

Source: *Red Herring*, October 1995, p. 54, from Software Publishers Association and PaineWebber.

★ 1803 ★
Software (SIC 7372)

Leading 2-D Video Capture Tools

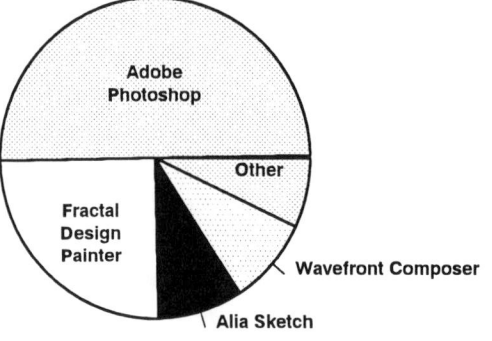

The table shows the 2-D video capture tools used by video game developers. Data are based on a survey.

Adobe Photoshop	50.0%
Fractal Design Painter	25.0
Alia Sketch	9.0
Wavefront Composer	9.0
Other	7.0

Source: *NewMedia*, October 1995, p. 29, from Computer Games Developers Association and 3Dfx Interactive Inc.

★ 1804 ★
Software (SIC 7372)

Leading Software Vendors - 1995

The table shows the top vendors ranked by sales in millions of dollars. Companies were included if they received over 50% of their revenues from software sales.

Microsoft	$ 7,419.0
Oracle	3,777.0
Computer Associates Intl.	3,196.0
Novell	1,986.0
SAP AG	1,887.0
Sybase	957.0
Adobe Systems	762.0
Informix	709.0
American Management Systems	632.0
Sterling Software	610.0
Compuware	580.0
SAS Institute	562.0
Software AG	552.0
Cadence Design Systems	548.0
Autodesk	544.0

Continued on next page.

★ 1804 ★ *Continued*

Software (SIC 7372)

Leading Software Vendors - 1995

The table shows the top vendors ranked by sales in millions of dollars. Companies were included if they received over 50% of their revenues from software sales.

Sunguard Data Systems	$ 533.0
Computervision	507.0
HBO & Co.	496.0
Intuit	490.0
Parametric Technology	441.0

Source: *Economist*, May 25, 1996, p. 4, from Broadview Associates.

★ 1805 ★

Software (SIC 7372)

Library Software by Platform

Data show the number of library automation software packages available by the leading operating systems.

	1994	1996
IBM PC	169	196
Macintosh	30	46
UNIX	24	26
DEC VAX	23	25
IBM mini/mainframe	12	19
HP	5	4

Source: *Computers in Libraries*, February 1996, p. 26.

★ 1806 ★

Software (SIC 7372)

Middleware Market

The market reached $1.0 billion in revenues in 1995.

Data access tools	47.5%
Messaging and transaction tools	46.5
Object request brokers	6.0

Source: *Informationweek*, May 13, 1996, p. 92, from International Data Corp.

★ 1807 ★

Software (SIC 7372)

Middleware Vendors

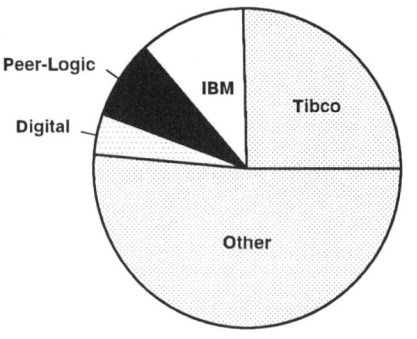

Message-oriented middleware vendors are ranked by 1995 revenues in millions of dollars.

	Rev. ($ mil.)	Share
Tibco	$ 29.0	25.4%
IBM	13.0	11.4
Peer-Logic	8.6	7.5
Digital	5.0	4.4
Other	58.4	51.2

Source: *Computerworld*, June 10, 1996, p. 61, from International Data Corp.

★ 1808 ★

Software (SIC 7372)

Net Browser Market

Shares are shown as of November 1995.

Netscape	79.0%
Microsoft	4.0
Mosaic	3.0
Other	14.0

Source: *Fortune*, January 15, 1996, p. 16, from Interse Corp.

★ 1809 ★
Software (SIC 7372)
Object Middleware Market

The market reached $42 million in 1995. Data are estimated.

Digital 33.0%
Iowa Technologies 25.0
IBM 17.0
Expersoft 14.0
PostModern Computing Technologies . . . 6.0
Hewlett-Packard 3.0
ICL 3.0

Source: *Computerworld*, April 22, 1996, p. 48, from Standish Group International Inc.

★ 1810 ★
Software (SIC 7372)
Office Suite Leaders - 1995

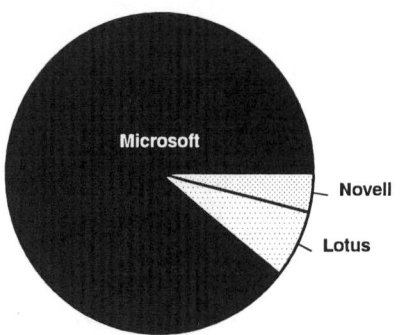

The market reached $3.02 billion.

Microsoft 89.0%
Lotus 7.0
Novell 4.0

Source: *Electronic Business Today*, April 1996, p. 26.

★ 1811 ★
Software (SIC 7372)
Operating Systems Market

Data are for 1996.

DOS 52.0%
Windows NT 37.0
UNIX 7.0
Other 16.0

Source: *Byte*, May 1996, p. 52, from Dataquest Inc.

★ 1812 ★
Software (SIC 7372)
Page-Layout Software Market

The most popular software used by designers.

QuarkXPress 88.6%
Adobe PageMaker 13.0
Ventura Publisher 2.4

Source: *Folio*, October 15, 1995, p. 56.

★ 1813 ★
Software (SIC 7372)
Presentation Graphics Software

Presentation graphics software brands for Windows are shown ranked by share of the market.

Lotus Freelance 29.8%
Harvard Graphics 29.2
Microsoft PowerPoint 26.6
WordPerfect Presentations 6.4
DeltaPoint DeltaGraph 2.3
Adobe Persuasion 2.0
Others 3.7

Source: *Nation's Business*, September 1995, p. 46, from International Data Corp.

★ 1814 ★
Software (SIC 7372)
Reference Software Makers

Microsoft 35.4%
Pro CD 16.2
SoftKey 14.7
American Business Information 7.4
Grolier 6.4
Digital Directory Assistance 4.9
Other 15.0

Source: *Investor's Business Daily*, March 13, 1996, p. A8, from PC Data.

★ 1815 ★
Software (SIC 7372)

Remote-Control Software

Vendor shares shown are based on 1995 remote-control software shipments.

Triton	55.7%
Symantec	9.9
Traveling Software	9.5
Farallon	8.3
Stac	6.5
Other	10.1

Source: *PC Week*, March 4, 1996, p. 33, from International Data Corp.

★ 1816 ★
Software (SIC 7372)

Resource Planning Producers

The table shows who supplied enterprise resource planning packages to North American automakers in 1995. Total sales reached $310 million.

SAP	22.0%
System Software Associates	21.0
Baan	10.0
Qad	8.0
Computer Associates	7.0
Oracle	7.0
JBA International	7.0
Others	18.0

Source: *Informationweek*, April 1, 1996, p. 16, from Martin Piszczalski & Co.

★ 1817 ★
Software (SIC 7372)

Support Software Market

Support software aids service professionals in dealing with customer problems. Brand shares are shown for 1994.

Astea	8.5%
Remedy	7.7
Inference	6.9
Software Artistry	5.4
Brock	4.2
Clarify	4.2
Magic	4.2
Scopus	4.2
Answer System	3.9

Vantive	3.9%
Bendata	3.5
AnswerSet	3.1
Target Systems	2.7
Quintus	1.9
Soft AD Group	1.5
Other	32.8

Source: *Software Magazine*, November 1995, p. 87, from Aberdeen Group.

★ 1818 ★
Software (SIC 7372)

Tax Preparation Software

Shares are estimated in percent. Producers include Intuit Inc., Block Financial Corp., Parsons Technology, and 4Home Production.

Turbo Tax & MacInTax	79.7%
Kiplinger TaxCut	19.2
Personal Tax Edge	1.0
Simply Tax	0.2

Source: *Kansas City Star*, February 4, 1996, p. F8, from PC Data.

★ 1819 ★
Software (SIC 7372)

Top IOS Software Vendors

Data are for 1994. IOS stands for Internetwork Operating System.

Cisco Systems	76.5%
Bay Networks	9.1
Digital Equipment	3.5
Ascom Timeplex	2.4
Proteon	1.6
Other	6.9

Source: *LAN Times*, September 11, 1995, p. 7.

★ 1820 ★
Software (SIC 7372)

Top Selling CD-ROMs by Type

Data are based on dollar sales.

Adventure/role playing/interactive drama	27.0%
Arcade/action games	17.0
Flight/war simulation games	15.0
Sports games	14.0

Continued on next page.

★ 1820 ★ *Continued*
Software (SIC 7372)

Top Selling CD-ROMs by Type

Data are based on dollar sales.

Strategy games	10.0%
Card/casino games	4.0
Multiple games	3.0
Board games	2.0
Puzzle games	1.0
Other simulation games	5.0
Other games	2.0

Source: *CD-ROM Professional*, May 1996, p. 34, from SofTrends.

★ 1821 ★
Software (SIC 7372)

Top Software Companies

The top independent software companies are ranked by 1995 revenues in millions of dollars. Shares of the group are shown in percent.

	Rev. ($ mil.)	% of Group
Microsoft	$ 7,419.0	51.4%
Novell	1,901.5	13.2
Adobe Systems	762.3	5.3
Autodesk	534.2	3.7
Intuit	502.6	3.5
Symantec	437.8	3.0
Attachmate	415.0	2.9
Softkey International	254.7	1.8
Borland International	207.8	1.4
GT Interactive Software	204.1	1.4
Santa Cruz Operation	199.3	1.4
Broderbund Software	189.5	1.3
Cheyenne Software	157.6	1.1
Davidson & Associates	147.2	1.0
Sierra On-Line	144.8	1.0
FTP Software	136.4	0.9
NetManage	125.4	0.9
Walker Richer & Quinn	111.6	0.8
Wall Data	110.7	0.8
Interplay Productions	99.6	0.7
Bentley Systems	96.9	0.7
Quarterdeck	95.0	0.7
McAfee Associates	90.1	0.6
Netscape Communications	80.7	0.6

Source: *Computer Reseller News*, May 13, 1996, p. 19, from *Softletter*.

★ 1822 ★
Software (SIC 7372)

Trip Planning Software

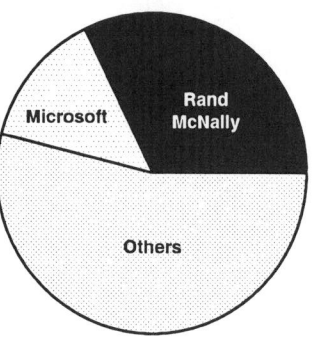

The top producers of trip planning software are shown in percent for 1995. Rand McNally produces TripMaker; Microsoft produces Automap.

Rand McNally	32.0%
Microsoft	14.0
Others	54.0

Source: *Forbes*, September 11, 1995, p. 86.

★ 1823 ★
Software (SIC 7372)

UNIX Market - 1995

UNIX market shares are shown in percent based on 1.4 million server and client licenses.

Solaris	22.9%
HP-UX	15.7
SCO Unix	14.0
AIX	8.4
Other Unix	39.0

Source: *Network World*, February 12, 1996, p. 12, from International Data Corp.

★ 1824 ★
Software (SIC 7372)

Web Browser Market

Market shares are shown in percent.

Netscape Navigator	85.0%
Microsoft Internet Explorer	7.5
Other	7.5

Source: *Newsweek*, April 29, 1996, p. 48, from Dataquest Inc. and company reports.

★ 1825 ★
Software (SIC 7372)

Web Server Software

Data are for the month of June 1996.

Apache	31.35%
NCSA	24.96
Netscape's Server line	16.09
CERN	7.79
WebSite	4.47
Microsoft Internet Information Server	2.55
Other	12.79

Source: *Web Week*, May 20, 1996, p. 33, from Webcraft.

★ 1826 ★
Software (SIC 7372)

Windows Office Suites

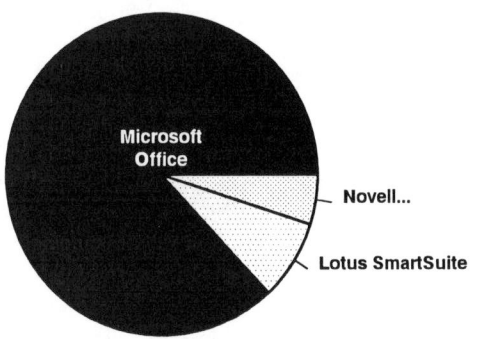

The office suite market for Windows and Windows 95 reached an estimated $2.94 billion.

Microsoft Office	86.8%
Lotus SmartSuite	8.1
Novell PerfectOffice	5.1

Source: *PC Week*, February 12, 1996, p. 29, from International Data Corp.

★ 1827 ★
Software (SIC 7372)

Word Processing Shipments - 1995

Shipments of standalone word processors reached 1.77 million units in 1995.

WordPerfect	53.0%
MS Word	35.0
WordPro	10.0
Other	2.0

Source: *Byte*, June 1996, p. 53, from Computer Intelligence InfoCorp.

★ 1828 ★
Integrated Systems (SIC 7373)

Airline Reservation Systems

Shares are shown based on installations at travel agencies across the United States.

Sabre	36.0%
Apollo	25.0
Worldspan	20.0
System One	19.0

Source: *USA TODAY*, April 10, 1996, p. B1, from AMR and Travel Distribution Board.

★ 1829 ★
Integrated Systems (SIC 7373)

Computer Systems in Body Shops

Data show the types of computer systems used in auto body repair shops.

Computerized damage estimation system	46.1%
Business management system	36.3
CD-ROM service information	26.5
Other	10.8

Source: *Automotive Body Repair News*, January 1996, p. 1.

★ 1830 ★
Integrated Systems (SIC 7373)

Healthcare Information Systems Market

The table shows the share of the market represented by the top three companies in 1994.

HBOC/Meditech/SMS 73.0%
Others 27.0

Source: *Healthcare Informatics*, May 1996, p. 24, from Charles J. Singer & Co.

★ 1831 ★
Integrated Systems (SIC 7373)

Top Systems Integrators

Companies are ranked by 1995 sales in billions of dollars.

IBM Global Services . . . . $ 12.7
EDS 5.8
Digital MCS Unit 3.7
Computer Sciences 3.7
Andersen Consulting 3.5
GTE 2.7
Unisys 2.4
SAIC 2.1
Entex 1.8
Vanstar 1.7

Source: *Computer Reseller News*, June 3, 1996, p. 112, from industry analysts and company reports.

★ 1832 ★
Integrated Systems (SIC 7373)

Top Systems Integrators - North America

Firms are ranked by systems integration revenues in millions of dollars.

Electronic Data Systems Corp. . . . . . $ 7,370.0
IBM Corp. 6,000.0
Computer Sciences Corp. 2,272.0
Andersen Consulting 1,678.0
AT&T Corp. 1,050.0
Digital Equipment Corp. 1,000.0
Hewlett-Packard Co. 903.0
Shared Medical Systems Corp. 434.7
Ernst & Young 410.0
American Management Systems, Inc. . . . 374.1

Price Waterhouse . . . . $ 357.0
Unisys Corp. 302.4
SHL Systemhouse Inc. 264.0
KPMG Peat Marwick 249.3
Deloitte & Touche 233.0

Source: *Computerworld*, February 26, 1996, p. SI/19, from ParaTechnology, Inc.

★ 1833 ★
Networks (SIC 7373)

Client/Server Licenses - 1995

Percentages are shown based on 880,000 client/ server tool licenses sold in 1995.

Microsoft Visual Basic 62.0%
Borland Delphi 16.0
Powersoft PowerBuilder 6.0
Centura SQL Windows 5.0
Other 11.0

Source: *Informationweek*, May 6, 1996, p. 30, from International Data Corp.

★ 1834 ★
Networks (SIC 7373)

Client/Server Suite Leaders

Shares of the integrated client/server suite market are estimated for 1995.

SAP 67.0%
Oracle 18.0
PeopleSoft 8.0
Baan 7.0

Source: *PC Week*, April 8, 1996, p. 22, from Oracle Corp.

★ 1835 ★
Networks (SIC 7373)

Client/Server Vendors

The leading vendors are ranked by annual application revenues in millions of dollars. Shares of the group are shown in percent.

	Rev. ($ mil.)	% of Group
SAP	$ 1,000	48.7%
Dun & Bradstreet Software . . .	350	17.0
Oracle	154	7.5

Continued on next page.

★ 1835 ★ *Continued*

Networks (SIC 7373)

Client/Server Vendors

The leading vendors are ranked by annual application revenues in millions of dollars. Shares of the group are shown in percent.

	Rev. ($ mil.)	% of Group
Hyperion Software	$ 137	6.7%
Baan	123	6.0
People Soft	113	5.5
Lawson Software	75	3.6
Platinum Software	60	2.9
Great Plains	43	2.1

Source: *Computerworld*, November 6, 1995, p. 52, from company reports.

★ 1836 ★

Networks (SIC 7373)

EDI VAN Makers

Shares are for 1994. VAN stands for value-added networks.

General Electric Information Services . . .	31.0%
Sterling Software	19.0
Advantis (IBM/Sears Joint Venture)	15.0
Kleinschmidt	7.0
RAILINC	5.0
Harbinger	3.0
AT&T	1.0
Others	19.0

Source: *Investext*, Thomson Financial Services, February 14, 1996, p. 8, from company reports.

★ 1837 ★

Networks (SIC 7373)

Embedded Database Market

Btrieve	70.0%
Other	30.0

Source: *PC Week*, May 6, 1996, p. 10, from Business Research Group.

★ 1838 ★

Networks (SIC 7373)

Enterprise Platform Market

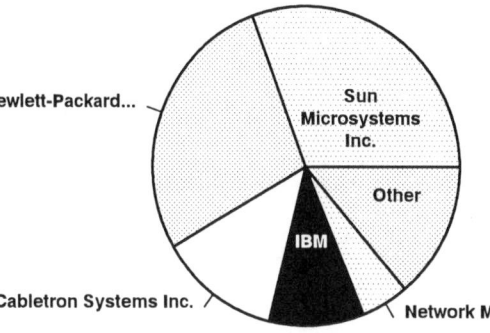

Shares are shown based on shipments of 21,196 units in 1994.

Sun Microsystems Inc.	30.7%
Hewlett-Packard Co.	27.8
Cabletron Systems Inc.	13.2
IBM	9.7
Network Managers Inc.	4.5
Other	14.1

Source: *InfoWorld*, October 23, 1995, p. 16, from International Data Corp.

★ 1839 ★

Networks (SIC 7373)

HIS Vendors

Firms are ranked by 1995 revenues in milllions of dollars. HIS stands for Healthcare Information Systems.

Shared Medical Systems	$ 650.6
HBO & Company	495.6
Medaphis Corp.	467.7
SAIC	275.0
PCS Health Systems Inc.	255.0
Cerner Corp.	186.9
Lanier Healthcare	150.0
Meditech	143.7
Medic Computer Systems Inc.	143.0

Source: *Healthcare Informatics*, June 1996, p. S6.

★ 1840 ★
Networks (SIC 7373)
Internetwork Hardware Vendors

Vendors are ranked by 1995 sales in millions of dollars.

Bay Networks	$ 1,300
3COM/Chipcom	972
Cabletron Systems	926
Digital	465
Cisco Systems	407
UB Networks	302
HP	277
IBM	176
Optical Data Systems	97
D-Link	94

Source: *Computer Reseller News*, June 3, 1996, p. 116, from industry analysts and company reports.

★ 1841 ★
Networks (SIC 7373)
LAN Operating System Shares

Shares are shown for 1995 based on node shipments.

NetWare 4x	62.8%
NT server	15.7
IBM Lan server	7.4
Banyan	4.1
Artisoft	2.7
Other	7.3

Source: *Computer Reseller News*, April 29, 1996, p. 89, from International Data Corp.

★ 1842 ★
Networks (SIC 7373)
Network Management Platform Market

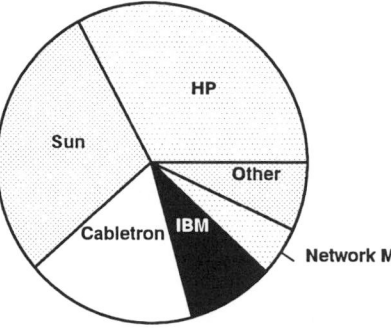

Company shares are shown as percentage of the 34.079 billion units shipped in 1995.

HP	32.9%
Sun	29.3
Cabletron	17.6
IBM	8.5
Network Managers (Microsoft)	4.8
Other	6.9

Source: *PC Week*, February 26, 1996, p. 39, from International Data Corp.

★ 1843 ★
Networks (SIC 7373)
Network Operating Systems

Data are for the first six months of 1995.

NetWare	63.0%
Windows NT	13.0
IBM LAN server	8.0
Banyan Vines	5.0
Other	9.0

Source: *Computer Reseller News*, April 8, 1996, p. 77, from International Data Corp.

★ 1844 ★
Networks (SIC 7373)
PC Server Market

Data are for 1995.

Compaq	46.6%
IBM	18.8

Continued on next page.

★ 1844 ★ *Continued*
Networks (SIC 7373)

PC Server Market

Data are for 1995.

Digital Equipment	8.5%
Dell	7.6
Hewlett-Packard	6.6
Apple	3.9
AST Research	1.6
Zenith Data Systems	1.1
Acer	1.1
AT&T GIS	1.0
Advanced Logic Research	0.9
Unisys	0.8
Everex Systems	0.4
CompuAdd	0.3
Sun Microsystems	0.2
Other	0.6

Source: *Computer Reseller News*, March 25, 1996, p. 21, from Computer Intelligence Corp.

★ 1845 ★
Networks (SIC 7373)

PC X Server Market

PC X server market shares are shown for 1993 and 1994. In the 1993 data shown, WRQ's figure is included under other.

	1993	1994
Hummingbird	32.0%	37.0%
NCD	17.0	18.0
Visionware	16.0	13.0
AGE Logic	8.0	9.0
WRQ	-	9.0
DEC	7.0	5.0
Apple	4.0	2.0
Other	16.0	7.0

Source: *Investor's Business Daily*, November 3, 1995, p. A6, from Zona Research.

★ 1846 ★
Networks (SIC 7373)

PC-to-Host Communications Market

Shares of the VAX-based PC-to-host communications market are shown in percent.

WRQ	31.2%
Attachmate	16.0
White Pine	14.6
Persoft	10.2
Other	28.0

Source: *DEC Professional*, August 1995, p. 19, from International Data Corp.

★ 1847 ★
Networks (SIC 7373)

SNA Network Leaders

Shares are shown based on 140,740 units sold in 1995.

Novell	30.9%
IBM	21.7
Microsoft	10.9
Attachmate	10.4
Eicon Tech	9.1
Other	17.0

Source: *Informationweek*, February 12, 1996, p. 71, from International Data Corp.

★ 1848 ★
Networks (SIC 7373)

Server Market

Shares are shown based on 1.9 billion units sold in 1995. "Other Unix" includes NextStep and UnixWare.

Netware	43.0%
Windows NT	19.0
All Unix	24.0
SCO Unix	8.0
HP-UX	3.0
IBM AIX	3.0
Sun Solaris	2.0
Other Unix	8.0
Other	14.0

Source: *Informationweek*, February 12, 1996, p. 30, from International Data Corp.

★ 1849 ★

Networks (SIC 7373)

Server Market - 1995

NetWare	42.1%
UNIX	24.8
Windows NT	18.7
OS/2	14.4

Source: *Datamation*, April 1, 1996, p. 57, from International Data Corp.

★ 1850 ★

Networks (SIC 7373)

Switched Token Ring Ports

Shares are shown based on total shipments of 9,600 units during the third quarter of 1995.

Madge Networks	49.6%
Bay Networks	22.8
Nashoba Networks	13.8
Xylan	11.3
Standard Microsystems (SMC)	2.5

Source: *Computerworld*, February 5, 1996, p. 14, from Dell'Oro Group.

★ 1851 ★

Networks (SIC 7373)

UNIX Server - 1994 Shipments

Percentages reflect the 513,000 UNIX servers shipped in 1994.

SCO Unix	34.0%
AIX	9.0
Solaris	9.0
HP-UX	7.0
UnixWare	5.0
NextStep	1.0
Other	35.0

Source: *Informationweek*, September 11, 1995, p. 78, from International Data Corp.

★ 1852 ★

Networks (SIC 7373)

Wireless LAN Market

AT&T GIS	28.0%
Motorola	22.0

Microwave Bypass	10.0%
InfraLAN/BICC	7.0
Telesystems SLW	5.0
AiroNet/Telxon	4.0
California Microwave	4.0
Proxim	4.0
Other	16.0

Source: *Telecommunications*, March 1996, p. 56, from Business Research Group.

★ 1853 ★

Information Technology (SIC 7375)

Consumer Internet Subscriptions

Subscriptions are shown in thousands of members.

NetCom	410
AT&T WorldNet	155
Global Network Navigator	140
PSINet	112
SpryNet	105
IDT	20

Source: *Wall Street Journal*, May 23, 1996, p. B4, from International Data Corp./ LINK.

★ 1854 ★

Information Technology (SIC 7375)

Imaging Market

The top imaging and workflow vendors are ranked by 1995 revenues in millions of dollars. Shares are shown based on a $3.0 billion industry.

	($ mil.)	Share
FileNet	$ 140.0	4.7%
IBM	50.0	1.7
ViewStar	23.0	0.8
Recognition	22.0	0.7
Optika	16.0	0.5
Wang	12.0	0.4
Sigma	10.0	0.3
Keyfile	8.0	0.3
Watermark	7.0	0.2
Westbrook	6.0	0.2
Other	2,706	90.2

Source: *Informationweek*, August 14, 1995, p. 71, from Rheinner Group.

★ 1855 ★
Information Technology (SIC 7375)

Information Services Market in Mexico

The information services market has a 31% share of the computer equipment and services market. The market is shown by end user. Financial companies use the services for communications and database management. "Other" includes schools, general public, and commercial companies.

Financial companies	37.0%
Petroleos Mexicanos (PEMEX)	17.0
Government agencies	13.0
Manufacturing	11.0
Retailers	9.0
Telecommunications	7.0
Other	5.0

Source: *National Trade Data Bank*, January 1, 1996, p. IS9509.643.

★ 1856 ★
Information Technology (SIC 7375)

Internet Service Providers

Internet service companies are ranked by revenues in millions of dollars for 1996.

MCI	$ 97.02
UUnet Technologies	96.50
Netcom	96.40
AT&T	90.72
PSInet	68.38

Source: *Computerworld*, May 20, 1996, p. 68, from Maloff Co.

★ 1857 ★
Information Technology (SIC 7375)

Net Use by Age

25-34	12.2%
35-44	23.5
45-54	35.7
55-64	22.4
65+	6.2

Source: *Today's Realtor*, June 1996, p. 22.

★ 1858 ★
Information Technology (SIC 7375)

On-Line Purchases

This table shows the percentage of Internet users who have purchased each item on-line.

Software	50.0%
Publications	26.0
Computer hardware	24.0
Entertainment	24.0
On-line information	21.0
Travel	16.0
Flowers	12.0
Clothes	11.0
Food	7.0
Home appliances	6.0
Event tickets	4.0
Jewelry	1.0
Other	11.0

Source: *St. Louis Post-Dispatch*, March 4, 1995, p. 11BP, from MasterCard.

★ 1859 ★
Information Technology (SIC 7375)

On-Line Service Providers

Commercial services are ranked by millions of subscribers.

America Online	4.0
CompuServe	3.7
Prodigy	2.2
Microsoft Network	0.2

Source: *U.S. News & World Report*, November 20, 1995, p. 104.

★ 1860 ★
Information Technology (SIC 7375)

On-line Market

Total on-line service subscribers are expected to grow from 7.2 million in 1995 to 9.5 million in 1996 to 10.0 million in 1997.

	1995	1996	1997
America Online	30.6%	28.4%	28.0%
CompuServe	30.6	25.3	25.0
Microsoft	9.7	22.1	24.0
Prodigy	19.4	15.8	15.0
Others	9.7	8.4	8.0

Source: *Inc. Technology*, no. 2, 1995, p. 16, from Forrester Research.

★ 1861 ★
Information Technology (SIC 7375)

On-line Service Shares

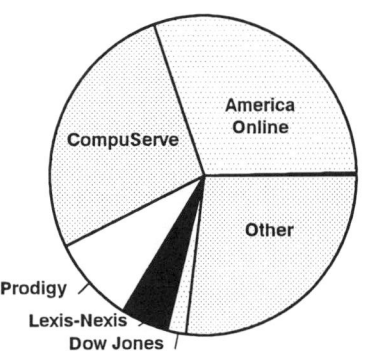

Services are ranked by 1995 subscribers.

	(000)	Share
America Online	4,500	30.2%
CompuServe	4,000	26.9
Prodigy	1,400	9.4
Lexis-Nexis	744	5.0
Dow Jones	233	1.6
Other	4,000	26.9

Source: *Computerworld*, March 25, 1996, p. 73, from Simba Information Inc.

★ 1862 ★
Information Technology (SIC 7375)

On-line Services Market

Shares of the market are shown in percent.

America Online	28.0%
CompuServe	25.0
Prodigy	20.0
Other	27.0

Source: *Computer*, January 1996, p. 12.

★ 1863 ★
Information Technology (SIC 7375)

Top I.T. Companies - Canada

Information technology (I.T.) companies are ranked by 1993 and 1994 revenues in millions of dollars.

	1993	1994
IBM Canada Ltd.	$ 6,700.0	$ 8,449.0
Northern Telecom Canada Ltd.	4,022.0	4,751.0
Digital Equipment of Canada Ltd.	1,213.0	1,563.0
SHL Systemhouse Inc.	546.0	647.0
Hewlett-Packard (Canada) Ltd.	496.0	603.0

Source: *Computing Canada*, August 16, 1995, p. 1, from International Data Corp. Canada.

★ 1864 ★
Information Technology (SIC 7375)

Web Server Market by Platform

Market is shown by operating system.

Sun	20.0%
Macintosh	17.0
Unix	16.0
Windows	10.0
Windows NT	5.0
Hewlett-Packard	4.0
Other	18.0

Source: *Investor's Business Daily*, April 22, 1996, p. A6, from Laidlaw Equities Inc. and Morgan Stanley.

★ 1865 ★
Computer Consulting (SIC 7379)

Computer Consulting - Tri-State Area

*Computer consulting firms shown do business in
Indiana, Ohio, and Kentucky and are ranked by tri-
state revenues in millions of dollars.*

Origin Technology in Business Inc.	$ 15.0
Computer Horizons Corp.	14.0
Keane Inc.	13.5
Cap Gemini America	13.0
CTG (Computer Task Group)	6.0
Shared Resources Inc.	2.6
Client Server Associates	2.5
LDA Systems Inc.	2.5
ComputerPeople Consulting Services	2.0
Whittman-Hart LP	2.0

Source: *Cincinnati Business Courier*, January 28, 1996, p.
30, from companies.

★ 1866 ★
Photofinishing (SIC 7384)

Photofinishing Services by Outlet

*Shares of the photofinishing market are shown in
percent for 1993 and 1994.*

	1993	1994
Discount/mass merchant	25.5%	28.3%
Drug store	26.5	26.4
Stand-alone minilab	15.0	13.8
Supermarket	14.1	13.4
Mail order	7.7	7.7
Camera store	8.1	7.3
Other	3.2	3.1

Source: *DM*, September 1995, p. 30, from
Photomarketing Association International.

★ 1867 ★
Business Services (SIC 7389)

Information Services by Industry

*Data show the types of clients for information
technology service firms.*

Financial services	36.0%
Telecommunications	19.4
Manufacturing	13.7
Health care	9.7
Utilities & agencies	8.0
Consumer product	6.3
Other	6.9

Source: *Computer Reseller News*, May 20, 1996, p. 43,
from Updata Group Inc.

★ 1868 ★
Business Services (SIC 7389)

Interior Designers - Retail

*The retail interior design firms are ranked by 1995
revenues in millions of dollars.*

Pavlik Design Team	$ 21.0
Frch Design Worldwide	16.3
Callison Architecture Inc.	16.0
Retail Planning Associates, L.P.	12.2
Walkergroup/CNI	8.2
Schafer Associates, Inc.	6.7
Design Forum	6.4
Jon Greenberg & Assoc. Inc.	6.0
Bergmeyer Associates. Inc.	5.5
Fitzpatrick Design Group Inc.	4.8
NBBJ Architects-Retail Concepts	4.2
Gensler	4.0

Source: *VM&SD*, February 1996, p. 78.

★ 1869 ★
Business Services (SIC 7389)

Meeting Facilities

*Meeting and banquet facilities are shown for the
Cincinnati area ranked by square feet.*

Dr. Albert B. Sabin Cincinnati Convention Center	88,000
Museum Center at Union Terminal	48,400
Omni Netherland Piaza	45,176
Drawbridge Estate	42,000
Westin Hotel Cincinnati	31,000
Children's Museum of Cincinnati	30,000

Continued on next page.

★ 1869 ★ *Continued*
Business Services (SIC 7389)

Meeting Facilities

Meeting and banquet facilities are shown for the Cincinnati area ranked by square feet.

Sharonville Convention Center 28,000
Receptions Conference and Convention
  Center 25,000
Regal Cincinnati Hotel 25,000
Shriners Oasis Conference & Banquet
  Center 21,178

Source: *Cincinnati Business Courier*, February 18, 1996, p. 16.

★ 1870 ★
Conventions (SIC 7389)

Computer Convention Market

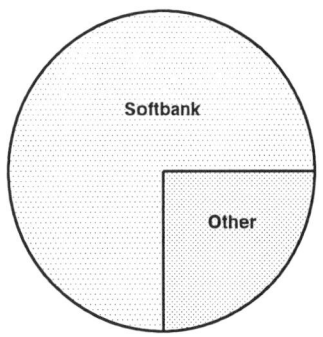

The market for computer trade show organizing is shown by company.

Softbank 75.0%
Other 25.0

Source: *Business Week*, August 12, 1996, p. 56.

★ 1871 ★
Conventions (SIC 7389)

Convention Market - 1994

The table shows who received the $82.81 billion in revenues generated by the U.S. convention business.

Hotels/meeting places 32.5%
Airlines 23.3
Restaurants 12.1
Ground transportation 8.6
Retail trade 6.7

Business services 6.6%
Entertainment 4.9
Equipment rental 0.6
Advertising 0.6
Other 4.1

Source: *The Baltimore Sun*, August 18, 1996, p. E2, from Convention Liason Center.

★ 1872 ★
Conventions (SIC 7389)

Top Trade Show Sites

Cities are ranked by number of shows booked in 1995.

Chicago 208
Atlanta 207
Montreal 184
New York City 173
Las Vegas 163
Dallas 144
San Francisco 143
Orlando 124
Toronto 124
Boston 116

Source: *Air Conditioning, Heating & Refrigeration News*, February 5, 1996, p. 10, from *Tradeshow Week*.

★ 1873 ★
Mergers & Acquisitions (SIC 7389)

Biggest Deals - 1995

The top deals are ranked by value in billions of dollars. Acquirers are shown in parentheses.

EDS shareholders (Electronic Data
  Systems) . . . . $ 21.00
Walt Disney (Capital Cities/ABC) 18.83
ITT shareholders (ITT) 11.60
First Bank System (First Interstate) 10.05
Chemical Banking (Chase Manhattan) . . . 9.87
Hoechst (Marion Merrell Dow) 7.12
Time Warner (Turner Broadcasting) . . . 6.88
Kimberly Clark (Scott Paper) 6.79
Pharmacia (Upjohn) 6.32
First Data (First Financial Management) . . 5.76

Source: *Wall Street Journal*, January 2, 1996, p. R8, from Securities Data Co.

★ 1874 ★
Mergers & Acquisitions (SIC 7389)

Largest U.S. Banking Deals

The largest mergers and acquisitions announced in the last year are shown based on value of the transaction. Acquirers are shown in parentheses. Figures are in millions of dollars.

First Interstate Bancorp (Wells Fargo) .	$ 11,600.0
Chase Manhattan (Chemical Banking) . .	9,866.0
First Fidelity Bancorp (First Union) . . .	5,555.0
First Chicago (NBD Bancorp)	5,136.0
Security Pacific (BankAmerica)	4,667.0
C&S Sovran (NCNB Corp)	4,457.0
Society (Keycorp)	4,040.0
Shawmut Natl (Fleet Financial Group) . .	3,646.0
NatWest USA (Fleet Financial Group) .	3,260.0
Meridian Bancorp (Core States Financial)	3,200.0

Source: *New York Times*, January 25, 1996, p. C1, from Keefe, Bruyette & Woods.

★ 1875 ★
Mergers & Acquisitions (SIC 7389)

Leading Chemical Deal Advisers

The leading advisers on mergers and acquisitions (M&A) in the chemicals industry are ranked by value of deals. Data are in millions of dollars for the last six months of 1995.

Lehman Brothers	$ 3,410.0
Merrill Lynch	2,610.0
CS First Boston	2,585.0
J.P. Morgan	1,990.0
Chase Manhattan	1,315.0
Donaldson, Lufkin & Jenrette	980.0
KPMG Peat Marwick	315.0
Rothschild	205.0
PaineWebber	100.0
Price Waterhouse	90.0

Source: *Chemicalweek*, March 6, 1996, p. 26, from Securities Data.

★ 1876 ★
Mergers & Acquisitions (SIC 7389)

Top Dealers in Bank Branches

This table shows the top advisors in bank branch sales in 1995. Figures are in millions of dollars.

J.P. Morgan	$ 8,138.6
CS First Boston	8,138.6
Berwind Financial Group	1,021.3
Montgomery Securities	961.0
Friedman, Billings & Ramsey	820.0
Smith Barney	739.0
Hovde Financial	635.8
M.A. Schapiro	390.0
Baxter Fentriss	348.0
McDonald & Co.	255.2

Source: *USBanker*, January 1996, p. 37.

★ 1877 ★
Mergers & Acquisitions (SIC 7389)

Top M&A Advisors

Data show M&A (mergers & acquisitions) advisors ranked by 1995 announced deals in millions of dollars.

Goldman Sachs	$ 45,438.1
Morgan Stanley	31,347.0
Merrill Lynch	16,566.4
Smith Barney	12,776.0
Lazard Freres & Co.	12,414.0
James D. Wolfensohn	11,500.0
CS First Boston	9,390.6
Salomon Brothers	7,385.7
Montgomery Securities	6,699.6
Keefe, Bruyette & Woods	6,340.0

Source: *USBanker*, March 1996, p. 44.

★ 1878 ★
Mergers & Acquisitions (SIC 7389)

Top M&A Industries - 1995

Distribution is shown based on $306.39 billion in mergers & acquisitions in 1995.

Banking & finance	21.4%
Broadcasting	14.6
Computer, software, supplies, services	14.1
Drugs, medical supplies and equipment	6.8
Insurance	4.3
Other	38.3

Source: *Business Marketing*, December 1995, p. 1, from Houlihan Lokey.

★ 1879 ★
Mergers & Acquisitions (SIC 7389)

Top Oil & Gas Advisors

Shares are shown for 1990-95 based on a total value of $62.097 billion in transactions. A total of 1,908 deals were conducted during this period, with full credit given to target and acquiror advisors.

Goldman Sachs	16.7%
Morgan Stanley	13.7
CS First Boston/Credit Suisse	10.3
Lehman Brothers	8.1
Salomon Brothers	7.4
Smith Barney	5.1
Merrill Lynch	4.6
Donaldson, Lufkin & Jenrette	4.4
Dillon, Read	3.7
Petrie Parkman	3.6
PaineWebber	3.2
Schroder Wagg	3.0
Simmons & Company	2.0
Bankers Trust	1.8
Wasserstein, Perella	1.7
Other	10.7

Source: *Petroleum Economist*, December 1995, p. 15, from Securities Data Co.

★ 1880 ★
Mergers & Acquisitions (SIC 7389)

Top Systems Sales - 1995

The top systems sales are shown ranked by value of transaction in millions of dollars. Acquirers are shown in parentheses.

Scripps (Comcast)	$ 1,575.0
Colony Communications & King Holding (Continental)	1,547.0
Chronicle Publishing (TCI)	654.0
Columbia International (TCI/Jones)	378.0
Gaylord Broadcasting (Charter Communications)	360.0
Summit Communications (Time Warner Inc.)	337.0

Source: *Broadcasting & Cable*, March 11, 1996, p. 42.

★ 1881 ★
Mergers & Acquisitions (SIC 7389)

Top U.S. Advisers

Firms are ranked by value of deals in the first six months of 1995. Data are in millions of dollars.

Morgan Stanley & Co.	$ 37,884.2
Goldman, Sachs & Co.	37,617.5
CS First Boston	34,607.1
Lazard Houses	25,486.4
Merrill Lynch & Co.	22,868.5
Salomon Brothers	18,149.5
Bear Stearns & Co.	14,990.0
Donaldson, Lufkin & Jenrette	13,298.0
Lehman Brothers	11,398.3
Dillon, Read & Co.	8,291.8

Source: *Corporate Growth Weekly Report*, December 4, 1995, p. 8184, from Securities Data Co.

★ 1882 ★
Mergers & Acquisitions (SIC 7389)

U.S. Merger Advisors

Firms are ranked by value of mergers & acquisitions deals in millions of British pounds in 1996.

Merrill Lynch	65,624.1
Morgan Stanley	50,336.3
Lazard Houses	48,760.7
Bear, Stearns	45,236.4
Salomon Brothers	33,473.0
Goldman, Sachs	29,752.6

Continued on next page.

★ 1882 ★ *Continued*

Mergers & Acquisitions (SIC 7389)

U.S. Merger Advisors

Firms are ranked by value of mergers & acquisitions deals in millions of British pounds in 1996.

Lehman Brothers 22,836.8
J.P. Morgan 16,129.1
Wasserstein, Perella 10,164.3
Donaldson, Lufkin & Jenrette 8,254.6
Smith Barney 7,209.2
PaineWebber 4,241.7
Montgomery Securities 4,076.2
CS First Boston/Credit Suisse 3,909.4
NatWest Markets Group 3,768.6

Source: *Financial Times*, May 22, 1996, p. 3, from Securities Data Co.

★ 1883 ★

Training (SIC 7389)

Corporate Training Spending - 1995

Training staff salaries 72.0%
Outside expenditures 20.0
Facilities/overhead 8.0
Seminars/conferences 6.0
Hardware 5.0
Off-the-shelf materials 4.0
Custom materials 3.0
Outside services 3.0

Source: *Training*, October 1995, p. 12.

SIC 75 - Auto Repair, Services, and Parking

★ 1884 ★
Auto Rental (SIC 7514)

Car Rental Market - San Francisco

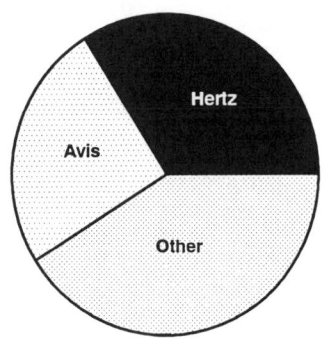

Shares of the airport market are shown in percent.

Hertz	34.1%
Avis	24.6
Other	41.3

Source: *USA TODAY*, April 23, 1996, p. 10B, from D.K. Shifflet & Associates.

★ 1885 ★
Auto Rental (SIC 7514)

Rental Car Leaders - Business Market

Shares of the market for business travelers are shown for 1995.

Hertz	30.1%
Avis	22.8
Budget	12.9
National	12.2
Alamo	9.2
Other	12.8

Source: *USA TODAY*, March 12, 1996, p. B5, from D.K. Shifflet.

★ 1886 ★
Auto Rental (SIC 7514)

Top Auto Rental Firms

Firms are ranked by number of cars in service for 1994 and 1995.

	1994	1995
Enterprise	213,985	263,000
Hertz	215,000	228,750
Avis	165,000	175,000
Alamo	150,000	150,000
Budget	135,000	135,000
National	111,000	125,000
Dollar	62,500	62,500
Value	25,000	18,000
Payless	15,000	15,000
Snappy	13,400	13,750

Source: *Travel Weekly*, May 9, 1996, p. 21, from *Auto Rental News*.

★ 1887 ★
Auto Rental (SIC 7514)

Top Car Rental Companies

Firms are ranked by 1994 revenues in billions of dollars. Figures refer to the airport or near airport market. Shares of the group are shown in percent.

	Rev. ($ bil.)	% of Group
Hertz	$ 2.10	25.3%
Avis	1.70	20.5
Budget	1.29	15.5
Alamo	1.28	15.4
National	1.04	12.5
Dollar	0.56	6.7
Thrifty	0.33	4.0

Source: *Wall Street Journal*, August 14, 1995, p. B4, from Alamo and *Auto Rental News*.

★ 1888 ★
Auto Rental (SIC 7514)

Top Car Rental Firms

Firms are ranked by 1994 sales in millions of dollars. Shares of the group are shown in percent.

	Sales ($ mil.)	% of Group
Hertz	$ 4,800	29.2%
Avis	3,000	18.3
Budget	2,900	17.7
Enterprise	1,975	12.0
Alamo	1,275	7.8
National	1,000	6.1
Dollar	650	4.0
Thrifty	452	2.8
Carey	222	1.4
Value	150	0.9

Source: *Brandweek*, August 21, 1995, p. 43, from *Business Travel News*.

★ 1889 ★
Auto Leasing (SIC 7515)

Car Leasing in Canada

Ontario
Quebec
Prairies
British Columbia
Atlantic

The table shows the percentage of one- to three- year old vehicles that are leased.

Ontario	21.1%
Quebec	17.0
Prairies	13.6
British Columbia	13.2
Atlantic	8.6

Source: *Macleans*, August 5, 1996, p. 43, from Desrosiers Automotive Consultants.

★ 1890 ★
Parking Lots (SIC 7521)

Commercial Parking Market - Canada

Imperial Parking	75.0%
Other	25.0

Source: *Forbes*, July 29, 1996, p. 51.

★ 1891 ★
Parking Lots (SIC 7521)

Leading Parking Lot Firms

Firms are ranked by 1995 revenues in millions of dollars.

Onex (Imperial Parking)	$ 6,516.7
ABM Inds.	965.4
Central Parking	126.2
Square Industries	66.2

Source: *Forbes*, July 29, 1996, p. 51.

★ 1892 ★
Auto Body Repair (SIC 7530)

Auto Repair Services - Mexico

Distribution is shown based on 40,000 independent repair services in the Mexican market.

General mechanical services	57.0%
Painting	25.0
Carwash and lubricating shops	5.0
Electrical	5.0
Tire repair/exhaust pipes/radiators	5.0
Tire balancing and alignment	2.0
Windshields	1.0

Source: *National Trade Data Bank*, March 2, 1996, p. IS9410.026.

★ 1893 ★
Auto Body Repair (SIC 7532)

Spray Equipment Market

The table shows the types of spray equipment used in collision shops.

HVLP	62.4%
Conventional high pressure	31.8
LVLP	4.7
Airless	0.8
Electrostatic	0.5

Source: *Automotive Body Repair News*, May 1996, p. 1.

★ 1894 ★

Auto Body Repair (SIC 7532)

Who Owns Straightening Equipment

The table shows the percentage of auto body repair firms that own each type of business or straightening equipment.

Pull pots	58.7%
Drive-on rack	45.0
Universal bench	21.3
Dedicated bench	15.7

Source: *BodyShop Business*, March 1996, p. 57, from *BodyShop Business Industry Profile, 1995.*

★ 1895 ★

Retreading Shops (SIC 7534)

Top Truck Tire Retreaders

Truck tire retreaders are ranked by millions of pounds of rubber used per year. Data shown are for 1994.

Goodyear	27.10
Treadco Inc.	15.09
Tire Centers Inc.	6.50
Purcell Tire & Rubber Co.	5.70
New Holland Tire Co. Inc.	5.62
Les Schwab Tire Centers Inc.	5.24
Brad Ragan Inc.	5.20
Pomp's Tire Service Inc.	5.04
GCR Truck Tire Centers	5.03
Southern Tire Mart Inc.	4.40
McGuriff Treading Co. Inc.	4.24
J.W. Brewer Tire Co. Inc.	4.13

Source: *Tire Business*, December 11, 1995, p. 22.

★ 1896 ★

Transmission Repair (SIC 7537)

Replacement Transmissions by Source

Data show the sources of replacement transmissions for construction equipment.

Supplier rebuilds	44.0%
Remanufactured	24.0
Owner rebuilds	19.0
New	10.0
Used	3.0

Source: *Construction Equipment*, November 1995, p. 29, from *Construction Equipment Lifecycle Survey, 1995.*

SIC 76 - Miscellaneous Repair Services

★ 1897 ★
Repair Services (SIC 7699)

Who Repairs Hospital Equipment

The service work market for the health care industry reached $3.7 billion in 1994. It is estimated to grow to $7.6 billion by 2000.

Equipment makers	65.0%
Hospitals	15.0
Top 5 service firms	7.0
Other service firms	13.0

Source: *Investor's Business Daily*, April 9, 1996, p. A6, from Wedbush Morgan Securities Inc.

SIC 78 - Motion Pictures

★ 1898 ★

Motion Pictures (SIC 7812)

Children's Video Market

The table shows who supplies the top 100 titles in the children's non-theatrical video market.

Barney	27.0%
Disney	20.0
Sony	14.0
UNI	14.0
WEA	11.0
Warner	3.0
Random	2.0
Other	11.0

Source: *Discount Store News*, July 17, 1996, p. 46, from *Videoscan*.

★ 1899 ★

Motion Pictures (SIC 7812)

Film Market by Segment

	1986	1995
Home video	36.0%	47.0%
Theatrical exhibition	40.0	33.0
Television	24.0	20.0

Source: *Investor's Business Daily*, March 25, 1996, p. A3, from Veronis, Suhler & Associates and Smith Barney Inc.

★ 1900 ★

Motion Pictures (SIC 7812)

Film Producers - 1996

Shares are as of August 11, 1996.

Walt Disney	21.4%
Warner Bros.	15.4
Fox	13.7
Universal	10.9
Paramount	10.4
Sony	9.1
MGM/UA	7.2
Other	11.9

Source: *Business Week*, August 26, 1996, p. 26, from Exhibitor Relations Ltd.

★ 1901 ★

Motion Pictures (SIC 7812)

Films Released by Rating

The table shows the number of feature films released during the first 8 months of 1995.

	No.	Share
R	98	50.0%
PG-13	46	23.4
PG	35	17.9
G	16	8.2
NC-17	1	0.5

Source: *USA TODAY*, September 25, 1995, p. A12, from Motion Picture Association of America.

★ 1902 ★
Motion Pictures (SIC 7812)

Home Video Market

Distribution is shown based on $16.2 billion in consumer spending in 1996, $17.3 billion in 1997, and $18.3 billion in 1998.

	1996	1997	1998
Rentals	54.9%	52.0%	50.3%
Sales	45.1	48.0	49.7

Source: *USA TODAY*, July 10, 1996, p. B4, from Adams Media Research.

★ 1903 ★
Motion Pictures (SIC 7812)

Motion Picture Producers

Shares of the market are shown in percent. There were $5.4 billion in ticket sales in 1995.

Disney	19.0%
Warner Brothers	16.3
Sony	12.8
Universal	12.5
Paramount	10.0
20th Century Fox	7.6
New Line	6.6
MGM/UA	6.2
Miramax	3.5
Gramercy	1.1
Other	4.4

Source: *Entertainment Weekly*, February 2, 1996, p. 29.

★ 1904 ★
Motion Pictures (SIC 7812)

Popular Video Purchases

The table shows the best-selling videos priced for rental. Sales are in thousands of units.

Pulp Fiction	715
Terminator 2	690
Dances With Wolves	648
Ghost	642
True Lies	602

Source: *USA TODAY*, September 26, 1995, p. D1, from Buena Vista Home Video.

★ 1905 ★
Motion Pictures (SIC 7812)

Top Films - 1996

Independence Day
Twister
Toy Story
Mission: Impossible
The Rock
The Birdcage
The Nutty Professor
Ace Ventura: When Nature Calls
GoldenEye
Jumanji

Films are ranked by box office in millions of dollars as of August 1996. Year begins with the 1995 Christmas season.

Independence Day	$ 241.8
Twister	231.9
Toy Story	191.5
Mission: Impossible	174.6
The Rock	126.5
The Birdcage	123.7
The Nutty Professor	109.9
Ace Ventura: When Nature Calls	108.3
GoldenEye	105.9
Jumanji	100.1

Source: *Hollywood Reporter*, August 6, 1996, p. 72.

★ 1906 ★
Motion Pictures (SIC 7812)

Top Movies - 1995

Films are ranked by box office receipts in millions of dollars as of December 18, 1995.

Batman Forever (Warner)	$ 184.0
Apollo 13 (Universal)	172.0
Pocahontas (Disney)	141.0
Ace Ventura - Where Nature Calls (Warner)	103.0
Die Hard With A Vengeance (Fox)	100.0
Casper The Friendly Ghost (Fox)	100.0

Continued on next page.

Motion Pictures (SIC 7812)

Top Movies - 1995

Films are ranked by box office receipts in millions of dollars as of December 18, 1995.

Crimson Tide (Disney)	$ 91.0
Waterworld (Universal)	88.0
Seven (New Line)	86.6
Toy Story (Disney)	86.0

Source: *Times*, December 29, 1995, p. 11, from *Variety*.

★ 1907 ★
Motion Pictures (SIC 7812)

Top Specialized Releases

The table shows the box office gross of the top specialized films of 1994. Figures are in millions of dollars. Specialized films refer to any film that screens at no more than 500 theaters at the height of its release.

The Madness of King George	$ 15.1
Bullets over Broadway	13.1
The Adventures of Priscilla, Queen of the Desert	11.0
The Inkwell	8.8
Fresh	8.0
Hoop Dreams	7.8
Sirens	7.8
Eat Drink Man Woman	7.3
Barcelona	7.2
Widows' Peak	6.2

Source: *Wired*, November 1995, p. 64, from *Variety*.

★ 1908 ★
Motion Pictures (SIC 7812)

Top States - Film Production

The top states for film and television production are ranked by millions of dollars in revenues generated in 1995.

California	$ 19,000.0
New York	2,410.0
Florida	500.0
North Carolina	391.0
Texas	146.0
Utah	74.0
New Mexico	57.5
South Carolina	$ 54.0
Arizona	50.0
Illinois	22.0

Source: *USA TODAY*, April 2, 1996, p. A11.

★ 1909 ★
Motion Pictures (SIC 7812)

Top Video Hits - 1996

Films are ranked by video rental revenues generated in millions of dollars for the first six months of 1996.

Braveheart	$ 43.0
Seven	39.9
The Net	38.9
Ace Ventura 2	34.1
Under Siege 2	33.8
Dangerous Minds	30.9
Babe	29.7
Copycat	29.2
Waterworld	27.9
Jumanji	27.8

Source: *Hollywood Reporter*, August 6, 1996, p. 7, from Vidtrac and Video Software Dealers Association.

★ 1910 ★
Television Production (SIC 7812)

Infomercial Billings

Billings are shown in millions of dollars for the third quarter of 1995.

Heath & fitness	$ 42.7
Cosmetics, hair care, personal products	27.6
Personal, self help, education	15.5
Automotive	13.0
Housewares and appliances	10.8
Entertainment, travel, psychic services	10.0

Source: *Direct Marketing*, March 1996, p. 14, from *Response TV*.

★ 1911 ★
Television Production (SIC 7812)

Leading Infomercials

Infomercials are ranked by gross sales in millions of dollars.

Psychic Friends	$ 250
Health Rider	200
Ab & Back Plus	150
Murad	80
Making Love Work	48
Power Foam	40

Source: *Consumers Research*, April 1996, p. 14, from Jordan Whitney Inc.

★ 1912 ★
Television Production (SIC 7812)

Spanish-Language TV Market

The table shows the Spanish-language TV market in the United States.

Univision	76.0%
Telemundo	24.0

Source: *Chicago Tribune*, November 10, 1995, p. C1, from Univision.

★ 1913 ★
Television Production (SIC 7812)

TV Syndication Leaders

King World	18.0%
Paramount	14.0
Time Warner	11.0
Disney	8.0
Columbia	7.0
Viacom	7.0
Other	35.0

Source: *Investext*, Thomson Financial Services, March 27, 1995, p. 14, from Baseline, *Variety*, Cabletelevision Advertising Bureau, and company reports.

★ 1914 ★
Film Distribution (SIC 7822)

Film Distribution - 1995

Shares of the market are shown in percent.

Buena Vista	19.4%
Warner Brothers	16.6
Sony	13.1
Universal	12.7
Paramount	10.1
20th Century Fox	8.0
Other	20.1

Source: *New York Times*, January 19, 1996, p. C1, from *Hollywood Reporter* and Nielsen Media Research.

★ 1915 ★
Film Distribution (SIC 7822)

Leading Film Distributors - 1996

Shares are shown for January 1 - March 21, 1996 based on gross revenues of $1.1652 billion.

Buena Vista	22.9%
Sony	12.7
Fox	10.7
Universal	9.9
Warner Bros.	9.6
MGM/UA	9.3
Paramount	7.7
Miramax	6.8
New Line	5.2
Gramercy	2.8
Other	2.4

Source: *Variety*, March 31, 1996, p. 10.

★ 1916 ★

Film Distribution (SIC 7822)

Movie Distribution - 1996

Shares are through August 4, 1996.

Buena Vista	21.5%
Warner Bros.	15.3
Fox	13.7
Universal	11.1
Paramount	10.4
Sony	9.0
MGM/UA	7.2
Miramax	3.6
New Line	3.3
Gramercy	2.1
Orion	1.0
Other	1.8

Source: *Hollywood Reporter*, August 6, 1996, p. 72.

★ 1917 ★

Film Distribution (SIC 7822)

Top Film Distributors

Shares of the 1995 market are shown in percent.

Buena Vista	19.4%
Warner Brothers	16.6
Sony	12.8
Universal	12.5
Paramount	10.0
20th Century Fox	7.6
New Line	6.6
MGM/UA	6.2
Miramax	3.5
Savoy	1.3
Other	3.5

Source: *Observer*, January 7, 1996, p. 14, from Screen International/EDI.

★ 1918 ★

Movie Theaters (SIC 7832)

Movie Theater Market - Canada

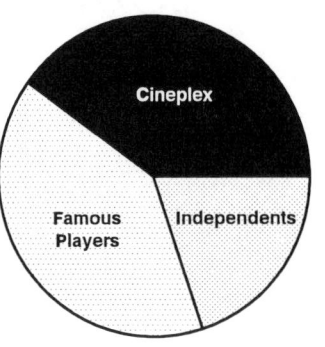

Shares of the market are shown in percent. Cineplex has 621 screens while Famous Players follows with 466 screens.

Cineplex	40.0%
Famous Players	40.0
Independents	20.0

Source: *Marketing Magazine*, April 15, 1996, p. 4.

★ 1919 ★

Movie Theaters (SIC 7832)

Movie Theaters - Mexico

Shares are shown based on number of theaters.

Theater Operating Company - COTSA	3.0%
RamArez Circuit	1.8
Hollywood Organization	1.3
Carlos Amador	0.3
Other	93.6

Source: *National Trade Data Bank*, March 2, 1996, p. IS9410.026.

★ 1920 ★

Movie Theaters (SIC 7832)

Top Movie Theater Operators

United Artists leads with 2,329 screens.

United Artists Theaters	9.0%
Carmike Cinemas	8.0
AMC Entertainment	6.0
Cineplex Odeon	6.0
Cinemark USA	5.0
GC Companies	5.0

Continued on next page.

★ 1920 ★ *Continued*
Movie Theaters (SIC 7832)

Top Movie Theater Operators

United Artists leads with 2,329 screens.

Sony Theaters	4.0%
National Amusements	3.0
Regal Cinemas	3.0
Act III Theaters	2.0
Other	50.0

Source: *Investext,* Thomson Financial Services, August 29, 1995, p. 19, from various sources.

★ 1921 ★
Movie Theaters (SIC 7832)

Top Theater Chains

Chains are ranked by number of screens in North America.

United Artists	2,295
Carmike Cinemas	2,037
AMC Entertainment	1,632
Cineplex Odeon	1,631
Cinemark Theaters	1,224

Source: *USA TODAY*, November 10, 1995, p. D1, from National Association of Theater Owners.

★ 1922 ★
Video Tape Rental (SIC 7841)

Home Video Market Shares

Shares of the home video market are shown in percent. Warner includes MGM/UA with a 3.0% share. Turner includes New Line Home Video with a 3.7% share.

	1994	1995
Disney	24.2%	27.0%
Warner	12.0	13.5
FoxVideo	9.8	11.5
MCA/Universal	11.0	9.0
Columbia	9.4	6.8
GoodTimes	7.2	6.4
Paramount	6.5	6.2
Turner	1.0	5.2
PolyGram	1.8	1.9
WarnerVision	1.8	1.9
Vidmark	1.0	1.5
Anchor Bay	1.5	1.3
LIVE	1.5	1.3

	1994	1995
Republic	1.0%	1.1%
HBO Video	1.3	0.9
Orion	1.0	0.9
Other	8.0	3.6

Source: *Billboard*, January 6, 1996, p. 43.

★ 1923 ★
Video Tape Rental (SIC 7841)

Leading Video Rental Chains

Chains are ranked by number of domestic outlets. Blockbuster Video leads with an estimated 20% of the market.

	1994	1995	1996
Blockbuster Video	2,196	2,566	2,866
Movie Gallery	292	613	993
Hollywood Entertainment . .	112	279	479
Moovies	80	115	165
Video Update	15	37	167

Source: *USA TODAY*, October 23, 1995, p. B1, from Veronis, Suhler & Associates.

★ 1924 ★
Video Tape Rental (SIC 7841)

Special Interest Video Market - 1994

The special interest video market had a 6.0% share of the $15.5 billion video market in 1994. Shares are shown by segment. "Other" includes how-to and fine arts videos.

Exercise & fitness	31.0%
Documentary	23.0
Sports	15.0
Travel	7.0
Other	24.0

Source: *Supermarket News*, October 30, 1995, p. 30, from Cambridge Associates.

★ 1925 ★
Video Tape Rental (SIC 7841)

Video Rental Market - 1996

Shares of the video rental market are shown for the first six months of 1996. PolyGram, Vidmark, and LIVE have less than 3% of the market.

	($ mil.)	Share
Warner	$ 642.8	17.1%
Buena Vista	638.9	16.9
Columbia/Tri-Star	570.1	15.4
MCA/Universal	392.9	10.6
Paramount	366.1	10.0
Fox	319.2	7.8
New Line	239.9	6.6
MGM/UA	193.4	4.8
PolyGram	101.5	3.0
Vidmark	46.0	3.0
LIVE	34.9	3.0
Other	179.9	5.3

Source: *Hollywood Reporter*, August 6, 1996, p. 1, from Vidtrac and Video Software Dealers Association.

★ 1926 ★
Video Tape Rental (SIC 7841)

Video Store Market - Mexico

Shares are shown in percent.

Videovisa	55.0%
Other	45.0

Source: *Mexico Business*, January/February 1996, p. 67.

SIC 79 - Amusement and Recreation Services

★ 1927 ★

Entertainment Facilities (SIC 7900)

Major Venues - Florida

The leading arenas are ranked by gross revenues for 1995.

Miami Arena	$ 5,045,054
Joe Robbie Stadium, Miami	4,385,725
Tampa Bay Performing Arts Center	4,292,119
Sunrise (Fla.) Musical Theater	3,734,327
ThunderDome, St. Petersburg	3,154,736
Tampa Stadium	2,993,280
Orlando Arena	2,664,820
Sun Dome, Tampa	1,646,820
Expo Hall, Fla. State Fairgrounds, Tampa	1,642,455
Pensacola Civic Center	1,530,912

Source: *Amusement Business*, March 3, 1996, p. 18, from Amusement Business Boxscore.

★ 1928 ★

Entertainment Facilities (SIC 7900)

Top Ampitheaters

Arenas are ranked by 1995 gross ticket sales in millions of dollars. Data are for the year ended November 1995.

Pine Knob Music Theater	$ 13.82
Shoreline Ampitheater	13.24
Jones Beach Theater	12.37
Riverport Ampitheater	10.63
Coca-Cola Star Lake Ampitheater	10.47
Garden State Arts Center	10.41
World Music Theater	9.45
Hardee's Walnut Creek Ampitheater	9.43
Sandstone Ampitheater	9.13
Universal Ampitheater	8.79

Source: *Amusement Business*, December 18, 1995, p. 50, from Amusement Business Boxscore.

★ 1929 ★

Entertainment Facilities (SIC 7900)

Top Facilities in the Northwest

The 1995 ranking is based on gross revenues. Data include venues on both sides of the U.S. and Canadian border.

Tacoma (Wash.) Dome	$ 8,550,142
Gorge, George, WA	7,213,445
Memorial Coliseum, Portland OR	3,825,276
Pacific Coliseum, Vancouver, B.C.	3,096,802
Olympic Saddledome, Calgary, Alta.	2,839,854
Edmonton (Alta.) Northlands	2,816,247
Mercer Arena, Seattle, WA	2,520,763
Portland (Ore.) Meadows	1,907,322
Pavilion, Boise (Idaho) State Un.	1,802,171
Seattle (WA) Center Mem. Stadium	1,742,656
Key Arena, Seattle, WA	1,654,164
Puyallup (Wash.) Fair	1,427,375
Thunderbird Stadium Un. of B.C., Vancouver	1,258,373
L.B. Day Amphitheatre, Salem, OR	1,050,572
Spokane (Wash.) Arena	881,331

Source: *Amusement Business*, February 25, 1996, p. 16, from Amusement Business Boxscore.

★ 1930 ★

Theatrical Entertainment (SIC 7922)

Amphitheater Promotors - 1995

Leading promoters are ranked by gross revenues.

PACE Concerts	$ 67,915,452
MCA Concerts	36,168,948
Cellar Door	30,390,112
Nederlander Organization	24,594,585
Bill Graham Presents	23,384,436
Contemporary Prods.	21,030,094
Sunshine Promotions	14,757,506
Delsener/Slater Enterprises	13,479,022
Belkin Prods.	13,383,003
Jam Prods./Tinley Park Jam Corp.	11,971,703

Continued on next page.

★ **1930** ★ *Continued*

Theatrical Entertainment (SIC 7922)

Amphitheater Promotors - 1995

Leading promoters are ranked by gross revenues.

Metropolitan Entertainment Group	.$ 8,739,852
New West Presentations	8,646,208
DiCesare-Engler Prods.	7,040,780
Bill Silva Presents	6,244,229
Avalon Attractions	6,158,836

Source: *Amusement Business*, April 14, 1996, p. 23.

★ **1931** ★

Theatrical Entertainment (SIC 7922)

Broadway Show Attendance

Data show the millions of people who attended Broadway shows each season. Ticket sales have increased from $290 million in 1991-92 to nearly $810 million in 1995-96. The increase in sales has generated an $810 million touring-show business.

1993-94	8.1
1994-95	9.0
1995-96	9.4

Source: *Business Week*, July 8, 1996, p. 8, from League of American Theaters & Producers Inc.

★ **1932** ★

Theatrical Entertainment (SIC 7922)

How Theaters Get Income

The sources of income are shown for 1995, based on a survey of 66 theaters.

Subscriptions	25.0%
Single tickets	23.4
Individuals	8.9
Foundations	7.1
Corporations	5.7
Fundraising events/guilds	3.0
In-kind donations	2.6
State	2.5
United Arts Funds	2.4
Federal	2.2
City/county	1.8
Other	1.4

Source: *American Theater*, April 1996, p. 11.

★ **1933** ★

Theatrical Entertainment (SIC 7922)

Largest Theatrical Events

Gross receipts are shown in millions of dollars for the period from December 5, 1994 to November 27, 1995.

Radio City Christmas Spectacular	$ 39.5
Joseph and the Amazing Technicolor Dreamcoat	10.0
National Finals Rodeo	9.4
Mighty Morphin Power Rangers	4.1
Radio City Easter Show	3.5
Jesus Christ Superstar	3.5
Moorer vs. Foreman	3.4
Walt Disney's World On Ice	3.1
Rob Becker's Defending the Caveman	3.0

Source: *Amusement Business*, December 18, 1995, p. 36, from Amusement Business Boxscore.

★ **1934** ★

Theatrical Entertainment (SIC 7922)

Popular Operas - North America

The table shows the most popular operas in North America, ranked by the number of stagings in the 1993-94 season.

Tosca by Puccini	22
La Boheme by Puccini	20
Carmen by Bizet	18
The Magic Flute by Mozart	18
Madama Butterfly by Puccini	16
La Traviata	16

Source: *USA TODAY*, April 19, 1996, p. D1, from *OPERA America's Field Report*.

★ **1935** ★

Theatrical Entertainment (SIC 7922)

Top Midwest Promoters

Top promoters are ranked by gross revenues in millions of dollars for April 1, 1995 - March 31, 1996.

Jam/MAJ/Tinley park	$ 47.26
Belkin Prods.	35.58
Cellar Door	34.12
Contemporary Prods.	32.42
Sunshine Promotions	19.47
Brass Ring Prods.	14.46

Continued on next page.

★ 1935 ★ *Continued*
Theatrical Entertainment (SIC 7922)

Top Midwest Promoters

Top promoters are ranked by gross revenues in millions of dollars for April 1, 1995 - March 31, 1996.

Live Entertainment	$ 13.78
Nederlander Organization	13.14
New West Presentations	9.84
Glass Palace Promotions	9.78

Source: *Amusement Business*, June 10, 1996, p. 20.

★ 1936 ★
Theatrical Entertainment (SIC 7922)

Top Talent Agencies

The top agencies are ranked by revenues in millions of dollars.

Creative Artists Agency	$ 175
William Morris Agency	125
International Creative Management	110
United Talent Agency	40

Source: *Wall Street Journal*, August 17, 1995, p. B1.

★ 1937 ★
Musical Entertainers (SIC 7929)

Concert Tour Leaders

Rod Stewart
Bob Seger & The Silver Bullet Band
Garth Brooks
AC/DC
Ozzy Osbourne
Bush
Eagles
George Strait
Jimmy Buffett
Reba McEntire

Entertainers are ranked by concert revenues in millions of dollars for the first six months of 1996. Total receipts for the leading 25 concert entertainers was $239 million.

Rod Stewart	$ 29.1
Bob Seger & The Silver Bullet Band	26.3

Garth Brooks	$ 18.0
AC/DC	15.9
Ozzy Osbourne	14.8
Bush	11.7
Eagles	10.3
George Strait	9.6
Jimmy Buffett	8.9
Reba McEntire	7.9

Source: *Philadelphia Inquirer*, July 4, 1996, p. D1, from *Pollstar*.

★ 1938 ★
Musical Entertainers (SIC 7929)

Leading Country Music Tours

The table shows the gross receipts in millions of dollars from December 5, 1994 - November 27, 1995.

Reba McEntire	$ 22.33
Alan Jackson	18.21
George Strait	12.92
Brooks & Dunn	10.78
Vince Gill	10.56
Tim McGraw	8.30
Little Texas	7.51
Alabama	6.50
Sawyer Brown	5.93
Mary Chapin Carpenter	4.77

Source: *Amusement Business*, December 18, 1995, p. 50, from Amusement Business Boxscore.

★ 1939 ★
Musical Entertainers (SIC 7929)

Top Concert Tours - 1995

The entertainers shown are ranked by ticket sales in millions of dollars. The number of shows performed is in parentheses.

Eagles (58)	$ 63.3
Boyz II Men (134)	43.2
R.E.M. (81)	38.7
Grateful Dead (45)	33.5
Page-Plant (68)	32.4
Van Halen (68)	32.7

Continued on next page.

★ 1939 ★ *Continued*

Musical Entertainers (SIC 7929)

Top Concert Tours - 1995

The entertainers shown are ranked by ticket sales in millions of dollars. The number of shows performed is in parentheses.

Tom Petty & the Heartbreakers (89) . . . $ 27.5
Reba McEntire (107) 27.4
Elton John (41) 22.5
Elton John-Billy Joel (12) 22.0

Source: *Detroit Free Press*, December 19, 1995, p. 3C, from *Pollstar*.

★ 1940 ★

Professional Baseball (SIC 7941)

Leading Baseball Teams

Major league baseball teams are ranked by franchise value in millions of dollars. Figures include gate receipts, media receipts, and venue revenues.

New York Yankees . . . . $ 209
Baltimore Orioles 168
Atlanta Braves 163
Toronto Blue Jays 152
Los Angeles Dodgers 147
Chicago White Sox 144
Boston Red Sox 143
Chicago Cubs 140
Texas Rangers 138
Colorado Rockies 133
New York Mets 131
Cleveland Indians 125
San Francisco Giants 122
St. Louis Cardinals 112
Detroit Tigers 106

Source: *Financial World*, May 20, 1996, p. 56.

★ 1941 ★

Professional Baseball (SIC 7941)

Minor League Game Attendance

| Kane County Cougars |
| Bowie Baysox |
| Trenton Thunder |
| Rancho Cucamonga Quakes |
| Wilmington Blue Rocks |

Attendance is shown for 1995.

Kane County Cougars 477,556
Bowie Baysox 463,976
Trenton Thunder 453,915
Rancho Cucamonga Quakes 446,146
Wilmington Blue Rocks 358,766

Source: *Wall Street Journal*, November 8, 1995, p. B1, from team reports, Howe SportsData International Inc., and Baseball America.

★ 1942 ★

Professional Basketball (SIC 7941)

Leading Basketball Teams

Leading professional basketball teams are ranked by franchise value in millions of dollars. Figures include gate receipts, media revenues, and venue revenues.

New York Knicks . . . . $ 205
Phoenix Suns 191
Detroit Pistons 186
Chicago Bulls 178
LA Lakers 171
Cleveland Cavaliers 151
Utah Jazz 142
Portland Trail Blazers 137
Boston Celtics 134
Seattle SuperSonics 129
San Antonio Spurs 126
Orlando Magic 121
Houston Rockets 116
Sacremento Kings 114
Charlotte Hornets 113

Source: *Financial World*, May 20, 1996, p. 57.

★ 1943 ★
Professional Football (SIC 7941)

Leading Pro Football Teams

Leading professional football teams are ranked by franchise value in millions of dollars. Figures include gate receipts, media revenues, and venue revenues.

Dallas Cowboys	$ 272
Miami Dolphins	214
Baltimore Ravens	201
San Francisco 49ers	196
St. Louis Rams	193
Philadelphia Eagles	192
Buffalo Bills	188
Kansas City Chiefs	188
New Orleans Saints	184
Washington Redskins	184
Chicago Bears	184
New York Giants	183
Cincinnati Bengals	171
San Diego Chargers	169
Minnesota Vikings	167

Source: *Financial World*, May 20, 1996, p. 58.

★ 1944 ★
Professional Hockey (SIC 7941)

Leading Pro Hockey Teams

Leading professional hockey teams are ranked by franchise value in millions of dollars. Figures include gate receipts, media revenues, and venue revenues.

Detroit Red Wings	$ 126
Chicago Blackhawks	122
New York Rangers	118
Boston Bruins	111
Philadelphia Flyers	102
Anaheim Mighty Ducks	99
Toronto Maple Leafs	96
Vancouver Canucks	91
Montreal Canadiens	86
Los Angeles Kings	78
San Jose Sharks	77
Pittsburgh Penguins	76
St. Louis Blues	74
Washington Capitals	70
Buffalo Sabres	65

Source: *Financial World*, May 20, 1996, p. 59.

★ 1945 ★
Professional Soccer (SIC 7941)

Professional Soccer Attendance

The attendance at the National Professional Soccer League games are shown for the 1994-95 season. The Cincinnati Silverbacks played in Dayton, OH as the Dynamos.

St. Louis Ambush	204,589
Cleveland Crunch	176,047
Buffalo Blizzards	159,611
Milwaukee Wave	146,479
Harrisburg Heat	141,469
Baltimore Spirit	119,467
Wichita Wings	116,343
Kansas City Ambush	96,880
Detroit Rockers	90,453
Chicago Power	66,668
Cincinnati Silverbacks	64,535
Canton Invaders	36,510

Source: *Amusement Business*, December 10, 1995, p. 9.

★ 1946 ★
Sports Promotion (SIC 7941)

Leading Corporate Sponsors

Anheuser-Busch	
Philip Morris	
Coca-Cola	
General Motors	
Pepsico	

Companies are ranked by sponsorship spending in millions of dollars. Total spending reached $3.05 billion in 1995.

Anheuser-Busch	$ 88.0
Philip Morris	77.0
Coca-Cola	54.0
General Motors	46.0
Pepsico	40.0

Source: *USA TODAY*, March 5, 1996, p. C3, from *IEG Sponsorship Report*.

★ 1947 ★
Sports Promotion (SIC 7941)

Top Athlete Endorsers

Athletes are ranked by total earnings, which include both salary and endorsements income. Data are in millions of dollars.

Michael Jordan	$ 43.9
Mike Tyson	40.0
Deion Sanders	22.5
Riddick Bowe	22.2
Shaquille O'Neal	21.9
George Foreman	18.0
Andre Agassi	16.0
Jack Nicklaus	15.1
Michael Schumacher	15.0
Wayne Gretzky	14.5
Arnold Palmer	14.1
Drew Bledsoe	13.9
Gerhard Berger	13.5
Evander Holyfield	13.0
Pete Sampras	11.2

Source: *Forbes*, December 18, 1995, p. 213.

★ 1948 ★
Fitness Centers (SIC 7991)

Hospital-Owned Fitness Centers

Hospital-owned fitness centers have grown from 175 units in 1990 to 240 centers in 1993 to 350 units in 1996.

Hospital only	94.0%
Hospital joint venture	3.0
Limited partnership	3.0

Source: *Modern Healthcare*, April 8, 1996, p. 40, from Association of Hospital Health and Fitness.

★ 1949 ★
Amusement Parks (SIC 7996)

Amusement Park Companies

Shares are shown based on a total of 265 million visitors to parks in 1994. Time Warner manages Six Flags; Anheuser-Busch manages Sea World; Paramount manages King's Island; Seagram Co. includes Universal City; Cedar Fair manages Cedar Point; Gaylord Entertainment includes Opryland.

Walt Disney Co.	24.6%
Time Warner	8.2
Anheuser-Busch Cos.	7.5%
Paramount	4.8
Seagram Co.	4.6
Cedar Fair	2.2
Silver Dollar City	1.9
Gaylord Entertainment	1.5
Knott's Berry Farm	1.4
Santa Cruz Seaside Co.	1.2
Other	42.1

Source: *Advertising Age*, September 27, 1995, p. 12, from *Amusement Business*.

★ 1950 ★
Amusement Parks (SIC 7996)

Top Theme Parks

Attendance is shown in millions.

Disneyland, California	14.1
Magic Kingdom, Florida	12.9
Epcot, Florida	10.7
Disney-MGM Studios, Florida	9.5
Universal Studios Florida	8.0
Sea World of Florida	4.9
Universal Studios Hollywood	4.7
Six Flags Great Adventure, N.J.	4.0
Busch Gardens Tampa	3.8
Sea World of California	3.7

Source: *Fortune*, April 15, 1996, p. 102, from *Amusement Business*.

★ 1951 ★
Amusement Parks (SIC 7996)

Top Waterparks

Attendance is shown for 1995, in thousands.

Wet 'N Wild	1,330
Typhoon Lagoon	1,200
Blizzard Beach	1,000
Schlitterbahn	753
Raging Waters	752
White Water	725

Source: *Amusement Business*, December 18, 1995, p. 88, from Amusement Business Boxscore.

★ 1952 ★

Amateur Sports (SIC 7997)

Soccer Team Membership - Canada

Registrations in the Canadian Soccer Association are shown by province in 1995. Approximately 85% of the registrations are for youths.

Ontario	196,487
Quebec	91,260
British Columbia	80,710
Alberta	51,107
Manitoba	18,553
Nova Scotia	17,172
Saskatchewan	9,512
Newfoundland	7,600
New Brunswick	6,514
Prince Edward Island	3,571
Northwest Territories	1,200
A-league	100

Source: *National Trade Data Bank*, March 2, 1996, p. IM951207.060, from Canadian Soccer Association.

★ 1953 ★

Gambling (SIC 7999)

Gaming Market - Atlantic City

Shares are shown for the first six months of 1995.

Trump Taj Mahal	14.2%
Caeser's Boardwalk	10.7
Bally's Park Place	10.4
Showboat	9.8
TropWorld	9.3
Harrah's Marina	9.2
Trump Plaza	8.4
Resorts International	7.9
Sands	7.9
Bally's Grand	7.5
Claridge	4.9
Other	8.8

Source: *Investext,* Thomson Financial Services, July 27, 1995, p. 13, from New Jersey Casino Control Commission.

★ 1954 ★

Gambling (SIC 7999)

Gaming Market by State

Nevada
New Jersey
Mississippi
Illinois
Lousiana

States are ranked by 1995 gambling revenues in billions of dollars. The figure for Illinois is for the fiscal year ended May 31, 1996.

Nevada	$ 7.03
New Jersey	3.75
Mississippi	1.72
Illinois	1.12
Lousiana	1.04

Source: *New York Times*, July 9, 1995, p. C1, from state governments and Mississippi Gaming Commission.

★ 1955 ★

Gambling (SIC 7999)

Indian Casinos - Michigan

Casinos are ranked by 1995 revenues. Figures are estimates based on industry averages that slot machines make up 75% of the income.

Saginaw Chippewa	$ 225,860,250
Sault Ste. Maries Chippewa	126,904,447
Bay Mills Indian Community	40,562,340
Lac Vieux Desert Tribe	23,659,968
Grand Travers Bay Band	19,497,849
Hannahville Indian Community	8,774,143
Keweenaw Bay Indian Community	7,837,773

Source: *Detroit Free Press*, March 21, 1996, p. 12A.

★ 1956 ★

Gambling (SIC 7999)

Top Casinos

Shares are shown based on total casino revenues of $14.1 billion.

Harrah's Entertainment	7.9%
Caesars World	5.6
Mirage Resorts	5.2
Bally Entertainment	5.1
Circus Circus Enterprises	4.3

Continued on next page.

★ **1956** ★ *Continued*

Gambling (SIC 7999)

Top Casinos

Shares are shown based on total casino revenues of $14.1 billion.

Hilton Hotels Corp.	3.4%
Trump Organization	3.3
Aztar Corp.	3.1
MGM Grand	3.1
Hollywood Casinos Corp.	3.0
Other	55.9

Source: *Advertising Age*, September 27, 1995, p. 12, from Salomon Brothers.

★ **1957** ★

Golf Courses (SIC 7999)

Largest Private Golf Courses

The largest San Diego area golf courses shown are ranked by 1995 membership.

Rancho Santa Fe Golf Club	619
Lomas Santa Fe Country Club	550
Shadowridge Country Club	525
La Costa Resort & Spa	518
Escondido Country Club	500
Fairbanks Ranch Country Club	485
La Jolia Country Club	420
Rancho Bernardo Golf Club	412
El Camino Country Club	400
Lake San Marcos Country Club	400
Stoneridge Country Club	400
Farms Golf Club	308
Vista Valley Country Club	303
De Anza Desert Country Club	241
Del Mar Country Club	130

Source: *San Diego Business*, June 12, 1995, p. 24, from course representatives.

★ **1958** ★

Golf Courses (SIC 7999)

Top States for Golf Courses

The table shows the top states for course development. Ranking is based on number of openings in 1995. In 1994, there were 1,189 daily fee courses, 242 municipal courses, and 241 private courses in development.

Michigan	32
New York	25
Illinois	24
Ohio	23
Wisconsin	22
Minnesota	21
Missouri	15
Indiana	14
California	13
Texas	13

Source: *Grounds Maintenance*, January 1996, p. 10, from *Golf Market Today*.

★ **1959** ★

Leisure Activities (SIC 7999)

How We Spend Our Free Time

The table shows how we spent our time per capita in 1994. Figures include the per capita dollars spent on each activity.

	Spent	Hours
Television	$ 110	1,560
Radio	--	1,102
Recorded music	56	294
Daily papers	49	169
Consumer books	79	102
Consumer mags	36	84
Home video	73	52
Home videogames	17	22
Movies in theaters	25	12
Consumer online and Internet services	7	3

Source: *Wired*, December 1995, p. 56, from Veronis, Suhler & Associates.

★ 1960 ★

Leisure Activities (SIC 7999)

Leisure Industry

Audio, video, computer	
Publications	
Gambling	
Commercial amusement	
Leisure hotels	
Recorded music	
Cruise ships	
Non-sports live entertainment	
Theme parks	
Spectator sports	
Film: box office totals	

The table shows the billions of dollars in revenues generated by each segment.

Audio, video, computer	$ 55.3
Publications	50.3
Gambling	40.0
Commercial amusement	29.1
Leisure hotels	17.8
Recorded music	12.0
Cruise ships	7.0
Non-sports live entertainment	6.3
Theme parks	6.1
Spectator sports	5.9
Film: box office totals	5.4

Source: *Sunday Oregonian*, March 17, 1996, p. G4, from *LaFleur's 1996 World Lottery Almanac* and *International Gaming & Wagering Business*.

★ 1961 ★

Leisure Activities (SIC 7999)

Popular Equipment-Related Sports

The table shows the most popular equipment related sports, ranked by millions of participants in 1994.

Billiards	46.9
Free weights exercise	35.9
Treadmill exercise	26.5
Stair-climbing exercise	20.5
In-line skating	18.8

Step aerobics	12.6
Home gym exercise	10.2
Mountain biking	9.2
Nordic ski exercise	9.2

Source: *Swimming Pool/Spa Age*, May 1996, p. 18, from *Sporting Goods Manufacturers Association Participation Trends Report*.

★ 1962 ★

Leisure Activities (SIC 7999)

Snowboard Industry

During the 1994-95 season, 52.46 million skiers took to the slopes. The table shows the percentage of total skier visits generated by snowboarders.

Pacific south	15.2%
Pacific north	14.7
Rocky Mts.	10.0
Northeast	9.6
Southeast	8.2
Midwest	7.3

Source: *Travel Weekly*, August 28, 1995, p. 95, from National Ski Areas Association.

★ 1963 ★

National Parks (SIC 7999)

Popular National Parks

Data show the millions of visitors in 1995.

Great Smoky Mountains National Park	9.0
Grand Canyon National Park	4.5
Yosemite National Park	3.9
Olympic National Park	3.9
Yellowstone National Park	3.1
Rocky Mountain National Park	2.8
Acadia National Park	2.8
Grand Teton National Park	2.7
Zion National Park	2.4
Mammoth Cave National Park	1.9

Source: *Christian Science Monitor*, August 13, 1996, p. 2, from National Park Service.

Tourist Attractions (SIC 7999)

Arkansas' Leading Attractions

Attendance is estimated for 1995. The figures for attractions that are free of charge such as the biblically-themed events are not always accurate.

Greers Ferry Lake	5,458,422
Hot Springs National Park	3,626,243
DeGray Lake Resort State Park	2,878,455
Great Passion Play & other Biblical attractions	1,200,000
Lake Quachita State Park	1,179,863
Oaklawn Park	1,091,403
Southland Greyhound Park	850,000
Buffalo National River	700,564
Pinnacle Mountain State Park	444,375
Arkansas State Fair & Livestock Show	423,178
Little Rock Zoo	392,000
Mammoth Spring State Park	304,698

Source: *Arkansas Business*, March 11, 1996, p. 31, from Arkansas Department of Parks and Tourism and the attractions.

★ 1965 ★
Tourist Attractions (SIC 7999)

Visitors to Monuments - Washington D.C.

Visitors to the major monuments are shown for January through July 1995. Some July figures are estimates.

Lincoln Memorial	823,000
Vietnam Memorial	740,400
Washington Monument	627,000
Jefferson Memorial	460,000

Source: *Wall Street Journal*, September 1, 1995, p. B1, from National Park Service.

SIC 80 - Health Services

★ 1966 ★
Health Care (SIC 8000)

Health Care Spending - 1995

This table shows the distribution of the $1.0 trillion spent on health care by receipient. Data are estimates for 1995.

Hospital care	36.2%
Doctors	19.7
Nursing home care	10.7
Drugs	8.4
Administration & private health ins.	5.2
Dental	4.3
Government public health activities	2.8
Other professional services	6.2
Others	6.5

Source: *Economist*, November 4, 1995, p. 67, from Health Care Financing Administration.

★ 1967 ★
Health Care (SIC 8000)

Health Care Users by State - Mexico

The table shows the thousands of health care users in selected states in 1993. A total of 60.146 million people in Mexico used health care facilities in 1993. There are expected to be 162.88 million medical visits in 1994, with the top types of service being general medical care with 109.9 million visits, 25.3 million specialized medical visits, and 17.9 million emergency medical visits.

Federal District	10,179.2
Mexico	6,135.3
Veracruz	4,054.1
Jalisco	3,058.8
Puebla	2,883.0
Nuevo Leon	2,639.8

Oaxaca	2,391.1
Chiapas	2,387.6
Michoacan	2,359.7
Guanajuato	2,161.3

Source: *National Trade Data Bank*, September 1, 1995, p. IS9504.246, from Mexico's Secretariat of Health.

★ 1968 ★
Health Care (SIC 8000)

Information Handling Market

The market for information handling in the health care industry is expected to grow from $20.3 billion in 1995 to $35.0 billion in 2000.

	1995	2000
Value added services	35.5%	37.4%
Software	29.1	30.0
Hardware	27.1	25.4
Information services	8.4	7.1

Source: *Health Management Today*, February 1996, p. 10, from Business Communications Company.

★ 1969 ★
Health Care (SIC 8000)

Physicians in San Diego

The table shows the types of physician specialties in San Diego County in 1995.

Specialists	73.0%
Primary care	27.0

Source: *Healthcare Financial Management*, May 1996, p. 31.

★ 1970 ★

Surgery (SIC 8011)

Cosmetic Surgery for Men

| Hair transplant |
| Liposuction |
| Chemical peel |
| Rhinoplasty |
| Eyelid surgery |

The table shows the number of men who had each surgery performed in 1994.

Hair transplant	197,276
Liposuction	37,743
Chemical peel	36,290
Rhinoplasty (nose)	22,204
Eyelid surgery	18,350

Source: *USA TODAY*, May 16,1 996, p. D1, from American Academy of Cosmetic Surgery.

★ 1971 ★

Surgery (SIC 8011)

U.S. Organ Registrations

Because patients can register with more than one transplant center, the number of registrations may exceed the number of people needing organs.

Kidney	29,753
Liver	5,039
Heart	3,371
Lung	1,836
Kidney/pancreas	1,220
Pancreas	255
Heart/lung	214
Intestine	78

Source: *Safety & Health*, May 1996, p. 75, from United Network for Organ Sharing.

★ 1972 ★

Surgery (SIC 8011)

U.S. Organ Transplants

The table shows the number of transplants performed in each year.

	1993	1994
Kidney	11,021	11,390
Liver	3,440	3,653
Heart	2,298	2,340
Pancreas	774	844
Lung	675	737
Heart-lung	59	70

Source: *USA TODAY*, October 19, 1995, p. D6, from United Network for Organ Sharing.

★ 1973 ★

Dentists (SIC 8021)

Dentists by Region - Canada

Ontario	764
Quebec	356
Prairie Provinces	266
British Columbia	190
Atlantic Provinces	104

Source: *National Trade Data Bank*, March 2, 1996, p. 111092517.

★ 1974 ★

Dentists (SIC 8021)

Dentists by Specialty in Canada

Orthodontics	31.9%
Oral/maxillofacial surgery	17.1
Periodontics	14.5
Pediatric dentistry	10.6
Prosthodontics	10.3
Endodontics	8.2
Dental public health	3.6
Oral pathology	2.5
Oral radiology	1.3

Source: *National Trade Data Bank*, March 2, 1996, p. 111092517.

★ 1975 ★
Podiatrists (SIC 8043)

Common Foot Problems

The table shows the most common foot problems, in millions, based on a survey of 46,676 households.

Infections	11.3
Toenail problems	11.3
Corns/calluses	11.2
Injuries	5.6
Flat feet/fallen arches	4.6
Bunions	4.4
Arthritis	3.9
Joint deformity	2.5

Source: *USA TODAY*, June 17, 1996, p. 5D, from National Health Interview Survey.

★ 1976 ★
Nursing Homes (SIC 8050)

Leading Nursing Home Operators

Companies are ranked by nursing facility beds owned, managed, or leased.

Beverly Enterprises Inc.	74,488
Vencor Inc.	39,518
Integrated Health Services	28,800
Living Centers of America	26,326
Manor Care Inc.	23,757
Life Care Centers of America Inc.	20,768
Evangelical Lutheran Good Samaritan Society	18,646
Horizon/CMS Healthcare Corp.	18,000
GranCare	16,557
United Health Inc.	16,278
Healthcare and Retirement Corp.	15,715
ServiceMaster Diversified Health Services	15,318
Sun Healthcare Group Inc.	14,535
Genesis Health Ventures Inc.	13,097
National HealthCare	12,493

Source: *Contemporary Long Term Care*, December 1995, p. 56.

★ 1977 ★
Nursing Homes (SIC 8051)

Baltimore's Top Nursing Homes

Nursing homes are ranked by available beds as of January 15, 1995.

Stella Maris Cardinal Shehan Center	448
Lorian Nursing & Rehabilitation Center	361
Seton Hill Manor	360
Deaton Specialty Hospital & Home	360
Riverview Nursing Center	308
Charlestown Care Center	270
Keswick-Multi Care Center	268
Johns Hopkins Geriatric Center	255
Maridian Nursing Center-Randallstown	250
Manor Care Ruxton	232

Source: *Baltimore Business Journal*, January 25, 1996, p. 26, from Dept. of Health & Mental Hygiene's Directory of Licensed Facilities and company representatives.

★ 1978 ★
Nursing Homes (SIC 8051)

Top Nursing Home Chains

Nursing home chains are ranked by available skilled nursing and subacute nursing beds as of June 30, 1995.

Beverly Enterprises Inc.	76,440
Hillhaven Corp.	37,331
Integrated Health Services Inc.	28,200
Living Centers of America	26,326
Manor HealthCare Corp.	23,763
Life Care Centers of America	20,729
Horizan/CMS Healthcare Corp.	18,000
Evangelical Lutheran Good Samaritan Society	17,952
GranCare Inc.	17,380
United Health Inc.	16,073

Source: *Provider*, February 1996, p. 45.

★ 1979 ★

Nursing Homes (SIC 8059)

Limited Care Facilities

Based on available beds, the top assisted living chains are shown as of June 30, 1995.

Evangelical Lutheran Good Samaritan Society	6,531
ARV Assisted Living	3,612
Sunrise Assisted Living	3,299
Adult Care Management	2,800
Beverly Enterprises Inc.	2,542
Retirement Care Associates Inc.	2,400
Advocate, Inc.	2,335
Leisure Care	2,200
Integrated Health Services Inc.	1,990
Forum Group Inc.	1,978
Manor HealthCare	1,800
Standish Care	1,659

Source: *Provider*, February 1996, p. 45.

★ 1980 ★

Hospitals (SIC 8060)

California Hospitals by Type

Nonprofit (not religious)	43.0%
Nonprofit (religious)	16.0
Country hospitals	11.8
For-profit, investor owned	10.2
Veterans Administration	6.8
University hospitals	4.2
Other	8.0

Source: *Los Angeles Times*, February 21, 1995, p. D1, from California Association of Hospitals and Health Systems.

★ 1981 ★

Hospitals (SIC 8060)

Largest Public Hospitals

Hospitals are ranked by number of licensed beds.

LAC + USC Medical Center	2,045
Jackson Memorial Hospital	1,567
Grady Health System	1,550
Bellevue Hospital Center	1,232
Kings County Hospital Center	1,204

Source: *AHA News*, November 13, 1995, p. 4.

★ 1982 ★

Hospitals (SIC 8060)

Public Hospital Admissions

The table shows the number of 1993 admissions to public hospitals in selected cities. Figures include the largest public hospital and its share of total city admissions.

	Adm.	City Share
Atlanta(Grady Memorial)	33,170	32.1%
Miami(Jackson Memorial)	50,832	29.5
Los Angeles(5 facilities)	133,247	28.7
Dallas(Parkland Memorial)	41,098	21.3
New York City(11 facilities)	202,746	18.4
Houston(2 facilities)	43,673	12.9
Washington D.C.(D.C. General)	14,755	9.4
Chicago(Cook County)	32,892	7.5

Source: *Washington Post National Weekly Edition*, October 3, 1995, p. 6, from National Association of Public Hospitals and American Hospital Association.

★ 1983 ★

Psychiatric Care (SIC 8063)

Juvenile Psychiatric Facilities - Michigan

Michigan's state run psychiatric facilities for children are ranked by available beds for 1995-1996. Capacity measurement is based on legislative appropriations.

Fairlawn	75
Hawthorn	60
Pheasant Ridge	16
Detroit Psychiatric Institute/children's unit	12

Source: *Detroit Free Press*, January 26, 1996, p. 6B, from Michigan Department of Mental Health.

★ 1984 ★

Dental Services (SIC 8072)

Leading Dental Advertisers

Firms are ranked by share of total dental advertising expenditures in 1995.

Dentsply International Incorporated	6.20%
Procter & Gamble	2.50
Ultradent Products Incorporated	2.48
Den-Mat Corporation	2.31
Ivoclar North America	1.98
Bisco Dental Products	1.97
Henry Schein Inc. Co.	1.69
Block Drug Company Inc.	1.56
Parkell Today	1.56
Glidewell Laboratories	1.54
Other	76.21

Source: *Medical Marketing & Media*, April 1996, p. 76, from HCI Medical Promotion Audit, 1995.

★ 1985 ★

Home Health Care (SIC 8082)

Home Care Spending - Canada

Ontario

British Columbia

Quebec

Alberta

Manitoba

Saskatchewan

Nova Scotia

New Brunswick

Newfoundland

Northwest Territories

Prince Edward Island

Yukon Territory

Spending is shown in millions of Canadian dollars in 1993.

Ontario	454
British Columbia	193
Quebec	163
Alberta	71
Manitoba	46
Saskatchewan	43
Nova Scotia	39
New Brunswick	35
Newfoundland	7
Northwest Territories	6
Prince Edward Island	4
Yukon Territory	1

Source: *National Trade Data Bank*, March 2, 1996, p. IS9503.165.

★ 1986 ★

Home Health Care (SIC 8082)

Home Infusion Industry

The home infusion therapy industry reached $4.0 billion in 1995. Data show the market by service.

Antibiotics	39.0%
Total parenternal nutrition therapy (TPN)	19.0
Pain management	16.0
Enteral nutrition	8.0
Chemotherapy	7.0
Hydration	5.0
Other therapies	6.0

Source: *Drug Topics*, June 12, 1995, p. 59, from National Alliance for Infusion Therapy.

★ 1987 ★

Home Health Care (SIC 8082)

Intravenous Drug/Nutrition Market

Shares of the $3.5 billion market are shown in percent.

Coram/Caremark	23.0%
National Medical Care - W.R. Grace	9.0
Apria Healthcare	7.0
American Home Patient	1.0
Rotech Medical	1.0
Other	59.0

Source: *New York Times*, September 15, 1995, p. C2, from Robertson, Stephens & Company.

★ 1988 ★

Kidney Dialysis Centers (SIC 8092)

Renal Dialysis Providers

Leaders in the dialysis business are ranked by revenues in millions of dollars. Data are for fiscal year 1994. Texas leads the nation with 72 dialysis clinics.

National Medical	$ 1,870.0
Vivra	284.6
Ren Corp. USA	131.8
Renal Treatment Centers	86.5
Total Renal Care	80.5

Source: *New York Times*, December 4, 1995, p. A12, from company reports.

SIC 81 - Legal Services

★ 1989 ★

Legal Services (SIC 8111)

Largest Law Firms - Detroit

Firms are ranked by number of attorneys.

Dykema Gossett	181
Dickinson, Wright, Moon, Van Dusen & Freeman	166
Honigman Miller Schwartz and Cohn	156
Miller, Canfield, Paddock and Stone	155
Butzel Long	137
Plunkett & Cooney	119
Clark Hill	112
Kitch, Drutchas, Wagner & Kenney . . .	110
Bodman, Longley & Dahling	90
Jaffe, Raitt, Heuer & Weiss	84

Source: *Crain's Detroit Business*, May 27, 1996, p. 12.

★ 1990 ★

Legal Services (SIC 8111)

Largest Law Firms - Mexico

Firms are ranked by number of employees.

Santamarina y Steta	57
Basham, Ringe y Correa	55
Goodrich Riqueline y Asociados	50
Baker & McKenzie	40
Barrera, Aiquieros Torres Landa	30
Jauregui, Navarrete Nader y Rojas	24
Noriega y Escobedo	24

Source: *Mexico Business*, May 1996, p. 52.

★ 1991 ★

Legal Services (SIC 8111)

Largest Law Firms - Minnesota

Law firms are ranked by the number of Minnesota attornies.

Dorsey & Whitney	258
Faegre & Benson	226
Oppenheimer Wolff & Donnelly	148
Robins, Kaplan, Miller & Ciresi	135
Briggs and Morgan	131
Leonard, Street and Deinard	127
Fredrikson & Byron	122
Popham, Haik, Schnobrich & Kaufman . .	122
Gray, Plant, Mooty, Mooty & Bennett . . .	110
Lindquist & Vennum	99
Doherty, Rumble & Butler	99
Rider, Bennett, Egan & Arundel	93

Source: *Corporate Report Minnesota*, February 1996, p. 52.

SIC 82 - Educational Services

★ 1992 ★
Universities (SIC 8221)

Business School Applications

Harvard	
Wharton	
Stanford	
Columbia	
NYU	
Duke	
MIT	

Universities are ranked by business school applications in 1995.

Harvard	7,000
Wharton	6,354
Stanford	6,000
Columbia	4,600
NYU	3,000
Duke	2,400
MIT	2,300

Source: *Wall Street Journal*, August 15, 1996, p. B1.

★ 1993 ★
Universities (SIC 8221)

Business School Enrollment

Schools are ranked by part-time student enrollment. Locations are in parentheses.

Webster University (St. Louis, MO)	4,152
Johns Hopkins University (Baltimore, MD)	2,850
University of St. Thomas (Minneapolis, MN)	2,802
New York University (New York, NY)	2,597
City University (Bellevue, WA)	2,579
Keller Graduate School of Mgmt. (Oakbrook Terrace, IL)	2,069
Bentley College (Waltham, MA)	1,880
Walsh College (Troy, MI)	1,838
Fairleigh Dickinson Un. (Teaneck, NJ)	1,828
Wayne State Univ. (Detroit, MI)	1,745

Source: *Business Week*, August 21, 1995, p. 83.

★ 1994 ★
Libraries (SIC 8231)

Largest NYC Libraries

The table shows the millions of people served by New York City's libraries. The three libraries have 230 branches.

New York Public Library	3.00
Brooklyn Public Library	2.30
Queens Borough Public Library	1.95

Source: *Library Journal*, June 1, 1996, p. 51.

★ 1995 ★
Libraries (SIC 8231)

Library Spending By Region

The table compares the per capita spending on library materials in each region, based on library systems serving more than 1.0 million people.

Orange County, California	$ 4.31
Philadelphia	3.47
Miami-Dade County, Florida	3.14
Montreal	3.09
Broward County, Florida	3.04
Queens, N.Y.	2.92
New York City	2.55
Detroit	2.34
Houston	2.33
Chicago	2.29
Brooklyn, N.Y.	2.07

Continued on next page.

★ 1995 ★ *Continued*
Libraries (SIC 8231)

Library Spending By Region

The table compares the per capita spending on library materials in each region, based on library systems serving more than 1.0 million people.

Phoeniz, AZ	$ 2.06
San Antonio	1.76
San Diego	1.70
Dallas	1.57

Source: *Dallas Morning News*, July 16, 1995, p. A26, from Public Library Data Service and Dallas Public Library.

SIC 83 - Social Services

★ 1996 ★

Child Care (SIC 8351)

Day Care Centers - Milwaukee

Child care centers in Milwaukee are ranked by capacity. Figures may include more than one location.

Children's World Learning Centers	2,878
KinderCare Learning Centers	1,800
YMCA Child Care Services	1,637
Day Care Services For Children	826
Milestones, Programs for Children	815
Ebenezer Child Care Centers Inc.	640
Children's Edu-Care	500
Grandma's House Day Care Center	478
Child & Family Centers	460
Carter Child Development Centers	435
Wauwatosa Day Care & Learning Cen. Inc.	356
Quad/Care	355

Source: *Business Journal*, January 20, 1996, p. 15, from Milwaukee & the Southeastern Region of the WI Div. of Community Services.

★ 1997 ★

Child Care (SIC 8351)

Leading Child Care Centers

Child care service providers are ranked by licensed capacity. Data include national chains (NC), franchising ventures (FV), employer focused (EF) organizations, and regional chains (RC).

KinderCare Learning Centers (NC)	140,956
La Petite Academy (NC)	95,000
Children's World Learning Centers (NC)	62,500
Children's Discovery Centers (NC)	23,600
Childtime Childcare Inc. (NC)	18,285
Nobel Education Dynamics Inc. (NC)	15,000
Tutor Time Child Care Learning Centers (FV)	13,800
Bright Horizons Children's Center (EF)	11,400
Corporate Family Solutions (EF)	10,132
Kids 'R Kids International (FV)	9,250
Children Today (NC)	8,100
New Horizons Child Care (RC)	7,327

Source: *Child Care Information Exchange*, March 1996, p. 62.

★ 1998 ★

Charities (SIC 8399)

Charitable Contributions - 1994

The table shows the sources of $129.88 billion in charitable giving in 1994.

Individuals	80.9%
Foundations	7.6
Bequests	6.8
Corporations	4.7

Source: *Association Management*, December 1995, p. 57, from American Association of Fund Raising Counsel.

★ 1999 ★

Charities (SIC 8399)

Most Efficient Charities

The table shows the leading charities ranked by 1994 income in millions of dollars. Figures include the program spending as a percentage of income.

	Income ($ mil.)	% of Income
Salvation Army	1,354.8	86.2%
Second Harvest	426.8	99.8
American Cancer Society . . .	391.8	72.3
Nature Conservancy	306.7	84.0
World Vision	278.9	76.8
Campus Crusade for Christ . .	189.4	84.9
United Negro College Fund . .	91.1	75.3

Source: *Money*, December 1995, p. 18, from *Nonprofit Times*.

★ 2000 ★

Charities (SIC 8399)

Top Charities

Firms are ranked by incomes in millions of dollars.

Catholic Charities USA	$ 1,900.0
YMCA of the USA	1,900.0
American Red Cross	1,700.0
Salvation Army	1,400.0
Goodwill Industries International	951.0
Girl Scouts of America	505.4
Shriners Hospital for Crippled Children . .	494.0
Boy Scouts of America	486.6
Planned Parenthood Federation of America	462.5
YWCA of the USA	409.1

Source: *U.S. News & World Report*, December 4, 1995, p. 89.

SIC 84 - Museums, Botanical, Zoological Gardens

★ 2001 ★

Arts Spending (SIC 8412)

Business Spending on the Arts

Distribution of the $875 million spent by businesses on the arts is shown in percent.

Symphony orchestras 15.0%
Performing arts centers 13.0
Museums 12.0
Theaters 11.0
Arts education 1.0
Other 48.0

Source: *New York Times*, October 12, 1995, p. B1, from Business Committee for the Arts.

★ 2002 ★

Museums (SIC 8412)

Popular Exhibits - Canada

Exhibits are ranked by attendance.

The Queen's Pictures: Old Masters . . . 100,558
Barbara Hepworth: A Retrospective . . . 87,433
A Private World: John Constable's
    Landscape 75,994
Thomas Gainsborough: The Harvest
    Wagon 65,506

Source: *Apollo*, December 1995, p. 15.

★ 2003 ★

Museums (SIC 8412)

Popular Science Museums

The nation's top science museums are ranked by millions of visitors in 1995.

National Air and Space Museum 8.2
National Museum of Natural History 5.8
National Museum of American History . . . 4.8
American Museum of National History . . . 3.0
Houston Museum of Natural Science 2.4

California Museum of Science and Industry . . 2.0
Museum of Science and Industry 2.0
Denver Museum of Natural History 1.6
St. Louis Science Center 1.3
Pacific Science Center 1.1

Source: *USA TODAY*, June 3, 1996, p. D6, from Association of Science-Technology Centers Inc.

SIC 86 - Membership Organizations

Business Associations (SIC 8611)

Independent Franchise Associations

Organizations are ranked by number of members.

American Franchisees Assn.	6,963
American Assn. of Franchisees & Dealers	6,000
Intl. Gay & Lesbian Franchise Assn.	262

Source: *Franchise Times*, June 1996, p. 3.

Business Associations (SIC 8611)

Largest Trade/Institutional Groups

| U.S. Chamber of Commerce |
| Distributive Education Clubs of America |
| National Association of Home Builders |
| Uniform Code Council |
| American Management Association |
| United States Hispanic Chamber of Commerce |
| American Hospital Association |
| National Futures Association |
| National Association of Wheat Growers |
| American Advertising Federation |

Membership is shown for 1996.

U.S. Chamber of Commerce	220,000
Distributive Education Clubs of America	186,000
National Association of Home Builders	185,000
Uniform Code Council	120,000
American Management Association	85,000
United States Hispanic Chamber of Commerce	70,000
American Hospital Association	55,000
National Futures Association	53,719
National Association of Wheat Growers	50,000
American Advertising Federation	40,000

Source: *Association Management*, May 1996, p. 120.

Labor Unions (SIC 8631)

Major Union Locals - Michigan

Union locals shown are ranked by gross receipts for 1995. Data are for Wayne, Oakland, Macomb, Washtenaw, and Livingston counties in Michigan. Figures shown pertain to union dues and other revenues collected.

United Food and Commercial Workers 876	$ 7,947,963
UAW Local 600	7,589,063
Service Employees Intl. Local 79	4,977,371
Operating Engineers Local 324	4,501,739
Electrical Workers Local 58	4,056,081
UAW Local 594	3,710,009
Iron Workers Local 25	3,218,994
UAW Local 653	3,170,936
Teamsters Local 337	3,133,051
UAW Local 400	2,918,823

Source: *Crain's Detroit Business*, December 25, 1995, p. 62, from United States Department of Labor and union locals.

Civic Organizations (SIC 8641)

Fraternal Organizations

Selected groups are ranked by thousands of members in 1995.

Moose Lodge	1,720
Shriners	609
Lions Club	485

Source: *Detroit News*, February 19, 1996, p. D4, from national organizations.

★ 2008 ★
Political Organizations (SIC 8651)

Leading Lobbyists - Detroit

Firms are ranked by number of Detroit-area clients as of October 1995.

Karoub Associates	39
Governmental Consultant Services Inc.	31
Muchmore Harrington Associates Inc.	30
Public Affairs Associates Inc.	17
Kheder and Associates Inc.	16
Cawthorne, McCollough & Cavanaugh	15

Source: *Crain's Detroit Business*, November 13, 1995, p. 21.

★ 2009 ★
Political Organizations (SIC 8651)

Popular Environmental Groups

Groups are ranked by number of members.

Ralph Nader Affiliates	4,100,000
National Wildlife Federation	1,719,000
Greenpeace	1,700,000
World Wildlife Fund	1,200,000
Sierra Club	570,000
National Wildlife Club	540,000
Environmental Defense Fund	250,000
Natural Resources Defense Council . .	170,000
Defenders of Wildlife	101,000
Union of Concerned Scientists	80,000

Source: *Mining Voice*, Jan./ Feb. 1996, p. 26.

★ 2010 ★
Religious Organizations (SIC 8661)

Church Membership by Denomination

Membership is shown in millions.

Roman Catholic	60.2
Southern Baptist	15.6
United Methodist	8.6
National Baptist, USA	8.2
Church of God in Christ	5.5
Evangelical Lutheran	5.2
Mormon	4.6
Presbyterian	3.7

Source: *Mirror*, July 12, 1996, p. 6, from *1996 Yearbook of American and Canadian Churches*.

SIC 87 - Engineering and Management Services

Engineering Services (SIC 8711)

Major Engineering Firms

Firms are ranked by revenues in millions of dollars.

Flour Daniel Inc.	$ 251.47
BE&K Inc.	170.13
Dames & Moore	120.00
Burns and Roe Enterprises	54.00
Raytheon Engineers & Constructors	43.02
Syska & Hennessy Inc.	37.90
Bechtel Group Inc.	36.30
Parsons Brinckerhoff Inc.	27.73
Martin Associates Group Inc.	25.63
Fru-Con Engineering Inc.	22.42

Source: *Building Design & Construction*, July 1995, p. 38.

★ 2012 ★

Architectural Services (SIC 8712)

Largest Architectural Firms - New York

Firms are ranked by number of architects.

Skidmore Owings & Merrill	103
Pei Cobb Freed & Partners	92
Kohn Pedersen Fox Associates	68
Davis Brody & Associates Architects	66
HLW International	62
Gwathmey Siegel & Associates Architects	60
Perkins Eastman Architects	54
Perkins & Will	53
Hellmuth Obata & Kassabaum	50
Brennan Beer Gorman/Architects	46

Source: *Crain's New York Business*, April 1, 1996, p. 22.

★ 2013 ★

Architectural Services (SIC 8712)

Leading Architects - Health Care Construction

The table ranks the architectural firms involved in the design of buildings for the health care industry. Fees are shown in millions of dollars for 1995.

NBBJ	$ 40.32
Henningson, Durham & Richardson	40.10
HKS Architects	35.28
Perkins & Will	34.15
Ellerbe Becket	23.38
Hansen Lind Meyer	22.93
RTKL Associates	22.10
Gresham Smith & Partners	20.30
Cannon	19.30
URS Consultants	17.65

Source: *Modern Healthcare*, April 1, 1996, p. 32.

★ 2014 ★

Architectural Services (SIC 8712)

Leading Architectural Firms

The top firms are ranked by revenues in millions of dollars. Figures exclude revenues from foreign projects.

Gensler & Associates/Architects	$ 63.45
NBBJ	43.10
Kohn Pedersen Fox Associates	31.00
The Hillier Group	24.76
Callison Architecture Inc.	23.20
Schenkel & Shultz	17.00
FRCH Design Worldwide	16.10
Kaplan/McLaughlin/Diaz	15.00
Smallwood, Reynolds	14.08
Shepley Bulfinch Richardson and Abbott	12.99

Source: *Building Design & Construction*, July 1995, p. 9.

★ 2015 ★
Accounting Services (SIC 8721)

Accounting Firms - Mountain States

Accounting firms are ranked by 1995 revenues in millions of dollars.

Galusha, Higgins & Galusha	$ 10.0
Hein & Associates, LLP	7.0
Ehrhardt Keefe Steiner & Hottman PC	6.0
Gelfond Hochstadt Pangburn & Co., PC	5.5
Anderson ZurMuehlen & Co., P.C.	5.1
Junkermier, Clark, Campanella, Stevens, P.C.	4.1
Rudd & Co. PLLC	3.1
Foote, Passey, Griffin & Company	3.0
Presnell Gage, PC	2.9
Hawkins Cloward Simister	2.8

Source: *Practical Accountant*, April 1996, p. 43.

★ 2016 ★
Accounting Services (SIC 8721)

Accounting Firms - North Central

Accounting firms are ranked by 1995 revenues in millions of dollars.

Crowe Chizek and Co. LLP	$ 76.0
Plante & Moran LLP	67.6
Altschuler, Melvoin & Glasser LLP	65.0
Clifton, Gunderson & Co.	61.9
Geo. S. Olive & Co. LLP	43.2
Friedman, Eisenstein, Raemer & Schwartz, LLP	41.0
Wipfli Ullrich Bertelson	25.5
Checkers Simon & Rosner LLP	23.9
Hausser & Taylor	21.7
Thomas Harvey & Co. LLP	21.5

Source: *Practical Accountant*, April 1996, p. 35.

★ 2017 ★
Accounting Services (SIC 8721)

Leading Accounting Firms - Northeast

Accounting firms are ranked by 1995 revenues in millions of dollars.

Richard A. Eisner & Co. LLP	$ 55.9
Goldstein Golub Kessler & Co. LLP	40.4
Anchin, & Block & Anchin LLP	28.0

Campos & Stratis LLP	$ 27.7
Resnick Fedder & Siverman	26.7
David Berdon & Co., LLP	26.5
M.R. Weiser & Co., LLP	25.0
Mitchell & Titus, LLP	24.9
Parente, Randolph, Orlando, Carey & Assoc., P.C.	23.3
Zelenkofske Axelrod & Co., Inc.	19.7

Source: *Practical Accountant*, April 1996, p. 18.

★ 2018 ★
Accounting Services (SIC 8721)

Leading National Accounting Firms

Accounting firms are ranked by 1995 revenues in millions of dollars.

Andersen Worldwide	$ 3,900.0
Ernst & Young LLP	3,000.0
Deloitte & Touche LLP	2,600.0
KPMG Peat Marwick LLP	2,300.0
Coopers & Lybrand LLP	1,900.0
Price Waterhouse LLP	1,800.0
Grant Thornton LLP	240.0
McGladrey & Pullen, LLP	230.0
BDO Seidman, LLP	203.0

Source: *Practical Accountant*, April 1996, p. 18.

★ 2019 ★
Accounting Services (SIC 8721)

Major Paycheck Processors

A total of 28 million payroll checks were outsourced in 1994. Percentages indicate the number of paychecks processed by each company.

ADP	60.0%
Ceridian	20.0
Paychex	8.0
Others	12.0

Source: *Informationweek*, August 28, 1995, p. 76, from Merrill Lynch.

★ 2020 ★
Accounting Services (SIC 8721)

Top Accounting Firms - Midwest

Accounting firms are ranked by 1995 revenues in millions of dollars.

Baird, Kurtz & Dobson	$ 75.4
Larson Allen Weishair & Co. LLP	39.8
Eide Helmeke P.L.L.P.	16.1
Charles Bailly & Company PLLP	16.1
Rubin Brown Gornstein & Co.	14.5
Kennedy & Coe LLC	14.2
Mayer Hoffman McCann, L.C.	13.5
Lurie, Besikof, Lapidus & Co., LLP	11.0
Brady Martz & Assoc., P.C.	9.5
Olsen, Thielsen & Co. Ltd.	8.5

Source: *Practical Accountant*, April 1996, p. 39.

★ 2021 ★
Accounting Services (SIC 8721)

Top Accounting Firms - Southwest

Accounting firms are ranked by 1995 revenues in millions of dollars.

Weaver and Tidwell L.L.P.	$ 9.7
Mann Frankfort Stein & Lipp, P.C.	7.8
Lane Goman Trubitt, L.L.P.	7.0
Postlethwaite & Netterville, APAC	6.8
Brousard Poche Lewis & Breaux	6.3
Toback CPAs, P.C.	5.9
Henry & Horne, P.L.C.	5.7
Bourgeois Bennett, L.L.C.	5.3
Heard, McElroy & Vestal, L.L.P.	5.2
Johnson Miller & Co.	5.0

Source: *Practical Accountant*, April 1996, p. 46.

★ 2022 ★
Accounting Services (SIC 8721)

Top Dallas Accounting Companies

Accounting companies are ranked by total number of professionals working in the Dallas area.

Arthur Andersen	1,200
Ernst & Young LLP.	710
Price Waterhouse	635
Coopers & Lybrand LLP.	524
KPMG Peat Marwick	500
Deloitte & Touche LLP.	405

Grant Thornton LLP.	85
Weaver and Tidwell LLP.	81
Lane Gorman Trubitt LLP.	73
Belew Averitt LLP.	52

Source: *Dallas Business Journal*, January 18, 1996, p. 17, from companies.

★ 2023 ★
Commercial Research (SIC 8732)

Market Research - Canada

The table shows the sources of $112.4 million in commercial research billings in Canada in 1994. The 20 members of the Canadian Association of Marketing Research Organizations do 80% of the research in Canada.

Private industry	77.4%
Government	9.3
Crown corporations	5.5
Advertising agencies	4.0
Other	3.7

Source: *Marketing Magazine*, January 15, 1996, p. 18, from Canadian Association of Marketing Research Organizations.

★ 2024 ★
Commercial Research (SIC 8732)

Market Research Companies - Silicon Valley

Firms are ranked by number of employees.

SRI Consulting	350
Gartner Group Inc.	300
Dataquest	250
Frost & Sullivan	175
Nichols Research Inc.	75
International Data Corp.	36
H&M Consulting	33
VLSI Research Inc.	25
Technology Marketing Resources	13
Macro Consulting Inc.	12

Source: *San Jose and Silicon Valley Business Journal*, April 21, 1996, p. 18.

★ 2025 ★

Commercial Research (SIC 8732)

Top Research Organizations

The top U.S. companies are ranked by research revenues in millions of dollars.

D&B Marketing Information Services . $ 2,388.1
Information Resources Inc. 399.9
The Arbitron Co. 137.2
Westat Inc. 124.0
Maritz Marketing Research Inc. 122.4
Walsh International/PMSI 111.6
The Kantar Group 91.9
The NPD Group 85.8
NFP Research Inc. 73.1
Market Facts Inc. 64.6
Audits & Aurveys Worldwide Inc. . . . 54.6
The M/A/R/C Group 52.1
Opinion Research Corp. 44.1
Abt Associates Inc. 42.9
The BASES Group 41.6
Intersearch Corp. 41.1
MAI Information Group 38.0
Macro International Inc. 37.8
Walker Information 37.7
Elrick & Lavidge 34.6

Source: *Marketing News*, June 3, 1996, p. H4, from Council of American Survey Research Organizations.

★ 2026 ★

Commercial Research (SIC 8732)

Top Research Parks

The parks are ranked by acreage.

Research Triangle Park 6,800
Cummings Research Park 3,800
University Research Park 3,200
Tri-Cities Science & Tech Park 2,600
Princeton Forrestal Center 2,150
Oakland Technology Park 1,800
Stanford Research Park 910
University of Utah Research Park 320
Louisiana Biomedical Research Park . . . 116
University City Science Center 17

Source: *World Trade*, January 1996, p. 46.

★ 2027 ★

Laboratories (SIC 8734)

Animal Use in Research

Distribution of the 1.6 million animals used in research in 1994 is shown by type. Less than 1.0% of dogs and cats and less than than 0.3% of primates were used in research.

Rats, mice, rodents 90.0%
Dogs and cats 1.0
Primates 0.3
Other 8.7

Source: *USA TODAY*, June 20, 1996, p. A14, from National Association for Biomedical Research.

★ 2028 ★

Laboratories (SIC 8734)

Leading Environmental Labs - Washington

Labs are ranked by 1995 billings in Washington state. Figures are in millions of dollars.

Columbia Environmental Services Inc. . . $ 17.5
Quanterra Environmental Services 7.0
Analytical Resources Inc. 5.2
Sound Analytical Services Inc. 4.7
North Creek Analytical 4.1
Laucks Testing Laboratories Inc. 4.0

Source: *Puget Sound Business Journal*, February 21, 1996, p. 24.

★ 2029 ★

Construction Management (SIC 8741)

Leading Construction Managers

Firms are ranked by fees in millions of dollars.

Turner Corp. . . . . $ 699.7
Centex Construction Group 524.0
McCarthy 489.0
Barton Malow Co. 303.5
Bovis 303.0
Morse Diesel International 302.0
Beers Construction Co. 232.0

Source: *Modern Healthcare*, April 1, 1996, p. 39.

★ 2030 ★

Management Services (SIC 8741)

Environmental Service Providers

The table shows the leading companies that provide consulting and engineering services, and conduct environmental impact studies in Mexico.

Corporacion	20.0%
Murad Asesores	15.0
Hart Crouser	10.0
Bufete Quimico	5.0
Other	50.0

Source: *National Trade Data Bank*, January 2, 1996, p. IS9506.647.

★ 2031 ★

Management Services (SIC 8741)

Health Care Program Managers

Firms are ranked by fees in millions of dollars.

American Medical Design Corp.	$ 164.0
Meta Associates	139.8
W.R. Adams Co.	130.0
Medical Cities	108.1
Healthcare Realty Management	63.4

Source: *Modern Healthcare*, April 1, 1996, p. 38.

★ 2032 ★

Management Services (SIC 8741)

Top Construction Managers

The top managers are ranked by 1994 revenues in millions of dollars.

Lehrer McGovern Bovis Inc.	$ 1,580.00
Gilbane Building Co.	1,182.19
Heery International Inc.	1,068.00
Sverdrup Corp.	902.00
Barton Malow Co.	612.00
URS Consultants Inc.	554.76
Tishman Realty & Construction Co.	521.36
3D/International	510.25
The Turner Corp.	495.59
Parsons Brinckerhoff Inc.	474.93

Source: *Building Design & Construction*, July 1995, p. 26.

★ 2033 ★

Management Services (SIC 8741)

Top Hotel Management Companies

Firms are ranked by sales in millions of dollars.

Interstate Hotels	$ 1,050
Carnival Hotels & Resorts	500
Richfield Hospitality	440
Tishman Hotel Corp.	418
American General Hospitality	324
Ocean Hospitalities	310
Prime Hospitality	306
John Q. Hammons	256
Winegardener & Hammons	250
Beck Summit Hotel Management	200
Gencom American Hospitality	200
Servico Hotels & Resorts	176
Remington Hotel Corp.	170
Hostmark Management	165
Sage Hospitality Resources	160

Source: *Hotel & Motel Management*, March 18, 1996, p. 28.

★ 2034 ★

Marketing Services (SIC 8741)

Top Marketing Agencies

Firms are ranked by 1995 revenues in millions of dollars.

Gage Marketing Group	$ 108.5
Wunderman Cate Johnson	101.0
Alcone Marketing Group	84.2
Rapp Collins Worldwide	80.0
Bronner Slosberg Humphrey	67.4
DIMAC Direct	64.7
Ogilvy & Mather Direct	52.0
DraftDirect Worldwide	51.6
Barry Blau & Partners	49.8
Frankel & Co.	47.5

Source: *Advertising Age*, August 5, 1996, p. S1.

★ 2035 ★
Pharmacy Management (SIC 8741)

Pharmacy Management - 1994

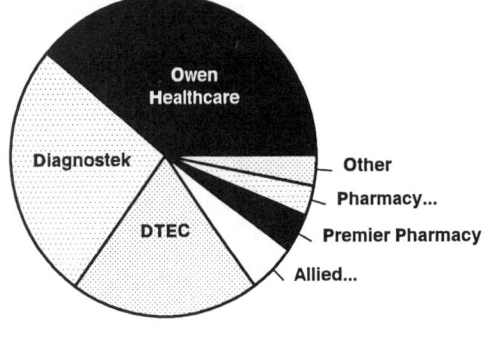

Owen Healthcare	39.0%
Diagnostek	26.0
DTEC	20.0
Allied Pharmacy Mgmt.	5.0
Premier Pharmacy	4.0
Pharmacy Systems	3.0
Other	3.0

Source: *Investor's Business Today*, January 18, 1996, p. A6, from *Modern Healthcare* and company reports.

★ 2036 ★
Management Services (SIC 8742)

Consulting Services in Mexico

"Other" includes planning, energy projects, installation services, and quality control analysis.

Management administration	20.1%
Environmentnal impact	14.4
Urban/architectural services	14.0
Project management	11.8
Technical support	11.4
Planning/design	8.9
Other	19.3

Source: *National Trade Data Bank*, March 2, 1996, p. 11108995.

★ 2037 ★
Public Relations Services (SIC 8743)

Public Relations Firms - Dallas

Companies are ranked by fee incomes.

Halcyon Associates	$ 2,017,843
Edelman Public Relations Worldwide	. 2,000,000
Temerlin McClain Public Relations	. 1,620,000
E. Bruce Harrison Co./Southwest Inc.	. 1,250,000
Stern, Nathan & Perryman	. 1,200,000
MCCommunications	1,175,650
Bustin & Co.	1,100,000
Meltzer & Martin Public Relations . . .	1,100,000
Publicis Public Relations	1,000,000
Hart Agency Inc.	986,261

Source: *Dallas Business Journal*, October 5, 1995, p. 10, from companies.

★ 2038 ★
Outsourcing (SIC 8744)

Outsourcing Market

Data are for 1994.

EDS	33.8%
IBM	11.3
CSC	9.0
Systematics	5.0
Martin Marietta	4.0
Unisys	3.1
Digital	2.4
PRC	2.1
Affiliated Computer Systems	2.0
Analyst International	1.8
Other	26.55

Source: *Chemicalweek*, December 13, 1995, p. 60, from International Data Corp.

★ 2039 ★
Prisons (SIC 8744)

Private Correctional Facilities

An estimated 57,600 adult beds have been awarded to private firms in 1995, a 4% share of the 1.6 million inmates housed in U.S. prisons. With the inclusion of foreign contracts in Australia and Britain, the number increases to 63,000. Shares are shown based on awarded beds.

CorrectionsCorp. of America 48.0%
Wackenhut Corrections 25.0
Other 27.0

Source: *Investor's Business Daily*, May 21, 1996, p. A4.

★ 2040 ★
Prisons (SIC 8744)

Private Prison Capacities

The table shows the capacities of private prisons by location. Data include facilities under construction and planned expansions.

	No.	Share
Texas	23,008	36.2%
Florida	5,915	9.3
Tennessee	5,112	8.0
Louisiana	2,948	4.6
Mississippi	2,034	3.2
Kentucky	1,750	2.8
Virginia	1,500	2.4
Rest of U.S.	15,342	24.1
Outside U.S.	5,986	9.4

Source: *Southern Exposure*, Summer 1996, p. 14, from Center for Studies in Criminology and Law.

★ 2041 ★
Construction Management (SIC 8748)

Leading At-Risk Construction Managers

The leading construction management at-risk firms are ranked by 1995 revenues in millions of dollars.

The Turner Corp. . . . . $ 2,627.3
Brown & Root Inc. 1,353.7
Jacobs Engineering Group Inc. 1,120.0
Gilbane Building Co. 1,000.3
Structure Tone Co. 838.0
Morrison Knudsen Corp. 756.0
Fluor Daniel Inc. 644.0
Skanska (USA) Inc. 627.0
The Whiting-Turner Contracting Co. . . . 548.0
Huber, Hunt and Nichols Inc. 532.0

Source: *ENR*, June 10, 1996, p. 42.

★ 2042 ★
Environmental Consulting (SIC 8748)

Environmental Consulting/ Engineering Firms

Firms are ranked by consulting/engineering revenues in millions of dollars.

CH2M Hill Companies . . . . $ 576.0
Metcalf & Eddy 522.5
Fluor Daniel Inc. 350.0
Parsons Engineering Services Inc. 327.7
Black & Vestch 325.0
Montgomery Watson 318.0
Camp Dresser & McKee Inc. 308.7

Source: *Environment Today*, July 1995, p. 12.

★ 2043 ★
Human Resource Consulting (SIC 8748)

Leading Benefit Consulting Firms

The leading firms are ranked by estimated benefit consulting revenues in 1995. Data are in millions of dollars.

William M. Mercer . . . . $ 417.6
Towers Perrin 371.3
Hewlett Associates 350.5
Watson Wyatt Worldwide 313.2
A. Foster Higgins 187.6
Coopers & Lybrand 169.4
Continued on next page.

★ 2043 ★ *Continued*

Human Resource Consulting (SIC 8748)

Leading Benefit Consulting Firms

The leading firms are ranked by estimated benefit consulting revenues in 1995. Data are in millions of dollars.

Buck Consultants	$ 147.0
Alexander Consulting Group	113.7
Goodwins Booke & Dickenson	109.4
Deloitte Touche	87.1

Source: *Business Insurance*, December 11, 1995, p. 14.

SIC 92 - Justice, Public Order, and Safety

★ 2044 ★
Crime (SIC 9220)

Crime in Mexico City

The table shows the types of crimes committed in Mexico City in the first six months of 1995.

	No.	Share
Assaults	10,750	24.9%
Car theft	9,419	21.8
Assault & battery	9,169	21.2
Robbery to delivery trucks	8,071	18.7
Violent assaults to companies	4,108	9.5
Rapes	627	1.5
Murders	583	1.4
Home breakins	430	1.0

Source: *National Trade Data Bank*, January 1, 1996, p. IS9505.637, from Mexico City Government, Secreteriat of Public Safety.

★ 2045 ★
Crime (SIC 9220)

Drug Seizures by State

The table compares the pounds of heroin and marijuana seized by U.S. authorities in selected states.

	Mar.	Heroin
South Texas	55	246,510
Arizona	11	131,855
California	178	124,440
West Texas	11	84,922
New Mexico	44	14,410

Source: *Washington Post National Weekly Edition*, May 6, 1996, p. 16.

★ 2046 ★
Crime (SIC 9220)

Piracy in China

The table shows the millions of dollars in U.S. trade losses from copyright piracy in China.

Entertainment software	$ 1,290
Records and music	300
Business software	250
Books	125
Motion pictures	124

Source: *Wall Street Journal*, May 17, 1996, p. A10, from American Chamber of Commerce, U.S. and Chinese governments, Intellectual Property Alliance, and Software Publishers Association.

★ 2047 ★
Crime (SIC 9220)

Piracy in Mexico - 1995

The table shows the millions of dollars in revenues U.S. companies lost to Mexico in 1995. Mexico ranks fourth among countries where the most piracy occurs.

Computer entertainment and software	$ 100.0
Records and music	85.0
Motion pictures	67.0
Books	33.0

Source: *New York Times*, April 20, 1996, p. 20, from Mexico's Special Prosecutor for Intellectual Property Crimes.

★ 2048 ★
Prisons (SIC 9223)

Largest U.S. Prisons

The prison population has grown by 90,000 in the last 12 months. The largest prison systems are shown by inmate population.

California 131,000
Texas 127,000
Federal system 99,500
New York 68,500
Florida 62,000
Ohio 43,000
Michigan 41,000
Illinois 37,800
Georgia 34,000
Pennsylvania 29,800

Source: *Detroit Free Press*, December 4, 1995, p. 7A, from United States Department of Justice.

★ 2049 ★

Taxation (SIC 9311)

U.S. Tax Collection

The United States is expected to gather $2.183 trillion in taxes in 1995. The table shows the leading sources.

Individual income	33.0%
Social insurance	30.0
Sales and excise	13.0
Corporate income	10.0
Property and other business	12.0
Other	2.0

Source: *Journal of Accountancy*, September 1995, p. 30, from Tax Foundation.

★ 2050 ★

Federal Programs (SIC 9441)

Food Stamp Households by State

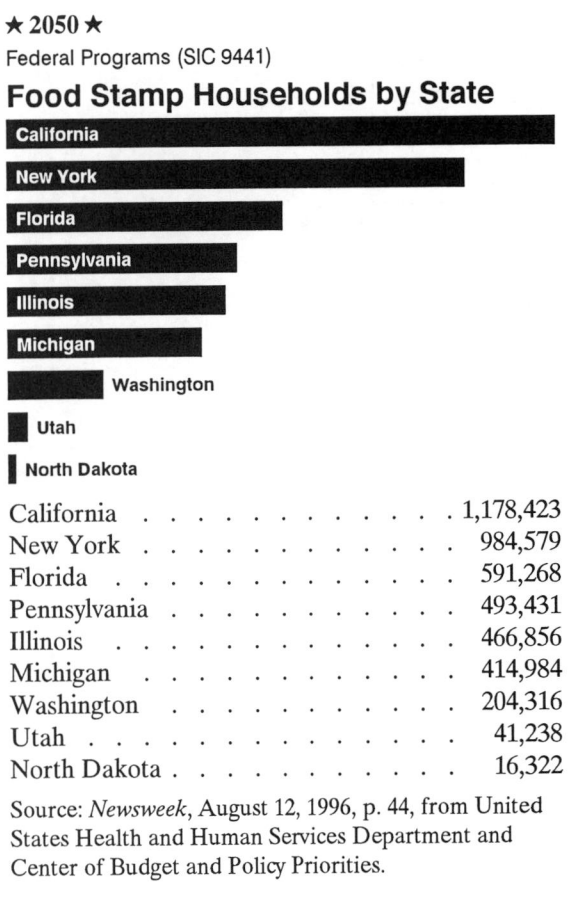

California	1,178,423
New York	984,579
Florida	591,268
Pennsylvania	493,431
Illinois	466,856
Michigan	414,984
Washington	204,316
Utah	41,238
North Dakota	16,322

Source: *Newsweek*, August 12, 1996, p. 44, from United States Health and Human Services Department and Center of Budget and Policy Priorities.

SIC 95 - Environmental Quality and Housing

★ 2051 ★

Environmental Services (SIC 9510)

Environmental Consulting Firms

The major environmental risk management consulting firms are shown ranked by 1994 revenues in millions of dollars.

ERM Group	$ 229.6
IT Corp.	212.0
Dames & Moore Inc.	148.4
Parsons Engineering Science Inc.	141.5
GroundWater Technology Inc.	127.3
Environmental Science & Eng. Inc. . . .	119.5
Radian Corp.	64.2
Law Eng. & Environmental Services Inc. . .	59.5
GZA Environmental Inc.	53.0
Environ International Corp.	38.2

Source: *Corporate Cashflow*, January 1996, p. 16, from *Business Insurance*.

★ 2052 ★

Land Conservation (SIC 9512)

Land Management Groups

The table shows the groups involved with land management and purchasing property for the conservation of the environment. Groups are ranked by membership.

The Nature Conservancy	819,000
Ducks Unlimited	550,000
The Wilderness Society	275,000
African Wildlife Foundation	100,000

Source: *Mining Voice*, Jan./ Feb. 1996, p. 26.

★ 2053 ★

Land Conservation (SIC 9532)

Who Owns U.S. Land

Data show that more than 6.6 million acres of agricultural land in the United States were owned by foreign companies and individuals. The table shows the owners who have at least 100,000 acres.

United Kingdom	17.34
Canada	15.72
Germany	7.59
Netherlands Antilles	3.56
Switzerland	2.91
Japan	2.00
Mexico	1.79
Liechtenstein	1.35
France	1.28
British Virgin Islands	1.24
Panama	1.21
Netherlands	1.12

Source: *Implement & Tractor*, July/August 1995, p. 11, from United States Department of Commerce.

★ 2054 ★

Space Research (SIC 9661)

Space Shuttle Cargo

The table shows the types of cargo on the Shuttle since the Challenger.

NASA Science	53.0%
U.S. Defense Dept.	16.0
Foreign payloads	8.0
Commercial	2.0
Other	21.0

Source: *Aviation Week & Space Technology*, April 8, 1996, p. 52, from NASA.

★ 2055 ★

Defense (SIC 9711)

U.S. Military Forces - Pacific

This table shows the deployment of military personnel in the Pacific by area. Army - 63,700; Air Force - 40,750; Marines - 24,900; Navy - 31,400.

Hawaii	52,400
Japan	45,500
South Korea	36,450
Alaska	19,600
Guam	6,800

Source: *Economist*, April 13, 1996, p. 18, from International Institute for Strategic Studies.

SOURCE INDEX

This index is divided into *primary sources* and *original sources*. Primary sources are the publications where the market shares were found. Original sources are sources cited in the primary sources. Numbers following the sources are entry numbers, arranged sequentially; the first number refers to the first appearance of the source in *Market Share Reporter*. All told, 1120 organizations are listed.

Primary Sources

Original Sources

Source Index: Original

PLACE NAMES INDEX

This index shows global regions, political entities, states and provinces, regions within countries, and cities. The numbers that follow listings are entry numbers; they are arranged sequentially so that the first mention of a place is listed first. The index shows references to more than 250 places.

PRODUCTS, SERVICES, AND ISSUES INDEX

This index shows, in alphabetical order, references to products, services, and issues covered in *Market Share Reporter*, 7th Edition. More than 2,500 terms are included. Terms include subjects not readily categorized as products and services, including such subjects as *crime* and *welfare*. The numbers that follow each term refer to entry numbers and are arranged sequentially so that the first mention is listed first.

2-D video tools, 1803
3-D video tools, 1785
Abrasive cleaners, 702, 705, 709-710
Abrasives, 134, 883-884
ABS (acrylonitrile butadiene styrene), 605-606, 609
Accounting services, 2015-2022
Acetaminophen, 665, 667
Acid & premetalized dyes, 792
Acid, phosphoric, 813
Acne remedies, 771
Acrylics, 626, 780
Acrylin resins, 607
Acrylonitrile butadiene styrene, 605-606, 609, 795
Action figures, 1236, 1575
Activewear, 437, 440
Actuators, 1016
Additives, 779
Adhesives, 818-819
Adventure CD-ROMs, 1820
Advertising, 561, 663, 1197, 1749-1773, 1775, 1911, 1984
Advertising supplements, 820
Advertising, design, 1792
Advertising, newspapers, 1763
Advertising, on-line, 1766
Advertising, outdoor, 1760
Advertising, radio, 1762, 1764
Advertising, television, 1761
Advertising, yellow pages, 1773
Aerosols, 585
Aerospace, 610, 924, 950, 953, 1104, 1183-1186
Agrichemicals, 806-810, 815-816
Agricultural banking, 1635-1636
Agriculture, 24, 26-28, 33, 38, 40-41, 44, 47, 59, 77, 79, 1635
Air cargo, 1326-1329
Air conditioners, 1005, 1008-1009
Air conditioning, 1003
Air terminals, 1004
Air transports, 1155
Airbags, 463
Aircraft, 610, 1155-1161, 1185

Aircraft parts, 1162-1164
Airlines, 1307-1326
Airlines, regional, 1315, 1319
Airlines, special services, 1311
Airports, 1330-1331
Alarms, 1089
Alcohol, 340, 344-350, 352-359, 361-365, 802
Alimentary drugs, 652
Alkalies and chlorine, 590-595
Allergy relief, 642, 653
Almonds, 334-335
Alphanumeric pagers, 1078
Alumina, 591, 899-900
Aluminum, 901
Aluminum cookware, 925
Aluminum products, 22
AM/FM receivers, 1052, 1055
Amateur sports, 1952
Ambulance services, 1283
Ambulatory care facilities, 1199
American cheese, 216
American Stock Exchange, 1664
Ammonia, 579, 814
Ammonium nitrate, 579, 814
Ammonium phosphate, 811
Ammonium sulfate, 814
Amphitheaters, 1928-1930
Ampuls & vials, 14
Amusement parks, 1949-1951
Analgesics, 659, 760
Anchovies, 385
Animal feed, 599
Animal products, 585
Animals, 62-63, 69, 72, 75-76, 2027
Antacids, 643, 665, 672
Anti-fungal products, 764
Anti-infectives, 652
Anti-lock brakes, 1149
Antiarthritics, 658
Antidepressants, 644
Antihistimines, 649

Products, Services, and Issues Index

Political organizations, 2008-2009
Polybutadiene, 631-632
Polychloroprene, 631-632
Polyethylene pipe, 849
Polyethylene terephthalate, 619-620, 627, 852
Polypropylene, 619, 622, 628
Polystyrene, 609, 619, 623
Polyurethane, 626
Polyvinyl acetate, 626
Polyvinyl chloride, 619, 621, 624
Pool sanitizers, 602
Popcorn, 392, 396, 400
Popcorn oil, 392
Pork, 60, 63-64, 201-202, 207
Pork rinds, 396
Porous point pens, 1258
Portable computers, 976-977
Postal service, 1294-1295
Potash, 140, 590
Potassium carbonate, 593
Potassium chloride, 814
Potato chips, 391, 393-394, 396, 398, 400-401
Potato crisps, 395
Potato products, 267
Potatoes, 34, 42, 237
Pots, 869
Potted flowering plants, 57
Poultry, 60, 64, 68-70, 72-73
Powdered detergents, 695
Powdered drinks, 383
Powdered metal, 928-929
Powdered milk, 254
Powders, 878
Power control devices, 1085
Power generation, 927
Power tools, 910, 951
PPOs, 1688-1689, 1703
Pre-cut homes, 474
Prefabricated buildings, 921-923
Preferred provider organizations, 1688-1689, 1703
Pregnancy kits, 678
Premarin, 660
Prerecorded music, 1058-1067, 1959-1960, 2047
Prerecorded video tapes, 1902, 1909, 1925
Preschool toys, 1233
Presentation graphics, 1802, 1813
Preserved wood, 475
Pretzels, 313-314, 316, 396, 400
Price/factory outlets, 1501
Prilosec, 660
Primary wood bonding, 818
Printers, 992, 1000-1001
Printers, computer, 998

Printers, dot matrix, 999
Printing, 544-545, 547, 572-574
Printing equipment, 956
Printing ink, 820-823
Prisons, 2039-2040, 2048
Private label goods, 18, 272, 442
Procardia XL, 660
Professional baseball, 1940-1941
Professional basketball, 1942
Professional football, 1943
Professional hockey, 1944
Professional soccer, 1945
Projectors, 1227-1228
Promoters, 1930
Promotional products, 19
Property development, 1721
Property insurance, 1697-1700
Proprietary fleets, 1301
Propylene, 579
Prosthodontics, 1974
Prozac, 660
Prune, 247
Psychiatric care, 1983
Psychic services, 1910
Public relations services, 2037
Public switched telephone networks, 1357
Public transit, 1277, 1279, 1281-1282, 1284
Publications, 1858, 1960
Publishing, 9, 546-548, 557, 559-560, 563, 565-566, 568-569, 571
Publishing & media, 1750
Pubs/taverns/lounges, 1540
Pudding, 232-233, 1584
Pull carts, 1243
Pulp, 778
Pulp & paper, 492-497, 591, 927
Pulp & paper machinery, 953
Pumpkins, 267
Pumps, 960, 1003, 1012
Pumps, medical, 1200
Purees, non-citrus, 266
Pushbuttons, 1045
Puzzles, 1234, 1820
PVC, 609, 621
Quick service, 1539
R&B music, 1066
R&D, 20-21
Radio advertising, 1749, 1751, 1762, 1764, 1959
Radio broadcasting, 1380-1390
Radios, 1050
Rail cars, 1278, 1281
Rail systems, 1279
Railroad equipment, 1172-1177

Products, Services, and Issues Index

Products, Services, and Issues Index

Products, Services, and Issues Index

COMPANY INDEX

The more than 5,450 companies and institutions in this book are indexed here in alphabetical order. Numbers following the terms are entry numbers. They are arranged sequentially; the first entry number refers to the first mention of the company in *Market Share Reporter*. Although most organizations appear only once, some entities are referred to under abbreviations in the sources and these have not always been expanded.

Company Index

Company Index

Company Index

Bartech Inc., 1783
Bartek Chemical, 794
Barton Inc., 362
Barton Malow Co., 2029, 2032
Bartow Homes Inc., 474
BASES Group, 2025
BASF, 584, 623, 785, 793, 796, 806, 822
Basha's, 1476
Basham, Ringe y Correa, 1990
Basin Electric Power Co-op (N.D.), 1417
Basis Inc., 1532
Baskin-Robbins, 210-211
Bass, 861-863
Bassett, 485
Bassett Furniture Ind., 484, 487
Bassett-Walker, 440, 450
Bates Worldwide, 1760-1762
Bath & Body Works, 724
Bath Iron Works, 1166
Bauer Built Inc., 1495, 1497
Bausch & Lomb, 653, 768-769, 1217
Baxter Fentriss, 1876
Baxter Health Care, 1206, 1208
Baxter International, 679, 1201, 1203
Bay Mills Indian Community, 1955
Bay Networks, 1068, 1088, 1819, 1840, 1850
Bayer, 637, 675, 679, 793-794, 806
Bayer Diagnostic Division, 1769
Bayer Pharmaceuticals, 1770
BB&T, 1612
BBDO Canada Inc., 1753
BBDO Mexico, 1752
BBDO Worldwide, 1759-1762
BC Tel, 1364
BCP Canada Inc., 1753
BDO Seidman, LLP, 2018
BE&K Inc., 169, 2011
Bean, 1796
Bear & Co., 571
Bear Stearns, 1649, 1651, 1661, 1881-1882
Bearings Inc., 1430
Beaton Cranberries Inc., 48
Beatrice Foods of Toronto, 227
Beaulieu, 434
Beaver Excavating Co., 187
Beazer, 156
Becher & Carlson Risk Mgmt. Inc., 1667
Bechtel Group Inc., 145, 167, 169-170, 2011
Beck Summit Hotel Management, 2033
Becker Group Inc., 462, 856
Becker Holding Corp., 53
Beckman Instruments Inc., 1769
Becton Dickinson, 1769

Beech Aircraft Corp., 1156
Beech Street Corp., 1688-1689, 1703
Beech-Nut Nutrition Group, 230
Beechcraft, 1311
Beers Construction Co., 2029
Behring Diagnostics Inc., 1769
Beiersdorf, 767-769
Bekins Van Lines Co., 1290
Belew Averitt LLP., 2022
Belk, 1464
Belk Stores, 1521
Belkin Prods., 1930, 1935
Bell Atlantic, 1070, 1073, 1362, 1371, 1373
Bell Atlantic Network, 5
Bell Atlantic/Nynex, 1352, 1359
Bell FCU, 1613
Bell Helicopter Textron, 1184
Bell Industries, 1437, 1439
Bell Microproducts Inc., 1437
Bell South, 1373
Bellco First FCU, 1610
Bellevue Hospital Center, 1981
BellSouth, 1070, 1073, 1361-1362, 1371
BellSouth Cellular, 1359
Belridge Farms, 52
Bemis Co., 846, 853
Ben & Jerry's, 224
Ben Hill Griffin, 53
Benckiser, 691, 724
Bendata, 1817
Bendix, 1146
Bendix/King (Allied Signal), 1155, 1192
Benetton, 1254
Benjamin Moore, 785
Bennigan's, 1549
Bentley Systems, 1821
Berg Electronics, 854
Bergen Brunswig, 1444
Berger Associates Inc., 1645
Bergmeyer Associates. Inc., 1868
Berkshire Hathaway, 1672
Bernard Hoods Group, 1763
Berol, 541
Berry Network, 1773
Bertelsmann Music Group, 1059, 1061-1062, 1066-1067
Bertino Brothers, 48
Berwind Financial Group, 1876
Besnier America, 210
Best Buy, 1527, 1529-1531, 1534, 1537
Best Foods, 297, 337
Best Group Inc., 188
Best Power/Sola, 1085
Best Software, 1799

Company Index

City Management Corp., 1427
City National, 1611
Claire's, 1503
Claridge, 1953
Clarify Inc., 1801, 1817
Clark Construction Group Inc., 167, 169
Clark Hill, 1989
Clayco, 166
Clayton Environmental Consultants Inc., 1427
Clear Channel, 1380-1381, 1387-1388
Cleveland Cavaliers, 1942
Cleveland Cement Contractors Inc., 184
Cleveland Crunch, 1945
Cleveland Indians, 1940
Cleveland Wrecking Co., 188
Client Server Associates, 1865
Clifton, Gunderson & Co., 2016
Clintec, 189
Clorox, 260, 681, 705-706, 787
Clougherty Packing Co., 64
Club Mediterrane, 1739
CML Group, 1581
CMS Energy, 1416
CMT, 1401
CNA Financial Corp., 1694
CNA Ins. Companies, 1680, 1701-1702, 1704-1705
CNA Managed Care, 1688
CNBC, 1401
CNN, 1401
CNN Headline, 1401
Coachmen, 1153, 1188
Coast, 697
Coast To Coast Vision Plan, 1683
Coastal, 121, 828
Coastal Oil & Gas, 125
Coastal Physician Services Inc., 1767
Coastal Towing Co., 1302, 1305
Coastland Construction Inc., 164
Cobra, 1188, 1241-1242
Coca-Cola Co., 197, 241, 342, 370, 377-378, 380, 852,
   1730, 1928, 1946
Coconuts, 1537
Coffee Beanery, 1559
COGEMA, 104
Cognos, 1788
Cohn & Wells, 1757
Colasanti Corp., 184
Coldwell Banker, 1724
Coleman, 1003, 1005, 1253-1254
Colgate-Palmolive, 293, 681-682, 689-690, 695, 702, 706,
   725, 749, 754-755, 1713
Colgate/Mennen, 724
Collins & Aikman, 427

Collins (Rockwell), 1155, 1192
Colonial Pipeline Co., 1334
Colony Communications & King Holding, 1880
Colony Homes, 153
Colorado Corporate, 1610
Colorado NB, 1610
Colorado Rockies, 1940
Columbia, 445, 860, 1254, 1913, 1922, 1992
Columbia Environmental Services Inc., 2028
Columbia International, 1880
Columbia Showcase, 491
Columbia/Tri-Star, 1392, 1925
Columbian Chemicals, 824
Columbus Life Insurance Co., 1676
Comair, 1319
Combe, 759
Comcast, 1400, 1406-1407, 1880
Comdisco, 1779
Comedy Central, 1401
Comercial Mexicana, 194
Comerica, 1606, 1634, 1642, 1728-1729
Comerical Mexicana, 1477
Cominco American, 603
Cominco Ltd., 90
Commander, 1311
Commercial Carriers, 1286
Commercial Federal, 1610, 1613
Commercial Furnishings Inc., 489
Commercial Metals, 887
Commercial Union Ins. Group, 1705
Commonwealth Edison, 1414
Community Bank, 1611
Community Care Network Inc., 1703
Community National Assurance Co., 1676
Commutair, 1319
Compaeia Papelera Maldonado, 502
Compaq, 964, 966-973, 976-978, 980, 982, 986, 1014, 1071,
   1844
Comphealth, 1767
Comprehensive Health Services, 1685
CompuAdd, 1844
CompUSA, 1532, 1534
CompuServe, 1859-1862
Computer 2000, 1432
Computer Associates, 1796, 1804, 1816
Computer Attic, 1532
Computer City, 1534
Computer Horizons Corp., 1865
Computer Sciences Corp., 5, 1831-1832
ComputerLand of Serramonte, 1532
ComputerPeople Consulting Services, 1865
Computertots, 1732
Computervision, 1804

Company Index

Ito Packing Co., 56
Itron, 1194
ITT, 1873
ITT Automotive, 1144, 1148
ITT Canon, 854
ITT Hartford Ins. Group, 1680-1681, 1694-1695,
    1697-1698, 1701, 1704-1705
ITT Industries, 1149
Ivex Packaging, 503
Ivoclar North America, 1984
Izod, 1242
J&J, 529, 1211-1212
J&L Farms, 51, 896
J. Walter Thompson Co., 1752, 1757, 1759-1762
J.A. Croson Co., 179
J.A. Jones Inc., 170
J.B. Edwards, 1796
J.B. Hunt Transport Services, 1286, 1291
J.C. Penney, 1458, 1461, 1463-1464, 1501-1502, 1507,
    1514, 1518, 1520, 1522-1523, 1530-1531, 1567, 1579,
    1581-1582, 1776
J.F. Afhern Co., 185
J.F. Aher Co., 179
J.F. Walker Co. Inc., 1445
J.H. Kelly Co., 176
J.L. Manta Inc., 177
J.M. Huber, 604
J.N. Mitchell, 768
J.P. Morgan, 1596, 1600, 1603, 1616, 1643, 1655,
    1659-1661, 1727, 1875-1876, 1882
J.P. Morgan Securities, 1651
J.R. Simplot, 811
J.R. Wood Inc., 56
J.S. Alberici, 166
J.S. McManus Produce Co. Inc., 41
J.T. Baker, 589
J.W. Brewer Tire Co., 1495, 1497, 1895
J.W. Messner, 1755
J.W. Yonce & Sons Farms Inc., 56
Jack in the Box, 1547
Jack M. Berry Inc., 53
Jackson Companies, 485
Jackson Hewitt Tax Service, 1731
Jackson Memorial Hospital, 1981-1982
Jacobs Engineering Group Inc., 143-145, 159, 167, 170,
    2041
Jacor, 1380-1381, 1387-1388
Jacques Monet, 452
Jaffe, Raitt, Heuer & Weiss, 1989
Jaguar, 1122, 1486
Jam Productions, 1930, 1935
James Beam, 362
James D. Wolfensohn, 1877

James River, 494, 504, 506, 513, 515-516, 522, 532, 537,
    539, 846, 853
Jani-King International Inc., 1731
Jannock (Canada), 857
JanSport, 445, 1253
Janssen Pharmaceuticals, 1770
Janus Capital Corp., 1645
Japan Travel Bureau Intl., 1345
Jasper Wyman & Son, 48
Jauregui, Navarrete Nader y Rojas, 1990
Jay's, 394
Jayco, 1188
JBA International, 1796, 1816
JCB, 937
Jean Coutu Group, 1465
Jean Phillipe, 747
Jefferson Memorial, 1965
Jefferson Smurfit, 499-500, 508-510, 516
Jennifer Convertibles, 1515
Jist Works, 571
Jitney-Jungle, 1474
JM Manufacturing Co., 850
Joe's Stone Club, 1558
John Brooks Company, 960
John Deere, 935
John E. Green Co., 179
John Hancock Mutual Life, 1678
John L. Scott Real Estate, 1724
John Q. Hammons, 2033
John Wieland Homes, 153
Johnathan's Landing Marina, 1306
Johns Hopkins, 5, 1977, 1993
Johnson & Higgins, 1665, 1667, 1671, 1699
Johnson & Johnson, 535, 675, 724, 738, 746, 759, 767-768,
    1217
Johnson & Johnson Clinical Diagnostics, 1769
Johnson Camping, 1253
Johnson Controls, 852, 908, 1143, 1147-1148
Johnson Miller & Co., 2021
Johnson Printing, 572
Johnston & Murphy, 862
Johnston Industries, 428-429
Jon Greenberg & Assoc. Inc., 1868
Jones Apparel Group, 438, 453
Jones Intercable Inc., 1406-1407
Jos. H. Stomel & Sons, 1445
Joseph A. Brooks, 1581
Joseph J. White Co., 48
JP Foodservice, 1545
JP Morgan & Co., 1607
JPMS, 744
JPS Textile Group, 429
Jugos Del Valle, 196

Company Index

National City, 1634
National Convenience Stores Inc., 1472
National Data, 1623
National Education Association, 1632
National Electric Information Corp., 1767
National Farms, 64
National Finals Rodeo, 1933
National Food Corp., 71
National Futures Association, 2005
National General, 1776
National Glass & Mirror Co. Inc., 186
National Gypsum, 882
National HealthCare, 1976
National Marine, 1300
National Marine Inc., 1302, 1305
National Medical Care, 1987-1988
National Museum of American History, 2003
National Museum of Natural History, 2003
National Oats, 278
National Processing, 1623
National Re, 1672
National Refractories & Minerals, 877
National RV, 1153
National Service, 1748
National Steel Corp., 888-889, 892, 895
National Tobacco Co., 424
National Wildlife Club, 2009
National Wildlife Federation, 2009
NationsBanc Mortgage, 1640
NationsBank, 79, 1592, 1594, 1596, 1600, 1607, 1612,
　　1614-1616, 1626, 1634-1635, 1652, 1725, 1727, 1729
NationsWay Transport Service, 1286
Nationwide Advertising Services, 1763
Nationwide Group, 1679-1681, 1697-1698, 1701,
　　1704-1705
Nationwide Homes, 473
Nationwide Life & Annuity Insurance, 1676
Nationwide Life Insurance Co., 1676
Natural Gas Pipeline of America, 1421
Natural Resources Defense Council, 2009
Nature Conservancy, 1999, 2052
Natuzzi, 485
Natwest Holdings, 1729
NatWest Markets Group, 1882
NatWest USA, 1874
Navajo Agricultural Products Industry, 41
Navistar, 908, 1133, 1136
NBBJ Architects, 1868, 2013-2014
NBC, 11, 1392, 1394-1395, 1626
NBD Bancorp, 1634, 1642, 1874
NCD, 983, 1845
NCI Building System, 923
NCNB Corp, 1874

NDL/Grid, 1249
NEBS, 1799
NEC, 964, 966, 968-970, 976-977, 982, 984, 986, 991, 1075,
　　1077, 1097, 1101, 1108
NECT, 995
NECX Direct, 1771-1772
Nederlander Organization, 1930, 1935
Neilson Dairy, 227
Neiman Marcus, 1464, 1521
Nelson & Schmidt, 1754
Nelson/Weather-Rite, 1253
Neoplan USA, 1132
Nesbitt Burns & Securities, 1657
Neste Resin, 801
Nestle, 218, 239, 254, 293, 319, 326, 342, 389-390, 399,
　　1583
NetCom, 1853, 1856
NetManage, 1821
Netscape, 1766, 1768, 1771-1772, 1808, 1821
Network Long Distance Inc., 1419
Network Managers Inc., 1838, 1842
Network Systems, 989
Neutrogena, 769, 772
New Balance, 837-838
New Berlin Industrial Park, 1712
New England Patriots, 1564
New Enterprise Associates, 1644, 1663
New Flyer, 1132
New Holland Tire Co. Inc., 935, 1895
New Horizons Child Care, 1997
New Horizons Computer Learning, 1732
New Jersey, 1706
New Jersey Transit Corp., 1282
New Line, 1903, 1915-1917, 1922, 1925
New Mexico Salt & Mineral, 826
New Orleans Saints, 1943
New Penn Motor Express, 1287
New Venture Partners, 1663
New West Presentations, 1930, 1935
New York Air Brake, 1172
New York Bancorp Inc., 1598
New York City Retirement, 1706
New York Coke, 1450
New York Giants, 1564, 1943
New York Knicks, 1942
New York Life, 1678, 1713
New York Mets, 1940
New York Public Library, 1994
New York Rangers, 1944
New York State Teachers, 1706
New York Times Co., 11, 557
New York University, 1993
New York Yankees, 1940

Company Index

Simmons, 455, 1518
Simmons & Company, 1879
Simon & Schuster, 568-569
Simon Property Group, 1716
Simpson, 508, 517
Simpson Farm Co., 51
Six Flags, 1949-1950
Six L's Packing Co. Inc., 40
Sizzler, 1552
Skanska (USA) Inc., 2041
Skechers USA, 859
Skidmore Owings & Merrill, 2012
Sklar-Peppler, 483
Skyline, 1188
SkyWest, 1319
Smallwood, Reynolds, 2014
Smith & Nephew, 1207, 1211-1212
Smith & Wollensky, 1558
Smith Barney, 1646, 1651, 1653, 1656, 1661-1662,
    1876-1877, 1879, 1882
Smith Brothers Office Environments Inc., 489
Smith Farms Inc., 71
Smith Optics, 1218
Smith's Food & Drug, 1476, 1479
Smithfield, 207
Smithfield Farms, 64
Smithfield Foods, 192
Smithfield/Morrell, 63
SmithKline Beecham, 675, 755, 759, 1770
Smithsonian, 560
Smitty's, 1469, 1476
SMS, 1830
Smurfit Cartan Papel de Mexico, 502
SMW Advertising Ltd., 1753
Snake River Farms, 45
Snapper, 940
Snappy, 1886
Snider Tire Co., 1497
Snider Tire Inc., 1495
Snyder's of Hanover Inc., 398, 1583
Societe Generale Mexico, 1603
Society, 1874
Society Bancorp of Mich. Inc., 1728
Sodexho, 1541, 1544
Soft AD Group, 1817
Soft-Tech, 1789
Softbank, 1870
Softdesk, 1789
Softkey, 1798, 1814, 1821
Software AG, 1804
Software Artisting Inc., 1801
Software Artistry, 1817
Software Plus, 1534

Software Services Corp., 1783
Soil and Materials Engineers Inc., 1427
Sola Optical USA, 1197
Solar Suncare, 772
Solarex, 916
Solec International, 916
Solo, 1530-1531
Solvay, 600, 612
Solvay Minerals, 595
Solvay Polymers, 615, 622, 628
Solver, 1426
Somerset Tire Service Inc., 1494
Sonat, 1332
Sonoco Products, 516
Sonoma County Showcase, 351
Sony, 975, 984, 991, 995, 1047-1049, 1052-1053, 1057,
    1059, 1061-1062, 1066-1067, 1109-1110, 1237, 1239,
    1898, 1900, 1903, 1914-1917
Sony Theaters, 1920
Soo Line, 1275
Sotheby's London, 355
Sound Analytical Services Inc., 2028
South Valley National Bank, 1602
Southam, 548
Southdown, 135, 865, 873
Southern Company, 1414
Southern Freight Lines, 1287
Southern Living, 560
Southern Methodist University Catering, 1538
Southern National, 1594, 1612
Southern Natural Gas Co., 1421
Southern Pacific, 1272-1273, 1276, 1611
Southern Plantations Group, 79
Southern Tire Mart Inc., 1495, 1497, 1895
Southgate Plaza, 1714
Southland, 940
Southland Corp., 1472
Southland Greyhound Park, 1964
Southtrust, 1592
Southtrust Bank of Central Carolina, 1612
Southwest Airlines, 1307, 1309-1310, 1312, 1317, 1320,
    1322-1324
Southwest B&TC of Omaha, 1613
Southwest Company Club, 1313
Southwest Dental Plan, 1687
Southwestern Bell, 1070, 1359, 1370
Spalding, 838, 1254
Spanish Broadcasting Systems Inc., 1388
Spar Aerospace Limited, 1184
Sparboe Companies, 71
Sparks Steakhouse, 1558
Spartan Stores Inc., 1449
Spartech Plastics, 847

Company Index

BRANDS INDEX

This index shows more than 1,650 brands—including names of periodicals, television programs, popular movies, and other "brand-equivalent" names. Each brand name is followed by one or more numerals; these are entry numbers; they are arranged sequentially, with the first mention of the brand shown first.

Brands Index

Molson Golden, 344
Molson Ice, 344
Mondo, 251
Money, 559
Monistat-7, 759, 764
Montgomery Ward, 1009, 1019, 1027-1028
Moosehead, 344
Mootown Snackers, 312
Mother's, 310
Motrin, 658-659
Motrin IB, 654
Mott's, 240, 249
Mountain Dew, 376, 382
Mountain Valley, 366
Mr. And Mrs. T, 360
Mr. Clean, 705
Mr. Phipps Tater Crisp, 395
Mrs. Smith's, 317-318
Mrs. Smith's Smart Style, 318
Mrs. T's, 271
Mrs. Winner's, 1554
MS Word, 1827
MTV, 1397
Mug, 374
Mule 20 Teram Borax, 708
Murad, 1911
Muriel, 422
Murine, 728
Musselman's, 240, 249
Mycelex-7, 759
Mycogen, 27, 807
Mylan, 674-675
Mylanta, 643, 671-672
MySoftware, 1799
Nabisco, 309, 311, 313, 339
Nabs, 312
Nalspan, 651
Naphcon-A, 653
Naprosyn + EC, 658
Naproxen, 658
National Enquirer, 556
National Geographic, 560
Natural Light, 349-350
Naturals, 534
Nature Made, 639
Nature Valley, 328
Nature's Bounty, 637, 639
Naturistics, 698
Navane, 645
NCSA, 1825
NECCO Plainmint, 322
Nestea, 371-373
Nestea Cool, 371

Nestle's Contadina, 406
Net, The, 1909
Netscape Navigator, 1824
Netscape's Server line, 1825
Netware, 1848
NetWare, 1843, 1849
NetWare 4x, 1841
Neutrogena, 698, 741-742, 769, 771-773, 775
Neutrogena Heatsafe, 739
New York Daily News, 554
New York Post, 551
New York Times, 547, 551-552, 554-555
New York Times Magazine, 559
Newark Star-Ledger, 552, 554
Newport, 415, 418, 421
Newsday, 551-552, 554-555
Newsweek, 559-560
Newtons, 310
NextStep, 1848, 1851
Nice, 325
Nice N Fluffy, 691
NICK, 1397
Nicodern, 664
Nicotrol, 664
Nifedipine, 661
Night Train Express, 354
Nine-Lives, 288
Nintendo, 1240
Nissan, 1485
Nissan Altima, 1127
Nissan Quest, 1125
Nissan Sentra, 1127
Nivea, 698, 769
Nivea Visage, 770
No-Ad, 772, 775
Norco, 1178
Norcom, 1256
Norelco, 1036
Norge, 1027-1028
North County Blade Citizen, 550
North Shore Herald, 549
Northern, 531, 539
Novell, 1795
Novell PerfectOffice, 1826
Noxzema, 766, 771
NT server, 1841
Nuprin, 654
NuSkin, 724
Nutra Nail, 747
Nutrament, 341
NutraSweet Spoonful, 411
Nutty Professor, 1905
Nyquil, 673

APPENDIX I

SIC COVERAGE

This appendix lists the Standard Industrial Classification codes (SICs) included in *Market Share Reporter*. Page numbers are shown following each SIC category; the page shown indicates the first occurrence of an SIC. *NEC* stands for not elsewhere classified.

Agricultural Production - Crops

0110 Cash grains, p. 7
0111 Wheat, p. 7
0115 Corn, p. 8
0119 Cash grains, nec, p. 8
0131 Cotton, p. 8
0132 Tobacco, p. 8
0133 Sugarcane and sugar beets, p. 9
0134 Irish potatoes, p. 9
0161 Vegetables and melons, p. 9
0170 Fruits and tree nuts, p. 12
0171 Berry crops, p. 12
0172 Grapes, p. 13
0173 Tree nuts, p. 14
0174 Citrus fruits, p. 14
0175 Deciduous tree fruits, p. 15
0181 Ornamental nursery products, p. 15

Agricultural Production - Livestock

0210 Livestock, except dairy and poultry, p. 17
0212 Beef cattle, except feedlots, p. 17
0213 Hogs, p. 17
0214 Sheep and goats, p. 18
0241 Dairy farms, p. 18
0251 Broiler, fryer, and roaster chickens, p. 19
0252 Chicken eggs, p. 19
0253 Turkeys and turkey eggs, p. 20
0272 Horses and other equines, p. 20
0279 Animal specialties, nec, p. 21
0291 General farms, primarily animal, p. 21

Agricultural Services

0762 Farm management services, p. 23
0783 Ornamental shrub and tree services, p. 23

Forestry

0811 Timber tracts, p. 24

Fishing, Hunting, and Trapping

0910 Commercial fishing, p. 25
0912 Finfish, p. 25
0913 Shellfish, p. 25
0921 Fish hatcheries and preserves, p. 25

Metal Mining

1000 Metal mining, p. 26
1011 Iron ores, p. 26
1021 Copper ores, p. 26
1031 Lead and zinc ores, p. 27
1041 Gold ores, p. 27
1044 Silver ores, p. 28
1061 Ferroalloy ores, except vanadium, p. 28
1094 Uranium-radium-vanadium ores, p. 29
1099 Metal ores, nec, p. 29

Coal Mining

1220 Bituminous coal and lignite mining, p. 30

Oil and Gas Extraction

1311 Crude petroleum and natural gas, p. 31
1321 Natural gas liquids, p. 33
1381 Drilling oil and gas wells, p. 34
1389 Oil and gas field services, nec, p. 35

Nonmetallic Minerals, Except Fuels

1400 Nonmetallic minerals, except fuels, p. 36
1420 Crushed and broken stone, p. 36
1440 Sand and gravel, p. 37
1455 Kaolin and ball clay, p. 38
1459 Clay and related minerals, nec, p. 38
1470 Chemical and fertilizer minerals, p. 38

Appendix: SIC Nomenclature

Instruments and Related Products

Miscellaneous Manufacturing Industries

Railroad Transportation

Local and Interurban Passenger Transit

Trucking and Warehousing

U.S. Postal Service

Water Transportation

Transportation by Air

Pipelines, Except Natural Gas

Transportation Services

Communications

Electric, Gas, and Sanitary Services

Wholesale Trade - Durable Goods

Wholesale Trade - Nondurable Goods

Appendix: SIC Nomenclature

APPENDIX II

ANNOTATED SOURCE LIST

The following listing provides the names, publishers, addresses, telephone and fax numbers (if available), and frequency of publications for the primary sources used in *Market Share Reporter*.

ABA Banking Journal, Simmons-Boardman Publishing Corp., 345 Hudson St., New York, NY 10014-4502, *Telephone:* (212) 620-7200.

AHA News, American Hospital Publishing Inc., 572 N. Michigan Ave., Chicago, IL. 60601, *Telephone:* (800) 621-6902, *Fax:* (312) 951-8491.

Advertising Age, Crain Communications, Inc., 220 E. 42nd St., New York, NY 10017, *Telephone:* (212) 210-0725, *Fax:* (212) 210-0111. *Published:* weekly.

Adweek, BPI Communications, Merchandise Mart, Suite 936, Chicago, IL 60654, *Telephone:* (800) 722-6658, *Fax:* (312) 464-8540. *Published:* weekly.

Aerospace America, American Institute of Aeronautics and Astronautics, Inc., 370 L'Enfant Promenade, S.W., Washington, DC 20024, *Telephone:* (202) 646-7171. *Published:* monthly, *Price:* $70 per year U.S. and Canada for non-members; included in membership dues.

Aftermarket Business, Advanstar Communications, Inc., 7500 Old Oak Blvd., Cleveland, OH 44130-3343. *Published:* monthly.

Agri Finance, Century Publishing Co., 990 Grove St., Evanston, IL 60201-4370, *Telephone:* (708) 491-6440, *Fax:* (708) 647-7055. *Published:* 9x/yr.

Agricultural Outlook, U.S. Govt. Printing Office, Superintendent of Documents, Washington DC 20402, *Telephone:* (202) 783-3238.

Air Conditioning, Heating and Refrigeration News, Business News Publishing Co., PO Box 2600, Troy, MI 48007, *Telephone:* (313) 362-3700, *Fax:* (313) 362-0317.

Air Transport World, Penton Publishing, Inc., 600 Summer St., P.O. Box 1361, Stanford, CT. 06904, *Telephone:* (203) 348-7531, *Fax:* (203) 348-4023. *Published:* monthly.

Aluminum, Bauxite and Alumina, Bureau of Mines, U.S. Dept. of the Interior, Superintendent of Documents, USGPO, Washington DC, 20402, *Telephone:* (202) 783-3238.

America's Textile International, Billian Publishing, 2100 Powers Ferry NW, Ste. 300, Atlanta, GA 30339, *Telephone:* (404) 955-5656, *Fax:* (404) 952-0669. *Published:* monthly.

American Banker, American Banker Inc., 1 State St. Plaza, New York, NY 10023, *Telephone:* (212) 408-1480, *Fax:* (212) 943-2984. *Published:* Mon.-Fri.

American Ceramic Society Bulletin, American Ceramic Society, 735 Ceramic Place, Westerville, OH 43081-8720. *Published:* monthly, *Price:* $50 per year for nonmembers and libraries; included in membership dues.

American Co-Op, American Trade Magazines, Inc., 500 N. Dearborn St., Chicago, IL 60610-4901. *Published:* monthly, *Price:* $33 per year.

American Demographics, P.O. Box 68, Ithaca, NY 14851-0068, *Telephone*: (607)273-6343, *Fax*: (607)273-3196. *Published*: monthly, *Price*: $62 a year.

American Health, 28 W. 23rd St., New York, NY 10010, *Telephone*: (212)366-8900, *Price*: $18 per year.

American Ink Maker, MacNair-Dorland Co., 445 Broadhollow Rd., Melville, NY 11747, *Telephone*: (212) 279-4456. *Published*: monthly.

American Medical News, American Medical Assn., 515 N. State St., Chicago, IL 60610, *Telephone*: (312) 464-4440, *Fax*: (312) 464-4184, *Price*: $45 a year.

American Metal Market, Capital Cities Media Inc., 825 7th Avenue, New York, NY 10019, *Telephone*: (800) 360-7600. *Published*: daily, except Saturdays, Sundays, and holidays, *Price*: $560 per year (U.S., Canada, and Mexico).

American Nurseryman, American Nurseryman Publishing Co., 77 W. Washington St., Ste. 2100, Chicago, IL 60602-2801, *Telephone*: (312) 782-5505, *Fax*: (312) 782-3232. *Published*: 2x/mo.

American Paint & Coatings Journal, American Paint Journal Co., 2911 Washington Ave., St. Louis MO 63103-1372, *Telephone*: (314) 534-0301. *Published*: weekly, except during 5-day convention.

American Printer, Maclean Hunter Publishing Co., 29 N. Wacker Dr., Chicago, IL 60606. *Published*: monthly.

American Theatre, Theatre Communications Group, 355 Lexington Ave, New York, NY 10017, *Published*: monthly (combined issues May/June and July/August), *Price*: $27 per year.

American Vegetable Grower, Meister Publishing Co., 37733 Euclid Ave., Willoughby, OH 44094-5992, *Telephone*: (216) 942-2000, *Fax*: (216) 942-0662. *Published*: monthly.

Amusement Business, BPI Communications Inc., Box 24970, Nashville, TN 37202, *Telephone*: (615) 321-4250, *Fax*: (615) 327-1575. *Published*: weekly.

Apollo, 29 Chesham Place, London SWIX 8HB.

Apparel Industry Magazine, Shore Communications, 6255 Barfield Rd., Ste. 200, Atlanta, GA 30328, *Telephone*: (800) 241-9034.

Appliance Industry Magazine, Dan Chase Publications Inc., 1110 Jorie Blvd., Oak Brook IL, 60522-9019, *Frequency*: monthly.

Appliance Manufacturer, Business News Publishing Co., 755 W. Big Beaver Rd., Ste. 1000, Troy, MI 48084-4900, *Telephone*: (313) 362-3700, *Fax*: (313) 244-6439. *Published*: monthly.

Architectural Record, McGraw-Hill Inc., 1221 Avenue of the Americas, New York, NY 10020, *Telephone*: (212) 512-2000. *Published*: monthly.

Arizona Business, Arizona State University, P.O. Box 874406, Tempe, AZ 85287-4406, *Telephone*: (602) 965-3961. *Published*: monthly, *Price*: $18 per year for residents; $24 per year nonresident.

Arizona Republic, 120 E. Van Buren, Phoenix, AZ 85004, *Telephone*: (602) 271-8000. *Published*: daily.

Arkansas Business, 201 E. Markham, P.O. Box 3686, Little Rock, AR 72203, *Telephone*: (501)372-1443 Fax: (501) 375-3623. *Published*: weekly, *Price*: $38 per year.

Asiaweek, 20th Floor, Trust Tower, 58 Johnston Road, Wanchal, Hong Kong. *Published*: weekly.

Assembly, Hitchcock Publishing Co., 191 S. Gary Ave., Carol Stream, IL 60188, *Telephone*: (708) 665-1000, *Fax*: (708) 462-2225. *Published*: 9X/yr. *Price*: $65 a year.

Asset Finance & Leasing Management, 700 19th St., NW, Washington D.C., 20431. *Published*: monthly.

Association Management, American Society of Asso-caition Executives, 1575 Eye St., Washington DC 20005. *Published:* monthly, *Price:* $24 per year to members, $30 per year for nonmembers.

Atlanta Constitution, 72 Marietta St. NW, Atlanta GA 30303, Frequency: daily, *Price:* $53 a year.

Automated Builder, 4371 Carpinteria Ave, Carpinteria CA 93013, *Telephone:* (805) 684-7659, *Fax:* (805)684-1765. *Published:* monthly, *Price:* $50 per year.

Automotive Body Repair News, Capital Cities/ABC/Chilton Co., Chilton Wy., Radnor PA 19089. *Published:* monthly.

Automotive Industry, Capitall Cities/ABC/Chilton Co., Chilton Way, Radnor, PA, *Telephone:* (215) 964-4255, *Fax:* (215) 964-4251.

Automotive Marketing, Capital Cities/ABC/Chilton Co., Chilton Way, Radnor, PA 19089, *Telephone:* (215) 964-4000. *Published:* monthly, *Price:* $36 per year.

Automotive News, Crain Communications Inc., 380 Woodbridge, Detroit, MI 48207 *Telephone:* (313) 446-6000, *Fax:* (313) 446-0347.

Aviation Week & Space Technology, McGraw-Hill, Inc., 1221 Avenue of the Americas, New York, NY 10020, *Telephone:* (212) 512-2294, *Fax:* (212) 869-7799. *Published:* weekly.

BC Business, Canada Wide Magazines Ltd., 40180 Lougheed Highway Burnaby BC V5C6A7, *Telephone:* (604)299-7311, *Fax:* (604)299-9188.

Bakery Production and Marketing, Cahners Publishing Co., 455 N. Cityfront Plaza Dr., Chicago, IL 60611, *Telephone:* (312) 222-2000.

Baltimore Business Journal, American City Business Journals, 117 Water St., Baltimore, MD 21202, *Telephone:* (410) 576-1161, *Fax:* (301) 383-3213. *Published:* weekly.

Baltimore Sun, 501 N. Calvert St., Baltimore, MD 21278-0001, *Telephone:* (410) 332-6000, *Fax:* (410)332-6670.

Bank Management, Faulkner & Gray for Bank Administration Institute, 118 S. Clinton St., Suite 700, Chicago, IL 60661, *Telephone:* (312) 648-0255, *Fax:* (312)648-9569. *Published:* monthly, *Price:* $59.00 per year; $5.00, single copies.

Banker, Greystoke Place, Feteer Lane, London EC4A 1ND, *Telephone:* (071)405-6969. *Published:* m onthly.

Battery Man, Independent Battery Manufacturers Association, 100 Larchwood Drive, Largo, FL 34640, *Telephone:* (813) 586-1408, *Fax:* (813) 586-1400. *Published:* monthly, *Price:* $20 per year.

Best's Review, A.M. Best Co. Inc., Ambest Rd., Oldwick, NJ 08858, *Telephone:* (908) 439-2200, *Fax:* (908) 439-3363. *Published:* monthly.

Beverage Industry, Advanstar Communications, Inc., 7500 Oald Oak Blvd., Cleveland OH 44130, *Telephone:* (216) 243-8100, *Fax:* (216) 891-2651. *Published:* monthly, *Price:* $40 per year.

Beverage World, Keller International Publishing Corp., 150 Great Neck Rd., Great Neck, NY 11021, *Telephone:* (516) 829-9210, *Fax:* (516) 829-5414. *Published:* monthly.

Beverage World's Periscope, Keller International Publishing Corp., 150 Great Neck Rd., Great Neck, NY 11021, *Telephone:* (516) 829-9210, *Fax:* (516) 829-5414. *Published:* monthly.

Billboard, BPI Communications, One Astor Plaza, 1515 Broadway, New York, NY 10036, *Telephone:* (212) 764-7300, *Price:* $239 a year.

Black Enterprise, Earl G. Graves Publishing Co., Inc., 130 Fifth Ave., New York, NY 10011, *Telephone:* (212) 242-8000. *Published:* monthly.

Black Issues in Higher Education, 1255 23rd St. NW. No. 700, Washington D.C., 20037, *Telephone:* (202) 466-1200, *Fax:* (202) 296-2691.

Boating Industry Annual Industry Review, Communication Channels, Inc., 6151 Powers Ferry Road, Atlanta, GA 30339, *Telephone:* (404) 955-2500.

Bobbin, Bobbin Blenheim Media, 1110 Shop Rd., P.O. Box 1986, Columbia, SC 29202, *Telephone:* (803) 771-7500. *Published:* monthly, *Price:* U.S.: $48 per year, $84 for 2 years, $117 for 3 years; Canada: $66 per year, $102 for 2years, $144 for 3 years.

Body Fashions/Intimate Apparel, Advanstar Communications Inc., 7500 Old Oak Blvd., Cleveland, OH 44130, *Price:* $35 a year.

BodyShop Business, Babcox Publications Inc., 11 S. Forge St., Akron, OH 44304, *Telephone:* (216) 535-7011.

Brake & Front End, Babcox Publications Inc., 11 S. Forge St., Akron, OH 44304, *Telephone:* (216) 535-7011, *Price:* $115 per year.

Brandweek, Adweek L.P., 1515 Broadway, New York, NY 10036, *Telephone:* (212) 536-5336. *Published:* weekly, except no issue in the last week of Dec.

Broadcasting & Cable, Cahners Publishing Co., 1705 DeSales Street, N.W., Washington, DC 20036, *Telephone:* (800) 554-5729 or (202) 659-2340, *Fax:* (202) 331-1732.

Broiler Industry, Watt Publishing Co., 122 S. Wesley Ave., Mount Morris, IL 61054-1497, *Telephone:* (815) 734-4171, *Fax:* (815) 734-4201. *Published:* monthly.

Builder, Hanley-Wood Inc., 655 15th St. N.W., Ste. 475, Washington, D.C. 20005, *Telephone:* (202) 737-0717, *Fax:* (202) 737-2439. *Published:* monthly.

Builders Hardware. Industry & Trade Summary, Superintendent of Documents, USGPO, Washington DC 20402, *Telephone:* (202) 783-3238.

Building Design & Construction, Cahners Publishing, 1350 E. Touhy Ave., Des Plaines, IL 60017-5080, *Telephone:* (708) 635-8800. *Published:* monthly.

Building Material Retailer, National Lumbermens Publishing Corp., 1405 Lilac Drive N, No. 131, Minneapolis, MN 55422. *Telephone:* (612) 544-1597, *Fax:* (612) 544-0820. *Published:* monthly.

Building Supply Business, Cahners Publishing, 1350 E. Touhy Ave., Des Plaines, IL 60018-3358.

Buildings, Stamats Communications Inc., 427 6th Ave., P.O. Box 1888, Cedar Rapids, IA 52406, *Telephone:* (319) 364-6167, *Fax:* (319) 364-4278. *Published:* monthly, *Price:* $50 per year.

Building & Operation Management, Trade Press Publishing Corp., 2100 W. Florist Ave., Milwaukee, WI 53209, *Telephone:* (414) 228-7701, *Fax:* (414) 228-1134. *Published:* monthly.

Business & Commercial Aviation, 4 International Dr., Ste. 260, Rye Brook, NY 10573-1065, *Telephone:* (914) 939-0300, *Fax:* (914) 939-1100. *Published:* monthly, *Price:* $42 per year.

Business & Health, Medical Economics Publishing Co., 5 Paragon Dr., Montvale, NJ 07645-1184, *Telephone:* (201) 358-7208. *Published:* 14x/yr.

Business Communications Review, BCR Enterprises, Inc., 950 York Rd., Hinsdale, IL 60521, *Telephone:* (800) 227-1324. *Published:* monthly.

Business First - Columbus, 200 E. Rich St., Columbus, OH 43215, *Telephone:* (614) 461-4040.

Business First of Buffalo, 472 Delaware Ave., Buffalo, NY 14202.

Business India, Living Media India, Connaught Place, New Delhi, 11001.

Business Insurance, Crain Communications, Inc., 740 N. Rush St., Chicago IL 60611, Published: monthly.

Business Journal, American City Business Journals, 2025 N. Summit Ave., Milwaukee, WI 53202.

Business Marketing, Crain Communications, 740 N. Rush St., Chicago, IL 60611, *Telephone:* (312) 649-5200. *Published:* monthly.

Business Mexico, American Chamber of Commerce, A.C., Lucerna 78, Col. Juarez, DEl. Cuauhtemoc, Mexico City, Mexico, *Telephone:* 705-0995. *Published:* monthly.

Business North Carolina, 5435 77 Center Dr., No. 50, Charlotte, NC 28217-0711 *Telephone:* (704) 523-6987 *Published:* monthly.

Business Week, McGraw-Hill Inc., 1221 Avenue of the Americas, New York, NY 10020. *Published:* weekly, *Price:* U.S.: $46.95 per year; Canada: $69 CDN per year.

Business & Society Review, 200 W. 57th St., 15th Fl., New York, NY 10019, *Telephone:* (212) 399-1088, *Fax:* (212) 245-1973. *Published:* quarterly, *Price:* $56 per year; $81 foreign.

Byte, Byte Publications, 1 Phoenix Mill Lane, Petersborough, NH 03458, *Telephone:* (212) 512-2000.

CD-ROM Professional, Pemberton Press Inc., 462 Danbury Road, Wilton, CT 06897-2126, *Published:* 6X per year.

Cablevision, Chilton Publications, P.O. Box 7698, Riverton, NJ 08077-7698, *Telephone:* (609) 786-0501. *Published:* twice monthly, *Price:* U.S.: $55 per year, $99 for 2 years; Elsewhere via surface mail: $85 per year, $159 for 2 years.

Canadian Banker, Canadian Bankers Assn., 2 1st Canadian Place, P.O. Box 348, Toronto, ON, Canada M5X 1E1, *Telephone:* (416) 362-6092, *Fax:* (416) 362-7705.

Canadian Geographic, Royal Canadian Geographic Society, 39 McArthur Ave., Vanier, Ont. K1L 8L7, *Telephone:* (613) 745-4629.

Canadian Mining Journal, Southam Magazine Group, PO Box 1144, Lewiston, NY 14092. *Published:* 4x/yr.

Canadian Plastics, Southam Magazine Group, 4703 Porter Ctr. Rd, Lewiston, NY 14092 .

Catalog Age, Cowles Business Media Inc., 911 Hope St., Six River Bend Center, Box 4949, Stanford CT 06907-0949, *Telephone:* (203) 358-9900. *Published:* monthly.

Ceramic Forum International, Bauverlag GmbH, Am Klingenweg 4, D-65396 Walluf, Germany.

Chain Store Age, Lebhar-Friedman Inc., 425 Park Ave., New York, NY 10022, *Telephone:* (212) 371-9400, *Fax:* (212) 319-4129. *Published:* monthly.

Chemical & Engineering News, American Chemical Society, Dept. L-0011, Columbus, OH 43210, *Telephone:* (800) 333-9511 or (614) 447-3776. *Published:* weekly, except last week in December, *Price:* U.S.: $100 per year, $198 for 2 years; elsewhere: $148 per year, $274 for 2 years.

Chemical Engineering, McGraw-Hill Inc., 1221 Avenue of the Americas, New York, NY 10020, *Telephone:* (212) 512-2000. *Published:* monthly.

Chemical Marketing Reporter, Schnell Publishing Co., Inc., 80 Broad St., New York, NY 1004-2203, *Telephone:* (212) 248-4177, *Fax:* (212) 248-4903. *Published:* weekly.

Chemical week, Chemical Week Associates, P.O. Box 7721, Riverton, NJ 08077-7721, *Telephone:* (609) 786-0401. *Published:* weekly, except four combination issues (total of 49 issues), *Price:* U.S.: $99 per year; Canada: $129 per year. Single copies $8 in U.S. and $10 elsewhere.

Chemistry & Industry, Society of Chemical Industry, 15 Belgrave Sq., London SW1X 8PS, UK, *Telephone:* 071-235-3681, *Fax:* 071-235-9410. *Published:* semi-monthly.

Chicago Crain's Business - Crain's Market Facts, Crain Communications Inc., 740 N. Rush St., Chicago, IL 60611, *Telephone:* (312) 649-5411.

Chicago Tribune, 435 N. Michigan Ave., Chicago, IL 60611, *Telephone:* (312) 222-3232. *Published:* daily.

Child Care Information Exchange, Exchange Press Inc., P.O. 2890, Redmond, WA 98073, *Telephone:* (800) 221-2864. *Published:* bimonthly, *Price:* $35 per year.

Christian Science Monitor, Christian Science Publishing Society, One Norway St., Boston, MA 02115, *Telephone:* (800) 456-2220. *Published:* daily, except weekends and holidays.

Chronicle of Higher Education, 1255 23rd St. NW. No. 700, Washington D.C., 20037, *Telephone:* (202) 466-1200, *Fax:* (202) 296-2691.

Cincinnati Business Courier, Standard Publishing, 4500 Carew Tower, Cincinnati, OH 45202, *Telephone:* (513) 621-6665, *Fax:* (513) 621-2462. *Published:* weekly.

Clay. U.S. Department of Interior, Bureau of Mines. Superintendent of Documents, USGPO, Washington, DC 20402, *Telephone:* (202) 783-3238.

Coal Data: A Reference, U.S. Department of Interior, Superintendent of Documents, USGPO, Washington, DC 20402, *Telephone:* (202) 783-3238.

Commercial Appeal, Memphis Publishing Co., 495 Union Ave., Memphis, TN 38103, *Telephone:* (901) 529-2211, *Fax:* (901) 529-2522, *Published:* daily.

Commercial Carrier Journal, Chilton Co., Chilton Wy., Radnor, PA 19089, *Telephone:* (215) 964-4000.

Communications, IGI Publishing, Inc., 214 Harvard Ave., Boston, MA 02134.

Computer, IEEE Computer Society, 10662 Los Vaqueros Circle, P.O. Box 3014, Los Alamitos, CA 90720-

3014, *Telephone:* (714) 821-8380, *Fax:* (714) 821-4010, *Frequency:* monthly.

Computer Design, PennWall Publishing Company, 1421 Sheridan, Tulsa, OK 74112, Published: monthly, *Price:* $88 per year.

Computer Reseller News, CMP Publications Inc., One Jericho Plaza, Jericho, NY 11753, *Telephone:* (516) 733-6700, *Published:* weekly.

Computers in Libraries, Meckler Corp., 11 Ferry Ln NW, Westport, CT, 06680.

Computerworld, P.O. Box 2043, Marion, OH 43305-2403, *Telephone:* (800) 669-1002.

Computing Canada, Plesman Publications Ltd., 2005 Sheppard Ave. E., 4th Fl., Willowsdale, ON, Canada M2J 5B1, *Telephone:* (416) 497-9562, *Fax:* (416) 497-9427. *Published:* biweekly.

Construction Equipment, Cahners Publishing Company, 8773 Ridgeline Blvd., Highlands Ranch, CO 80126-2329, *Telephone:* (303) 470-4445.

Consumers Research, 800 Maryland Ave., Washington D.C. 20002. *Published:* monthly, *Price:* $24 per year.

Contemporary Long Term Care, Bill Communications Inc., PO Box 3599, Akron, OH 44309-3599, *Telephone:* (216) 867-4401, *Fax:* (216) 867-0019, *Publsihed:* monthly.

Contractor, Cahners Publishing Co., 44 Cook St., Denver, CO. 80206-5800, *Telephone:* (708) 390-2676, *Fax:* (708) 390-2690, *Published:* monthly.

Cornell Hotel and Restaurant Administration Quarterly, Cornell University, Statler Hall, Ithaca, NY 14853, *Telephone:* (607) 255-5093, *Fax:* (607) 257-1204, *Published:* 6x/yr.

Corporate Cashflow, Intertec Publishing Corp., 6151 Powers Ferry Rd., Atlanta, GA 30339, *Telephone:*

(770) 955-2500, *Published:* monthly, *Price:* $98 per year.

Corporate Growth Weekly Report, Quality Services Co., 5290 Overpass Rd., Santa Barbara, CA 93111 Telephone: (805) 964-7841.

Corporate Report Minnesota, Corporate Report Inc., 5500 Wayzata Blvd., Suite 800, Minneapolis, MN 55416, *Telephone:* (612) 591-2531. *Published:* monthly, *Price:* $29 per year, $47 for 2 years, $63 for three years. Back issues $3.95 each.

Crain's Chicago Business, Crain Communications Inc., 740 N. Rush St., Chicago, IL 60611, *Telephone:* (312) 649-5411.

Crain's Cleveland Business, Crain Communications, Inc., 1725 Merriman Rd., Ste. 300, Akron, OH 44313-5251, *Telephone:* (216) 836-9180, *Fax:* (216) 836-1005. *Published:* weekly.

Crain's Detroit Business, Crain Communications Inc., 1400 Woodbridge, Detroit, MI 48207-3187, *Telephone:* (313) 446-6000. *Published:* weekly, except semiweekly the fourth week in May.

Crain's New York Business, Crain Communications, Inc., 220 E. 42nd St., New York, NY 10017, *Telephone:* (212) 210-0100, *Fax:* (212) 210-0799. *Published:* weekly.

DCI (Drug & Cosmetic Industry), Advanstar Communications, Inc., 7500 Old Oak Blvd., Cleveland, OH 44310. *Published:* monthly.

DEC Professional, Cardinal Business Media Inc., 101 Winer Rd., Horsham, PA 19044, *Telephone:* (215) 957-1500, *Fax:* (215) 957-1050, *Published:* monthly.

DM (Discount Merchandiser), Schwartz Publications, 233 Park Ave. S., New York, NY 10003, *Telephone:* (212) 979-4860, *Fax:* (212) 979-7431. *Published:* monthly.

DNR (Digital News & Review), Cahners Publishing Co., 275 Washington St., Newton, MA 02158, *Tele-*

phone: (617) 558-4243, *Fax:* (617) 558-4759. *Published:* 2x/mo.

Dairy Foods, Gorman Publishing Co., 8750 W. Bryn Mawr Ave., Chicago, IL 60062, *Telephone:* (312) 693-3200. *Published:* monthly, except semimonthly in Aug.

Dairy Goat Journal, Duck Creek Publications, 128 E. Lake St., Lake Mill, WI 53551, *Telephone:* (414) 648-8285, *Fax:* (414) 648-3770.

Dairy Herd Management, Miller Publishing, 12400 Whitewater Dr., Minnetonka, MN 55345, *Telephone:* (612) 931-0211.

Dallas Business Journal, American City Business Journals, 4131 N. Central Expy, Ste. 310, Dallas, TX 75204, *Telephone:* (214) 520-1010, *Fax:* (214) 528-4686.

Dallas Morning News, 508 Young St., P.O. Box 655237, Dallas, TX 75265, *Telephone:* (214) 977-8222, *Fax:* (214) 977-8776. *Published:* daily.

Data Communications, McGraw-Hill Inc., 1221 Avenue of the Americas, New York, NY 10020, *Telephone:* (212) 512-2699, *Fax:* (212) 512-6833. *Published:* monthly.

Datamation, Cahners Publishing Co., 275 Washington Street, Newton, MA 02158, *Telephone:* (617) 558-4281.

Daytona Beach Sunday News Journal, News-Journal Corp., 901 Sixth Street, Daytona Beach, FL 32117-8099.

Dealerscope, North American Publishing Co., 401 N. Broad St., Philadelphia, PA 19108, *Telephone:* (215) 238-5300. *Published:* semi-monthly.

Denver Business Journal, 1700 Broadway, Ste. 515, Denver, CO 80290, Telephone: (303) 837-3500, Fax: (303) 837-3535, *Published:* weekly.

Design News, 275 Washington St., Weston, MA 02158-1630, *Telephone:* (617) 964-3030, *Fax:* (617) 558-4402.

Detroit Free Press, Knight-Ridder, Inc., 1 Herald Plaza, Miami, FL 33132, *Telephone:* (305) 376-3800. *Published:* daily.

Detroit News, Gannett Co. Inc., 1 Gannett Dr., White Plains, NY 10604-3498, *Telephone:* (914) 694-9300, *Published:* daily.

Diesel Progress Engines & Drives, Diesel & Gas Turbine Publications, 13555 Bishop's Court, Brookfield, WI 53005-6286, Published: monthly, *Price:* $60 per year.

Direct Marketing, Hoke Communications Inc., 224 7th St., Garden City, NY 11530, *Telephone:* (516) 746-6700, *Fax:* (516) 294-8141. *Published:* monthly, *Price:* $56 per year; $6 single issue.

Discount Store News, Lebhar-Friedman Inc., 425 Park Ave, New York, NY 10022, *Telephone:* (212) 756-5100, *Fax:* (212) 756-5125. *Published:* weekly.

Drug Topics, Medical Economics Publishing Co., 5 Paragon Dr., Montvale, NJ 07645-1742, *Telephone:* (201) 358-7200. *Published:* semimonthly, only once in December.

ENR (Engineering News-Record), McGraw-Hill Inc., Fulfillment Manager, ENR, P.O. Box 518, Highstown, NJ 08520, *Telephone:* (609) 426-7070 or (212) 512-3549, *Fax:* (212) 512-3150. *Published:* weekly, *Price:* U.S.: $89 per year; Canada: $75 per year. Single copies $5 in U.S.

Ebony, Johnson Publishing Co., 820 S. Michigan Ave., Chicago, IL 60605. *Published:* monthly, *Price:* $16 per year.

Economist, 111 West 57th Street, New York, NY 10019, *Telephone:* (212) 541-5730, *Fax:* (212) 541-9378, *Published:* weekly.

Editor & Publisher, 11 W. 19th St., New York, NY 10011, *Telephone:* (212) 675-4380, *Fax:* (212) 929-1259, *Published:* weekly.

Egg Industry, Watt Publishing Co., 122 S. Wesley Ave., Mount Morris, IL 61054-1497, *Telephone:* (815) 734-4171, *Fax:* (815) 734-4201. *Published:* bimonthly

Electronic Business Today, CMP Publications, Inc., 8773 South Ridgeline Blvd., Highlands Ranch, CO, 80126-2329, *Telephone:* (516) 562-5000, *Fax:* (516) 562-5409. *Published:* monthly, *Price:* $65 per year.

Electronic Design, 222 Rosewood Drive, Danvers, MA 01923.

Electronic News, Electronic News Publishing Corp., 488 Madison Ave., New York, NY 10022, *Telephone:* (212) 909-5924. *Published:* weekly, except last week of Dec.

Engineering & Mining Journal, Maclean Hunter Publishing Co., 29 Wacker Dr., Chicago, IL 60606, *Fax:* (312) 726-2574. *Published:* monthly.

Entertainment Weekly, 1675 Broadway, New York, NY 10019. *Published:* weekly.

Environment Today, Enterprise Communications Inc., 1165 Northchase Parkway, Ste. 350, Marietta GA 30067, *Telephone:* (404) 988-9558. *Published:* monthly.

Environmental Progress, 225 New Rd., Waco, TX 76798.

EPRI Journal, Electric Power Research Institute, P.O. Box 10412, Palo Alto, CA 94303, *Telephone:* (415) 855-2730, *Fax:* (415) 855-2041.

European Rubber Journal, Crain Communications Ltd., 20-22 Bedford Row, London WC1R 4EW, UK- *Telephone:* 071-831 9511, *Fax:* 071-430 2176, *Published:* monthly, except Aug.

Facts About Newspapers, Newspaper Association of America, The Newspaper Center, 11600 Sunrise Valley

Drive, Reston, VA 22091-1412, *Telephone*: (703) 648-1000, *Fax:* (703) 620-4557.

Farm Journal, 230 W. Washington Sq., Philadelphia, PA 19106, *Telephone:* (215) 829-4700. *Published:* 13x/yr. *Price:* $14 per year.

Farms and Land in Farms, Superintendent of Documents, USGPO, Washington, DC 20402, *Telephone:* (202) 783-3238.

Field and Stream, Times Mirror Magazines, Inc., 2 Park Ave., New York, NY 10016, *Telephone:* (212) 779-5000, *Fax:* (212) 725-3836. *Published:* monthly.

Financial Post, The Financial Post Company, 333 King St., East, Toronto M5A 4N2, Canada, *Telephone:* (800) 387-9011. *Published:* monthly with 5-day per week newspaper, *Price:* $182 per year; weekend mail subscription $49.95 includes magazine and annual issues.

Financial Times, FT Publications Inc., 14 East 60th Street, New York, NY 1022, *Telephone:* (212) 752-4500, *Fax:* (212) 319-0704. *Published:* daily,e xcept Sundays and some holidays.

Financial World, 1328 Broadway, Ste. 3, New York, NY 10001-2132, *Telephone:* (212) 594-5030, *Fax:* (212) 629-0021. *Published:* biweekly.

Floriculture Crops, Superintendent of Documents, USGPO, Washington, DC 20402, *Telephone:* (202) 783-3238.

Folio, Cowles Business Media, P.O. Box 4294, Stamford, CT 60907-0294, *Price:* U.S.: 24 issues for $96, 48 issues for $152, 72 issues for $199; Canada/Mexico: 24 issues for $116, 48 issues for $184, 72 issues for $240.

Food Engineering, Chilton Co., One Chilton Way, Radnor, PA 19089, *Telephone:* (215) 964-4000. *Published:* monthly, *Price:* solicited only from professionals in field: $55 per year, $100 for 2 years; educational rate: $28 per year.

Food Technology, Institute of Food Technologies, 221 N. LaSalle ASt., Chicago, IL 60601.

Footwear News, Fairchild Publications, 7 West 34th Str., New York, NY 10001-8191.

Forbes, Forbes, Inc., P.O. Box 10048, Des Moines, IA 50340-0048, *Telephone:* (800) 888-9896. *Published:* 27 issues per year, *Price:* U.S.: $54 per year; Canada: $95 per year (includes GST).

Forces, 500 Rue Sherbroke Ouest, Bureau 1270, Montreal, Quebec H3A 3C6, *Telephone*: (514) 286-7600.

Forest Products Journal, Forest Products Society, 2801 Marshall Court, Madison, WI 53705-2295. *Published:* monthly, except combined issues in July/August and November/December, *Price:* U.S.: $115 per year; Canada/Mexico: $125; single copies $12 each plus shipping and handling.

Fortune, Time Inc., Time & Life Building, Rockefeller Center, New York, NY 10020-1393. *Published:* twice monthly, except two issues combined into a single issue at year-end, *Price:* U.S.: $57 per year; Canada: $65 per year.

Franchise Times, 1350 New York Ave., NW, 9th Fl., Washington D.C. 20005. *Published:* monthly.

Fruit Grower, Meister Publishing Co., 37733 Euclid Ave., Willoughsby, OH 44094-5992.

Furniture Today, Cahners Publishing Co., 200 S. Main St., P.O. Box 2754, High Point, NC 27261, *Telephone:* (919) 889-0113. *Published:* weekly.

Glass Industry, Ashlee Publishing Co., Inc., 310 Madison Avenue, New York, NY 10017-6098, *Telephone:* (212) 682-7681, *Fax:* (212) 697-8331. *Published:* monthly, except 2 issues in February, *Price:* U.S./Canada/Mexico: $40 per year, $50 for 2 years, $60 for 3 years.

Globe and Mail, 444 Front St. W., Toronto, ON, Canada M5V 2S9, *Telephone:* (416) 585-5000, *Fax:* (416) 585-5085. *Published:* Mon.-Sat. (morn.).

Globe and Mail's Report on Business Magazine, 444 Front St. W., Toronto, ON, Canada M5V 2S9, *Telephone:* (416) 585-5000, *Fax:* (416) 585-5085.

Graphic Arts Monthly, Cahners Publishing Company, 44 Cook St., Denver, CO 80206-5800, *Telephone:* (800) 637-6089. *Published:* monthly, *Price:* U.S.: $84.95 per year, $143.95 for 2 years, single copies $20 each; Canada: $164.95 per year, $279.95 for 2 years (includes GST); Mexico: $153.95 per year, $261.95 for 2 years.

Grocery Marketing, Gorman Publishing Co., 8750 W. Bryn Mawr Ave., Chicago, IL 60631, *Telephone:* (312)693-2300.

Grounds Maintenance, Intertec Publishing Co., 9800 Metcalf Ave., Overland Park, KS 66212-2215. *Published:* monthly.

HFN, 7 E. 12th St., New York, NY 10003. *Published:* weekly.

HR Magazine, Society For Human Resource Managment, 105 N. Washington St., Alexandria, VA 22314, *Telephone:* (703) 548-3440, *Fax:* (703) 836-0367.

Hardware Age, Chilton Company, One Chilton Way, Radnor, PA 19089, *Telephone:* (215) 964-4287, *Fax:* (215) 964-4284. *Published:* monthly.

Health Care Strategic Management, Business Word Inc., 5350 S. Roslyn St., Englewood, CO 8011-2125, *Telephone:* (800) 328-3211, *Fax:* (303) 290-9025.

Health Management Today, 200 Orchard Ridge, Gaithersburg, MD 20878.

Healthcare Financial Management, 2 West Brook Corp., Wetshester, IL 60154.

Healthcare Informatics, Wiesner Inc., 7009 S. Potomac, Englewood, CO 80112.

High Volume Printing, Innes Publishing Co., 425 Huehl Rd., Bldg. 11, Northbrook, IL 60062-2319, *Published:* monthly, *Price:* $45 per year.

Hoard's Dairyman, W.D. Hoard & Sons Co., 28 Milwaukee Ave., Fort Atkinson, WI 53538, *Telephone:* (414) 563-5551.

Hollywood Reporter, H.R. Industries Inc., 5055 Wilshire Blvd, Los Angeles, CA 90036-4396, *Price:* $190 per year.

Home Improvement Market, Chilton Co. , Chilton Wy., Radnor, PA 19089. *Published:* monthly.

Home Mechanix, Times Mirror Magazines, 2 Park Ave., New York, NY 10016, *Telephone:* (212) 779-5000, *Fax:* (212) 779-5468.

Hospital Pharmacy, Lippincott Publishing, 12107 Insurance Way, Hagerstown, MD 21740. *Published:* monthly.

Hotel & Motel Management, Advanstar Communications, Inc., 7500 Old Oak Blvd., Cleveland, OH 44130, *Telephone:* (216) 826-2839.

Household and Personal Products Industry, Rodman Publishing, 17 S. Franklin Turnpike, Box 555, Ramsey, NJ 07446, *Telephone:* (201) 825-2552, *Fax:* (201) 825-0553. *Published:* monthly.

Implement & Tractor, Farm Press Publications, Inc., PO Box 1420, Clarksdale, MS 38614, *Telephone:* (601) 624-8503, *Fax:* (601) 627-1977. *Published:* monthly, *Price:* $15 per year.

IN-PLANT Graphics, North American Publishing Co., 401 N. Broad St., Philadelphia, PA 19108, *Telephone:* (215) 238-5300, *Fax:* (215) 238-6490. *Published:* monthly.

In-Tech, ISA Services Inc., 67 Alexander Dr., PO Box 12277, Research Triangle Park, NC 27709, *Telephone:* (919) 549-8411, *Fax:* (919) 549-8288.

INC. Technology, Inc. Publishing Co., 38 Commercial Wharf, Boston, MA 02110, *Telephone:* (617) 248-8426. *Published:* monthly, with a bonus issue in the fall.

Incentive, Bill Communciations Inc., 355 Park Ave. South, New York, NY 10010, *Telephone:* (212) 592-6459, *Fax:* (212) 592-6459.

Industrial Distribution, Cahners Publishing Company, 275 Washington Street, Newton, MA 02158, *Telephone:* (617) 964-3030. *Published:* monthly.

Industrial Minerals, 220 Fifth Ave., New York, NY 1001, *Telephone:* (212) 213-6202, *Published:* monthly.

Industrial Paint & Powder, Chilton Publications, 191 S. Gary Ave., Carol Stream, IL 60188, *Telephone:* (708) 665-1000, *Fax:* (708) 462-2225. *Published:* monthly.

Informationweek, CMP Publications Inc., P.O. Box 1093, Skokie, IL 60076-8093. *Published:* weekly, except for double issue at the end of December, *Price:* $120 per year.

Infoworld, InfoWorld Publishing Co., 155 Bovet Rd., Ste. 800, San Mateo, CA 94402, *Telephone:* (415) 572-7341. *Published:* weekly.

Institutional Investor, Institutional Investor Inc., 488 Madison Avenue, New York, NY 10022, *Telephone:* (212) 303-3300.

Interavia, Swissair Centre, 31 Route de l'Aeroport, P.O. Box 437, 1215 Geneva 15, Switzerland, *Telephone:* (022) 788 27 88, *Fax:* (022) 788 27 26. *Published:* monthly, Price: $128 per year (in U.S.).

International Business, 500 Mamaroneck Ave., Ste. 314, Harrison, NY 10528-1600, *Telephone:* (914) 381-7700.

International Journal of Powder Metallurgy, APMI Intl., 105 College Road, Princeton, NJ 08540-6692, *Telephone:* (609) 452-7700. *Published:* quarterly, *Price:* $75 individuals, $150 institutions to non-members.

International Water Power & Dam Construction, Reed Business Publishing, Quadrant House, The Quadrant, Sutton, Surrey SM2 5A5.

Internet World, 20 Ketchum St., Westport, CT 06880, *Telephone:* (612) 633-0578, *Fax:* (612) 633-1862.

Investext, The Investext Group, 22 Pittsburgh Street, Boston, MA 02210. Investext is an online database of full-text company and industry research reports produced by more than 385 investment banks and brokerage firms around the globe. Approximately 400 new reports are added daily. The Investext database is available on the Investext Group's online and CD-ROM products and via most major online business providers. Reports and research services may also be ordered by phone. *Telephone:* 800-662-7878 (US), +44-171-815-3860 (UK/Europe), 852-2522-4159 (Hong Kong), 03-5213-7300.

Investor's Business Daily, P.O. Box 661750, Los Angeles, CA 90066-8950. *Published:* daily ,except weekends and holidays, *Price:* $128 per year.

JEMS (Journal of Emergency Medical Services), Jems Communications, 1947 Camino Vida Roble, Ste. 200, Carlsbad, CA 92008, *Telephone:* (619) 431-9797. *Published:* monthly, *Price:* $24 per year.

Jewelers' Circular Keystone, Chilton Co., Chilton Way, Radnor, PA 19089, *Telephone:* (212) 887-8452, *Fax:* (212) 887-8348. *Published:* monthly.

Journal of Accountancy, American Institute of Certified Public Accountants, 1211 Avenue of the Americas, New York, NY 10036, *Telephone:* (212) 596-6200, *Fax:* (212) 596-6213. *Published:* monthly.

Journal of Applied Corporate Finance, Stern Stewart Management Services Inc., 450 Park Ave., New York, NY 10022. Published: quarterly, *Price:* $95 per year.

Journal of Commerce, Journal of Commerce, Inc., Two World Trade Center, 27th Floor, New York, NY 10048, *Telephone:* (212) 837-7000, *Fax:* (212) 837-7035.

Journal of Retail Banking Services, American Banker Inc., One State Street Plaza, New York, NY 10004, *Price:* $125 per year, $40 single copy.

Kansas City Star, Kansas City Star Co., 1729 Grand Ave., Kansas City, MO 64108, *Telephone:* (816) 234-4141, *Fax:* (816) 234-4464. *Published:* daily.

Kiplingers Personal Finance, Washington Editors Inc., 1729 H. St., Washington D.C., *Telephone:* (202) 887-6400, *Fax:* (202) 331-1200. *Published:* monthly, *Price:* $18 per year, $2.50 single issue.

LAN Times, Miller Freeman Inc., 600 Harrison St., San Francisco, CA 94107.

Lakeland Boating, O'Meara-Brown Publications Inc., 1560 Sherman ave., Ste. 1220, Evanston, IL 60201, *Telephone:* (847) 869-5400. *Published:* monthly, except Nov., *Price:* $28 per year.

LandUse Digest, ULI - the Urban Land Institute, 625 Indiana Avenue, N.W., Washington, DC 20004-2930, *Price:* subscription included in annual membership fees.

Library Journal, Cahners Publishing Company, P.O. Box 59690, Boulder, CO 80322-9690, *Telephone:* (800) 677-6694. *Published:* 21 times per year, semimonthly, except January, July, and August, *Price:* U.S.: $79 per year; Canada: $99 per year (includes GST).

Lightwave, PennWell Publishing Co., 1421 S Sheridan, Tulsa, OK 74112, *Telephone:* (918) 832-9349. *Published:* monthly, with two issues in March, *Price:* U.S.: $54 per year, $78 per year for libraries; Canada: $74 per year.

Lodging Hospitality, Penton Publishing, 1100 Superior Ave., Cleveland, OH 44114-2543, *Telephone:* (216) 696-7000, *Fax:* (216) 696-7658. *Published:* monthly.

Los Angeles Times, The Times Mirror Company, Times Mirror Square, Los Angeles, CA 90053, *Telephone:* (800) LA TIMES.

Macleans, Maclean Hunter Ltd., 777 Bay St., Toronto, ON, Canada M5W 1A7, *Telephone:* (416) 596-5311, *Fax:* (416) 596-6001. *Published:* weekly.

Management Today, Management Publications Limited, 174 Hammersmith Road, London, UK W6 7JP *Telephone:* 0171-413 4566.

Manufacturing Confectioner, The Manufacturing Confectioner Publishing Company, 175 Rock Rd., Glen Rock, NJ 07452, *Telephone:* (201) 652-2655, *Fax:* (201) 652-3419. *Published:* 12 times per year, *Price:* $25 per year, single copies $10 each, except $25 for April and July issues.

Manufacturing Systems, 191 South Gary Avenue, Carol Stream, IL 60198, *Telephone:* (708) 665-1000, *Fax:* (708) 462-2225. *Published:* monthly.

Marine Log, Simmons-Boardman Publishing, 345 Hudson St., New York, NY 10014, *Telephone:* (212) 620-7200, *Fax:* (212) 633-1165. *Published:* monthly.

Marketing Magazine, Maclean Hunter Canadian Publishing, P.O. Box 4541, Buffalo, NY 14240-4541, *Telephone:* (800) 567-0444, *Fax:* (416) 946-1679, *Price:* Canada: $59.50 per year, $98.50 for 2 years, $125 for 3 years; U.S.: $90 per year.

Marketing News, American Marketing Assn., 250 S. Wacker Dr., Ste. 200, Chicago, IL 60606-5819, *Telephone:* (312) 993-9517, *Fax:* (312) 993-7540. *Published:* biweekly.

Mediaweek, ADWEEK, L.P., P.O. Box 1976, Danbury, CT 06813-1976, *Telephone:* (800) 722-6658. *Published:* weekly, except first week of July, last week of August, and Last two weeks of December, *Price:* U.S.: $95 per year, $170 for 2 years; Canada: $230 per year.

Medical Marketing & Media, CPS Communications, Inc., 7200 West Camino Real, Suite 215, Boca Raton, FL 33433, *Telephone:* (407) 368-9301, *Fax:* (407) 368-7870. *Published:* monthly, *Price:* U.S.: $75 per year; Canada: $90 per year.

Metro Magazine, Bobit Publishing Co., 2512 Artesia Boulevard, Redondo Beach, CA 90278, *Published:* bimonthly, with an extra issue in October, *Price:* $25 per year. $4 single issue.

Metro Magazine Fact Book, Bobit Publishing Co., 2512 Artesia Boulevard, Redondo Beach, CA 90278.

Mexico Business, 3033 Chimney Rd., Suite 300, Houston, TX 77056, *Published:* monthly , combined issues in Jan./Feb. and July/Aug.

Milwaukee Business Journal, 2025 N. Smmit Ave., Milwaukee, WI 53209.

Mineral Commodity Summaries. U.S. Dept. of the Interior, Superintendent of Documents, USGPO, Washington, DC 20402, *Telephone:* (202) 783-3238.

Mineral Industries of Latin America and Canada, Superintendent of Documents, USGPO, Washington, DC 20402, *Telephone:* (202) 783-3238.

Mining Engineering, Society for Mining, Metallurgy, and Exploration, Inc., 8307 Shaffer Parkway, Littleton, CO 80127-5002, *Telephone:* (303) 973-9550, *Fax:* (303) 973-3845. *Published:* monthly, *Price:* $80 per year, single copies $7 each, except special issues $9 each and July issue $135; subscription included in membership dues.

Mining Voice, National Mining Association, 1130 17th Street, NW, Washington D.C. 20036-4677. *Published:* bimonthly, *Price:* $36 per year.

Mirror, Diocese of Springfield-Cape Girardeau, P.O. Box 847, Springfield, MO 65801, *Telephone:* (417) 866-0841, *Fax:* (417) 866-1140. *Published:* weekly, *Price:* $10 per year.

Modern Healthcare, Crain Communications, Inc., 740 N. Rush St., Chicago, IL 60611-2590, *Telephone:* (312) 649-5350, *Fax:* (312) 280-3189. *Published:* weekly.

Modern Materials Handling, Cahners Publishing Co., 275 Washington St., Newton, MA 02158, *Telephone:* (617) 964-3030, *Fax:* (617) 558-4402. *Published:* 14x/yr.

Modern Paint & Coatings, Argus Business, 6151 Powers Ferry Road, N.W., Atlanta, GA 30339-2941, *Telephone:* (404) 955-2500. *Published:* monthly, plus an extra issue in July, *Price:* $48 per year, $76 for 2 years; Outside U.S. surface: $68 per year.

Modern Plastics, McGraw-Hill, Inc., Attn. Fulfillment Manager, P.O. Box 481, Highstown, NJ 08520, *Telephone:* (800) 525-5003. *Published:* monthly, *Price:* U.S.: $41.75 per year, $62.70 for 2 years, $83.50 for 3 years; Canada:$CDN 53 per year, $CDN 80 for 2 years, $CDN 106 for 3 years.

Molybdenum, Bureau of Mines, Superintendent of Documents, USGPO, Washington, DC 20402, *Telephone:* (202) 783-3238.

Money, Time Warner Inc., Time & Life Bldg., Rockefeller Center, New York, NY 10020, *Telephone:* (212) 522-1212, *Fax:* (212) 522-0332. *Published:* monthly, *Price:* $32 per year.

Mortgage Banking, Mortgage Bankers Association of America, MBA Dept. 0021, Washington, DC 20073-0021, *Telephone:* (202) 861-6992. *Published:* monthly, *Price:* U.S.: $40 per year, $95 for 3 years; Canada: $42 per year.

Motor Boating and Sailing, 250 W. 55th St., New York, NY 10019, *Telephone:* (212) 649-4092, *Fax:* (212) 489-9258.

NAFTA. International Trade and Agricultural Reports, Superintendent of Documents, USGPO, Washington, DC 20402, *Telephone:* (202) 783-3238.

NARD Journal, 205 Daingerfield Road, Alexandria, VA 22314, *Telephone:* (703) 683-8200. *Published:* monthly, *Price:* $50 per year; $70 foreign.

Nation's Business, 1615 H Street, NW, Washington D.C., 20062-2000, *Telephone:* (800) 638-6582. *Published:* monthly, *Price:* $22 per year, $35 for 2 years.

Nation's Restaurant News, Lebhar-Friedman, Inc., Subscription Dept., P.O. Box 31179, Tampa, FL 33631-3179, *Telephone:* (800) 447-7133. *Published:* weekly on Mondays, except the first Monday in July and the last Monday in December, *Price:* $34.50 per year and $55 for 2 years for professionals in the field; $89 per year for those allied to field.

National Petroleum News, Hunter Publishing Limited Partnership, Circulation Dept., National Petroleum News, 25 Northwest Point Blvd., Suite 800, Elk Grove Village, IL 60007, *Telephone:* (708) 427-9512. *Published:* monthly, except semimonthly in June, *Price:* U.S.: $60 per year for those in petroleum marketing industry, $75 per year for others; Canada: $69 per year for those in petroleum marketing industry, $84 per year for others.

National Real Estate Investor, Intertec Publishing Co., 6151 Powers Ferry Road, NW, Atlanta, GA 30339, *Telephone:* (770) 955-2500, *Published:* monthly, *Price:* $84 per year, $136 for 2 years.

National Trade Data Bank - The Export Connection, STAT-USA, Superintendent of Documents, USGPO, Washington, DC 20402, *Telephone:* (202) 783-3238.

National Underwriter, The National Underwriter Co., 505 Gest St., Cincinnati, OH 45203, *Telephone:* (800) 543-0874, *Fax:* (800) 874-1916. *Published:* weekly, except last week in December, *Price:* U.S.: $77 per year, $130 for 2 years; Canada: $112 per year, $130 for 2 years.

Network Computing, CMP Publications, Inc., 600 Community Dr., Manhasset, NY 11030, *Telephone:* (708) 647-6834, *Fax:* (708) 647-6838.

Network World, Network World, Inc., 161 Worcester Rd., Framingham, MA 01701-9172, *Telephone:* (508) 875-6400. *Published:* weekly.

New York Times, New York Times Co., 229 W. 43rd St., New York, NY 10036, *Telephone:* (212) 556-1234. *Published:* daily.

NewMedia, Hyper Media Communications Inc., 901 Mariners Island Blvd., Ste. 365, San Mateo, CA 94404. *Published:* 2x/a month, *Price:* $24 per year.

Newsweek, The Newsweek Building, Livingston, NJ 07039-1666, *Telephone:* (800) 631-1040. *Published:* weekly, *Price:* U.S.: $41.08 per year; Canada: $61.88 per year (send to P.O. Box 4012, Postal Station A, Toronto, ON M5W 2K1).

Nonfoods Merchandising, Intl. Thomson Retail Press, 22 W. 21st. St., Box 640, New York, NY 10011, *Telephone:* (212) 741-7210. *Published:* monthly.

Oakland Press, Great Lakes Media Inc., 48 W. Huron, Pontiac, MI 48342. *Published:* daily.

Observer, Guardian Newspapers Limited, 119 Farringdon Road, London EC1R 3ER, Telephone: (0171) 278-2332.

Oil & Gas Journal, PennWell Publishing Co., Circulation Services Manager, P.O. Box 2002, Tulsa, OK 74101, *Telephone:* (800) 633-1656. *Published:* weekly, *Price:* industry rates - U.S.: $69 per year, $120 for 2 years, $161 for 3 years; Canada/Latin America: $76 per year, $132 for 2 years, $180 for 3 years; non-industry rates: $127 per year.

PC Magazine, Ziff-Davis Publishing Co., One Park Ave., New York , NY 10016-5802, *Published:* biweekly, except July and August.

PC WEEK, Ziff-Davis Publishing Company L.P., Customer Service Dept., PC WEEK, P.O. Box 1770, Riverton, NJ 08077-7370, *Telephone:* (609) 461-2100. *Published:* weekly, except combined issue at year-end, *Price:* U.S.: $160 per year; Canada/Mexico: $200 per year.

PIMA Magazine, Paper Industry Management Assn., 2400 East Oakton Street, Arlington Heights, IL 60005-4898. *Published:* monthly, *Price:* Canada/Mexico/U.S. military: $35 per year; all others: $75 per year.

Paperboard Packaging, Advanstar Communications Inc., 131 West First Street, Duluth, MN 55802, *Telephone:* (218) 723-9477, *Fax:* (218) 723-9437. *Published:* monthly, *Price:* U.S.: $39 per year, $58 for 2 years; Canada: $59 per year, $88 for 2 years.

Pensions & Investments, Crain Communications, Inc., 220 E. 42nd St., New York, NY 10017, *Telephone:* (212) 210-0227, *Fax:* (212) 210-0117. *Published:* monthly.

Pet Product News, Fancy Publications, Inc., P.O. Box 6050, Mission Viejo, CA 92690, *Telephone:* (714) 855-8822, *Fax:* (714) 855-3045. *Published:* monthly.

Petroleum Economist, Hart Publications Inc., 1900 Grant St., Suite 400, P.O. Box 1917, Denver, CO 80201. *Published:* monthly, *Price:* North America: petroleum industry - $49 per year, $77 for 2 years; outside petroleum industry - $75 per year.

Philadelphia Inquirer, Philadelphia Newspapers Inc., 400 N. Broad St., Box 8263, Philadelphia, PA 19101, *Telephone:* (215) 854-2000. *Published:* daily.

Photo Marketing, Photo Marketing Association International, 3000 Picture Place, Jackson, MI 49201, *Telephone:* (517) 788-8100, *Fax:* (517) 788-8371. *Published:* monthly, *Price:* U.S.: $35 per year/with Newsline $50, $55 for 2 years/$65 with Newsline; Canada: $35 per year/$50 with Newsline, $55 for 2 years/$70 with Newsline (payable in Canadian funds plus GST).

Photonics Spectra, Laurin Publishing Co., Inc., Berkshire Common, PO Box 4949, Pittsfield, MA 01202, *Telephone:* (413) 499-0514, *Fax:* (413) 442-3180, *Published:* monthly.

Plastics News, Crain Communications, 965 E. Jefferson, Detroit, MI 48207-3185. *Published:* weekly.

Platinum Group Metals. Mineral Industry Surveys, Bureau of Mines, U.S. Dept. of the Interior, Superintendent of Documents, USGPO, Washington, DC 20402, *Telephone:* (202) 783-3238.

Playthings, Geyer-McAllister Publications, Inc., 51 Madison Ave., New York, NY 10010, *Telephone:* (212) 689-4411, *Fax:* (212) 683-7929. *Published:* monthly, except semimonthly in May.

Potato Stocks, U.S. Dept of Agriculture, Superintendent of Documents, USGPO, Washington, DC 20402, *Telephone:* (202) 783-3238.

Practical Accountant, Faulkner & Gray, Inc., 11 Penn Plaza, 17th Floor, New York, NY 10001, *Telephone:* (800) 535-8403 or (212) 967-7060. *Published:*

monthly, *Price:* U.S.: $60 per year; Elsewhere: $79 per year.

Prepared Foods, Cahners Publishing Company, 44 Cook St., Denver, CO 80217-3377, *Telephone:* (303) 388-4511. *Published:* monthly, except semimonthly in April, *Price:* qualified manufacturers - $41 per year; all others in U.S. - $84 per year.

Professional Builder, Cahners Publishing Co., 275 Washington Street, Newton, MA 02158-1630. *Published:* monthly, *Price:* U.S.: $140 for 1 year, $238 for 2 years; Canada: $193 for 1 year; Mexico: $180 for one year.

Progressive Grocer, 263 Tresser Blvd., Stamford, CT 06901, *Telephone:* (203) 325-3500. *Published:* monthly, *Price:* U.S.: $75 per year; Canada: $86 per year; single copies $9 each.

Provider, American Health Care Association, 5615 W. Cermak Rd., Cicero, IL 60650. *Published:* monthly.

Public Utilities Fortnightly, 2111 Wilson Blvd., Ste. 200, Arlington, VA 22204.

Publishers Weekly, Cahners Publishing Company, ESP Computer Services, 19110 Van Ness Ave., Torrance, CA 90501-1170, *Telephone:* (800) 278-2991. *Published:* weekly, *Price:* U.S.: $129 per year; Canada: $177 per year (includes GST).

Puget Sound Business Journal, 101 Yesler Way, Ste. 200, Seattle, WA 98104, *Telephone:* (206) 583-0701, *Fax:* (206) 447-8510. *Published:* weekly, *Price:* $48 per year.

Pulp & Paper, Miller Freeman Inc., P.O. Box 1065, Skokie, IL 60076-8065, *Telephone:* (800) 682-8297. *Published:* monthly, *Price:* free to those in pulp, paper, and board manufacturing and paper converting firms; Others in U.S.: $100 per year.

Purchasing, Cahners Publishing Company, 44 Cook St., Denver, CO 80217-3377, *Telephone:* (303) 388-4511. *Published:* semimonthly, except monthly in January, February, July, August, December, and one extra issue in March and September, *Price:* U.S.:

$84.95 per year; Canada: $133.95 per year; Mexico: $124.95 per year.

Quick Facts From the Census of Agriculture, U.S. Dept of Agriculture, Superintendent of Documents, USGPO, Washington, DC 20402, *Telephone:* (202) 783-3238.

Quick Frozen Foods International, E.W. Williams Publications Co., 2125 Center Ave., Ste. 305, Fort Lee, NJ 07024, *Telephone:* (201) 592-7007, *Fax:* (201) 592-7171. *Published:* quarterly.

RCR (Radio Communications Report), RCR Publications, Inc., 777 East Speer Blvd., Denver, CO 80203. *Published:* semimonthly.

RV Business, TL Enterprises, Inc., 29901 Agoura Rd., Agoura Hills, CA 91309, *Telephone:* (818) 991-4980, *Fax:* (818) 597-2403. *Published:* 2x/mo.

Railway Age, Simmons-Boardman Publishing, 345 Hudson St., New York, NY 10014, *Telephone:* (212) 620-7200, *Fax:* (212) 633-1165. *Published:* monthly.

Red Herring, Flipside Communications, 1550 Bryant St., Suite 950, San Francisco, CA 94103, *Telephone:* (415) 865-2277, *Fax:* (415) 865-2277. *Published:* monthly.

Restaurant Business, 355 Park Ave., New York, NY 10010. *Published:* monthly, except semimonthly in Jan., Mar., May, July, Sept., and Nov.

Restaurants & Institutions, Cahners Publishing Co., 1350 Touhy Ave., Cahners Plaza, Des Plaines, IL 60017-5080, *Telephone:* (312) 635-8800.

Rock Products, Maclean Hunter Publishing Co., 29 N. Wacker Dr., Chicago, IL 60606, *Telephone:* (312) 726-2802.

Rough Notes, Rough Notes Co. Inc., 11690 Technology Dr., Carmel, IN 46032-5600, *Published:* monthly, Price:$25 per year

Rubber & Plastics News, Crain Communications, 1725 Merriman Road, Ste. 300, Akron, OH 44313, *Telephone:* (330) 836-9180, *Fax:* (330) 836-1005.

Rubber World, 1867 W. Market St., PO Box 5485, Akron, OH 44313, *Telephone:* (216) 864-2122, *Fax:* (216) 836-1005.

Rural Builder, Krause Publications, 700 East State St., Ola, WI 54990. *Published:* monthly.

Rural Electrification, National Rural Electric Cooperative Assn., 1800 Massachusetts Ave., NW, Washington D.C. 20036.

STN/Skiing Trade News, Times Mirror Magazines, Inc., 2 Park Ave., New York, NY 10016, *Telephone:* (212) 779-5019, *Fax:* (212) 779-5466. *Published:* 8x/yr. *Price:* $15 per year.

Safety & Health, American Safety Council, 121 Spring Lake Drive, Itasca, IL 60143-3201, *Telephone:* (708) 285-1121, *Fax:* (708) 285-9114.

Sales & Marketing Management, Times Mirror Magazines, Inc., 2 Park Ave., New York, NY 10016, *Telephone:* (212) 592-6300, *Fax:* (212) 592-6309. *Published:* 15x/yr.

San Diego Business Journal, 4909 Murphy Canyon Rd., No. 200, San Diego, CA 92123, *Telephone:* (619) 277-6359, *Fax:* (619) 571-3628. *Published:* weekly.

San Francisco Business Times, San Francisco Business Times, Inc., Embarcadero Center West, 275 Battery Street, Suite 940, San Francisco, CA 94111. *Published:* weekly, *Price:* $49 per year.

San Jose Mercury News, Knight-Ridder Inc., 1 Herald Plaza, Miami, FL 33132, *Telephone:* (305) 376-3800, *Published:* daily.

San Jose and Silicon Valley Business Journal, 56 N. 3rd St., San Jose, CA 95112, *Telephone:* (408) 295-3800, *Fax:* (408) 295-5028. *Published:* weekly, *Price:* $55 per year, $1.25 a single copy.

School Foodservice & Nutrition, School Foodservice Assn., 1600 Duke Street, 7th Floor, Alexandria, VA *Telephone:* (703) 739-3900, *Fax:* (703) 739-3915. *Published:* monthly, *Price:* $125 for nonmembers.

Secondary Mortgage Markets, 8200 Jones Branch Drive, McLean, Virginia 22102.

Shopping Center World, Communications Channels, Inc., 6255 Barfield Rd., Altanta, GA 30328, *Telephone:* (404) 256-9800.

Site Selection, Conway Data, Inc., 40 Technology Park/Atlanta, Norcross, GA 30092-9990, *Telephone:* (404) 446-6996.

Skillings Mining Review, 1st Bank Pl., Ste. 278, 130 W. Superior St., Duluth, MN 55802, *Telephone:* (218) 722-2310, *Fax:* (218) 722-0134. *Published:* weekly.

Snack Food, Stagnito Publishing Co., 1935 Shermer Rd., Ste. 100, Northbrook, IL 60062-5354, *Telephone:* (708) 205-5660, *Fax:* (708) 205-5680. *Published:* monthly, *Price:* free to qualified subscribers; $45 per year to all others.

Soap/Cosmetics/Chemical Specialties, 445 Broad Hollow Road, Melville, NY 11747-4722.

Software Magazine, Sentry Publishing Co., One Research Drive, Suite 400B, Westborough, MA 01581, *Telephone:* (508) 366-2031. *Published:* monthly, *Price:* U.S. $65 per year, *Canada:* $75 per year.

Solid State Technology, PennWell Publishing Company, 1421 S. Sheridan Road, Tulsa, OK 74112, *Telephone:* (603) 891-0123. *Published:* monthly.

South Florida Business Journal, American City Business Journals, 7950 NW 53 St., Ste. 210, Miami, FL 33166, *Telephone:* (305) 594-2100, *Fax:* (305) 594-1892.

Southern Exposure, Institute for Southern Studies, P.O. Box 531, Durham NC 27702, *Telephone:* (919) 419-8311.

Spice Market in the United States, U.S. Dept. of Agriculture, Superintendent of Documents, USGPO, Washington, DC 20402, *Telephone:* (202) 783-3238.

Sporting Goods Business, Gralla Publications, Inc., 1515 Broadway, New York, NY 10036, *Telephone:* (212) 869-1300.

Sporting Goods Dealer, Times Mirror Magazines, Inc., 2 Park Ave., New York, NY 10016, *Telephone:* (212) 779-5000, *Fax:* (212) 213-3540. *Published:* monthly.

Sportstyle, Fairchild Publications, 7 W. 34th St., New York, NY 10001, *Telephone:* (212) 630-4000, *Fax:* (212) 630-3726.

Spray Technology & Marketing, Industry Publications, Inc., 389 Passaic Ave., Fairfield, NJ 07004, *Telephone:* (201) 227-5151, *Fax:* (201) 227-9211. *Published:* monthly.

St. Louis Post-Dispatch, 900 N. Tucker Blvd., Saint Louis, MO 63101, *Telephone:* (314) 340-8000, *Fax:* (314) 340-3050.

Star Tribune, 425 Portland Ave., Minnepolis, MN 55488, *Telephone:* (612) 673-4000, *Fax:* (612) 673-4359. *Published:* daily.

Stores, NRF Enterprises Inc., 100 West 31st St., New York, NY 10001. *Published:* monthly, *Price:* U.S./Canada: $49 per year, $80 for 2 years, $120 for 3 years.

Successful Farming, Meredith Corp., 1716 Locust St., Des Moines, IA 50309, *Telephone:* (515) 284-3000, *Fax:* (515) 284-2700.

Sugar and Sweetener, U.S. Dept. of Agriculture, Superintendent of Documents, USGPO, Washington, DC 20402, *Telephone:* (202) 783-3238.

Sunday Journal Sentinel, Star Printing, P.O. Box 270, Edina, MO 63537.

Sunday Oregonian, Eagle Newspapers, 558 N. Main St., Prineville, OP 97754, *Telephone:* (503) 447-6205, *Fax:* (503) 447-1754.

Supermarket Business, Howfrey Communications, Inc., 1086 Teaneck Rd., Teaneck, NJ 07666, *Telephone:* (201) 833-1900. *Published:* monthly.

Supermarket News, Fairchild Publications, 7 W. 34th St., New York, NY 10001, *Telephone:* (212) 630-4750, *Fax:* (212) 630-4760.

Survey of Current Business, Superintendent of Documents, USGPO, Washington, DC 20402, *Telephone:* (202) 783-3238, *Price:* $41 U.S.; $52 foreign; single copies are $11 U.S. and $14 foreign..

Swimming Pool/Spa Age, Intersec Publishing Co., 6151 Powers Ferry Road, NW, Atlanta, GA 30339, *Telephone:* (770) 955-2500. *Published:* monthly.

TV Digest, Warren Publishing, Inc., 215 Ward Ct. NW, Washington, DC 20037, *Telephone:* (202) 872-9200.

Tampa Bay Business Journal, American City Business Journals, 405 Reo St., Ste. 210, Tampa, FL 33609, *Telephone:* (813) 289-8225.

Target Marketing, North American Publishing Co., 401 N. Broad St., Philadelphia, PA 19108, *Telephone:* (215) 238-5300, *Fax:* (215) 238-5457. *Published:* monthly.

Telecommunications, Horizon House Publications, Inc., 685 Canton St., Norwood, CA 02062, *Telephone:* (617) 769-9750, *Fax:* (617) 762-9071.

Telephony, Intersec Publishing Corp., 9800 Metcalf, Overland Park, KS 66282-2960. *Published:* monthly.

Textile Asia, Tak Yan Commercial Bldg., 11th Fl., 30-32 D'Aguilar St., Hong Kong, *Telephone:* (5) 247467. *Published:* monthly.

Textile Rental, Textile Rental Services Association of America, 1130 E. Hallandale Beach Blvd., Hallandale, FL 33009, *Published:* monthly, *Price:* $90 per year.

Textile World, Maclean Hunter Publishing Co., Circulation Dept., 29 N. Wacker Dr., Chicago, IL 60606, *Price:* U.S./Canada: $45 per year, $75 for 2 years, $105 for 3 years.

Time, Time Inc., Time & Life Bldg., Rockefeller Center, New York, NY 10020-1393, *Telephone:* (800) 843-8463. *Published:* weekly.

Times, Times Newspapers, P.O. Box 495, Virginia Street, London E1 9XY, *Telephone:* 0171- 782-5000.

Times Picayune, Times-Picauyne Publishing Co., 800 Howard Ave., New Orleans, LA 70140, *Telephone:* (504) 826-3300. *Published:* daily.

Tire Business, Crains Communcations, Inc., 1725 Merriman Rd., Ste. 300, Akron, OH 44313-5251, *Telephone:* (216) 836-9180, *Fax:* (216) 836-1005.

Today's Realtor, National Association of Realtors, 430 N. Michigan Ave., Chicago, IL 60611-4087. *Published:* monthly.

Tooling & Production, Huebcore Communications Inc., 29100 Aurora Rd., Ste. 200, Solon, OH 44139. *Published:* monthly, *Price:* U.S.: $90 per year, Canada/Mexico $125 per year.

Toronto Star, One Yong Street, Toronto, Ontario M5E 1E6, *Telephone:* (416) 367-2000.

Traffic Management, Cahners Publishing Co., 275 Washington St., Newton, MA 02158, *Telephone:* (617) 964-3030, *Fax:* (617) 558-4327.

Traffic World, Journal of Commerce Inc., TRAFFIC WORLD, Two World Trade Center, New York, NY 10048. *Published:* weekly, except last week of December, *Price:* $159 per year, single copies $5 each.

Training, American Society for Training and Development Inc., 1640 King Street, P.O. Box 1443, Alexandria, VA 22313-2043, *Telephone:* (703) 683-8100.

Transport Topics, American Trucking Assn., 2200 Mill Road, Alexandria, VA 22314, *Telephone:* (703) 838-1770.

Travel Weekly, Reed Travel Group, 500 Plaza Dr., Secaucus, NJ 07096, *Telephone:* (201) 902-2000, *Fax:* (201) 319-1947. *Published:* 2 times/week (Mon. and Thurs.).

U.S. Distribution Journal, BMT Publications Inc., 7 Penn Plaza, New York, NY 10001, *Telephone:* (212) 594-4120. *Published:* monthly, plus one additional issue in Dec.

U.S. News & World Report, 2400 N. St. NW, Washington, D.C. 20037, *Telephone:* (202) 955-2000. *Published:* weekly.

Urban Land, Urban Land Institute, 625 Indiana Avenue, N.W., Suite 400, Washington, DC 20004-2930, *Telephone:* (202) 624-7000. *Published:* monthly, *Price:* $60 per year as part of membership.

US Banker, Kalo Communications, 60 E. 42nd St., Ste. 3810, New York, NY 10165, Telephone: (212) 599-3310.

USA TODAY, Gannett Co., Inc., 1000 Wilson Blvd., Arlington, VA 22229, *Telephone:* (703) 276-3400. *Published:* Mon.-Fri.

VM + SD (Visual Merchandising and Store Design), ST Publications Inc., 407 Gilbert Ave., Cincinnati, OH 45202, *Telephone:* (513) 421-2050. *Published:* monthly, *Price:* $39 per year.

Vanadium, Bureau of Mines, Superintendent of Documents, USGPO, Washington, DC 20402, *Telephone:* (202) 783-3238.

Variety, 475 Park Ave., South, New York, NY 10016, *Telephone:* (212) 779-1100, *Fax:* (212) 779-0026. *Published:* weekly.

Vegetables, U.S. Dept. of Agriculture, Superintendent of Documents, USGPO, Washington, DC 20402, *Telephone:* (202) 783-3238.

Vegetables and Specialties. Situation and Outlook Yearbook, U.S. Dept. of Agriculture, Superintendent of Documents, USGPO, Washington, DC 20402, *Telephone:* (202) 783-3238.

Vending Times, Vending Times Inc., 545 8th Ave., New York, NY 10018, *Telephone:* (212) 714-0101, *Fax:* (212) 564-0196, *Published:* monthly.

WARD's Auto World, Ward's Communications, 28 W. Adams, Detroit, MI 48226, *Telephone:* (313) 962-4456. *Published:* monthly.

Wall Street Journal, Dow Jones & Co. Inc., 200 Liberty St., New York, NY 10281, *Telephone:* (212) 416-2000. *Published:* Mon.-Fri.

Washington Post, The Washington Post, 1150 15th St., N.W., Washington, DC 20071. *Published:* weekly, *Price:* $48 per year.

Washington Post National Weekly Edition, The Washington Post, 1150 15th St., N.W., Washington, DC 20071. *Published:* weekly, *Price:* $48 per year.

Water & Environment & Technology, 601 Wythe Street, Alexandria, VA 22314-1994.

Web Week, Mecklemedia Corp., 20 Ketchum Street, Westport, CT 06880. *Published:* monthly.

Welding Design & Fabrication, Penton Publishing Inc., 1100 Superior Ave., Cleveland, OH 44114-2543, *Telephone:* (216) 696-7000, *Fax:* (216) 696-7658.

Wine Spectator, Shanken Communications Inc., 587 Park Ave. S, 8th Fl., New York, NY 10016, *Telephone:* (212) 684-4224, *Fax:* (212) 684-5424, *Published:* 2x/mo.

Wines & Vines, Hiaring Co., 1800 Lincoln Ave., San Rafael, CA 94901-1298, *Telephone:* (415) 453-9700, *Fax:* (415) 453-2517. *Published:* monthly, *Price:* $32 per year without directory; $77.50 per year including directory.

Wired, 24 3rd Street, San Francisco, CA 94111, *Published:* monthly.

Wirtschaftwoche, 40045 Dusseldorf, Postfach 1054 65, Kasermanstrabe, Germany 67 40213.

Women's Wear Daily, Fairchild Publications, 7 E. 12th St., New York, NY 10003, *Telephone:* (212) 741-4000, *Fax:* (212) 337-3225. *Published:* daily.

Wood & Wood Products, Vance Publishing Corp., 400 Knightsbridge Pkway., Lincolnshire, IL 60069, *Telephone:* (708) 634-4347, *Fax:* (708) 634-4379. *Published:* monthly, except semimonthly in March.

Wood Technology, Miller Freeman Inc., 600 Harrison St., San Francisco, CA 94107, Published: 9x/yr.

World Horticultural Trade & U.S. Export Opportunities, U.S. Department of Agriculture. Superintendent of Documents, USGPO, Washington, DC 20402, *Telephone:* (202) 783-3238.

World Oil, Gulf Publishing Co., 3301 Allen Parkway, Houston, TX 77019. *Published:* monthly.

World Trade, Freedom Magazines, 17702 Cowan, Ste. 100, Irvine, CA 92714-6035.